MAKING THE TEAM
A GUIDE FOR MANAGERS

Fourth Edition

MAKING THE TEAM
A GUIDE FOR MANAGERS

Leigh L. Thompson

Kellogg School of Management
Northwestern University

Prentice Hall

Boston   Columbus   Indianapolis   New York   San Francisco   Upper Saddle River
Amsterdam   Cape Town   Dubai   London   Madrid   Milan   Munich   Paris   Montreal   Toronto
Delhi   Mexico City   Sao Paulo   Sydney   Hong Kong   Seoul   Singapore   Taipei   Tokyo

Editorial Director: Sally Yagan
Editor in Chief: Eric Svendsen
Director of Editorial Services: Ashley Santora
Editorial Project Manager: Meg O'Rourke
Editorial Assistant: Carter Anderson
Director of Marketing: Patrice Lumumba Jones
Marketing Manager: Nikki Ayana Jones
Marketing Assistant: Ian Gold
Senior Managing Editor: Judy Leale
Project Manager: Holly Shufeldt
Art Director: Jayne Conte
Cover Designer: Bruce Kenselaar
Cover Image: Fotolia: Teamwork © Finnegan
Media Director: Denise Vaughn
Lead Media Project Manager: Lisa Rinaldi
Full-Service Project Management and Composition: Integra
Text and Cover Printer: Courier
Text Font: 10/12 Times

Credits and acknowledgments borrowed from other sources and reproduced,
with permission, in this textbook appear on appropriate page within text.

Library of Congress Cataloging-in-Publication Data
Thompson, Leigh L.
   Making the team : a guide for managers / Leigh L. Thompson.—4th ed.
      p. cm.
   Includes bibliographical references and index.
   ISBN-13: 978-0-13-609003-8
   ISBN-10: 0-13-609003-6
   1. Teams in the workplace.   2. Performance.   3. Leadership.   4. Organizational effectiveness.   I. Title.
   HD66.T478 2011
658.4'022—dc22

2010036125

10 9 8 7 6 5 4 3 2 1

Prentice Hall
is an imprint of

www.pearsonhighered.com

ISBN 10:   0-13-609003-6
ISBN 13: 978-0-13-609003-8

For my home team: Bob, Sam, Ray, and Anna

BRIEF CONTENTS

CONTENTS

PREFACE

When I wrote *Making the Team* in 2000, my intent was to introduce leaders, managers, and executives to practical research on groups and teams. This enterprise required an integration of theory, research, and application. Five professors—Jeanne Brett, Tanya Menon, Keith Murnighan, Mark Rittenberg, and I—offer a 3-day course for executives in team leadership at the Kellogg School of Management at Northwestern University. Moreover, Kellogg offers a full-term course on teamwork to our MBA students. This book is dedicated to the students of Kellogg's executive program and MBA program.

Making the Team has two audiences: leaders and team members. For the leader, the book directs itself toward how teams can be designed to function optimally; for those people who are members of teams, the book focuses on the skills necessary to be a productive team member.

Since the publication of the first three editions, many advances have occurred in team and group research. Every chapter has new information, new research, updated examples, and more. Specifically, I have made the following major changes to the fourth edition of *Making the Team:*

1. **New, updated research:** True to the book's defining characteristic—providing managers with the most up-to-date research in a digestible fashion—I have included the latest research on teamwork and group behavior, thus keeping the book up-to-date and true to its strong research focus and theory-driven approach.
2. **Surveys of managers and executives:** The updated research also reports on the survey of executives that we have conducted at Kellogg for the past 14 years. The survey in the first edition reported the responses of 149 managers and executives; the fourth edition has a database of more than 1,000 team managers.
3. **New research studies:** More than 184 new research studies have been cited.
4. **More case studies:** I have included more examples and illustrations of effective (as well as ineffective) teamwork. More than 162 new case studies and examples of actual company teams have been added. Each chapter has a new, updated opening example.
5. **Illustrations and examples:** Many of the concepts and techniques in the chapters are supplemented with illustrations and examples from real teams, both contemporary and historical. I do not use these examples to prove a theory; rather, I use them to illustrate how many of the concepts in the book are borne out in real-world situations.
6. **New exercises, cases, and supplemental material:** The supplemental material and teaching support materials have been greatly improved so as to complement the text. This allows students to have a more integrated experience inside and outside of the classroom. The book strongly advocates experientially based teaching, and the instructor now has even more options for making the concepts come alive in the classroom.

In addition to the changes discussed, which affect all chapters and sections of the book, several chapters have undergone updates as new theory and research have broken ground and as our world has been shaped by events such as the economic crisis that began in 2008, the election of President Obama, H1N1 flu outbreak, and the averted Christmas day "underwear" bomber. The revision was sparked not only by advances—as well as calamities—in the corporate world but also, even more so, by the great scientific research on teamwork that my colleagues have relentlessly contributed to the field of management science in the years since the first edition went to press.

One of the reasons why I love this field is that there are so many wonderful people with whom to collaborate. The following people have had a major impact on my thinking and have brought joy and meaning to the word *collaboration*: Cameron Anderson, Linda Babcock, Max Bazerman, Terry Boles, Jeanne Brett, Susan Brodt, John Carroll, Hoon-Seok Choi, Taya Cohen, Jennifer Crocker, Susan Crotty, Hal Ersner-Hershfield, Gary Fine, Craig Fox, Adam Galinsky, Wendi Gardner, Dedre Gentner, Robert Gibbons, Kevin Gibson, James Gillespie, Rich Gonzalez, Deborah Gruenfeld, Brian Gunia, Reid Hastie, Andy Hoffman, Molly Kern, Peter Kim, Shirli Kopelman, Rod Kramer, Laura Kray, Terri Kurtzburg, Geoffrey Leonardelli, John Levine, Allan Lind, George Loewenstein, Jeff Loewenstein, Bob Lount, Denise Lewin Loyd, Beta Mannix, Kathleen McGinn, Vicki Medvec, Tanya Menon, Dave Messick, Terry Mitchell, Don Moore, Michael Morris, Keith Murnighan, Janice Nadler, Maggie Neale, Erika Petersen, Kathy Phillips, Robin Pinkley, Jo-Ellen Pozner, Mark Rittenberg, Ashleigh Rosette, Ken Savitsky, Elizabeth Seeley, Vanessa Seiden, Marwan Sinaceur, Ned Smith, Harris Sondak, Tom Tyler, Leaf Van Boven, Kimberly Wade-Benzoni, Cindy Wang, Juinwen Wang, Laurie Weingart, and Judith White.

The revision of this book would not have been possible without the dedication, organization, and creativity of Larissa Tripp and Joel Erickson, who created the layout, organized the information, edited the hundreds of drafts, mastered the figures, organized the permissions for the exhibits in each chapter, and researched many of the case studies for this book.

In this book, I talk quite a bit about the "power of the situation" and how strongly the environment shapes behavior. The Kellogg School of Management is one of the most supportive, dynamic environments that I have ever had the pleasure to be a part of. My colleagues across the Kellogg School are uniquely warm, constructive, and generous. Directing the KTAG (Kellogg Teams and Groups) Center has been a pleasure beyond compare. I am very grateful for the generous grants I have received through the years from the National Science Foundation's Decision, Risk and Management Program, the Kellogg Teams and Groups Center, and its sister, the Dispute Resolution Research Center.

This book is very much a team effort of the people I have mentioned here; their talents are diverse, broad, and extraordinarily impressive. I am deeply indebted to my colleagues and students, and I feel very grateful that they have touched my life and this book.

The Basics of Teamwork

1

Teams in Organizations

Facts and Myths

Jeffrey D. Zients became first chief performance officer of the United States on June 29, 2009. His job is to make sure the government's 24 major agencies and departments "make the government more effective and efficient by making it faster, smarter and cheaper" (p. 45). Known as the "SWAT team," Zients and his team swoop in to put out fires, such as embarrassing delays in GI Bill payments and the Cash for Clunkers program. Zients does not believe in radical reorganization of government; rather he believes in execution and results. For example, in the fall of 2009, nearly 280,000 U.S. veterans applied for an improved GI Bill education benefit that essentially brought the antiquated computer system to a halt. By 5:30 a.m. the next morning, Zients' SWAT team caught a flight from Washington to a VA processing center in St. Louis and paired off with claims processors for three hours. On the return flight, a dozen members of the SWAT team gathered in the aisle and divided up tasks. Zients came up with a breakthrough solution that involved outsourcing simpler tasks to a private firm. The result was faster payments for the veterans.[1]

Zients arguably faces the toughest team challenge in the United States, being responsible for 1.8 million employees and more than 10,000 computing systems. Instead of becoming mired in technology, structure, and systems, Zients focuses on the essentials of effective teamwork: goal setting, deliverables, processes, and timelines. Every Thursday, Zients and his SWAT team gather in his office for a "divide and conquer" meeting in which they set operational goals, determine deadlines, measure results, and split up tasks. These elements—a shared goal and an interdependent group of people—are the defining characteristics of teams.

Virtually everyone who has worked in an organization has been a member of a team at one time or another. Good teams are not a matter of luck; they result from hard work, careful planning, and commitment from the sponsoring organization. Designing effective teams is

---

[1]Hamm, S. (2009, December 7). Obama's big gov SWAT team. *Business Week, 4158*, 44–46.

a skill that requires a thorough understanding of teams to ensure that the team works as designed. Although there are no guarantees, understanding what makes teams work will naturally lead to better and more effective teams. This book introduces a systematic approach that allows leaders, managers, executives, trainers, and professionals to build and maintain excellent teams in their organizations.

Our systematic approach is based upon scientific principles of learning and change. Implementing change requires that managers audit their own behavior to see where mistakes are being made, consider and implement new techniques and practices, and then examine their effects. Unfortunately, accomplishing these tasks in a typical organizational setting is not easy. This chapter sets the stage for effective learning by defining what a team is—it's not always clear! We distinguish four types of teams in organizations in terms of their authority. We expose the most common myths about teamwork and share some observations from team leaders. We provide the results of our survey on how teams are used in organizations and the problems with which managers are most concerned. The problems cited by these managers cut across industries, from doughnut companies to high-tech firms.

WHAT IS A TEAM?

A **work team** is an interdependent collection of individuals who share responsibility for specific outcomes for their organizations. Not everyone who works together or is in proximity belongs to a team. A team is a group of people who are interdependent with respect to information, resources, and skills and who seek to combine their efforts to achieve a common goal. As is summarized in Exhibit 1-1, teams have five key defining characteristics. First, teams exist to achieve a *shared goal*. Simply put, teams have work to do. Teams produce outcomes for which members have collective responsibility and reap some form of collective reward. Second, team members are interdependent regarding a common goal. Interdependence is the hallmark of teamwork. **Interdependence** means that team members cannot achieve their goals single-handedly, but instead, must rely on each other to meet shared objectives. There are several kinds of interdependencies, as team members must rely on others for information, expertise, resources, and support. Third, teams are bounded and remain relatively stable over time. **Boundedness** means the team has an identifiable membership; members, as well as nonmembers, know who is on the team. **Stability** refers to the tenure of membership. Most teams work together for a meaningful length of time—long enough to accomplish their goal. Fourth, team members have the *authority* to manage their own work and internal processes. We focus on teams in which

---

EXHIBIT 1-1 Five Key Characteristics of Teams

- Teams exist to achieve a shared goal.
- Team members are interdependent regarding some common goal.
- Teams are bounded and stable over time.
- Team members have the authority to manage their own work and internal processes.
- Teams operate in a social system context.

Source: Alderfer, C. P. (1977). Group and intergroup relations. In J. R. Hackman & J. L. Suttle (Eds.), *Improving life at work* (pp. 227–296). Palisades, CA: Goodyear; Hackman, J. R. (1990). Introduction: Work teams in organizations: An oriented framework. In J. Hackman (Ed.), *Groups that work and those that don't*. San Francisco, CA: Jossey-Bass.

individual members can, to some extent, determine how their work gets done. Thus, although a prison chain gang may be a team in some sense, the prisoners have little authority in terms of managing their own work. Finally, teams operate in a larger **social system context**. Teams are not islands unto themselves. They do their work in a larger organization, often alongside other teams. Furthermore, teams often need to draw upon resources from outside the team and vice versa—something we discuss in Part III of this book.

A **working group**, by contrast, consists of people who learn from one another and share ideas but are not interdependent in an important fashion and are not working toward a shared goal. Working groups share information, perspectives, and insights; make decisions; and help people do their jobs better, but the focus is on individual goals and accountability. For example, a group of researchers who meet each month to share their new ideas is a working group.

WHY SHOULD ORGANIZATIONS HAVE TEAMS?

Teams and teamwork are not novel concepts. In fact, teams and team thinking have been around for years at companies such as Procter & Gamble and Boeing. In the 1980s, the manufacturing and auto industries strongly embraced a new, team-oriented approach when U.S. companies retooled to compete with Japanese companies that were quickly gaining market share.[2] During collaboration on the B-2 stealth bomber between the U.S. Air Force, Northrop, and 4,000 subcontractors and suppliers in the early 1980s, teams were employed to handle different parts of the project.[3]

Managers discovered the large body of research indicating that teams can be more effective than the traditional corporate hierarchical structure for making decisions quickly and efficiently. Even simple changes such as encouraging input and feedback from workers on the line can make a dramatic improvement. For instance, quality control (QC) circles and employee involvement groups encourage employee participation.[4] It is a mark of these programs' success that this kind of thinking is considered conventional wisdom nowadays. But, although these QC teams were worthy efforts at fostering the use of teams in organizations, the teams needed for the restructuring and reengineering processes of the future may be quite different. According to one study, team-based projects fail 50 to 70 percent of the time.[5]

At least four challenges suggest that building and maintaining effective teams is of paramount importance.

Customer Service Focus

The first challenge has to do with *customer service*. Businesses and companies all over the world have moved from a transactional, economic view of customers and clients to a relational view of customers. **Transactional** models of teamwork are characterized by discrete exchanges, are short-term in nature, and contain little interaction between the customer and the vendor. In contrast, **relational** models of teamwork occur over time, are more intense, and are built upon a relationship between the people involved. There is good reason to care about the customer from a relational point of view, given that 74 percent of consumers blame customer

[2]Nahavandi, A., & Aranda, E. (1994). Restructuring teams for the re-engineered organization. *Academy of Management Review, 8*(4), 58–68.

[3]Kresa, K. (1991). Aerospace leadership in a vortex of change. *Financier, 15*(1), 25–28.

[4]Cole, R. E. (1982). Diffusion of participating work structures in Japan, Sweden and the United States. In P. S. Goodman et al. (Eds.), *Change in organizations* (pp. 166–225). San Francisco, CA: Jossey-Bass.

[5]Greenberg, J., & Baron, R. A. (2008). *Behavior in organizations* (9th ed.). Upper Saddle River, NJ: Pearson Education.

service as a major factor in their decision to stop using a product or service.[6] Sixty-five percent of a company's business comes from existing customers, and it costs five times as much to attract a new customer than to keep an existing one satisfied.[7] To the extent that teams are positioned to care about the customer from a relational perspective, this can add tremendous value for the organization.

Competition

The second challenge has to do with *competition*. A few large companies often emerge as the dominant players in the biggest markets. These industry leaders often enjoy vast economies of scale and earn tremendous profits. The losers are often left with little in the way of a market—let alone a marketable product.[8] Think, for example, of Microsoft's Windows operating system and Office Products' market share dominance. The division that develops the Office Products software—which includes Word, Excel, PowerPoint, Outlook, and Access—employs thousands of people. Those products share a lot of code, and so teamwork is critical to coordinate the activities of the various component groups that make up the Office Products Division.[9] With so much at stake, companies aggressively compete in a winner-take-all battle for market share. Thus, bringing out the best in teams within the company has become even more important. This means that people can be expected to specialize more, and these areas of expertise will get ever more narrow and interdependent. Both companies and people have to increasingly rely on others to get access to their expertise. This is the core structure of a team-based approach to work.

Information Age

A third factor is the presence of the *information age*. In the knowledge era, employees are knowledge workers and teams are knowledge integrators.[10] One of the challenges of the information era is in finding the information that is located within the company. Activities and interactions that occur in blogs, wikis, and social networks provide information that is often missing from expertise search systems.[11] Surveys of people in companies reveal that the following is what they look for in experts: extent of expertise, trustworthiness, communication skills, willingness to help, years of experience, and awareness of other resources. Companies such as Warner Brothers and General Motors have used the software programs (like Crowdcast) to predict revenue, ship dates, or new products from competitors, using their own employee knowledge base. Using Crowdcast, employees start out with a certain amount of virtual money. When people inside the company pose a question—such as when a new game will be ready to ship or whether a competitor's new drug will get regulatory approval—employees offer a response and choose an amount to bet on its accuracy. They can anonymously explain their reasoning. Then, if they are right, they get more money and a louder voice in the future; if they are wrong, they lose

---

[6]Thompson, B. (2005, March). *The loyalty connection: Secrets to customer retention and increased profits.* Rightnow.com

[7]U.S. Small Business Administration. (2010). *Customer service—An imperative.* sba.gov

[8]Frank, R. H., & Cook, P. J. (1995). *The winner-take-all society.* New York: Penguin.

[9]Anonymous. (1996). Microsoft teamwork. *Executive Excellence, 13*(7), 6–7.

[10]Fisher, K., & Fisher, M. D. (1998). *The distributed mind: Achieving high performance through the collective intelligence of knowledge work teams.* Chicago, IL: AMACOM American Management Association.

[11]Dorit, N., Izak, B., & Yair, W. (2009, October 29). Who Knows What? *The Wall Street Journal*, p. R4.

money and do not have as much to "bet" in the future. Star predictors get real prizes, like gift cards or lunch with the boss.[12]

The role of managers has shifted accordingly; they are no longer primarily responsible for gathering information from employees working below them in the organizational hierarchy and then making command decisions based on this information. Their new role is to identify the key resources that will best implement the team's objectives and then to facilitate the coordination of those resources for the company's purposes.

The jobs of the team members have also changed significantly. This can be viewed as a threat or a challenge. For example, in 2008, 33.7 million Americans worked from home or another out-of-office location at least one day per month.[13] Decisions may now be made far from their traditional location; indeed, sometimes they are even made by contractors, who are not employees of the company. This dramatic change in structure requires an equally dramatic reappraisal of how companies structure the work environment.

Globalization

The fourth challenge is *globalization*. An increasingly global and fast-paced economy requires people with specialized expertise, yet the specialists within a company need to work together. As acquisitions, restructurings, outsourcing, and other structural changes take place, the need for coordination becomes all the more salient. Changes in corporate structure and increases in specialization imply that there will be new boundaries among the members of an organization. Boundaries both separate and link teams within an organization, although the boundaries are not always obvious.[14] These new relationships require team members to learn how to work with others to achieve their goals. Team members must integrate through coordination and synchronization with suppliers, managers, peers, and customers. Teams of people are required to work with one another and rarely (and, in some cases, never) interact in a face-to-face fashion. With the ability to communicate with others anywhere on the planet (and beyond!), people and resources that were once remote can now be reached quickly, easily, and inexpensively. This has facilitated the development of the virtual team—groups linked by technology so effectively that it is as if they were in the same building. Furthermore, cultural differences, both profound and nuanced, can threaten the ability of teams to accomplish shared objectives.

TYPES OF TEAMS IN ORGANIZATIONS

Organizations rely on team-based arrangements to improve quality, productivity, customer service, and the experience of work for their employees. However, teams differ greatly in their degree of autonomy and control vis-à-vis the organization. Specifically, how is authority distributed in

---

[12]Miller, C. C. (2009, June 25). Start-up's software goes to employees for company forecasts [Web log post]. bits.blogs.nytimes.com

[13]Telework Revs Up as More Employers Offer Work Flexibility. (2009, February 17). World at Work press release from Dieringer Research Group's random digit dialed (RDD) telephone survey between November 6, 2008 and December 2, 2008.

[14]Alderfer, C. P. (1977). Group and intergroup relations. In J. R. Hackman & J. L. Suttle (Eds.), *Improving life at work* (pp. 227–296). Palisades, CA: Goodyear; Friedlander, F. (1987). The design of work teams. In J. W. Lorsch (Ed.), *Handbook of organizational behavior*. Upper Saddle River, NJ: Prentice Hall.

EXHIBIT 1-2 Authority of Four Illustrative Types of Work Teams

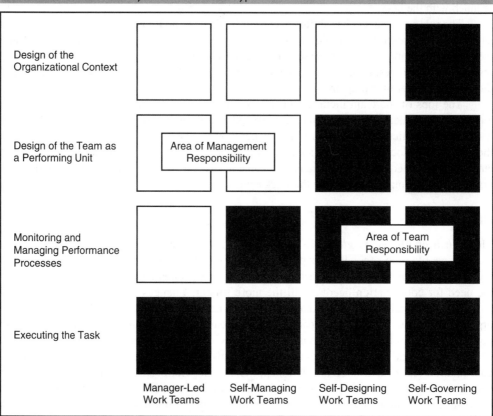

Source: Hackman, J. R. (1987). The design of work teams. In J. W. Lorsch (Ed.), *Handbook of organizational behavior.* Upper Saddle River, NJ: Prentice Hall.

the organization? Who has responsibility for the routine monitoring and management of group performance processes? Who has responsibility for creating and fine-tuning the design of the group?[15] Consider the four levels of control depicted in Exhibit 1-2.

Manager-Led Teams

The most traditional type of team is the **manager-led team**. In the manager-led team, the manager acts as the team leader and is responsible for defining the goals, methods, and functioning of the team. The team itself is responsible only for the actual execution of their assigned work. Management is responsible for monitoring and managing performance processes, overseeing design, selecting members, and interfacing with the organization. Examples of manager-led work teams include automobile assembly teams, surgery teams, sports teams, and military teams. A manager-led team typically has a dedicated, full-time, higher-ranking supervisor, as in a coal-mining crew.

---

[15]Hackman, J. R. (1987). The design of work teams. In J. W. Lorsch (Ed.), *Handbook of organizational behavior.* Upper Saddle River, NJ: Prentice Hall.

Manager-led teams provide the greatest amount of control over team members and the work they perform; they allow the leader to have control over the process and products of the team. In addition, they can be efficient, in the sense that the manager does the work of setting the goals and outlining the work to be done. In manager-led teams, managers don't have to passively observe the team make the same mistakes they did. These teams also have relatively low start-up costs. However, there can be some key disadvantages, such as diffusion of responsibility and conformity to the leader. In short, members have less autonomy and empowerment. Manager-led teams may be ideally suited for simple tasks in which there is a clear goal, such as task forces or fact-finding teams. Other examples include military squads, flight crews, and stage crews.

Self-Managing Teams

In **self-managing** or **self-regulating teams**, a manager or leader determines the overall purpose or goal of the team, but the team is at liberty to manage the methods by which to achieve that goal. Self-managed teams are increasingly common in organizations. Examples include executive search committees and managerial task forces. Self-managing teams improve productivity, quality, savings, and employee morale, as well as contribute to reductions in absenteeism and turnover.[16] These benefits have been observed in both manufacturing and service settings.

Wageman studied 43 self-managing teams in the Xerox service organization.[17] According to Wageman, seven defining features emerged in the superbly performing teams but not in the ineffective teams, including: clear direction, a team task, rewards, material resources, authority to manage their work, goals, and strategic norms (see Exhibit 1-3).

At Suma, a British grocery co-op, day-to-day operations are carried out by self-managing teams of employees, all of whom have an equal stake in the business, are responsible for multiple job functions, and are paid the same hourly wage. There's no chief executive or chairman. Decisions are made by the management committee, a team of six appointed to make the business plan work. The company holds quarterly board meetings where staff can raise any points. Also, all new staff work for 6 months in the warehouse, picking orders and driving trucks.[18] Self-managing teams build commitment, offer increased autonomy, and often enhance morale. The disadvantage is that the manager has much less control over the process and products, making it difficult to assess progress. Self-managing teams can also be more time consuming.

Self-Directing Teams

Self-directing or **self-designing teams** determine their own objectives and the methods by which to achieve them. Management has responsibility only for the team's organizational context. Self-directed teams offer the most potential for innovation, enhance goal commitment, and motivation and provide opportunity for organizational learning and change. However,

---

[16]Stewart, G. I., & Manz, C. C. (1995). Leadership and self-managing work teams: A typology and integrative model. *Human Relations, 48*(7), 747–770.
[17]Wageman, R. (1997). Critical success factors for creating superb self-managing teams. *Organizational Dynamics*, Summer, pp. 49–61.
[18]Wholesaler profile Suma. (2008, June 14). Thegrocer.com

EXHIBIT 1-3 Critical Success Factors for Self-Managing Teams

1. **Clear direction**
   * Can team members articulate a clear direction, shared by all members, of the basic purpose that the team exists to achieve?
2. **A real team task**
   * Is the team assigned collective responsibility for all the team's customers and major outputs?
   * Is the team required to make collective decisions about work strategies (rather than leaving it to individuals)?
   * Are members cross-trained, able to help each other?
   * Does the team get team-level data and feedback about its performance?
   * Is the team required to meet frequently, and does it do so?
3. **Team rewards**
   * Counting all reward dollars available, are more than 80 percent available to teams only and not to individuals?
4. **Basic material resources**
   * Does the team have its own meeting space?
   * Can the team easily get basic materials needed for work?
5. **Authority to manage the work**
   * Does the team have the authority to decide the following (without first receiving special authority):
   —How to meet client demands
   —Which actions to take and when
   —Whether to change their work strategies when they deem necessary
6. **Team goals**
   * Can the team articulate specific goals?
   * Do these goals stretch their performance?
   * Have they specified a time by which they intend to accomplish these goals?
7. **Strategy norms**
   * Do team members encourage each other to detect problems without the leader's intervention?
   * Do members openly discuss differences in what members have to contribute to the team?
   * Do members encourage experimentation with new ways of operating?
   * Does the team actively seek to learn from other teams?

Source: Wageman, R. (1997, Summer). Critical success factors for creating superb self-managing teams. *Organizational Dynamics, 26*(1), 49–61.

self-directed or self-designing teams are extremely time consuming, have the greatest potential for conflict, and can be very costly to build. (For a step-by-step guide to setting up self-designing teams, see *The New Self-Directed Work Teams*.[19]) Furthermore, it can be extremely difficult to monitor their progress. Other disadvantages include marginalization of the team and lack of team legitimacy. However, self-directed teams are often capable of great accomplishments (see Exhibit 1-4 for an example).

---

[19]Orsburn, J. D., Moran, L., Musselwhite, E., & Zenger, J. H. (2000). *The new self-directed work teams*. New York: McGraw-Hill.

EXHIBIT 1-4 An Example of a Self-Directing Team

It's Wednesday evening at Carnegie Hall. The air is charged with the excitement generated when people know that they are about to experience an event that will stimulate their senses and challenge their minds. As the Orpheus Chamber Orchestra takes the stage to warm applause, the musicians exude confidence. There's something different about this orchestra: There is no conductor. Founded in 1972 by cellist Julian Fifer, Orpheus gives every person great power to direct great music. Orpheus is designed to rely on the skills, abilities, and passionate commitment of the members, rather than on the monolithic leadership of a conductor. The decision to give power to the musicians—a radical innovation in the orchestra world—required a structural model that was fundamentally different from the rigid command-and-control hierarchy universally employed by traditional orchestras. The original members of Orpheus found their inspiration in chamber music, a world grounded in democratic values, where small ensembles (generally fewer than 10 musicians) function as self-directing teams, and where power, responsibility, leadership, and motivation rest entirely with the team.

Source: Seifter, H., & Economy, P. (2001). *Leadership ensemble: Lessons in collaborative management from the world's only conductorless orchestra.* New York: Henry Holt & Company, Inc.

Self-designing teams may be ideally suited for complex, ill-defined, or ambiguous problems and next-generation planning. Some companies have "free time" policies that allow employees to pursue novel projects they feel passionate about. Biotechnology company Genentech has a policy of "discretionary time," and there are no set limits. At Google, employees have "20 percent time" for their projects. Both Genentech and Google have codified a degree of employee freedom, but employees are expected to get approval for their projects from managers. Independent projects that sprouted led to the Gmail electronic mail service, the Google News service, and social networking site, Orkut. At MySpace, executives create an environment that stimulates innovation by taking down walls in-between cubicles and providing "designing areas" equipped with white boards where employees can draw or display their ideas as they talk to coworkers over coffee.[20]

In 2004, RL Wolfe, a midsize plastic pipe manufacturing company introduced self-directing teams. By 2007, the plant was outperforming other plants that still enforced a hierarchical model.[21] Self-directing teams decide who does which work; they schedule training, vacations, and overtime and monitor their own performance issues, such as lack of productivity or lack of work ethic. However, this is seldom a problem. Even though there are no incentives other than promotion on the basis of skills, technicians are often motivated by the work itself, the drive for perfection, and pride in being industry leaders. The leader of these teams is responsible for listening, informing, and focusing on costs.

---

[20]Steel, E. (2009, October 15). MySpace's Reboot, From Exec Suite to Cubicles. *Wall Street Journal.* online.wsj.com; Frauenheim, E. (2006, April 24). On the clock but off on their own: Pet-project programs set to gain wider acceptance. *Workforce Management,* pp. 40–41.
[21]Garvin, D., & Collins, E. (2009, November 30). RL Wolfe: Implementing self-directed teams. *The Harvard Business Review.* Boston, MA: Harvard Business Publishing.

Self-Governing Teams

Self-governing teams and boards of directors are usually responsible for executing a task, managing their own performance processes, designing the group, and designing the organizational context. They have a wide latitude of authority and responsibility. In many companies, the president or chief operating officer has been replaced with an executive, self-governing team.[22] Movie studio Metro-Goldwyn-Mayer Inc. replaced CEO Harry Sloan in 2009 with a three-member team.[23] In certain cases, organizations set up a self-governing (autonomous) team to investigate serious problems. The Securities and Exchange Commission did this after failing to learn of the ponzi scheme perpetrated by investor Bernie Madoff until after his former investors lost a combined $18 billion.[24]

There are trade-offs involved with each of these four types of teams. Self-governing and self-directed teams provide the greatest potential in terms of commitment and participation, but they are also at the greatest risk of misdirection. When decisions are pushed down in organizations, team goals and interests may be at odds with organizational interests. Unless everyone in the organization is aware of the company's interests and goals, poor decisions (often with the best of intentions) may be made. An organization that chooses a manager-led group is betting that a manager can run things more effectively than a team can. If it is believed that the team can do the job better, a self-governing or self-designing team may be appropriate. One implication of this is that the manager's traditional role as a collector of information is less and less important.

SOME OBSERVATIONS ABOUT TEAMS AND TEAMWORK

There is a lot of folklore and unfounded intuition when it comes to teams and teamwork. We want to set the record straight by exposing some of the observations that managers find most useful. This is not an exhaustive list, obviously, but we believe the factors on this list have the most value for leaders when it comes to understanding how teams perform, change, and grow.

Teams Are Not Always the Answer

When companies are in trouble, they often restructure into teams. However, organizing people into teams does not solve problems; if not done thoughtfully, this may even cause more problems. For every case of team success, there is an equally compelling case of team failure. Teams can outperform the best member of the group, but there are no guarantees. Admitting the inefficiency of teams is hard, especially when most of us would like to believe the Gestalt principle that the whole is greater than the sum of its parts! Teams are not a panacea for organizations; they often fail and are frequently overused or poorly designed. In the best circumstances, teams provide insight, creativity, and cross-fertilization of knowledge in a way that a person working independently cannot. In the wrong circumstances, teamwork can lead to confusion, delay, and poor decision making.

---

[22]Ancona, D. G., & Nadler, D. A. (1989). Top hats and executive tales: Designing the senior team. *Senior Management Review, 31*(1), 19–28.
[23]Wilkerson, D. B. (2009, August 18). *MGM's CEO out in reshuffle.* MarketWatch.com
[24]U.S. Securities and Trade Commission. (2008, September16). *Statement regarding Madoff investigation.* sec.gov

Managers Fault the Wrong Causes for Team Failure

Imagine yourself in the following situation: The wonderful team that you put together last year has collapsed into lethargy. The new product line is not forthcoming, conflict has erupted, and there is high turnover. What has gone wrong? If you are like most managers, you place the blame on one of two things: (1) external, uncontrollable forces (e.g., a bad economy) or (2) the people on the team (e.g., difficult personalities). Conveniently for the manager, both of these problems do not directly implicate poor leadership. However, according to most research investigations, neither of these causes is the actual culprit. Most team problems are not explained by external problems or personality problems. Faulty team design is a key causal factor in underperforming teams.

The misattribution error is the tendency for managers to attribute the causes of team failure to forces beyond their personal control. Leaders may blame individual team members, the lack of resources, or a competitive environment. When the leader points to a problem team member, the team's problems can be neatly and clearly understood as emanating from one source. This protects the leader's ego (and, in some cases, the manager's job), but it stifles learning and destroys morale. It is more likely that the team's poor performance is due to a structural, rather than personal, cause. Furthermore, it is likely that several things, not just one, are at work.

Managers Fail to Recognize Their Team-Building Responsibilities

Many new managers conceive of their role as building the most effective relationships they can with each individual subordinate; they erroneously equate managing their team with managing the individual people on the team.[25] These managers rarely rely on group-based forums for problem solving and diagnosis. Instead, they spend their time in one-on-one meetings. Teamwork is expected to be a natural consequence. As a result, many decisions are based upon limited information, and decision outcomes can backfire in unexpected and negative ways. Leaders need to help managers learn about teamwork.

Experimenting with Failures Leads to Better Teams

It may seem ironic, but one of the most effective ways to learn is to experience failure. Evidence of this is provided by the letdown that followed the attempt of Intuit Inc. of Mountain View, California to target young tax filers by combining tax-filing with hip-hop style. Using a specifically designed Web site, RockYourRefund.com, Intuit offered discounts to Expedia Inc. and Best Buy Co. as well as depositing tax refunds into prepaid Visa cards that were issued by hip-hop mogul Russell Simmons. This attempt generated very few returns. The campaign team learned that young people don't visit advertising look-a-like Web sites, and, later, the team received an award from Chairman Scott Cook, who said, "It's only a failure if we fail to get the learning." Even more, Intuit started sessions that focused on learning from failures.[26] A failed team effort should be viewed as a critical source of information from which to learn. However, when you are the one failing, failure is hard to embrace: Our defense systems go into overdrive at the inkling that something we do is not

[25]Hill, M. (1982). Group versus individual performance: Are N + 1 heads better than one? *Psychological Bulletin, 91*, 517–539.
[26]How failure breeds success. (2006, July 10). *BusinessWeek*. Cover story.

above average. The true mark of a valued team member is a willingness to learn from mistakes. However, this learning can come only when people take personal responsibility for their actions.

Teams have a flatter learning curve than do most individuals; it takes teams longer to "get on their feet." However, teams have greater potential than do individuals. We discuss this further in Chapter 2.

Conflict Among Team Members Is Not Always a Bad Thing

Many leaders naively boast that their teams are successful because they never have conflict. However, it is a fallacy to believe that conflict is detrimental to effective teamwork. In fact, conflict may be necessary for effective decision making in teams. Conflict among team members can foment accuracy, insight, understanding, trust, and innovation.

Strong Leadership Is Not Always Necessary for Strong Teams

A common myth is that to function effectively, teams need a strong, powerful, and charismatic leader. In general, leaders who control all the details, manage all the key relationships in the team, have all the good ideas, and use the team to execute their "vision" are usually overworked and underproductive. Teams with strong leaders sometimes succumb to flawed and disastrous decision making.

As we discuss in Chapter 11, a leader has two main functions: a design function, meaning that the leader structures the team environment (working conditions, access to information, incentives, training, and education), and a coaching function, meaning that the leader has direct interaction with the team.[27]

Good Teams Can Still Fail Under the Wrong Circumstances

Teams are often depicted as mavericks: bucking authority, striking out on their own, and asking for permission only after the fact. Such cases do occur, but they are rare and tend to be one-shot successes. Most managers want consistently successful teams.

To be successful in the long run, teams need ongoing resources and support. By resources, we mean more than just money. Teams need information and education. In too many cases, teams tackle a problem that has already been solved by someone else in the company, but a lack of communication prevents this critical knowledge from reaching the current task force.

To lay the best groundwork for teams, it is important to consider the goals and resources of the team: Are the team's goals well defined? Does everyone know them? Are the goals consistent with the objectives of other members of the organization? If not, how will the inevitable conflict be managed? Does everyone on the team have access to the resources necessary to successfully achieve the goal? Is the organizational hierarchy designed to give team members access to these resources efficiently? If not, it might be necessary to reconsider the governance structure within which the team must operate. What are the rights of the team members in pursuing their duties, who can they contact, and what information can they command? It is also important to assess the incentive structure existing for team members and for those outside the team with whom team members must interact. Are the team members' incentives aligned? Are team members'

---

[27]Hackman, J. R. (2002). *Leading teams: Setting the stage for great performances*. Boston, MA: Harvard Business School Press.

incentives aligned with those of the group and the organization, for instance, to cooperate with one another and to fully share information and resources? There is no cookie-cutter solution to team structure. For instance, it may be appropriate for team members to compete with one another (in which case, cooperation may not be an achievable feature of the group dynamic). Choosing the structure of the group and the incentives that motivate the individuals inside it are essential factors contributing to the success of any team.

Retreats Will Not Fix All the Conflicts Between Team Members

Teams often get into trouble. Members may fight, slack off, or simply be unable to keep up with their responsibilities, potentially resulting in angry or dissatisfied customers. When conflict arises, people search for a solution to the team problem. A common strategy is to have a "team-building retreat," "corporate love-in," or "ropes and boulders course" where team members try to address underlying concerns and build trust by engaging in activities—like rock climbing—that are not part of what they ordinarily do as a team. Perhaps this is why one review of the Fish! Movement, posted on Amazon.com, says of such retreats, "What's sad is that companies actually think that throwing fish around is something that should be done. [The company] I worked for had a fish throw...an actual afternoon dedicated to throwing dead fish at each other....I was burned out on the philosophy after two days of training and I voluntarily left the company two months after being hired."[28]

A team retreat is a popular way for team members to build mutual trust and commitment. A retreat may involve team members spending a weekend camping and engaging in cooperative, shared, structured activities. This usually results in a good time had by all. However, unless retreats address the structural and design problems that plague the team day to day in the work environment, they may fail. At San Francisco's Skyline Construction, one employee from every department is selected each fall to participate in a 2-day retreat at a hotel where the company develops its strategic goals for the coming year. Employees are encouraged to come forward with problems—and then brainstorm solutions together. When some project managers reported that they felt overworked and burned-out due to juggling multiple duties, they introduced an internship program.[29]

Design problems are best addressed by examining the team in its own environment while team members are engaged in actual work. For this reason, it is important to take a more comprehensive approach to analyzing team problems. Retreats are often insufficient because they encourage managers to attribute team failures to interpersonal dynamics, rather than examining and changing deeper, more systemic issues.

WHAT LEADERS TELL US ABOUT THEIR TEAMS

To gain a more accurate picture of the challenges leaders face in their organizations when designing, leading, and motivating teams, we conducted a survey, spanning 13 years, of over 1,000 executives and managers from a variety of industries.[30] Here are some highlights of what they told us.

---

[28]Walker, R. (2002, August). Hook, line, sinker. *Inc.*, pp. 85–88.
[29]Spors, K. K. (2009, September 28). Top small workplaces 2009. *Wall Street Journal*, p. R1.
[30]Thompson, L. (2010). Leading high impact teams survey. Kellogg Executive Programs.

Most Common Type of Team

The most common type is the management team, followed by cross-functional, operations, and service teams. Cross-functional teams epitomize the challenges outlined earlier in this chapter. They represent the greatest potential, in terms of integrating talent, skills, and ideas, but because of their diversity of training and responsibility, they provide fertile ground for conflict.

Team Size

Team size varies dramatically, from 3 to 80 members, with an average of 15.20. However, the modal team size is 8. These numbers can be compared with the optimum team size. As we discuss later in the book, teams should generally have fewer than 10 members—more like 5 or 6.

Team Autonomy Versus Manager Control

Most of the managers in our survey were in self-managing teams, followed by manager-led teams, with self-directing teams distinctly less common (see Exhibit 1-5). There is an inevitable tension between the degree of manager control in a team and the ability of team members to guide and manage their own actions. Manager-led teams provide more control, but less innovation than stems from autonomy. We do not suggest that all teams should be self-directing. Rather, it is important to understand the trade-offs and what is required for each type of team to function effectively.

Team Longevity

Teams vary a great deal in terms of how long they have been in existence. On average, teams are in existence for 1 to 2 years (see Exhibit 1-6).

The Most Frustrating Aspect of Teamwork

Managers considered several possible sources of frustration in managing teams. The most frequently cited cause of frustration and challenge in teams is developing and sustaining high motivation, followed by minimizing confusion and coordination problems (see Exhibit 1-7). We discuss issues of motivation in Chapter 2; also, we focus on team compensation and incentives in

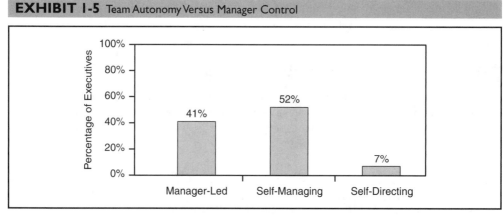

EXHIBIT 1-5 Team Autonomy Versus Manager Control

Source: Thompson, L. (2010). Leading high impact teams: Tools for teams. Kellogg Executive Program.

EXHIBIT 1-6 Team Longevity

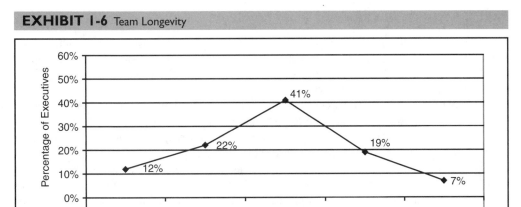

Source: Thompson, L. (2010). Leading high impact teams: Tools for teams. Kellogg Executive Program.

EXHIBIT 1-7 The Most Frustrating Aspects of Teamwork

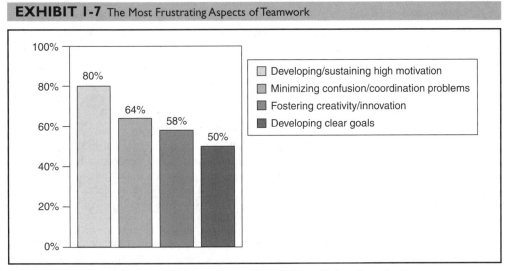

Source: Thompson, L. (2010). Leading high impact teams: Tools for teams. Kellogg Executive Program.

Chapter 3. We analyze conflict (and ways to effectively manage it within a team) in Chapter 8 and address creativity in Chapter 9. Not surprisingly, among the skills on the most-wanted list for managerial education are developing and sustaining high motivation, developing clear goals, fostering creativity and innovation, training, and minimizing confusion and coordination problems. Consequently, we designed this book to prepare managers and reeducate executives in how to effectively deal with each of these concerns.

DEVELOPING YOUR TEAM-BUILDING SKILLS

This book focuses on three skills: accurate diagnosis of team problems, research-based intervention, and expert learning.

Skill 1: Accurate Diagnosis of Team Problems

It is difficult to identify a single measure of team functioning because team effectiveness is hard to define. For example, perhaps your organization beat the competition in winning a large contract, but the contract was ultimately not very profitable. Was this a victory or a failure? What will be the implications for future competition?

Many people make the mistake of looking for causes *after* they find effects. In the scientific literature, this is known as **sampling on the dependent variable**. For example, if your goal is to identify the determinants of a successful team, it may appear useful to look for effective teams in your organization and then try to determine what is common among them. This sounds logical, until you realize that there may be many common factors that have nothing to do with making a team successful. Or there may be common features that interfere with good teamwork, but are nonetheless difficult to detect—perhaps precisely because they are common to all the teams, successful or not. One important example of this is the institutional background of the company, for example, taking certain established practices for granted, such as operating procedures, information sources, and even contractual relationships. In this case, the team may be effective, but not as effective as it might otherwise be. A manager who is also entrenched in the institutional framework of the company may perceive a team as effective, while overlooking its shortcomings. Thus, it is essential to be as independent and critical as possible when analyzing team effectiveness.

How do you avoid the trap of sampling on the dependent variable? From a methodological point of view, you can do one of two things: (1) identify *a preexisting baseline or control group*—that is, a comparison group (in this case, unsuccessful teams)—and look for differences between the two; or (2) do an experiment in which you provide different information, education, communication, and so on to one group (randomly assigned) but not the other. Then look for differences. Unfortunately, most executives do not have the time or resources to do either of these things. This book provides insights based upon research that has done these things before drawing conclusions. However, nothing can substitute for a thoughtful understanding of the environment in which the team operates, the incentives facing team members, and so on. We discuss these factors throughout this book.

Another problem is called **hindsight bias**, or the "I knew it all along" fallacy.[31] This is the tendency to believe that something seems obvious, even inevitable, after you learn about it when you have not predicted (or cannot predict) what will happen. This can result in an unfortunate form of overconfidence: Managers think they know everything, when in fact they don't. We often see managers engage in post hoc justification rather than careful reasoning. The best way to avoid this trap is to read actively to learn about other possibilities, critically examine your assumptions, and be open to a change of mind once you have the facts. As you read this book, some things will surprise you, but much will seem obvious. As a general principle, do not rely on your intuition; rather, test your assumptions.

Skill 2: Research-Based Intervention

For every managerial problem, there are a dozen purported solutions and quick fixes. How can a manager knowledgeably choose among them? The answer, we think, is the science of teamwork.

Team and group-related research is based on scientific theory. Group-related research accounts for over one-sixth of all the research in social psychology and one-third of the most

---

[31]Fischhoff, B. (1975). Hindsight does not equal foresight: The effect of outcome knowledge on judgment under uncertainty. *Journal of Experimental Psychology: Human Perception and Performance, 1,* 288–299.

cited papers in social psychology journals focus on groups and teams.[32] The interventions presented in this book have a key quality going for them: They are all theory based and empirically sound. This means that they are not based on naive, intuitive perceptions; rather, they have been scientifically examined. This is known as **evidence-based management**.[33] This book was written to provide managers with up-to-date, scientifically based information about how best to manage their teams.

Skill 3: Expert Learning

Effective managers make mistakes, but they don't make the same mistakes twice. Expert learning involves the ability to continually learn from experience. One of the great fallacies about learning is that people reach a point where they have acquired all the knowledge they need; in contrast, great leaders are always learning. In this book, we use a model that we call **expert learning** to refer to how managers can continually benefit, even from the most mundane experiences. Consider Chris Argyris's distinction between single-loop versus double-loop learning.[34] According to Argyris, **single-loop learning** is learning that is primarily one-dimensional. For example, a leader may believe that she has nothing to learn from a subordinate but that the subordinate can learn from her. Therefore, the interactions between the leader and the subordinate will be primarily one-directional, or single loop. In contrast, Argyris argues that effective leaders engage in **double-loop learning** processes, which involve a reciprocal interchange between leaders and teams. This means, of course, that leaders not only coach and direct and instruct their teams, but that teams also help their leaders learn.

Another important aspect of learning is the use of examples to illustrate and convey concepts. Experiential and example-based learning is more effective than didactic (lecture-based) learning.[35] An important key to whether knowledge is actually used or remains inert is what Whitehead, over 80 years ago, called the **inert knowledge problem**.[36] The key to unlocking the pervasive inert knowledge problem lies in how the manager processes the information, and when managers link examples to concepts, they learn better.[37] Thus, in this book, we attempt to provide several ways of looking at the same problem via a combination of theory, research, and real business practices.

A WARNING

We believe that teamwork, like other interdependent social behaviors, is best perfected in an active, experimental, and dynamic environment. Thus, to fully benefit from this book, it is necessary for you to actively engage in teamwork and examine your own behavior. It may seem somewhat heretical to make the point in a textbook that team-building skills cannot be learned exclusively from a textbook, but we do so anyway.

---

[32]Abrams, D. A., De Moura, G. R., Marques, J. M., & Hutchison, P. (2008). Innovation credit: When can leaders oppose their group's norms? *Journal of Personality and Social Psychology, 95*(3), 662–678.

[33]Pfeffer, J., & Sutton, R. (2006). Evidence- based management. *Harvard Business Review, 84*(1), 62–74.

[34]Argyris, C. (1977a). Double loop learning. *Harvard Business Review, 55*(5), 115–125.

[35]Nadler, J., Thompson, L., & Van Boven, L. (2003). Learning negotiation skills: Four models of knowledge creation and transfer. *Management Science, 49*(4), 529–540; Gentner, D., Loewenstein, J., & Thompson, L. (2003). Learning and transfer: A general role for analogical encoding. *Journal of Educational Psychology, 95*, 393–408.

[36]Whitehead, A. N. (1929). *The aims of education.* New York: MacMillan.

[37]Thompson, L., Loewenstein, J., & Gentner, D. (2000). Avoiding missed opportunities in managerial life: Analogical training more powerful than individual case training. *Organizational Behavior and Human Decision Processes, 82*(1), 60–75.

We strongly urge you to work through the models and ideas presented here in the context of your own experience. We can think of no better way to do this than in a classroom setting that offers the opportunity for online, applied, experiential learning. It is easy to watch, analyze, and critique other teams, but much more challenging to engage in effective team behavior yourself. We hope that what you gain from this book, and the work you do on your own through team-building exercises, is the knowledge of how to be an effective team member, team leader, and team designer. In the long run, we hope this book will help you in developing your own experience, expertise, and models of how you can best function with teams.

Conclusion

There is no foolproof scientific formula for designing and maintaining an effective team. If there were, it would have been discovered by now. In some ways, a team is like the human body: No one knows the exact regimen for staying healthy over time. However, we have some very good information about the benefits of a lean diet, exercise, stress reduction, wellness maintenance, and early detection of disease. The same goes for teamwork. Just as we rely on science to cure disease and to advance health, this book takes an unabashedly scientific approach to the study and improvement of teamwork in organizations. There is a lot of misperception about teams and teamwork. Intuition and luck can only take us so far; in fact, if misapplied, they may get us into trouble. In the next chapter, we undertake a performance analysis of teamwork, asking these questions: How do we know a healthy and productive team when we see it? What are the biggest "killers" and "diseases" of teams? And, more important, what do we need to do to keep a team functioning effectively over time? In Chapter 3, we deal with the question of incentives and rewards for good teamwork. Part II focuses on internal team dynamics, and Part III focuses on the bigger picture—the team in the organization.

2

Performance and Productivity

Team Performance Criteria and Threats to Productivity

Prior to April 2009 no one had ever heard of "swine flu" (H1N1). However, on April 26, 2009, the U.S. Department of Health and Human Services (HHS) declared a nationwide public health emergency when the extremely virulent form of the flu began claiming lives of young and old across the globe. Working as part of a team led by the HHS, the Food and Drug Administration (FDA) stood ready with a plan in place as soon as the spread of H1N1 became evident. A disparate and talented group of laboratory scientists, medical reviewers, epidemiologists, product experts, and field inspectors used an incident management system and cross-cutting teams to act speedily. The FDA readied seven cross-cutting teams, whose members overlapped and shared critical information and updates, including the vaccine team, the antiviral team, the in vitro diagnostics team, the personal protective equipment team, the blood team, the drug shortage team, and the consumer protection team.[1]

Most teams do not have to operate in life-or-death situations like the FDA and the HHS, but they do need to work together in a productive fashion for their companies to survive. Ideally, teams could benefit from a model or set of guidelines that would tell them how to organize and how to deal with inevitable threats to their goal achievement. Such a model would serve two purposes: *description*, or the interpretation of events so that managers can come up with an accurate analysis of the situation, and *prescription*, or a recommendation on what to do to fix the situation.

In this chapter, we introduce a model of team performance. The model tells us the conditions that have to be in place for teams to function effectively and how to address problems with performance. The remainder of the chapter focuses on different parts of the model and provides choices to enact change.

---

[1]U.S. Department of Health and Human Services. U.S. Food and Drug Administration. (2009, May 12). *H1N1 Flu: FDA Responds Quickly to Protect the Public's Health.* fda.gov

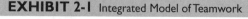

EXHIBIT 2-1 Integrated Model of Teamwork

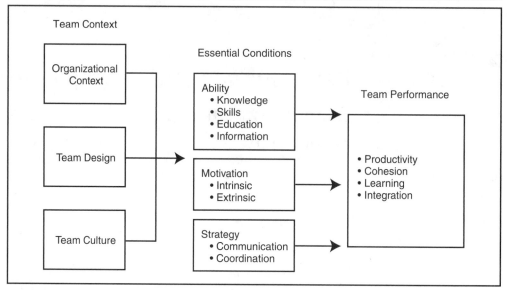

AN INTEGRATED MODEL OF SUCCESSFUL TEAM PERFORMANCE

The best models of teamwork focus on the internal processes of teams as well as how the team works with other units.[2] Exhibit 2-1 is a descriptive–prescriptive model of team performance. It tells us what to expect in terms of team performance and suggests ways to improve the functioning of teams. As promised in Chapter 1, the model in Exhibit 2-1 is based upon empirical research. This chapter steps through each element of the model.

The message of the model is actually quite simple: the context of the team (referring to its internal processes and external constraints and opportunities) affects the team's ability to do three essential things: perform effectively, build and sustain motivation, and coordinate people. These essential conditions are the causal determinants of the team's performance—that is, whether it succeeds or fails. The remainder of the chapter is divided into three key sections corresponding to the three pieces of the model: team context, essential conditions, and team performance. We begin with the team context.

Team Context

The **team context** includes the larger organizational setting within which the team does its work, the design of the team in terms of its internal functioning, and the culture of the team. Teams rely on their organization to provide resources, funding, and individuals for membership, and so on.

---

[2]Hackman, J. R. (1987). The design of work teams. In J. W. Lorsch (Ed.), *Handbook of organizational behavior.* Upper Saddle River, NJ: Prentice Hall; Hackman, J. R. (1990). Introduction: Work teams in organizations: An oriented framework. In J. Hackman (Ed.), *Groups that work and those that don't.* San Francisco, CA: Jossey-Bass; Hill, S. (1995). The social organization of boards of directors. *British Journal of Sociology, 46*(2), 245–278.

In Chapter 1, we stated that teams operate in a social context that shapes and confines behavior. As we discuss in Parts II and III, the team leader must think not only about the internal functioning of the team (i.e., ability, motivation, and coordination among team members) but also about the external functioning of the team, including the organizational context, team design, and group norms.

ORGANIZATIONAL CONTEXT   The organizational context includes the basic structure of the organization (e.g., lateral, hierarchical), the information system, the education system, and the reward system. It includes organizational policy and material and physical resources required to accomplish group tasks. Even if a team possesses spectacular skills, motivation, and coordination, lack of critical organizational infrastructure such as information, tools, equipment, space, raw materials, money, and human resources will hurt team performance. Teams ideally need a supportive organizational context—one that recognizes and welcomes their existence; responds to their requests for information, resources, and action; legitimizes the team's task and how they are achieving it; and expects the team to succeed.[3]

TEAM DESIGN   Team design refers to the observable structure of the team (e.g., manager led or self-managing). It refers to the leadership style within the team, functional roles, communication patterns, composition of the team, and training of members. In contrast to the team's culture, the team design is the deliberate aspect of teamwork. Although the team's culture evolves and grows and is not under the direct control of a manager, the design of a team is a deliberate decision or choice made by managers. Some managers may not realize that by not making a choice or leaving teamwork up to natural forces, they are, in fact, designing their team. We urge the leaders and managers of teams to carefully think through their options when designing their team.

TEAM CULTURE   *Culture* is the personality of a team. Team culture includes the unstated, implicit aspects of the team that are not discussed in a formal fashion but that nevertheless shape behavior. Member roles, norms, and patterns of behaving and thinking are influenced by the team's culture. One way in which teams develop their culture is by imposing ways of thinking and acting that are considered acceptable. A *norm* is a generally agreed-upon set of rules that guides behavior of team members. Norms differ from organizational policies in that they are informal and unwritten. Often, norms are so subtle that team members are not consciously aware of them. Team norms regulate behaviors such as honesty, manner of dress, punctuality, and emotional expression. Norms can either be prescriptive, dictating what should be done, or proscriptive, dictating behaviors that should be avoided.

Norms that favor innovation[4] or incorporate shared expectations of success[5] may foster team effectiveness. Often, culture is more a property of work units than the entire organization. This means that certain norms may exist in teams but not the larger organization. The attitudes of one's closest peers (known as referent groups) strongly affect behaviors like absenteeism, more so than the norms established by the formal organizational units in which such referent groups are nested.[6] In the classic study of organizational norm setting, two teams in the

---

[3]Bushe, G. R. (1984). Quality circles in quality of work life projects: Problems and prospects for increasing employee participation. *Canadian Journal of Community Mental Health, 3*(2), 101–113.

[4]Cummings, T. G., & Mohrman, S. A. (1987). Self-designing organizations: Towards implementing quality-of-work-life innovations. In R. W. Woodman & W. A. Pasmore (Eds.), *Research in organizational change and development* (Vol. 1, pp. 275–310). Greenwich, CT: JAI Press.

[5]Shea, G. P., & Guzzo, R. A. (1987, Spring). Group effectiveness: What really matters? *Sloan Management Review, 28*(3), 25–31.

[6]Bamberger, P., & Biron, M. (2007). Group norms and excessive absenteeism: The role of peer referent others. *Organizational Behavior and Human Decision Processes, 103,* 179–196.

Western Electric Company's Hawthorne Works developed highly different norms, even though they were in the same shop. One group spent much time in conversation and debate, played games involving small bets, and maintained uniformly high output. In contrast, the other group traded jobs (a prohibited activity), engaged in joking, and maintained uniformly low output.[7]

Norms develop as a consequence of precedent. The behaviors that emerge at a team's first meeting often define how the team operates in the future—just look at the consistency of seating arrangements in business meetings. Norms also develop because of carryovers from other situations or in response to an explicit statement by a superior or coworker. They may also result from critical events in the team's history. **Goal contagion** is a form of norm setting in which people adopt a goal held by others.[8] Goal contagion is more likely between people who belong to the same group.[9] We cover norms in greater detail in Part II.

Essential Conditions for Successful Team Performance

A number of factors must be in place for a team to be successful.[10] The team members must:

1. Bring adequate knowledge and skill to bear on the task.
2. Exert sufficient motivation and effort to accomplish the task at an acceptable level of performance.
3. Coordinate their activities and communication.

Next, we discuss each of these essential conditions in greater detail.

KNOWLEDGE, SKILL, AND ABILITY   For teams to perform effectively, members must have the requisite teamwork knowledge, skill, and ability, or **KSA**s, to perform the task.[11] This requires that the manager appropriately match people with the right skills to the tasks at hand and to the organizational human resource structure itself. There are five crucial skills for team members:[12]

1. *Conflict resolution* (recognize and encourage desirable team conflict, but discourage undesirable ones)
2. *Collaborative problem solving* (recognize the obstacles to collaborative group problem solving and implement appropriate corrective actions)
3. *Communication* (listen nonevaluatively, and appropriately use active listening techniques)
4. *Goal setting and performance management* (establish specific, challenging, and accepted team goals)
5. *Planning and task coordination* (coordinate and synchronize activities, information, and task interdependencies between team members)

---

[7]Homans, G. (1950). *The human group.* New York: Harcourt Brace.

[8]Aarts, H., Gollwitzer, P. M., & Hassin, R. R. (2004). Goal contagion: Perceiving is for pursuing. *Journal of Personality and Social Psychology, 87,* 23–37.

[9]Loersch, C., Aarts, H., Payne, B. K., & Jefferis, V. E. (2008). The influence of social groups on goal contagion. *Journal of Experimental Social Psychology, 44,* 1555–1558.

[10]Steiner, I. (1972). *Group process and productivity.* New York: Academic Press; Hackman, "Design of work teams."

[11]Stevens, M. A., & Campion, M. J. (1994). The knowledge, skill, and ability requirements for teamwork: Implications for human resource management. *Journal of Management, 20,* 503–530; Chen, G., Donahue, L. M., & Klimoski, R. J. (2004). Training undergraduates to work in organizational teams. *Academy of Management: Learning and Education, 3*(1), 27–40.

[12]Stevens & Campion, "The knowledge, skill, and ability requirements for teamwork."

Team Member Skills   One consistent predictor of team effectiveness is team members' cognitive ability. For example, the average level of team members' cognitive abilities in military tank crews, assembly and maintenance teams, and service teams directly predicts their effectiveness. Conscientiousness, as a trait, also predicts effective team performance in assembly and maintenance teams and service teams.[13]

An effective team needs people not only with the technical skills necessary to perform the work but also with interpersonal skills, decision-making skills, and problem-solving skills. Team members who demonstrate greater mastery of teamwork knowledge are also those who perform better on their teams. Field data from 92 teams in a U.S. Air Force officer development program revealed that teamwork knowledge increased task proficiency.[14] Anyone who is a member of a team fully understands that not all of the work of teams is accomplished in the physical presence of the other group members. What types of work are best performed as a team, in the presence of a team, or independently? Teams are superior to individuals at analyzing information, convergent thinking, and assimilating information. However, teams are worse than individuals at divergent thinking.

Moreover, because teams increase performance pressure and performance anxiety, the performance of well-intentioned team members may be hindered. For experts, the physical presence of the team can be a great benefit, because the presence of others increases motivation to perform, and the expert knows the skill sets required. However, for people who are not experts, the presence of others can hinder performance. For example, Barb Linquist, a swimmer at the U.S. Open, "choked" when she heard the announcer reciting the accomplishments of her competitors. "I was next to a swimmer that I had read about. I got really flustered by hearing her accomplishments. . . . I didn't concentrate on my race and. . .I finished last."[15]

Choking under pressure occurs when a person's performance declines despite incentives for optimal performance.[16]

Learning Curves and Expertise   The physical presence of other people is stimulating, and this greater arousal acts as a motivator on behavior. Whatever we might be doing, we do with more "gusto" when in the presence of other people, especially our team. However, there is a catch: The presence of other people enhances performance for well-learned behaviors (but hinders performance for less well-learned behaviors). Thus, greater arousal or stimulation enhances our performance on tasks that are well learned, but hinders our performance on novel tasks. The presence of other people triggers one of two responses: challenge (if someone is an expert) or threat (if someone is not an expert). Moreover, the cardiovascular responses of people while they perform a well-learned task in the presence of others provide

---

[13]Tziner, A., & Eden, D. (1985). Effects of crew composition on crew performance: Does the whole equal the sum of its parts? *Journal of Applied Psychology, 70*, 85–93; Barrick, M. R., Stewart, G. L., Neubert, M. J., & Mount, M. K. (1998). Relating member ability and personality to work-team processes and team effectiveness. *Journal of Applied Psychology, 83*, 377–391; Neuman, G. A., & Wright, J. (1999). Team effectiveness: Beyond skills and cognitive ability. *Journal of Applied Psychology, 84*(3), 376–389; Neuman, G. A., Wagner, S. H., & Christiansen, N. D. (1999). The relationship between work-team personality composition and the job performance of teams. *Groups and Organization Management, 24*, 28–45.

[14]Hirschfeld, R., Jordan, M., Field, H., Giles, W., & Armenakis, A. (2006). Becoming team players: Team members' mastery of teamwork knowledge as a predictor of team task proficiency and observed teamwork effectiveness. *Journal of Applied Psychology, 91*(2), 467–474.

[15]Hudepohl, D. (2001, March 1). Face your fears. *Sports Illustrated for Women*, p. 53.

[16]Baumeister, R. F., & Steinhilber, A. (1984). Paradoxical effects of supportive audiences on performance under pressure: The home field disadvantage in sports championships. *Journal of Personality and Social Psychology, 47*(1), 85–93.

physiological evidence that experts feel challenged—increased cardiac response and decreased vascular resistance.[17] However, if people are performing an unlearned task in the presence of others, they go into "threat mode"—increased cardiac response and increased vascular resistance. Consider, for example, what happens to pool players when they are observed by others in pool halls.[18] Novice players perform worse when someone is watching. In contrast, expert players' games improve dramatically when they are observed. Similarly, joggers speed up on paths when someone is watching them and slow down when no one appears to be in sight.[19] Additionally, people giving impromptu speeches perform worse in the presence of others than when alone.

Social Facilitation Versus Social Inhibition   **Social facilitation** is the predictable enhancement in performance that occurs when people are in the presence of others. **Social inhibition** occurs when people are the center of attention and are concerned with discrepancies between their performance and standards of excellence. Thus, team leaders will actually make the performance of their team suffer if they apply performance pressure to people who are not yet expert.

How can team players ensure that their behavior is the optimal response? There are two routes. Expertise is one way: Experts are trained to focus on what matters most. For example, Olympiad Nordic Combined athlete Todd Lodwick, says, "I've learned to focus on what I can control, like my training, my equipment, my race strategy, and be aware of what I can't control, like weather, the quality of the snow, or my competitors. I use the image of bricks on a balance: I want the 'bricks' from the things I can control to outweigh the 'bricks' on the other side of the scale."[20] Practice and rehearsal is another strategy: It modifies the behavioral response hierarchy, so that the desired response becomes second nature. However, being an expert does not completely protect people from choking. Just look at professional players on sports teams. In the championship series in professional baseball and basketball, the home team is significantly more likely to lose the decisive game than it is to lose earlier home games in the series. Why? Expertise is the result of overlearning. The pressure to perform well causes people to focus their attention on the process of performing—the focus of attention turns inward. The more pressure, the more inwardly focused people become. When people focus on overlearned or automated responses, it interferes with their performance.[21] It is best to avoid trying to learn difficult material or perform complex tasks in groups, because peer pressure will obstruct performance. However, if team members are experts, they will likely flourish under this kind of pressure. Practice not only makes perfect but it also makes performance hold up under pressure. Not all teamwork needs to be done in a team setting; sometimes it is beneficial to allow team members to complete work on their own and bring it back to the group.

Flow: Between Boredom and Choking   At a precise point between boredom with a task and intense pressure is a state that psychologist Mihaly Csikszentmihalyi calls flow.[22] See Exhibit 2-2.

[17]Blascovich, J., Mendes, W. B., Hunter, S. B., & Salomon, K. (1999). Social "facilitation" as challenge and threat. *Journal of Personality and Social Psychology, 77*(1), 68–77.
[18]Michaels, S. W., Brommel, J. M., Brocato, R. M., Linkous, R. A., & Rowe, J. S. (1982). Social facilitation in a natural setting. *Replication in Social Psychology, 4*(2), 21–24.
[19]Worringham, C. J., & Messick, D. M. (1983). Social facilitation of running: An unobtrusive study. *Journal of Social Psychology, 121,* 23–29.
[20]Citrin, J. M. (2009, October 2). Performance lessons from Olympians. *Wall Street Journal.* online.wsj.com
[21]Lewis, B. P., & Linder, D. E. (1997). Thinking about choking? Attentional processes and paradoxical performance. *Personality and Social Psychology Bulletin, 23*(9), 937–944.
[22]Csikszentmihalyi, M. (2003). *Good business: Leadership, flow, and the making of meaning.* New York: Viking Press.

EXHIBIT 2-2 The Flow Experience

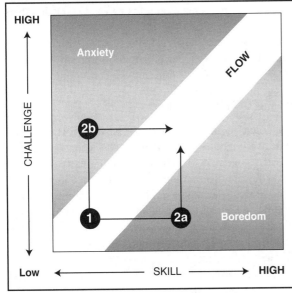

A person (1) will move out of flow and become bored as his or her skills for a specific task increase (2a), unless the challenge to succeed also increases. Likewise, a person (1) will move out of flow if the demand on them is too great (2b). To stay in flow, they must increase their level of skill.

Source: Based on Csikszentmihalyi, M. (1990). *Flow: The psychology of optimal experience* (p. 74). New York: HarperCollins.

Flow is a psychological state in which a person is highly engaged in a task—so interested, in fact, that the person loses track of time, and the process of engaging the task is its own reinforcement. Engagement is critical for flow. A Gallup study of 32,400 business units found that those in the top quartile on engagement had 18 percent higher productivity, 16 percent higher profitability, and 49 percent fewer safety incidents compared with those in the bottom quartile on engagement.[23]

Stress Versus Challenge   There is a fine line between challenge and stress. For example, people who strive to accomplish difficult goals may perceive their goal as a challenge, rather than a threat, and perform quite well. Challenge is experienced when there is an opportunity for self-growth with available coping strategies; threat is experienced when the situation is perceived as leading to failure with no available strategies for coping. For example, in one investigation, people evaluated companies' stocks and had to make decisions quickly and accurately.[24] The same level of goal difficulty impaired performance and adaptation to change when people appraised the situation as a "threat," but it improved adaptation to change when people appraised the situation as a "challenge."

MOTIVATION AND EFFORT   It is not enough for members of a team to be skilled; they must also be motivated to use their knowledge and skills to achieve shared goals. Motivation comes both from within a person and from external factors. People by nature are goal directed, but a

[23]Frauenheim, E. (2009, November 16). Commitment issues—restoring employee engagement. *Workforce Management*, pp. 20–25.
[24]Drach-Zahavy, A., & Erez, M. (2002). Challenge versus threat effects on the goal-performance relationship. *Organizational Behavior and Human Decision Processes, 88,* 667–682.

poorly designed team or organizational environment can threaten team dedication and persistence. At certain times, members of a team may feel that their actions do not matter, that something always goes wrong to mess things up (e.g., a sports team on a losing streak), or that their input is not listened to. This can also happen if team members feel they are unable to affect their environment or cannot rely on others. The belief that the group has in themselves, or their **group potency**, is a significant predictor of actual performance.[25] For example, in one investigation, officer cadets completed a task in teams. Group potency, or "thinking we can," contributed to group performance over and above measures of pure cognitive ability.[26] Next, we introduce two motivational effects in groups: motivation gains and motivation losses.

Motivation Gains   Motivation gains refer to circumstances that increase the effort expended by group members in a collective task. Motivational gains in which the less capable member works harder is known as the **Köhler effect**.[27] In some investigations, athletes curled a bar attached to a pulley system until exhaustion. They did this first individually and then in groups of two. Motivation gains happened when the athlete pairs had moderately different abilities. Conversely, motivation gains did not emerge when athletes had equal or very unequal abilities. It was the weaker member of the group who was responsible for the motivation gain. The psychological mechanisms underlying the Köhler effect are social comparison (particularly when someone thinks that their teammate is more capable) and the feeling that one's effort is indispensable to the group.[28] Group members are willing to exert effort on a collective task when they expect their efforts to be instrumental in obtaining outcomes that they value personally.[29] Moreover, in particular, the weakest member of a team is more likely to work harder when everyone is given feedback about people's performance in a timely fashion.[30] Although, motivation gains gradually start to attenuate, they remain higher when people work with several different partners (as opposed to the same people).[31] And, motivation gains were significantly greater when people worked in the physical presence of their coworker (as opposed to the virtual presence).[32]

Social Loafing   A more common observation in groups is motivation losses, also known as social loafing. A French agricultural engineer named Max Ringelmann was interested in the relative efficiency of farm labor supplied by horses, oxen, machines, and men. In particular, he was curious about their relative abilities to pull a load horizontally, such as in a tug-of-war. In one of his experiments, groups of 14 men pulled a load, and the amount of force they generated was measured. The force that each man could pull independently was also measured. There was a steady decline in the average pull-per-member as the size of the rope-pulling team increased.

---

[25]Shea & Guzzo, "Group effectiveness."

[26]Hecht, T. D., Allen, N. J., Klammer, J. D., & Kelly, E. C. (2002). Group beliefs, ability and performance: The potency of group potency. *Group Dynamics: Theory, Research and Practice, 6*(2), 143–152.

[27]Stroebe, W., Diehl, M., & Abakoumkin, G. (1996). Social compensation and the Köhler effect: Toward a theoretical explanation of motivation gains in group productivity. In E. H. White & J. H. Davis (Eds.), *Understanding group behavior, Vol. 2: Small group processes and interpersonal relations.* Mahwah, NJ: Erlbaum.

[28]Kerr, N. L., Messé, L. M., Seok, D., Sambolec, E., Lount, R. M., & Park, E. S. (2007). Psychological mechanisms underlying the Köhler motivation gain. *Personality and Social Psychology Bulletin, 33*(6), 828–841.

[29]Karau, S., Markus, M., & Williams, K. (2000). On the elusive search for motivation gains in groups: Insights from the collective effort model. *Zeitschrift fur Sozialpsychologie, 31*(4), 179–190.

[30]Kerr, N., Messé, L., Park, E., & Sambolec, E. (2005). Identifiability, performance feedback and the Köhler effect. *Group Processes and Intergroup Relations, 8*(4), 375–390.

[31]Lount, R. M., Kerr, N. L., Messé, L. M., Seok, D., & Park, E. S. (2008). An examination of the stability and persistence of the Köhler motivation gain effect. *Group Dynamics: Theory, Research, and Practice, 12*(4), 279–289.

[32]Lount, R. B., Park, E. S., Kerr, N. L., Messe, L. A., & Seok, D. (2008). Evaluation concerns and the Kohler effect: The impact of physical presence on motivation gains. *Small Group Research, 39*(6), 795–809.

One person pulling on a rope alone exerted an average of 63 kilograms of force. However, in groups of three, the per-person force dropped to 53 kilograms, and in groups of eight, it plummeted to only 31 kilograms—less than half of the effort exerted by people working alone.[33] This detailed observation revealed a fundamental principle of teamwork: People in groups often do not work as hard as they do when alone. This is known as **social loafing**.

Team performance increases with team size, but the rate of increase is negatively accelerated, such that the addition of new members to the team has diminishing returns on productivity. Similar results are obtained when teams work on intellectual puzzles,[34] creativity tasks,[35] perceptual judgments, and complex reasoning.[36] Social loafing has been demonstrated in many cultures, including India,[37] Japan,[38] and Taiwan.[39] The general form of the social loafing effect is portrayed in Exhibit 2-3.

Free Riders   People's motivations often diminish in a team. Also, the larger the team, the less likely it is that any given person will work hard. For many team tasks, there is a possibility that others can and will do most or all of the work necessary for the team to succeed. This means that free riders benefit from the efforts of others while contributing little or nothing themselves. Team members are sensitive to how important their efforts are perceived to be. When they think their contributions are not going to have much impact on the outcome, they are less likely to exert themselves on the team's behalf.

How do teams react once a free rider has been detected? If someone is not contributing, the other team members might attempt to reduce that person's reward (e.g., not allow someone to put his or her name on the group report if he or she has not contributed) or reduce their own inputs (i.e., the other members of the group might stop working hard). Obviously, one free rider can undermine the overall effectiveness of the team. However, the company itself bears the greatest cost from this kind of behavior. When everyone stops working hard in retaliation against someone else's bad conduct, ultimately the work does not get done or done well. Among National Football League teams, fines are often leveled toward individual players for tardiness or other team disruptions. Under former Dallas Cowboys coach Bill Parcells, players were fined $5,000 for being late to meetings and as much as $12,000 for missing an injury treatment session.[40] Meaningful consequences emphasize the team's core values: showing up and contributing. The leaders of these teams correctly recognize that free riding and social loafing, if unchecked, can be a serious threat to team productivity.

Three Main Causes of Free Riding   Why do people loaf and free ride? Three reasons: diffusion of responsibility, a reduced sense of self-efficacy, and the "sucker aversion."

---

[33]Ringelmann, M. (1913). *Aménagement des fumiers et des purins.* Paris: Librarie agricole de la Maison rustique. Summarized by Kravitz, D. A., & Martin, B. (1986). Ringelmann rediscovered: The original article. *Journal of Personality and Social Psychology, 50*(5), 936–941.

[34]Taylor, D. W., & Faust, W. L. (1952). Twenty questions: Efficiency of problem-solving as a function of the size of the group. *Journal of Experimental Social Psychology, 44*, 360–363.

[35]Gibb, J. R. (1951). *Dynamics of participative groups.* Boulder, CO: University of Colorado.

[36]Ziller, R. C. (1957). Four techniques of group decision-making under uncertainty. *Journal of Applied Psychology, 41*, 384–388.

[37]Werner, D., Ember, C. R., & Ember, M. (1981). *Anthropology: Study guide and workbook.* Upper Saddle River, NJ: Prentice Hall.

[38]Williams, K. D., & Williams, K. B. (1984). *Social loafing in Japan: A cross-cultural development study.* Paper presented at the Midwestern Psychological Association Meeting, Chicago, IL.

[39]Gabrenya, W. K., Latané, B., & Wang, Y. (1983). Social loafing in cross-cultural perspective: Chinese on Taiwan. *Journal of Cross-Cultural Psychology, 14*(3), 368–384.

[40]Watkins, C. (2009, January 20). Sources: Dallas cowboys often tardy, undisciplined in '08. *The Dallas Morning News.* Dallasnews.com

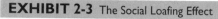

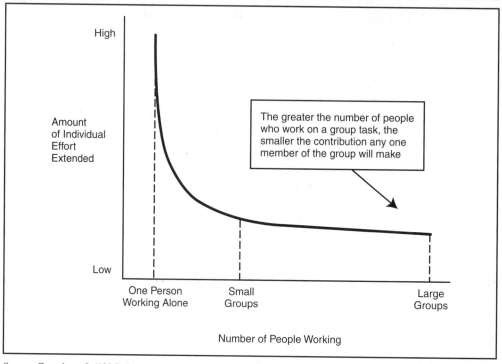

EXHIBIT 2-3 The Social Loafing Effect

Source: Greenberg, J. (1996). *Managing behavior in organizations* (p. 189). Upper Saddle River, NJ: Prentice Hall.

Diffusion of Responsibility.   In a team, a person's effort and contributions are less identifiable than when that person works independently. This is because everyone's efforts are pooled
into the team enterprise and the return is a function of everyone's contribution. It is difficult (or
impossible) to distinguish one person's contribution from another. At an extreme, this can lead
to **deindividuation**—a psychological state in which a person does not feel individual responsibility. As a result, the person is less likely to perform or contribute. Consider, for example, a real-
world case. A woman named Kitty Genovese was on her way home from work late one evening
in New York.[41] She was attacked by a man and stabbed to death. Thirty-eight of her neighbors in
the apartment building where she lived saw the attacker approach and slay her, but not a single
person so much as called the police.

Most people attribute the neighbors' lack of assistance to insensitivity. We might look at
this, however, from another perspective: People are more likely to free ride as the number of others in the group increases. Perhaps this is one reason why many people employed by companies
that regularly committed accounting fraud did not blow the whistle. Observers in Kitty
Genovese's apartment building who knew that others were also watching felt less responsible
and so less inclined to intervene. In effect, they told themselves, "Someone else has probably
already called for help." Why inconvenience yourself when it is likely the woman will receive

---

[41]Discussed by Latané, B., & Darley, J. M. (1968). Group inhibition of bystander intervention in emergencies. *Journal of
Personality and Social Psychology, 10,* 215–221.

help from someone else? Of course, if everyone thinks this way, the probability that the victim eventually gets help decreases dramatically.

Dispensability of Effort. In some cases, it is not diffusion of responsibility that hinders people from contributing to a team effort, but rather the feeling that our contributions will not be as valuable, efficacious, or worthwhile as they might be in a smaller group. We believe our contributions will not be sufficient to justify the effort. Consider, for example, the problem of voting. Most everyone agrees that voting is necessary for democracy. Why then did only 65.7 percent of the eligible U.S. population turn out to vote during the presidential election of 2008?[42] People may feel that their vote has such a small impact on the outcome that voting is not worthwhile. Similarly, team members may feel they lack the ability to positively influence a team's outcome. Indeed, when the least capable member of a team feels particularly indispensable for group success, the group actually experiences a sort of **social striving** effect, meaning that they work harder to achieve their goals.[43]

Sucker Aversion. A common concern held by team members is whether someone will be left doing all of the work and getting little or no credit.[44] Because everyone wants to avoid being taken advantage of, team members hedge their efforts and wait to see what others will do. Of course, when everyone does this, no one contributes. When people see others not contributing, it confirms their worst fears. The sucker effect becomes a self-fulfilling prophecy. In contrast, the Protestant Work Ethic (PWE) holds that hard work leads to economic success.[45] People with strong PWEs are not affected by the reasons for their partner's low output. Whether it is a lack of ability or lack of motivation, people with high PWE work hard, even if that means they are the "sucker."[46]

Suggestions for Enhancing Successful Team Performance Suppose you are managing a team that processes insurance claims. Prior to the formation of teams, you measure the average claim processing time and find it to be three days. After forming the teams, you find the average has increased to about 9 days. Has your team fallen victim to social loafing? Your manager advises you to immediately dismantle the teams. Someone else tells you that the company's incentive system needs to be overhauled. What do you think?

Before you dismantle the teams or restructure the company's entire pay structure, consider the following strategies:

Increase Identifiability. When each member's contribution to a task is displayed where it can be seen by others (e.g., weekly sales figures posted on a bulletin board or e-mail), people are less likely to loaf, or slack off, than when only overall group (or companywide) performance is made available.[47] People often regard their fellow group members as a collective

---

[42]Hunt, T. (2008, November). Triumphant Obama turns to sobering challenges. *WSBT (Weather, Sport, West Bend)*. Wsbt.com

[43]Hertel, G., Kerr, N. L., & Messe, L. A. (2000). Motivation gains in performance groups: Paradigmatic and theoretical developments on the Köhler effect. *Journal of Personality and Social Psychology, 79*(4), 580–601.

[44]Kerr, N. L. (1983). Motivation losses in small groups: A social dilemma analysis. *Journal of Personality and Social Psychology, 45*, 819–828.

[45]Furnham, A. (1990a). *The Protestant work ethic.* New York: Routledge.

[46]Abele, S., & Diehl, M. (2008). Finding team mates who are not prone to sucker and free-rider effects: The Protestant Work Ethic as a moderator of motivation losses in group performance. *Group Processes and Intergroup Relations, 11*, 39–54.

[47]Kerr, N. L., & Bruun, S. (1981). Ringelmann revisited: Alternative explanations for the social loafing effect. *Journal of Personality and Social Psychology, 37*, 224–231; Williams, K. D., Harkins, S. G., & Latané, B. (1981). Identifiability as a deterrent to social loafing: Two cheering experiments. *Journal of Personality and Social Psychology, 40*(2), 303–311.

rather than as individuals; if people think about the contributions made by each person in their group, they will be less likely to act in a self-interested fashion.[48] At Worthington Industries, a Columbus, Ohio-based steel processing company, digital clocks are mounted in the manufacturing floor so that everyone can see how long team members take to complete tasks. Displaying the clocks was an idea that came from a worker on the floor.[49] However, the key is not identifiability per se, but rather the evaluation that identifiability makes possible.[50]

Promote Involvement.   Social loafing may be eliminated if the task is sufficiently involving,[51] attractive,[52] or intrinsically interesting.[53] When tasks are highly specialized and routinized, monotony sets in; in contrast, when team members are responsible for all pieces of a work product or service, they feel more responsibility for the work. In one investigation in a fund-raising organization, callers in an intervention group briefly interacted with a beneficiary; callers in two control groups read a letter from a beneficiary or had no exposure to him. One month later, the intervention group displayed significantly greater persistence (142 percent more phone time) and job performance (171 percent more money raised) than the control groups.[54]

Challenging tasks may be particularly important for teams composed of people who are good at what they do or who believe that they are superior. Most people regard themselves to be superior on a number of intellective and social tasks. For example, the majority of people regard themselves to be better-than-average drivers;[55] they also believe that they are more likely to have a better job.[56] However, the **positive illusion bias**, unwarranted beliefs in one's own superiority, can wreak havoc in teams. Work teams composed of people with strong motives to view themselves as distinctly more talented than others are likely to suffer from social loafing when the task is unchallenging. In particular, people from individualistic cultures are most likely to have such motives.[57] People who see themselves as above average are the most likely to engage in social loafing, because they have a false sense of the value of their contributions. Indeed, people who feel uniquely superior expend less effort when working collectively on easy tasks. However, they actually work harder when the task is challenging.

---

[48]Savitsky, K., Van Boven, L., Epley, N., & Wight, W. (2005). The unpacking effect in allocations of responsibility for group tasks. *Journal of Experimental Social Psychology, 41*, 447–457.

[49]Gearino, D. (2009, November 5). Beat the clock. *The Columbus Dispatch*. dispatch.com

[50]Harkins, S. G., & Jackson, J. M. (1985). The role of evaluation in eliminating social loafing. *Personality and Social Psychology Bulletin, 11*, 457–465; Harkins, S. G., & Szymanski, K. (1987). *Social loafing and social facilitation: New wine in old bottles.* Beverly Hills, CA: Sage.

[51]Brickner, M. A., Harkins, S. G., & Ostrom, T. M. (1986). Effects of personal involvement: Thought-provoking implications for social loafing. *Journal of Personality and Social Psychology, 51*(4), 763–770.

[52]Zaccaro, S. J. (1984). Social loafing: The role of task attractiveness. *Personality and Social Psychology Bulletin, 10*, 99–106.

[53]Petty, R. E., Cacioppo, J. T., & Kasmer, J. (1985). *Effects of need for cognition on social loafing.* Paper presented at the Midwestern Psychology Association Meeting, Chicago, IL.

[54]Grant, A. M., Campbell, E. M., Chen, G., Cottone, K., Lapedis, D., Lee, K. (2007). Impact and the art of motivation maintenance: The effects of contact with beneficiaries on persistence behavior. *Organizational Behavior and Human Decision Processes, 103*, 53–67.

[55]Svenson, O. (1981). Are we all less risky and more skillful than our fellow drivers? *Acta Psychologica, 47*, 143–148.

[56]Taylor, S. E., & Brown, J. D. (1988). Illusion of well-being: A social psychological perspective on mental health. *Psychological Bulletin, 103*, 193–210.

[57]Huguet, P., Charbonnier, E., & Monteil, J. (1999). Productivity loss in performance groups: People who see themselves as average do not engage in social loafing. *Group Dynamics: Theory, Research, and Practice, 3*(2), 118–131.

Reward Team Members for Performance.   Team members should recognize and reward contributions by individuals. When Andrew Schuman bought Hammond's Candies in 2007, he knew nothing about the candy business. So, he rewarded team members for their insights by offering a $50 bonus to assembly-line workers who came up with successful ideas to cut manufacturing costs. One worker suggested a tweak in a machine gear that reduced workers needed on an assembly line to four from five. Another employee devised a new way to protect candy canes while en route to stores, which resulted in a 4 percent reduction in breakage.[58]

Rewarding team members need not mean large financial incentives: Symbolic rewards can be more important than money. Sales managers may strategically use symbolic rewards, such as high-performer sales clubs or plaques and ceremonies honoring exemplary service, to deliver messages to the sales force. It is important for team members to feel appreciated and acknowledged by the members of their team as well as by the organization. There can be serious consequences if people feel they are not valued and respected, so much so that people are more likely to cheat and steal from the organization when they feel they have been unfairly treated.[59] When people feel that they are respected by their superiors, they are more likely to contribute to the group's welfare.[60] Feeling respected is most important for members who feel least included.

Strengthen Team Cohesion.   Cohesive teams are less inclined to loaf.[61]

Increase Personal Responsibility.   When teams set their own performance goals, they are less likely to loaf.[62]

Use Team Charters.   At the outset of teamwork, members should develop a written statement of objectives and practices. This should be collectively written, posted, and, most important, regularly revisited. In a study of MBA students competing in a business strategy simulation, those students who developed a team charter and invested in taskwork (performance strategies) outperformed teams that did not develop charters or strategies.[63] Referred to as "stacking the deck," laying a solid foundation of teamwork and taskwork is essential for sustained performance.

Provide Team Performance Reviews and Feedback.   People often don't realize that they are not doing their fair share. And, they overestimate how much they contribute to collaborative endeavors.[64] It is common practice for people to receive regular performance feedback from their supervisors. Why shouldn't we do the same for teams? As we noted in Chapter 1, team leaders often fail to manage their team as an entity, preferring to manage the individual relationships with each team member. Team leaders should meet with the entire team on a regular basis to talk about how the team is performing. And the communication should be double loop, such that the team leader is asking questions in addition to providing feedback.

---

[58]Evans, T. (2009, December 21). Entrepreneurs seek ways to draw out workers' ideas. *Wall Street Journal*, p. 22.
[59]Greenberg, J. (1988). Equity and workplace status: A field experiment. *Journal of Applied Psychology, 75*, 561–568.
[60]De Cremer, D. (2002). Respect and cooperation in social dilemmas: The importance of feeling included. *Personality and Social Psychology Bulletin, 28*(10), 1335–1341.
[61]Williams, K. D. (1981). The effects of group cohesiveness on social loafing in simulated word-processing pools. *Dissertation Abstracts International, 42*(2-B), 838.
[62]Brickner, Harkins, & Ostrom, "Effects of personal involvement."
[63]Mathieu, J. E., & Rapp, T. L. (2009). Laying the foundation for successful team performance trajectories: The roles of team charters and performance strategies. *Journal of Applied Psychology, 94*(1), 90–103.
[64]Savitsky, Van Boven, Epley, & Wight, "The unpacking effect in allocations of responsibility for group tasks."

Maintain the "Right" Staffing Level.   As the team gets larger and larger, personal contributions to the team become less important to the team's chances of success.[65] As team size increases, feelings of anonymity increase.

Suppose that you implement the preceding steps, and your team's performance is still less than what you think is possible. What should you do? Consider the third source of threats to productivity: coordination problems.

COORDINATION STRATEGIES   Ability and motivation are essential and desirable for effective teamwork but insufficient for effective team functioning. A team needs to coordinate the skills, efforts, and actions of its members in order to effectively enact team strategy. Consider the coordination within the Barack Obama team when Obama aides heard a verbal gaffe by Republican opponent John McCain. Late in the campaign, they jumped into action within minutes. They coordinated with Dan Pfeiffer, Obama's communications director, about the McCain blunder, and Obama quickly inserted the comments into his speech delivered moments later. By nightfall, the Obama team produced an advertisement that included video of McCain making the statement that would shadow him for the rest of the campaign.[66]

Coordination problems must be surmounted for a team to be effective. Team members may be individually good at what they do, but unless they coordinate their activities, they will not meet their team objectives. Coordination is the combined synchronization of the strategies of all members. Teams vary in terms of their coordination or synchrony. Consider a football team—the slightest misunderstanding about a play can lose the game. Another example is a rowing team or a dance troupe—unless everyone is synchronized, they cannot achieve their performance goals, no matter how skilled and motivated the individuals. This is why teams often sing or chant to synchronize their movements and actions.

Sir Adrian Cadbury, former chairman of Cadbury Schweppes, rowed in the 1952 Olympics. Sir Adrian took more than the lesson of timing from the world of rowing when he entered corporate life. "What has always been important to me is the team— rowing taught me that. More importantly, trust." Rowing is certainly a sport that places more emphasis on team harmony than others—there's less scope for those with individual flare to shine. "The beauty of racing in a crew is that you learn that any victory is the combined effort of everyone. In the same way company results reflect the performance of the whole firm."[67]

Coordination problems increase with team size and do so in an accelerating manner. The number of ways in which a team can organize itself (e.g., divide responsibilities, combine contributions, and coordinate efforts) increases rapidly as the team gets larger.[68] Most of the threats to team productivity are attributable to coordination problems, but managers, used to thinking in terms of ability and motivation, fail to realize this—an example of the misattribution problem discussed in Chapter 1.

---

[65]Kerr, N. L. (1989). Illusions of efficacy: The effects of group size on perceived efficacy in social dilemmas. *Journal of Experimental Social Psychology, 25,* 287–313; Olson, M. (1965). *The logic of collective action.* Cambridge, MA: Harvard University Press.

[66]Nagourney, A., Rutenberg, J., & Zeleny, J. (2008, October 5). Obama campaign team rarely stumbled. *New York Times.* nytimes.com

[67]Phelps, R. (1996, September). Cadbury trusts in teamwork. *Management Today,* p. 110.

[68]Kelley, H. H. (1962). *The development of cooperation in the minimal social situation.* Washington, DC: American Psychological Association.

Most people take coordination and communication in teams for granted. In other words, they do not anticipate that their handwriting will be misread by a teammate or that an e-mail will be directed to a spam folder. People have a biased sense about the clarity of their own messages and intentions. They may not be as clear as they think they are. The problems in communication and coordination are compounded when the medium of communication is less rich, such as in e-mail, fax, and videoconferencing (a topic discussed in Part III on global teamwork).

What are some practical steps to ensure coordination of effort within teams?

Use Single-Digit Teams   Most teams are too large. As the number of people on a team increases, it is that much harder to schedule meetings, move paperwork, and converge on ideas. The incidence of unanticipated failure increases. As a rule of thumb, teams should have fewer than 10 members and just enough to cover all needed skill areas.

Have an Agenda   Members need a clear sense of where they are going and how they will get there. If the team does not know where it is going, its efforts will be fragmented and members will waste time and energy.

Train Team Members Together   Team members who train together, as opposed to separately, work more effectively. This is because they have an opportunity to coordinate their strategies. A side benefit of training team members together is that training provides the opportunity to build trust.

Practice   Teams are low on the learning curve when the team members begin to work with one another. A team might be motivated and highly skilled but naive in terms of communicating with one another in a highly synchronized and coordinated fashion. Teams require more practice than do individuals.

Minimize Links in Communication   For most tasks, it is better for team members to directly communicate rather than going through others. For example, at ATA Engineering, Inc., when it comes to team decision making, 8 to 10 ATA employees interview every job candidate.[69]

Set Clear Performance Standards   Every team needs clear performance standards. In the absence of performance standards, it is impossible to evaluate the effectiveness of a team. The most common means by which people are evaluated by organizations is through a performance appraisal, which we discuss in detail in the next chapter. Many performance appraisals are routine and occur on a regular basis. Ideally, they are objective, based upon hard facts, and deliverables. People receive clear and informative feedback about what they are doing well and what they need to work on. We've argued that performance appraisals should be used when evaluating team performance.

How does a manager know whether a team is performing effectively? If this question is hard to answer, then it will be difficult to pull together a high-performance team and diagnose problems before they threaten team performance. Furthermore, even if you happen to be in the fortunate position of working on a successful team, unless you understand what makes your team effective, you may make the wrong choices or be indecisive at inopportune times.

Team performance evaluation is more difficult than individual performance evaluation. Teams are harder to track, and higher turnover can blur the relationship between the actions

---

[69]Spors, K. (2009, February 22). Top small workplaces 2008 creating great workplaces has never been more important. *Wall Street Journal*, p. R1.

that people take and the results achieved by the team. Nevertheless, it is still possible to do a rigorous performance evaluation on teams, just as it is with individual employees. In this chapter, we consider the factors important to consider in assessing team performance. In the next chapter, we deal with the thornier issue of how to measure performance and structure the incentive system.

Performance Criteria

What are the criteria by which we should evaluate team effectiveness? By performance criteria, we mean those factors used to evaluate the success or failure of a team effort. Hackman identified three key criteria in his model of group effectiveness: productivity, cohesion, and learning.[70] We add a fourth criterion, integration, suggested by Gruenfeld.[71]

PRODUCTIVITY   Productivity is arguably the most important measure of team success. Did the team achieve its goals? According to LaFasto and Larson, the most important determinant of team success is whether the team has a clear and elevating goal.[72] Team productivity requires that the team have a clear goal and adapt accordingly as new information arrives, goals change, and organizational priorities shift. This also holds true for changes in the marketplace—for example, the entrance or exit of a competitor or a stock market plunge. There are many dimensions to productivity: What was the team's output? How does the output correspond to the team's original goals? How quickly or timely were results achieved? How effective was the outcome? What is the correspondence between the team output and a measurable accomplishment (such as improved market share and new product development) by the organization? Efficiency is also important. If the team's goals were accomplished, at what cost did this happen? Was it worth it? The productivity of a team is highly correlated with its goals, as well as the ability of the team to adapt, change, and accommodate the goals in the face of new information, changing organizational priorities, and the changing marketplace.

The productivity criterion asks whether the team's output meets the standards of those who have to use it—that is, the end user. It is not enough that the team is satisfied with the output or even that it meets some objective performance measure. If the team's output is unacceptable to those who have to use it, the team is not effective. For these reasons, it is important to identify the legitimate clients of the team. The various end users who depend on the team's output may focus on different performance standards (e.g., quantity, quality, cutting costs, innovation, and timeliness). At the world-famous Mayo Clinic, the best interest of the patient is the only interest to be considered. All employees know the needs of the patient come first and the entire organization is dedicated toward that goal.[73]

COHESION   A second major criterion on team performance is team cohesion. The word *cohesion* derives from the Latin word *cohaesus,* meaning to cleave or stick together. In physics and chemistry, cohesion refers to the force(s) binding molecules of a substance together. For teams, cohesion refers to the processes that keep members of a team (e.g., military unit and work

---

[70]Hackman, "Design of work teams."

[71]D. H. Gruenfeld, personal communication, 1998.

[72]Lafasto, F. M. J., & Larson, C. E. (2001). *When teams work best: 6,000 team members and leaders tell what it takes to succeed.* Newbury Park, CA: Sage.

[73]Lee, A. (2008, September 8). How to build a brand. *Fast Company.* fastcompany.com

group) united.[74] Did the team work together well, and are its members better able to work together in the future as a result of this experience? Are team members' needs more satisfied than frustrated by the group experience,[75] and "is the capacity of members to work together on subsequent group tasks enhanced or maintained"?[76] Cohesion is a consistent predictor of team performance within project teams,[77] but not necessarily service teams (for a review, see Sundstrom et al., 2000[78]). Sometimes teams meet their goals, but relationships suffer and are not dealt with in a way that allows members to work productively together in the future: "Mutual antagonism could become so high that members would choose to accept collective failure rather than to share knowledge and information with one another."[79] In an effectively functioning team, the capability of members to work together on future projects is maintained and strengthened.

It is worthwhile to ask why team cohesion is important, as opposed to being just a nice side benefit. For example, if a team puts a person on the moon, is this not a success regardless of whether the team was cohesive? If the team effort is really and truly a one-time effort, then maximizing team cohesion may not be necessary. However, most of us want to build teams that will last for some meaningful length of time. If team members do not enjoy working on a team, future performance will suffer.

Learning

In addition to the functioning of the team as a whole, learning is also important. As anyone who has attended an executive education course can testify, cohesion may be present but learning may be absent. Simply stated, teams should represent growth and development opportunities for the individual needs of the members. People have a need for growth, development, and fulfillment. Some teams operate in ways that block the development of individual members and satisfaction of personal needs. In short, members' needs should be more satisfied than frustrated by the team experience. Teams should be sensitive to members and provide opportunities for members to develop new skills. This does not mean that teams or, for that matter, organizations exist to serve individual needs; rather, successful organizations create opportunities that challenge individual members.

Integration

Another perspective is that of the larger organization. Thus, a fourth criterion of team performance is integration. Does the organization benefit from the team? In many instances, the team becomes so self-serving that it loses sight of the organization's larger goals. (This is most likely

---

[74]Dion, K. (2000). Group cohesion: From "field of forces" to multidimensional construct. *Group Dynamics: Theory, Research, and Practice, 4*(1), 7–26.

[75]Sundstrom, E. D., Demeuse, K. P., & Futrell, D. (1990). Work teams: Applications and effectiveness. *American Psychologist, 45*(2), 120–133.

[76]Hackman, J. R., & Oldham, G. R. (1980). *Work redesign*. Menlo Park, CA: Addison-Wesley Publishing.

[77]Gillespie, D. F., & Birnbaum-More, P. H. (1980). Status concordance, coordination and success in interdisciplinary research teams. *Human Relations, 33*(1), 41–56; Greene, C. N. (1989). Cohesion and productivity in work groups. *Small Group Behavior, 20*, 70–86; Keller, R. T. (1986). Predictors of the performance of project groups in R&D organizations. *Academy of Management Journal, 29*, 715–725.

[78]Sundstrom, E. D., Mcintyre, M., Halfhill, T., & Richards, H. (2000). Work groups: From the Hawthorne studies to work teams of the 1990s and beyond. *Group Dynamics, 4*, 44–67.

[79]Hackman, "Introduction: Work teams in organizations."

the case with teams that have greater autonomy.) This can occur when the team's goals are incompatible with those of other departments or areas. If, for instance, a company's sales force dramatically improves sales over a short time, this does the company no good. In fact, it could even hurt the company if the manufacturing group cannot fulfill the promises made by the sales force or if the technical support group cannot handle the new customer calls. This is an example where the sales strategy backfires at the organizational level.

In other cases, different teams in the organization may reinvent things already developed by the organization because they are not able to learn from outside their group. It is important for teams to understand the organization's goals to work effectively toward them. Teams need to integrate with other units in the organization. Practically, this means that teams must disseminate information, results, status reports, failures, expertise, and ideas in a timely and efficient manner. Achieving integration requires solid planning and coordination with the rest of the company. Exhibit 2-4 summarizes the team performance analysis, which can be performed by team members or team leaders. The relative importance of each of the four criteria varies across circumstances, and there is no single best set of conditions for optimizing performance. There are many ways a team can perform work well and, unfortunately, more ways for it to be ineffective. Teams are governed by the principle of **equifinality**[80]—a team can reach the same outcome from various initial conditions and by a variety of means.

It is important for every team leader to think about which criteria are important when evaluating teamwork and to specify those in an a priori fashion.

THE TEAM PERFORMANCE EQUATION

Now that we have discussed the four critical measures of team performance and the three key ingredients for team success, we can put them together in a single equation for the leader to use when assessing team performance:

$$AP = PP + S - T$$

Where   AP = Actual productivity

   PP = Potential productivity

   S = Synergy

   T = Performance threats

The actual productivity of a team is a function of three key factors: The potential productivity of the team, synergy, and threats. The first factor, the potential productivity of a team, depends on three subfactors: task demands, the resources available to the team, and the team process.

Task demands are the requirements imposed on the team by the task itself and the rules governing task performance. Task demands determine both the resources needed for optimal performance and how to combine resources. **Resources** are the relevant abilities, skills, and tools possessed by people attempting to perform the task. **Process** concerns the way teams use resources to meet task demands. Team process describes the steps taken by the team when attempting the task and includes nonproductive as well as productive actions. The task demands reveal the kinds of resources needed, the resources determine the team's potential productivity, and the process determines the degree of potential realized.

---

[80]Katz, D., & Kahn, R. L. (1978). *The social psychology of organizations* (2nd ed.). New York: John Wiley & Sons.

EXHIBIT 2-4 Team Performance Analysis

Conduct a performance analysis of your team using the following four criteria as a baseline. Remember, you don't have to wait until the team is finished with its task to begin an evaluation. It is actually best to continually assess performance as the team is working toward its goal.

PRODUCTIVITY

- Does the team have a clear goal?
- What objective performance measures have been established at the outset of teamwork?
- Who are the legitimate clients of the team?
- Does the team's output (e.g., decisions, products, and services) meet the standards of those who have to use it?
- Under what conditions should the goal change?
- What sources of information should the team consider to assess whether the initial goal might need to be changed?

COHESION

- Do the team members enjoy working together?
- What conditions could lead to feelings of resentment?

- What conditions could prevent team members from working together in the future?
- How can team members best learn from one another?
- How are team members expected to accommodate changes, such as additions to the team, growth, and turnover?

LEARNING

- Do the individual team members grow and develop as a result of the team experience?
- Do team members have a chance to improve their skills or affirm themselves?
- What factors and conditions could block personal growth?
- Are individuals' growth needs understood and shared by group members?

INTEGRATION

- How does the team benefit the larger organization?
- Are the team's goals consistent with those of the larger organization?
- What other groups, departments, and units are affected by the team?
- What steps has the team taken to integrate its activities with those of others?

source: Thompson, L. (2010). Leading high impact teams. Executive Programs Course, Kellogg School of Management.

 Synergy refers to everything that can and does go better in a team compared with individuals working independently.[81] **Performance threats** refer to everything that can go wrong in a team. Unfortunately, teams often fall below their potential; there is considerable process loss, or underperformance, due to coordination problems and motivational problems.[82] Leaders can more easily control threats than synergies. Synergies can emerge, but they usually take more time than anyone expects. Therefore, the leader's job is to set the stage for synergies by attempting to minimize all possible threats.

[81]Collins, E. G., & Guetzkow, H. (1964). *A social psychology of group processes for decision making.* New York: Wiley.
[82]Davis, J. (1969). *Group performance.* Reading, MA: Addison-Wesley; Laughlin, P. R. (1980). Social combination processes of cooperative problem-solving groups on verbal interactive tasks. In M. Fishbein (Ed.), *Progress in social psychology* (Vol. 1). Mahwah, NJ: Lawrence Erlbaum & Associates; Steiner, *Group process and productivity.*

Conclusion

Unless a team has a clear goal, success will be impossible to achieve. However, having a clear goal does not guarantee successful team performance. Successful team performance is a multidimensional concept. To be sure, leaders want their teams to satisfy the end user or client, but they also need to make sure that teamwork is satisfying and rewarding for the members. If the team does not enjoy working together, sustaining long-term productivity will be impossible. Moreover, managing a team successfully must include managing and investing in the individual team members. Thus, teamwork ultimately needs to be a rewarding experience for team members. Finally, as organizations move toward flatter structures and greater team empowerment, the possibility arises that team goals may become superordinate to those of the larger organization. A successful team is integrated with the larger organization. Putting teams on a course to achieve these four markers of success requires a combination of managing the internal dynamics of teams (ability, motivation, and coordination), as well as the external relations of teams within the larger organization. One of the most effective things a manager can do to ensure team success is to take a proactive approach and undertake an analysis of the essential conditions affecting team performance. One of the biggest managerial shortcomings in terms of teamwork is a failure to account for threats to team performance. This is unfortunate because managers can more easily control threats than synergies.

3

Rewarding Teamwork

Compensation and Performance Appraisals

In October 2006, movie rental company Netflix launched a competition for engineers and scientists around the world to solve a rather simple-looking problem: improve Netflix's ability to predict what movies users would like by 10 percent. After 3 years and 40,000 teams from 186 countries competing for the prize, Netflix awarded the $1million. However, it took an international brain trust led by a team of AT&T labs researchers 36 months to solve the problem. The team, called BellKor's Pragmatic Chaos, was made up of a cross-cultural group of researchers and computer scientists from the United States, Austria, Canada, and Israel. And it came down to seconds. The winning algorithm was submitted 30 minutes before the contest deadline. The submission improved Netflix's existing system by 10.06 percent. With the success and excitement of the first contest, Netflix held a second contest and awarded $1 million to the winning team.[1]

Not all companies offer this level of reward for great ideas. Netflix executives want to build a "Ferrari," and they believe that establishing a meaningful prize is a first step. The move to self-managing teams begs the question of reward and compensation in teams because hierarchical pay plans centered on individuals may not make sense in the context of teams and may, in fact, be detrimental.[2] If pay plans reward the individual but the corporate message is teams, then teamwork may be undermined.

Variable performance among team members means differentiated pay. Even though teams may be perfectly capable of allocating pay or rewards to individuals in the team, this may sometimes mean that superstars are not rewarded unless other teammates forgo part of their own profit sharing. (For an example of these difficulties, see Exhibit 3-1).

---

[1]Sarno, D. (2009, September 21). Netflix awards $1M prize to recommendation wizards, announces 2nd contest [Web log post]. latimesblogs.latimes.com
[2]Lawler, E. E. (2000). *Rewarding excellence: Pay strategies for the new economy.* San Francisco, CA: Jossey-Bass.

EXHIBIT 3-1 Compensating Company Talent

Most Americans had likely never heard of a retention bonus before the furor over the 165 million dollars in executive bonus pay at federally bailed out American International Group in the spring of 2009. But when at least 19 of the companies that received government bailouts (including giants such as Citibank and SunTrust banks in Atlanta) promised to pay their executives millions of dollars in bonuses just for staying in their jobs—irrespective of how executives or their companies perform—the term was suddenly well known, and not in a positive way.

Companies had routinely defended retention bonuses as a way to retain employees in rough economic times, but during a severe recession the idea of being paid extra to show up for work struck many Americans as absurd.

Source: Based on Dash, E., & Glater, J. (2009, March 26). Paid handsomely to stay. *New York Times*, p. B1.

Even if a compensation system can be set up that appropriately rewards team effort, some team members may be unwilling to determine their coworkers' pay. As we discuss in this chapter, team members feel more comfortable when performance criteria are based on objective standards. Some companies such as Siemens and Jelly Belly, use software to log employee's progress and goals.[3]

This chapter examines types of team pay and the choices companies have for rewarding their teams. We discuss the advantages and disadvantages of each method. In the second section of the chapter, we take up the question of performance appraisals: What are they? What should be measured? Who should do the measuring? We examine 360-degree evaluations. In the third section of the chapter, we examine the types of biases that can play havoc on performance appraisals and discuss what to do about these biases. We conclude the chapter by providing a step-by-step guide for implementing a variable team-based pay structure.

TYPES OF TEAM PAY

We consider four types of team pay or reward: incentive pay, recognition, profit sharing, and gainsharing (see Exhibit 3-2). Pay is a communication device. According to salary.com, compensation is the most important factor for employees when choosing to leave a job.[4] People tend to behave according to the way they are evaluated and paid. Therefore, if the organization values teamwork, team members must be ultimately recognized and compensated for teaming. For example, at ATA Engineering, Inc., bonuses have an egalitarian flavor: All workers receive an equal percentage of their salary as an annual bonus. ATA leaders believe that every employee should reap the rewards of the whole team. Managers also feel it's too hard to accurately assess how much one employee deserves a bonus over another; singling people out could result in unfairness and resentment. "It's a controversial topic, but what we've found is it's extremely difficult to be fair and consistent if your bonus policies are too differential," says General Manager and Chairman Jeff Young. "Someone who made a big splash may be compensated, but someone who was silent and didn't speak up wouldn't be."[5] Most important, employees must understand how the incentive system works in their company. Generally, the simpler, the better.

---

[3]Kanaracus, C. (2009, July 20). Success factors aims for small business with new HR app. *PCWorld*. pcworld.com; A sweet employee performance appraisal system for jelly belly. (n.d.). HalogenSoftware.com.

[4]Employee job satisfaction & retention survey 2007/2008. (2008). Salary.com

[5]Spors, K. (2008, October 13). Top small workplaces 2008: Creating great workplaces has never been more important for small businesses; nor more difficult; here are 15 companies that do it well. *Wall Street Journal*, p. R1.

EXHIBIT 3-2 Team-Based Pay

Type	Description/Types	Advantages/Applications	Disadvantages
Incentive pay	A team of employees receives money based on increased performance against predetermined targets	• Can combine a focus on individual and team performance • Team can be given opportunity to allocate	• Employees averse to thinking of selves as team members • Risky if base pay is reduced • Guided by upper management and corporate initiative
Recognition	One-time award for a limited number of employees or groups for performing well beyond expectations or for completing a project, program, or product	• Easy to implement • Distributed at the local (team) level • Introduced easily, quickly, and inexpensively without layers of approval • Comparatively simple	• Employees concerned they won't be recognized for own contributions • Risky if base pay is reduced • Carry less front-end motivation
Profit sharing	A share of corporate profits is distributed in cash on a current basis to all employees (driven by financial factors)	• Serves communication purpose by signaling that rewards are in balance across the organization • Informs and educates employees about financial well-being of organization	• May be too far removed from workers' control to affect performance
Gainsharing	A percentage of the value of increased productivity is given to workers under a prearranged formula (driven by operational factors [e.g., quality, productivity, customer satisfaction])	• Geared toward production-oriented workers • Add-on to compensation, so easily accepted by employees	• May be too far removed from workers' control to affect performance

For example, burying incentives and recognition for team membership in the company's basic compensation package can dampen the intended motivating effect on individuals. Second, an incentive system should be comprehensive enough that people feel fairly treated. Employees compare their pay with that of others. At Whole Foods Market, employees vote on their benefits package every three years, which includes 100 percent health coverage.[6] An incentive system that appears unfair can result in trouble (see Exhibit 3-3).

---

[6]Whole Foods Market. (2010). *Whole Foods Market benefits*. Wholefoodsmarket.com.

In the traditional model of compensation, base pay was designed to attract and retain employees. Incentives and bonuses were reserved for managers, salespeople, and higher executives. More companies are applying some form of variable pay for all levels of employees. Individual incentives, commissions, profit sharing, and gainsharing are methods of variable pay designed to motivate and reward performance. However, they are not designed to motivate and reward teams. Two common practices for rewarding and motivating team performance are team incentives and recognition.

Incentive Pay

In terms of salary and pay, **base pay** is how companies determine an individual's base salary. This is an integration of internal equity (based on job evaluation) and external equity (based on market data). The second issue in pay is **variable pay**. One type of variable pay is incentive pay. According to a 2008 study by Employers Resource Council, the average percentage of incentive pay rewards allocated annually by most organizations is between 4 percent and 10 percent, with nearly 79 percent of organizations reporting rewards in that range. Seventy-one percent of organizations surveyed used productivity measures to determine who receives variable pay.[7]

As employees move up the organizational chart, the proportion of variable pay should increase—along with their amount of control over the situation. Many organizations have incentive-based pay plans based on individual performance. Because the focus of this book is on teams, we focus on team-based pay. When teams are an organization's choice approach to job design, it often makes little sense for the organization to use systems that reward individual performance. Eighty-one percent of employees in one survey indicated that their compensation packages were based on individual performance, while only 58 percent were based on collaboration and teamwork.[8] However, performance appraisal systems for individuals that require a fixed number of positive and negative rations or provide fixed pots of budget money to be divided within a group are destructive because they put team members in competition for rewards.[9] The "cutthroat cooperation effect" refers to the fact that it is more difficult for teams to move from competitive to cooperative reward structures than vice versa.[10] Indeed, teams with a history of

---

EXHIBIT 3-3 Women Are Still Paid Less Than Men for the Same Work

It is well known that women earn significantly less money for doing the same work as men: The 2008 American Community Survey stated that the median earnings of full-time, year-round men in the United States were $45,556. For women, the median earnings were $35,471, or 77.9 percent of men's earnings.

Source: Semega, J. (2009). Men's and women's earnings by state: 2008 American Community survey. Washington, DC: Department of Commerce, Economics and Statistics Administration, U.S. Census Bureau.

---

[7]Employers Resource Council. (2008). *Variable pay plans.* www.ercnet.org.
[8]Scott, D., McMullen, T., & Shields, J. (2009, May). Alignment of business strategies, organization structures and reward programs: A survey of policies, practices and effectiveness. *Worldatwork.* worldatwork.org
[9]Lawler, E. E. (1992). *The ultimate advantage: Creating the high-involvement organization.* San Francisco, CA: Jossey-Bass.
[10]Johnson, M. D., Hollenbeck, J. R., Humphrey, S. E., Ilgen, D. R., Jundt, D., & Meyer, C. J. (2006). Cutthroat cooperation: Asymmetrical adaptation to changes in team reward structures. *Academy of Management Journal, 49,* 103–119.

competitive reward structures performed worse than teams with a history of cooperative reward structures.[11] Incentive systems combine individual performance and team performance to reflect the degree to which a job calls for individual work and teamwork. For example, a bonus pool may be created based on the performance of the overall team. The bonus pool can be divided among the individuals who are members of the team based on how well the individuals performed. (For an example of the implementation of bonus pay, see Exhibit 3-4.) To ensure that team members do not compete in a destructive fashion, a 360-degree feedback method can be used (we discuss the method in detail in the next section). Another alternative is to have two reward systems operating in tandem. One system provides bonuses to teams based on their performance; the second rewards individuals, based on how well they have performed. These systems can be based on separate budgets so that they do not compete. Hybrid rewards lead to higher levels of team performance than do individual and shared rewards.[12] The reason why hybrid rewards are more effective is due to improvements in information allocation and reductions in social loafing (free riding).

A critical question is whether to reward behavior or to reward results. Traditional thinking may lead managers to link team performance to their results. For goals such as cost reduction, this is easy to quantify, but for other areas it is much more difficult. One solution is to redefine or broaden the meaning of success, much as the previous chapter reviewed the four measures of team productivity (productivity, cohesion, learning, and integration). Thus, many managers reward competencies rather than results—for example, does the person participate? Does the person empower others? Does the person listen in a team environment? The Calgon brand created an annual award for the best idea that didn't work and presented it at the company's annual awards dinner.[13]

Although team incentives offer significant advantages, there are some potential drawbacks. Incentives may create unintended behavior. For example, when Ken O'Brien was an NFL

EXHIBIT 3-4 Team Bonus Pay

After working in the profession primarily on a solo level, some real estate agents are following the lead of profitable medical practices by joining forces as teams. Agents are pitching the team concept to home buyers and sellers, suggesting that around-the-clock coverage will give them an edge with competition. The team relationship proposes a win-win situation; real estate teams typically operate under a separate banner under the company, dividing the commission among members based on each agent's role, and as with solo agents, give a share of the team's commission to the firm. The only potential drawback to this arrangement is whether a larger company feels slighted by a team receiving greater recognition than the firm. To ensure success for the team, individual skills of team member must be taken into consideration, as not everyone can do everything well. Also, although some workers may not make as much money per deal as they would have working alone, they realize that it is better to bring in any piece of a deal than nothing at all.

Source: Based on Brenner E. (2009, November 1). Agents find benefits in teaming up. *New York Times*, p. RE5.

---

[11]Beersma, B., Hollenbeck, J. R., Conlon, D. E., Humphrey, S. E., & Moon, h. (2009). Cutthroat cooperation: The effects of team role decisions on adaption to alternative reward structures. *Organizational Behavior and Human Decision Process, 108*, 131–142.

[12]Pearsall, M. J., Christian, M. S., & Ellis, A. P. J. (2010). Motivating interdependent teams: Individual rewards, shared rewards, or something in between? *Journal of Applied Psychology, 95*(1), 183–191.

[13]Tynan, D. (n.d.). 25 ways to reward employees (without spending a dime). *HRWorld*. hrworld.com.

quarterback, he threw a lot of interceptions, and one team attorney wrote a clause into O'Brien's contract penalizing him for each one he threw.[14] The incentive plan worked: O'Brien's interceptions plummeted, but he also stopped throwing the ball! The use of team-based rewards may create the potential for motivational loss (i.e., social loafing and free riding). This may result from perceptions of inequity when other team members are perceived as free riders, but rewards are nevertheless allocated based on equality. Moreover, team rewards may not foster cooperation in teams.[15] Team rewards may foster competition between teams, leading to suboptimization of the organizational goals.[16]

Recognition

The power of positive recognition often is severely underestimated. "Firms are overly focused on rewards and punishments," says Dan Pink, author of *Drive: The Surprising Truth About What Motivates Us*. Companies "should move past their outdated reliance on carrots and sticks," Pink says. "That was fine for simple, routine 20th-century tasks. But for creative, conceptual 21st-century work, companies are much better off ensuring that people have ample amounts of autonomy and that their individual efforts are hitched to a larger purpose."[17] Making sure that employees are happy and feel that they are appreciated builds loyalty and productivity. Leaders should not approach this passively. Furthermore, in companies with team environments where people's identities are incorporated into teams, employees may feel a greater need for recognition.[18] It can cost virtually nothing—just a little time, energy, and forethought. For example, Pride@Boeing has four elements: formal appreciation, instant appreciation, service awards, and cash awards.[19] Both managers and employees can nominate employees and teams for exceptional performance. Formal appreciation awards are given as points redeemable online for merchandise. Instant appreciation includes items such as pens, mugs, and bags that managers have on hand and can give out at any time to reward some specific behavior, event, or accomplishment. Recognition, rewards, spot cash awards, or "celebrations of success" reward contributions after the fact, when performance is known. With regard to fairness, people view it as less fair to distribute resources equally when the resource is a medium of exchange (i.e., cash and tokens) rather than a good that holds value (tickets, plaque, etc.).[20]

The idea behind team recognition is that money is not everything. There are infinite sources of nonmonetary recognition—plaques, trophies, small gifts, vacations, and dinners with company officers. The most important feature of any of these is to give the gift respectfully, personally, and sincerely. First and foremost, this means that people and teams are singled out— if everyone gets the same recognition, it doesn't work. Bob Nelson, author of *1001 Ways to Reward Employees* and *1001 Ways to Energize Employees*, notes that recognitions such as

---

[14]Heath, D., & Heath, C. (2009, February). The curse of incentives. *Fast Company, 132*, 48–49.

[15]Wageman, R. (1995). Interdependence and group effectiveness. *Administrative Science Quarterly, 40*(1), 145–180.

[16]Mohrman, S. A., Lawler, E. E., & Mohrman, A. M. (1992). Applying employee involvement in schools. *Educational Evaluation and Policy Analysis, 14*(4), 347–360.

[17]Frauenheim, E. (2009, November 16). Commitment issues—restoring employee engagement. *Workforce Management*, pp. 20–25.

[18]Gross, S. E. (2000). Team-based pay. In L. A. Berger & D. R. Berger (Eds.), *The compensation handbook: A state-of-the-art guide to compensation strategy and design* (4th ed., pp. 261–273). New York: McGraw-Hill.

[19]www.boeing.com

[20]DeVoe, S. E., & Iyengar, S. S. (2010). Medium of exchange matters: What's fair for goods is unfair for money. *Psychological Science, 21*(2), 159–162.

"employee of the month programs" don't work because, eventually, everyone is going to receive the award.[21] The reward should be chosen with the people in mind. Not everyone likes sporting events or ballet, for example. It is important to clearly tie the recognition to team performance; it will lose its effect if the organization waits two months to reward the team. (For some general guidelines for implementing recognition awards, consult Exhibit 3-5.)

EXHIBIT 3-5 Implementing Recognition Awards: A Guide

To have maximum possible impact, recognition awards should have the following features:

Purpose/objective	The program should clearly recognize what has been accomplished by the team and how that effort is linked to the company's values.
Eligibility	Companies must clearly determine whether teams or individuals will be recognized; lower, middle, and upper management; and how frequently employees are eligible for awards.
Program award levels	Use a few levels to recognize different accomplishments and different degrees of contributions: (a) application noncash awards (up to $250); (b) awards for significant financial contribution ($250 to $2,500) for team members whose efforts significantly exceed expectations, support the unit's efforts, and produce measurable results; (c) awards for "extraordinary financial results" ($2,500 to $10,000) for team members whose efforts have exceptional bottom-line impact.
Benefit implications	Recognition awards are not considered benefit bearing.
Funding	Recognition programs are typically funded out of the expense budget of the business unit and department and are often stated as a percentage of the payroll.
Types of awards	(Noncash versus cash)
Nomination procedures	For appreciation award level, nomination procedure should be as simple as possible; for companywide rewards, nomination procedures may be much more elaborate with peers, customers, and supervisors all having opportunity for input.
Timing	All awards should be given as close to the event as possible to reinforce the actions that led to the event.
Award presentation	This should be a positive experience, that makes the winner(s) feel proud; comments should be personalized and refer to details of the achievement; the connection between the accomplishment and the company's business strategy should be made clear; never present the award in passing; publicize the award (e.g., via memo, e-mail, bulletin board, or newsletter).
Program evaluation	Annually, a rewards and recognition committee should be chartered to evaluate the program in terms of its effectiveness.

Source: Adapted from Gross, S. E. (1995). *Compensation for teams: How to design and implement team-based reward programs.* New York: AMACOM.

---

[21]Nelson, B. (2005). *1001 ways to reward employees* (2nd ed.). New York: Workman Publishing.

CASH AND NONCASH   Spot awards (also known as lightning bolts) can either be cash or noncash. Noncash awards, which are the most common, are given out for a job well done and are usually of nominal value. Cash awards can be far more substantial, although usually they are small bonuses. At J.A. Frate trucking, one driver is designated "Driver of the Year" and wins a cash prize. This trucker receives nearly $4,000 of embellishments that drivers usually don't get, such as satellite radio, power windows, and chrome wheels. Employees are also encouraged to suggest changes, with the top three suggestion makers each quarter awarded $100, $50, and $25, respectively. Retention rates are high; the average tenure of current employees is 7.3 years.[22]

There is an infinite variety of noncash rewards that companies can give to teams to recognize contributions, ranging from thank-you notes to time off to all-expenses-paid trips for two to exotic places. Nearly 90 percent of organizations have employee recognition programs in place; 90 percent of organizations surveyed continue all of their existing recognition programs from year to year.[23] PricewaterhouseCoopers has a points-based program called "Acclaim" in which employees are given points for noteworthy accomplishments or results at work. These points can be redeemed for merchandise or services.[24] Such rewards often reinforce the company image and strengthen the connection between the employer and the employee. In Symantec's "Applause" program, employees reward their team members with applause certificates with values from $25 to $1,000.[25] To be effective, recognition needs to be clearly focused on the team whose achievements are being celebrated, rather than on a general self-congratulatory party for the entire unit or organization.

An especially thorny issue is whether recognition awards to teams should equally recognize all team members. Managers often think they're giving their team quality recognition, but it turns out to be meaningless due to a lack of respect. For instance, perhaps one employee has a great relationship with her manager and asks him for a day off. When the manager tells her she's too valuable to take any time off, she actually views this as recognition. Another employee with a poor relationship with his boss sees his $1,000 bonus as a ploy and asks, "What is my manager trying to get out of me now?"[26] Similarly, giving team members tickets to an evening ball game in reward for putting in long hours on a project may be deflating to team members with families.

For these reasons, many consultants believe that teams should be given a role in distributing recognition awards—letting the team decide which members get how much. This practice is consistent with the whole idea of self-managing teams: autonomy and self-management (see Exhibit 3-6).

Two types of incentive pay systems that are not designed specifically for teams but are popular in participative management companies and are consistent with many team-based approaches are profit sharing and gainsharing. They can be tailored for teams.

Profit Sharing

Many companies use profit sharing schemes, wherein a portion of the bottom-line economic profits is given to employees. These internally distributed profits may be apportioned according to equality or equity. In the typical profit sharing plan, profit sharing bonuses are put into retirement plans. This makes it more difficult to clearly relate rewards to controllable performance. Thus, most profit sharing plans have little impact on the motivation and behavior of employees.[27]

---

[22]Spors, Top small workplaces 2008.

[23]Trends in employee recognition. (2008, April). Retrieved on January 29, 2010, worldatwork.org.

[24]PriceWaterhouseCoopers. (2010). *Reward and recognition*. pwc.com.

[25]Palmer, A. (2009, December 9). Global Engagement. *Incentive, 183*(11), 16–23.

[26]Ohngren, K. (2009, May 13). *Cheap ways to motivate you team*. Entrepreneur.com

[27]Lawler, *Rewarding excellence*.

EXHIBIT 3-6 Seven Ways to Praise Teams

Bob Nelson, author of *1001 Ways to Reward Employees*, suggests these seven methods of recognizing the accomplishments of a team, as well as the achievements of individual team members:

1. Have managers pop in at the first meeting of a special project team and express their appreciation for the members' involvement.
2. When a group presents an idea or suggestion, managers should thank members for their initiative.
3. Encourage a lunch meeting with project teams once they've made interim findings. Have managers express their appreciation. Encourage continued energy. Provide the lunch.
4. Promote writing letters to every team member at the conclusion of a project thanking them for their contribution.
5. Encourage creative symbols of a team's work, such as T-shirts or coffee cups with a motto or logo.
6. Have managers ask the boss to attend a meeting with the employees during which individuals and groups are thanked for their specific contributions.
7. Suggest catered lunches or breakfasts for high-performing groups.

Source: Excerpted from *1001 Ways to Reward Employees*. Copyright © 2005, 1994 by Bob Nelson. Used by permission of Workman Publishing Co., Inc., New York. All rights reserved.

Profit sharing plans serve an important communication purpose by signaling to everyone that rewards are in balance across the organization. Second, they inform and educate employees about the financial health of the organization. Finally, profit sharing makes the labor costs of an organization variable, thus adjusting them to the organization's ability to pay.[28]

Gainsharing

Gainsharing involves a measurement of productivity, combined with the calculation of a bonus, designed to offer employees a mutual share of any increases in total organizational productivity. In gainsharing plans, an organization uses a formula to share financial gains with all employees in a single plant or location. The organization establishes a historical base period of performance and uses this to determine whether gains in performance have occurred. Typically, only controllable costs are measured for the purpose of computing gain. Unless a major change takes place in the company's products or technology, the historical base stays the same during the entire history of the plan. Thus, the organization's performance is always compared with the time period before it started the gainsharing plan. When the organization's performance is better than it was in the base period, the plan funds a bonus pool. When its performance falls short, no bonus pool is created; when performance is met or exceeded, the typical plan pays about half of the bonus pool to employees and the rest is kept by the company. Payments are usually made on a monthly basis, with all employees receiving the same percentage of their regular base pay. A trend of large corporations that have their own gainsharing plans has led more companies to adopt gainsharing.

Gainsharing enhances coordination and information sharing among teams, instigates attitude change, raises performance standards, and enhances idea generation and flexibility. (For an in-depth discussion of gainsharing, see Chapter 12 in Martocchio's *Strategic Compensation: A Human Resource Management Approach*).[29] Gainsharing plans are more than just pay incentive plans; they are a way of managing and a technology for organizational development.

---

[28]Weitzman, M. (1984). *The share economy*. Cambridge, MA: Harvard University Press.
[29]Lawler, *Rewarding excellence*.

For gainsharing to work successfully, it should be developed in collaboration with the people it will affect. It is important that employees understand the formula and how to influence it, that the standards seem credible, that bonuses be timely, and that some mechanism exists for change. A company needs a participative management system, because the plan requires employees to take ownership of the success of the company.[30]

Profit sharing plans are typically less effective than gainsharing plans in influencing employee motivation and changing culture than are gainsharing plans.[31] This lack of effectiveness is largely attributable to the disconnection between individual performance and corporate profits—even with high-level involvement. This depends on how salient profit sharing benefits are made to the workers. Consider the company that boldly posts its stock value for all employees to view in public areas—people see the value literally.

These four systems for rewarding employees—incentive pay, recognition, profit sharing, and gainsharing—should not be looked at as competing approaches, but rather as compatible systems that accomplish different, important objectives. For example, the combination of gainsharing and profit sharing deals directly with an organization's need to have variable labor costs and helps to educate the workforce about financial information.

TEAMS AND PAY FOR PERFORMANCE

For teams to be optimally effective, a reward system should be attuned to the behaviors and skills that are needed for team success.[32] And even in a recession, companies still must track how employees perform, manage their development, and figure out how much to pay them. "During an economic downturn, it's imperative that you institute more frequent reviews where employee goals are similar across similar roles, are tied directly to revenue generating tasks, and are reviewed consistently," says Zach Thomas, an analyst at research firm Forrester.[33]

Lawler distinguishes four types of teams: parallel teams, production and service teams, project teams, and management teams. Exhibit 3-7 suggests the best possible pay for performance schemes, according to each type of team.

One investigation examined the effect of "cooperative" versus "competitive" reward structures on team performance.[34] Eighty-four-person teams participated in a challenging distributed dynamic decision-making task developed for the Department of Defense. The teams all did the simulation two times: time 1 and time 2; each time, they operated under a different reward and compensation structure. One reward structure was "cutthroat competition" in which in order to win a cash prize, they would need to be a top performer in their group; the other reward structure was cooperation, in which all team members would share the cash reward equally. Some of the teams operated under "cutthroat cooperation," in which they first participated under a competitive reward structure at time 1 and then a cooperative reward structure at time 2. Another group operated under "friendly competition," in which they first operated under a cooperative reward structure at time 1 and then a competitive reward structure at time 2. It was more difficult for teams to shift from competition to cooperation than vice versa. These teams had lower accuracy and less information sharing. "Without team goals, you may find that one of your employees refuses to help out a fellow

[30]Blinder, A. S. (1990). Pay, participation, and productivity. *Brookings Review, 8*(1), 33–38.
[31]Ibid.
[32]Lawler, *Rewarding excellence.*
[33]Frauenheim, E. (2009, April 20). Talent tools still essential. *Workforce Management*, p. 20.
[34]Johnson et al., "Cutthroat cooperation."

EXHIBIT 3-7 Pay Strategies for Four Types of Teams

Type of Team	Work Focus	Pay for Performance
Parallel	Supplement regular organizational structure and perform problem-solving and work-improvement tasks (e.g., problem-solving teams, quality circles, and employee participation teams)	Gainsharing or other business unit plan to reward savings Recognition rewards
Production and Service	Responsible for producing a project or service and are self-contained, identifiable work units (e.g., manufacturing teams, assembly teams, tactical teams, and customer sales or service teams)	Team bonuses or business unit bonuses if teams are interdependent Use individual bonuses that are based on peer evaluations
Project	Often involve diverse group of knowledge workers, such as design engineers, process engineers, programmers (e.g., new project development teams)	Use bonuses based on project success Profit sharing and stock plans
Management	Composed of well-trained managers; often have stable membership; teams usually permanent; expected to provide integration, leadership, and direction to organization	Team or business unit bonuses Profit sharing and stock-based options

Source: Adapted from Lawler, E. E. (2000). *Rewarding excellence: Pay strategies for the new economy* (p. 217). San Francisco, CA: Jossey-Bass.

colleague. That type of behavior is counterproductive to business growth and needs to be nipped in the bud. The best way to encourage teamwork is to pay the entire team when they hit team goals."[35]

TEAM PERFORMANCE APPRAISAL

Individual performance appraisal is an evaluation of a person's behaviors and accomplishments in terms of the person's work in an organization. Performance appraisals are a source of feedback, a basis for personal development, and a determination of pay. The rise of teams presents special challenges for performance appraisal. It is difficult for a supervisor to conduct a traditional performance appraisal of an individual who is serving at least part time on a team. When the individual is part of a self-managed, self-directing, or self-governing team, it is virtually impossible, because supervisors are rarely close enough to the teams to evaluate them. The catch-22 is that if they were, they might hinder the performance of the team. The overarching purpose of a measurement system should be to help a team, rather than to employ top management to gauge its progress.[36] Moreover, a truly empowered team should play a lead role in designing its own measurement system. We address how performance should be measured and by whom.

---

[35]Alter, M. (2008, January 1). Performance based pay. *Inc Magazine.* inc.com
[36]Meyer, C. (1994, May–June). How the right measures help teams excel. *Harvard Business Review,* pp. 95–103.

What Is Measured?

A change in traditional performance appraisals, precipitated by the rise of teams, concerns what is measured in performance reviews. In many traditional control-oriented organizations, the major determinant of employees' pay is the type of work they do or their seniority. The major alternative is competency-based pay. Companies are increasingly recognizing that dynamic factors, such as competencies and skills, may be a better way to measure success than static measures, such as experience and education. In the following paragraphs, we review job-based pay, skill-based pay, and competency-based pay.

JOB-BASED PAY   Job-based pay is determined by a job evaluation system, which frequently takes a point factor approach to evaluating jobs.[37] The point factor approach begins with a written job description that is scored in terms of duties. The point scores are then translated into salary levels. A key advantage of job-based pay systems is that organizations can determine what other companies are paying and can assess whether they are paying more or less than their competitors. Another advantage of job evaluation systems is that they allow for centralized control of an organization's pay system.

SKILL-BASED PAY   To design a skill-based pay system, a company must identify the tasks that need to be performed in the organization. Next, the organization identifies skills that are needed for those tasks to be performed and develops tests or measures to determine whether a person has learned these skills. For this reason, it is important to specify the skills that an individual can learn in a company. Employees need to be told what they can learn given their position in the organization and how learning skills will affect their pay. People are typically paid only for the skills that they have and are willing to use. Many skill-based plans give people pay increases when they learn a new skill. One system of skill-based pay is a technical ladder, in which individuals are paid for the depth of skill they have in a particular technical specialty. IBM's Professional Marketplace program provides IBM consultants with access to a database of 68,000 company employees who are available to work. Consultants can search for the right person for any job by sifting through 100 job classifications (such as account technical representative or Web specialist) and 10,000 skills (such as "mentoring" or specific experience with health-care regulations). The program provides information on who is available, where they are located, and how much it will cost the company to use them. Based on their skills, the program's software adjusts the figure by taking into account how far away from home the employee will be working and how long he or she is needed. Since the programs' inception, job fulfillment is 20 percent faster and better matched to the exact qualifications needed.[38] (For an example of the importance of acquiring skills, see Exhibit 3-8.)

COMPETENCY-BASED PAY   Competency-based pay differs from skill-based pay in that employees prove they can use their skills. After all, it is possible for people to attain skills (e.g., training and mentoring programs) but never use them—or be ineffective when using them. It is important for organizations to focus on demonstrated competencies, rather than accumulated accreditations.

Competency-based pay is regarded as a much more sensible and ultimately profitable approach to use in a team-based organization. Competency-based pay systems promote

---

[37]Lawler, *Rewarding excellence.*
[38]IBM professional marketplace matches consultants with clients. (n.d.). IBM.com

EXHIBIT 3-8 Skill Acquisition

Jeff Koeze, a law professor with no business experience, took over the then 86-year-old family business from his father after only two months of training. The younger Koeze found himself the leader of a $7 million company, armed only with knowledge acquired from books. Initially Koeze approached the situation by hiring an array of professionals and soaking up every behavioral book and seminar available, in an attempt to challenge both the workers and him. Over the course of his first 12 years with the company, Koeze advanced by learning to trust his instincts, changing his own behavior, and applying critical thinking skills. To build confidence in his employees, he focused on improving communication, facing up to service problems, and diminishing service anxieties and errors.

Source: Based on Baily, J. (2008, December). The education of an educated CEO. *Inc., 30*(12), 100–106.

flexibility in employees: When employees can perform multiple tasks, organizations gain tremendous flexibility in using their workforce. This, of course, is the concept of cross-training. In addition to the benefits of cross-training, individuals who have several skills have an advantage in terms of developing an accurate perspective on organizational problems and challenges. When employees have an overview of the entire company, they are more committed. When they are broadly knowledgeable about the operations of an organization, they can increase their self-managing, coordinate with others, use organizational resources, and communicate more effectively.

However, competency-based pay systems are not perfect. An organization using a competency-based pay system typically commits to giving everyone the opportunity to learn multiple skills and then to demonstrate them; thus, the organization has to make a large investment in training and evaluation. There is a trade-off between getting the work done and skill acquisition and demonstration.

Who Does the Measuring?

The standard is the employee's supervisor or some set of top-level persons. With the increasing use of teams, peer review is becoming more common and more necessary in organizations. Popularly known as **360-degree** or **multirater feedback** methods, the peer review procedure involves getting feedback about an employee from all sides: top (supervisors), bottom (subordinates), coworkers, suppliers, and end-user customers or clients (see Exhibit 3-9). Typically, several people (ideally 5 to 10) participate in the evaluation, compared with a traditional review in which only one person, usually a supervisor, provides feedback. At Wyeth Healthcare, employees negotiate with their manager who their reviewers will be on the 360-degree evaluation. They are advised to select a broad a range of people whom they work with on a regular basis and also consider choosing someone with whom their relationship could be improved. The reviewers complete a short online questionnaire and the results form part of a report discussed at the review, along with their own views and those of their manager.[39] In 360 program, the highest paid should be the highest ranked when the results are plotted on a graph. Anonymity is the key to building a nonbiased feedback system, especially for peers and subordinates. Otherwise, the entire system is compromised.

---

[39]Carmichael, M. (2009, July 1). Case study Wyeth consumer healthcare an all-round appraisal success. *Human Resources*, 74.

EXHIBIT 3-9 360-Degree or Multirater Feedback

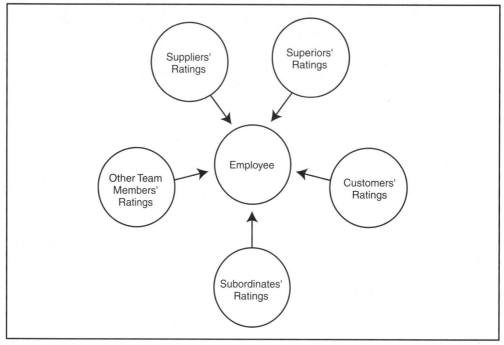

Source: Novak, C. J. (1997, April). Proceed with caution when paying teams. *HR Magazine, 42*(4), 73–78. Copyright 1997 by Society for Human Resource Management (SHRM). Reproduced with permission of Society for Human Resource Management (SHRM) in the format Textbook via Copyright Clearance Center.

A big disadvantage of the top-down performance review is evaluation bias. The multiple data points and aggregate responses provided by 360-degree feedback make the bias of a single person less of a problem. A second major disadvantage of single-source evaluation is that it is easy to dismiss the information. As an example of how companies put 360-degree feedback in place, Goldman Sachs Group Inc. "insists on minimizing the use of the first-person pronoun," says former chairman Stephen Friedman. To make sure that employees serve the firm on the whole, it uses comprehensive 360-degree reviews in which feedback is solicited from as many as 15 coworkers, supervisors, and underlings alike, including subordinates several levels down on the flowchart.[40]

In theory, the 360-degree process provides a multifaceted view of the team member. However, putting it into practice can be difficult: If the number of feedback sources is limited, raters are not guaranteed anonymity and may fear retaliation. The system is subject to abuse if members make side deals to rate one another favorably. However, despite its difficulties, 360-degree or multirater feedback is usually regarded to be a more fair assessment of performance than is top-down review. Although team members are often best qualified to rate one another, there are some weaknesses to this approach. Team members unpopular for reasons other than performance can suffer. Team members do not always grasp the big picture in terms of organizational goals. As raters, peers can suffer from evaluation biases.

---

[40]BW 50 Interactive Scoreboard. (2008). *Business Week.* bwnt.businessweek.com; Weber, J. (2006, June 12). The leadership factory. *Business Week, 3988*, p. 60.

Developing a 360-Degree Program

It is impossible to develop a 360-degree evaluation program overnight. Most teams are not ready to base all of their pay on multisource performance management, especially when teams are relatively new. Most teams are hesitant to have all of their pay tied to team member evaluations; at the same time, they scoff at individual pay performance systems. The key is to set up a system of feedback that is anonymous and private and slowly build into an open feedback, public knowledge system.

There is no standard method for 360-degree implementation. Some companies administer and develop the whole system. Some allow outside consultants to prepare and analyze feedback to ensure anonymity. As a start for developing 360-degree evaluation systems, consider the steps outlined in Exhibit 3-10.[41]

The practices put into place to address the issues in Exhibit 3-10 will be different for every organization. Duplicating systems used by world-class companies is not necessarily the best approach. Each organization should develop the 360-degree system that will optimize effectiveness within its organizational design. Companies should first use a pilot 360-degree program that is not tied to compensation and that is not public. In the beginning stages, only the employee sees all of the feedback; gradually, the supervisor is brought into the loop. Eventually, it is important to tie employee compensation to the 360-degree evaluation.

As companies begin to challenge old assumptions about performance appraisals, they need to be careful not to cross the line of legal liability (see Exhibit 3-11). If people other

---

EXHIBIT 3-10 Things to Think about before Developing a 360-Degree Program in Your Company

The following questions should be considered before implementing 360-degree evaluation programs:
- Should other evaluation systems be utilized in addition to 360-degree feedback?
- Should the organization consider hiring an outside consultant?
- Should the organization purchase a generic program or create a customized evaluation?
- Should the evaluation be computer based or consist of a paper-and-pencil form?
- How many raters should be involved? (Ideally, 5 to 10; less than 5 provides limited viewpoints, and more than 10 consumes time and adds unnecessary complexity.)
- Who should be involved in the rating?
- Who should choose the raters?
- How are terms like *peer*, *supervisor*, and *subordinate* defined by the organization?
- How many questions or items should be incorporated into the evaluation?
- Should the feedback remain anonymous?
- How should employees be educated on the use of constructive criticism and the characteristics of 360-degree feedback?

Source: Adapted from Hoffman, R. (1995, April). Ten reasons you should be using 360-degree feedback. *HR Magazine, 40*(4), 82–85; Milliman, J. F., Zawacki, R. F., Norman, C., Powell, L., & Kirksey, J. (1994, November). Companies evaluate employees from all perspectives. *Personnel Journal, 73*(11), 99–103.

---

[41]Hoffman, R. (1995, April). Ten reasons you should be using 360-degree feedback. *HR Magazine, 40*(4), 82–85; Milliman, J. F., Zawacki, R. F., Norman, C., Powell, L., & Kirksey, J. (1994, November). Companies evaluate employees from all perspectives. *Personnel Journal, 73*(11), 99–103.

EXHIBIT 3-11 Prescriptions for Legally Defensible Appraisal Systems

1. Job analysis to identify important duties and tasks should precede development of a performance appraisal system.
2. The performance appraisal system should be standardized and formal.
3. Specific performance standards should be communicated to employees in advance of the appraisal period.
4. Objectives and uncontaminated data should be used whenever possible.
5. Ratings on traits such as dependability, drive, or attitude should be avoided.
6. Employees should be evaluated on specific work dimensions rather than on a single, global, or overall measure.
7. If work behaviors rather than outcomes are to be evaluated, evaluators should have ample opportunity to observe ratee performance.
8. To increase the reliability of ratings, more than one independent evaluator should be used whenever possible.
9. Behavioral documentation should be prepared for ratings.
10. Employees should be given an opportunity to review their appraisals.
11. A formal system of appeal should be available for appraisal disagreements.
12. Raters should be trained to prevent discrimination and to evaluate performance consistently.
13. Appraisals should be frequent, offered at least annually.

Source: Adapted from Bernardin, H. J., & Cascio, W. F. (1988). Performance appraisal and the law. In R. S. Schuler, S. A. Youngblood, & V. L. Huber (Eds.), *Readings in personnel and human resource management* (3rd ed., p. 239). St. Paul, MN: West.

than management are involved in the appraisal process, then they must be trained on the legal issues involved with discrimination law, the Americans with Disabilities Act, and other relevant legislation. Whereas the use of multiple raters has become more popular as many firms move toward team-based management systems, gender and race affect performance reviews, with evaluations more positive for underlings whose managers share their social demographic. Ingrained expectations, about what types of people perform better, also subtly influence the process.[42] For a detailed look at actual items used in 360-degree evaluations, consult Appendix 4.

Wageman, Hackman, and Lehman developed a team diagnostic survey (TDS) to identify conditions that increase the likelihood that teams will perform well.[43] The TDS can be used on a 360-degree or peer-feedback format. It assesses the effectiveness of team task processes, the quality of members' work relationships, and team members' motivation and satisfaction. As can be seen in Exhibit 3-12, the TDS is organized into eight sections: Section 1 captures the general description of the team, and sections 2–7 assess the conditions for team effectiveness. Section 8 provides measures of three effectiveness criteria.

---

[42]Pfeffer, J. (2009, July 23). Managers and employees alike sense the truth: Workplace appraisals aren't working. *Business Week*, p.24.
[43]Wageman, R., Hackman, J. R., & Lehman, E. V. (2005). The team diagnostic survey: Development of an instrument. *The Journal of Applied Behavioral Science, 41*(4), 373–398.

EXHIBIT 3-12 Team Diagnostic Survey

Part 1: Real Team

1a. *Bounded*
- Team membership is quite clear—everybody knows exactly who is and isn't on this team.
- There is so much ambiguity about who is on this team that it would be nearly impossible to generate an accurate membership list [R].
- Anyone who knows this team could accurately name all its members.

1b. *Interdependent*
- Members of this team have their own individual jobs to do, with little need for them to work together [R].
- Generating the outcome or product of this team requires a great deal of communication and coordination among members.
- Members of this team have to depend heavily on one another to get the team's work done.

1c. *Stable*
- Different people are constantly joining and leaving this team [R].
- This team is quite stable, with few changes in membership.

Part 2: Compelling Direction

2a. *Clear*
- There is great uncertainty and ambiguity about what this team is supposed to accomplish [R].
- This team's purposes are specified so clearly that all members should know exactly what the team exists to accomplish.

2b. *Challenging*
- This team's purposes are so challenging that members have to stretch to accomplish them.
- This team's purposes are not especially challenging—achieving them is well within reach [R].

2c. *Consequential*
- The purposes of this team don't make much of a difference to anybody else [R].
- This team's purposes are of great consequence for those we serve.

2d. *Ends versus means*
- Which best describes your team with respect to purpose and means?
- The purposes of our team are specified by others, but the means and procedures we use to accomplish them are left to us.
- The means or procedures we are supposed to use in our work are specified in detail by others, but the purposes of our team are left unstated.
- Both the purposes of our team and the means or procedures we are supposed to use in our work are specified in detail by others.
- Neither the purposes nor the means are specified by others for our team.

Part 3: Enabling Structure

3a. *Size*
- This team is larger than it needs to be [R].
- This team has too few members for what it has to accomplish [R].
- This team is just the right size to accomplish its purposes.

3b. *Diversity*
- Members of this team are too dissimilar to work together well [R].
- This team does not have a broad enough range of experiences and perspective to accomplish its purpose [R].

(cont.on p. 58)

- This team has a nearly ideal "mix" of members—a diverse set of people who bring different perspectives and experiences to the work.

3c. *Skills*

- Members of this work team have more than enough talent and experience for the kind of work that we do.
- Everyone in this team has the special skills that are needed for teamwork.
- Some members of this team lack the knowledge and skills that they need to do their parts of the team's work [R].

3d. *Whole task*

- We do a whole, identifiable piece of work.
- Our team does such a small part of the overall task that it is hard to point specifically to our special contribution [R].
- This team's work is inherently meaningful.

3e. *Autonomy/Judgment*

- The work of this team leaves little room for the exercise of judgment or initiative [R].
- The work we do requires the team to make many "judgment calls" as we carry it out.

3f. *Knowledge of results*

- Carrying out our team's task automatically generates trustworthy indicators of how well we are doing.
- The work itself provides almost no trustworthy feedback about our team's performance [R].
- The only way we can figure out how well we are performing is for other people in the organization to tell us [R].

3g. *Group norms*

- Standards for member behavior in this team are vague and unclear [R].
- It is clear what is—and what is not—acceptable member behavior in this team.
- Members of this team agree about how members are expected to behave.

Part 4: Supportive Organizational Context

4a. *Rewards/Recognition*

- Excellent team performance pays off in this organization.
- Even teams that do an especially good job are not recognized or rewarded by the organization [R].
- This organization recognizes and reinforces teams that perform well.

4b. *Information*

- It is easy for teams in this organization to get any data or forecasts that members need to do their work.
- This organization keeps its teams in the dark about information that could affect their work plans [R].
- Teams in this organization can get whatever information they need to plan their work.

4c. *Education/Consultation*

- Teams in this organization have to make do with whatever expertise members already have—technical training and support are not available even when needed [R].
- When something comes up that team members do not know how to handle, it is easy for them to obtain the training or technical advice they need.
- In this organization, teams do not receive adequate training for the work they have to do [R].

(cont.on p. 59)

4d. *Material Resources*
- Teams in this organization can readily obtain all the material resources that they need for their work.
- Scarcity of resources is a real problem for teams in this organization [R].

Part 5: Available, Expert Coaching

5a. *Focus of leader's attention*
- The leader coaches individual team members.
- The leader helps team members learn how to work well together.
- The leader gets the team set up right: clarifying its purpose, picking members, structuring the task, and setting expectations.
- The leader runs external interference for the team—getting resources, security in outside assistance, removing roadblocks.

5b. *Coaching availability*
- When members of teams in this organization have trouble working together, there is no one available to help them out [R].
- Teams in this organization have access to "coaches" who can help them learn from their successes and mistakes.
- Expert coaches are readily available to teams in this organization.

5c. *Task-focused coaching*
- The team leader helps the team build a high shared commitment to its purposes.
- The team leader helps the team sustain the motivation of all members.
- The team leader works with the team to develop the best possible approach to its work.
- The team leader keeps the team alert to anything that might require a change of work strategy.
- The team leader helps members learn from one another and from the team's work experiences.
- The team leader helps the team identify and use each member's unique talents.

5d. *Operant coaching*
- The team leader provides positive feedback when the team behaves or performs well.
- The team leader provides corrective feedback when needed.
- The team leader gives inappropriate or undeserved praise or criticism [R].

5e. *Interpersonal coaching*
- The team leader helps members resolve any conflicts that may develop among them.
- The team leader helps members work on improving their interpersonal relationships.

5f. *Unhelpful directives*
- The team leader micromanages the content and process of team discussions.
- The team leader instructs the team in detail about how to solve its problems.
- The team leader tells the team everything it is doing wrong.

5g. *Task-focused peer coaching*
- Regular team members take initiative to promote high shared motivation and commitment.
- Regular team members take initiative to make sure the team develops and uses the best possible approach to its work.
- Regular team members take initiative to help the team build and use members' knowledge and skills.

5h. *Interpersonal peer coaching*
- Regular team members take initiative to constructively resolve any problems or conflicts that develop among members.

(cont. on p. 60)

5i. *Unhelpful peer interventions*
- Regular team members tell other members what to do and how they should do it.

Part 6: Process Criteria of Team Effectiveness

6a. *Effort-related process criteria*
- Members demonstrate their commitment to our team by putting in extra time and effort to help it succeed.
- Everyone on this team is motivated to have the team succeed.
- Some members of our team do not carry their fair share of the overall workload [R].

6b. *Strategy-related process criteria*
- Our team often comes up with innovative ways of proceeding with the work that turn out to be just what is needed.
- Our team often falls into mindless routines, without noticing any changes that may have occurred in our situation [R].
- Our team has a great deal of difficulty actually carrying out the plans we make for how we will proceed with the task [R].

6c. *Knowledge and skill–related process criteria*
- How seriously a members' ideas are taken by others on our team often depends more on who the person is than on how much he or she actually knows [R].
- Members of our team actively share their special knowledge and expertise with one another.
- Our team is quite skilled at capturing the lessons that can be learned from our work experience.

Part 7: Team Interpersonal Processes

7a. *Quality of Team interaction*
- There is a lot of unpleasantness among members of this team [R].
- The longer we work together as a team, the less well we do [R].
- Working together energizes and uplifts members of our team.
- Every time someone attempts to correct a team member whose behavior is not acceptable, things seem to get worse rather than better [R].

7b. *Satisfaction with Team Relationships*
- My relations with other team members are strained [R].
- I very much enjoy talking and working with my teammates.
- The chance to get to know my teammates is one of the best parts of working on this team.

Part 8: Individual Learning and Well-Being

8a. *Internal work motivation*
- I feel a real sense of personal satisfaction when our team does well.
- I feel bad and unhappy when our team has performed poorly.
- My own feelings are not affected one way or the other by how well our team performs [R].
- When our team has done well, I have done well.

8b. *Satisfaction with Growth Opportunities*
- I learn a great deal from my work on this team.
- My own creativity and initiative are suppressed by this team [R].
- Working on this team stretches my personal knowledge and skills.

8c. *General Satisfaction*
- I enjoy the kind of work we do in this team.
- Working on this team is an exercise in frustration [R].
- Generally speaking, I am very satisfied with this team.

Note: [R] = reverse-scored item.

Source: Adapted from Wageman, R., Hackman, J. R., & Lehman, E. (2005). Team diagnostic survey: Development of an instrument. *Journal of Applied Behavioral Science, 41*(4), 373–398.

RATER BIAS

Peers are often best qualified to evaluate a team member's performance; peer assessment is a valid and reliable evaluation procedure.[44] In addition, the team's supervisor and the team's customers or clients (either internal or external, if available) are also valuable sources of input. These information sources are valuable, but they can also be biased. Raters are not perfect; below, we discuss several serious biases that can threaten the quality of peer evaluation.

Inflation Bias

Candid performance evaluation and feedback are essential for team members because these allow them to adjust their behavior and motivation and to seek training.[45] However, raters frequently positively distort performance ratings when they anticipate giving feedback to ratees.[46] Inflation appears to stem from two sources: empathic buffering and fear of conflict. People are generally reluctant to transmit bad news to a poorly performing employee.[47] And, when doing so, they feel bad themselves.[48] A second reason is that raters want to avoid interpersonal conflict, particularly with someone they expect to respond defensively to criticism.[49]

Extrinsic Incentives Bias

Most managers believe that employees are primarily motivated by extrinsic incentives (e.g., job security and pay) and less motivated by intrinsic incentives (e.g., learning new things). For example, Douglas McGregor explicitly acknowledged this tendency when he described a social fault line between managers who inferred motivations incorrectly and those who inferred them correctly.[50] He bemoaned the commonness of Theory X managers (who believe that employees dislike work, wish to avoid responsibility, and desire security above all) and the scarcity of Theory Y managers (who believe that employees like work, wish to develop their skills, and desire to participate in tasks that advance worthy organizational goals). Consider a survey of 486 prospective lawyers who were questioned by Kaplan Educational Centers during a preparation course for the Law School Admissions Test.[51] The prospective lawyers were asked to describe their own motivations for pursuing a legal career and then those of their peers. Although 64 percent said that they were pursuing a legal career because it was intellectually appealing or because they had always been interested in the law,

[44]Huber, V. L., Neale, M. A., & Northcraft, G. B. (1987). Judgment by heuristics: Effects of ratee and rater characteristics and performance standards on performance-related judgments. *Organizational Behavior and Human Decision Processes, 40,* 149–169.

[45]Ashford, S. J., & Cummings, L. L. (1983). Feedback as an individual resource: Personal strategies of creating information. *Organizational Behavior and Human Decision Processes, 32,* 370–398.

[46]Antonioni, D. (1994). The effects of feedback accountability on upward appraisal ratings. *Personnel Psychology, 47,* 349–356.

[47]Tesser, A., & Rosen, S. (1975). The reluctance to transmit bad news. In L. Berkowitz (Ed.), *Advances in experimental social psychology* (Vol. 8). New York: Academic Press.

[48]Longnecker, C. O., Sims, H. P., & Gioia, D. A. (1987). Behind the mask: The politics of employee appraisal. *Academy of Management Executive, 1,* 183–193.

[49]Bond, C. F., & Anderson, E. L. (1987). The reluctance to transmit bad news: Private discomfort or public display? *Journal of Experimental Psychology, 23,* 176–187.

[50]McGregor, D. (1960). *The human side of enterprise.* New York: McGraw-Hill.

[51]Lawler, E. E., Mohrman, S. A., & Ledford, G. E., Jr. (1995). *Creating high performance organizations: Practices and results of employee involvement and total quality management in Fortune 1000 companies.* San Francisco: Jossey-Bass.

only 12 percent thought this about their peers. Instead, 62 percent thought that their peers were pursuing a legal career because of the financial rewards. Indeed, most of us have claimed that "*they're* only in it for the money" many more times than we have claimed "*I'm* only in it for the money."[52]

According to Frederick Taylor, "What workers want most from their employers beyond anything else is high wages."[53] In contrast, McGregor and other members of the human relations school of management argued that intrinsic features motivated employees.[54]

The **extrinsic incentives bias** states that people believe that others are more motivated than themselves by situational or extrinsic factors and less motivated than themselves by dispositional or intrinsic factors.[55] For example, in one survey, 74 MBA students ranked the importance of eight motivations (benefits, pay, job security, learning new skills, praise from manager, developing skills, accomplishing something worthwhile, and feeling good about oneself) for themselves and predicted the rank order that would be provided by their classmates and by actual managers and employees.[56] The MBA students overestimated how highly Citibank managers would rank extrinsic incentives. They predicted that the top four incentives would be primarily extrinsic (pay, security, benefits, and praise); however, the actual Citibank employees listed only one extrinsic incentive in their top four (benefits). Another survey of 235 managers identified only two goals—increased sales and more customer referrals—that were thought to be influenced by cash incentives. Numerous other goals, such as better customer satisfaction, improving teamwork, and employee retention, were believed to be better achieved with noncash awards.[57]

If managers falsely assume that others' motives are less noble than their own, then they may fail to communicate the importance and relevance of the organization's goals.[58] Corporate managers may spend too little time highlighting the satisfaction of solving customer problems; nonprofit managers may spend more time describing the joys of charity balls than the pleasures of community service. When managers fall prey to the extrinsic incentives bias, they may overlook the importance of feedback, neglect opportunities to make jobs more interesting, and underestimate the employee's desire to participate in team and organizational decisions. Managers could substantially improve their ability to understand the motivations of others if they assume that others are motivated exactly as they are.[59]

People work hard for a lot of reasons. It is a mistake to think that the only thing that drives performance is monetary incentives and that people hoard effort until incentives justify greater contributions. Many managers incorrectly believe that people are primarily motivated by monetary reward. However, they view themselves as having loftier reasons. For example, most people overestimate the impact that financial reward exerts on their peers' willingness to donate blood.[60]

---

[52]Heath, C. (1999). On the social psychology of agency relationships: Lay theories of motivation overemphasize extrinsic rewards. *Organizational Behavior and Human Decision Processes, 78*(1), 25–62.

[53]Taylor, F. W. (1911). *Shop management.* New York: Harper & Brothers.

[54]Lawler et al. *Creating high performance organizations.*

[55]Taylor, *Shop management.*

[56]Customer service representatives at Citibank; Heath, "On the social psychology of agency relationships."

[57]Huff, C. (2006, September 11). Recognition that resonates. *Workforce Management,* pp. 25–27.

[58]Bennis, W., & Nanus, B. (1985). *Leaders.* New York: Harper & Row.

[59]Taylor, *Shop management.*

[60]Miller, D. T., & Ratner, R. (1998). The disparity between the actual and assumed power of self-interest. *Journal of Personality and Social Psychology, 74*(1), 53–62.

In sum, evolutionary biology, neoclassical economics, behaviorism, and psychoanalytic theory all assume that people actively and single-mindedly pursue their self-interest.[61] However, organizational science research tells a different story. People often care more about the fairness of procedures they are subjected to than the material outcomes these procedures yield;[62] they often care more about a group's collective outcomes than about their personal outcomes;[63] and their attitudes toward public policies are often shaped more by values and ideologies than by the impact they have on material well-being.[64]

Homogeneity Bias

Generally, appraisers rate appraisees who are similar to themselves more favorably than those who are different from them. This means that, in general, white male superiors tend to favor white male subordinates over females and minority supervisees.[65]

Halo Bias

Once we know one positive (or negative) fact about someone, we tend to perceive other information we learn about that person in line with our initial perceptions. This has several serious implications, the most obvious of which is the fact that physically attractive people are evaluated more positively than are less attractive people—even when holding constant their skills and competencies.

Fundamental Attribution Error

We tend to perceive people's behaviors as reflecting their personality rather than temporary, situational factors. This can obviously be a good thing for someone who seems to be doing well, but it can be problematic for a person who seems to be performing under par.

Communication Medium

Performance appraisers give poor performers substantially higher ratings when they have to give face-to-face feedback as opposed to anonymous written feedback. In one investigation, managers were asked to give feedback to a poorly performing employee, either in a face-to-face mode or via tape-recorded message.[66] In all cases, the objective information about the poorly performing employee was identical. However, managers using direct, face-to-face communication gave more positive performance feedback than managers who used the indirect mode (the tape recorder).

---

[61]Schwartz, B. (1986). *The battle for human nature: Science, morality, and modern life.* New York: Norton.

[62]Tyler, T. R. (1990). *Why people obey the law.* New Haven, CT: Yale University Press.

[63]Dawes, R., Orbell, J., & van de Kragt, A. (1988). Not me or thee but we: The importance of group identity in eliciting cooperation in dilemma situations. *Acta Psychologica, 68,* 83–97.

[64]Sears, D. O., & Funk, C. L. (1990). The limited effect of economic self-interest on the political attitudes of the mass public. *Journal of Behavioral Economics, 19*(3), 247–271; Sears, D. O., & Funk, C. L. (1991). Graduate education in political psychology. Annual meeting of International Society of Political Psychology, Washington, DC. *Political Psychology, 12*(2), 345–362.

[65]Kraiger, K., & Ford, J. K. (1985, February). A meta-analysis of ratee race effects in performance ratings. *Journal of Applied Psychology, 70*(1), 56–65.

[66]Waung, M., & Highhouse, S. (1997). Fear of conflict and empathic buffering: Two explanations for the inflation of performance feedback. *Organizational Behavior and Human Decision Processes, 71*(1), 37–54.

Experience Effect

Experienced appraisers tend to render higher-quality appraisals, and training and practice can reduce error in ratings.[67]

Reciprocity Bias

People feel a strong social obligation to return favors. Thus, a potential flaw of 360-degree programs is that they are subject to collusion: "I'll give you a good rating if you give me one." Providing for anonymous rating may reduce both biases. However, this is difficult to achieve when team size is relatively small.

Bandwagon Bias

People want to "jump on the bandwagon," meaning that they will want to hold the same opinion of someone as does the rest of the group. Consider, for example, the question of how a team leader might react if he were to learn that his opinion of a team member differed from that of another member. In one investigation, people with organizational supervisory experience made an initial performance judgment about a profiled employee.[68] These leaders then received additional information that was discrepant from their initial judgment (either positive or negative) from one of two sources (the profiled employee himself or one of his peers). Leaders were more likely to use discrepant information to alter their performance judgments in a consistent direction when the source was a peer (but not the profiled employee).

Primacy and Recency Bias

People tend to be overly affected by their first impression of someone (primacy) or their most recent interaction with this person (recency).

There is no simple solution to overcoming these biases. Awareness is an important first step. We suggest that everyone in the business of providing performance evaluations be made aware of these biases. Employees in companies probably do receive some form of training on conducting performance appraisals, but hardly anyone receives training on the biases that afflict ratings. As a second step, we suggest that only objective behavior and productivity measures be used—they are less susceptible to biases than are traits and attitudes. A rule of thumb: If you can't observe it directly, then don't measure it.

Conflict of Interest Bias

Conflicts of interest can lead experts to give biased and corrupt advice.[69] Whereas simple disclosure of the conflict of interest by the rater is often suggested as a solution, people generally fail to discount advice from biased advisors. Moreover, the advisor who discloses a conflict of interest then feels morally licensed and strategically encouraged to exaggerate the advice even

---

[67]Klimoski, R., & Inks, L. (1990, April). Accountability forces in performance appraisal. *Organizational Behavior and Human Decision Processes, 45*(2), 194–208.

[68]Makiney, J. D., & Levy, P. E. (1998). The influence of self-ratings versus peer ratings on supervisors' performance judgments. *Organizational Behavior and Human Decision Processes, 74*(3), 212–228.

[69]Cain, D., Loewenstein, G., & Moore, D. (2005). The dirt on coming clean: Perverse effects of disclosing conflicts of interest. *Journal of Legal Studies, 34*, 1–25.

further. In one investigation, people making estimates of the value of a jar of coins were allowed to listen to "advisors." Advisors who disclosed their initial biases gave advice that was more distorted.[70]

RATEE BIAS

In addition to the rater biases discussed earlier, the quality of a 360-degree process can be compromised by the ratees themselves. Although countless articles and books have dealt with sources of rater bias, virtually no attention has been paid to the biases that ratees might have when receiving feedback. The more managers know about ratee bias, the better able they will be to anticipate the impact of a performance review on the employee.

Egocentric Bias

Most people feel underrecognized for the work they do and the value they bring to their company. The human cognitive system is primarily egocentric in nature. In short, people give themselves greater credit than do others. This means that in a typical 360-degree evaluation, no matter how positive it may be, people will feel underappreciated by others. There is no perfect solution to dealing with this. The supervisor (or person providing the feedback) should present as many facts as possible to justify the ratings and feedback. It is important to focus on behaviors rather than attitudes when assessing others, because it is more difficult to misinterpret objective information (e.g., "you've been late 18 out of the last 20 days"). Undoing egocentric biases in groups can backfire. For example, team members who contribute a lot are less satisfied and less interested in future collaborations when they are instructed to consider others' contributions.[71]

Intrinsic Interest

As we noted earlier, people are strongly motivated by intrinsic interest, rather than by extrinsic rewards. However, this is not to say that people don't care about extrinsic rewards. Furthermore, this does not mean that intrinsic interest will always flourish. In fact, even positive feedback, if not carefully administered, may undermine intrinsic interest.[72] That is, employees may do something for purely intrinsic reasons, such as the joy of learning new things or expressing themselves; however, if a supervisor or a person of obvious importance praises the work and administers large extrinsic rewards for the work, this may lead the employees to believe that they are doing the work for the money (or other extrinsic rewards). In some cases, external reward may undermine intrinsic interest. For example, incentive or pay-for-performance systems tend to make people less enthusiastic about their work.[73] And, massive bonuses actually cause employees to perform worse. Specifically, in one investigation, people were asked to perform various tasks involving memory, attention, concentration, and creativity.[74] One-third were promised a small bonus if they did well (one day's pay), one-third were promised a medium bonus (two weeks'

---

[70]Ibid.

[71]Caruso, E., Epley, N., & Bazerman, M. (2006). The costs and benefits of undoing egocentric responsibility assessments in groups. *Journal of Personality and Social Psychology, 91*(5), 857–871.

[72]Freedman, J. L., Cunningham, J. A., & Krismer, K. (1992). Inferred values and the reverse incentive effect in induced compliance. *Journal of Personality and Social Psychology, 62*, 357–368.

[73]Kohn, A. (1993, September–October). Why incentive plans cannot work. *Harvard Business Review, 71*, 54–63.

[74]Ariely, D. (2009, March 4). Massive bonuses might actually cause poor performance. *New York Times.* nytimes.com

pay), and one-third were promised a very high bonus (5 months' pay). The group offered the highest bonus did worse in every single task because they were focused on their bonus, rather than the actual work.[75]

We are not suggesting that companies should never offer extrinsic rewards to their employees. Rather, the manager should emphasize, when providing the reward, what is valued about the work and how the company views the employee. The research evidence supports this: When high effort is rewarded, people are more industrious. Just as people can be reinforced for working hard, they can be reinforced for creativity.[76] Thus, for fabulous work effort, a supervisor or company may give the team a special cash reward or noncash recognition and clearly communicate to the team that the company values their inspiring motivation, creativity, and attention to detail. It is important to clearly indicate what is being rewarded.

Social Comparison

Ideally, raters' evaluations should be objective and based on defined standards. However, teams and leaders often make comparative rather than absolute performance judgments.[77] This is why students feel less value in receiving an A if they find out that everyone has received an A. Thus, supervisors must anticipate that team members will talk and compare notes, one way or another, about the feedback they receive. It is often these comparisons that drive how employees interpret feedback. Saavedra and Kwun examined how a rater's relative performance affects their ratings of peers.[78] Self-evaluations were higher than ratings given to the self by one's peers, and high performers were the most likely to be discriminating. Below-average and average contributors tended to make external attributions for their low performance.[79]

Supervisors should be frank about feedback to employees and team members. For example, it would be wrong to imply that an employee was the only stellar performer if, in fact, over 60 percent performed at the same level. (For this reason, it may be useful to provide information about averages and standard deviations to employees.)

Fairness

People evaluate the quality of their organizational experiences by how fair they regard them to be. For example, CEOs use their own power to increase their salaries as well as those of their subordinates.[80] Moreover, salaries of CEOs serve as a key referent for employees in determining whether their own situation is "fair" and influences their reactions to their own compensation, including how long they will stay at the organization. Non-CEO top management team members receive higher pay when they work for a high-status CEO.[81] However, "star" CEOs retain most of the compensation benefits for themselves.

[75]Ariley, D. (2008). *Predictably irrational: The hidden forces that shape our decisions.* New York: HarperCollins.

[76]Eisenberger, R., & Selbst, M. (1994). Does reward increase or decrease creativity? *Journal of Personality and Social Psychology, 49,* 520–528.

[77]Ilgen, D. R., & Feldman, J. M. (1983). Performance appraisal: A process focus. In L. L. Cummings & B. M. Staw (Eds.), *Research in Organizational Behavior* (Vol. 5, pp. 141–197). Greenwich, CT: JAI Press.

[78]Saavedra, R., & Kwun, S. K. (1993). Peer evaluation in self-managing work groups. *Journal of Applied Psychology, 78*(3), 450–462.

[79]Ibid.

[80]Wade, J. B., O'Reilly, C. A., III, & Pollock, T. G. (2006). Overpaid CEOs and underpaid managers: Fairness and executive compensation. *Organization Science, 17*(5), 527–544.

[81]Graffin, S. D., Wade, J. B., Porac, J. F., & McNamee, R.C. (2008). The impact of CEO status diffusion on the economic outcomes of other senior managers. *Organization Science, 19*(3) 457–474.

In addition, people care about the fairness of procedures and processes. People are more likely to accept the outcome if they think the procedure has been fair. The fairness of procedures is determined by the extent to which the employee has a voice in the system.[82] Supervisors should actively involve the employee in the performance review, because people who are invited to participate regard procedures and systems to be fairer than those who are not invited. Superiors may ask employees to anticipate the feedback they will receive and to suggest how to best act upon it.

Listening to Advice

People often underweight advice they get from others.[83] However, how much people actually use the advice they receive depends on the difficulty of the task. People overweight advice when they perform difficult tasks and underweight advice on easy tasks.[84] This is true regardless of whether advice is automatically provided or deliberately sought. People often fall victim to a **curse of knowledge** effect, such that once they receive advice or information, they find it difficult or impossible to take the perspective of someone who does not have that information.[85] In a team environment, this means that people who know the answer to problems find it difficult to take the perspective of someone who does not have that information.

Although there is no surefire way to eliminate the biases on the part of the ratee, awareness of the bias is key. A second step is to recognize that many ratee biases are driven by a need to maintain or enhance self-esteem. Put evaluations in a positive light and help employees view them as opportunities to grow, rather than as marks of failure. A third step is to involve employees actively in the evaluation procedure before they receive their results. For this reason, an early planning meeting months ahead of the evaluation can be an ideal opportunity for teams and leaders to identify and clarify goals. Finally, recognize that performance appraisals, in any form, tend to be stressful for all involved. However, they provide an opportunity for everyone to gain feedback about what otherwise might be an "undiscussable problem." Tools such as 360-degree evaluations have the power to break down the barriers of fear in the organization. However, this can be effective only if managers are trained and skilled at using the information to break down barriers instead of building new ones.

GUIDING PRINCIPLES

An organization that wants to institute some kind of variable team-based pay structure needs to follow a step-by-step approach. However, even before that, the organization needs to adhere to some basic guiding principles.[86]

---

[82]Lind, E. A., & Tyler, T. R. (1988). *The social psychology of procedural justice*. New York: Plenum.

[83]Yaniv, I. (2004). The benefit of additional opinions. *Current Directions in Psychological Science, 13*, 75–78.

[84]Gino, F., & Moore, D. (2007). Effects of task difficulty on use of advice. *Journal of Behavioral Decision Making, 20*(1), 21–35.

[85]Camerer, C., Loewenstein, G., & Weber, M. (1989). The curse of knowledge in economic settings: An experimental analysis. *Journal of Political Economy, 97*, 1232–1254.

[86]Gross, S. E. (1995). *Compensation for teams: How to design and implement team-based reward programs* (p. 129). New York: AMACOM.

Principle 1: Goals Should Cover Areas That Team Members Can Directly Affect

Otherwise, the team is disempowered. Compensation won't motivate employees unless there is a direct line of sight between performance and results. For example, when incentives are tied only to the final profit of a company or group, which can be affected by all sorts of market forces, the connection between performance and reward is weakened. At the same time, pay should bear some kind of relationship to the company's bottom line. If the company is in the red, team rewards appear nonsensical—unless management is confident that ultimately the team's superior productivity and quality will help turn the company around.[87]

In effective programs, rewards are contingent upon performance. This is in perfect contrast to a Las Vegas slot machine, in which payouts are contingent upon luck. Furthermore, a system that always pays out is ineffective. The key is to devise a system that equitably spreads the risk between the team and the company, offers a potential gain that makes the risk worth taking, and gives employees a fair shot at making more by working harder, more intelligently, and in a more coordinated fashion.

Principle 2: Balance the Mix of Individual and Team-Based Pay

For many teams, a thoughtful balance of individual and group incentives may be most appropriate. A good rule of thumb is to balance this proportion in line with the amount of individual and team-based work an employee is expected to do or the percentage of control and responsibility the individual and the team have.

Principle 3: Consult the Team Members Who Will Be Affected

The process by which an organization introduces a program is more important than the program itself. The programs with the greatest likelihood of success are those that have input from all levels of the organization, including members of the team, teams that support or interface with the team, those who will administer the plan, management, and customers. The feasibility of the team pay program is determined through a full understanding of the business, the wants and needs of the management and employees, the impact of the current compensation program, and the company's ambitions for the new plan.

If people remain ignorant or uninformed about a process, they are more likely to reject it out of hand when they see it—even if it is perfectly compatible with their interests. In short, people want to be involved. The team members who are affected will have greater buy-in to the program if they had a hand in shaping it, and they can be valuable sources of information. In addition, employees need to feel that nothing is set in stone—if something does not work, employees will feel better knowing it can be changed.

Principle 4: Avoid Organizational Myopia

Many programs fail not because they are inherently flawed, but rather because they create problems with other teams, groups, and units within the organization. Managers often are myopic about their own team issues; good leaders are able to ask the question of how the particular team

---

[87]Ibid.

compensation system fits into the larger organization. This is the heart of what we referred to in Chapter 2 as "integration."

Principle 5: Determine Eligibility (Who Qualifies for the Plan)

Every member of the team should be eligible for the plan, and the plan should indicate when someone becomes eligible or loses eligibility. (Another complication concerns full- and part-time membership.)

Principle 6: Determine Equity Method

There are two basic variations: same dollar amount (wherein each team or each member is given the same amount of pay) and same percentage amount (wherein each team or each member is given the same percentage of pay).

Principle 7: Quantify the Criteria Used to Determine Payout

There are two main ways to measure team results: financial and operational. Financial measures tend to be "bigger," encompassing profit and loss (measured either companywide or in terms of the teams' contribution) or revenues. Operational measures are typically productivity based (e.g., cycle time). There are several drawbacks to financial measures that primarily stem from the inability of team members to control the corporate-level decisions that will affect their micro-finances. Operational measures are more firmly within the team's grasp.

Principle 8: Determine How Target Levels of Performance are Established and Updated

Goals can be based on either past performance or projected performance. There are advantages and disadvantages to each. The most immediate advantage of the historical approach is that people can readily accept it. However, many managers like to set stretch goals. One popular compromise is raising the bar, in which the baseline is increased and employees are given a one-time payment to compensate them for lost incentive opportunity. However, there is likely to be conflict over the amount of the payout. The rolling average method sets the baseline against which performance is measured as an average of some relevant period of time. (For a detailed discussion of payment options, see Gross).[88]

Principle 9: Develop a Budget for the Plan

All plans should pay for themselves, with the exception of safety plans. This means that the improvements must be quantifiable.

Principle 10: Determine Timing of Measurements and Payments

Shorter measurement periods and faster payouts motivate employees more and—particularly when pay is at risk—are fairer. However, the disadvantages with a short turnaround system include administrative overhead and manipulation of results.

---

[88]Gross, S. E. (2000). Team-based pay. In L. A. Berger & D. R. Berger (Eds.), *The compensation handbook: A state-of-the-art guide to compensation strategy and design* (4th ed., pp. 261–273). New York: McGraw-Hill.

Principle 11: Communicate with Those Involved

As stated earlier in the chapter, it is important for companies to be completely straightforward about what counts and how things are going.

Principle 12: Plan for the Future

As teaming becomes more developed and the organization experiences shifts in culture or focus, a new mix of rewards needs to be defined to keep the organization in alignment.

Conclusion

Many organizations promote and value teamwork, yet they pay people based upon individual accomplishments. Individuals operating under this system feel the tension. Just as college basketball players who feed their teammates instead of shooting will not compile impressive scoring statistics and are less likely to be drafted by the pros, managers who devote energy to organizational goals will often not enhance their own career. Viewed in this sense, it is rational for team members to think of themselves first and the team second. The organization that wants otherwise had better align its incentive system with the stated goals. This chapter does not provide easy answers to team compensation problems because there are none. However, there are some fundamental questions to think about, and there exist choices for managers and organizations when it comes to rewarding teams. Lawler perhaps sums it up best.[89] First, he emphasizes paying the individual instead of the job. And, second, he asserts that pay for performance should focus on collective performance more than individual performance. These two guiding principles encourage team members to learn the right skills to make teams effective and, more importantly, motivate the right type of performance focus.

---

[89]Lawler, *Rewarding excellence.*

PART TWO

Internal Dynamics

4

Designing the Team

Tasks, People, and Processes

Teamwork in the operating room is mission critical for patient safety. The correct diagnosis is either missed or delayed in 5 to 14 percent of urgent hospital admissions, and autopsies indicate diagnostic error rates between 10 percent and 20 percent. Communication errors are the most common cause of wrong-site surgeries in the United States. One among them is the "Are you sure?" problem: When weekend nurses and pharmacists noticed that the physician's prescription did not appear to fit the patient's condition, they asked the doctor, "Are you sure this is the right medicine?" The doctor said yes, and they continued with what was ultimately the wrong chemo plan. A better question is, "I didn't know about combining X and Y..." Such a question forces more than an automated yes–no response. In one investigation, operating room personnel in 60 hospitals were surveyed using the Safety Attitudes Questionnaire. Surgeons, anesthesiologists, certified registered nurse anesthetists, and operating room nurses rated their own peers and each other using a 5-point scale (1 = very low; 5 = very high). The ratings of teamwork differed dramatically among the team roles, with surgeons giving the lowest ratings and anesthesiologists giving the highest ratings. In short, physicians consider the teamwork to be good, but nurses perceive it to be mediocre. There were also differences in peer ratings, with surgeons rating other surgeons "high" or "very high" 85 percent of the time, but nurses rating their collaboration with surgeons as "high" or "very high" only 48 percent of the time.[1]

The opening example raises the critical issue of communication and effective teamwork. In this chapter, we focus on how to build effective teams and how to evaluate their performance. Managing an effective team involves two sets of responsibilities: (1) managing the internal dynamics of the

---

[1]Makary, M., Sexton, B., Freischlag, J., Holzmueller, C. G., Millman, E. A., Rowen, L. A. & Pronovost, P. J. (2006). Operating room teamwork among physicians and nurses: Teamwork in the eye of the beholder. *Journal of the American College of Surgeons, 202*(5), 746–752; Price, M. (2010, January). The antidote to medical errors. *Monitor on Psychology, 41*(1), 50–53.

team itself—that is, specifying the task, selecting the members, and facilitating the team process; and (2) managing the external dynamics of the team—navigating the organizational environment and managing relationships with those on whom the team is interdependent.[2] We refer to these dual processes as "internal team management" and "external team management." In Part II, we focus on internal team dynamics. The starting point presumes that the manager has determined that teams are necessary to do the work required. For expositional purposes, we take the point of view of the manager when we discuss building the team. However, all of our messages can be extended to the team as its own manager (i.e., as in the case of self-managing and self-designing teams). This chapter takes you through the steps involved in building a team and keeping it running smoothly. The goal of this chapter is to create a tool kit for the busy manager to use in developing and maintaining teams. In Part III, we focus on external team dynamics.

BUILDING THE TEAM

Contrary to popular wisdom, it is more important to have a well-designed team than a team with a good leader. In an intensive study of customer service teams at Xerox with, team sizes ranging from 3 to 12 persons, well-designed teams were more successful on a number of key organizational effectiveness criteria—assuming collective responsibility, monitoring their own performance, managing their own task strategies, and customer approval—than were poorly designed teams.[3] Poorly designed teams, even under good leadership, were significantly less effective. In the case of Xerox, team effectiveness was judged by supervisors as well as customers, thus providing a comprehensive view of team effectiveness. For these reasons, it may be more important to have excellent team members than to have an excellent leader to achieve success. This is why many leaders prefer to hire people smarter than they are.

Once it is determined that a team is desirable for the work and viable within the organization, then the manager must focus intently on three aspects: the work that the team will do, the people who will do the work, and the procedures and processes that the team will follow to achieve their goal. These three critical internal dynamics are illustrated in Exhibit 4-1.

These three factors—tasks, people, and processes—form the basic, internal system of teamwork. Just like Rome, the building and maintenance of a team is not something that is accomplished in a day. We begin by discussing the task, then we move to the people, and we conclude by discussing the processes and procedures.

The Task: What Work Needs to Be Done?

Teams are goal-directed entities. Some teams make products, some teams provide services, other teams make decisions, and still others provide advice and consultation.

Optimal team design depends on the type of work the team is doing, the structure of the organization, and so on. However, managers often do not think carefully about team design, leaving it up to the team to work out on their own or rely on traditional, functional practices.

---

[2]Ancona, D. G. (1990). Outward bound: Strategies for team survival in an organization. *Academy of Management Journal, 33*(2), 334–365.
[3]Wageman, R. (1997). Case study: Critical success factors for creating superb self-managing teams at Xerox. *Compensation and Benefits Review, 29*(5), 31–41.

| **EXHIBIT 4-1** Internal Dynamics: Key Questions to Ask When Building the Team |

Task Analysis	**People**	**Processes and Procedures**
• What work needs to be performed? • Is the goal clearly defined • How much authority does the team have to manage its own work? • What is the focus of work the team will do? • What are the roles and responsibilities of the team? • What is the degree of interdependence among team members? • Is there only one correct solution? • Are team members' interests aligned or competitive? • How big should the team be? • What is the time allotted to accomplish the task?	• Who is ideally suited to do the work? • What technical, task management, and interpersonal skills are required? • What motivates individuals to join teams? • What types of diversity are optimal in the team?	• How much structure is the group given? • What are the explicit (spoken) norms of the groups? • What are the implicit (unspoken) norms of the groups? • Which norms are conducive for performance? • What is the process by which ineffective norms can be revised?

If left to their own devices, teams rarely make explicit plans or develop performance strategies.[4] Those that do, however, usually perform better, especially when the appropriate performance strategy is not obvious.[5] For example, when surgical teams follow a checklist, patient-mortality rates are cut almost in half and complications reduce by more than a third.[6]

It is useful to distinguish **preplanning** (before actually performing the task) and **on-line planning** (during the task itself).[7] Teams permitted to plan between periods of task completion perform better than those that plan only during periods of task completion or do not have opportunities to discuss and develop plans.[8] In one investigation, the efficacy of four different "team aids" for articulating and representing knowledge in teams was tested: individual clipboards, team checklists, team clipboards, and a control condition that contained no

[4]Hackman, J. R., Brousseau, K. R., & Weiss, J. A. (1976). The interaction of task design and group performance strategies in determining group effectiveness. *Organizational Behavior and Human Performance, 16*, 350–365; Weingart, L. R. (1992). Impact of group goals, task component complexity, effort, and planning on group performance. *Journal of Applied Psychology, 77*, 682–693.

[5]Hackman, Brousseau, & Weiss, "Interaction of task design and group performance," p. 81.

[6]Szalavitz, M. (2009, January 14). Study: A simple surgery checklist saves lives. *Time*. time.com

[7]Weingart, "Impact of group goals," p. 81.

[8]Shure, G. H., Rogers, M. S., Larsen, I. M., & Tasson, J. (1962). Group planning and task effectiveness. *Sociometry, 25*, 263–282.

clipboards, or checklists. Teams were challenged with a complex task regarding target identification in a military operation in which a target could be peaceful or hostile, military or civilian, and approach by air, surface, or submarine. Team aids (i.e., team checklists and team clipboards) enhanced team performance more than individual aids (i.e., individual clipboards).[9]

Is the Goal Clearly Defined?

Teams often do not have a goal or the goal is clear to some members but not to others. Whether the team is assigned a goal or it articulates its own goal, the goal needs to be clear. Goals should be articulated in the form of a team charter (mission statement). Wageman's analysis of teams at Xerox revealed two common errors when it came to goal setting: Some teams failed to set any direction at all, and some teams set a direction that focused exclusively on means (the how), but did not specify the ends (the why).[10] The first error occurs when teams assume that everyone knows why they are there and launch the team into action without a thoughtful discussion of the purpose. The second error occurs when there is excessive focus on how a team should function.

According to Wageman, team goals should be: (1) clear and simple and (2) specify ends but not means.[11] In terms of clear and simple, the best team mission statements contain only a few objectives. But, those objectives orient the team and allow members to make thoughtful decisions. For example, in Wageman's analysis of teams at Xerox, successful teams continually referred to their goals when making tough decisions: "Would this action please the customer and would it do so without excessive cost to Xerox?"[12] Wageman also cautions that successful teams specify their ends, but not the means.[13] Their mission statement is clear about the team's purpose, but does not prescribe the steps on how the team should get there.

With respect to goals, some team members have a **high-performance orientation,** whereas other team members have a **high-learning orientation.**[14] A performance orientation reflects a desire to gain favorable judgments of performance or avoid negative judgments of competence. A learning orientation reflects the desire to understand something novel or to increase competence in a task. In one investigation, the effectiveness and performance and learning orientation was examined. Halfway through a 3-hour simulation in which teams needed to make a series of decisions, their communication channel began to deteriorate. To perform effectively, they needed to adapt their roles. Teams with difficult goals and a high-*performance* orientation were the least able to adapt. Teams with difficult goals and a high-*learning* orientation were most likely to adapt.

How Much Authority Does the Team Have?

In Chapter 1, we considered four types of teams: manager led, self-managing, self-directing, and self-governing. The more authority team members have to manage their own work, the more likely they are to be motivated and highly involved in the work. However, this comes at a loss of control for the manager. Furthermore, when teams set and carry out their own objectives, they may not be aligned with those of the larger organization. In one investigation of 121 service

---

[9]Sycara, K., & Lewis, M. (2004). Integrating intelligent agents into human teams. In E. Salas & S. Fiore (Eds.), *Team Cognition: Understanding the Factors that Drive Process and Performance*. Washington, DC: American Psychological Association.
[10]Wageman, "Case study."
[11]Ibid.
[12]Ibid.
[13]Ibid.
[14]LePine, J. (2005). Adaptation of teams in response to unforeseen change: Effects of goal difficulty and team composition in terms of cognitive ability and goal orientation. *Journal of Applied Psychology, 90*(6), 1153–1167.

technician teams, empowered teams developed team processes that effectively increased quantitative performance and indirectly increased customer satisfaction.[15]

What Is the Focus of the Work the Team Will Do?

Teams do one of three types of tasks: tactical, problem solving, and creative. Exhibit 4-2 describes tactical, problem solving, and creative teams and the disadvantages and advantages of each team.

Tactical teams execute a well-defined plan. Some examples of tactical teams include cardiac surgery teams, many sports teams, and other teams that are tightly organized.[16] For tactical teams to be successful there must be a high degree of task clarity and unambiguous role definition. One type of tactical team is a crew. A crew is a group of expert specialists each of whom has specific role positions, perform brief tasks that are closely synchronized with each other, and repeat those events across different environmental conditions.[17] When NASA trains astronauts to work in teams, crew members are forced to work in a confined craft in an underwater environment similar to the physical and psychological stress of space. Astronaut Ron Garan says that teamwork is important because, "You could be the best pilot, scientist, or astronaut in the world, but if you can't work as part of a team or live with people for 6 months, you're no good to NASA."[18] To assess whether a particular team is a "work crew," complete the survey in Exhibit 4-3.

EXHIBIT 4-2 Types of Work That Teams Do			
Broad Objective	**Dominant Feature**	**Process Emphasis**	**Threats**
Tactical	Clarity	• Directive, highly focused tasks • Role clarity • Well-defined operational standards • Accuracy	• Role ambiguity • Lack of training • Communication barriers
Problem solving	Trust	• Focus on issues • Separate people from problem • Consider facts, not opinions • Conduct thorough investigation • Suspend judgment	• Failure to stick to facts • Fixate on solutions • Succumb to political pressures • Confirmatory information search
Creative	Autonomy	• Explore possibilities and alternatives	• Production blocking • Uneven participation

Source: Adapted from Larson, C. E., & LaFasto, F. M. (1989). *Teamwork: What must go right/what can go wrong.* Newbury Park, CA: Sage.

---

[15]Mathieu, J., Gilson, L., & Ruddy, T. (2006). Empowerment and team effectiveness: An empirical test of an integrated model. *Journal of Applied Psychology, 91*(1), 97–108.

[16]LaFasto, F. M. J., & Larson, C. E. (2001). *When teams work best: 6,000 team members and leaders tell what it takes to succeed.* Newbury Park, CA: Sage.

[17]Klimoski, R., & Jones, R. G. (1995). Staffing for effective group decision making. In R. A. Guzzo & E. Salas (Eds.), *Team effectiveness and decision making* (pp. 9–45). San Francisco, CA: Jossey-Bass; Sundstrom, E. D., DeMeuse, K. P., & Futrell, D. (1990). Work teams: Applications and effectiveness. *American Psychologist, 45*(2), 120–133.

[18]Levine, R. (2006, June 12). The new right stuff. *Fortune, 153*(11), 116.

EXHIBIT 4-3 The Crew Classification Scale

1. In general, when you joined your group, how clear were your roles and responsibilities?

   1————————2————————3————————4————————5

   extremely unclear   extremely clear

2. To what extent does your group recruit for specific job positions that need to be filled for the group to be successful?

   1————————2————————3————————4————————5

   no specific job positions   all are specific job positions

3. To what extent does your group need to be in a specific work environment or setting to complete its tasks?

   1————————2————————3————————4————————5

   we can meet in just   we can only do our work if
      about any place   we have the right work layout and
                                              equipment/tech

4. In general, to what extent do the *same* group members need to be present for the group's task(s) to be completed successfully? (R)

   1————————2————————3————————4————————5

   need none of the same
      team members   need all of the same team
                                                      members

5. To what extent do *all* of the group members need to be present for your group to accomplish its task or goals?

   1————————2————————3————————4————————5

   need only one group member   need all of the group members

6. To what extent is the workflow (i.e., how the work will get done) in your group well established before anyone joins the team?

   1————————2————————3————————4————————5

   no extent   very large extent

7. To what extent does each group member need to coordinate carefully with others in the group for the group to effectively accomplish its task(s)?

   1————————2————————3————————4————————5

   no extent   very large extent

8. To what extent would your activities in the group (including the task(s) that you are responsible for) change if you were to move to another group that might be assigned to the same task or mission? (R)

   1————————2————————3————————4————————5

   does not change   complete change

9. To what extent can your group complete its assigned task(s) if one or more of the people in the group are not there? (R)

   1————————2————————3————————4————————5

   cannot complete any of the task(s)   can complete all of the task(s)

10. In general how frequently do people come and leave as members of your group? (R)

   1————————2————————3————————4————————5

   daily   Never

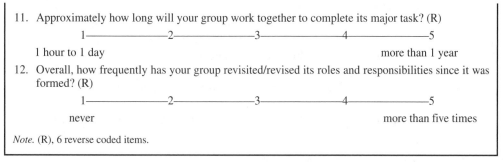

11. Approximately how long will your group work together to complete its major task? (R)

    1————————2————————3————————4————————5

    1 hour to 1 day   more than 1 year

12. Overall, how frequently has your group revisited/revised its roles and responsibilities since it was formed? (R)

    1————————2————————3————————4————————5

    never   more than five times

Note. (R), 6 reverse coded items.

Source: Webber, S. S., & Klimoski. (2004). Crews: A distinct type of work team. *Journal of Business and Psychology, 18*(3), 261–279.

Problem-solving teams are those that attempt to resolve problems, usually on an ongoing basis. To be effective, each member of the team must expect and believe that interactions among members will be truthful and of high integrity. Some examples of problem-solving teams include the Centers for Disease Control and Prevention and Sandia Laboratory's nuclear weapons team.[19]

Creative teams are those in which the key objective is to create something, think out of the box, and question assumptions. The process focus of creative teams is that of exploring possibilities and alternatives. We discuss creative teams in much more depth in Chapter 9. Examples of creative teams include the IDEO design teams, Hallmark's creative advisory group, and the teams responsible for HBO's original programming.

Teams often contain some blend of all three elements, but there is a dominant focus. Sometimes, teams are mischaracterized—for example, a team that is supposed to be creative uses a problem-solving perspective, or a team that really requires problem solving is organized as a tactical team. This may happen when the goals of the team are not clear. This can also happen when teams are not apprised of the goal.

ROLES AND RESPONSIBILITIES   According to the theory of the **strategic core** of teams, certain team roles are most important for team performance, and the characteristics of the role holders in these "core" roles are more important than others for overall team performance.[20] A field investigation of 778 teams drawn from 29 years of major league baseball (1974–2002) demonstrated that whereas high levels of experience and job-related skill are important predictors of team performance, the link between career experience, job-related skill and ultimate performance is much stronger when the characteristic is possessed by core role holders (as opposed to non–core role holders). Absence of role clarity was the key reason cited for the abysmal performance of the 2008 U.S. Olympic boxing team.[21] Several U.S. boxers did not seem to know whom to listen to: the Olympic coach, Dan Campbell, or their longtime personal coaches. In short, the athletes did not understand the core roles of coaches.

---

[19]LaFasto & Larson, *When teams work best.*

[20]Humphrey, S., Morgeson, F., & Mannor, M. (2009). Developing a theory of the strategic core of teams: A role composition model of team performance. *Journal of Applied Psychology, 94*(1), 48–61.

[21]Wartzman, R. (2008, August 29). Organizations need structure and flexibility. *Business Week.* Businessweek.com

Backing-up behavior is defined as "the discretionary provision of resources and task-related effort to another member of one's team that is intended to help that team member obtain the goals as defined by his or her role."[22] However, there are some costs of back-up behavior, most notably, the team member providing back up neglects their own taskwork, especially when workload is evenly distributed.[23] Moreover, it leads to free riding, as team members who receive high amounts of backing-up behavior decrease their taskwork in subsequent tasks.

What Is the Degree of Task Interdependence Among Team Members?

Many types of task interdependence affect the way teams get their work done[24] (see Exhibit 4-4). Consider three types of task interdependence:

- *Pooled interdependence*   occurs when group members work independently and then combine their work. Consider a department store's furniture department. It comprises

---

EXHIBIT 4-4 Levels of Interdependence

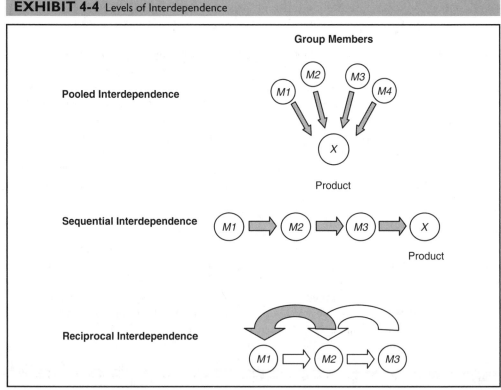

Source: Thompson, J. (1967). *Organizations in action.* New York: McGraw-Hill.

---

[22]Porter, C., Hollenbeck, J., Ilgen, D., Ellis, A., West, B., & Moon, H. (2003). Backing up behaviors in teams: The role of personality and legitimacy of need. *Journal of Applied Psychology, 88*(3), 391–403.
[23]Barnes, C., Hollenbeck, J., Wagner, D., DeRue, S., Nahrgang, J., & Schwind, K., (2008). Harmful help: The costs of backing-up behavior in teams. *Journal of Applied Psychology, 93*(3), 529–539.
[24]Thompson, J. (1967). *Organizations in action.* New York: McGraw-Hill.

several salespeople, each of whom is compensated based on sales performance. On an interdepartmental level, the sales of each salesperson are totaled and compared across departments, so that cosmetics, furniture, and men's accessories can all be compared and added together to determine overall store profit. Throughout this process, each salesperson is independent. Another example is a team of sprinters, each running as fast as they can; the team's output is simply the average time.

- *Sequential interdependence* is the classic assembly line or division of labor; each member of the team has a particular skill or task to perform. Members are more interdependent, with those further down the line more dependent on others. For example, a relay race in which each runner needs to "hand off" to the other team member.
- *Reciprocal interdependence* is the highest form of interdependence. Every member is dependent on others at all levels—not just in a simple linear fashion, as in sequential interdependence. Consider a cycling team in which members ride in a pace line and change position every few seconds to maintain a high, steady speed. Similarly, when software developers are writing code, each person must have a high degree of familiarity with the other pieces of the program; otherwise the likelihood of bugs increases significantly.

High levels of task interdependence, which require interactions among group members to obtain crucial resources, consistently enhance performance.[25] Highly interdependent members generate solutions faster, complete more tasks, and perform better than teams whose members are not highly dependent upon one another. Top management teams with higher interdependence experienced higher team and firm performance when their team was cohesive and had greater communication; however, teams with low interdependence had higher performance when communication and cohesion were lower.[26]

The degree of interdependence has design implications for teamwork. To the extent that tasks are easily divisible and threats to performance (Chapter 2) have been adequately resolved, pooled interdependence may be very effective for groups. For example, in a customer service call center, members do roughly the same type of work. However, pooled interdependence often cannot work for teams because completing the tasks requires specialization and division of labor. Thus, sequential or reciprocal interdependence is necessary. To a large degree, greater specialization means greater interdependence, because team members must rely on others to complete their portion of the work. The start-up times for reciprocal interdependence may seem daunting, but it may be especially important for highly complex tasks that require high levels of customer satisfaction. Another advantage of reciprocal interdependence is that all team members know the overall objectives of the team and may feel more accountable (thus reducing the motivational problems discussed in Chapter 2). Team values also influence the nature of their interdependence. A longitudinal field study of 39 project teams revealed that teams whose members shared **egalitarian values** (i.e., desire to create a shared sense of membership) develop highly interdependent task approaches and patterns of interaction. In contrast, groups whose members hold **meritocratic values** (i.e., individuals are motivated to demonstrate their unique abilities to other group members) develop low-interdependence task approaches.[27]

[25]Fan, E. T., & Gruenfeld, D. H. (1998). When needs outweigh desires: The effects of resource interdependence and reward interdependence on group problem solving. *Basic and Applied Social Psychology, 20*(1), 45–56.

[26]Barrick, M. R., Bradley, B. H., Kristof-Brown, A. L., & Colbert, A. E. (2007). The moderating role of top management team interdependence: Implications for real teams and working groups. *Academy of Management Journal, 50*, 544–577.

[27]Wageman, R., & Gordon, F. (2006). As the twig is bent: How group values shape emergent task interdependence in groups. *Organization Science, 16*(6), 687–700.

Is There a Correct Solution That Can Be Readily Demonstrated and Communicated to Members?

Some tasks have one correct solution; other tasks have several possible solutions. Consider a team building a house in which each component (the framework, the windows, the insulation, etc.) has to conform to a blueprint, versus a consulting team outlining a strategy proposal for a company. In the case of the construction team, the blueprint is the criterion by which the team will be judged. This kind of team task is known as a **demonstrable** task.[28]

In contrast, no single best answer exists for the consulting team. This kind of team task is known as a **nondemonstrable** task. In nondemonstrable tasks, it is important for team members to discuss the indices they will use to assess their performance as a team. Otherwise, there could be considerable disagreement after the work is completed—not only among team members but also between the team and the client!

Are Team Members' Interests Perfectly Aligned (Cooperative), Opposing (Competitive), or Mixed in Nature?

In many team-based organizations, reward structures are constructed so that some portion of team members' pay is contingent on the performance of the team as a whole, to promote cooperation and reduce the incentive for competition among team members.

It is important to determine the extent to which members have an incentive to work with one another or compete with other group members for monetary gain (such as might exist within some sales teams), promotion, and so on. At Whole Foods, the team is the foundation of the store and encourages creativity and a sense of ownership. Individual teams participate in selecting new employees, bosses, and customer products. No one at the company is allowed a salary more than 19 times what an average team member earns. The chief executive, John Mackey, pays himself a salary of $1 per year.[29]

How Big Should the Team Be?

Leaders consistently struggle with the question of how many people to put on the team. Obviously, this depends on the nature of the work to be done and the level and overlap of skills among team members. It also depends on the budget. Generally, teams should be fewer than 10 members. It is wise to compose teams using the smallest number of people who can do the task.[30] Unfortunately, there is a pervasive tendency for managers to err on the side of making teams too large. There are many reasons for this—it is easier to include others than to exclude them. Unfortunately, managers seriously underestimate how coordination problems geometrically increase as team members are added.

Teams that are overgrown have a number of disadvantages.[31] Larger teams are less cohesive,[32] and members of large teams are less satisfied with team membership, participate less often

---

[28]Steiner, I. (1972). *Group process and productivity*. New York: Academic Press.

[29]Paumgarten, N. (2010, January 4). Food Fighter. *The New Yorker*, pp. 36–47.

[30]Hackman, J. R. (1987). The design of work teams. In J. W. Lorsch (Ed.), *Handbook of organizational behavior*. Upper Saddle River, NJ: Prentice Hall.

[31]Nieva, V. F., Myers, D., & Glickman, A. S. (1979, July). An exploratory investigation of the skill qualification testing system. *U.S. Army Research Institute for the Behavioral and Social Sciences,* TR 390.

[32]McGrath, J. E. (1984). *Groups: Interaction and performance*. Upper Saddle River, NJ: Prentice Hall.

in team activities, and are less likely to cooperate with one another.[33] People are more likely to behave in negative and socially unacceptable ways in larger teams, perhaps because team members feel more anonymous or are less self-aware.[34]

As team size increases, the frivolity of conversation increases and people tend to avoid serious subjects. People in large groups are more self-conscious and concerned about projecting the right image. It is safer for people to avoid serious topics. As group size increases, conformity increases in a negatively accelerating fashion, such that each additional person who agrees with the majority has less overall influence.[35] Another problem of large teams concerns the equality of participation. For example, in a team of two to three, one person may do more of the talking, but all may participate. As the size of the team grows, more people do less talking relative to others. Sometimes, a few members say and do nothing.

In contrast, there are advantages to smaller (even understaffed) teams. Members of understaffed teams work harder, engage in a wider variety of tasks, assume more responsibility for the team's performance, and feel more involved in the team.[36]

If smaller teams are more advantageous, why are they relatively rare? The problem is that managers of teams appear to have an **overstaffing bias.** When team leaders are asked whether their teams could ever become too small or too large, 87 percent believe that understaffing is possible, but only 62 percent believe overstaffing is possible.[37]

The question of how to downsize is critical in teams. One study investigated three types of downsizing on task focus: downsizing that eliminates the leader, downsizing that maintains the hierarchy (leader), and downsizing that integrates hierarchy. Only the teams that lost their leader (and hierarchy) increased their effort on task-related behaviors.[38]

Time Pressure? Good or Bad?

Another contextual factor is time and the organization's norms of marking time—in particular, deadlines. How much time should a group devote to completing its work? A typical response might be "as long as it takes." This answer is neither good nor practical. When a work group is given a specific amount of time to do a job, its members adjust their behavior to "fit" whatever time is available. When time is scarce, team members work harder, worry less about the quality

[33]Kerr, N. L. (1989). Illusions of efficacy: The effects of group size on perceived efficacy in social dilemmas. *Journal of Experimental Social Psychology, 25,* 287–313; Markham, S. E., Dansereau, F., & Alutto, J. A. (1982). Group size and absenteeism rates: A longitudinal analysis. *Academy of Management Journal, 25*(4), 921–927.

[34]Latané, B. (1981). The psychology of social impact. *American Psychologist, 36,* 343–356; Prentice-Dunn, S., & Rogers, R. W. (1989). Deindividuation and the self-regulation of behavior. In P. B. Paulus (Ed.), *Psychology of group influence* (2nd ed.), Mahwah, NJ: Lawrence Erlbaum & Associates.

[35]Latané, "Psychology of social impact," p. 89.

[36]Arnold, D. W., & Greenberg, C. I. (1980). Deviate rejection within differentially manned groups. *Social Psychology Quarterly, 43*(4), 419–424; Perkins, D. V. (1982). Individual differences and task structure in the performance of a behavior setting: An experimental evaluation of Barker's manning theory. *American Journal of Community Psychology, 10*(6), 617–634; Petty, R. M., & Wicker, A. W. (1974). Degree of manning and degree of success of a group as determinants of members' subjective experiences and their acceptance of a new group member. *Catalog of Selected Documents in Psychology, 4,* 43; Wicker, A. W., Kermeyer, S. L., Hanson, L., & Alexander, D. (1976). Effects of manning levels on subjective experiences, performance, and verbal interaction in groups. *Organizational Behavior and Human Performance, 17,* 251–274; Wicker, A. W., & Mehler, A. (1971). Assimilation of new members in a large and a small church. *Journal of Applied Psychology, 55,* 151–156.

[37]Cini, M., Moreland, R. L., & Levine, J. M. (1993). Group staffing levels and responses to prospective and new members. *Journal of Personality and Social Psychology, 65,* 723–734.

[38]DeRue, D. S., Hollenbeck, J. R., Johnson, M. D., Ilgen, D. R., & Jundt, D. K. (2008). How different team downsizing approaches influence team-level adaptation and performance. *Academy of Management Journal, 51,* 182–196.

of their output, and focus on the task rather than social or emotional issues. However, if more time becomes available, these employees continue to work as though time was still scarce, rather than relaxing. It is important to properly manage how teams are initially introduced to their tasks.

Consider an investigation in which three groups were evaluated according to their ability to solve puzzles.[39] Each group had a different task load (completing 20, 40, or 80 anagrams), time limit (5, 10, or 20 minutes), and group size (1, 2, or 4 persons). Each group had three work periods. The task load remained the same for all periods for any given group, but the time interval either increased, decreased, or remained constant. Groups of all sizes, and over all possible time intervals, solved more anagrams per member-minute the higher the assigned task load; groups of any size and for any given task load solved more anagrams per member-minute the shorter the time limit; and for any given load and time limit, productivity was higher the smaller the size of the group. Thus, the more the work load per member-minute, the more work gets done. The point is clear: Teams adapt themselves to the constraints presented to them, such as the amount of time they have to perform a task.

Not only is team performance susceptible to arbitrary "norming" cues, but team communication and interaction and some aspects of product quality are also affected by these factors.[40] For example, short time limits on an initial task induce teams to spend more time on task-oriented behaviors and less time on interpersonal interaction, whereas teams with a longer time period engage in more interpersonal interactions.

Kelly et al. outlined two kinds of problems related to this issue: capacity problems and capability problems.[41] **Capacity problems** occur when there is not enough time to do all of the required tasks, although each task is easy. **Capability problems** occur when the task is difficult, even though there is plenty of time in which to do it. Capacity problems lead to a faster rate of task activity on subsequent trials regardless of the actual time limits set for those later trials; capability problems lead to more extensive processing of information, hence a slower rate of production on subsequent trials regardless of the actual time limits set for those trials.

Time limits are important from the standpoint of organizational planning and budget considerations. The **Attentional Focus Model (AFM)** predicts how time pressure affects team performance.[42] The AFM model suggests that time pressure narrows group members' attention to the most salient features of the task. As time pressure increases, the things that appear most central to completing the task become more salient and other factors are not considered. Time pressure can either enhance or reduce performance depending on the requirements for successful task performance. Specifically, when teams are under time pressure, they filter what they judge to be less important information.[43]

---

[39]McGrath, J. E., Kelly, J. R., & Machatka, D. E. (1984). The social psychology of time: Entrainment of behavior in social and organizational settings. *Applied Social Psychology Annual, 5,* 21–44.

[40]Kelly, J. R., Futoran, G. C., & McGrath, J. E. (1990). Capacity and capability: Seven studies of entrainment of task performance rates. *Small Group Research, 21*(3), 283–314; Kelly, J. R., & McGrath, J. E. (1985). Effects of time limits and task types on task performance and interaction of four-person groups. *Journal of Personality and Social Psychology, 49*(2), 395–407.

[41]Kelly, Futoran, & McGrath, "Capacity and capability," p. 91.

[42]Karau, S., & Kelly, J. (1992). The effects of time scarcity and time abundance on group performance quality and interaction process. *Journal of Experimental Social Psychology, 28,* 542–571.

[43]Kelly, J., & Loving, T. (2004). Time pressure and group performance: Exploring underlying processes in the Attentional Focus Model. *Journal of Experimental Social Psychology, 40,* 185–198.

THE PEOPLE: WHO IS IDEALLY SUITED TO DO THE WORK?

Once managers have some idea of the task design issues facing them, they are ready to turn to the people part of team building—how to best select members for their team. Obviously, the freedom to select team members is constrained in many ways: Managers may be limited to selecting members from a particular department, of a particular status, and so on. In other cases, managers may go outside the organization to recruit. At the opposite extreme, some managers do not have a choice about who is on their team; existing departmental structures determine team membership. Many teams are built by accretion and swapping members, not just created from scratch.

The first step is to carefully think about the task in terms of the work to be done, and then choose people on the basis of their skills relevant to that work. For example, consider the three basic purposes of teamwork described earlier: tactical, problem solving, and creative. Obviously, creative types are not as well suited for tactical teams as are highly organized, results-driven people, and vice versa.

The following skills are important to think about when forming any team:

- *Technical or functional expertise* If the task calls for open-heart surgery, a chemist or a lawyer will not suffice, no matter how great they are at what they do. Team members must demonstrate competence to perform what they need to do for the team to accomplish its goals. In most team tasks, it is necessary to recruit members with diverse skills. In an age of increasing specialization, it is rare for one person to be knowledgeable in all aspects of a complex task.
- *Task-management skills* It is not enough for team members to simply perform their functional area of expertise. They need to coordinate the efforts of the team, set goals, and enact plans. Task-management skills involve planning the work, monitoring performance, dealing with disappointments and unknowns, and surmounting coordination problems (see Exhibit 4-5). The left-hand side focuses on task-management skills; the right-hand side focuses on interpersonal skills.
- *Interpersonal skills* People on teams are not just automatons who simply carry out their tasks according to some predetermined plan. Because members of teams are people first— with their own issues, problems, and agendas—and team members second, the people side of teams is always present and a powerful influence on productivity. Interpersonal skills include the ability to give constructive criticism, be objective, give recognition, learn from others, and so on. Consult the right-hand side of Exhibit 4-5 for examples of interpersonal skills in groups.

The type and blend of skills needed on a team depend largely on the task the team does. For example, problem-solving tasks often require more interpersonal skills; tactical teams require more organizational skills. Consider the following:

- *Self-report* What do employees regard to be their key strengths (and weaknesses)?
- *Past accomplishments* What projects have employees been involved with that called for these skills?
- *360-degree reports* What do employees' peers, supervisors, and subordinates regard to be their key strengths and weaknesses vis-à-vis these tasks? (See the discussion in Chapter 3.)

It is rare for one person to have all the three skills. Thus, a key task of the manager is not to search for "Jacks and Jills of all team skills," but rather to focus on the task of *diversifying* the team so as to meet and exceed performance objectives.

EXHIBIT 4-5 Task-Management and Interpersonal Skills

Task-Management Skills	Interpersonal Skills
• **Initiating:** Suggesting new goals or ideas	• **Encouraging:** Fostering team solidarity by reinforcing others
• **Information seeking:** Clarifying key issues	• **Harmonizing:** Mediating conflicts
• **Opinion seeking**: Clarifying attitudes, values, and feelings	• **Compromising:** Shifting one's own position on an issue to reduce conflict in the team
• **Elaborating:** Giving additional information—examples, rephrasing, implications—about points made by others	• **Gatekeeping:** Encouraging all team members to participate
• **Energizing:** Stimulating the team to continue and working when progress wanes	• **Reflecting:** Pointing out the positive and negative aspects of the team's dynamics and calling for change if necessary
• **Coordinating:** Pulling together ideas and suggestions	• **Following:** Accepting the ideas offered by others and serving as an audience for the team
• **Orienting:** Keeping the team headed toward its stated goals	• **Standard setting:** Expressing, or calling for discussion of, standards for evaluating the quality of the team process
• **Detailing:** Caring for operational details	
• **Recording:** Performing a "team memory" function by documenting discussion and outcomes	
• **Challenging:** Questioning the quality of the team's methods, logic, and results	

Source: Adapted from Benne, K. D., & Sheats, P. (1948). Functional roles of group members. *Journal of Social Issues, 4*, 41–49.

MEMBER-INITIATED TEAM SELECTION   The preceding discussion took the point of view of the leader in assembling a team. What factors motivate a person to join a particular team? Potential group members make decisions to join groups based on group attributes (characteristics of the group itself, including its status, past success, and member composition) as well as relationship attributes (e.g., their personal relationship with group members).[44] Member-initiated groups are not necessarily exclusive of others. In one investigation, participants played four rounds of "social poker" (a card game in which self-selected groups compete for money). Some people were not chosen to be on any team; nevertheless, when "isolates" earned nothing, self-organized groups frequently included isolates, even at their own expense.[45]

Diversity

Left to their own instincts, most leaders and most teams opt for homogeneity, not diversity. In a large-scale study, spanning 33 project groups over 4 years, work partner choice was biased toward others of the same race.[46] When people in actual work groups had an opportunity to select future group members, their choices were biased toward those who were from the same racial

[44]Barsness, Z., Tenbrunsel, A., Michael, J., & Lawson, L. (2002). Why am I here? The influence of group and relational attributes on member-initiated team selection. In Neale, M. A., Mannix, E., & Sondak, H., *Toward phenomenology of groups and group membership* (Vol. 4, pp. 141–171). Kidlington, Oxford: Elsevier Limited.

[45]Arrow, H., & Crosson, S. (2003). Musical chairs: Membership dynamics in self-organized group formation. *Small Group Research, 34*(5), 523–556.

[46]Hinds, P., Carley, K. M., Krackhardt, D., & Wholey, D. (2000). Choosing workgroup members: The balance of similarity, competence, and familiarity. *Organizational Behavior and Human Decision Making Processes, 81*(2), 226–251.

group as themselves, but also toward those who had a reputation for being competent and hard-working and those with whom they had developed strong working relationships. People strive for predictability when choosing future work group members.[47] United States Air Force Major General Larry Spencer says of diversity, "You wouldn't line up 11 quarterbacks or 11 linemen on a football field to make a play. You need diversity. People have their own unique backgrounds and skill sets that help them accomplish the mission. We need all those talents and only when we work together do we find success."[48]

What are the key advantages of having teams composed of diverse members?

- *Expanded talent pool*   First and foremost, the company that does not tolerate or promote diversity has access to a smaller amount of corporate talent—the less diversity, the less likelihood of recruiting and maintaining talented individuals.
- *Multiple viewpoints*   Diverse (or heterogeneous) teams are more likely to generate creative solutions and solve problems more accurately than homogeneous teams—a topic we take up in Chapter 9 (creativity). Heterogeneous groups are more effective than homogeneous groups at solving complex problems (for a review, see Shaw).[49] Groups whose charter members are ethnically diverse socialize newcomers more readily than groups with all Anglo-American founders.[50]

When we refer to a minority viewpoint, we are not describing the views held by a demographic minority; rather, we are referring to the presence of a statistical minority. The mere presence of a minority opinion has beneficial effects in terms of prompting others to make sounder judgments and in launching better discussions. Minority opinions can arise from one of two sources—from a member of one's own team (an ingroup member) or a member of another group (an outgroup member). Both can be effective; however, a minority opinion offered by an ingroup member is often more influential.[51] Yet, people in an ingroup may be particularly unlikely to offer a different viewpoint because of the strong pressure to conform and not express views that effectively threaten the group.[52] Indeed, when two people on the same team disagree with one another, there is more uncertainty, greater stress and anxiety, and more concern about social relationships.[53] In short, people on the team may want to repair the relationships, rather than discuss the issues. Indeed, disagreement with outgroup members is more tolerable than disagreement with ingroup members. Perhaps this is why ingroup minorities use the phrases "I don't know" and "I'm not sure" much more often when expressing a different view than do outgroup members.[54]

[47]Ibid.

[48]Buzanowski, J. G. (2009, February 5). Generals reflect on importance of diversity. Secretary of the Air Force Public Affairs.af.mil

[49]Shaw, M. E. (1981). *Group dynamics: The psychology of small group behavior* (3rd ed.). New York: McGraw-Hill.

[50]Arrow, H. (1998). Standing out and fitting in: Composition effects on newcomer socialization. *Research on Managing Groups and Teams, 1,* 59–80.

[51]David, B., & Turner, J. C. (1996). Studies in self-categorization and minority conversion: Is being a member of the outgroup an advantage? *British Journal of Social Psychology, 35,* 179–199.

[52]Phillips, K. W. (2003). The effects of categorically based expectations on minority influence: The importance of congruence. *Personality Sociology and Psychology Bulletin, 29,* 3–13.

[53]Moscovici, S. (1985a). Innovation and minority influence. In S. Moscovici, G. Mugny, & E. Van Avermaet (Eds.), *Perspectives on minority influence* (pp. 9–52). Cambridge, England: Cambridge University Press; Moscovici, S. (1985b). Social influence and conformity. In G. Lindzey & E. Aronson (Eds.), *Handbook of social psychology* (3rd ed., Vol. 2, pp. 347–412). New York: Random House.

[54]Phillips, "The effects of categorically based expectations on minority influence."

Members in the majority exhibit greater integrative complexity than do those in the minority.[55] For example, consider opinions rendered by the U.S. Supreme Court.[56] The authors of majority opinions tend to concern themselves with specifying all imaginable contingencies under which the law should and should not apply to ensure the longevity of their precedent. In contrast, the authors of minority opinions often focus on arguments that could eventually facilitate the precedent's overruling. This suggests that people who are exposed to members who hold a majority view experience an increase in their own levels of integrative thought; in contrast, people exposed to minority opinions or unanimous groups actually experience a decrease in integrative thinking.[57]

- ***Better decision making***   Diverse decision-making teams make better decisions than teams that lack diversity. For example, all-male or male-dominated teams make decisions that are overaggressive.[58]
- ***Competitive advantage***   The key reason why diversity is so advantageous is that by sampling from a larger pool of potential team members, teams increase their competitive advantage. Nondiverse teams have a smaller talent pool to recruit from, which can only hurt their performance.

CHALLENGES OF DIVERSITY   Diversity is not without its challenges, however. The following are some key challenges in creating and managing diversity within a team:

Surface- Versus Deep-Level Diversity   Consider the distinction between **surface-level diversity** (features that are immediately apparent, such as age, gender, and race) and **deep-level diversity** (features such as attitudes, opinions, information, and values).[59] Surface-level diversity is based on social categories (e.g., race and gender); deep-level diversity is based on attitudes, opinions, information, and values. It is often assumed that surface-level characteristics are a proxy for deep-level characteristics.[60] Groups whose members differ on the surface as well as in their attitudes and information discuss information more thoroughly and perform better than do groups who do not have surface- as well as deep-level similarity.[61] Surface-level diverse groups are perceived to be more positive and accepting of others, engaged in more persistent and confident articulation of divergent perspectives, and are more engaged in the task than are surface-level homogeneous groups.[62] Surface-level diversity (whether it is task

---

[55]Gruenfeld, D. H. (1995). Status, ideology and integrative complexity on the U.S. Supreme Court: Rethinking the politics of political decision making. *Journal of Personality and Social Psychology, 68*(1), 5–20.

[56]Ibid.

[57]Gruenfeld, D. H., Thomas-Hunt, M. C., & Kim, P. (1998). Cognitive flexibility, communication strategy, and integrative complexity in groups: Public versus private reactions to majority and minority status. *Journal of Experimental Social Psychology, 34*, 202–226.

[58]LePine, J., Hollenbeck, J. R., Ilgen, D. R., Colquitt, J. A., & Ellis, A. (2002). Gender composition, situational strength, and team decision-making accuracy: A criterion decomposition approach. *Organizational Behavior and Human Decision Processes, 88*(1), 445–475.

[59]Jehn, K. A., Northcraft, G. B.. & Neale, M. A. (1999). Why differences make a difference: A field study of diversity, conflict, and performance in workgroups. *Administrative Science Quarterly, 44*, 741–763; Phillips, K. W., & Loyd, D. (2006). When surface and deep-level diversity collide: The effects on dissenting group members. *Organizational Behavior and Human Decision Processes, 99*(2), 143–160.

[60]Chatman, J. A., Polzer, J. T., Barsade, S. G., & Neale, M. A. (1998). Being different yet feeling similar: The influence of demographic composition and organizational culture on work processes and outcomes. *Administrative Science Quarterly, 43*, 749–780.; Phillips, "Effects of categorically based expectations," p. 95; Phillips, K. W., Mannix, E. A., Neale, M. A., & Gruenfeld, D. H. (2004). Diverse groups and information sharing: The effects of congruent ties. *Journal of Experimental Social Psychology, 40*(4), 497–510.

[61]Phillips, Mannix, Neale, & Gruenfeld, "Diverse groups and information sharing," p. 96.

[62]Phillips & Loyd, "When surface and deep-level diversity collide," p. 96.

relevant or not) may be beneficial for groups in stimulating thoughtful discussion and analysis. Educational diversity refers to heterogeneity in terms of education; national diversity refers to differences in culture. Both types of diversity provide teams with information-processing benefits that outweigh the limitations associated with social categorization processes.[63] In general, groups with greater educational diversity are more likely to use information. In contrast, national diversity tends to raise issues of social categorization, which hinders information use.[64]

Perceived Versus Actual Diversity   When team members perceive themselves to be diverse in terms of information, conflict increases.[65] However, informational diversity increases information sharing in teams, which eventually increases perceived work style similarity. When the effects of *actual* dissimilarity are controlled for, *perceived* deep-level diversity predicts negative job attitudes, decreases helping behavior, increases turnover, and leads to withdrawal.[66]

Fault Lines   If group members fall into two distinct, nonoverlapping subgroups, based on demographic characteristics, such as young Hispanic women and old Caucasian men, a strong "fault line" is present.[67] These fault lines may split a group into subgroups and provide an informal structure for intragroup conflict.[68] Groups with strong fault lines are more likely to identify not with their group as a whole, but rather, with subgroups inside the team.[69] Moreover, people evaluate work groups with strong fault lines to be less effective than groups with weaker fault lines.[70] Teams in which reward structures are "faultlined" with diversity perform worse than do teams in which reward structures cut across differences between group members or focus on a shared, superordinate identity.[71]

How Much Diversity?   The question of how much diversity to have on a team is not always clear. A team that is so diverse that it has little or no overlap in terms of interpersonal style or disciplinary or strategic background and training will have a difficult time getting anything done. However, managers usually err in the direction of not diversifying enough. Managers should specify those skills they see as necessary to perform the job and then sample from all persons who meet those requirements. The optimal degree of diversity may depend on "interpersonal congruence"—the

---

[63]Dahlin, K., Weingart, L., & Hinds, P. (2005). Team diversity and information use. *Academy of Management Journal, 48*(6), 1107–1123.
[64]Ibid.
[65]Zellmer-Bruhn, M., Maloney, M., Bhappu, A., & Salvador, R. (2008). When and how do differences matter? An exploration of perceived similarity in teams. Organizational Behavior and Human Decision Processes, *107*(1), 41–59.
[66]Liao, H., Chuang, A., & Joshi, A. (2008). Perceived deep-level dissimilarity: Personality antecedents and impact on overall job attitude, helping, work withdrawal, and turnover. *Organizational Behavior and Human Decision Processes, 106*, 106–124.
[67]Lau, D., & Murnighan, K. (1998). Demographic diversity and faultlines: The compositional dynamics of organizational groups. *Academy of Management Review, 23*, 325–340.
[68]Thatcher, S., Jehn, K., & Zanutto, E. (2003). Cracks in diversity research: The effects of diversity faultlines on conflict and performance. *Group Decision and Negotiation, 12*, 217–241; Gibson, C., & Vermeulen, F. (2003). A healthy divide: Subgroups as a stimulus for team learning behavior. *Administrative Science Quarterly, 48*, 202–239.
[69]Lau, D., & Murnighan, K. (2005). Interactions within groups and subgroups: The effects of demographic faultlines. *Academy of Management Journal, 48*(4), 645–659.
[70]Oudenhoven-van der Zee, K., Paulus, P., Vos, M., & Parthasarathy, N. (2009). The impact of group composition and attitudes towards diversity on anticipated outcomes of diversity in Groups. *Group Processes and Intergroup Relations, 12*(2), 257–280.
[71]Homan, A. C., Hollenbeck, J. R., Humphrey, S., van Knippenberg, D., Ilgen, D. R., & van Kleef, G. A. (2008). Facing differences with an open mind: Openness to experience, salience of intragroup differences, and performance of diverse work groups. *Academy of Management Journal, 51*, 1204–1222.

degree to which we see ourselves as others see us. A longitudinal study of 83 work groups revealed that diversity improved performance on creative tasks—provided that interpersonal congruence was high.[72] Yet, diversity undermined the performance of groups with low interpersonal congruence.

Conflict   Diverse teams will often (but not always) experience more conflict than will homogeneous groups, as individuals attempt to reconcile one another's views or simply decide upon a single course of action. In an investigation of 45 teams from the electronics divisions of three major corporations, functional background diversity drove task conflict, but multiple types of diversity drove emotional conflict.[73] Race and tenure diversity are positively associated with emotional conflict, whereas age diversity is negatively associated with emotional conflict. Similarly, in an investigation of 92 work teams in a household goods moving company, three types of team diversity were explored: social category diversity (e.g., gender and race), value diversity, and informational diversity.[74] Informational diversity positively influenced group performance; social category diversity positively increased team morale; and value diversity decreased satisfaction, intent to remain, and commitment to the group. In a study of top management teams in bank holding companies, heterogeneity with respect to age and experience outside the industry was positively related to turnover rates.[75] If improperly managed, culturally diverse groups may not reach their potential. In a study of culturally diverse work groups over a 15-week period,[76] homogeneous groups reported more process effectiveness than did heterogeneous groups during the early period (the first few weeks). The diverse groups (composed of one Caucasian American, one African American, one Hispanic American, and one foreign national) reported more difficulty in agreeing on what was important and in working together, and they frequently had members who tried to be too controlling. The result was lower total task performance for the culturally diverse groups over the first 9 weeks. Diverse groups were good at generating ideas, but homogeneous groups were superior in overall task performance. However, at 9 weeks, the diverse and homogeneous groups performed about the same.

Bias in Performance Reviews   One of the most important responsibilities of a team leader is to conduct performance reviews. Overly harsh performance reviews should be avoided, but failing to give team members honest, straightforward feedback is another problem. In the absence of clear, straightforward, thoughtful feedback, it is not possible for people to change. The leader of diverse teams faces a particular challenge: how to provide constructive, critical feedback along racial and other demographic divides. Harber's investigation of job performance feedback revealed that the feedback Caucasian Americans offer to African Americans is significantly less critical than when evaluating the identical performance by a Caucasian American. Moreover, the tendency toward what Harber terms a **positive bias**[77] becomes even more pronounced as the task grows increasingly subjective—for example, evaluations of the "content" of written essays led to more positive bias than evaluations of the "mechanics" of essays. Whereas the more positive feedback may derive from a

---

[72]Polzer, J. T., Milton, L. P., & Swann, W. B. (2002). Capitalizing on diversity: Interpersonal congruence in small work groups. *Administrative Science Quarterly, 47*, 296–324.

[73]Pelled, L. H., Eisenhardt, K. M., & Xin, K. R. (1999). Exploring the black box: An analysis of work group diversity, conflict, and performance. *Administrative Science Quarterly, 44*, 1–28.

[74]Jehn, Northcraft, & Neale, "Why differences make a difference," p. 96.

[75]Jackson, S. E., Brett, J. F., Sessa, V. I., Cooper, D. M., Julin, J. A., & Peyronnin, K. (1991). Some differences make a difference: individual dissimilarities and group heterogeneity as correlates of recruitment, promotions, and turnover. *Journal of Applied Psychology, 76*(5), 675–689.

[76]Watson, W. E., Kumar, K., & Michaelsen, L. K. (1993). Cultural diversity's impact on interaction process and performance: Comparing homogeneous and diverse task groups. *Academy of Management Journal, 36*(3), 590–602.

[77]Harber, K. D. (1998). Feedback to minorities: Evidence of a positive bias. *Journal of Personality and Social Psychology, 74*(3), 622–628.

norm to be kind[78] or sympathy motives,[79] the recipients of such "kindness" may, in fact, be robbed of important learning opportunities. Inflated praise and insufficient criticism may dissuade minority team members from striving toward greater achievement levels and may misrepresent the level of effort and mastery that professional advancement in the organization actually entails.[80] Biased feedback may deprive minority team members of the mental challenge that educators have cited as critical for intellectual growth.[81] Moreover, African Americans are wary of praise from a Caucasian supervisor, so much so that the receipt of it can actually depress their self-esteem.[82]

What is the best approach that team leaders should follow? The key lies in the delivery of the feedback. In particular, when African Americans receive "unbuffered" critical feedback, they respond less favorably to the feedback than do Caucasian Americans who receive identical feedback, both in terms of how they evaluate the person delivering the feedback and how motivated they feel about the task.[83] However, when the critical feedback is accompanied by an invocation of high standards and by an assurance of that person's capacity to reach those standards, African Americans respond as positively as Caucasian Americans, and both groups show more identification with their skills and their careers.

Solo Status   Individuals experience solo status when they are the only member of their social category (e.g., gender and race) present in a group. The smaller the number of other (disadvantaged, minority) group members present, the more negative the experience for the individual. Solos are more visible in a group and are more likely to be isolated and experience role entrapment.[84] The increased visibility pressures create performance pressure on the "token." Because they are more likely to be stereotyped according to their group membership, they experience isolation and are essentially trapped into whatever role is expected of them. An investigation comparing men's and women's job performance ratings revealed that women's performance evaluations worsened as their proportion in the work group declined, whereas men's performance evaluations were independent of their relative numbers in the work group.[85] In a testing situation, solos performed more poorly during an oral examination.[86] Moreover, men, particularly solos and nonsolos, appear to merit positive evaluations simply by being men.[87] When women are active in groups, they may overcome the solo stigma.[88]

[78]Hastorf, A. H., Northcraft, G. B., & Picciotto, S. R. (1979). Helping the handicapped: How realistic is the performance feedback received by the physically handicapped? *Personality and Social Psychology Bulletin, 5,* 373–376.

[79]Jones, E. E., Farina, A., Hastorf, A. H., Markus, H., Miller, D. T., & Scott, R. A. (1984). *Social stigma: The psychology of marked relationships.* New York: W. H. Freeman.

[80]Massey, G. C., Scott, M. V., & Dornbusch, S. M. (1975). Racism without racists: Institutional racism in urban schools. *The Black Scholar, 7*(3), 2–11.

[81]Sommers, N. (1982). Responding to student writing. *College Composition and Communication, 33,* 148–156.

[82]Crocker, J., Voelkl, K., Testa, M., & Major, B. (1991). Social stigma: The affective consequences of attributional ambiguity. *Journal of Personality and Social Psychology, 60,* 218–228.

[83]Cohen, G. L., Steele, C. M., & Ross, L. D. (1999). The mentor's dilemma: Providing critical feedback across the racial divide. *Personality and Social Psychology Bulletin, 25*(10), 1302–1318.

[84]Kanter, R. M. (1977). Some effects of proportions on group life: Skewed sex ratios and responses to token women. *American Journal of Sociology, 82,* 465–490.

[85]Sackett, P. R., DuBois, C. I. Z., & Wiggins-Noe, A. (1991). Tokenism in performance evaluation: The effects of work group representation on male-female and white-black differences in performance ratings. *Journal of Applied Psychology, 76,* 263–267.

[86]Sekaquaptewa, D., & Thompson, M. (2002). The differential effects of solo status on members of high- and low-status groups. *Personality and Social Psychology Bulletin, 28*(5), 694–707.

[87]Williams, C. L. (1992). The glass escalator: Hidden advantages for men in "female" professions. *Social Forces, 39,* 253–267.

[88]Fuegen, K., & Biernat, M. (2002). Reexamining the effects of solo status for women and men. *Personality and Social Psychology Bulletin, 28*(7), 913–925.

Low-status minorities in high-prestige work groups are expected to act as role models and mentor demographically similar others.[89] However, role modeling is a threat to these group members because it highlights their low status and other members may perceive them to be coalition builders.[90]

CREATING DIVERSE TEAMS   Fortunately, there are several opportunities—almost more than ever—to capitalize on diversity. Changing workforce demographics mean that work teams can be diversified in terms of gender, race, ethnicity, national origin, area of expertise, and organizational affiliation.

In terms of age and gender diversity, variability in age may create conflict, because team members with different training and experience are more likely to have different perspectives about their jobs.[91] Teams whose members vary more widely in age have greater turnover.[92] Age diversity correlates highly with performance only in groups solving complex decision tasks.[93] The same study of 4,538 employees working in 222 teams found that groups with a high proportion of female employees performed worse and reported more health disorders than did gender-diverse teams. When people are the minority member of a gendered group, their performance is enhanced in sex-typical (versus sex-atypical) tasks.[94]

Diversity may raise challenges for the managers, but these are not insurmountable problems. In contrast, the problems associated with a lack of diversity may be insurmountable. A properly managed workplace meets these challenges, and it is worth the effort that it will take to address these problems because a diverse workforce greatly benefits the firm and the team. However, it would be inaccurate to imply that once diverse teams are created, everything is fine. Managing diversity is an ongoing process. We outline a four-pronged plan:

Publicly Commit to Valuing Diversity   An important first step is for companies to publicly commit themselves to valuing diversity. When groups are persuaded of the value of diversity (versus the value of similarity) for their team's performance, diverse groups perform better when they hold prodiversity (versus prosimilarity) beliefs.[95]

Solicit Ideas and Best Practices from Employees on How to Diversify   Managers should pay attention to what team members say and implement at least some of these ideas. Part of this plan also includes asking team members to suggest ways to deal with conflict before it erupts. It is less useful to ask members how to deal with conflict after it erupts, because once embroiled in conflict

[89]Brown, R. (1986). *Social Psychology* (2nd ed.). New York: Free Press.
[90]Ragins, B. R., & Sundstrom, E. (1989). Gender and power in organizations: a longitudinal perspective. *Psychological Bulletin, 105,* 51–88; Duguid, M., Loyd, D. L., & Tolbert, P. S. Dimensions of status: How categorical, numeric, and work group status interact to affect preference for demographically similar others. Under review at *Organization Science*.
[91]Pfeffer, J. (1983). Organizational demography. In B. M. Staw & L. L. Cummings (Eds.), *Research in organizational behavior* (Vol. 5, pp. 299–359). Greenwich, CT: JAI Press.
[92]Wagner, G., Pfeffer, J., & O'Reilly, C. (1984). Organizational demography and turnover in top management groups. *Administrative Science Quarterly, 29,* 74–92.
[93]Wegge, J., Roth, C., Neubach, B., Schmidt, K., Kanfer, R. (2008). Age and gender diversity as determinants of performance and health in a public organization: The role of task complexity and group size. *Journal of Applied Psychology, 93*(6), 1301–1313.
[94]Chatman, J., Boisnier, A., Spataro, S., Anderson, C., & Berdahl, J. (2008). Being distinctive versus being conspicuous: The effects of numeric status and sex-stereotyped tasks on individual performance in groups. Organizational Behavior and Human Decision Processes, 107(2), 141–160.
[95]Homan, A., van Knippenberg, D., Van Kleef, G., & De Dreu, C. (2007). Bridging faultlines by valuing diversity: Diversity beliefs, information elaboration, and performance in diverse work groups. *Journal of Applied Psychology, 92*(5), 1189–1199.

people are less objective and more egocentric in their suggestions. Asking members to identify the causes of conflict will inevitably lead to finger pointing or blame-finding attributions.

Educate Members on the Advantages of Diversity   Rather than just stating the advantages of diversity, managers should explain the facts. Instead of preaching to the team (e.g., "you should diversify because it is the right thing to do"), managers should explain why diversity is in members' best interests.

Diversify at All Levels   Organizations cannot simply hire more diverse people and hope they interact. Organizations must commit to and work toward diversity at the team level and the governing level. At Kaiser Permanente, over 5,000 employees have been assessed, trained, and certified as qualified bilingual staff, receiving pay increases for their additional language skill. Five of the eight regional health presidents are women, and of nearly 160,000 nonphysician staff, 77 percent are women and 57 percent are people of color. Half of the organization's 14 governing board members are people of color, and 36 percent are women.[96]

Left to their own devices, top management teams will tend toward "homosocial reproduction" (i.e., selecting people in their own image) rather than diversity. In a longitudinal analysis of a major Dutch newspaper publisher of 25 years, poor performance and high diversification caused teams to select "likes," and this tendency was even stronger when competition increased.[97] When pressure increases, top management teams tend to "hire likes and fire unlikes."

PROCESSES: HOW TO WORK TOGETHER?

In this section, we focus on team norms and team processes.

Team Structure

Team structure refers to how tightly the group's processes are articulated by team leaders and the organization and the extent to which they are closely adhered to by team members. Groups that are high in structure have specialized roles and routines; groups that are low in structure do not have set roles and routines. Groups with low structure are often allowed to allocate work and organize themselves in any way that they please. They are often not assigned roles and not given specific routines to do a given task. They are simply asked to deliver. In contrast, highly structured teams are asked to assume specialized roles and take on distinct jobs. They are often told how to engage in the processes in order to deliver. Switching jobs or roles is usually not permitted. Rao and Argote examined how high- and low-structure groups perform when there is high turnover.[98] They hypothesized that organizational turnover would affect the performance of low-structure groups more than high-structure groups; in an analysis of 80 small groups that performed a production task, those with low structure suffered the most when turnover occurred.

[96]Frauenheim, E. (2008, October 20). Kaiser permanente: Optimas award winner for ethical practice. *Workforce Management,* 35
[97]Boone, C., Olffen, W., Van Witteloostuijn, A., & Brabander, B. (2004). The genesis of top management team diversity: Selective turnover among top management teams in Dutch newspaper publishing, 1970–1994. *Academy of Management Journal, 47*(5), 633–656.
[98]Rao, R. D., & Argote, L. (2006). Organizational learning and forgetting: The effects of turnover and structure. *European Management Review, 3,* 77–85.

Team Norms

"[People] cannot help producing rules, customs, values, and other sorts of norms whenever they come together in any situation that last for any considerable time."[99] **Norms** are shared expectations that guide behavior in groups. Just as role negotiation and status competition occur early on in the development of groups, so do norms, or the ideas and expectations that guide appropriate behavior for members. Norms differ from formal rules in that they are not written down. Norms are critical for team and organizational performance. Because norms are expectations about appropriate behavior, they embody information about what people should do under various conditions. This makes it easier for people to respond appropriately under new or stressful conditions and helps ensure that everyone is working toward the same goal. Thus, norms reduce threats to productivity, and, in particular, they reduce coordination problems. Precious time is not lost while staff members brainstorm about what to do. For example, at Nordstrom, it is well known by employees as well as shoppers that customer service is the number one priority. At many employee entrances there are signs that say: "Through these doors pass the world's most courteous people."[100]

DEVELOPMENT AND ENFORCEMENT   People in new groups rely on their definition of the situation to retrieve an appropriate script.[101] A **script** is a highly prescriptive sequence of behaviors that dictate appropriate behavior in any given situation. For example, there is a script for behavior at restaurants (e.g., speak with hostess about how many are in your party, review menu, order, and pay bill at table). Many norms develop within the first few minutes of a team's first meeting—such as whether it is appropriate to come a few minutes late, seating arrangements, and so on.[102] "Lasting patterns can appear as early as the first few seconds of a group's life."[103] As soon as the group members act collectively, they have established a new behavior, which serves as a precedent.[104] All group members now have a shared script for "how we do this in a group." The issue for the group when they face their next task or decision is not "what shall we do?" but "shall we proceed as before?"[105] This precedent shapes members' shared beliefs about appropriate behavior.

When norms are left strictly to natural processes and interaction patterns among members, those individuals who are most disruptive and least self-conscious may set unfavorable norms. This is because people who are the most outspoken and the least self-conscious do the most talking. One of the best ways to counteract undesirable norms is to introduce some kind of structure to the team early on (see Appendix 1 on meeting management); structure is the opposite of free-form interaction, where anything goes.

Menlo Innovations uses a process called "Extreme Interviewing," to examine how people interact in small groups, ensuring they have exactly the right fit for the company's unique norms. Norms involving social skills and technical ability are honed through weekly learning lunches, in

---

[99]Sherif, M. (1936). *The psychology of social norms* (p. 3). New York: Harper & Bros.
[100]100 best companies to work for, 2010. (2010, January 21). money.cnn.com
[101]Bettenhausen, K., & Murnighan, J. K. (1985). The emergence of norms in competitive decision-making groups. *Administrative Science Quarterly, 30*, 350–372.
[102]Bettenhausen & Murnighan, "Emergence of norms," p. 102; Gersick, C. J. C. (1988). Time and transition in work teams: Toward a new model of group development. *Academy of Management Journal, 31*, 9–41; Schein, E. H. (1988). *Process consultation: Its role in organization development* (Vol. 1). Reading, MA: Addison-Wesley.
[103]Gersick, "Time and transition in work teams."
[104]Arrow, H., & Burns, K. (2004). Self-organizing culture: How norms emerge in small groups. In M. Schaller & C. S. Crandall (Eds.), *The psychological foundations of culture*. Mahwah: NJ: Lawrence Erlbaum.
[105]Ibid.

which staff make presentations on a compendium of topics; and a "Daily Stand Up" meeting, where employees take turns giving short project reports.[106]

Still other norms may focus on improving group cohesion (e.g., team members regularly arriving with specialty coffee and breakfast items to share with others, technical engineers bringing their dogs to work at companies in Silicon Valley, office birthday parties, and casual Fridays).

Although some level of agreement is necessary for an expectation to be a norm, this does not mean that norms may not be in conflict. For example, in one hospital, nurses might think that the amount of work administrators expect the nurses to do is about right, whereas in another, nurses might think administrators expect the nurses to do too much paperwork.[107] It may be that the norm within one department of a company is to allow its employees to take time during the workday to handle personal matters as long as the time is made up later, but this may not be considered acceptable behavior in another department within the same company.

NORM VIOLATION   Like rules, norms may often be broken. What are the consequences of norm violation in a team? Contrary to naive intuition, the first response of a team to a norm violator is not exclusion, but rather to persuade that person to change. When regularity is interrupted, or violated, the "injured" parties frequently attempt to regain regularity by appealing to the norm (e.g., "Why didn't you circulate the report—we always do that!"). When a team member repeatedly violates a norm, there are serious repercussions, even if the behavior in question is useful for the organization. Consider, for example, the studies conducted at the Hawthorne Works plant in the 1940s. Strong norms developed among work group members concerning the rate of acceptable productivity. That is, members in a particular work group developed a pace at which to work; it was just enough to produce the desired output requested by the supervisor but not enough to overly tax the group's members. Consequently, when members of the work group failed to produce at the level displayed by their peers, they were sharply reprimanded. Furthermore, when members of the group overproduced (worked harder than other members of the group), they were harshly punished. In the Hawthorne Works plant, researchers observed a behavior called "binging," in which the "rate buster" (i.e., the overproducer) was given a sharp blow to the arm so as to reprimand the employee and decrease the level of output.

Certainly, not all cases of norm violation in organizational work groups are met with physical aggression. The first response of a team is usually to attempt to correct the misbehavior with some reminding. Teams will often persist in this kind of corrective activity for a long period before they move to more drastic measures. Indeed, other forms of punishment and aggression are perhaps even more detrimental to individual and organizational well-being, such as ostracism, in which people are excluded from certain social or professional activities.[108] Ostracism can have negative repercussions for the company as well if the isolated individual is not given sufficient information to effectively do the job.

CHANGING NORMS   Once established, norms are not easily changed. Norms are often maintained over several "generations," during which old members gradually leave the team and

[106]2008 Top small workplaces finalists. (n.d.). Winningworkplaces.org

[107]Argote, L. (1989). Agreement about norms and work-unit effectiveness: Evidence from the field. *Basic and Applied Social Psychology, 10*(2), 131–140.

[108]Williams, K. D. (1997). Social ostracism. In R. Kowalski (Ed.), *Aversive interpersonal behaviors* (pp. 133–170). New York: Plenum Publishers.

new members join.[109] Teams' efforts to transmit their norms are particularly strong when newcomers are involved.[110] Teams are highly motivated to provide newcomers with the knowledge, ability, and motivation they will need to play the role of a full member. Consequently, newcomers are usually receptive to these influence attempts because they feel a strong need to learn what is expected of them.[111]

Behavioral Integration

Behavioral integration refers to the extent to which the team's collaborative behavior is integrated, the quantity and quality of their information exchange, and their joint decision making.[112] In essence, behavioral integration refers to the degree to which the group engages in mutual and collective interaction. Survey data from 402 companies revealed that the extent to which top management teams are integrated is a function of three key factors: qualities of the CEO, the team, and the firm (company) itself.

With regard to the CEO, two factors reliably predict top management team integration: (1) the extent to which the CEO has a collectivistic orientation (i.e., focusing on team level rewards rather than individual-level rewards) and (2) CEO tenure.

With respect to team-level factors, two things were significant: (1) goal preference diversity and educational diversity. Specifically, teams that had more diverse goals (i.e., lack of agreement on a single goal) were less integrated. Moreover, teams that were of different educational levels were less integrated. Larger teams tended to be less integrated.

Finally, with respect to firm-level considerations, the overall performance of the company was positively associated with behavioral integration, and the size of the company was negatively related to behavioral integration.

In sum, this field investigation of top management teams underscores the key point of this chapter: Team leaders need to focus not only on internal (i.e., team-level) factors, but they also need to take a wider-lens approach by considering firm-level factors.

Prescriptive Model of Necessary Conditions for Effective Teamwork

Larson and LaFasto specify eight necessary conditions for effective teamwork:[113]

- A clear and elevating goal
- A results-driven structure that includes the following:
  - Clear roles and accountabilities
  - An effective communication system

---

[109]Jacobs, R. C., & Campbell, D. T. (1961). The perpetuation of an arbitrary tradition through several generations of a laboratory microculture. *Journal of Abnormal and Social Psychology, 62,* 649–658; Weick, K. E., & Gilfillan, D. P. (1971). Fate of arbitrary traditions in a laboratory microculture. *Journal of Personality and Social Psychology, 17,* 179–191.

[110]Levine, J. M., & Moreland, R. L. (1991). Culture and socialization in work groups. In L. B. Resnick, J. M. Levine, & S. D. Teasley (Eds.), *Perspectives on socially shared cognition* (pp. 585–634). Washington, DC: American Psychological Association; Moreland, R. L., & Levine, J. M. (1989). Newcomers and oldtimers in small groups. In P. Paulus (Ed.), *Psychology or group influence* (2nd ed., pp. 143–186). Mahwah, NJ: Lawrence Erlbaum.

[111]Louis, M. R. (1980). Surprise and sense making: What newcomers experience in entering unfamiliar organizational settings. *Administrative Science Quarterly, 25,* 226–251; Van Maanen, J. (1977). Experiencing organization: Notes on the meaning of careers and socialization. In J. Van Maanen (Ed.), *Organizational careers: Some new perspectives* (pp. 15–34). New York: John Wiley & Son.

[112]Simsek, Z., Veiga, J. F., Lubatkin, M., & Dino, R. (2005). Modeling the multilevel determinants of top management team behavioral integration. *Academy of Management Journal, 48*(1), 69–84.

[113]Larson, C. E., & LaFasto, F. M. J. (1989). *Teamwork: What must go right/what can go wrong.* Newbury Park, CA: Sage.

- Monitoring of individual performance and providing feedback to members
- Fact-based judgments
- Competent team members (including technical as well as personal competency)
- Unified commitment
- Collaborative climate
- Standards of excellence
- External support and recognition
- Principled leadership

To the extent that these eight conditions are in place, the team is in a good position to perform well. However, there is no guarantee that performance will be optimal.

Conclusion

We have focused on some of the important dimensions of creating and managing teams in a direct fashion. Much planning needs to precede the construction of teams, and, once constructed, teams need fairly continual maintenance. To the extent that the teams are manager led, this work is the purview of the leader or manager; the more self-directing the team becomes, the more the team must do this for itself. When the team is built—in terms of the task, the people, and the process—the leader's work does not stop. During this time, the leader needs to also assess the physical, material, economic, and staffing resources necessary for performing the work to be done. The focus of the leader should not be to presume that everything is fine, but rather to coach the team to work through the issues of task, people, and processes systematically.

5

Team Identity, Emotion, and Development

The CEO of Seagate Technology, Bill Watkins, modifies his employees' behavior by putting them in unfamiliar and downright uncomfortable situations. Watkins believes that when team members are facing a 17 km trek through a bog, on an 18 km bike ride down treacherous descents, or are dangling by cables over gorges, they are more apt to ask for help and work as a team. At Seagate, it all happens in Eco week with a budget of $2 million. Watkins taunts, "What would you do if you knew you could not fail? This week is about doing what you want to do for every week for the rest of your life." Of the 55,000 Seagate employees worldwide, approximately 200 go to Eco week. They are split into 40 teams, with each team comprising four men and a woman. All of the teams are balanced in terms of physical prowess, but each team has a weakness (that they don't know about). For example, one team containing a salesman from Hong Kong, a Malaysian engineer, California attorney, VP from Colorado, and a writer from San Francisco doesn't know that no one on the team can read a map. At the opening ceremony, Watkins plaintively says that they are all going to die. Of course, he is not trying to kill his employees; rather, he is making them uncomfortable as a way to open their minds.[1]

Most companies don't have $2 million budgets to engage in exotic treks, but they do care about the psychology of their teamwork. This chapter focuses on team development, mood, and culture. These dynamics form the personality of a team.

ARE WE A TEAM?

Just because senior management decides to create a team, it does not mean that the team members feel like a team.

---

[1]O'Brien, J. (2008, May 26). Team building in paradise. *Fortune International, 157*(10), 74–82.

Group Entiativity

Group entiativity refers to the degree to which people perceive themselves (and others) to be a team or collective. People are more likely to see people as a team when they are close together, resemble one another, and move together.[2] When people identify with their team, they think and behave in terms of "we" instead of "I."[3] And, when people think about their team, they assume that they should act in accord with the principles of the team.[4] When group members agree on which principle is most fundamental to them, their perceived entiativity will be greater than when they do not agree about that principle, regardless of how many other principles they might agree about.[5]

Group Identity

Group identity is the extent to which people feel their group membership is an important part of who they are. Membership in teams provides people with a sense of belonging. People who have been rejected from groups judge their own groups to be more meaningful and cohesive.[6] People who are strongly identified with their groups feel particularly stressed when their attitudes differ from those of their group; and they avoid attempting to change the behavior of their group.[7]

RELATIONAL AND COLLECTIVE IDENTITY   Gabriel and Gardner distinguished two types of identities people might have to their groups: relational and collective.[8] **Relational identity** is based on important relationships to particular people. **Collective identity** is based on group memberships. Collective identity affects the ability of teams to perform. In teams with low collective identification, diversity in expertise is negatively related to team learning and performance; however, in teams with high collective identification, diversity in expertise promotes team learning and performance.[9]

Men and women differ in terms of their attachment styles, with women's attachments being primarily relational (based on one-on-one relationships) and men's attachments being strongly collective (based on team and group memberships) as well as a relational[10] (see Exhibit 5-1). Attachment style and strength predicts how important teams are for employees.[11]

---

[2]Campbell, D. T. (1958). Common fate, similarity, and other indices of the status of aggregates of persons as social entities. *Behavioral Science, 3*, 14–25.

[3]Tajfel, H., & Turner, J. C. (1986). The social identity theory of intergroup behavior. In S. Worchel & W. Austin (Eds.), *Psychology of intergroup relations* (pp. 7–24). Chicago, IL: Nelson-Hall.

[4]Turner, J. C., Hogg, M. A., Oakes, P. J., Reicher, S. D., & Wetherell, M. S. (1987). *Rediscovering the social group: A self-categorization theory.* Oxford, UK: Blackwell.

[5]Sani, F., Todman, J., & Lunn, J. (2005). The fundamentality of group principles, and perceived group entiativity. *Journal of Experimental Social Psychology, 41*(6), 567–573.

[6]Knowles, M., & Gardner, W. (2008). Benefits of membership: The activation and amplification of group identities in response to social rejection. *Personality and Social Psychology Bulletin, 34*(9), 1200–1213.

[7]Glasford, D., Dovidio, J., & Pratto, F. (2009). I continue to feel so good about us: In-group identification and the use of social identity—enhancing strategies to reduce intragroup dissonance. *Personality and Social Psychology Bulletin, 35*(4), 415–427.

[8]Gabriel, S., & Gardner, W. L. (1999). Are there "his" and "hers" types of interdependence? The implications of gender differences in collective versus relational interdependence for affect, behavior, and cognition. *Journal of Personality and Social Psychology, 77*, 642–655.

[9]Van der Vegt, G., & Bunderson, S. (2005). Learning and performance in multidisciplinary teams: The importance of collective team identification. *Academy of Management Journal, 48*, 532–547.

[10]Gabriel & Gardner, "Are there 'his' and 'hers' types of interdependence?

[11]Seeley, E. A., Gardner, W. L., Pennington, G., & Gabriel, S. (2003). Circle of friends or members of a group? Sex differences in relational and collective attachment to groups. *Group Processes and Intergroup Relations, 6*, 251–263.

EXHIBIT 5-1 Relational and Collective Attachment Styles

Part 1: Your task is to indicate the extent to which you agree with each statement. In the space next to each statement, please write the number that best indicates how you feel about the statement.

1	2	3	4	5	6	7

strongly disagree   strongly agree

1. My close relationships are an important reflection of who I am. _____
2. I usually feel strong sense of pride when someone close to me has an important accomplishment. _____
3. When I think of myself, I often think of my close friends or family as well. _____
4. My sense of pride comes from knowing I have close friends. _____
5. My close relationships are important to my sense of what kind of person I am. _____

Part 2: We are all members of different groups, some of which we choose (such as sports teams and community groups) and some of which we do not (such as racial and religious groups). We would like you to consider your various group memberships and respond to the following questions with them in mind. Please use the same scale as above.

1	2	3	4	5	6	7

strongly disagree   strongly agree

1. When I am in a group, it often feels to me like that group is an important part of who I am. _____
2. When I join a group, I usually develop a strong sense of identification with that group. _____
3. I think one of the most important parts of who I am can be captured by looking at groups I belong to and understanding who they are. _____
4. In general, groups I belong to are an important part of my self-image. _____
5. If a person insults a group I belong to, I feel personally insulted myself. _____

Source: Table 2 (adapted) from page 795 from Cross, S. E., Bacon, P. L., & Morris, M. L. (2000). The relational-interdependent self-construal and relationships. *Journal of Personality and Social Psychology, 78*(4), pp. 791–808. Reprinted by permission of American Psychological Association.

Common Identity and Common Bonds

The attachment that people feel for their groups is rooted in one of two bonds: bonds based on the group as a whole (common identity) and bonds felt for particular group members (common bond).[12] In an investigation of selective and nonselective university eating clubs, the people in common-identity groups were more attached to the group than to any particular member of the group, whereas people in common-bond groups were as attached to particular members as to the group itself.

IDENTITY FUSION   When group members' personal identities become fused with their social identities, their sense of self becomes nearly indistinct from their view of themselves as a group member. **Identity fusion** refers to a blurring of the self-other barrier in a group, and group membership is intensely personal.[13] Fused people are more likely to endorse extreme behaviors on

[12]Prentice, D. A., Miller, D. T., & Lightdale, J. R. (1994). Asymmetries in attachments to groups and to their members: Distinguishing between common-identity and common-bond groups. *Personality and Social Psychology Bulletin, 20*, 484–493.
[13]Swann, W. B., Jr., Gomez, A., Seyle, D. C., Morales, J. F., & Huici, C. (2009). Identity fusion: The interplay of personal and social identities in extreme group behavior. *Journal of Personality and Social Psychology, 5*, 995–1011.

behalf of their group, and they are more willing to fight or die for their groups than a nonfused person, especially when their personal or social identities are activated.

Group-serving Attributions

Group-serving judgments offer a self-protective function for the team member, by enhancing the ego. In a study of 81 simulated top management teams, superior firm performance was attributed to excellent teamwork, whereas inferior firm performance was attributed to external factors.[14] The more cohesive the teams were, the more likely they were to make internal attributions, regardless of firm performance. When people make positive self-affirmations, they are less likely to show a group-serving judgment.[15] Another form of group-serving attributions is **retroactive pessimism**, which occurs when people lower their evaluations of a group's chances for success after a failed competition.[16] Indeed, when supporters of two college basketball teams evaluated the chances for victory for each team, the most avid supporters of the losing team were the most likely to engage in retroactive pessimism.[17]

GROUP POTENCY AND COLLECTIVE EFFICACY

Group potency is "the collective belief of group members that the group can be effective."[18] Similarly, **collective efficacy** refers to an individual's belief that a team can perform successfully.[19] The results of a large meta-analysis of 6,128 groups revealed that groups with higher collective efficacy performed better than groups with lower collective efficacy.[20] Group potency may be a more important predictor of group performance than actual ability. In one investigation, 143 officer cadets working in 51 groups participated in a team simulation in which performance was measured. Group potency predicted group performance over and above actual ability.[21] Similarly, in an investigation of 648 military officers working in 50 self-managed teams over a 5-week period, team performance was assessed via two objective criteria (mental task performance and physical task performance) and one subjective criterion (commander team performance ratings).[22] Group potency had more predictive power in explaining team performance than did cohesion. Thus, thinking "we can" is often more important than actual ability. Over time, group members develop more homogeneous (similar) perceptions of their efficacy.[23]

[14]Michalisin, M. D., Karau, S. J., & Tangpong, C. (2004). Top management team cohesion and superior industry returns: An empirical study of the resource-based view. *Group and Organization Management, 29*, 125–140.

[15]Sherman, D. K., & Kim, H. S. (2005). Is there an "I" in "team"? The role of the self in group-serving judgments. *Journal of Personality and Social Psychology, 88*, 108–120.

[16]Tykocinski, O., Pick, D., & Kedmi, D. (2002). Retroactive pessimism: A different kind of hindsight bias. *European Journal of Social Psychology, 32*, 577–588.

[17]Wann, D., Grieve, F., Waddill, P., & Martin, J. (2008). Use of retroactive pessimism as a method of coping with identity threat: The impact of group identification. *Group Processes and Intergroup Relations, 11*(4), 439–450.

[18]Shea, G. P., & Guzzo, R. A. (1987, Spring). Group effectiveness: What really matters? *Sloan Management Review, 28*(3), 25–31.

[19]Guzzo, R. A., Yost, P. R., Campbell, R. J., & Shea, G. P. (1993). Potency in groups: Articulating a construct. *British Journal of Social Psychology, 32*, 87–106.

[20]Stajkovic, A., Lee, D., & Nyberg, A. (2009). Collective efficacy, group potency, and group performance: Meta-analyses of their relationships, and test of a mediation model. *Journal of Applied Psychology, 94*(3), 814–828.

[21]Hecht, T. D., Allen, N. J., Klammer, J. D., & Kelly, E. C. (2002). Group beliefs, ability and performance: The potency of group potency. *Group Dynamics: Theory, Research and Practice, 6*(2), 143–152.

[22]Jordan, M. H., Field, H. S., & Armenakis, A. A. (2002). The relationship of group process variables and team performance: A team-level analysis in a field setting. *Small Group Research, 33*(1), 121–150.

[23]Jung, D. I., & Sosik, J. J. (2003). Group potency and collective efficacy: Examining their predictive validity, level of analysis, and effects of performance feedback on future group performance. *Group and Organization Management, 28*, 366–391.

People can hold positive or negative beliefs about groups. The beliefs about groups (BAG) scale (Exhibit 5-2) identifies four factors that collectively form a person's beliefs about groups: group preference, positive performance beliefs, negative performance beliefs, and effort beliefs.[24]

GROUP MOOD AND EMOTION

People express moods and so do teams. And, just as people have chronic moods, so do teams. **Group emotion** is a group's affective state that arises from the combination of its bottom-up components (e.g., the moods of particular team members) and its top-down components (e.g., the overall mood of the company).[25] Team members bring their individual-level emotional experiences, such as their chronic moods, emotions, and emotional intelligence, to the team interaction. This emotional information is communicated to other group members. Similarly, the organization's norms and group's emotional history set the stage for the expression and feeling of emotion. For example, following a downsizing or restructuring, the overall mood of the organization or industry might be severely dampened.

Group emotion serves an important role in promoting group survival.[26] The emotions that are felt and displayed in groups coordinate the group's behaviors, particularly in response to threat or stress. In particular, expressed emotion in groups provides the group with information about the environment (e.g., "a layoff has been announced"). Also, shared emotions in groups foster group bonds and group loyalty. For example, happiness felt about one's own group (or collective anger about a rival group) increases the identification that people feel with their own team.[27]

How Emotions Get Shared in Groups

Group emotion can be reliably recognized by group members and outsiders, both on-site and through video ratings.[28] Individual emotions get shared and spread among group members, much like a cold or flu spreads among people who live or work together. There are implicit methods by which this happens, such as emotional contagion, vicarious affect, and behavioral entrainment, as well as conscious, deliberate processes, such as affective influence and affective impression management.[29]

EMOTIONAL CONTAGION   **Emotional contagion** is the process whereby moods and emotions of people around us influence our emotional state. It is the process by which we "catch" other people's emotions. Because people automatically mimic the facial, movement, and vocal rhythms of others, the physiological feedback from such movements often leads them to feel the accompanying emotions. The mere manipulation of facial muscles involved in a particular expression

[24]Karau, S., Moneim, A., & Elsaid, M. (2009). Individual differences in beliefs about groups. *Group Dynamics: Theory, Research and Practice, 13*(1), 1–13.

[25]Barsade, S. G., & Gibson, D. E. (1998). Group emotion: A view from the top and bottom. In D. Gruenfeld, B. Mannix, & M. Neale (Eds.), *Research on managing groups and teams* (pp. 81–102). Stamford, CT: JAI Press.

[26]Spoor, J. R., & Kelly, J. R. (2004). The evolutionary significance of affect in groups: Communication and group bonding. *Group Processes and Intergroup Relations, 7*, 398–416.

[27]Kessler, T., & Hollbach, S. (2005). Group-based emotions as determinants of ingroup identification. *Journal of Experimental Social Psychology, 41*(6), 677–685.

[28]Barsade, S. G. (2000). *The ripple effect: Emotional contagion in groups.* New Haven, CT: Yale University Yale School of Management; Bartel, C., & Saavedra, R. (2000). The collective construction of work group moods. *Administrative Science Quarterly, 45*, 197–231; Totterdell, P., Kellet, S., Teuchmann, K., & Briner, R. B. (1998). Evidence of mood linkage in work groups. *Journal of Personality and Social Psychology, 74*, 1504–1515.

[29]Kelly, J. R., & Barsade, S. G. (2001). Mood and emotions in small groups and work teams. *Organizational Behavior and Human Decision Processes, 86*, 99–130.

EXHIBIT 5-2 BAG: Beliefs about Groups Scale

Item	Group Preferences	Positive Performance Beliefs	Negative Performance Beliefs	Effort Beliefs
1. I'd rather work alone than work with others.[a]	X			
2. I'm more comfortable working by myself rather than as part of a group.[a]	X			
3. I generally prefer to work toward group goals rather than individual goals.	X			
4. I prefer group work to individual work.	X			
5. Whenever possible, I like to work with others rather than by myself.	X			
6. Groups usually outperform individuals.		X		
7. Groups often produce much higher-quality work than individuals.		X		
8. Generally speaking, groups are highly effective.		X		
9. Assigning work to a group is a recipe for disaster.[a]			X	
10. Group projects usually fail to match the quality of those done by individuals.[a]			X	
11. It would be foolish to expect a group to outperform the same number of individuals working alone.[a]			X	
12. I trust other people to work hard on group tasks.				X
13. I am always reluctant to put my fate in the hands of other group members.[a]				X
14. Most people can be trusted to do their fair share of the work.				X
15. Most people loaf when working on a group task.[a]				X
16. It is naive to think that other group members will live up to their promises.[a]				X

Note. All items are assessed on five-point scales ranging from *strongly disagree* to *strongly agree*.
[a] Item was reverse scored.

Source: Karau, S., Moneim, A., & Elsaid, M. (2009). Individual differences in beliefs about groups. *Group Dynamics: Theory, Research and Practice, 13*(1), 1–13.

(e.g., a smile or frown) stimulates emotional feelings.[30] For example, people in conversation converge on a conversational rhythm,[31] nonverbal behaviors,[32] and facial movements.[33]

Some people, however, are more susceptible to "catching" the emotions of others in their groups. Similarly, some people are better at "spreading" emotions than are others. For example, people who are high in feelings of interrelatedness and good decoders of emotional expressions, and score high on emotional contagion scales are more likely to catch the emotions of those around them.[34] People who categorize themselves as "group members" are more likely to converge toward what they believe are their group's emotional experience.[35] When people are explicitly asked about the emotions they experience as members of a particular group, their reported emotions converge toward a profile typical for that group.[36] Identifying with a group produces convergence for emotions as well as attitudes and behaviors.[37] The process of emotional contagion implies that group members will converge in their emotional states over time, leading to a homogeneous group composition.[38] The average affective state of team members was related to a given team member's affect over time, even after controlling for team performance.[39] Group leaders, especially those who are high in expressiveness, may be particularly likely to influence the emotional state of the group.[40]

A group's overall emotional tone, or group affective tone,[41] can affect a variety of team behaviors and performance. For example, in a study of sales teams, group affective tone predicted absenteeism (groups with chronically worse moods were absent more often) and customer-directed prosocial behavior (groups with chronically worse moods were less helpful to customers).[42] Similarly, a field sample of 61 work teams revealed that negative affective tone in teams served a critical link between dysfunctional team behavior and performance when nonverbal negative expressivity was high.[43] Just as group members influence one another to form an overall affective tone, people can be drawn to groups that have members with similar emotions as

---

[30]Duclos, S. E., Laird, J. D., Schneider, E., Sexter, M., Stern, L., & Van Lighten, O. (1989). Categorical vs. dimensional effects of facial expressions on emotional experience. *Journal of Personality and Social Psychology, 57,* 100–108.

[31]Warner, R. (1988). Rhythm in social interaction. In J. E. McGrath (Ed.), *The social psychology of time* (pp. 63–88). Newbury Park, CA: Sage.

[32]Tickle-Degnen, L., & Rosenthal, R. (1987). Group rapport and nonverbal behavior. In C. Hendrick (Ed.), *Review of personality and social psychology: Vol. 9. Group processes and intergroup relations* (pp. 113–136). Newbury Park, CA: Sage.

[33]Bavelas, J. B., Black, A., Lemery, C. R., & Mullett, J. (1987). Motor mimicry as primitive empathy. In N. Eisenberg & J. Strayer (Eds.), *Empathy and its development* (pp. 317–338). Cambridge, England: Cambridge University Press; Hatfield, E., Cacioppo, J. T., & Rapson, R. (1994). *Emotional contagion.* New York: Cambridge University Press.

[34]Hatfield, Cacioppo, & Rapson, *Emotional contagion.*

[35]Moons, W. G., Leonard, D. J., Mackie, D. M., & Smith, E. R. (2009). I feel our pain: Antecedents and consequences of emotional self-stereotyping. *Journal of Experimental Social Psychology, 45(4),* 760–769.

[36]Smith, E. R., Seger, C., & Mackie, D. M. (2007). Can emotions be truly group-level? Evidence regarding four conceptual criteria. *Journal of Personality and Social Psychology, 93,* 431–446.

[37]Smith, E. R., Seger, C., & Mackie, D. M. (2009). Subtle activation of a social categorization triggers group-level emotions. *Journal of Experimental Social Psychology, 45(3),* 460–467.

[38]Kelly, J. R. (2001). Mood and emotion in groups. In M. Hogg & S. Tindale (Eds.), *Blackwell handbook in social psychology. Vol. 3: Group processes* (pp. 164–181). Oxford, UK: Blackwell.

[39]Ilies, R., Wagner, D., & Morgeson, F. (2007). Explaining affective linkages in teams: Individual differences in susceptibility to contagion and individualism-collectivism. *Journal of Applied Psychology, 92(4),* 1140–1148.

[40]Barsade & Gibson, "Group emotion."

[41]George, J. M. (1996). Group affective tone. In M. A. West (Ed.), *Handbook of work group psychology* (pp. 77–93). Chichester, UK: Wiley.

[42]George, J. M. (1990). Personality, affect, and behavior in groups. *Journal of Applied Psychology, 75,* 107–116.

[43]Cole, M., Walter, F., & Bruch, H. (2008). Affective mechanisms linking dysfunctional behavior to performance in work teams: A moderated mediation study. *Journal of Applied Psychology, 93(5),* 945–958.

their own.[44] And, to the extent to which a group displays homogeneity of affect, they are more effective.[45]

VICARIOUS AFFECT   **Vicarious affect**, or socially induced affect, refers to situations in which a person's emotions are induced or caused by another person's emotions. Moreover, the strength of emotional experience is often a function of how similar or well liked the source of the emotion is.[46]

BEHAVIORAL ENTRAINMENT   **Behavioral entrainment** refers to the processes whereby one person's behavior is adjusted or modified to coordinate or synchronize with another person's behavior. Synchrony often happens with both micro (small) and macro (large) body movements.[47] Usually, the outcome of synchronizing movement is positive affect, which can take the form of liking the other person,[48] satisfaction with the interaction,[49] and greater group rapport.[50]

Emotional Intelligence in Teams

Emotional intelligence is the ability to recognize emotions in ourselves and others and to use emotional knowledge in a productive fashion. Emotional intelligence in teams is positively linked to team performance.[51] In one investigation, 139 respondents were administered the Workgroup Emotional Intelligence Profile, a measure of group members' emotional intelligence when working in teams (see Exhibit 5-3 for the 2009 version of this scale). The results consistently showed that individuals with high emotional intelligence preferred to seek collaborative solutions when confronted with conflict.[52]

Leadership and Group Emotion

As emotional intelligence becomes recognized as a leadership skill, leaders are encouraged to both recognize emotions and manage them in their teams. Leaders' emotions strongly influence group emotion and performance. In addition, leaders' ability to recognize emotions in their team members determines the effectiveness of their leadership. **Emotional aperture** is the ability to recognize diverse emotions in a team.[53] The leaders who are the most likely to be effective at

---

[44]George, "Group affective tone."

[45]Ibid.; George, "Personality, affect, and behavior in groups."

[46]McIntosh, D. N., Druckman, D., & Zajonc, R. B. (1994). Socially induced affect. In D. Druckman & R. A. Bjork (Eds.), *Learning, remembering, believing: Enhancing human performance* (pp. 251–276). Washington, DC: National Academy Press.

[47]Siegman, A. W., & Reynolds, M. (1982). Interviewer-interviewee nonverbal communications: An interactional approach. In M. A. Davis (Ed.), *Interaction rhythms: Periodicity in communication behavior* (pp. 249–278). New York: Human Sciences Press.

[48]Kelly, J. R. (1987). *Mood and interaction.* Unpublished doctoral dissertation, University of Illinois, Urbana-Champaign, IL.

[49]Bernieri, F., Reznick, J. S., & Rosenthal, R. (1988). Synchrony, pseudosynchrony, and dissynchrony: Measuring the entrainment process in mother-infant dyads. *Journal of Personality and Social Psychology, 54,* 243–253.

[50]Hecht, Allen, Klammer, & Kelly, "Group beliefs, ability and performance."

[51]Jordan, P. J., & Troth, A. C. (2004). Managing emotions during team problem solving: Emotional intelligence and conflict resolution. *Human Performance, 17,* 195–218.

[52]Jordan, P. J., & Troth, A. C. (2002). Emotional intelligence and conflict resolution: Implications for human resource development. *Advances in Developing Human Resources, 4*(1), 62–79.

[53]Sanchez-Burkes, J., & Huy, Q. (2009). Emotional aperture and strategic change: The accurate recognition of collective emotions. *Organization Science, 20*(1), 22–34.

EXHIBIT 5-3 Workgroup Emotional Intelligence Profile

The questions on the Work Group Emotional Intelligence Profile (WEIP) ask you about your feelings when working in your team. When thinking about your team, please think of your immediate work unit. Please indicate your level of agreement with each of the following statements using a 1-7 scale, ranging from 1 (strongly disagree) to 7 (strongly agree).

Awareness of Own Emotions (Own Aware)

1. I can explain the emotions I feel to team members.
2. I can discuss the emotions I feel with other team members.
3. If I feel down, I can tell team members what will make me feel better.
4. I can talk to other members of the team about the emotions I experience.

Management of Own Emotions (Own Manage)

5. I respect the opinion of team members, even if I think they are wrong.
6. When I am frustrated with fellow team members, I can overcome my frustration.
7. When deciding on a dispute, I try to see all sides of the disagreement before I come to a conclusion.
8. I give a fair hearing to fellow team members' ideas.

Awareness of Others' Emotions (Other Aware)

9. I can read fellow team members 'true' feelings, even if they try to hide them.
10. I am able to describe accurately the way others in the team are feeling.
11. When I talk to a team member I can gauge their true feelings from their body language.
12. I can tell when team members don't mean what they say.

Management of Others' Emotions (Other Manage)

13. My enthusiasm can be contagious for members of a team.
14. I am able to cheer team members up when they are feeling down.
15. I can get fellow team members to share my keenness for a project.
16. I can provide the 'spark' to get fellow team members enthusiastic.

Source: Jordan, P.J., & Lawrence, S.A. (2009). Emotional intelligence in teams: Development and initial validation of the short version of the Workgroup Emotional Intelligence Profile (WEIP-S). *Journal of Management & Organization, 15*, 452–469

transformational leadership are those who can accurately recognize emotions, exude positive emotions, and are agreeable in nature.[54]

GROUP COHESION

Group cohesion or cohesiveness might be considered to be a special type of group affective tone or emotion.[55] **Group cohesiveness** refers to emotional attraction among group members. Indeed, most people who have been a part of a team will claim that there are ties that bind the group together.[56]

---

[54]Rubin, R. S., Munz, D. C., & Bommer, W. H. (2005). Leading from within: The effects of emotion recognition and personality on transformational leadership behavior. *Academy of Management Journal, 48*(5), 845–858.

[55]Kelly, J. B. (1991). Parent interaction after divorce: Comparison of mediated and adversarial divorce processes. *Behavioral Sciences and Law, 9*, 387–398.

[56]Hogg, M. A. (1992). *The social psychology of group cohesiveness: From attraction to social identity.* London/New York: Harvester Wheatsheaf/New York University Press.

Cohesion and Team Behavior

Members of cohesive teams sit closer together, focus more attention on one another, show signs of mutual affection, and display coordinated patterns of behavior. Furthermore, members of cohesive teams who have a close relationship are more likely to give due credit to their partners. In contrast, those who do not have a close relationship are more likely to take credit for successes and blame others for failure.[57] Cohesive groups are easier to maintain. Members of cohesive teams are more likely to participate in team activities, stay on the team and convince others to join, and resist attempts to disrupt the team.[58] Cohesion increases conformity to team norms.[59] This effect can be helpful when deviance endangers the team or harmful when innovation is required. Cohesive teams are more likely to serve team rather than individual interests.[60] Most important, members of cohesive teams are more productive on a variety of tasks than are members of noncohesive groups.[61] In a study of 81 simulated teams of competing airlines, top management cohesion was associated with superior returns.[62]

Cohesive teams are more productive than are less cohesive teams, but it could very well be that (1) more productive teams become more cohesive, (2) something other than cohesion is responsible for increased productivity, or (3) both. The link of cohesion with performance may depend on team norms: Cohesion amplifies norms favoring both high and low productivity.[63] There are many ways to promote cohesion (see Exhibit 5-4).

Building Cohesion in Groups

Building cohesion in teams is often easier than we think.

- *Help the team build identity*   Simply assembling people into a team is enough to produce some cohesion,[64] and the more time people spend together (in a face-to-face fashion), the more cohesive they become.[65] When team members think about their identity (i.e., what they stand for) and what they have in common, they become more cohesive.[66]

---

[57]Sedekides, C., Campbell, W. K., Reeder, G. D., & Elliot, A. J. (1998). The self-serving bias in relational context. *Journal of Personality and Social Psychology, 74*(2), 378–386.

[58]Brawley, L. R., Carron, A. V., & Widmeyer, W. N. (1988). Exploring the relationship between cohesion and group resistance to disruption. *Journal of Sport and Exercise Psychology, 10*(2), 199–213; Carron, A. V., Widmeyer, W. N., & Brawley, L. R. (1988). Group cohesion and individual adherence to physical activity. *Journal of Sport and Exercise Psychology, 10*(2), 127–138.

[59]O'Reilly, C. A., & Caldwell, D. F. (1985). The impact of normative social influence and cohesiveness on task perceptions and attitudes: A social-information processing approach. *Journal of Occupational Psychology, 58*, 193–206; Rutkowski, G. K., Gruder, C. L., & Romer, D. (1983). Group cohesiveness, social norms, and bystander intervention. *Journal of Personality and Social Psychology, 44*(3), 545–552.

[60]Thompson, L., Kray, L., & Lind, A. (1998). Cohesion and respect: An examination of group decision making in social and escalation dilemmas. *Journal of Experimental Social Psychology, 34*, 289–311.

[61]Dion, K. L., & Evans, C. R. (1992). On cohesiveness: Reply to Keyton and other critics of the construct. *Small Group Research, 23*(2), 242–250; Michel, J. G., & Hambrick, D. C. (1992). Diversification posture and top management team characteristics. *Academy of Management Journal, 35*(1), 9–37; Smith, K., Smith, K., Olian, J., Sims, H., O'Bannon, D., & Scully, J. (1994). Top management team demography and process: The role of social integration and communication. *Administrative Science Quarterly, 39*, 412–438.

[62]Michalisin, Karau, & Tangpong, "Top management team cohesion and superior industry returns."

[63]Stogdill, R. M. (1972). Group productivity, drive, and cohesiveness. *Organizational Behavior and Human Performance, 8*(1), 26–43.

[64]Hogg, M. A. (1987). Social identity and group cohesiveness. In J. C. Turner, M. A. Hogg, P. J. Oakes, S. D. Reicher, & M. Wetherell (Eds.), *Rediscovering the social group: A self-categorization theory* (pp. 89–116). Oxford, UK: Basil Blackwell.

[65]Manning, J. F., & Fullerton, T. D. (1988). Health and well-being in highly cohesive units of the U.S. Army. *Journal of Applied Social Psychology, 18*, 503–519.

[66]Prentice, Miller, & Lightdale, "Asymmetries in attachments to groups and to their members."

EXHIBIT 5-4 Fostering Cohesion in Teams

Just inside the door of the men's room was a rack that held sweaty biking shirts, damp bathing suits, and clammy running shoes. The aroma seemed to belong more to a high school locker room than to a corporate headquarters. But this was the house of Patagonia, the apparel company that prides itself on letting its employees take their play every bit as seriously as they take their work. At lunchtime many days, Patagonia employees go surfing for 2 hours, while half-dozen others take a 100-minute, 27-mile bike loop in the hills overlooking the Pacific. One of the sweaty biking shirts belongs to Andy Welling, a sales manager at Patagonia's headquarters in Ventura, California. At 41, Welling is a fiend about staying in shape—he bikes several days a week at lunchtime and joins Patagonia's weekly pick-up soccer game. He often makes up for his lunchtime cycling by working a few hours at home in the evening. Patagonia is so mellow about flextime that the receptionist at headquarters, an 11-time world Frisbee champion, is allowed to take 3 months off each summer to run a surfing school. "I could make quite a bit more money working somewhere else," Welling said. "But to have the quality of life and to remain physically fit, by cycling or going surfing, you can't put a dollar amount on it."

At Fahrenheit 212, an innovation consultancy located in Manhattan, every 100 days every-one gets together, locks the doors, ditches the cell phones, and sits down to a companywide strat-egy session. Together, they set the company's goals for the next 100 days. And they go around the table to hear how each staffer—execs included—did on his personal deliverables over the last 100 days. They ask each other questions, weigh in with their own perspectives on their colleagues' work, and do lots of ribbing, reflecting, and cheering. And if the fear of being embar-rassed in front of rowdy colleagues wasn't enough, staffers work directly with their managers to lay out their individual plans for the next 100 days and actually grade themselves on their last 100-day plan. At the end of the year, the scores are added up to help determine incentive bonuses and future compensation.

In May of 2009, employees of Student Media Group in Newark, Delaware, started noticing a few things popping up in the office: a 50-inch plasma television screen, a ping-pong table, a Wii videogame player, and a fridge stocked with free soda and snacks. They wondered what was going on. After three salespeople were laid off during the spring and revenue fell 40 percent year-to-year in the first 4 months of 2009, the owner of the college advertising company sensed a bad vibe among the 19 remaining employees that he didn't want to continue. So, he invested $3,000 on perks to motivate his staff. "Let's show our employees that we're not scared," says Paul Alford, chief executive of Springboard Inc., which owns Student Media Group. "Let's see if this inspires them. It did." By the end of the month, sales were at $1.5 million for the year, up 10 percent from the same period last year. Mr. Alford says the action had a big impact on the staff. "It really was the catalyst that got people believing," he says.

Sources: Greenhouse, S. (2008, April 20). Working Life (High and Low). *New York Times*, p. BU, p. 1. *Also*, Hira, N. (2009, December 16). A management strategy that works for young employees. *Fortune Magazine*. money.cnn.com. *Also*, Flandez, R. (2009, July 7). Rewards Help Soothe Hard Times. *Wall Street Journal*, p. B4.

- ***Make it easy for the team to be close together***   Physical proximity and real or perceived similarity strengthen team cohesion.[67]
- ***Focus on similarities among team members***   Team members feel more cohesive when they focus on their similarities, rather than their differences.

---

[67]Ruder, M. K., & Gill, D. L. (1982). Immediate effects of win-loss on perceptions of cohesion in intramural and inter-collegiate volleyball teams. *Journal of Sport Psychology, 4*(3), 227–234; Stokes, J. P. (1983). Components of group cohesion: Inter-member attraction, instrumental value, and risk taking. *Small Group Behavior, 14*, 163–173; Sundstrom, E. D., & Sundstrom, M. G. (1986). *Work places: The psychology of the physical environment in offices and factories.* Cambridge, UK: Cambridge University Press.

• *Put a positive spin on the team's performance*   Teams are more cohesive when they succeed rather than fail, though some teams can preserve (if not strengthen) cohesion even when they fail.[68]
• *Challenge the team*   External pressure and rewards for team performance also increase team cohesion.[69]

Many factors that produce greater cohesion in teams contradict those that promote diversity. We suggest that the manager first consider strategies for building diversity and then focus on building cohesion within the diverse team.

TRUST

Trust and respect are both important for teams, but they are not the same thing. **Respect** is the level of esteem a person has for another, whereas **trust** is the willingness of a person to rely on another person in the absence of monitoring.[70] (See Exhibit 5-5 for measures of trust and respect in teams.) Trust is very important for teams. Among the characteristics of "ideal members" of teams and relationships is trustworthiness, which is the most important attribute for all interdependent relationships.[71]

A high level of trust among team members can make members of self-managing work teams reluctant to monitor one another. In a study of 71 self-managing teams, when low monitoring combined with high individual autonomy, team performance suffered.[72] Autonomy, in a team context, is defined as the amount of freedom and discretion that a person has in carrying out assigned tasks.[73] It was only when high trust in the team was combined with low individual autonomy that performance improved. The dangerous combination was high trust combined with high individual autonomy.

According to Cronin and Weingart, teams high in both trust and respect should be desirable, as team members begin with the belief that their fellow teammates have something valuable to add to the team.[74] Teams high in respect but low in trust might appear as collections of individualists, afraid of exposing their vulnerabilities for fear they might be exploited. Conversely, teams high in trust but low in respect are safe but ineffective, such that members don't see much value in the contributions of their teammates, even if they are well intentioned. In a simulation study of top management teams, higher respect increased task conflict and decreased relationship conflict. Trust decreased process conflict.[75]

---

[68]Brawley, Carron, & Widmeyer, "Exploring the relationship between cohesion and group resistance," p. 114.

[69]Glickman, A. S., Zimmer, S., Montero, R. C., Guerette, P. J., & Campbell, W. J. (1987). The evolution of teamwork skills: An empirical assessment with implications for training. *US Naval Training Systems Center Technical Reports*, No. 87–016; Shea & Guzzo, "Group effectiveness," p. 110.

[70]Mayer, R. C., Davis, J. H., & Schoorman, F. D. (1995). An integrative model of organizational trust. *Academy of Management Review, 20*, 709–734; Rousseau, D. M., Sitkin, S. B., Burt, R. S., & Camerer, C. (1998). Not so different after all: Across-discipline view of trust. *Academy of Management Review, 23*(3), 393–404.

[71]Cottrell, C., Neuberg, S., & Li, N. (2007). What do people desire in others? A sociofunctional perspective on the importance of different valued characteristics. *Journal of Personality and Social Psychology, 92*(2), 208–231.

[72]Langfred, C. W. (2004). Too much of a good thing? Negative effects of high trust and individual autonomy in self-managing teams. *Academy of Management Journal, 47*(3), 385–399.

[73]Hackman, J. R. (1983). Designing work for individuals and for groups. In J. R. Hackman (Ed.), *Perspectives on Behavior in Organizations* (pp. 242–256). McGraw-Hill, New York.

[74]Cronin, M., & Weingart, L. (2007). The differential effects of trust and respect on team conflict. In K. Behfar & L. Thompson (Eds.), *Conflict in organizational groups: New directions in theory and practice*. Chicago, IL: NU Press.

[75]Langfred, "Too much of a good thing?"

EXHIBIT 5-5 Trust and Respect in Teams

Trust in teams can be measured by . . .	Respect in teams can be measured by . . .
• I trust my teammates. • I have little faith that my teammates will consider my needs when making decisions. (R) • I believe my teammates are truthful and honest.	• I think highly of my teammates' character. • This team sets a good example. • Our team does things the right way. • My team deserves my consideration. • I admire my teammates. • I am proud to be part of my team. • I think my teammates have useful perspectives. • My teammates usually have good reasons for their beliefs. • People on my team have well-founded ideas. • I hold my team in high regard. • I think highly of my team members. • Our team has a reason to be proud. • I respect my teammates.

Note. (R), Reverse-scaled item.

Source: Cronin, M., & Weingart, L. (2007). The differential effects of trust and respect on team conflict. In K. Behfar & L. Thompson (Eds.), *Conflict in organizational groups: New directions in theory and practice.* Chicago, IL: NU Press. *Also,* Cronin, M. A. (2004). The effect of respect on interdependent work. *Unpublished doctoral dissertation,* Pittsburgh, PA: Carnegie Mellon University.

TRUST OR FAITH?   Business is built on relationships of all sorts, and almost nothing is truly guaranteed in writing. No contract can be so complete as to specify, for instance, what an employee must actually do at a given time on a given day in a particular instance, because at some level just about every situation is unique. Faith in other team members' integrity to do things that cannot be specified in a contract or monitored after the fact is an essential feature of a successful team—or for that matter, any business relationship. It is the integrity of the individual team members, and the members' trust in this integrity, that allows for successful teamwork.

The absence of a positive, trusting relationship can undermine teamwork, and so fostering trust is one of the most important tasks of a manager. One key type of trust is the confidence we have in the ability or knowledge of others. The absence of trust need not be associated with anything malicious; a lack of trust can stem from a lack of experience working with others, such as when a cross-functional team is assembled to establish organizational policy or to hire key executives to lead the company. The next few sections elaborate on the issue of trust—how to get a better understanding of it and its role in working relationships and, most important, where and when to find it.

INCENTIVE-BASED TRUST   Incentive-based or calculated trust involves designing incentives to minimize breaches of trust. When an arrangement, such as a contract, is made on favorable terms for the other party, it is easier to trust that they will fulfill their end of the deal. Companies often pay bonuses, in fact, to ensure just this kind of outcome.

TRUST BASED ON FAMILIARITY   As people become more familiar with one another, they are more likely to trust one another. For this reason, group turnover presents special challenges for trust within the team. For example, distrust of new members places extra burdens on full members, who must work harder to make sure that the team's expectations are clear and that new members' behaviors are monitored.[76]

TRUST BASED ON SIMILARITY   Oftentimes, trust can develop based on commonalities, such as being alumni of the same school, belonging to the same religious institution, or having kids who play on the same Little League team. People who are similar to one another in beliefs, attitudes, and interests tend to like one another more.

TRUST BASED ON SOCIAL NETWORKS   Trusting relationships in organizations are often based upon social networks. **Social embeddedness** refers to the idea that transactions and opportunities take place as a result of social relationships that exist between organizational actors.[77] This is conducive to organizational teamwork in that trust and shared norms of reciprocal compliance have beneficial governance properties for the people involved. In short, embedding commercial exchange in social attachments creates a basis for trust that, if accepted and returned, crystallizes through reciprocal coinvestment and self-enforcement for use in future transactions. Trust based on social networks offers several advantages.[78] "Embedded ties" reduce the time needed to reach and enforce agreements. Second, the expectations and trust associated with embedded ties increases risk taking and coinvestments in advanced technology. Third, the transfer of proprietary information through embedded ties leads to more win-win types of arrangements. Finally, embedded ties promote cooperation, even when groups will not work together very long.

IMPLICIT TRUST   Sometimes, we put our trust in others even in the absence of any rational reason or obvious similarity. Trust, in this sense, is based upon highly superficial cues. In every social interaction, there are subtle signals that we attend to even though we are not aware of their influence. They operate below our conscious awareness. Some examples follow.

Instant Attitudes   Near-immediate, intense likes or dislikes for a novel object based on a first encounter with it.[79]

Mere Exposure: "He Grew on Me."   The more we see someone, the more we like them.[80] This even goes for people that we initially do not like. However, most people do not realize that their liking for people is driven by how often they see them.

Schmoozing: "Let's Have Lunch Sometime."   Small talk might not appear to be relevant to accomplishing a work task. The exchange of pleasantries about the weather or our

[76]Moreland, R. L., & Levine, J. M. (2002b). Socialization and trust in work groups. *Group Processes and Interpersonal Relations, 5*(3), 185–201.
[77]Uzzi, B. (1997). Social structure and competition in interfirm networks: The paradox of embeddedness. *Administrative Science Quarterly, 42*, 35–67.
[78]Ibid.
[79]Greenwald, A. G., & Banaji, M. (1995). Implicit social cognition: Attitudes, self-esteem, and stereotypes. *Psychological Review, 102*(1), 4–27.
[80]Zajonc, R. (1968). Attitudinal effects of mere exposure. *Journal of Personality and Social Psychology* (monograph supplement, No. 2, Part 2).

favorite basketball team seems to be purposeless, except for conforming to social etiquette. However, on a preconscious level, schmoozing has a dramatic impact on our liking and trust of others. For example, even a short exchange can lead people to develop considerably more trust in others than in the absence of interaction.

Mirroring   People involved in a face-to-face interaction tend to mirror one another in posture, facial expression, tone of voice, and mannerisms. Mirroring helps people to develop rapport.[81] On the surface, it might seem that mimicking others would be extremely annoying—almost like a form of mockery. However, the type of mimicry that is involved in everyday social encounters is quite subtle. When two people are mimicking each other, their movements are like a choreographed dance. Their behavior becomes synchronized. To the extent that our behaviors are synchronized with those of others, we feel more rapport, and this increases our trust in them.

"Flattery Can Get You Anywhere."   We like people who appreciate us and admire us. We tend to trust people more who like us. Many people believe that for flattery to be effective in engendering trust, it must be perceived as genuine. However, even if people suspect that the flatterer has ulterior motives, this can still increase liking and trust under some conditions.[82]

Face-to-Face Contact   We are more likely to trust other people in a face-to-face encounter than when communicating via another medium, such as phone or fax machine. Perhaps this is why people often choose to travel thousands of miles for a face-to-face meeting when it would be more efficient to communicate via phone, e-mail, or videoconference.

Psychological Safety

People in teams size up how "safe" they feel bringing up certain subjects and seeking assistance from the team.[83] **Psychological safety** reflects the extent to which people feel that they can raise issues and questions without fear of being rebuffed. Psychological safety is important in teams that need to communicate knowledge about new technological procedures to one another and learn from one another.[84] Team members in one hospital intensive care unit were asked three questions: (1) How comfortable do you feel checking with others if you have a question about the right way to do something? (2) How much do people in your unit value others' unique skills and talents? (3) To what extent can people bring up problems and tough issues? When combined, these questions were used to create a measure of psychological safety. Team members who expressed greater psychological safety were more likely to engage in learning about how to use new technological procedures, which in turn predicted the success of implementation in the neonatal intensive care units.

---

[81]Drolet, A., Larrick, R., & Morris, M. W. (1998). Thinking of others: How perspective-taking changes negotiators' aspirations and fairness perceptions as a function of negotiator relationships. *Basic and Applied Social Psychology, 20*(1), 23–31.

[82]Jones, E. E., Stires, L. K., Shaver, K. G., & Harris, V. A. (1968). Evaluation of an ingratiator by target persons and bystanders. *Journal of Personality, 36*(3), 349–385.

[83]Edmondson, A. (1999). Psychological safety and learning behavior in work teams. *Administrative Science Quarterly, 44*, 350–383.

[84]Tucker, A. T., Nembhard, I. M., & Edmondson, A. C. (2007). Implementing new practices: An empirical study of organizational learning in hospital intensive care units. *Management Science, 53*(6), 894–907.

TEAM DEVELOPMENT AND SOCIALIZATION

Teams are not permanent entities. The average lifespan of a team is approximately 24 months.[85] Teams are constantly being reconfigured, and people need to quickly transition into new teams.

Group Socialization

Teams are not built from scratch. Instead, a member or two is added to a team that is changing its direction; members leave teams for natural (and other) reasons. Members of teams are continually entering and exiting; as a consequence, the team itself is constantly forming and reconfiguring itself. **Group socialization** is the process of how individuals enter into and then (at some point) leave teams. The process is disruptive, to be sure, yet it need not be traumatic or ill advised. When people begin to work together as a team, they begin a process of **socialization**, such that members of the team mutually shape each other's behavior. More often, teams may undergo changes in membership, such that some members may leave and new ones may enter. The process of socialization is essential for team members to be able to work together and coordinate their efforts.

Most people think of socialization as a one-way process, wherein the team socializes the individual member—usually a newcomer—in the norms and roles of the team. However, as any leader can attest, the introduction of a new team member is a process of joint socialization. Facilitating newcomer effectiveness in teams is particularly important in high-technology industries in which knowledge workers transition frequently and the cost of integrating new employees is high.[86] Three predictors of newcomer performance include newcomer empowerment, team expectations, and team performance.[87] In an investigation of 65 project teams, newcomer performance improved over time, particularly early in socialization.[88] Newcomer empowerment and the team's expectation of the newcomer positively predicted newcomer's performance. Moreover, newcomers who were empowered and performed well were less likely to express intentions to leave the team.

The Phases of Group Socialization

Think about a time when you joined an existing team. Perhaps you joined a study group that had been previously formed, took a summer internship with a company that had ongoing teams already in place, or moved to a different unit within your organization. In all of these instances, you went through a process of group socialization.[89] Three critical things go on during group socialization that can affect the productivity of teams: evaluation, commitment, and role transition.

EVALUATION   Teams evaluate individual members, and individual members evaluate teams. In short, the individuals on the team "size each other up." People conduct a cost-benefit analysis

---

[85]Thompson, L. (2010). *Leading high impact teams*. Team leadership survey from the Kellogg School of Management Executive Program. Evanston, IL: Northwestern University.

[86]Chen, G., & Klimoksi, R. J. (2003). The impact of expectations on newcomer performance in teams as mediated by work characteristics, social exchanges, and empowerment. *Academy of Management Journal, 46*(5), 591–607.

[87]Ibid.

[88]Chen, G. (2005). Newcomer adaptation in teams: Multilevel antecedents and outcomes. *The Academy of Management Journal, 48*(1), 101–116.

[89]Moreland, R. L., & Levine, J. M. (2000). Socialization in organizations and work groups. In M. Turner (Ed.), *Groups at work: Theory and research* (pp. 69–112). Mahwah, NJ: Lawrence Erlbaum.

when it comes to evaluating team members. If team members receive (or expect to receive) relatively high returns from team membership while enduring few costs, they probably like their team. Teams, too, evaluate a member positively who makes many contributions to the collective while exacting few costs.[90] People with either little experience or negative experiences in teams often avoid working in groups.[91]

COMMITMENT   Commitment is a person's "enduring adherence" to the team and the team's adherence to its members.[92] The key factor that affects commitment is the alternatives that are available to the individual and the team. For example, if a team has its choice of several highly qualified candidates, its level of commitment to any one candidate is less than if a team does not have as many alternatives.

ROLE TRANSITION   A person usually moves through a progression of membership in the team, going from nonmember to quasi-member to full member (see Exhibit 5-6). One key to gaining full member status is to be evaluated positively by the team and to gain the team's commitment. This can often (but not always) be achieved by learning through direct experience with the team, and also through observations of others in the team. Indeed, newcomers in teams feel a strong need to obtain information about what is expected of them;[93] simultaneously, teams communicate this knowledge through formal and informal indoctrination sessions.[94] However, newcomers may not learn crucial information they need to perform their jobs, such as information about the preferences of supervisors or administrative procedures, until they are trusted by their coworkers.[95]

According to Swann, Milton, and Polzer, people who join groups can engage in either **self-verification** or **appraisal effects**.[96] Self-verification occurs when group members persuade others in the team to see them as they see themselves. In contrast, appraisal occurs when groups persuade members to see themselves as the group sees them. Of the two, self-verification is more prevalent than appraisal. When team members encourage their group to see them the way they

[90]Kelley, H. H., & Thibaut, J. (1978). *Interpersonal relations: A theory of interdependence.* New York: Wiley; Thibaut, J., & Kelley, H. (1959). *The social psychology of groups.* New York: John Wiley & Sons.

[91]Bohrnstedt, G. W., & Fisher, G. A. (1986). The effects of recalled childhood and adolescent relationships compared to current role performances on young adults' affective functioning. *Social Psychology Quarterly, 49*(1), 19–32; Gold, M., & Yanof, D. S. (1985). Mothers, daughters, and girlfriends. *Journal of Personality and Social Psychology, 49*(3), 654–659; Hanks, M., & Eckland, B. K. (1978). Adult voluntary association and adolescent socialization. *Sociological Quarterly, 19*(3), 481–490; Ickes, W. (1983). A basic paradigm for the study of unstructured dyadic interaction. *New Directions for Methodology of Social and Behavioral Science, 15,* 5–21; Ickes, W., & Turner, M. (1983). On the social advantages of having an older, opposite-sex sibling: Birth order influences in mixed-sex dyads. *Journal of Personality and Social Psychology, 45*(1), 210–222.

[92]Kelley, H. H. (1983). The situational origins of human tendencies: A further reason for the formal analysis of structures. *Personality and Social Psychology Bulletin, 9*(1), 8–36.

[93]Louis, M. R. (1980). Surprise and sense making: What newcomers experience in entering unfamiliar organizational settings. *Administrative Science Quarterly, 25,* 226–251; Van Maanen, J. (1977). Experiencing organization: Notes on the meaning of careers and socialization. In J. Van Maanen (Ed.), *Organizational careers: Some new perspectives* (pp. 15–45). New York: John Wiley & Sons; Wanous, J. P. (1980). *Organizational entry: Recruitment, selection, and socialization of newcomers.* Reading, MA: Addison-Wesley.

[94]Gauron, E. F., & Rawlings, E. I. (1975). A procedure for orienting new members to group psychotherapy. *Small Group Behavior, 6,* 293–307; Jacobs, R. C., & Campbell, D. T. (1961). The perpetuation of an arbitrary tradition through several generations of a laboratory microculture. *Journal of Abnormal and Social Psychology, 62,* 649–658; Zurcher, L. A. (1965). The sailor aboard ship: A study of role behavior in a total institution. *Social Forces, 43,* 389–400; Zurcher, L. A. (1970). The "friendly" poker game: A study of an ephemeral role. *Social Forces, 49,* 173–186.

[95]Feldman, D. C. (1977). The role of initiation activities in socialization. *Human Relations, 30,* 977–990.

[96]Swann, W. B., Milton, L. P., & Polzer, J. T. (2000). Should we create a niche or fall in line? Identity negotiation and small group effectiveness. *Journal of Personality and Social Psychology, 79*(2), 238–250.

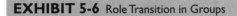

EXHIBIT 5-6 Role Transition in Groups

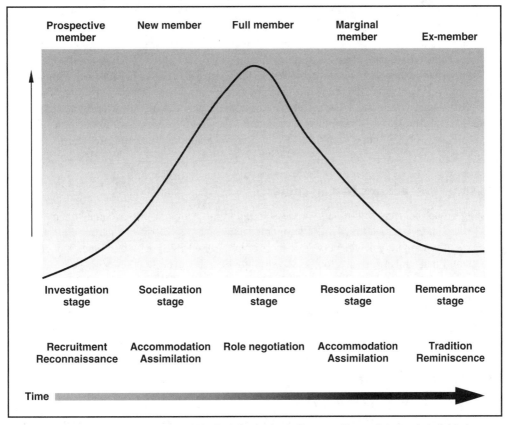

Source: Moreland, R. L., & Levine, J. M. (1982). Socialization in small groups: Temporal changes in individual-group relations. In L. Berkowitz (Ed.), *Advances in experimental social psychology* (Vol. 15, pp. 137–192). New York: Academic Press.

see themselves, this heightens the feelings of connection to the team, lessens A-type (unhealthy) conflict, and improves performance on creative tasks. In contrast, when groups beseech individuals to see themselves as the group sees them, this improves performance on computational tasks (e.g., tasks that have a single correct answer).

The following strategies are especially useful for integrating new members into teams.

Upper Management and Leaders: Make It Clear Why the New Member Is Joining the Team   Many times, the introduction of a new team member is threatening for individuals, when it need not be. The manager should not assume that everyone is fully aware of why the newcomer is joining the team. Simple, clear, straightforward statements about how upper management sees the relationship between the individual and the team are needed early on before an unnecessary cycle of paranoia is set in motion.

Existing Team Members: Explain What You Regard to Be the Strengths and Weaknesses of the Team   It can be very revealing for existing team members to talk about their strengths and weaknesses when a new member joins. The new member can "see" the team through the eyes of each team member.

New Members: Understand the Team's Goals and Processes   Existing members often expect newcomers to be anxious, passive, dependent, and conforming. Further, new members who take on those characteristics are more likely to be accepted by old-timers.[97] What newcomers may not realize is that they inevitably pose some threat to the team. This is often because newcomers have a fresh and relatively objective view of the team, which causes them to ask questions or express opinions that are unsettling. New members can take initiative by demonstrating an interest in learning about the team. Remember that the team may be hypersensitive about past failures. Therefore, it is often a good idea to deflect defensive reactions by noting the team's positive qualities.

Old-timers' Reactions to Newcomers

Existing group members (old-timers) are less accepting of "temporary" newcomers than "permanent" newcomers because they expect temporary newcomers to be different from their group.[98] Paradoxically, temporary newcomers share more unique knowledge in groups than permanent newcomers and thus enhance their group's decision quality. However, temporary newcomers cause teams to experience more conflict and less group identification.[99] When newcomers criticize their workplace, their profession, or Internet community, they arouse more resistance in old-timers.[100] Newcomers reduce old-timer resistance when newcomers distance themselves from their previous group. Groups with out-group (i.e., diverse) newcomers are less confident about their performance, but yet perform better than groups with in-group (homogeneous) newcomers.[101]

Newcomer Innovation

Contrary to popular opinion, turnover might benefit a group—through the exit of "old-timers" who lack the skills or motivation to help the group attain its goals and the entry of newcomers who possess needed skills.[102] Three factors determine the extent to which newcomers can introduce change: (1) their commitment to the team; (2) their belief that they can develop good ideas for solving team problems; and (3) their belief that they will be rewarded. For turnover to have positive effects, it must outweigh the substantial benefits that group members derive from working together.[103] In one investigation of turnover, teams worked on an air surveillance task

---

[97]Moreland, R. L., & Levine, J. M. (1989). Newcomers and old-timers in small groups. In P. Paulus (Ed.), *Psychology of group influence* (2nd ed., pp. 143–186). Hillsdale, NJ: Erlbaum.

[98]Rink, F., & Ellemers, N. (2009). Temporary versus permanent group membership: how the future prospects of newcomers affect newcomer acceptance and newcomer influence. *Personality and Social Psychology Bulletin, 35*(6), 764–775.

[99]Ibid.

[100] Hornsey, T., Grice, J., Jetten, N., Paulsen, V., & Callan, V. (2007). Group-directed criticisms and recommendations for change: Why newcomers arouse more resistance than old-timers. *Personality and Social Psychology Bulletin, 33*(7), 1036–1048.

[101]Phillips, K., Liljenquist, K., & Neale, M. (2009). Is the pain worth the gain? The advantages and liabilities of agreeing with socially distinct newcomers. *Personality and Social Psychology Bulletin, 35*(3), 336–351.

[102]Levine, J. M., Choi, H.-S., & Moreland, R. L. (2003). Newcomer innovation in work teams. In P. B. Paulus & B. A. Nijstad (Eds.), *Group creativity: Innovation through collaboration* (pp. 202–224). New York: Oxford University Press.

[103] Argote, L., & Kane, A. (2003). Learning from direct and indirect organizations: The effects of experience content, timing, and distribution. In P. Paulus & B. Nijstad (Eds.), *Group creativity*. New York: Oxford University Press; Hollenbeck, J. R., Ilgen, D. R., LePine, J. A., Colquitt, J. A., & Hedlund, J. (1998). Extending the multilevel theory of team decision making: Effects of feedback and experience in hierarchical teams. *Academy of Management Journal, 41*, 269–282.

over 2 days.[104] On both days, specialists monitored changes in plane information (e.g., airspeed and altitude) and transmitted it to the commander, who integrated this information and assigned threat values to the planes. At the beginning of day 2, there was turnover: In some teams, one of the specialists was replaced with a specialist from another team; in other teams, the commander was replaced with a commander from another team. Teams performed better when newcomers had high rather than low ability; this was particularly pronounced when newcomers had high status (commander) rather than low status (specialist).

There are several "newcomer" roles: visitors, transfers, replacements, and consultants.[105] Visitors are people who are expected to remain on the team for a short time and not viewed as instrumental to attaining long-term goals. Because they are viewed as lacking in commitment, their ability to change the team is muted.[106] Transfers have recently belonged to a similar team and have expertise. Replacements take the place of former members. Consultants join the team to observe its work practices and suggest improvements.

Turnover and Reorganizations

One of the most frequently occurring but daunting challenges for teams is personnel turnover, defined as the entry of new members and/or the exit of old members.[107] Turnover represents a change in team composition that can have profound consequences for team performance, because it alters the technical knowledge of the team, as well as the interpersonal dynamics. As might be expected, turnover disrupts group performance, especially when group members are reciprocally interdependent;[108] when the group has high, rather than low, structure;[109] and when the task is complex rather than simple.[110]

TIME IN TEAMS

A key issue in team design concerns how to optimally balance the amount of group work versus the amount of individual work. A purely linear view of time would suggest that teams given more hours to do their work will be more productive. However, this is not always the case. There are three theories of how time is viewed in teams:[111]

---

[104]Levine, J. M., & Choi, H.-S. (2004). Impact of personnel turnover on team performance and cognition. In E. Salas & S. M. Fiore (Eds.), *Team cognition: Understanding the factors that drive process and performance* (pp. 153–176). Washington, DC: American Psychological Association.

[105]Arrow, H., & McGrath, J. E. (1995). Membership dynamics in groups at work: A theoretical framework. In B. M. Staw & L. L. Cummings (Eds.), *Research in organizational behavior, 17*, 373–411. Greenwich, CT: JAI Press.

[106]Gruenfeld, D. H., & Fan, E. T. (1999). What newcomers see and what oldtimers say: Discontinuities in knowledge exchange. In L. Thompson, J. Levine, & D. Messick (Eds.), *Shared cognition in organizations: The management of knowledge*. Mahwah, NJ: Lawrence Erlbaum; Gruenfeld, D. H., Martorana, P., & Fan, E. T. (2000). What do groups learn from their worldliest members? Direct and indirect influence in dynamic teams. *Organizational Behavior and Human Decision Processes, 82*(1), 45–59.

[107]Levine, J. M., Choi, H.-S., & Moreland, R. L. (2003). Newcomer innovation in work teams. In P. B. Paulus & B. A. Nijstad (Eds.), *Group creativity: Innovation through collaboration* (pp. 202–224). New York: Oxford University Press.

[108] Naylor, J. C., & Briggs, G. E. (1965). Team-training effectiveness under various conditions. *Journal of Applied Psychology, 49*, 223–229.

[109] Devadas, R., & Argote, L. (1995, May). *Collective learning and forgetting: The effects of turnover and group structure*. Paper presented at the meeting of the Midwestern Psychological Association, Chicago, IL.

[110]Argote, L., Insko, C. A., Yovetich, N., & Romero, A. A. (1995). Group learning curves: The effects of turnover and task complexity on group performance. *Journal of Applied Social Psychology, 25*, 512–529.

[111]Ancona, D. G., Okhuysen, G. A., & Perlow, L. A. (2001). Taking time to integrate temporal research. *Academy of Management Review, 26*, 512–529; Mathieu, J. E., & Schulze, W. (2006). The influence of team knowledge and formal plans on episodic team process-performance relationships. *The Academy of Management Journal, 49*(3), 605–619.

- *Clock time*   Clock-based time depicts a linear continuum of team development as infinitely divisible into objective, quantifiable units.
- *Developmental or growth patterns*   Teams are viewed as qualitatively evolving over time as they move through various stages toward maturity. For example, Tuckman's forming, storming, norming, performing, adjourning model[112] and Gersick's punctuated equilibrium conception are examples of team development.[113] Similarly, Wheelan proposed a model of group development in which groups pass through five stages:[114]
  - *Stage 1: Dependency and inclusion:* Members are dependent on the leader.
  - *Stage 2: Counterdependency and fight:* Conflict exists among members and the leader.
  - *Stage 3: Trust and structure:* There is a more mature determination of the elements of group structure and norms.
  - *Stage 4: Work:* There is effective progress toward group goals.
  - *Stage 5: Termination:* There is evaluation of past work, feedback, and the expression of feelings about fellow group members.
- *Performance cycles or episodes*   Cyclical theories of team functioning suggest that events unfold in a recurring fashion over time in cycles or episodes related to performance. Performance episodes are distinguishable periods over which performance accrues and feedback becomes available.[115]

How groups think about time affects how they treat time.[116] For example, in one investigation, four men counteracted the monotony of long hours of tedious machine work (objective time) by reconstructing time into a series of recurrent daily events, mostly organized around the procurement, sharing, stealing, and consumption of food and drink.[117] In this sense, the team of men reconstructed how they think about the time spent on their task.

ROLE NEGOTIATION

In all teams, task-management and people-management skills are required. Task-related roles focus on getting the work done and accomplishing the task at hand; interpersonal roles focus on how the work gets done and satisfying the emotional needs of team members. However, unlike traditional functional roles, such as finance, sales, and manufacturing, the roles of task management and people management are not necessarily played by one particular person.

Over time, through the process of role negotiation, various roles emerge.[118] Most often these roles and the negotiations for them are not talked about in an explicit fashion; rather, people engage in actions designed to take on that role, which are either accepted or rejected by

---

[112]Tuckman, B. W. (1965). Developmental sequence in small groups. *Psychological Bulletin, 63*(6), 384–399.

[113]Gersick, C. J. G. (1988). Time and transition in work teams: Toward a new model of group development. *Academy of Management Journal, 31*, 9–41.

[114]Wheelan, S. A. (1990). *Facilitating training groups.* New York: Praeger; Wheelan, S. A. (1994). *Group processes: A developmental perspective.* Boston, MA: Allyn & Bacon.

[115]Marks, M. A., Mathieu, J. E., & Zaccaro, S. J. (2001). A temporally based framework and taxonomy of team processes. *Academy of Management Review, 26*, 356–376.

[116]Arrow, H., Poole, M. S., Henry, K. B., Wheelan, S., & Mooreland, R. L. (2004). Time, change, and development: The temporal perspective on groups. *Small Group Research, 35*(1), 73–105.

[117]Roy, D. F. (1960). "Banana time": Job satisfaction and informal interaction. *Human Organization, 18*, 158–168.

[118]Bettenhausen, K., & Murnighan, J. K. (1985). The emergence of norms in competitive decision-making groups. *Administrative Science Quarterly, 30*, 350–372.

other members of the team. First, there is no one set of ideal roles for any particular team. Roles are unique to each team. However, some roles are more common than others.

Second, few people can simultaneously fulfill both the task and interpersonal needs of the team.[119] When taskmasters move troops toward their goals, they often appear domineering, controlling, and unsympathetic. These actions may be conducive to goal attainment, but team members may react negatively. Because team members believe the task specialist is the source of the tension, someone other than the task leader must often assume a role aimed at reducing interpersonal hostilities and frustrations.[120] The diplomat who intervenes to restore harmony and cohesion is the socioemotional master. An example of this on a corporate scale is evident in the management styles of the former and current CEOs of Yahoo, Jerry Yang and Carol Bartz, respectively. Bartz has a candid and decisive style. Conversely, Yang's leadership was regarded to be more passive.[121]

Status Competition

Role negotiation may take the form of status competition within the team. **Status competition** is the process by which people acquire the authority and legitimacy to be the taskmaster or the relationship coordinator of the team. Even in teams with established status roles, status competition can emerge as certain members attempt to compete with the leader. Team members intuitively take note of one another's personal qualities they think are indicative of ability or prestige (years on the job, relevant connections, etc.). People consider two types of cues or information into consideration: real status characteristics and pseudostatus characteristics. **Real status characteristics** are qualities that are relevant to the task at hand (e.g., previous experience with the decision domain). **Pseudostatus characteristics** include factors such as sex, age, ethnicity, status in other groups, and cultural background. Typically, pseudostatus characteristics are those that are highly visible. Pseudostatus characteristics have little to do with ability, but people act as if they do.

Status systems develop very quickly, often within minutes after most teams are formed.[122] Soon after meeting one another, team members form expectations about each person's probable contributions to the achievement of the team's goals.[123] These expectations are based on personal characteristics that people purposely reveal to one another (real status characteristics such as intelligence, background, and education) or that are readily apparent (pseudostatus characteristics such as sex, age, race, demeanor, size, musculature, and facial expression).[124] Personal characteristics that are more relevant to the achievement of team goals have more impact on expectations, but even irrelevant factors are evaluated. People who possess more valuable characteristics evoke more positive expectations and are thus assigned higher status in

---

[119]Bales, R. F. (1955). How people interact in conferences. *Scientific American, 192,* 31–55; Bales, T. (1958). Task roles and social roles in problem-solving groups. In E. E. Maccoby, T. M. Newcomb, & E. I. Hartley (Eds.), *Readings in Social Psychology.* New York: Holt, Rinehart & Winston; Parsons, T., Bales, R. F., & Shils, E. (1953). *Working paper in the theory of action.* Glencoe, IL: Free Press.

[120]Burke, P. J. (1967). The development of task and social-emotional role differentiation. *Sociometry, 30,* 379–392.

[121]Letzing, J. (2009, December 3). For battle-tested Bartz, how hard could running yahoo be? *Wall Street Journal Market Watch.* marketwatch.com

[122]Barchas, P. R., & Fisek, M. H. (1984). Hierarchical differentiation in newly formed groups of rhesus and humans. In P. R. Barchas (Ed.), *Essays toward a sociophysiological perspective* (pp. 23–33). Westport, CT: Greenwood Press.

[123]Berger, J., Rosenholtz, S. J., & Zelditch, M. (1980). Status organizing processes. *Annual Review of Sociology, 6,* 479–508.

[124]Mazur, A. (1985). A biosocial model of status in face-to-face groups. *Social Forces, 64,* 377–402.

the team. An action plan for a manager who suspects that pseudostatus characteristics may supplant more relevant qualifications would be to provide clear information to team members about others' qualifications well in advance of the team meeting (e.g., circulating members' resumes). In addition to this, the leader should structure the first meeting of the team so as to ensure that relevant factors are made known to all members (e.g., a round-robin discussion in which members review their experiences).

It is critical for team members to not overestimate their status in their group. Disconcertingly, most people overestimate their status in groups, and, as a consequence, they are liked less by others and paid less for their work.[125] Status enhancers are socially punished because people think they are disruptive to the group's process.

Solo Status

When everyone in a group shares a common social identity except one person, the one who is different from the majority has solo status. Solo status increases that team member's visibility and performance pressure, which often results in stress. When the solo regards the task to be a challenge and the person's resources exceed demands, solo status improves performance. However, when the solo regards the task to be threatening (the task demands exceed the person's resources), the solo's performance is hurt.[126]

Conclusion

Teams have their own personality, moods, and emotions. Teams differ in terms of how attached they feel to one another, and these attachment styles can affect the behavior and performance of the team. Teams feel and express emotions and, over time, team members develop similar chronic emotions due to the process of contagion. We've focused on how to build cohesion in teams, and we've examined the types of trust that characterize relationships. Finally, we explored the socialization process by which teams admit newcomers and how time may be studied in teams.

---

[125]Anderson, C., Ames, D., & Gosling, S. (2008). Punishing hubris: The perils of overestimating one's status in a group. *Personality and Social Psychology Bulletin, 34*(1), 90–101.
[126]White, J. (2008). Fail or flourish? Cognitive appraisal moderates the effect of solo status on performance. *Personality and Social Psychology Bulletin, 34*, 1171–1184.

6

Sharpening the Team Mind
Communication and Collective Intelligence

On Christmas day, 2009, Umar Farouk Abdulmutallab attempted to blow up a Northwest Airlines flight. Umar, a Nigerian, was listed in a U.S. terrorism database the previous month after his father told the U.S. State Department officials that he was worried about his son's radical beliefs and extremist connections. However, Umar was not placed on any watch list for flights into the United States because there was "insufficient derogatory information available." Umar told FBI agents that he received training and explosive materials from al-Qaeda-linked terrorists in Yemen. Umar, who studied engineering at University College London, was issued a 2-year U.S. tourist visa in June 2008, and no red flags were raised before he boarded the Northwest flight. Senior U.S. officials spoke critically of the apparent failure of aviation security measures to detect a dangerous and common military explosive brought on board. U.S. officials acknowledged that Umar's name was added to the Terrorist Identities Datamart Environment (TIDE), which contains 550,000 individuals and is maintained by the Office of the Director of National Intelligence at the National Counterterrorism Center. The Transportation Security Administration has a "no-fly" list of 4,000 people who are prohibited from boarding any domestic or U.S.-bound aircraft. However, Umar's name never made it past the TIDE list. President Obama said that the government had sufficient information to uncover the error plot, but that intelligence officials had "failed to connect the dots." After meeting with his national security team for 2 hours, Obama declared, "This was not a failure to collect intelligence. It was a failure to integrate and understand the intelligence we already had."[1]

In hindsight, it seems preposterous that the information known about Umar was not shared with key aviation personnel. As teamwork grows more specialized, teams and their leaders must deal with overcoming communication obstacles and integrating knowledge. The question of how to

---

[1]Eggen, D., DeYoung, K., & Hsu, S. (2009, December 27). Plane suspect was listed in terror database after father alerted US officials. *The Washington Post*, p. AO1; Zeleny, J., & Cooper, H. (2010, January 6). Obama says plot could have been disrupted. *New York Times*, p. A11.

collect and assimilate data, analyze it and transform it into knowledge, and collaborate with other teams and groups is often left to intuition rather than science.

This chapter examines how team members communicate and develop team intelligence. We discuss communication within teams, the possible problems that can occur, and how to effectively treat them. We describe the information-dependence problem—the fact that team members depend on one another for critical information. After this, we build a model of team-level collective intelligence. We suggest that teams develop mental models, which are causal structures that influence how they solve problems. We then explore the team mind in depth and the nature of **transactive memory systems (TMS)**, which are the ways in which teams encode, store, and retrieve critical information necessary for doing their work. Next, we undertake a case analysis of the effects of different types of training on TMS. Finally, we make some recommendations for team development and review some evidence pointing to the effects of group longevity, particularly in creative teams.

TEAM COMMUNICATION

Communication among team members is subject to biases that afflict even the most rational of human beings with the best of intentions (see Exhibit 6-1).

In a perfect communication system, a sender transmits or sends a message that is accurately received by a recipient. There are at least three points of possible error, however: The

---

EXHIBIT 6-1 Communication Failures

- A breakdown in communication can make even the largest retailers blue. All Frank Maurer wanted was some fresh blueberries from a Port Richey, Florida, Walmart Supercenter. But when the store ran out of the blueberries advertised at $2.50 a pint, the 65-year-old local resident found himself in a fight over rain checks. When a customer service rep told him that Walmart doesn't have rain checks, Maurer pointed to the fine print in the advertising circular that spells out Walmart's longstanding policy: "If an advertised item is out-of-stock at your Walmart, upon request, we will issue you a rain check so that you can purchase the item at the advertised price when it becomes available." Despite the evidence, the rep didn't budge. Maurer asked to talk to someone in management. The assistant manager didn't budge, either. A frustrated Maurer began stopping shoppers and telling them of Walmart's "fraud" and "false advertising." Walmart called the police. They threatened Maurer with a trespassing arrest if he didn't leave the store. They then talked with him in the parking lot. Maurer left and tried another Walmart in nearby Hudson, which also echoed the "no rain check" mantra. "I was right. But they bullied, then humiliated me in public for 45 minutes in the parking lot." When Maurer called up the *St. Petersburg Times* with his story, Walmart realized it had a serious break-down in communication. "We screwed up," said Dan Fogleman, spokesman for the world's largest retailer. "We are taking this very seriously." In the wake of the blueberry bungle, all Florida district managers were told in a conference call to be sure workers understand rain checks are available for any advertised special that is out of stock. Reminders to ensure the policy is understood in stores were made part of the weekly corporate instructions dispatched to all store managers coast to coast.
- In 2009, numerous questions emerged about the Securities and Exchange Commission's (SEC's) failure to detect the multibillion-dollar fraud conducted for more than a decade by convicted investor Bernard L. Madoff. According to SEC inspector general David Kotz, the agency bungled five investigations of Mr. Madoff's business from June 1992 to December 2008, when the disgraced financer confessed. During that time span, the SEC. received six "substantive complaints that raised significant red flags" regarding Mr. Madoff's operations, but "a thorough and competent investigation or examination was never performed." Its failure to pursue the most obvious leads, disputes among inspection staffers, and lack of communication among SEC. offices cleared the

way for Mr. Madoff to continue for 16 years what is considered the biggest Ponzi scheme in U.S. history. Providing further embarrassment for the SEC., William Galvin, Secretary of the Commonwealth of Massachusetts, released a transcript of a 2005 telephone call during which Mr. Madoff coached a potential witness about fooling federal regulators, saying "you don't have to be too brilliant" to get away with it.

- When two Northwest airline pilots overshot the Minneapolis airport by more than 100 miles in October 2009, the Federal Aviation Administration (FAA) admitted that air-traffic controllers and their supervisors took an hour longer than they should have to alert the military about the plane that had lost radio contact with controllers, putting hundreds of passengers at risk. The failure to quickly notify the North American Aerospace Defense Command, or NORAD, was among a series of communication missteps by air-traffic controllers during Northwest Flight 188 from San Diego to Minneapolis-St. Paul. According to FAA Administrator Randy Babbitt, who added that flights lose radio contact briefly with controllers about seven times a day but rarely do they lose contact for 77 minutes, as the Northwest flight did. Air-traffic controllers typically are supposed to notify NORAD authorities after 10 minutes of lost radio contact with a given flight.

Source: Albright, M. (2010, February 23). Man vs. Walmart in blueberry battle; Fight for cheap berries brings clarity on policy from HQ. *St. Petersburg Times*, p. A1; Congress to investigate Madoff failure as tape is released [Web log post]. dealbook.blogs.nytimes.com; Mitchell, J. (2009, November 14). Alert on errant jet took too long, FAA says. *Wall Street Journal*, p. A3.

sender may fail to send a message; the message may be sent, but it is inaccurate or distorted; or, an accurate message is sent, but it is distorted or not received by the recipient. In a team environment, the complexity grows when teams of senders transmit messages and teams of recipients receive them. We examine some of these biases and then take up the question of how to effectively deal with their existence.

Message Tuning

People who send messages (e.g., "I have no fuel"; "I did not receive the attached file") convey their messages in a way that they think best suits the recipient. **Message tuning** refers to how senders tailor messages for specific recipients. For example, people give longer and more elaborate street directions and instructions to people whom they presume to be nonnatives or unfamiliar with a city.[2] Also, senders capitalize on the knowledge that they believe the recipient already holds (e.g., "Turn right when you see that big tree that the city pruned last week"). For this reason, team members send shorter, less complete messages to one another because they believe that they can capitalize on an existing shared knowledge base. However, team members often overestimate the commonality of information they share with others. Consequently, the messages they send become less clear.

Message Distortion

Message senders present information that they believe will be favorably received by the recipient and, therefore, distort messages.[3] For example, when people present a message to an audience whom they believe has either a pro- or antistance on a particular topic, they err in the

---

[2]Krauss, R. M., & Fussell, S. R. (1991). Perspective-taking in communication: Representations of others' knowledge in reference. *Social Cognition, 9*, 2–24.

[3]Higgins, E. T. (1999). "Saying is believing" effects: When sharing reality about something biases knowledge and evaluations. In L. Thompson, J. M. Levine, & D. M. Messick (Eds.), *Shared cognition in organizations: The management of knowledge.* Mahwah, NJ: Lawrence Erlbaum & Associates.

direction of adopting the audience's point of view. Because senders who bring bad news are not welcome, they often modify the news. A former senior executive at Xerox says, "I was never allowed to present to the board unless things were perfect. [I] could only go in with good news. Everything was prettied up."[4] Unfortunately, message distortion can wreak havoc on effective teamwork.

Saying is Believing

The saying-is-believing (SIB) effect occurs when a speaker tunes a message to suit an audience and in the course of tuning the message, the speaker's subsequent memories and impressions about the topic change.[5] The SIB effect is even more pronounced when the audience validates the communicator's message.[6]

Biased Interpretation

Senders are not the only ones who distort messages. Recipients often hear what they want to hear when receiving messages, especially ambiguous ones. For example, when people are given neutral information about a product, they interpret it in a way that is favorable toward their own position. Furthermore, they selectively attend to information that favors their initial point of view and ignore or misinterpret information that contradicts their position.

Perspective-Taking Failures

People are remarkably poor at taking the perspective of others. For example, people who are privy to information and knowledge that they know others are not aware of still act as if others are aware of it, even though it would be impossible for the receiver to have this knowledge.[7] This problem is known as the **curse of knowledge**.[8] For example, in one simulation, traders who possessed privileged information that could have been used to their advantage behaved as if their trading partners also had access to the privileged information. Perspective-taking deficiencies also explain why some instructors who understand an idea perfectly are unable to teach students the same idea. Perspective-taking deficiencies explain why teams fail, even though every team member really wants to succeed. Emotional states play a role in effective knowledge transfer. Happy receivers are more likely to absorb and act on new information than angry or frustrated receivers.[9] Moreover, knowledge transfer is greater when receivers and senders are in the same high-arousal, affective state, regardless of whether it is positive or negative.

---

[4]Charan, R., & Useem, J. (2002, May 27). Why companies fail. *Fortune, 145*(11), 50–62.
[5]Higgins, T., & McCann, D. (1984). Social encoding and subsequent attitudes, impressions, and memory: "Context-driven" and motivational aspects of processing. *Journal of Personality and Social Psychology, 47*(1), 26–39.
[6]Hausmann, L., Levine, J., & Higgins, E. (2008). Communication and group perception: Extending the "saying is believing" effect. *Group Processes and Intergroup Relations, 11*(4), 539–554.
[7]Keysar, B. (1998). Language users as problem solvers: Just what ambiguity problem do they solve? In S. R. Fussell & R. J. Kreuz (Eds.), *Social and cognitive approaches to interpersonal communication* (pp. 175–200). Mahwah, NJ: Lawrence Erlbaum & Associates.
[8]Camerer, C. F., Loewenstein, G., & Weber, M. (1989). The curse of knowledge in economic settings: An experimental analysis. *Journal of Political Economy, 97*, 1232–1254.
[9]Levin, D., Kurtzberg, T., Phillips, K., & Lount, R. (2010). The role of affect in knowledge transfer. *Group Dynamics, 14*(2), 123–142.

Transparency Illusion

People believe that their thoughts, attitudes, and reasons are much more transparent—that is, obvious to others—than is actually the case.[10] Yet, members of teams often have no idea what their leaders are thinking, but the leaders believe they are being perfectly clear. Part of the reason for the **illusion of transparency** is that people find it impossible to put themselves in the position of the receiver. For example, when people are told to "tap out with their fingers" famous songs such as "Happy Birthday," they significantly overestimate the likelihood that a listener will understand which song they are tapping—but the listeners hardly ever do![11] Perhaps it is for this reason that most communicators overestimate their effectiveness. In short, people expect others to understand them more often than others actually do.[12]

Indirect Speech Acts

Indirect speech acts are the ways in which people ask others to do things—but in indirect ways. For example, consider the various ways of requesting that a person shut a door (see Exhibit 6-2). Each statement can serve as a request to perform that act, although (except for "close the door") the sentence forms are not requests but assertions and questions. Thus, statements 2 through 9 are indirect speech acts; a listener's understanding of the intention behind a communicator's intention requires an extra cognitive step or two—and can often fail, especially in cases of stress.

Indirect speech acts are a function of the magnitude of the request being made (i.e., trivial requests, such as asking someone for the time of day, are easy to accommodate; asking someone if you can have a job is much more difficult to accommodate), the power the recipient has over the sender, and the social distance in the culture.[13] Thus, as the magnitude of requests increases, the power distance increases, and the social distance increases, requests made by team members will become more indirect.

Uneven Communication

The **uneven communication problem** refers to the fact that in virtually any group, a handful of people do the majority of the talking. For example, in a typical five-person group, two people do over 70 percent of the talking; in a six-person group, three people do over 70 percent of the talking; and in a group of eight, three people do 67 percent of the talking.[14] This would not ordinarily be a problem, except for the fact that the people who do the majority of the talking may not be the people who are the most informed about the problem. Exhibit 6-3 plots the percentage of communication attributed to each member in groups of four, six, and eight members; in all cases, communication is uneven and skewed.

---

[10]Gilovich, T., Savitsky, K., & Medvec, V. H. (1998). The illusion of transparency: Biased assessments of others' ability to read one's emotional states. *Journal of Personality and Social Psychology, 75*(2), 332–346.

[11]Griffin, D. W., & Ross, L. (1991). Subjective construal, social inference, and human misunderstanding. In M. P. Zanna (Ed.), *Advances in experimental social psychology* (Vol. 24, pp. 319–359). San Diego, CA: Academic Press.

[12]Keysar, B., & Henly, A. (2002). Speakers' overestimation of their effectiveness. *Psychological Science, 13*(3), 207–212.

[13]Brown, P., & Levinson, S. (1987). *Politeness: Some universals in language use.* Cambridge, UK: Cambridge University Press.

[14]Shaw, M. E. (1981). *Group dynamics: The psychology of small group behavior* (3rd ed.). New York: McGraw-Hill.

EXHIBIT 6-2 Direct Vs. Indirect Communication

Direct

1. Close the door.
2. Can you close the door?
3. Would you close the door?
4. It might help to close the door.
5. Would you mind awfully if I asked you to close the door?
6. Did you forget the door?
7. How about a little less breeze?
8. It's getting cold in here.
9. I really don't want the cats to get out of the house.

Indirect

1. Dan, leave the project team.
2. Dan, we're wondering whether it might be best if you left the team.
3. Dan, we're thinking that we don't need your involvement in the team at this point.
4. Dan, we're wondering if your talents might be best utilized elsewhere.
5. Dan, we're thinking that the team is ahead of schedule and does not require its original staffing.
6. Dan, have you thought about involving yourself in some of the new projects and lessening your involvement in others?
7. Dan, many of the original projects are being reconfigured; yours might be the one that is affected.
8. Dan, the team has been able to take on the project, thanks to your early involvement.
9. Dan, can you help us out with some of these new projects?

Source: Adapted from Krauss, R. M., & Fussell, S. R. (1996). Social psychological models of interpersonal communication. In E. T. Higgins & A. W. Kruglanski (Eds.), *Social psychology: Handbook of basic principles* (pp. 655–701). New York: Guilford; Levinson, S. C. 1983. Pragmatics (p. 264). Cambridge, England: Cambridge University Press.

ABSORPTIVE CAPACITY

Absorptive capacity is a person's ability to transform new knowledge into useable knowledge. **Experienced community of practice** is the extent to which a person is engaged with the given practice community[15] (see Exhibit 6-4). Field studies reveal that teams high in knowledge-sharing practices have higher customer satisfaction and better performance.[16] A meta-analysis of 4,795 groups revealed that information sharing in groups predicted team performance.[17]

THE INFORMATION DEPENDENCE PROBLEM

By pooling their different backgrounds, training, and experience, team members have the potential to work in a more informed fashion than would be the case if the decision were relegated to any single person. The fact that team members are dependent on one another for information is the

---

[15]Cadiz, D., Sawyer, J. E., & Griffith, T. L. (2009). Developing and validating field measurement scales for absorptive capacity and experienced community of practice. *Educational and psychological measurement, 20*(1), 1–23.

[16]Griffith, T., & Sawyer, J. (2009). Multilevel knowledge and team performance. *Journal of Organizational Behavior.*

[17]Mesmer-Magnus, J., & DeChurch, L. (2009). Information sharing and team performance: A meta-analysis. *Journal of Applied Psychology, 94*(2), 535–546.

EXHIBIT 6-3 Distribution of Participation as a Function of Group Size

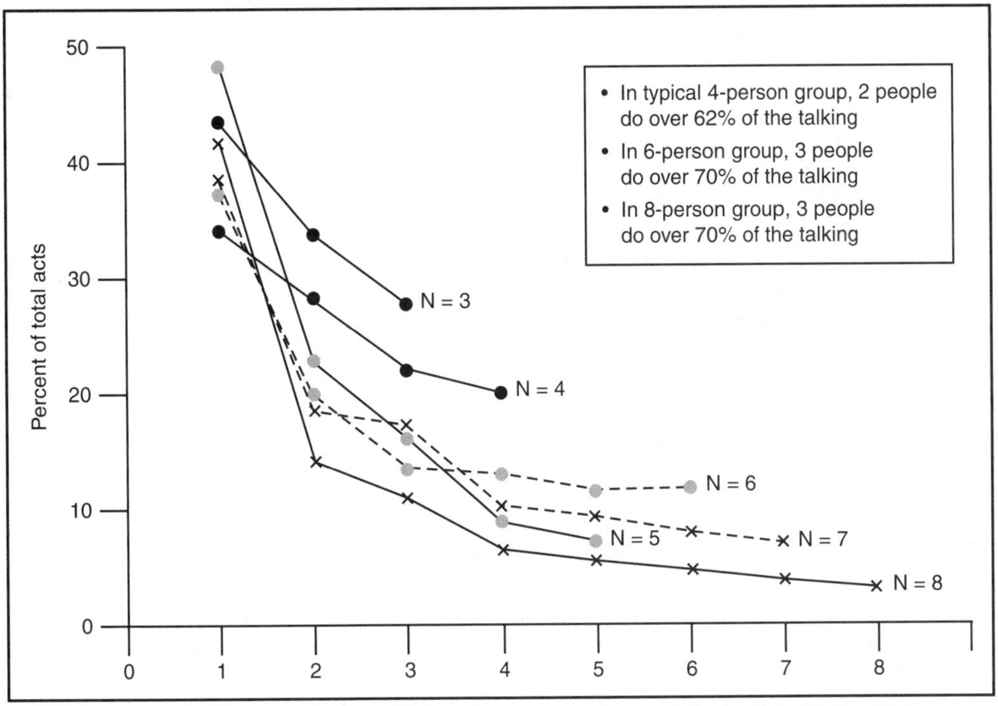
Percent of total acts
50
40
30
20
10
0
0 1 2 3 4 5 6 7 8
• In typical 4-person group, 2 people do over 62% of the talking
• In 6-person group, 3 people do over 70% of the talking
• In 8-person group, 3 people do over 70% of the talking
N = 3
N = 4
N = 5
N = 6
N = 7
N = 8

Source: Shaw, M. E. (1981). *Group dynamics: The psychology of small group behavior* (3rd ed.). New York: McGraw-Hill.

information dependence problem. As an example of information dependence in groups and the dire consequences it can have, consider the case in Exhibit 6-5.

When the team consists of members who come from different functional areas—with different areas of expertise, different information, different priorities, and different perceptions of problems and opportunities—the information dependence problem is exacerbated. Thus, a central issue facing any group charged with making a collective decision is how to get the ideas, information, and expertise in each person's head onto the table for all to see.

The Common Information Effect

Consider a typical group decision-making task in the ABC Company. A three-member top-executive committee, Allen, Booz, and Catz, is charged with the task of hiring a new manager for an important division within ABC. The company has determined that six pieces of information are critical to evaluate for this position:

- Previous experience (A)
- Academic grades (B)
- Standardized test scores (C)
- Performance in round 1 interview (D)
- Cultural and international experience (E)
- Letters of recommendation (F)

EXHIBIT 6-4 Absorptive Capacity and Experienced Community of Practice

I. Absorptive Capacity

A. Assessment
   1. People in my team are able to decipher the knowledge that will be most valuable to us.
   2. It is easy to decide what information will be most useful in meeting our customer's needs.
   3. We know enough about the technology we use to determine what new information is credible and trustworthy.

B. Assimilation
   1. The shared knowledge within my team makes it easy to understand new material presented within our technical areas.
   2. It is easy to see the connections among the pieces of knowledge held jointly within our team.
   3. Many of the new technological developments coming to the team fit well into the current technology.

C. Application
   1. It is easy to adapt our work to make use of the new technical knowledge made available to us.
   2. My technical knowledge can be quickly applied to our work.
   3. My customers can immediately benefit from new technical knowledge learned from the team.

II. Experienced Community of Practice

A. Open Communication
   1. I feel comfortable communicating freely with others in my technical specialty.
   2. In my technical specialty, there is an open environment for free communication.
   3. It is easy to communicate with others in my technical specialty.

B. Shared vocabulary
   1. My technical specialty has a unique vocabulary.
   2. There is a common understanding within my technical specialty of the words and meanings that are used within the technical specialty.
   3. People outside my technical specialty might have difficulty understanding the vocabulary members of my technical specialty use to talk about the technology.

C. Remembering Previous Lessons
   1. Collaborating with other members of my technical specialty helps me remember things we have learned.
   2. Participating in meetings with members of my technical specialty helps me to remember things we have learned.
   3. Lessons learned from past experienced shared within my technical specialty are easily remembered.

D. Learning from each other
   1. I interact with others in my technical specialty with the intention of learning from them.
   2. I learn new skills and knowledge from collaborating with others in my technical specialty.
   3. Learning is shared among members of my technical specialty.

Source: Cadiz, D., Sawyer, J. E., & Griffith, T. L. (2009). Developing and validating field measurement scales for absorptive capacity and experienced community of practice. *Educational and Psychological Measurement, 20*(1), 1–23.

Allen, Booz, and Catz have narrowed the competition down to three candidates: Kate, Ken, and Kerry. As is standard practice in the company, members of the hiring committee specialize in obtaining partial information about each candidate. Stated another way, each member of the

EXHIBIT 6-5 Information Dependence

In 1955, the Centers for Disease Control (CDC) took the responsibility of evaluating the polio vaccine developed by Jonas Salk. In late 1954, six vaccine manufacturers met with the Division of Biological Standards, with Jonas Salk, and others. Some of them had been having problems with inactivation of the virus during the process of vaccine manufacture. While one of the manufacturers was explaining that his company had been more efficient and successful at inactivating the virus, a representative from one of the other manufacturers had a telephone call, left the room, and came back after the discussion. Within 2 weeks after the beginning of the nationwide vaccination program, in April 1955, CDC began to get reports of polio. What was significant was that these children had received the vaccine 6–8 days earlier and had developed polio, almost invariably in the arm or leg where they received the shot. Of the six reported cases, the vaccine contaminated with the live virus was manufactured by the laboratory whose representative took the phone call during the discussion on inactivating the virus.

Source: Larson, C. E., & LaFasto, F. M. J. (1989). *Teamwork: What must go right/what can go wrong.* Newbury Park, CA: Sage. Copyright 1989 by Sage. Reprinted by permission of Sage Publications.

hiring committee has some of the facts about each candidate, but not all of the facts. Thus, Allen, Booz, and Catz are information dependent on one another.

What will happen when they discuss various candidates for the job? Consider three possible distributions of information (see Exhibit 6-6):

- *Nonoverlapping case*   Each partner, Allen, Booz, and Catz, has unique information about each candidate.
- *Distributed, partial overlap*   Each partner knows something about each candidate that others also know (common information), but also knows some unique information.
- *Fully shared case*   Each partner knows full information about each candidate. In this sense, the partners are informational clones of one another.

The only difference among these three cases is the information redundancy, or how equally the information is distributed among decision makers. The collective intelligence of the partners is identical in all three cases. Does the distribution of information affect the way the partners make decisions? In a rational world, it should not, but in real teams, it does.

The impact of information on the aggregate decision of the team is directly related to the number of members of the team who know the information prior to making a group decision. Stated simply, *information held by more members before team discussion has more influence on team judgments than information held by fewer members, independent of the validity of the information*. This team fallacy is known as the **common information effect**.[18]

This means that even though (in an objective sense) the six pieces of information are really equally important, the top management group will tend to overemphasize information (such as A and C in the distributed case) more than is warranted.

The common information effect has several important consequences. First, team members are more likely to discuss information that everyone knows, as opposed to unique information that each may have. This often means that technical information (which is often not fully shared) is not

---

[18]Gigone, D., & Hastie, R. (1997). The impact of information on small group choice. *Journal of Personality and Social Psychology, 72*(1), 132–140.

EXHIBIT 6-6 Three Possible Distributions of Information

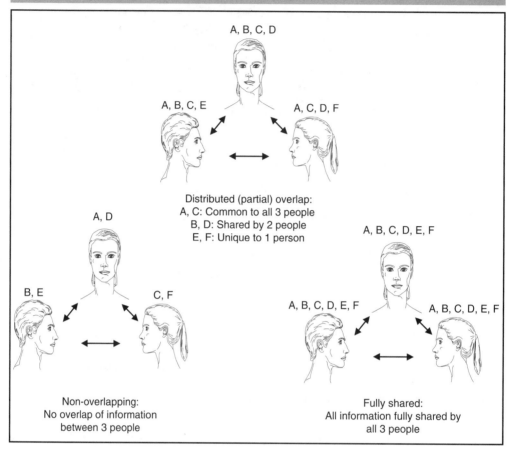

A, B, C, D

A, B, C, E

A, C, D, F

Distributed (partial) overlap:
A, C: Common to all 3 people
B, D: Shared by 2 people
E, F: Unique to 1 person

A, D

B, E

C, F

Non-overlapping:
No overlap of information
between 3 people

A, B, C, D, E, F

A, B, C, D, E, F

A, B, C, D, E, F

Fully shared:
All information fully shared by
all 3 people

given the weight that experts believe it should have. Information that people have in common is not only more likely to be discussed, but it also gets discussed for a longer period of time, and this too can exert a significant bias on the integrity of decision making. People are better at remembering information they have read or described more than information they hear from others.[19]

The result is that teams often fail to make the decision that would be supported if all the team members had full information about the choices.

Hidden Profile

A **hidden profile** is a superior decision alternative, but its superiority is hidden from group members because each member has only a portion of the information that supports this superior alternative.[20] Stated another way, the information held in common by group members favors a particular choice, whereas the unshared information contradicts the choice.

---

[19]Larson, J. R., & Harmon, V. M. (2007). Recalling shared vs. unshared information mentioned during group discussion: Toward understanding differential repetition rates. *Group Processes and Intergroup Relations, 10*(3), 311–322.
[20]Stasser, G. (1988). Computer simulation as a research tool: The DISCUSS model of group decision making. *Journal of Experimental Social Psychology, 24*(5), 393–422.

Let's consider an executive meeting, in which three candidates (Alva, Jane, and Bill) are under consideration for promotion to partner in the organization—obviously, an extremely important decision. Each of the three candidates has been with the company for some number of years; each has made a different number and type of accomplishments. The executive group can promote only one person for the position at this time.

The group can benefit the organization by pooling individual members' information so as to gain a complete picture of the qualifications of each candidate. This is particularly important when individual members of the decision-making team are biased by virtue of their own agendas.

Information that is known to only one or a few members will often be omitted from discussion.[21] Team members are more likely not only to mention information if it was known to all before discussion but also to bring it up repeatedly and dwell on it throughout the discussion. Thus, the team decision will often reflect the common knowledge shared by members before discussion rather than the diverse knowledge emanating from their unique perspectives and experiences.

Consider the scenario in Exhibit 6-7. In this situation, the initial bias favors Bill. At the outset of the meeting, each team member has more information about him (five pieces of information). The information the team has about Bill is fully shared, meaning that all team members are apprised of this candidate's qualifications prior to the meeting. Obviously, Bill has done an excellent job of marketing his own achievements within the organization!

However, consider Alva, who has a combined total of eight pieces of favorable information supporting his candidacy for the partnership. However, each member of the executive team is privy only to three pieces of information about this candidate, and the information is not redundant. In an objective sense, Alva is by far the most qualified; yet his accomplishments are not fully shared among the top management team—a factor that will not be corrected with discussion (at least unstructured discussion).

If this team were immune to the common information effect, and the members optimally combined and pooled their unique information, a hidden profile would emerge. *A hidden profile is a conclusion that is apparent only after team members have fully shared information.* In this case, Alva would prevail.

Common information also affects people's memory for team discussions. People recall fewer unshared arguments from team discussion.[22] Moreover, analysis of tape-recorded discussions reveals that unshared arguments are less likely to be expressed.[23]

The reliance on previously shared information is not an optimal use of team resources because uniquely held or previously unshared information may be most enlightening for the team as a whole. Unstructured, free-style discussion, even among trained professionals who have every motivation to make an accurate diagnosis, is insufficient for ensuring the quality of outcomes. (For an illustration of the inability of professionals to share relevant information, see Exhibit 6-8.)

---

[21]Stasser, G., & Titus, W. (1985). Pooling of unshared information in group decision making: Biased information sampling during discussion. *Journal of Personality and Social Psychology, 48,* 1467–1478.

[22]Gigone & Hastie, "The impact of information on small group choice," p. 140; Stasser, G., & Titus, W. (1987). Effects of information load and percentage of shared information on the dissemination of unshared information in group discussion. *Journal of Personality and Social Psychology, 53,* 81–93.

[23]Stasser, G., Taylor, L. A., & Hanna, C. (1989). Information sampling in structured and unstructured discussions of three- and six-person groups. *Journal of Personality and Social Psychology, 57,* 67–78.

EXHIBIT 6-7 Hidden Profiles

Best Practices for Optimal Information Sharing

We want to point out some plausible-appearing solutions that do not work, either because they actually reinforce the problem or do not address the problem adequately.

THINGS THAT DON'T WORK

Increase the Amount of Discussion Even when teams are explicitly told to spend more time discussing information, they still fall prey to the common information effect.[24]

---

[24]Parks, C. D., & Cowlin, R. A. (1996). Acceptance of uncommon information into group discussion when that information is or is not demonstrable. *Organizational Behavior and Human Decision Processes, 66*(3), 307–315.

EXHIBIT 6-8 Hidden Profiles in Medical Diagnosis

Professional teams are created for a number of important reasons. For example, in medicine, the use of teaching rounds, interdisciplinary consults, and case conferences serves both clinical and educational functions. Collaborative efforts of this sort are designed to ensure that relevant information is brought to bear on important clinical decisions, to facilitate the coordinated action of experts toward appropriate treatment goals, and to train novices. Consider how clinical teams composed of a resident, intern, and third-year medical student arrive at patient diagnoses on the basis of case information. (For example, the management of a seriously ill geriatric patient may require input from specialties and subspecialties such as internal medicine, pulmonology, and oncology, as well as from nurses and nutritionists.) Prior to discussion, team members may individually review different versions of a videotaped interview with a patient actor. Each videotape contains some information that is present in all three versions (shared information) and some that is present in only that version (unique information).

In addition, some patient case profiles are constructed so that unique information that appeared in only one tape was crucial for a correct diagnosis (i.e., "hidden profile" situation). After viewing the tapes, the team members meet to discuss the case and develop a differential diagnosis for the patient.

These medical specialists were not immune to the common information effect. Shared information about the patient was mentioned more often (67 percent) than was unique information (46 percent). More disconcerting, teams offered incorrect diagnoses substantially more often for the "hidden profile" patient case than for the "standard" patient cases: Overall, 17 of the 24 hidden profile cases were diagnosed correctly (a hit rate of about 70 percent), whereas all of the shared information cases were correctly diagnosed. Clearly, the medical teams' overreliance on previously shared information and the inability to appropriately utilize unique information were detrimental when a correct diagnosis demanded the inclusion of such information.

Source: Christensen, C., Larson, J. R., Jr., Abbott, A., Ardolino, A., Franz, T., & Pfeiffer, C. (2000). Decision-making of clinical teams: Communication patterns and diagnostic error. *Medical Decision Making, 20,* 45–50.

Separate Review and Decisions   In one investigation, team members were given instructions intended to curb the common information effect.[25] Team members avoided stating their initial preferences and were encouraged to review all relevant facts. However, the discussion primarily favored those facts initially shared by team members (67 percent of all shared facts were discussed in contrast to 23 percent of unshared facts).

Increase the Size of the Team   As team size increases but the distribution of information stays the same, the tendency to discuss common information increases. For example, the common information effect is more pronounced in six-person groups than in three-person groups. In a typical three-person group, 46 percent of shared information is mentioned, in contrast to only 18 percent of unshared information. This difference is even larger for six-person groups.[26] Moreover, if unique information is held by racially diverse members, even less information is shared.[27]

Increase Information Load   If members of the team are given additional information but the relative distribution of information remains the same, the common information effect still

---

[25]Stasser, Taylor, & Hanna, "Information sampling in structured and unstructured discussions of three- and six-person groups."

[26]Ibid.

[27]Sawyer, J. E., Houlette, M., & Muzzy, E. L. (2002). Decision performance in racially diverse cross-functional teams: The effect of convergent versus crosscut diversity structure. Working Paper, University of Delaware, Newark, NJ.

plagues the team.[28] In fact, the bias to discuss shared information is most likely to occur when there is a large number of "shared" facts to discuss. Groups perform better when they can reduce their cognitive load.[29]

Accountability Accountability refers to the extent to which people and teams feel responsible for their actions and decisions. Surprisingly, accountable teams are less likely to focus on unshared information than groups that are not held accountable.[30] For example, the medical teams described in Exhibit 6-8 were videotaped and told to make a diagnosis that would be evaluated, yet they still overrelied on previously shared information and consequently misdiagnosed the case. In contrast, when groups are made to be accountable for their *process* (rather than outcome), they are more likely to repeat unshared information and make better decisions.[31]

Prediscussion Polling One of the most common strategies for beginning a discussion is polling the group. However, this strategy can have extremely negative effects on the quality of the discussion that follows if the initial preferences of the team members are based on insufficient information. If the group is unanimous, it is inevitably concluded that there is little or no need for discussion. Furthermore, the very act of polling triggers conformity pressure, such that lower-status group members, eager to secure their position in the organization, may agree with the majority. In teams deciding which of two cholesterol-reducing drugs to market, initial preferences were the major determinants of the group's final decision.[32] Moreover, people tend to regard the information that they "own" to be more valid than other information.[33]

EFFECTIVE INTERVENTIONS Fortunately, there are ways to defeat the common information effect. They have one thing in common: They put the team leader in the position of an **information manager**. In fact, having a leader in the team can be an advantage in itself: Team leaders are consistently more likely than are other members to ask questions and repeat unshared (as well as shared) information.[34] Leaders play an important information management role during team discussion by focusing the team's attention, facilitating communication, stimulating member contributions, and ensuring that critical information brought out during discussion is "kept alive" and factored into the team's final decision. The type of leader is also important. Directive leaders are more likely than participative leaders to repeat unshared information and,

---

[28]Stasser & Titus, "Effects of information load," p. 142; Stasser, G. (1992). Information salience and the discovery of hidden profiles by decision-making groups: A "thought" experiment. *Organizational Behavior and Human Decision Processes, 52,* 156–181.

[29]Tindale, S., & Sheffey, S. (2002). Shared information, cognitive load, and group memory. *Group Processes and Intergroup Relations, 5*(1), 5–18.

[30]Stewart, D. D., Billings, R. S., & Stasser, G. (1998). Accountability and the discussion of unshared, critical information in decision making groups. *Group Dynamics: Theory, Research, and Practice, 2*(1), 18–23.

[31]Scholten, L., van Knippenberg, D., Nijstad, B. A., & De Dreu, C. K. W. (2007). Motivated information processing and group decision making: Effects of process accountability on information processing and decision quality. *Journal of Experimental Social Psychology, 33,* 539–552.

[32]Kelly, J. R., & Karau, S. J. (1999). Group decision making: The effects of initial preferences and time pressure. *Personality and Social Psychology Bulletin, 25*(11), 1342–1354.

[33]van Swol, L. M., Savadori, L., & Sniezek, J. A. (2003). Factors that may affect the difficulty of uncovering hidden profiles. *Group Processes & Intergroup Relations, 6*(3), 285–304.

[34]Larson, J. R., Christensen, C., Franz, T. M., & Abbott, A. S. (1998). Diagnosing groups: The pooling, management, and impact of shared and unshared case information in team-based medical decision making. *Journal of Personality and Social Psychology, 75*(1), 93–108.

consequently, identify the best options.[35] Leaders with more experience are also more effective.[36] The common information effect can be substantially reduced when leaders and teams actively do the following:

Redirect and Maintain the Focus of the Discussion to Unshared (Unique) Information   The more team members repeat common information, the less likely they are to uncover hidden profiles.[37] The leader should be persistent in directing the focus of the discussion to unique information. Furthermore, the leader must reintroduce noncommon information after it has been dismissed. The longer the delay in mentioning unique items of information, the lower the team's performance.[38]

Approach the Task as a "Problem" to Be Solved, Not a "Judgment" to Be Made   Leaders should define the task as a "problem" to be solved with "demonstrable evidence" and explicitly state that they are not interested in personal opinion and judgment. Teams are less likely to overlook unshared information if they believe that their task has a demonstrably correct answer.[39]

As an example, consider the instructions given to a panel of jurors. Members of the jury are explicitly told to pay attention to the facts and evidence. They are cautioned that the lawyers representing the parties in the case are not witnesses but rather are attempting to sway members of the jury to adopt a particular belief. It is precisely for this reason that trial lawyers have an opportunity to dismiss potential jurors who are regarded as unable to consider the facts because their mind is already made up—that is, they enter the courtroom with a particular bias or belief.

Rank Rather Than Choose   When teams are instructed to "rank" candidates or alternatives, they are more likely to make the best decision than when they are simply told to "choose."[40] When teams are asked to choose, people make comparisons among candidates, and if the best candidate is a hidden profile, teams are likely to choose the wrong candidate.

Consider the Decision Alternatives One at a Time   Leaders should make sure their team discusses one alternative fully before turning to the next.[41]

Heighten Team Members' Awareness of the Types of Information Likely to Be Possessed by Different Individuals   When team members are personally identified, the likelihood that unshared clues will be mentioned during discussion increases.[42] When team members know who

---

[35]Larson, J. R., Foster-Fishman, P. G., & Franz, T. M. (1998). Leadership style and the discussion of shared and unshared information in decision-making groups. *Personality and Social Psychology Bulletin, 24*(5), 482–495.

[36]Wittenbaum, G. M. (1998). Information sampling in decision-making groups: The impact of members' task-relevant status. *Small Group Research, 29*, 57–84.

[37]van Swol, Savadori, & Sniezek, "Factors that may affect the difficulty of uncovering hidden profiles."

[38]Kim, P. (1997). When what you know can hurt you: A study of experiential effects on group discussion and performance. *Organizational Behavior and Human Decision Processes, 69*(2), 165–177.

[39]Laughlin, P. R. (1980). Social combination processes of cooperative problem-solving groups on verbal interactive tasks. In M. Fishbein (Ed.), *Progress in social psychology* (Vol. 1). Mahwah, NJ: Lawrence Erlbaum & Associates; Stasser, G., & Stewart, D. D. (1992). Discovery of hidden profiles by decision-making groups: Solving a problem versus making a judgment. *Journal of Personality and Social Psychology, 63*, 426–434.

[40]Hollingshead, A. B. (1996b). The rank-order effect in group decision making. *Organizational Behavior and Human Decision Processes, 68*(3), 181–193.

[41]Larson, C. E., Foster-Fishman, P. G., & Keys, C. B. (1994). Discussion of shared and unshared information in decision-making groups. *Journal of Personality and Social Psychology, 67*(3), 446–461.

[42]Stasser, G., Stewart, D. D., & Wittenbaum, G. M. (1995). Expert roles and information exchange during discussion: The importance of knowing who knows what. *Journal of Experimental Social Psychology, 31*, 244–265.

has expertise in specific knowledge domains, the amount of unshared information discussed increases significantly.[43] Moreover, when groups are prompted to reflect upon who-knows-what, they make better decisions.[44] In studies of groups that contain a "minority" information holder, groups make more profitable use of that knowledge when the minority information holder also possesses different information; in this sense, the social category differences signal important informational differences.[45]

Suspend Initial Judgment   One of the most effective strategies for avoiding the common information effect is to caution team members against arriving at a judgment prior to the team discussion. The common information effect is a direct result of the biases that people bring to discussion, not the team discussion itself.[46] The more group members choose the same alternative prior to the group discussion, the more strongly the group prefers information supporting that alternative.[47]

Build Trust and Familiarity Among Team Members   Members who are familiar with one another are less likely to make poor decisions resulting from the common information effect than members of those teams who are unacquainted.[48] The more team members perceive themselves to be cooperatively interdependent with others on their team, the more they share information, learn, and are effective.[49] Team members who are competitive with one another withhold unique information compared to members who are cooperative.[50] Groups who realize that they share a goal of elaborating on information are more likely to make better decisions than groups who do not elaborate.[51]

Team Reflexivity   This is the process of discussing the groups' tasks and goals and the way in which those goals can be reached.[52] When not all group members initially realize the importance of elaborating on information, team reflexivity increases the degree to which the team understands the importance of information elaboration.[53] Team reflexivity encourages information elaboration and enhances decision quality.

---

[43]Stasser, "Computer simulation as a research tool," p. 142; Stasser, Stewart, & Wittenbaum, "Expert roles and information exchange during discussion," p. 147.

[44]Van Ginkel, W. P., & Knippenberg, D. (2009). Knowledge about the distribution of information and group decision making: When and why does it work? *Organizational Behavior and Human Decision Processes, 108(2)*, 218–229.

[45]Phillips, K. W., Mannix, E. A., Neale, M. A., & Gruenfeld, D. H. (2004). Diverse groups and information sharing: The effects of congruent ties. *Journal of Experimental Social Psychology, 40(4)*, 497–510; Dahlin, K., Weingart, L., & Hinds, P. (2005). Team diversity and information use. *Academy of Management Journal, 48(6)*, 1107–1123.

[46]Gigone, D., & Hastie, R. (1993). The common knowledge effect: Information sharing and group judgment. *Journal of Personality and Social Psychology, 65(5)*, 959–974.

[47]Schulz-Hardt, S., Frey, D., Lüthgens, C., & Moscovici, S. (2000). Biased information search in group decision making. *Journal of Personality and Social Psychology, 78(4)*, 655–669.

[48]Gruenfeld, D. H., Mannix, E. A., Williams, K. Y., & Neale, M. A. (1996). Group composition and decision making: How member familiarity and information distribution affect process and performance. *Organizational Behavior and Human Decision Processes, 67(1)*, 1–15.

[49]De Dreu, C. K. W. (2007). Cooperative outcome interdependence, task reflexivity, and team effectiveness: A motivated information processing perspective. *Journal of Applied Psychology, 92(3)*, 628–638.

[50]Toma, C., & Butera, F. (2009). Hidden profiles and concealed information: Strategic information sharing and use in group decision making. *Personality and Social Psychology Bulletin, 35(6)*, 793–806.

[51]van Ginkel, W., & van Knippenberg, D. (2008). Group information elaboration and group decision making: The role of shared task representations. *Organizational Behavior and Human Decision Processes, 105*, 82–97.

[52]West, M. A. (1996). *Handbook of work group psychology.* Chichester: John Wiley & Sons.

[53]Van Ginkel, W., Tindale, R. S., & van Knippenberg, D. (2009). Team reflexivity, development of shared task representations, and the use of distributed information in group decision making. *Group Dynamics: Theory, Research, and Practice, 13(4)*, 265–280.

Communicate Confidence   Teams whose members are encouraged to express confidence about their decisions and judgments perform more effectively and learn significantly more from their interaction than do teams whose ability to communicate confidence during interaction is reduced.[54] Team members who self-servingly attribute a group's past successes to themselves are more likely to share unique information and consider more divergent alternatives.[55]

Minimize Status Differences   In one investigation, groups contained either equal-status members or unequal-status members.[56] In some of these groups, the critical information required to make the best decision was given only to the low-status member. As compared with equal-status groups, mixed-status groups made poorer decisions and made fewer references to the critical information than the equal-status groups.

COLLECTIVE INTELLIGENCE

Team Mental Models

Mental models are mental representations of the world that allow people to understand, predict, and solve problems in a given situation.[57] Mental models can be models of a simple physical system, such as the trajectory of a thrown object; mental models also can represent a complex social system, such as an organization or financial system.

A **team mental model** is a common understanding that members of a group or team share about how something works.[58] From this, members form expectations about what others will do in a given situation. Team members have mental models not only about the work they do but also about the operation of their team. Mental models do not develop naturally; rather, team mental models develop through the process of role identification behaviors (through which team members share information regarding their specialized knowledge, skills, and abilities).[59] Teams with a cognitive foundation, like a mental model, perform better than teams that lack a cognitive foundation.[60]

There are two key considerations in terms of the mental models that members have about their actual work: the **accuracy** of the model and the degree of **correspondence** (or noncorrespondence) between members' models.

---

[54]Bloomfield, R., Libby, R., & Nelson, M. W. (1996). Communication of confidence as a determinant of group judgment accuracy. *Organizational Behavior and Human Decision Processes, 68*(3), 287–300.

[55]Goncalo, G. A., & Duguid, M. D. (2008). Hidden consequences of the group-serving bias: Casual attributions and the quality of group decision making. *Organizational Behavior and Human Decision Processes, 107*, 219–233.

[56]Hollingshead, A. B. (1996a). Information suppression and status persistence in group decision making: The effects of communication media. *Human Communication Research, 23*, 193–219.

[57]Gentner, D., & Gentner, D. R. (1983). Flowing waters or teeming crowds: Mental models of electricity. In D. Gentner & A. Stevens (Eds.), *Mental models*. Mahwah, NJ: Lawrence Erlbaum & Associates; Johnson-Laird, P. N. (1980). Mental models in cognitive science. *Cognitive Science, 4*(1), 71–115; Rouse, W., & Morris, N. (1986). On looking into the black box: Prospects and limits in the search for mental models. *Psychological Bulletin, 100*, 359–363.

[58]Klimoski, R., & Mohammed, S. (1997). Team mental model: Construct or metaphor? *Journal of Management, 20*(2), 403–437.

[59]Pearsall, M. J., Ellis, A. P. J., & Bell, B. S. (2010). Building the infrastructure: The effects of role identification behaviors on team cognition development and performance. *Journal of Applied Psychology, 95*(1), 192–200.

[60]DeChurch, L. A., & Mesmer-Magnus, J. R. (2010). The cognitive underpinnings of effective teamwork: A meta-analysis. *Journal of Applied Psychology, 95*(1), 32–53.

ACCURACY   Suppose that you are asked to explain how the thermostat in your house operates.[61] According to one (erroneous) model, the "valve" model, the thermostat works much like the accelerator in a car. People who hold a valve mental model of a thermostat reason that just as greater depression of the accelerator causes the car's speed to increase at a faster rate, turning the thermostat setting to high temperatures causes the room temperature to increase at a faster rate.

A different (and correct) mental model is the "threshold" model, in which the heat is either on or off and the thermostat setting determines the duration for which the heat is on. The greater the discrepancy between the current room temperature and the thermostat setting, the longer the heat will be on. These two models have different implications for how people set the thermostat in their homes. People with valve models will continually adjust their thermostat setting in an effort to reach a comfortable room temperature. In contrast, those with threshold models will determine at what temperature they are comfortable and set the thermostat to only one or two settings per day, a nighttime setting and a daytime setting. Thermostat records reveal that people's models of how thermostats operate predicted the stability of their actual thermostat settings.

This simple analogy illustrates an important aspect of the use of mental models in problem solving: The use of an incorrect mental model can result in inefficient or undesirable outcomes. People with an incorrect mental representation of a thermostat as a valve will spend greater time and effort adjusting the thermostat setting. In addition, they will be perpetually uncomfortable because they will be either too warm or too cold.

If team members hold erroneous mental models concerning the task at hand (because they either lack technical training or communicate poorly), their well-intentioned behaviors could produce disastrous results.

CORRESPONDENCE   Effective teams adapt to external demands and anticipate other members' information needs because of shared or compatible knowledge structures or team mental models. For example, when novel or unexpected events are encountered (such as when one airplane enters another's airspace), teams that cannot strategize overtly must rely on preexisting knowledge and expectations about how the team must perform to cope with task demands. The greater the overlap or commonality among team members' mental models, the greater the likelihood that team members will predict the needs of the task and team, adapt to changing demands, and coordinate activity with one another successfully.[62] For example, the negative effects of fatigue on air crew performance can be overcome when crews develop interaction patterns over time.[63] An investigation of 69 software development teams revealed that "expertise coordination"—the shared knowledge of who knows what—was a key predictor of team performance over and above expertise and administrative coordination.[64]

The following example, taken from Perrow's book on normal accidents, illustrates the concepts of accuracy and correspondence:[65]

[61]Kempton, W. (1986). Two theories of home heat control. *Cognitive Science, 10,* 75–90; Kempton, W. (1987). *Two theories of home heat control.* New York: Cambridge University Press.

[62]Cannon-Bowers, J. A., Salas, E., & Converse, S. A. (1993). Shared mental models in expert team decision making. In N. J. Castellan (Ed.), *Individual and group decision making* (pp. 221–246). Mahwah, NJ: Lawrence Erlbaum & Associates; Cannon-Bowers, J. A., Tannenbaum, S. I., Salas, E., & Converse, S. A. (1991). Toward an integration of training theory and technique. *Human Factors, 33*(3), 281–292.

[63]Foushee, H. C., Lauber, J. K., Baetge, M. M., & Comb, D. B. (1986). *Crew factors in flight operations: III. The operational significance of exposure to short-haul air transport operations* (NASA TM 88322). Moffett Field, CA: NASA Ames Research Center.

[64]Faraj, S., & Sproull, L. (2000). Coordinating expertise in software development teams. *Management Science, 46*(12), 1554–1568.

[65]Perrow, C. (1984). *Normal accidents: Living with high-risk technologies* (p. 215). New York: Basic Books.

On a beautiful night in October, 1978, in the Chesapeake Bay, two vessels sighted one another visually and on radar. On one of them, the Coast Guard cutter training vessel Cuyahoga, the captain (a chief warrant officer) saw the other ship up ahead as a small object on the radar, and visually he saw two lights, indicating that it was proceeding in the same direction as his own ship. He thought it possibly was a fishing vessel. The first mate saw the lights, but saw three, and estimated (correctly) that it was a ship proceeding toward them. He had no responsibility to inform the captain, nor did he think he needed to. Since the two ships drew together so rapidly, the captain decided that it must be a very slow fishing boat that he was about to over-take. This reinforced his incorrect interpretation. The lookout knew the captain was aware of the ship, so did not comment further as it got quite close and seemed to be nearly on a collision course. Since both ships were traveling full speed, the closing came fast. The other ship, a large cargo ship, did not establish any bridge-to-bridge communication, because the passing was routine. But at the last moment, the captain of the Cuyahoga realized that in overtaking the supposed fishing boat, which he assumed was on a near parallel course, he would cut off that boat's ability to turn as both of them approached the Potomac River. So he ordered a turn to the port.

The two ships collided, killing 11 sailors on the Coast Guard vessel. Clearly, the captain's mental model was incorrect. In addition, there was a lack of correspondence between the captain and the first mate's mental models.

In one investigation of 83 teams working on a complex skill task over a 2-week training protocol, both mental model accuracy and mental model correspondence were tested.[66] Accuracy was the stronger predictor of team performance. And, the teams' ability was more strongly related to accuracy than to mental model correspondence.

The Team Mind: Transactive Memory Systems

Many people supplement their own memories, which are known to be highly limited and unreliable, with various external aids. For example, PDAs and GPSs allow us to store and retrieve important information externally rather than in our own long-term memory. Similarly, other people (e.g., friends, family, coworkers, and teammates) also function as external memory aids.

A TMS is a shared system for attending to, encoding, storing, processing, and retrieving information.[67] Think of TMS as a division of mental labor. When each person learns in some general way what the other persons on the team may know in detail, team members can share detailed memories. In essence, each team member cultivates the other members as external memory, and, in doing so, they become part of a larger system. A TMS develops implicitly in many teams to ensure that important information is not forgotten. A TMS is a combination of two things: knowledge possessed by particular team members and awareness of who knows what. In this way, a TMS serves as an external storage device, such as a library or computer that

[66]Edwards, B., Day, E., Arthur, W., & Bell, S. (2006). Relationships among team ability composition, team mental models, and team performance. *Journal of Applied Psychology, 91*(3), 727–736.

[67]Wegner, D. M. (1986). Transactive memory: A contemporary analysis of the group mind. In B. Mullen & G. Goethals (Eds.), *Theories of group behavior* (pp.185–208). New York: Springer-Verlag; Wegner, D. M., Giuliano, T., & Hertel, P. (1995). Cognitive interdependence in close relationships. In W. J. Ickes (Ed.), *Compatible and incompatible relationships* (pp. 253–276). New York: Springer-Verlag.

can be visited to retrieve otherwise unavailable information. Teams that have a TMS have access to more and better information than any single group member does alone. A TMS is more beneficial to small groups that use quality as a performance measure, but more beneficial to large groups, groups in dynamic tasks environments, and groups in volatile knowledge environments that involve time as a critical performance measure.[68]

To see how a TMS might work within a team, consider a team composed of a finance, marketing, and production manager. The team members would expect that the person from finance would remember details concerning costs or profitability; the person from marketing would remember the results of a study concerning how customers responded to test marketing; and the production person would remember details about the mechanics of making the product. In other words, the other members of the team instinctively expect that the "experts" on the team will remember the details most closely associated with their area of expertise. Even when the experts are not so clearly defined, people specialize in remembering certain kinds of information, and it is generally understood by all members of the team (although often implicitly) which person is to remember what. This way of processing information provides an advantage to teams because they collectively remember and use more information than individuals acting on their own—even the same number of individuals considered separately.

The main disadvantage is that team members depend on one another for knowledge and information. Teams who have been working together for years find it nearly impossible to reconstruct interactions with clients and other shared experiences without the other team members present.

What does a TMS do for teams? How does it affect productivity in terms of the key dimensions of performance criteria? More important, how can the manager best capitalize on the strengths of a TMS while minimizing the liabilities?

TACIT COORDINATION   Tacit coordination is the synchronization of members' actions based on assumptions about what others on the team are likely to do. Task-oriented groups rarely discuss plans for how to perform their tasks unless they are explicitly instructed to do so.[69] Consider the results of an analysis of 14 years of the National Basketball Association.[70] Teams on which players had played together longer won more games. The teamwork effect was shown even for bad teams—if bad teams played together a lot, they won more than they should have based on other criteria. Berman attributed the gains to "tacit knowledge," for example, anticipating where a teammate will be on a fast break.[71] Team members' attempts to coordinate tacitly begin prior to interaction. Evaluating the competence of other team members can be difficult, however. Claims of personal competence by coworkers cannot always be trusted, because they may reflect members' desires to impress one another.[72] Accepting coworkers' evaluations of one another's competence can be risky as well because these secondhand evaluations are often based on limited information[73] and may reflect impression-management efforts by the people who

---

[68]Ren, Y., Carley, K., & Argote, L. (2006). The contingent effects of transactive memory: When is it more beneficial to know what others know? *Management Science, 52*(5), 671–682.
[69]Hackman, J. R., & Morris, C. G. (1975). Group tasks, group interaction process and group performance effectiveness. A review and proposed integration. In L. Berkowitz (Ed.), *Advances in experimental social psychology* (Vol. 8, pp. 45–99). New York: Academic Press.
[70]Berman, S. L., Down, J., & Hill, C. W. H. (2002). Tacit knowledge as a source of competitive advantage in the National Basketball Association. *The Academy of Management Journal, 45*, 13–31.
[71]Ibid.
[72]Gardner, W. L. (1992). Lessons in organizational dramaturgy: The art of impression management. *Organizational Dynamics, 21*(1), 33–46.
[73]Gilovich, T. (1987). Secondhand information and social judgment. *Journal of Experimental Social Psychology, 23*(1), 59–74.

provide them.[74] Knowing who is good at what improves the team's performance in several ways. For instance, it becomes easier to plan activities so that the people most suited for a particular task actually become responsible for that task. Similarly, coordinating actions and dealing with unexpected problems is easier when team members know who is good at what.

The TMS and Team Performance

TMS eliminates a lot of the coordination loss that can plague team effectiveness.[75] Teams that have a transactive memory structure because their members are familiar with one another are less likely to fall prey to the common information effect compared with teams composed of previously unacquainted persons.[76] Thus, the key question for the manager is how to ensure that teams develop an accurate TMS.

Probably the most straightforward way is to simply ask members of the team to indicate what knowledge bases the other members of the group possess. If there is high intrateam agreement, the TMS is higher than if there is low agreement about who knows what.

In one investigation, the completion times of teams of doctors performing total joint replacements in hospital surgeries were examined.[77] Three types of learning were examined: organizational experience (i.e., the number of times that kind of procedure had been performed); individual experience (i.e., the number of times a given person on a given team had performed the surgery); and team experience (i.e., the number of times any two people on a team had performed the surgery together). If successful surgical procedures were simply a function of accumulated expertise, then "team learning" should not matter. However, it does: The more times people have worked together as a team, the faster (and smoother) is their surgery. For example, holding all other sorts of experience constant, a team whose members have performed ten total knee replacements together takes 5 percent less time to complete the procedure when compared to a team that is just as accomplished but that has no experience in working together.

DEVELOPING A TMS IN TEAMS   The American Society for Training and Development (ASTD) estimates that U.S. organizations spend $134.07 billion annually on workplace learning and performance. Training expenditures (averaged across large Fortune 500 companies and public-sector organizations that share data) were $1,068 per employee in 2008, a 3 percent decrease from 2007, according to the 2009 ASTD State of the Industry Report.[78] Training is one of the most effective ways of ensuring that groups quickly and accurately develop a TMS.

A fundamental question that companies face is whether to train individuals independently or as part of a team. As a guiding principle, there should be a high degree of correspondence between workers' experiences during training and their experiences on the job. The key reason is that similar conditions will facilitate the transfer of knowledge learned in training to how individuals actually carry out their job. This type of state-dependent learning can be a strength of teamwork. Too often, learning is decontextualized from what the work teams are doing.

---

[74]Cialdini, R. B. (1989). *Indirect tactics of image management: Beyond basking*. Mahwah, NJ: Lawrence Erlbaum & Associates.

[75]Moreland, R. L., Argote, L., & Krishnan, R. (1998). Training people to work in groups. In R. S. Tindale, J. Edwards, E. J. Posavac, F. B. Bryant, Y. Suarez-Balcazar, E. Henderson-Kling, & J. Myers (Eds.), *Theory and research on small groups*. New York: Plenum Press.

[76]Gruenfeld, Mannix, Williams, & Neale, "Group composition and decision making."

[77]Reagans, R., Argote, L., & Brooks, D. (2005). Individual experience and experience working together: Predicting learning rates from knowing who knows what and knowing how to work together. *Management Science, 51*(6), 869–881.

[78]Rivera, R. J., & Paradise, A. (2009, November 12). ASTD's 2009 state of the industry report. www.astd.org

People perform their work differently when they are working in teams than when they are alone. This means that individuals require different kinds of training when they work in teams than when they work alone or apart. People who will work together as a team should train together, because (among other reasons) even during training, a TMS will ensure that the right structure of information sharing and responsibility will develop. Training can be specifically geared toward developing specific TMS structures. For example, teams can plan who will be responsible for what types of information; they can also make explicit efforts to discern expertise and then make that information known to members. Transactive memory training may be especially important when team members will work together only for a single project or when the team interacts with several other teams across the organization. It is important to align the unit of work—for example, individual, small team, large group—with the unit that is being trained. Therefore, when small teams work together, they should train together; when large groups work together, they should train together; when individuals work alone, it may be best to train them individually.

In Chapter 4, we reviewed three types of competencies for team members: technical skills, task-related skills, and interpersonal skills. If a company has limited resources for training, it is important that employees who will work together receive their technical training together. If that is not feasible, the training that they do undergo together should be directly connected to the work they will do together. Merely having workers undergo interpersonal skills training together (which is largely divorced from the real work they will do together) can undermine performance. The key to effective learning in most situations is the receipt of timely and effective feedback.

EXAMPLE OF TRAINING IN WORK GROUPS   As an illustration of the effect of a TMS on performance, simulated work groups were asked to assemble AM radios as part of a training experience.[79] Training was organized in two ways: (1) individually based training (as is common in many companies) and (2) group training, in which groups of three people worked together. In the training phase, all individuals and groups received identical information. Groups were not given any instructions in terms of how they should organize themselves. The only difference was whether people were trained alone or as part of a group.

Exactly one week later, the participants were asked to assemble the radios again. This was more difficult, because no written instructions were provided, as had been the case in the training phase. In this part of the investigation, everyone was placed into a three-person team, given the parts of the radio, and asked to assemble it from memory. This meant that some of the groups were composed of people who had trained individually and others of those who had trained with a team. Thus, any difference in performance between the two types of groups would be attributable to the differences in training.

Not surprisingly, the groups that had trained together performed dramatically better. They were more likely to complete the assembly and did so with fewer errors. The intact groups performed better than did the ad hoc groups because they were able to tap into the TMS that had spontaneously developed during training.

A TMS and an emphasis on team training are most relevant to tactical teams (i.e., teams that carry out a procedure) as opposed to creative or problem-solving teams. Thus, if a team is assembling radio parts, operating machinery in a coal mine, flying a jetliner, or performing heart surgery, it helps a lot for the members to have trained together on the job. However, as we saw in the last chapter, teams do more than perform routinized procedures; sometimes teams need to solve problems or create things. (See Exhibit 6-9 for a case analysis of training effectiveness.)

---

[79]Moreland, R. L., Argote, L., & Krishnan, R. (1996). Socially shared cognition at work. In J. L. Nye & A. M. Brower (Eds.), *What's social about social cognition?* Thousand Oaks, CA: Sage.

EXHIBIT 6-9 Case Analysis of Different Types of Training Effectiveness

PRELIMINARY INVESTIGATION

At a certain factory that assembles radios, a consultant was called in to assess variations in performance. To create healthy within-company competition, workers were organized into self-managing teams. There were four such teams in the plant, but performance varied dramatically across the four teams. What was the problem?

The consultant began her investigation by asking for information about how the different teams were trained. She uncovered four distinct training programs used by each of the teams. Upon interviewing each team in the plant, she found that each team was convinced that its method was the best one. When the consultant confronted teams with the evidence pointing to clear differences in performance, the team pointed to a number of countervailing factors that could have affected their performance. The managers were particularly concerned because the company was about to hire and train four new plant teams and they did not know which method would be best. The consultant devised the following test using the radio assembly task previously described.* Everyone in the entire plant received identical technical training and ultimately performed in a three-person group. However, certain aspects of the training were systematically varied. The consultant tracked the following teams:

- **Red team**: Members of the red team were trained individually for 1 day.
- **Blue team**: Members of the blue team were given individual training for one day and then, the entire team participated in a two-day team-building workshop, designed to improve cohesion and communication.
- **Yellow team**: Members of the yellow team were given group training for one day but were reassigned to different teams on the test day.
- **Green team**: Members of the green team were given group training for one day and remained in the same team on test day.

TEST DAY

On test day, the consultant wanted to capture the four key measures of team performance outlined in Chapter 2. Whereas the hiring organization seemed primarily interested in productivity—as measured by number of units successfully completed—the consultant was also interested in assessing other signs of team performance, such as cohesion, learning, and integration.

The consultant first asked each team to recall as much as they could about the training. In short, each team was asked to reconstruct the assembly instructions from memory. The consultant used this as a measure of organizational memory.

The consultant then asked each team to assemble the radios without the benefit of any kind of written instructions. Thus, each team was forced to rely on the training principles they had learned and (hopefully) remembered. Results were timed so that each team could be evaluated with respect to both efficiency and how accurately they met specifications.

Then, the consultant asked each team member to evaluate other team members in terms of their task expertise. This was a measure of the tendency to specialize in remembering distinct aspects of the task, as well as who was regarded by all team members as having a certain, relevant skill. The consultant videotaped each team during the critical test phase and documented how smoothly members worked together in terms of the principles of coordination (discussed in Chapter 2). Specifically, did members drop things unintentionally on the floor? Lose parts? Bump elbows? Have to repeat questions and directions? Question each others' expertise and knowledge? Or, alternatively, did the team work together seamlessly?

The tapes revealed the level of team motivation and also allowed the consultant to document things like how close members of the team sat to one another and the tone of their conversation. Finally, the consultant recorded the "we-to-I" ratio, or the number of times team members said "we" versus "I"—an implicit measure of team identity and cohesion. What do you think happened?

OUTCOME

The green team outperformed all of the other teams in terms of accuracy of completion.

DEBRIEFING WITH MANAGERS

One of the managers found it difficult to believe that team training received by the blue team in the area of cohesion and interpersonal skills did not make an appreciable difference. "We spend a lot of money every year trying to build trust and cohesion in our teams. Is this going to waste?" The consultant then shared the information shown in "Effects of Various Training Methods on Assembly Errors."

(cont.on p.144)

The results in displayed graph directly compare teams with a total of six weeks of working intensively with one another oncohesion-building (non-technical-skill building) tasks with teams who are virtual strangers, with the exception of having trained together. As you can see, the fewest number of errors were made by groups who trained with one another and then worked with one another; having special training in cohesion on top of that does not seem to matter much.

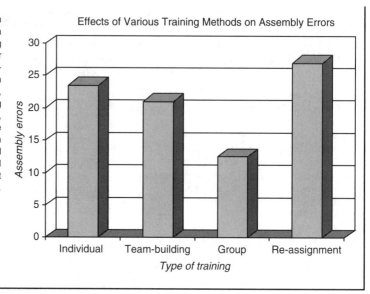

Source: Moreland, R. L., Argote, L., & Krishnan, R. (1996). Socially shared cognition at work. In J. L. Nye & A. M. Brower (Eds.), *What's social about social cognition?* Thousand Oaks, CA: Sage.

* Liang, D. W., Moreland, R. L., & Argote, L. (1995). Group versus individual training and group performance: The mediating role of transactive memory. *Personality and Social Psychology Bulletin, 21*(4), 384–393.

RECOMMENDATIONS FOR TEAM DEVELOPMENT   What are the ways to maximize team performance through a TMS?

Work Planning   Teams whose members will work together should plan their work. Teams spend a disproportionate amount of their time together doing the task, rather than deciding how it should be done.

Optimizing Human Resources   Teams should assess relevant areas of expertise among team members. Teams perform better when their members know who is good at what.[80] For example, when bank loan officers review the financial profiles of various companies and predict whether each company will go bankrupt, diversity in expertise and the ability of groups to recognize expertise improve predictions.[81] Unexpected problems can be solved more quickly and easily when members know who is good at what.[82] Such knowledge allows team members to match problems with the people most likely to solve them. People learn and recall more information in their own area of expertise when their partner has different, rather than similar, work-related expertise.[83]

---

[80]Stasser, Stewart, & Wittenbaum, "Expert roles and information exchange during discussion."
[81]Libby, R., Trotman, K. T., & Zimmer, I. (1987). Member variation, recognition of expertise, and group performance. *Journal of Applied Psychology, 72*(1), 81–87.
[82]Moreland, R. L., & Levine, J. M. (1992). The composition of small groups. In E. J. Lawler, B. Markovsky, C. Ridgeway, & H. A. Walker (Eds.), *Advances in group processes* (Vol. 9, pp. 237–280). Greenwich, CT: JAI Press.
[83]Hollingshead, A. B. (2000). Perceptions of expertise and transactive memory in work relationships. *Group Processes and Intergroup Relations, 3*(3), 257–267.

Monitor Stress and Pressure   Ellis examined how acute stress affects mental models and transactive memory in teams.[84] As might be predicted, the performance of 97 teams working on a command-and-control simulation was negatively affected when teams were under acute stress. However, if the stressor is regarded as a challenge (challenge stressor), this improves performance and transactive memory; hindrance stressors negatively affect performance (even when combined with a challenge stressor).[85] When nuclear power plant control room crews were examined in a simulated crisis, higher-performing crews were more adaptable in terms of exhibiting fewer, shorter, and less complex interaction patterns.[86]

Teams That Will Work Together Should Train Together   Teams whose members work and train together perform better than teams whose members are equally skilled but do not train together.[87] Team training increases performance by facilitating recognition and utilization of member expertise.

The importance of work group familiarity vis-à-vis training is hard to overestimate. For example, familiarity among team members is associated with fewer accidents and fatalities among pairs of crew members working closely together in coal mines (e.g., roof bolters and bolter helpers).[88] Although familiarity with the terrain has somewhat more impact than personnel similarity, the latter factor is clearly important, especially when teams work in less familiar terrain. Familiarity is associated with higher levels of crew productivity, even after labor, technology, and environment factors are taken into account.[89]

Plan for Turnover   At some point, teams dissolve; a member leaves or is transferred, and the team is left to find a replacement. Sometimes turnover is planned; other times it is unanticipated. Turnover can be a disruptive factor in teams, largely because newcomers and old-timers are unfamiliar with one another. However, much of the potential damage of turnover can be averted by strengthening team structure, such as assigning roles to members and prescribing work procedures.[90]

TEAM LEARNING

Group learning involves the basic process of sharing knowledge, storing knowledge, and retrieving knowledge.[91] How do teams learn from their environment, "newcomers," and outsiders?

---

[84]Ellis, A. (2006). System breakdown: The role of mental models and transactive memory in the relationships between acute stress and team performance. *Academy of Management Journal, 49*(3), 576–589.

[85]Pearsall, M., Ellis, A., & Stein, J. (2009). Coping with challenge and hindrance stressors in teams: Behavioral, cognitive, and affective outcomes. *Organizational Behavior and Human Decision Processes, 109(1)*, 18–28.

[86]Stachowski, A., Kaplan, S. A., & Waller, M. J. (2009). The benefits of flexible team interaction during crises. *Journal of Applied Psychology, 94*(6), 1536–1543.

[87] Hollingshead, A. B. (1998). Group and individual training. *Small Group Research, 29*(2), 254–280; Littlepage, G., Robison, W., & Reddington, K. (1997). Effects of task experience and group experience on group performance, member ability, and recognition of expertise. *Organizational Behavior and Human Decision Processes, 69*(2), 133–147.

[88]Goodman, P. S., & Garber, S. (1988). Absenteeism and accidents in a dangerous environment: Empirical analysis of underground coal mines. *Journal of Applied Psychology, 73*(1), 81–86.

[89]Goodman, P. S., & Leyden, D. P. (1991). Familiarity and group productivity. *Journal of Applied Psychology, 76*(4), 578–586.

[90]Devadas, R., & Argote, L. (1995). *Organizational learning curves: The effects of turnover and work group structure.* Invited paper presented at the annual meeting of the Midwestern Psychological Association, Chicago, IL.

[91]Argote, L., McEvily, B., & Reagans, R. (2003). Managing knowledge in organization: An integrative framework and review of emerging themes. *Management Science, 49*(4), 571–582.

Learning from the Environment

In an analysis of organizational learning in improvement project teams in hospital neonatal intensive care units, two distinct factors emerged as key: **learn-what** (activities that identify current best practices) and **learn-how** (activities that operationalize practices in a given setting).[92] The hospital teams had greater success when they implemented practices that were supported by extensive evidence and when project team members engaged in learning activities designed to promote engagement by the unit. Thus, both learn-what (content) and learn-how (means) are important.

Learning from Newcomers and Rotators

Many groups are "porous" in the sense that newcomers join groups and people rotate in and out of the group. Groups are more likely to adopt the routine of a rotator when they share a superordinate identity with that member.[93] A group is also more likely to adopt a routine from a rotator when it is superior to their own. When groups do not share a superordinate identity, they fail to adopt the rotator's ideas and knowledge, even when it is superior to their own and would have improved their performance.

Team Longevity: Routinization Versus Innovation Trade-Offs

Teams whose members work together for longer periods are more likely to develop a TMS and will, therefore, be more productive. However, there is a countervailing force at work in teams that have been together for long periods of time, namely, routinization. That is, because a TMS is basically a set of expectations, certain working relationships may become entrenched over time. For example, groups that experience partial membership change tend to rely on the TMS structure that their old-timers developed in their original group; this is ultimately detrimental to performance.[94] However, when old-timers are instructed to reflect upon their collective knowledge, these negative effects are minimized. When delegation is optional (which a TMS does not ensure), and in a world in which the team's expectations about what is needed (e.g., consumer demand) are accurate, then more TMS should basically lead to more routinization of the task and, hence, to a more efficient channeling of efforts by team members (because there will be less coordination loss involved in understanding each team member's role). Such expectations would seem to be best when there is little need for innovation. Thus, there is a precarious trade-off of sorts between routinization and innovation.

For much of the work that organizations do, routinization is a good thing; however, for a large part of what organizations do, innovation is desirable and necessary to meet the competitive challenges we outlined in Chapter 1. Thus, a well-defined TMS could hinder the team's ability to be adaptive.

For these reasons, there may be significant problems associated with extended team longevity. As a case in point, let's examine an R&D facility of a large American corporation.[95] The division,

---

[92]Tucker, A., Nembland, I., & Edmondson, A. (2006, April). *Implementing new practices: An empirical study of organizational learning in hospital intensive care units.* Working paper No. 06-049, Harvard Business School.

[93]Kane, A., Argote, L., & Levine, J. (2005). Knowledge transfer between groups via personnel rotation: Effects of social identity and knowledge quality. *Organizational Behavior and Human Decision Processes, 96,* 56–71.

[94]Lewis, K., Belliveau, M., Herndon, B., & Keller, J. (2007). Group cognition, membership change, and performance: Investigating the benefits and detriments of collective knowledge. *Organizational Behavior and Human Decision Processes, 103*(2), 159–178.

[95]Katz, R. (1982). The effects of group longevity on project communication and performance. *Administrative Science Quarterly, 27,* 81–104.

which included 345 engineers and scientific professionals, was geographically isolated from the rest of the organization. Katz examined 50 project groups in this division that varied greatly in terms of their longevity—that is, how long members of one group had worked with one another.

To keep informed about relevant developments outside the organization as well as new requirements within the organization, project groups must collect and process information from a variety of outside sources. The preferred means for obtaining such information for engineering professionals is interpersonal communication, rather than technical reports, publications, or other written documentation.

Therefore, for a period of 15 weeks, professionals kept records of their work-related communication; any time that a group member consulted or spoke with others, whether at the water cooler or in the parking lot, this was recorded.

As a final step, the department managers (a total of seven) and the two lab directors evaluated the performance of each project produced by each group with which they were technically familiar. The managers considered the following criteria: schedule, budget and cost performance, innovation, adaptability, and ability to cooperate. A consultant then computed a correlation between the longevity of teams and their performance. The results were startling.

As may be seen in Exhibit 6-10, the performance of these groups increased as they gained longevity, but only up to a point. After 5 years of working together, team project performance declined steeply, as did intraproject communication, organizational communication, and external professional communication—basically all the types of communication that serve to bring fresh ideas to the group.

Four behavioral changes took place in groups that worked together for over 5 years:

- *Behavioral stability*   Project members interacting over a long time develop standard work patterns that are familiar and comfortable. This can happen very rapidly—for instance, the way people in a group tend to sit in the same places in meeting after meeting, even when there may be no logical reason for doing so. Over time, this behavioral stability leads to isolation from the outside. The group can grow increasingly complacent, ceasing to question the practices that shape their behavior.
- *Selective exposure*   There is a tendency for group members to communicate only with people whose ideas agree with their own. It is related to the homogeneity bias—the tendency to select new members who are like members in the existing group. Over time, project members learn to interact selectively to avoid messages and information that conflict with their established practices and disposition.
- *Group homogeneity*   Groups that are separated from the influence of others in the organization develop a homogeneous set of understandings about the group and its environment.
- *Role differentiation*   Groups that work and train together become increasingly specialized in project competencies and roles. This results in greater role differentiation, which in turn results in less interaction among group members because the roles and expectations held by each are so well entrenched. Consequently, they lose access to much of the internal talent, and their ability to learn new ideas from one another is diminished.

Thus, in terms of actual task performance, as team longevity increases, certain social processes conspire to lower levels of project communication, which in turn decrease project performance. Project groups become increasingly isolated from key information sources both within and outside their organizations with increasing stability in their membership. Reductions in project communication adversely affect the technical performance of project groups. Variations in communication activities are more associated with the tenure composition of the

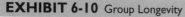

EXHIBIT 6-10 Group Longevity

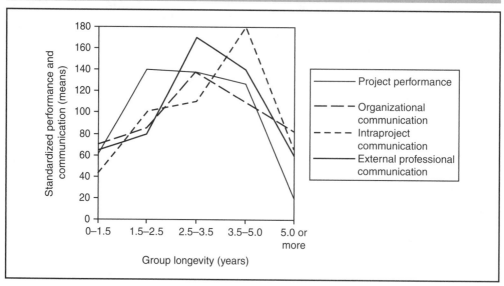

Source: Katz, R. (1982). The effects of group longevity on project communication and performance. *Administrative Science Quarterly, 27,* 81–104.

project group than with the project tenures of the individual engineers. Stated another way, it is not the age of the employee that is of critical importance, but the age of the team. Furthermore, individual competence does not account for differences in performance. Thus, it is not the case that the older, less skilled members were working in teams that were of greater longevity. Furthermore, the longevity of project groups does not appear to be part of the mental models of the managers—virtually no one was aware of the tenure demographics of their project groups.

What does all of this mean for team longevity? A certain amount of familiarity is necessary for teams to work together in a productive fashion. The effect of working together tends to make team members grow more familiar with each other's relevant knowledge base, and, hence, a TMS can develop. A TMS can be helpful in tasks where coordination losses need to be reduced and tactical precision is key. Although a certain amount of routinization is desirable in any team, the overly routinized team hinders communication and obstructs innovation. We don't have a precise answer as to how long teams should work together on a particular task; it simply depends too much on the nature of the task and the membership of the team.

Looking at this question from a team design standpoint might offer some insights. It may be desirable, for example, to design some teams whose primary objective is to act as innovation experts for the creation and transfer of the organization's best practices. According to Kane and Argote, groups are more likely to benefit from the knowledge and ideas brought by a newcomer when they share a superordinate identity with one another.[96] Moreover, when members sit in an integrated fashion (versus sitting on opposite sides of a table), a superordinate identity is more likely to be established.

---

[96]Kane, A., & Argote, L. (2002). *Social identity and knowledge transfer between groups.* Paper presented at the Annual Meeting of the Academy of Management, Denver, CO.

Conclusion

For teams to be effective in their work, they need to have a shared knowledge base. The knowledge base allows teams to more efficiently process and encode relevant information and then act upon it in a thoughtful and appropriate fashion. However, the shared knowledge base that governs a team is only as adequate as its communication system. Communication among team members is a collaborative effort. Natural biases in communication can play havoc with effective teamwork. It is the responsibility of team leaders to ensure that successful communication occurs among team members. The development of accurate team mental models and a TMS can partially combat the threat of the common information effect and hidden profiles.

7

Team Decision Making
Pitfalls and Solutions

On March 20, 2003, the United States invaded Iraq. The United States was working with the knowledge that Iraq not only possessed weapons of mass destruction (WMDs) but was also prepared to use them against the United States. The invasion was expected to be quick, and just weeks later, on May 1, 2003, the Bush White House announced that major combat in Iraq had ended. U.S. troops greeted the news with cheers. However, the proclamation was premature. In June 2008, after more than 5 years of combat in Iraq, the Senate Select Committee on Intelligence released two reports: one stating that on numerous occasions the George W. Bush administration misrepresented the intelligence and the threat from Iraq; the second report detailing inappropriate, sensitive intelligence activities conducted by the Department of Defense Office of the Undersecretary of Defense for Policy, without the knowledge of the intelligence community or the State Department. "Before taking the country to war, this Administration owed it to the American people to give them a 100 percent accurate picture of the threat we faced. Unfortunately, our Committee has concluded that the Administration made significant claims that were not supported by the intelligence," committee member Senator John Jay Rockefeller IV said. "In making the case for war, the Administration repeatedly presented intelligence as fact when in reality it was unsubstantiated, contradicted, or even nonexistent. As a result, the American people were led to believe that the threat from Iraq was much greater than actually existed."[1] By December 2009, U.S. casualties in Iraq totaled over 4,300.[2]

Whenever teams make decisions, they rely on information and judgment. Sometimes the information is insufficient and sometimes it is erroneous. When the consequences of decision making are disastrous, we try to find the root of the problem, which may be due to a faulty process or erroneous "facts." As we will see in this chapter, teams can follow a vigilant process and still reach bad decisions; in some cases, teams that seem to do all the wrong things still manage to succeed. (See Exhibit 7-1 for a model of team process and outcomes.)

---

[1]U.S. Senate Select Committee on Intelligence. (2008, June 5). *Senate Intelligence Committee Unveils Final Phase II Reports on Prewar Iraq Intelligence.* intelligence.senate.gov
[2]United States Department of Defense. (2010). *Operation Iraqi freedom military.* siadapp.dmdc.osd.mil

EXHIBIT 7-1 Team Process and Outcomes

	Failure Outcome	**Successful Outcome**
Flawed process	Predictable failure	"Lucky" • Nonreplicable success
Vigilant process	"Unlucky"	Predictable Success • Best condition for replicable success

DECISION MAKING IN TEAMS

Decision making is an integrated sequence of activities that includes gathering, interpreting, and exchanging information; creating and identifying alternative courses of action; choosing among alternatives by integrating differing perspectives and opinions of team members; and implementing a choice and monitoring its consequences.[3] For a schematic diagram of an idealized set of activities involved in a decision-making process, see Exhibit 7-2.

We begin by discussing how a variety of well-documented decision-making biases affect individual decision making and how these biases are ameliorated or exacerbated in groups. We identify five decision-making pitfalls that teams often encounter. For each, we describe the problem and then provide preventive measures. We focus on groupthink, the tendency to conform to the consensus viewpoint in group decision making and then discuss escalation of commitment, the Abilene paradox, group polarization, and unethical decision making.

INDIVIDUAL DECISION-MAKING BIASES

A variety of decision-making biases plague individual decision making (for reviews, see Bazerman's *Judgment in Managerial Decision Making*, 2009).[4] In this section, we briefly review three of the most well-documented individual decision-making biases and discuss their implications for teams.

Framing Bias

Consider the following problem:[5]

Imagine that the United States is preparing for the outbreak of an unusual disease, which is expected to kill 600 people in the United States alone. Two alternative programs to combat the disease have been proposed. Assume that the exact scientific estimates of the consequences of the programs are as follows:

Plan A: If program A is adopted, 200 people will be saved.

Plan B: If program B is adopted, there is a one-third probability that 600 people will be saved and a two-third probability that no one will be saved.

If forced to choose, which plan would you select?

---

[3]Guzzo, R. A., Salas, E., & Associates. (1995). *Team effectiveness and decision making in organizations.* San Francisco, CA: Jossey-Bass.
[4]Bazerman, M. H. (2009). *Judgment in managerial decision making* (7th ed.). Hoboken, NJ: John Wiley & Sons.
[5]Tversky, A., & Kahneman, D. (1981). The framing of decisions and the psychology of choice. *Science, 211,* 453–458.

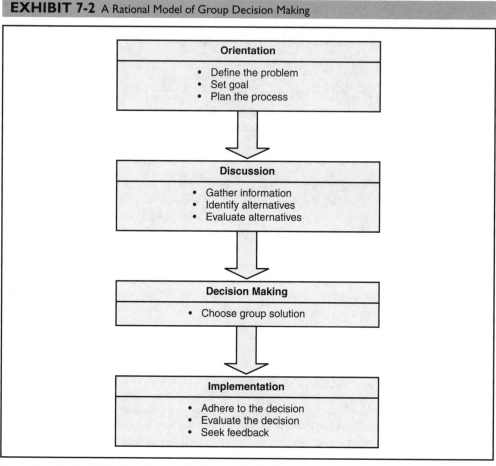

EXHIBIT 7-2 A Rational Model of Group Decision Making

Orientation
- Define the problem
- Set goal
- Plan the process

Discussion
- Gather information
- Identify alternatives
- Evaluate alternatives

Decision Making
- Choose group solution

Implementation
- Adhere to the decision
- Evaluate the decision
- Seek feedback

Source: Forsyth, D. (1990). *Group dynamics* (2nd ed., p. 286). Pacific Grove, CA: Brooks/Cole.

When given this choice, most individual decision makers choose program A (72 percent). Now, consider the following options:

>   Plan C: If program C is adopted, 400 people will die.

>   Plan D: If program D is adopted, there is a one-third probability that nobody will die and a two-thirds probability that 600 people will die.

When given the identical problem with the same options worded in terms of "lives lost," the majority of respondents choose the risky course of action (Plan D, 78 percent).[6] This inconsistency is a preference reversal and reveals the framing effect.

Almost any decision can be reframed as a gain or a loss relative to something.[7] Decision makers' reference points for defining gain and loss are often arbitrary. Several investigations

---

[6]Milch, K. F., Weber, E. U., Appelt, K. C., Handgraaf, M. J., & Krantz, D. H. (2009). From individual preference construction to group decisions: Framing effects and group processes. *Organizational Behavior and Human Decision Processes, 108*(2), 242–255.
[7]Tversky, & Kahneman, "The framing of decisions and the psychology of choice."

have compared individuals' versus groups' susceptibility to the framing effect. The results are mixed: Sometimes groups are less susceptible to framing, but in some investigations, they are just as fallible as individuals.[8]

Overconfidence

Ninety-four percent of college professors believe they are above-average teachers; 90 percent of drivers believe they are above average; when computer executives were given quizzes about their industry, they estimated they got 5 percent of the answers wrong—in fact, they had gotten 80 percent wrong.[9] Consider the questions in Exhibit 7-3. Many organizational situations require decision makers to assess the likelihood that judgments about someone or something will be correct. The overconfidence bias is the tendency for people to place unwarranted confidence in their judgments. For example, even though the instructions in Exhibit 7-3 ask decision makers to choose an upper and lower bound such that they are 98 percent sure that the actual answer falls within their bounds, most decision makers only have four answers that fall within their lower and upper confidence bounds. In a study of 100 people, 42 percent fell outside the 90 percent confidence range. In a team,

---

EXHIBIT 7-3 Overconfidence in Judgment

Instructions: Listed below are 10 questions. Do not look up any information on these questions. For each, write down your best estimate of the answer. Next, put a lower and an upper bound around your estimate, such that you are 98 percent confident that your range surrounds the actual answer.

Question	Your best estimate	Lower bound	Upper bound
1. The median age for the total U.S. population in 2009*			
2. The median U.S. household income in 2009*			
3. Percentage of the U.S. population under 5 years old in 2008			
4. U.S. Federal Government spending (in fiscal year 2009 in $ per capita) on health care			
5. Total 2009 federal spending per household			
6. Annual company cost of lost productivity per employee due to reading/deleting *spam* mails at work in 2009			
7. Number of all endangered and/or threatened animals and plants in U.S. in 2009			
8. Number of Global 500 Companies in U.S. in 2009			
9. Exxon Mobile 2009 revenue, which is the highest among Global 500 companies in U.S.			
10. Highest paid CEO in 2008 in the U.S. (including salary, bonus, perks, and estimated stock awards and stock options on the day of grant last year) Stephen Schwarzman (The Blackstone Group)*			

Answers: (1) 36.7 years; (2) $52,029; (3) 6.9%; (4) $2,328; (5) $33,932; (6)$1,250; (7) 747; (8) 190; (9) $442,851,000,000; (10) $702,440,573

---

[8]Milch, Weber, Appelt, Handgraaf, & Krantz, "From individual preference construction to group decisions."
[9]Brooks, D. (2009, October 27). The fatal conceit. *New York Times*, p. A31.

EXHIBIT 7-4 Card Test

Imagine that the following four cards are placed in front of you and are printed with the following symbols on one side:

Card 1	Card 2	Card 3	Card 4
E	K	4	7

Now, imagine you are told that a letter appears on one side of each card and a number on the other. Your task is to judge the validity of the following rule, which refers only to these four cards: "If a card has a vowel on one side, then it has an even number on the other side." Your task is to turn over only those cards that have to be turned over for the correctness of the rule to be judged. Which cards do you want to turn over? (Stop here and decide which cards to turn over before reading on.)

Averaging over a large number of investigations,* 89 percent of people select E, which is a logically correct choice because an odd number on the other side would disconfirm the rule. However, 62 percent also choose to turn over the 4, which is not logically informative because neither a vowel nor a consonant on the other side would falsify the rule. Only 25 percent of people elect to turn over the 7, which is a logically informative choice because a vowel behind the 7 would falsify the rule. Only 16 percent elect to turn over K, which would not be an informative choice.

Thus, people display two types of logical errors in the task. First, they often turn over the 4, an example of the confirmation bias. However, even more striking is the failure to take the step of attempting to disconfirm what they believe is true—in other words, turning over the 7.**

Source: *Oaksford, M., & Chater, N. (1994). A rational analysis of the selection task as optimal data selection. *Psychological Review, 101*, 608–631.

**Wason, P. C., & Johnson-Laird, P. N. (1972). *Psychology of reasoning: Structure and content.* Cambridge, MA: Harvard University Press.

overconfidence leads people to myopically focus on their teammates' strengths, as opposed to their weaknesses and neglect the strength and weaknesses of members of competitor teams.[10]

Confirmation Bias

The **confirmation bias** is the tendency for people to consider evidence that supports their position, hypothesis, or desires and disregard or discount (equally valid) evidence that refutes their beliefs. When people are ego invested in a project, the confirmation bias is stronger. Even upon the receipt of unsupportive data, people who have fallen prey to the confirmation bias will maintain, and in some cases increase, their resolve. (As a quick demonstration of the confirmation bias, take the test in Exhibit 7-4.)

INDIVIDUAL VERSUS GROUP DECISION MAKING IN DEMONSTRABLE TASKS

A **demonstrable task** is a task that has an obvious, correct answer. Many management and executive education courses challenge businesspeople with simulations in which they find themselves stranded in inhospitable environments—arctic tundra, scorched desert, treacherous jungles—and together, they must plan and enact strategies to ensure their survival.[11] Some

[10]Krizan, Z., & Windschitl, P. D. (2007). Team allegiance can lead to both optimistic and pessimistic predictions. *Journal of Experimental Social Psychology, 43*, 327–333.
[11]One such simulation is *Desert Survival*, available from Human Synergistics International, 39819 Plymouth Road, C8020, Plymouth, MI 48170–8020, USA.

companies actually place people in such situations (see Exhibit 7-5), popular television shows are based on "survival," and some teams excel at adventure sports—but in the management laboratory and classroom, teammates are simply asked to rank (in order of importance) the usefulness of several objects (e.g., flashlight, canteen of water, and knives). The team's rank order can be benchmarked against that of an expert and against the individual rankings made by each member of the team.

When this is done, an interesting phenomenon emerges: The performance of the team is inevitably better than the simple, arithmetic average of the group. Recall from Chapter 2 the

---

EXHIBIT 7-5 Decision Making with Real Stakes

- A young woman walks into a trendy restaurant on a busy city corner. She sets down a purse and leaves. Moments later a bomb explodes. The restaurant is engulfed in flames, people are screaming and hurt. Fire trucks and police cars quickly arrive, and working together the emergency responders rescue patrons, perform triage on the injured, and put out the flames. This is an emergency-response training scenario developed by Play2Train, a virtual training environment that operates in the online game, Second Life. The training scenarios support emergency response training initiatives as part of the Idaho Bioterrorism Awareness and Preparedness Program. In the virtual world, which includes a town and two hospitals, trainees meet in 3-D interactive virtual environments and participate in educational projects relevant to health care and emergency preparedness. They participate virtually and remotely in scenarios that include terrorist attacks, flu pandemics, or other disasters in which they are expected to jump in, in character, and respond as the event takes place. Regardless of their location, they all interact in real time and are expected to work together as a team responding without scripts. If they don't react to what's going on in the simulation, characters die, and other team members are directly affected by their choices. Trainers study how people establish teams, develop systems, and react in different environments.

- When the Soldiers of Headquarters and Headquarters Battery, 210th Fires Brigade, 2nd Infantry Division took to the field, the enemy force was stationary targets, but the rounds were anything but fake. Live ammunition made the stakes higher and the training very real. More than just shooting at targets, the training integrated firing live rounds with reacting to an ambush. The soldiers fired from moving vehicles in a convoy before being ambushed by an improvised explosive device (IED). Once the IED was detonated, some of the soldiers laid down suppressive fire. While the soldiers reacted to the enemy's attack, the observer/controllers threw curve balls at the troops. Soldiers were deemed wounded or killed in action to add realism to the scenario. Vehicles became inoperable. Soldiers shared ammunition as needed.

- At St. Joseph's Hospital and Medical Center in Phoenix, a diagnosis of a malignant tumor not shared with a patient's wife led to the hospital revamping its entire communication and decision-making process. In 2009, the hospital began working with the patient's widow to discuss how to improve the lines of communication between doctors, staff, and patients. "Immediate, ongoing communication is key," said Jackie Aragon, senior director of quality in the risk and regulatory division at the hospital. Not answering a patient's questions upfront "puts up a wall. You need everyone at the table." The 738-bed hospital involves patients in various procedures, including having them serve on advisory boards and committees. Clinicians also conduct safety rounds in which they ask patients and families how their hospital stay is going. Feedback from patients and employees through a safety culture survey are used to ensure the hospital is taking steps to prevent miscommunication and errors.

Source: Fisher Gale, S. (2008, December). Virtual training with real results. *Workforce Management.* workforce.com; Edgar, K. (2008, June 18). 210th Fires conducts convoy training. *United States Army.* army.mil; DerGurahian, J. (2009, November 2). Changing course. A few well-publicized cases of medical errors have led the hospitals involved to transform how they approach patient safety. *Modern Healthcare*, p. 6.

team performance equation, wherein: Actual Productivity (AP) of a team = Potential Productivity (PP) + Synergy (S) – Performance Threats (T). In this case, the arithmetic average of the team represents the potential productivity of the group. If the actual productivity of the team exceeds this, it suggests that the group has experienced a synergistic process (i.e., working together has allowed the group to outperform how they could have performed by simply aggregating their own decisions). If the actual productivity of the team is worse, it suggests that the group process is flawed. However, the team leader is justified in asking whether the team's performance exceeds that of the best member of the team.[8] Perhaps team decision making is best served by putting the trust of the group into one knowledgeable and competent group member. Michaelsen et al. studied individual versus group decision making in 222 project teams, ranging in size from three to eight members.[12] In most instances, groups outperformed their most proficient group member 97 percent of the time.

Groups perform better than independent individuals on a wide range of demonstrable problems. For example, groups of three, four, or five people perform better than the best individual in letters-to-numbers problems (e.g., "A + D = ?"),[13] and groups outperform individuals on estimation problems.[14] Groups perform at the level of the second-best individual or group member on world knowledge problems, such as vocabulary, analogies, and ranking items for usefulness. Groups who use a structured approach for making decisions perform better than those without structure.[15] People who have experience solving demonstrable problems in a group are able to transfer their performance to individual tasks,[16] and people who anticipate group discussion are more accurate.[17]

However, groups are much more overconfident than are individuals, regardless of their actual accuracy. For example, in one investigation, groups were asked to make stock price predictions. The actual accuracy of the group was 47 percent, but their confidence level was 65 percent.[18] Three days before the disintegration of the space shuttle *Columbia* in 2003, NASA officials met to discuss ways to monitor and minimize the amount of falling debris during liftoff (one probable cause of *Columbia*'s breakdown), but concluded that repair work in flight—a possible solution—would be too costly, creating "more damage than what [they] were trying to

---

[12]Michaelsen, L. K., Watson, W. E., & Black, R. H. (1989). A realistic test of individual versus group consensus decision making. *Journal of Applied Psychology, 74*(5), 834–839.

[13]Laughlin, P., Hatch, E., Silver, J., & Boh, L. (2006). Groups perform better than the best individuals on letters-to-numbers problems: Effects of group size. *Journal of Personality and Social Psychology, 90*(4), 644–651; Laughlin, P. R., Bonner, B. L., & Miner, A. G. (2002). Groups perform better than the best individuals on letters-to-numbers problems. *Organizational Behavior and Human Decision Processes, 88*, 605–620; Laughlin, P., Zander, M., Knievel, E., & Tan, T. (2003). Groups perform better than the best individuals on letters-to-numbers problems: Informative equations and effective strategies. *Journal of Personality and Social Psychology, 85*(4), 684–694.

[14]Laughlin, P., Gonzalez, C., & Sommer, D. (2003). Quantity estimations by groups and individuals: Effects of known domain boundaries. *Group Dynamics: Theory, Research and Practice, 7*(1), 55–63; Laughlin, P., Bonner, B., Miner, A., & Carnevale, P. (1999). Frames of references in quantity estimations by groups and individuals. *Organizational Behavior and Human Decision Processes, 80*(2), 103–117; Laughlin, P. R., Carey, H. R., & Kerr, N. L. (2008). Group-to-individual problem-solving transfer. *Group Processes & Intergroup Relations, 11*(3), 319–330.

[15]Whitte, E. H. (2007). Toward a group facilitation technique for project teams. *Group Processes & Intergroup Relations, 10*(3), 299–309; Bonner, B., Sillito, S., & Baumann, M. (2007). Collective estimation: Accuracy, expertise, and extroversion as sources of intra-group influence. *Organizational Behavior and Human Decision Processes, 103*(1), 121–133.

[16]Laughlin, Carey, & Kerr, "Group-to-individual problem-solving transfer."

[17]Roch, S. R. (2007). Why convene rater teams: An investigation of the benefits of anticipated discussion, consensus, and rater motivation. *Organizational Behavior and Human Decision Processes, 104*(1), 14–29.

[18]Fischhoff, B., Slovic, P., & Lichtenstein, S. (1977). Knowing with certainty: The appropriateness of extreme confidence. *Journal of Experimental Psychology: Human Perception and Performance, 3*(4), 552–564.

repair."[19] Groups are also more likely to exacerbate some of the shortcomings displayed by individuals, namely, groups are more likely than individuals to (faultily) neglect case-specific information and ignore base-rate information.[20]

Group Decision Rules

Given the pervasiveness of group decision making, teams need a method by which to combine individuals' decisions to yield a group decision. There are several kinds of group decision rules. The objective of decision rules may differ, such as finding the alternative that the greatest number of team members prefer, the alternative the fewest members object to, or the choice that maximizes team welfare. In an extensive test of the success of several types of decision rules, majority and plurality rules did quite well, performing at levels comparable to much more resource-demanding rules, such as individual judgment averaging rule (see Exhibit 7-6).[21] Thus, groups are well served in using majority or plurality voting in truth-seeking group decisions. Yet, they often avoid majority rule when given a choice. For example, groups tend to choose the alternative that is acceptable to all group members, even when a majority of members prefer a different alternative.[22]

The most common decision rule is majority rule. Teams may often use majority rule as a decision heuristic because of its ease and familiarity.[23] However, despite its demographic appeal, majority rule presents several problems in the attainment of consensus. First, majority rule ignores members' strength of preference for alternatives. The vote of a person who feels strongly about an issue counts only as much as the vote of a person who is virtually indifferent. Consequently, majority rule may not promote creative trade-offs among issues.[24] Majority rule may also encourage the formation of coalitions, or subgroups within a team. A coalition is a group of two or more members who join together to affect the outcome of a decision involving at least three parties.[25]

Although unanimous decision making is time consuming, it encourages team members to consider creative alternatives to satisfy the interests of all members. Teams required to reach consensus have greater accuracy than those that are not.[26]

DECISION-MAKING PITFALL 1: GROUPTHINK

Groupthink occurs when team members place consensus above all other priorities—including using good judgment when the consensus reflects poor judgment or improper or immoral actions. Groupthink involves a deterioration of mental efficiency, reality testing, and moral judgments as a result of group pressures toward conformity of opinion. For a list of groupthink fiascos in the

---

[19]Associated Press. (2003, February 14). *Before Columbia, NASA mulled space repairs.*
[20]Hinsz, V. B., Tindale, R. S., & Nagao, D. H. (2008). Accentuation of information processes and biases in group judgments integrating base-rate and case specific information. *Journal of Experimental Social Psychology, 44*(1), 116–126.
[21]Hastie, R., & Kameda, T. (2005). The robust beauty of majority rules in group decisions. *Psychological Review, 112*(2), 494–508.
[22]Ohtsubo, Y., & Miler, C. E. (2008). Test of a Level of Aspiration model of group decision making: Non-obvious group preference reversal due to an irrelevant alternative. *Journal of Experimental Social Psychology, 44*(1), 105–115.
[23]Hastie, R., Penrod, S., & Pennington, N. (1983). *Inside the jury.* Cambridge, MA: Harvard University Press; Ordeshook, P. (1986). *Game theory and political theory: An introduction.* Cambridge, UK: Cambridge University Press.
[24]Mannix, E., Thompson, L., & Bazerman, M. H. (1989). Negotiation in small groups. *Journal of Applied Psychology, 74*, 508–517; Thompson, L., Mannix, E., & Bazerman, M. (1988). Group negotiation: Effects of decision rule, agenda, and aspiration. *Journal of Personality and Social Psychology, 54*, 86–95; Castore, C. H., & Murnighan, J. K. (1978). Determinants of support for group decisions. *Organizational Behavior and Human Performance, 22*, 75–92.
[25]Komorita, S., & Parks, C. (1994). *Social dilemmas.* Madison, WI: Brown & Benchmark.
[26]Roch, "Why convene rater teams."

EXHIBIT 7-6 Group Decision Rules

Group Decision Rule	Description	Individual cognitive effort	Social (group) effort
Average winner	Each member estimates the value of each alternative and the group computes each alternative's mean estimated value and chooses the alternative with the highest mean	High	High
Median winner	Each member estimates the value of each alternative, and the group computes each alternative's median estimated value and chooses the alternative with the highest median	High	High
Davis's weighted average winner	Each member estimates the value of each alternative, and the group assigns a weighted average value to each alternative and chooses the alternative with the highest weighted average rule	High	High
Borda rank winner	Each member ranks all alternatives by estimated value, and the group assigns a Borda rank score to each location (the sum of individual ranks for each alternative) and chooses the alternative with the lowest (most favorable) score	High	High
Condorcet majority rule	All pairwise elections are held (e.g., 45 for 10 candidates) and the alternative that wins all elections is the Condorcet winner (it is possible for there to be no unique, overall winner)	Low	High
Majority/plurality rule	Each member assigns one vote to the alternative with the highest estimated value, and the alternative receiving the most votes is chosen	Low	Low
Best member rule	Member who has achieved the highest individual accuracy in estimating alternative values is selected and this member's first choices become the group's choices	High	Medium
Random member rule	On each trial, one member is selected at random, and this member's first choices become the group's choices	Low	Low
Group satisficing rule	On each trial, alternatives are considered one at a time in a random order; the first alternative for which all members' value estimates exceed aspiration thresholds is chosen by the group	Medium	Medium

Source: Hastie, R., & Kameda, T. (2005). The robust beauty of majority rules in group decisions. *Psychological Review,* *112*(2), 494–508.

political and corporate world, see Exhibit 7-7. The desire to agree can become so dominant that it can override the realistic appraisal of alternative courses of action.[27] The causes of groupthink may stem from group pressures to conform or a sincere desire to incorporate and reflect the views of all team members. Such pressure may also come from management if the directive is to reach a

[27]Janis, I. L. (1972). *Victims of groupthink* (2nd ed.). Boston: Houghton Mifflin.

EXHIBIT 7-7 Instances of Groupthink in Politics and the Corporate World

Examples from Politics

- The US invasion of Iraq in 2002 on the belief that Iraq possessed weapons of mass destruction (WMDs).
- Neville Chamberlain's inner circle, whose members supported the policy of appeasement of Hitler during 1937 and 1938, despite repeated warnings and events that indicated it would have adverse consequences.[a]
- President Truman's advisory group, whose members supported the decision to escalate the war in North Korea, despite firm warnings by the Chinese Communist government that U.S. entry into North Korea would be met with armed resistance from the Chinese.[a]
- President Kennedy's inner circle, whose members supported the decision to launch the Bay of Pigs invasion of Cuba, despite the availability of information indicating that it would be an unsuccessful venture and would damage U.S. relations with other countries.[a]
- President Johnson's close advisors, who supported the decision to escalate the war in Vietnam, despite intelligence reports and information indicating that this course of action would not defeat the Viet Cong or the North Vietnamese, and would generate unfavorable political consequences within the United States.[a]
- The decision of the Reagan administration to exchange arms for hostages with Iran and to continue commitment to the Nicaraguan Contras in the face of several congressional amendments limiting or banning aid.

Examples from the Corporate World

- Enron's board of directors was well informed about (and could therefore have prevented) the risky accounting practices, conflicts of interest, and hiding of debt that led to the company's downfall; likewise, Arthur Andersen (Enron's accounting firm) did nothing to halt the company's high-risk practices.[b, c]
- Gruenenthal Chemie's decision to market the drug thalidomide.[d]
- The price-fixing conspiracy involving the electrical manufacturing industry during the 1950s.
- The decision by Ford Motor Company to produce the Edsel.[e]
- The American Medical Association's (AMA's) decision to allow Sunbeam to use the AMA name as a product endorsement.[f]
- The selling of millions of jars of "phony" apple juice by Beech-Nut, the third largest baby food producer in the United States.
- The involvement of E. F. Hutton in "check kiting," wherein a money manager at a Hutton branch office would write a check on an account in Bank A for more money than Hutton had in the account. Because of the time lag in the check-collection system, these overdrafts sometimes went undetected, and Hutton could deposit funds to cover the overdraft in the following day. The deposited money would start earning interest immediately. The scheme allowed Hutton to earn a day's interest on Bank A's account without having to pay anything for it—resulting in $250 million in free loans every day.[g]
- The illegal purchases by Salomon Brothers at U.S. Treasury auctions in the early 1990s.[h]

[a]Janis, I. L., & Mann, L. (1977). *Decision making: A psychological analysis of conflict, choice, and commitment* (p. 130). New York: The Free Press, a Division of Simon & Schuster. Reprinted with permission.
[b]Byrne, J. A. (2002a, July 29). No excuses for Enron's board. *BusinessWeek*, pp. 50–51.
[c]Byrne, J. A. (2002b, August 12). Fall from grace. *BusinessWeek*, pp. 51–56.
[d]Raven, B. H., & Rubin, J. Z. (1976). *Social psychology: People in groups.* New York: John Wiley & Sons.
[e]Huseman, R. C., & Driver, R. W. (1979). Groupthink: Implications for small group decision making in business. In R. Huseman & A. Carroll (Eds.), *Readings in Organizational Behavior* (pp. 100–110). Boston: Allyn & Bacon.
[f]Wolinsky, H. (1998, November 11). Report calls AMA a house divided. *Chicago Sun-Times*, p. 72.
[g]ABA Banking Journal (1985, July). Hutton aftermath: A violation of business ethics or downright fraud? Computers and operations section, p. 30.
[h]Sims, R. R. (1992). Linking groupthink to unethical behavior in organizations. *Journal of Business Ethics, 11*(9), 651–662.

decision that all can agree to.[28] Conformity pressures can lead decision makers to censor their misgivings, ignore outside information, feel too confident, and adopt an attitude of invulnerability.

Symptoms of groupthink cannot be easily assessed by outside observers. Rather, most groupthink symptoms represent private feelings or beliefs held by group members or behaviors performed in private. Three key symptoms of groupthink take root and blossom in groups that succumb to pressures of reaching unanimity:

- *Overestimation of the group:* Members of the group regard themselves as invulnerable and, at the same time, morally correct. This lethal combination can lead decision makers to believe they are exempt from standards.
- *Close-mindedness:* Members of the group engage in collective rationalization, often accompanied by stereotyping outgroup members. Teams that develop norms of open-mindedness create more knowledge.[29]
- *Pressures toward uniformity:* There is a strong intolerance in a groupthink situation for diversity of opinion. Dissenters are subject to enormous social pressure. This often leads group members to suppress their reservations.

Deficits arising from groupthink can lead to many shortcomings in the decision-making process. Consider, for example, the following lapses that often accompany groupthink:

- Incomplete survey of alternatives
- Incomplete survey of objectives
- Failure to reexamine alternatives
- Failure to examine preferred choices
- Selection bias
- Poor information search
- Failure to create contingency plans

Each of these behaviors thwarts rational decision making.

Learning from History

Consider two decisions made by the same U.S. presidential cabinet—the Kennedy administration. The Kennedy cabinet was responsible for the Bay of Pigs operation in 1961 and the Cuban Missile Crisis in 1962. The Bay of Pigs was a military operation concocted by the United States in an attempt to overthrow Fidel Castro, the leader of Cuba. The Bay of Pigs is often seen as one of the worst foreign policy mistakes in U.S. history. The operation was regarded as a disaster of epic proportions, resulting in the loss of lives and the disruption of foreign policy. It is also puzzling because the invasion, in retrospect, seemed to have been poorly planned and poorly implemented, yet it was led by people whose individual talents seemed to make them eminently qualified to carry out an operation of that sort. In contrast, Kennedy's response to the Cuban Missile Crisis was regarded as a great international policy success. These examples, from the same organizational context and team, make an important point: Even smart and highly motivated people can make disastrous decisions under certain conditions. Kennedy's cabinet fell prey to groupthink in the Bay of Pigs decision, but not in the Cuban Missile Crisis.

---

[28]Ibid.
[29]Mitchell, R., Boyle, B., & Nicholas, S. (2009). The impact of goal structure in team knowledge creation. *Group Processes & Intergroup Relations, 12*(5), 639–651.

A number of detailed historical analyses have been performed comparing these two histor-ical examples, as well as several others.[30] Some sharp differences distinguish groupthink from vigilant decision making.

Exhibit 7-8 summarizes three kinds of critical evidence: (1) factors that may lead to group-think; (2) factors that may promote sound decision making; and (3) factors that do not seem to induce groupthink. We focus on leader behavior and team member behavior. Leader behavior that is associated with too much concern for political ramifications, or the analysis of alternatives in terms of their political repercussions, is a key determinant of groupthink. Similarly, when groups are overly concerned with their political image, they may not make sound decisions.

In terms of preventive conditions, the behavior of the team has a greater impact on the development of groupthink than does leader behavior. Sound group decision making can be achieved through task orientation, flexibility, less centralization, norms of openness, encouraging dissent, focus on shared goals, and realizing that trade-offs are necessary.

How to Avoid Groupthink

The empirical evidence for groupthink does not support some of the key predictions of the model.[31] Most of the "groupthink" phenomena (e.g., close-mindedness) occur in a far wider range of settings than originally believed. In this section, we identify some specific steps leaders can take to prevent groupthink. Prevention is predicated on two broad goals: The stimulation of constructive, intellectual conflict and the reduction of concerns about how the group is viewed by others—a kind of conformity pressure. We focus primarily on team design factors because those are the ones managers have the greatest control over. None of these can guarantee success, but they can be effective in encouraging vigilant decision making.

MONITOR TEAM SIZE   Larger teams are more likely to fall prey to groupthink.[32] People grow more intimidated and hesitant as team size increases. Teams with more than 10 members may feel less personal responsibility for team outcomes.

PROVIDE A FACE-SAVING MECHANISM FOR TEAMS   A small team that has the respect and support of their organization would seem to be in an ideal position to make effective decisions. Yet often, they fail to do so. One reason is that they are concerned with how their decision will be viewed by others. Many teams are afraid of being blamed for poor decisions—even decisions for which it would have been impossible to predict the outcome. Often, face-saving concerns pre-vent people from changing course, even when the current course is clearly doubtful. Teams that are given an excuse for poor performance before knowing the outcome of their decision are less likely to succumb to groupthink than teams that do not have an excuse.[33]

[30]Kramer, R. M. (1999). Social uncertainty and collective paranoia in knowledge communities: Thinking and acting in the shadow of doubt. In L. Thompson, J. Levine, & D. Messick (Eds.), *Social cognition in organizations: The manage-ment of knowledge.* Mahwah, NJ: Lawrence Erlbaum Associates; Peterson, R. S., Owens, P. D., Tetlock, P. E., Fan, E. T., & Martorana, P. (1998). Group dynamics in top management teams: Groupthink, vigilance, and alternative models of organizational failure and success. *Organizational Behavior and Human Decision Processes, 73,* 272–305.

[31]Baron, R. (2006). So right it's wrong: Groupthink and the ubiquitous nature of polarized group decision making. University of Iowa, manuscript.

[32]McCauley, C. (1998). Groupthink dynamics in Janis's theory of groupthink: Backward and forward. *Organizational Behavior and Human Decision Processes, 73*(2–3), 142–162.

[33]Turner, M. E., Probasco, P., Pratkanis, A. R., & Leve, C. (1992). Threat, cohesion, and group effectiveness: Testing a social identity maintenance perspective on groupthink. *Journal of Personality and Social Psychology, 63,* 781–796.

EXHIBIT 7-8 Precipitating and Preventative Conditions for the Development of Groupthink

Conditions	Leader Behavior and Cognition	Team Behavior and Cognition
Precipitous conditions *(likely to lead to group-think)*	• Narrow, defective appraisal of options • Analysis of options in terms of political repercussions • Concern about image and reputation • Loss-avoidance strategy	• Rigidity • Conformity • View roles in political terms (protecting political capital and status) • Large team size • Team members feel sense of social identification with team** • Group interaction and discussion must produce or reveal an emerging or dominant group norm** • Low self-efficacy, in which group members lack confidence in their ability to reach a satisfactory resolution** • Perceived threat to social identity
Preventative conditions *(likely to engender effective decision making)*	• Being explicit and direct about policy preferences allows the team to know immediately where the leader stands	• Task orientation • Intellectual flexibility • Less consciousness of crisis • Less pessimism • Less corruption (i.e., more concerned with observing correct rules and procedures) • Less centralization • Openness and candidness • Adjustment to failing policies in timely fashion • Genuine commitment to solving problems • Encouraging dissent • Acting decisively in emergencies • Attuned to changes in environment • Focus on shared goals • Realization that trade-offs are necessary • Ability to improvise solutions to unexpected events
Inconclusive conditions *(unlikely to make much of a difference)*	• Strong, opinionated leadership	• Risk taking • Cohesion • Internal debate

Source: Derived from: Tetlock, P., Peterson, R., McGuire, C., Chang, S., & Feld, P. (1992). Assessing political group dynamics: The test of the groupthink model. *Journal of Personality and Social Psychology, 63,* 403–425.

** Derived from: Baron, R. (2006). So right its wrong: Groupthink and the ubiquitous nature of polarized group decision making. Manuscript, University of Iowa, Iowa.

THE RISK TECHNIQUE   The risk technique is a structured discussion situation designed to reduce group members' fears about making decisions.[34] The discussion is structured so that team members talk about the dangers or risks involved in a decision and delay discussion of potential gains. Following this is a discussion of controls or mechanisms for dealing with the risks or dangers. The goal is to create an atmosphere in which team members can express doubts and raise criticisms without fear of rejection or hostility from the team. One way is to have a facilitator play the role of devil's advocate for a particular decision. The mere expression of doubt about an idea or plan by one person may liberate others to raise doubts and concerns. A second method may be to have members privately convey their concerns or doubts and then post this information in an unidentifiable manner. Again, this liberates members to talk about their doubts.

INVITE DIFFERENT PERSPECTIVES   In this technique, team members assume the perspective of other constituencies with a stake in the decision.[35] In 1986, the space shuttle *Challenger* exploded after liftoff due to a major malfunction regarding the booster rockets and, in particular, O-ring failure. Roger Boisjoly, an engineer who tried to halt the flight in 1986 because he was aware of the likely trouble, said later, "I received cold stares . . . with looks as if to say, 'Go away and don't bother us with the facts.' No one in management wanted to discuss the facts; they just would not respond verbally to . . . me. I felt totally helpless and that further argument was fruitless, so I, too, stopped pressing my case."[36] In the Challenger incident, the federal government, local citizens, space crew families, astronomers, and so on, all assumed the roles of "group members." Although the Challenger disaster happened in large part because of poor understanding of how to interpret statistical data, the key point of adopting different perspectives is to create a mechanism that will instigate thinking more carefully about problems, which could prompt these groups to reconsider evidence.

The absence of differing perspectives has also been identified as a root cause of the political corruption in Illinois. Democratic Governor Rod Blagojevich was arrested in 2008 on federal charges in which he conspired to sell his office as well as sell the U.S. Senate seat vacated by President Barack Obama. The governor and his chief of staff, John Harris, were simultaneously charged with conspiracy to commit wire fraud and solicitation to commit bribery as part of a scheme to shakedown campaign donors and politicians for high-paying posts and millions of dollars in campaign contributions.[37]

When it comes to different perspectives, those persons offering the counterpoint should prepare as they would if they were working on a court case—in other words, they should assemble data and evidence, as opposed to personal opinions.[38] The naysayers should not point fingers or say that someone has "screwed up." Rather, it is better to take the "we have a problem" approach.[39]

---

[34]Maier, N. R. F. (1952). *Principles of human relations, applications to management.* New York: John Wiley & Sons.
[35]Turner, M. E., & Pratkanis, A. R. (1998). A social identity maintenance model of groupthink. *Organizational Behavior and Human Decision Processes, 73*(2–3), 210–235.
[36]Boisjoly, R. M. (1987, December 13–18). *Ethical decisions—Morton Thiokol and the space shuttle Challenger disaster* (p. 7). Speech presented at the American Society of Mechanical Engineers, Winter Annual Meeting, Boston, MA, USA.
[37]Coen, J., Pearson, R., Chase, J., & Kidwell, D. (2008, December 10). Feds arrest Gov. Blagojevich to stop . . . —A political "crime spree"—Governor faces shocking array of charges—topped by accusations he tried to auction a U.S. Senate seat. *Chicago Tribune*, p. 1.
[38]Kirsner, S. (2002, September). How to get bad news to the top. *Fast Company,* p. 56.
[39]Ibid.

APPOINT A DEVIL'S ADVOCATE   By the time that upper management is wedded to a particular plan or point of view, they are often impervious to evidence that is questionable or even downright contradictory. To make matters worse, those around them—often subordinates—don't want to challenge management's beliefs. This is why some teams institute a special "devil's advocate" responsibility to members of the team. Teams that anticipate having to refute counterarguments are less likely to engage in confirmatory information processing as compared to teams that anticipate having to give reasons for their decision.[40] Winston Churchill knew how to combat groupthink and yes-men. Worried that his larger-than-life image would deter subordinates from bringing him the truth, he instituted a unit outside his chain of command, called the "statistical office," whose key job was to bring him the bleakest, most gut-wrenching facts. Similarly, authors of the book *How Companies Lie* suggest that "counterpointers" be appointed in teams, whose chief function is to ask the rudest possible questions.[41]

Whereas a devil's advocate procedure can be effective, it is **contrived** dissent. It is better for a team to have **genuine** dissent.[42] For example, when businesspeople made investment decisions, genuine dissent was more effective than contrived dissent in avoiding confirmatory decision making.[43] Genuine dissent is superior to contrived dissent or no dissent at all in terms of stimulating original ideas, considering opposing positions, and changing attitudes.[44]

STRUCTURE DISCUSSION PRINCIPLES   The goal of structured discussion principles is to delay solution selection and to increase the problem-solving phase. This prevents premature closure on a solution and extends problem analysis and evaluation. For example, teams may be given guidelines that emphasize continued solicitations of solutions, protection of individuals from criticism, keeping the discussion problem centered, and listing all solutions before evaluating them.[45]

ESTABLISH PROCEDURES FOR PROTECTING ALTERNATIVE VIEWPOINTS   Although teams can generate high-quality decision alternatives, they frequently fail to adopt them as preferred solutions.[46] Most problems that teams face are not simple, "eureka" types of decisions, in which the correct answer is obvious once it is put on the table. Rather, team members must convince others about the correctness of their views. This is difficult when conformity pressure exists and when team members have publicly committed to a particular course of action. For these reasons, it can be useful to instruct members to record all alternatives suggested during each meeting.

---

[40]Mojzisch, A., Schulz-Hardt, S., Kerschreiter, R., & Frey, D. (2008). Combined effects of knowledge about others' opinions and anticipation of group discussion on confirmatory information search. *Small Group Research, 39*(2), 203–223.

[41]Schroth, R. J., & Elliott, A. L. (2002). *How companies lie: Why Enron is just the tip of the iceberg.* New York: Crown Business.

[42]Schulz-Hardt, S., Jochims, M., & Frey, D. (2002). Productive conflict in group decision making: Genuine and contrived dissent as strategies to counteract biased decision making. *Organizational Behavior and Human Decision Processes, 88*, 563–586.

[43]Ibid.

[44]Nemeth, C., Connell, J., Rogers, J., & Brown, K. (2001). Improving decision making by means of dissent. *Journal of Applied Social Psychology, 31*(1), 48–58; Nemeth, C., Brown, K., & Rogers, J. (2001). Devil's advocate versus authentic dissent: Simulating quantity and quality. *European Journal of Social Psychology, 31*, 707–720.

[45]Maier, *Principles of human relations, applications to management.*

[46]Janis, *Victims of groupthink* (2nd ed.), p. 172; Turner, Probasco, Pratkanis, & Leve, "Threat, cohesion, and group effectiveness," p. 176.

SECOND SOLUTION   This technique requires teams to identify a second solution or decision recommendation as an alternative to their first choice. This enhances the problem-solving and idea-generation phases, as well as performance quality.[47]

BEWARE OF TIME PRESSURE   Time pressure acts as a stressor on teams, and stress impairs the effectiveness of team decision making.[48]

Moral principles are more likely to guide decisions for the distant future than for the immediate future, whereas difficulty, cost, and situational pressures are more likely to be important in near future decisions. Managers are more likely to compromise their principles in decisions regarding near future actions compared with distant future actions.[49]

DECISION-MAKING PITFALL 2: ESCALATION OF COMMITMENT

Coca-Cola's decision to introduce New Coke in 1985 was eventually recognized as a mistake and reversed. Do such clear failures prompt teams to revisit their decision-making process and improve upon it? Not necessarily. In fact, under some conditions, teams will persist with a losing course of action, even in the face of clear evidence to the contrary. This is known as the **escalation of commitment** phenomenon.

Consider the following decision situations.

- A senior marketing manager at a major pet food corporation continued to promote a specific brand, despite clear evidence that the brand was losing market share to its competitors.
- A company continued to invest in a manager who was known to have handled many situations poorly and received consistently subpar 360-degree evaluations.
- Quaker Oats continued to push Snapple, even though its market share dropped staggeringly.
- When the stock market tide is running, wildly enthusiastic investors will bid up companies' stock prices to levels known to be too high, in the certainty that they can "only go up."

EXHIBIT 7-9 New Product Investment Decision

As the president of an airline company, you have invested $10 million of the company's money into a research project. The purpose was to build a plane that would not be detected by conventional radar, in other words, a radar-blank plane. When the project is 90 percent completed, another firm begins marketing a plane that cannot be detected by radar. Also, it is apparent that their plane is much faster and far more economical than the plane your company is building. The question is: Should you invest the last 10 percent of the research funds to finish your radar-blank plane?

☐ Yes, invest the money.
☐ No, drop the project.

Source: Arkes, H. R., & Blumer, C. (1985). The psychology of sunk cost. *Organizational Behavior and Human Decision Process, 35*(1), 124–129.

---

[47]Hoffman, L. R., & Maier, N. R. F. (1966). An experimental reexamination of the similarity-attraction hypothesis. *Journal of Personality and Social Psychology, 3*, 145–152.
[48]Morgan, B. B., & Bowers, C. A. (1995). Teamwork stress: Implications for team decision making. In R. A. Guzzo & E. Salas (Eds.), *Team effectiveness and decision making in organizations* (pp. 262–290). San Francisco, CA: Jossey-Bass.
[49]Liberman, N., & Trope, Y. (1998). The role of feasibility and desirability considerations in near and distant future decisions: A test of temporal construal theory. *Journal of Personality and Social Psychology, 75*(1), 5–18.

Two years later, they dump these companies at any price, believing with equal certainty that they are becoming worthless.[50]

- A company continued to drill for oil, despite being unable to turn a profit on drilling efforts in the past 3 years.
- John R. Silber, a previous president of Boston University, decided to invest in Seragen, a biotechnology company with a promising cancer drug. After an investment of $1.7 million over 6 years, the value was $43,000.[51]

In all these situations, individuals and teams committed further resources to what eventually proved to be a failing course of action. In most cases, the situation does not turn into a problem for a while. The situation becomes an escalation dilemma when the persons involved in the decision would make a different decision if they had not been involved up until that point, or when other objective persons would not choose that course of action. In escalation situations, a decision is made to commit further resources to "turn the situation around." This process may repeat and escalate several times as additional resources are invested. The bigger the investment and the more severe the possible loss, the more prone people are to try to turn things around. Consider the situation faced by Lyndon Johnson during the early stage of the Vietnam War. Johnson received the following memo from George Ball, then undersecretary of state:

> The decision you face now is crucial. Once large numbers of U.S. troops are committed to direct combat, they will begin to take heavy casualties in a war they are ill-equipped to fight in a noncooperative if not downright hostile countryside. Once we suffer large casualties, we will have started a well-nigh irreversible process. Our involvement will be so great that we cannot—without national humiliation—stop short of achieving our complete objectives. Of the two possibilities I think humiliation will be more likely than the achievement of our objectives—even after we have paid terrible costs.[52]

The escalation of commitment process is illustrated in Exhibit 7-10. In the first stage of the escalation of commitment, a decision-making team is confronted with questionable or negative outcomes (e.g., a price drop, decreasing market share, poor performance evaluations, or a malfunction). This external event prompts a reexamination of the team's current course of action, in which the utility of continuing is weighed against the utility of withdrawing or changing course. This decision determines the team's commitment to its current course of action. If commitment is low, the team may withdraw from the project and assume its losses. If commitment is high, however, the team will continue commitment and continue to cycle through the decision stages. There are four key processes involved in the escalation of commitment cycle: project-related determinants, psychological determinants, social determinants, and structural determinants.[53]

---

[50]Train, J. (1995, June 24). Learning from financial disaster. *Financial Times,* p. II.

[51]Barboza, D. (1998, September 20). Loving a stock, not wisely, but too well. *New York Times,* Section 3, p. 1.

[52]Sheehan, N. (1971). The Pentagon papers: As published by the *New York Times,* based on the investigative reporting by Neil Sheehan, written by Neil Sheehan [and others] (p. 450). Articles and documents edited by G. Gold, A. M. Siegal, & S. Abt. New York, Toronto: Bantam.

[53]Ross, J., & Staw, B. M. (1993, August). Organizational escalation and exit: Lessons from the Shoreham Nuclear Power Plant. *Academy of Management Journal, 36*(4), 701–732.

EXHIBIT 7-10 Escalation of Commitment

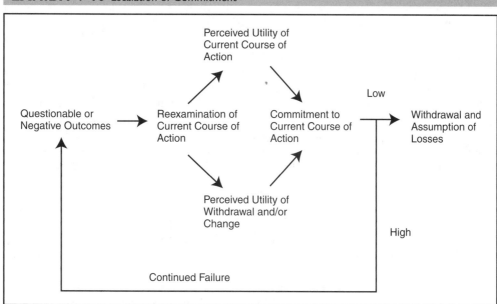

Source: Adapted from Ross, J., & Staw, B. M. (1993). Organizational escalation and exit: Lessons from the Shoreham Nuclear Power Plant. *Academy of Management Journal, 36*(4), 701–732.

Project Determinants

Project determinants are the objective features of the situation. Upon receiving negative feed-back, team members ask whether the perceived setback is permanent or temporary (e.g., is reduced market share a meaningful trend or a simple perturbation in a noisy system?). If it is perceived to be temporary, there may appear to be little reason to reverse course. Then, when considering whether to increase investment in the project or commit more time and energy, the team is essentially asking whether it wishes to escalate its commitment. Of course, this may often be the right choice, but it should be clear that such decisions also make it harder for the team to terminate that course of action if results continue to be poor.

Psychological Determinants

Psychological determinants refer to the cognitive and motivational factors that propel people to continue with a chosen course of action. When managers or teams learn that the outcomes of a project may be negative, they should ask themselves the following questions regarding their own involvement in the process:

WHAT ARE THE PERSONAL REWARDS FOR ME IN THIS PROJECT?   In many cases, the process of the project itself, rather than the outcome of the project, becomes the reason for continuing the project. This leads to a self-perpetuating reinforcement trap, wherein the rewards for continuing are not aligned with organizational objectives. Ironically, people who have high, rather than low, self-esteem are more likely to become victimized by psychological forces—people with high self-esteem have much more invested in their ego and its maintenance than those with low self-esteem.

ARE MY EGO AND THE TEAM'S REPUTATION ON THE LINE?   "If I pull out of this project, would I feel stupid? Do I worry that other people would judge me to be stupid?" Ego protection often becomes a higher priority than the success of the project. When managers feel personally responsible for a decision, monetary allocations to the project increase at a much higher rate than when managers do not feel responsible for the initial decision.[54]

When managers personally oversee a project, they attempt to ensure that the project has every chance of success (e.g., by allocating more resources to it). After all, that is their job. A manager who works on a project from beginning to end is going to know more about it and may be in a better position to judge it. Furthermore, personal commitment is essential for the success of many projects. Whereas it is certainly good to nurture projects so that they have their best chance of survival, it is nearly impossible for most managers to be completely objective. This is where it is important to have clear, unbiased criteria by which to evaluate the success of a project.

Social Determinants

Most people want others to approve of them, accept them, and respect them. Consequently, they engage in actions and behaviors that they think will please most of the people most of the time, perhaps at the expense of doing the right thing, which may not be popular.

The need for approval and liking may be especially heightened among groups composed of friends. Indeed, groups of longtime friends are more likely to continue to invest in a losing course of action (41 percent) than groups composed of unacquainted persons (16 percent) when groups do not have buy-in from relevant organizational authorities. In contrast, when they are respected by their organization, groups of friends are extremely deft at extracting themselves from failing courses of action.[55] The greater the group's sense of social identity, the more likely the group is to escalate commitment to an unreasonable course of action. For example, teams in a city council simulation, faced with an important budget allocation decision regarding a playground project, wore either team name tags (high social identity) or personal name tags (low social identity).[56] Groups that were stronger in social identity showed greater escalation of commitment to the ill-fated playground project.

Structural Determinants

A project can itself become institutionalized, removing it from critical evaluation. It becomes impossible for teams to consider removal or extinction of the project. Political support can also keep a project alive that should be terminated.

Avoiding Escalation of Commitment to a Losing Course of Action

Most teams do not realize that they are in an escalation dilemma until it is too late. In most escalation dilemmas, the team might have some early "wins" that reinforce the initial decision. How can a team best exit an escalation dilemma?

---

[54]Staw, B. H. (1976). Knee-deep in the big muddy: A study of escalating commitment to a chosen course of action. *Organizational Behavior and Human Decision Processes, 16*(1), 27–44.

[55]Thompson, L., Kray, L., & Lind, A. (1998). Cohesion and respect: An examination of group decision making in social and escalation dilemmas. *Journal of Experimental Social Psychology, 34*, 289–311.

[56]Dietz-Uhler, B. (1996). The escalation of commitment in political decision making groups: A social identity approach. *European Journal of Social Psychology, 26*, 611–629.

The best advice is to adopt a policy of risk management: Be aware of the risks involved in the decision, learn how to best manage these risks, and set limits, effectively capping losses at a tolerable level. It is also important to find ways to get information and feedback on the project from a different perspective. More specifically:

SET LIMITS   Ideally, a team should determine at the outset what criteria and performance standards justify continued investment in the project or program in question.

AVOID THE BYSTANDER EFFECT   In many situations, especially ambiguous ones, people are not sure how to behave, and do nothing because they don't want to appear foolish. This dynamic explains the bystander effect, or the tendency to not help others who obviously need help in emergency situations.[57] If team members have well-defined, predetermined limits, they need not try to interpret others' behavior; they can refer to their own judgment and act upon it.

AVOID TUNNEL VISION   Get several perspectives on the problem. Ask people who are not personally involved in the situation for their appraisal. Be careful not to bias their evaluation with your own views, hopes, expectations, or other details, such as the cost of extricating the team from the situation, because that will only predispose them toward the team's point of view.

RECOGNIZE SUNK COSTS   Probably the most powerful way to avoid escalation of commitment is to simply recognize and accept sunk costs. **Sunk costs** are resources, such as money and time, previously invested that cannot be recovered. If you were making the initial decision today, would you make the investment currently under consideration (as a continuing investment), or would you choose another course of action? If the decision is not one that you would choose anew, you might want to start thinking about how to terminate the project and move to the next one. For example, Microsoft accepted their sunk costs when they pulled the plug on "Windows Live Expo" in 2008 (after launching it 2 years before to compete with Craigslist). A hard look at the numbers revealed that the decision was not paying off.[58]

AVOID BAD MOOD   Unpleasant emotional states are often implicated in poor decision making.[59] Negative affect (such as bad mood, anger, and embarrassment) leads to nonoptimal courses of action—holding out the hope for some highly positive but risky outcome. When people are upset, they tend to choose high-risk, high-payoff options.[60]

EXTERNAL REVIEW   In some cases, it is necessary to remove or replace the original decision makers from deliberations precisely because they are biased. One way to do this is with an external review of departments.

---

[57]Latone, B., & Darley, J. M. (1970). *The unresponsive bystander: Why doesn't he help?* New York: Appleton-Century-Crofts.
[58]King, R. (2008, July 11). 10 web 2.0 ideas that failed. *Fast Company.* fastcompany.com
[59]Baumeister, R. F., & Scher, S. J. (1988). Self-defeating behavior patterns among normal individuals. *Psychological Bulletin, 104,* 3–22.
[60]Leith, K. P., & Baumeister, R. F. (1996). Why do bad moods increase self-defeating behavior? Emotion, risk-taking, and self-regulation. *Journal of Personality and Social Psychology, 71*(6), 1250–1267.

DECISION-MAKING PITFALL 3: THE ABILENE PARADOX

The **Abilene paradox** results from group members' desire to avoid conflict and reach consensus at all costs.[61] The Abilene paradox is a form of **pluralistic ignorance:** Group members adopt a position because they feel other members desire it; team members don't challenge one another because they want to avoid conflict or achieve consensus. Although this is a kind of "expectational

---

EXHIBIT 7-11   The Abilene Paradox

The July afternoon in Coleman, Texas (population 5,607), was particularly hot—104 degrees as measured by the Walgreen's Rexall Ex-Lax temperature gauge. In addition, the wind was blowing fine-grained West Texas topsoil through the house. But the afternoon was still tolerable—even potentially enjoyable. There was a fan going on the back porch; there was cold lemonade; and finally, there was entertainment. Dominoes. Perfect for the conditions. The game required little more physical exertion than an occasional mumbled comment, "Shuffle 'em," and an unhurried movement of the arm to place the spots in the appropriate perspective on the table. All in all, it had the markings of an agreeable Sunday afternoon in Coleman—that is, it was until my father-in-law suddenly said, "Let's get in the car and go to Abilene and have dinner at the cafeteria."

I thought, "What, go to Abilene? Fifty-three miles? In this dust storm and heat? And in an un-air-conditioned 1958 Buick?"

But my wife chimed in with "Sounds like a great idea. I'd like to go. How about you, Jerry?" Since my own preferences were obviously out of step with the rest I replied, "Sounds good to me," and added, "I just hope your mother wants to go."

"Of course I want to go," said my mother-in-law. "I haven't been to Abilene in a long time."

So into the car and off to Abilene we went. My predictions were fulfilled. The heat was brutal. We were coated with a fine layer of dust that was cemented with perspiration by the time we arrived. The food at the cafeteria provided first-rate testimonial material for antacid commercials.

Some four hours and 106 miles later we returned to Coleman, hot and exhausted. We sat in front of the fan for a long time in silence. Then, both to be sociable and to break the silence, I said, "It was a great trip, wasn't it?"

No one spoke. Finally my mother-in-law said, with some irritation, "Well, to tell the truth, I really didn't enjoy it much and would rather have stayed here. I just went along because the three of you were so enthusiastic about going. I wouldn't have gone if you all hadn't pressured me into it."

I couldn't believe it. "What do you mean 'you all'?" I said. "Don't put me in the 'you all' group. I was delighted to be doing what we were doing. I didn't want to go. I only went to satisfy the rest of you. You're the culprits."

My wife looked shocked. "Don't call me a culprit. You and Daddy and Mama were the ones who wanted to go. I just went along to be sociable and to keep you happy. I would have had to be crazy to want to go out in heat like that."

Her father entered the conversation abruptly. "Hell!" he said.

He proceeded to expand on what was already absolutely clear. "Listen, I never wanted to go to Abilene. I just thought you might be bored. You visit so seldom I wanted to be sure you enjoyed it. I would have preferred to play another game of dominoes and eat the leftovers in the icebox."

After the outburst of recrimination we all sat back in silence. Here we were, four reasonably sensible people who, of our own volition, had just taken a 106-mile trip across a godforsaken desert in a furnace-like temperature through a cloud-like dust storm to eat unpalatable food at a hole-in-the-wall cafeteria in Abilene, when none of us had really wanted to go. In fact, to be more accurate, we'd done just the opposite of what we wanted to do. The whole situation simply didn't make sense.

Source: Harvey, J. (1974). The Abilene paradox: The management of agreement. *Organizational Dynamics, 3*(1), 63–80. © American Management Association International. Reprinted with permission.

---

[61]Harvey, J. (1974). The Abilene paradox: The management of agreement. *Organizational Dynamics, 3*(1), 63–80.

bubble"—a set of expectations about other people's expectations that could be burst if even one person expressed a contrary view—it can have a dramatic impact on the actual decision-making behavior of the team. The story in Exhibit 7-11 illustrates this dilemma.

To the extent that team members are more interested in consensus than debate, they may end up "in Abilene." Indeed, the mismanagement of agreement can be more problematic than the management of disagreement. This may seem counterintuitive, but the consequences are very real.

It may seem strange to think that intelligent people who are in private agreement may somehow fail to realize the commonality of their beliefs and end up in Abilene. However, it is easy to see how this can happen if members fail to communicate their beliefs to each other.

Quandaries like the Abilene paradox are easy to fall into. Strategies to avoid the situation include playing devil's advocate, careful questioning, and a commitment on the part of all team members to fully air their opinions as well as respectfully listen to others. Note that none of these requires team members to abandon consensus seeking as a goal—if that is indeed their goal. However, it does require that consensus actually reflect the true beliefs of the team.

What factors lead to problems like the Abilene paradox? In general, if individual team members are intimidated or feel that their efforts will not be worthwhile, then they are less likely to air or defend their viewpoints. This is called self-limiting behavior. According to a survey of 569 managers, there are six key causes of self-limiting behavior in teams:[62]

- *The presence of someone with expertise:* When team members perceive that another member of the team has expertise or is highly qualified to make a decision, they will self limit.
- *The presentation of a compelling argument:* Frequently, the timing of a coherent argument influences decision making, such as when the decision is made after a lot of fruitless discussion.
- *A lack of confidence in one's ability to contribute:* If team members feel unsure about their ability to meaningfully contribute to the decision, they will be inclined to self limit.
- *An unimportant or meaningless decision:* Unless the decision is seen as vital or important to the individual's well-being, there is a powerful tendency to adopt a "who cares" attitude.
- *Pressure from others to conform to the team's decision:* Roger Boisjoly reported that he felt incredible pressure from the NASA management team to conform.
- *A dysfunctional decision-making climate:* When team members believe that others are frustrated, indifferent, disorganized, or generally unwilling to commit themselves to making an effective decision, they are likely to self limit. Such a climate can be created in the early stages of a decision by inadvertent remarks such as, "this is a ridiculous task," "nothing's going to change, so why bother," and so on.

How to Avoid the Abilene Paradox

The following suggestions are taken from Harvey and Mulvey et al.[63]

---

[62]Mulvey, P. W., Veiga, J. F., & Elsass, P. M. (1996). When teammates raise a white flag. *Academy of Management Executive, 10*(1), 40–49.
[63]Harvey, "Abilene paradox," p. 186; Mulvey, Veiga, & Elsass, "When teammates raise a white flag," p. 188.

CONFRONT THE ISSUE IN A TEAM SETTING   The most straightforward approach involves meeting with the organization members who are key figures in the problem and its solution. The first step is for the individual who proposes a solution to state it and then be open to any and all feedback. For example:

> I want to talk with you about the research project. Although I have previously said things to the contrary, I frankly don't think it will work and I am very anxious about it. I suspect that others may feel the same, but I don't know. Anyway, I am concerned that we may end up misleading one another, and if we aren't careful, we may continue to work on a problem that none of us wants and that might even bankrupt us. That's why I need to know where the rest of you stand. I would appreciate any of your thoughts about the project. Do you think it can succeed?[64]

CONDUCT A PRIVATE VOTE   People often go along with what they think the team wants to do. Dissenting opinions are easier to express privately—distribute blank cards and ask team members to privately write their opinions. Guarantee them anonymity and then share the overall outcomes with the team.

MINIMIZE STATUS DIFFERENCES   High-status members are often at the center of communication, and lower-status members are likely to feel pressures to conform more quickly. Although this can be difficult to avoid, reassurances by senior members about the importance of frank and honest discussion reinforced by the elimination of status symbols, like dress, meeting place, and title, may be helpful. This did not happen during the collapse of Wall Street in September 2008. Before Bank of America lawyers signed off on the sale of Merrill Lynch to Bank of America, they told Merrill's lawyers that they wanted to know the size of the bonuses that Thain and his Merrill Lynch colleagues would collect at the end of the year. A page was ripped from a notebook, and the Merrill team scribbled eight-digit figures for each of Merrill's top five executives, including $40 million for Thain alone. Thain felt he deserved a hefty payout for his deal-making heroics. Then, an internal debate erupted, and high-ranking employees at Merrill were antagonized by Thain's overblown sense of entitlement. The episode revealed the rampant hubris and sense of entitlement embedded on Wall Street, foreshadowing the myriad problems that would eventually threaten the merger of the two beleaguered financial giants.[65]

UTILIZE THE SCIENTIFIC METHOD   When team members use the scientific method, they let the evidence make the decision, not their own beliefs.

PROVIDE A FORMAL FORUM FOR CONTROVERSIAL VIEWS   This may be achieved by segmenting the discussion into pros and cons. Debate must be legitimized. Members should not have to worry about whether it is appropriate to bring up contrary views; it should be expected and encouraged.

TAKE RESPONSIBILITY FOR FAILURE   It is important to create a climate in which teams can make mistakes, own up to them, and then move on without fear of recrimination. For example,

---

[64]Ibid.
[65]Story, L., & Creswell, J. (2009, February 8). For bank of America and Merrill, love was blind. *New York Times*, p. BU1.

Zappos leaders encourage their team to make mistakes.[66] The company employs a full-time life coach who will listen to grievances and gripes, or even offer career advice on how to move up—or out.

DECISION-MAKING PITFALL 4: GROUP POLARIZATION

Consider the case in Exhibit 7-12. Most people independently evaluating the problem state that the new company would need to have nearly a two-thirds probability of success before they would advise Mr. A to leave his current job and accept a new position.[67] What do you think happens when the same people discuss Mr. A's situation and are instructed to reach consensus?

You might expect the outcome of the team to be the same as the average of the individuals considered separately. However, this is not what happens. The group advises Mr. A to take the new job, even if it only has slightly better than a 50–50 chance of success! In other words, groups show a **risky shift**. After a group discussion, people who are already supportive of war become more supportive, people with an initial tendency toward racism become more racist, and people with a slight preference for one job candidate will advocate for that person more strongly.[68] In a field investigation that analyzed the decisions of federal district court judges, in the 1,500 cases where judges sat alone, they took an extreme course of action only 30 percent of the time, but when sitting in groups of three, extreme decision making doubled to 65 percent.[69]

Now consider a situation in which a company is deciding the highest odds of a drug contraindication that could be tolerated on the release of a new medicine. In this case, individual advisors are cautious, but when the same people are in a group, they collectively insist on even lower odds. Thus, they exhibit a **cautious shift**. Nearly 4 years after Merck & Co. took

---

EXHIBIT 7-12 Advice Question

Mr. A., an electrical engineer who is married and has one child, has been working for a large electronics corporation since graduating from college 5 years ago. He is assured of a lifetime job with a modest, though adequate, salary and liberal pension benefits upon retirement. On the other hand, it is very unlikely that his salary will increase much before he retires. While attending a convention, Mr. A. is offered a job with a small, newly founded company that has a highly uncertain future. The new job would pay more to start and would offer the possibility of a share in the ownership if the company survived the competition with larger firms.

    Imagine that you are advising Mr. A. What is the <u>lowest</u> probability or odds of the new company proving financially sound that you would consider acceptable to make it worthwhile for Mr. A. to take the new job? Before reading on, indicate your response on a probability scale from zero to 100 percent.

Wallach, M. A., & Kogan, N. (1961). Aspects of judgment and decision making: Interrelationships and change with age. *Behavioral Science, 6,* 23–31.

---

[66]O'Brien, J. M. (2009, January 22). The 10 commandments of zappos. Money.cnn.com
[67]Stoner, J. A. F. (1961). *A comparison of individual and group decisions involving risk.* Thesis, Massachusetts Institute of Technology.
[68]Main, E. C., & Walker, T. G. (1973). Choice shifts and extreme behavior: Judicial review in the federal courts. *Journal of Social Psychology. 91*(2), 215–221.
[69]Ibid.

the painkiller Vioxx off the market because of links to heart attacks and strokes, the new regulatory climate altered the landscape of drug development. In 2008, the FDA approved just 19 new medicines, the fewest in the previous 24 years, and announced about 75 new or revised "black-box" warnings about potential side effects—the agency's strongest—twice the number in 2004.[70]

Why are teams both more risky and more cautious than are individuals, considering the identical situation? The reason for this apparent disparity has to do with some of the peculiarities of group dynamics. Teams are not inherently more risky or cautious than individuals; rather they are more *extreme* than individuals. **Group polarization** is the tendency for group discussion to intensify group opinion, producing more extreme judgment than might be obtained by pooling the individuals' views separately (see Exhibit 7-13).

Group polarization is not simply a case of social compliance or a bandwagon effect. The same individuals display the polarization effect when queried privately after group discussion. This means that people really believe the group's decision—they have conformed inwardly! The polarization effect does not happen in nominal groups. The polarization effect grows stronger with time, meaning that the same person who was in a group discussion 2 weeks earlier will be even more extreme in his or her judgment.

There are two psychological explanations for group polarization: the need to be right and the need to be liked.

The Need to Be Right

Groups are presumed to have access to a broader range of decision-making resources and, hence, to be better equipped to make high-quality decisions than any person can alone. By pooling their different backgrounds, training, and experience, group members have at least the potential for working in a more informed fashion than would be the case were the decision left to an individual. People are **information dependent**—that is, they often lack information that another member

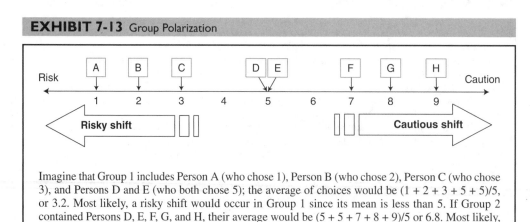

EXHIBIT 7-13 Group Polarization

Imagine that Group 1 includes Person A (who chose 1), Person B (who chose 2), Person C (who chose 3), and Persons D and E (who both chose 5); the average of choices would be (1 + 2 + 3 + 5 + 5)/5, or 3.2. Most likely, a risky shift would occur in Group 1 since its mean is less than 5. If Group 2 contained Persons D, E, F, G, and H, their average would be (5 + 5 + 7 + 8 + 9)/5 or 6.8. Most likely, a conservative shift would occur in Group 2 since its mean is closer to the caution pole.

Source: Adapted from Forsyth, D. R. (1983). *Group dynamics* (2nd ed.). Pacific Grove, CA: Brooks/Cole.

[70]Johnson, A., & Winslow, R. (2008, June 30). Drug makers say FDA safety focus is slowing new-medicine pipeline. *Wall Street Journal*, p. A1.

has. Consequently, individuals look to the team to provide information that they do not know. However, it can lead to problems when people treat others' opinions as facts and fail to question their validity. The need to be right, therefore, is the tendency to look to the group to define what reality is—and the more people who hold a particular opinion, the more right an answer appears to be. Whereas this information-seeking tendency would seem to be contradictory to the common information effect that we discussed in the previous chapter, the two processes are not inconsistent. The common information effect (and all of its undesirable consequences) are driven by a biased search for information. Conformity, or the adoption of group-level beliefs, is strongest when individuals feel unsure about their own position. **Informational influence** is likely to be stronger when people make private responses and communicate with the majority indirectly.[71]

The Need to Be Liked

Most people have a fundamental need to be accepted and approved of by others. One of the most straightforward ways to gain immediate acceptance in a group is to express attitudes consistent with those of the group members. Stated another way, most people like others who conform to their own beliefs. This means that people in groups will become more extreme in the direction of the group's general opinion, because attitudes that are sympathetic toward the group are most likely to be positively rewarded. The need to be liked refers to the tendency for people to agree with a group so that they can feel more like a part of that group. Statistical minority group members are much more preoccupied with their group membership and less happy than majority members.[72] **Normative influence**, or the need to be liked, is stronger when people make public responses and are face-to-face with a majority.[73]

Simply stated, people want to make the right decision and they want to be approved of by their team. Take the case concerning Mr. A, an electrical engineer. Most people are positively inclined when they agree to recommend to Mr. A that he seriously consider a job change. However, they vary greatly in their reasons for why Mr. A should change jobs. Someone in the group may feel that Mr. A should leave the secure job because it does not represent a sufficient challenge; others may think that Mr. A should leave the company because he should increase his standard of living. Thus, people feel that Mr. A should consider a move, but they have different (yet complementary) reasons supporting their belief. This is the rational type of conformity we discussed earlier. At the same time, members of the team want to be accepted—part of the socialization process we outlined in Chapter 4.

Conformity Pressure

The group polarization effect is related to conformity pressure. **Conformity** occurs when people bring their behavior into alignment with a group's expectations and beliefs. Although many people think their beliefs and behavior are based on their own free will, social behavior is strongly influenced by others. For a clear and surprising demonstration of the power of conformity pressure, see Exhibit 7-14.

---

[71]Bond, R. (2005). Group size and conformity. *Group Processes and Intergroup Relations, 8*(4), 331–354.
[72]Lucken, M., & Simon, B. (2005). Cognitive and affective experiences of minority and majority members: The role of group size, status, and power. *Journal of Personality and Social Psychology, 41*, 396–413.
[73]Bond, "Group size and conformity."

EXHIBIT 7-14 Conformity Pressure

Suppose that you are meeting with your team. The question facing your team is a simple one: Which of the three lines in panel 2 of Figure 6-5 is equal in length to the line in panel 1? The team leader seeks a group consensus. She begins by asking the colleague sitting to your left for his opinion. To your shock, your colleague chooses line 1; then, each of the other four team members selects line 1—even though line 2 is clearly correct. You begin to wonder whether you are losing your mind. Finally, it's your turn to decide. What do you do?

Most people who read this example find it nearly impossible to imagine that they would choose line 1, even if everyone else had. Yet 76 percent make an erroneous, conforming judgment (e.g., choose line 1) on at least one question; on average, people conform one-third of the time when others give the obviously incorrect answer.

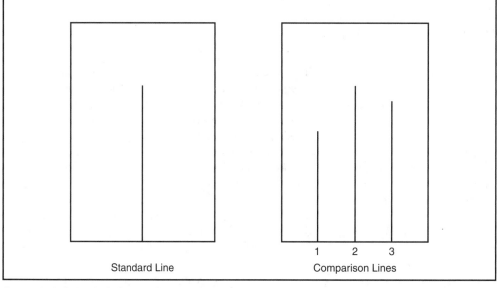

Standard Line   Comparison Lines

Source: Asch, S. E. (1956). Studies of independence and conformity: A minority of one against a unanimous majority. *Psychological Monographs, 70*(9), Whole No. 416.

Conformity is greater when the judgment or opinion issue is difficult and when people are uncertain. People are especially likely to conform if they face an otherwise unanimous group consensus.[74] Conformity is greater when people value and admire their team—rejection from a desirable group is very threatening.[75] When people are aware that another member of their team advocated an inferior solution to a problem, they are less likely to intervene if they are motivated to be *compatible* than if they are motivated to be *accurate*.[76] People are more willing to take a

[74]Asch, S. E. (1956). Studies of independence and conformity: A minority of one against a unanimous majority. *Psychological Monographs, 70*(9), Whole No. 416; Wilder, D. A., & Allen, V. L. (1977). Veridical social support, extreme social support, and conformity. *Representative Research in Social Psychology, 8*, 33–41.
[75]Back, K. W. (1951). Influence through social communication. *Journal of Abnormal Social Psychology, 46*, 9–23.
[76]Quinn, A., & Schlenker, B. (2002). Can accountability produce independence? Goals as determinants of the impact of accountability and conformity. *Personality and Social Psychology Bulletin, 28*(4), 472–483.

stand when they feel confident about their expertise, have high social status,[77] are strongly committed to their initial view,[78] and do not like or respect the people trying to influence them.[79]

Coupled with the need to be liked is the desire not to be *ostracized* from one's team. There is good reason for concern, because individuals who deviate from their team's opinion are more harshly evaluated than are those who conform.[80] A group may reject a deviant person even when they are not under pressure to reach complete consensus.[81] Apparently, holding a different opinion is enough to trigger dislike even when it does not directly block the group's goals. For this reason, people are more likely to conform to the majority when they respond publicly,[82] anticipate future interaction with other group members,[83] are less confident,[84] find the question under consideration to be ambiguous or difficult,[85] and are interdependent concerning rewards.[86] Ostracized team members experience a variety of deleterious effects; they don't like and trust their team, and this may ultimately harm group functioning.[87] Most managers dramatically underestimate the conformity pressures that operate in groups. Perhaps this is because people like to think of themselves as individualists who are not afraid to speak their own minds. However, conformity pressures in groups are real, and they affect the quality of team decision making. The key message for the manager is to anticipate conformity pressures in groups, to understand what drives it (i.e., the need to be liked and the desire to be right), and then to put into place group structures that will not allow conformity pressures to endanger the quality of group decision making.

DECISION-MAKING PITFALL 5: UNETHICAL DECISION MAKING

Unethical decision making can be small scale or affect the lives and welfare of hundreds of thousands of people. Financier Bernie Madoff defrauded thousands of people by committing fraud, theft, and money laundering in a huge ponzi scheme. At the time of his arrest, he claimed to manage $65 billion of investor money, but in reality there was just $1 billion.[88] Thousands of people were affected and lost their entire life savings. Unethical decision making shares many of the

---

[77]Harvey, O. J., & Consalvi, C. (1960). Status and conformity to pressure in informal groups. *Journal of Abnormal and Social Psychology, 60,* 182–187.

[78]Deutsch, M., & Gerard, H. B. (1955). A study of normative and informational social influence upon individual judgment. *Journal of Abnormal and Social Psychology, 51,* 629–636.

[79]Hogg, M. A. (1987). Social identity and group cohesiveness. In J. C. Turner, M. A. Hogg, P. J. Oakes, S. D. Reicher, & M. Wetherell (Eds.), *Rediscovering the social group: A self-categorization theory* (pp. 89–116). Oxford, UK: Basil Blackwell.

[80]Levine, J. M. (1989). Reaction to opinion deviance in small groups. In P. Paulus (Ed.), *Psychology of group influence* (2nd ed., pp. 187–231). Mahwah, NJ: Lawrence Erlbaum & Associates.

[81]Miller, C. E., Jackson, P., Mueller, J., & Schersching, C. (1987). Some social psychological effects of group decision rules. *Journal of Personality and Social Psychology, 52,* 325–332.

[82]Main & Walker, "Choice shifts and extreme behavior."

[83]Lewis, S. A., Langan, C. J., & Hollander, E. P. (1972). Expectation of future interaction and the choice of less desirable alternatives in conformity. *Sociometry, 35,* 440–447.

[84]Allen, V. L. (1965). Situational factors in conformity. In L. Berkowitz (Ed.), *Advances in experimental social psychology* (Vol. 2, pp. 267–299). New York: Academic Press.

[85]Tajfel, H., (Ed.). (1978). *Differentiation between social groups: Studies in the social psychology of intergroup relations.* New York: Academic Press.

[86]Deutsch & Gerard, "A study of normative and informational social influence upon individual judgment."

[87]Jones, E. E., Carter-Sowell, A. R., Kelly, J. R., & Williams, K. D. (2009). "I'm out of the loop": Ostracism through information exclusion. *Group Processes & Intergroup Relations, 12*(2), 157–174.

[88]Teather, D. (2009, June 30). Madoff case: Damned by judge and victims, fraudster will die behind bars: 150-year prison sentence for financier who cheated investors of $65B in one of Wall Street's biggest frauds. *The Guardian,* p. 2.

same dynamics involved in the other concepts we have discussed in this chapter, such as group-think. Groupthink can lead to a culture of unethical behavior within a company.[89] Groups lie more than individuals when deception is guaranteed to result in financial profit.[90] And, groups are more strategic than individuals in that they will adopt whatever course of action—deception or honesty—serves their financial interests.[91] However, teams are concerned about ethics; and value group morality more than competence or sociability.[92] Below, we consider some of the sit-uational triggers of unethical decision making. We resist the urge to explain all such occurrences of unethical decision making as a simple manifestation of evil personalities. Rather, we believe that certain conditions may act as enabling conditions for unethical behavior.

Rational Expectations Model

Undergirding virtually all economic theory and practice is the rational expectations model, also known as the **rational man model**. According to this model, people are fundamentally moti-vated to maximize their own utility, which has become equivalent to maximizing self-interest. So entrenched is this model in modern business analysis that to make any other assumption about human behavior is irrational, illogical, and flawed. However, the lay perception of the economic model has become somewhat of a caricature of the actual model in two important ways. First, people assume that others are more self-interested than they actually are. Second, people begin to view their own motivations as more driven by self-interest than is actually the case. This is referred to as the "norm of self interest and is so pervasive that people often 'invent' self-interested explanations of why they perform non-self-serving (or altruistic) acts, such as giving money to charity."[93] Even more disconcerting, people who take business courses are signifi-cantly more likely to engage in questionable and potentially unethical behaviors—for example, failing to return money that they find in the street, behaving competitively in a prisoner's dilemma game, and so on—than people who don't take business courses.[94]

Pluralistic Ignorance

Pluralistic ignorance, as discussed earlier in the Abilene paradox section, is the widely held belief that everyone else knows or believes something that we do not. A major reason that uneth-ical behavior is promulgated is the belief that "everyone else is doing it."

DESENSITIZATION   Another problem concerns desensitization of behavior. When someone first crosses the line of appropriate behavior, that person is extremely sensitized. However, once the line is crossed, the individual is desensitized, and the normal system of internal checks and balances is turned off. For example, despite the presence of a formal whistle-blowing policy at Apex Bank in Ireland, chairman William Trome borrowed huge amounts of money from the bank that he did not disclose. However, no one at the bank reported any suspicions of the

---

[89]Sims, R. R. (1992). Linking groupthink to unethical behavior in organizations. *Journal of Business Ethics, 11*(9), 651–662.
[90]Cohen, T. R., Gunia, B. C., Kim-Jun, S. Y., & Murnighan, J. K. (2009). Do groups lie more than individuals? Honesty & deception as a function of strategic self-interest. *Journal of Experimental Social Psychology, 45*, 1321–1324.
[91]Ibid.
[92]Leach, C. W., Ellemers, N., & Barreto, M. (2007). Group virtue: The importance of morality (vs. competence and sociability) in the positive evaluation of ingroups. *Journal of Personality and Social Psychology, 93*, 234–249.
[93]Miller, D. T. (1999). The norm of self-interest. *American Psychologist, 54*(12), 1053–1060.
[94]Frank, R. H., Gilovich, T., & Regan, D. T. (1993). Does studying economics prohibit cooperation? *Journal of Economic Perspectives, 7*(2), 159–171.

refinancing transactions that occurred shortly before and after the balance sheet date; and none of the random sampling of loans selected for audit ever included directors' loans.[95] The question, of course, is how to remedy or, ideally, prevent this situation. Consider the five steps below.

ACCOUNTABILITY FOR BEHAVIOR   To the extent that groups feel accountable for their behavior, they are more likely to behave ethically. For example, group members are more likely to compensate for the ethical transgression of an ingroup member when they are observed by others.[96] The committee on governmental affairs of the U.S. Senate discovered that there were almost no consequences for company directors who fail on the job. Their liability insurance is paid for by shareholders, but they are not held responsible for any damages. Perhaps this is why days before becoming the largest bankruptcy in U.S. history, Lehman Brothers rewarded departing executives with millions, and executives who feared for their bonuses in the company's last months were told not to worry. "Lehman was a company in which there was no accountability for failure," said Rep. Henry Waxman, D-Calif., chairman of the House Oversight and Government Reform Committee. Lehman Brothers CEO Richard Fuld depleted Lehman's capital reserves by over $10 billion through year-end bonuses, stock buybacks, and dividend payments. The federal government allowed Lehman to collapse on September 15, 2008, part of a series of financial failures that led to $700 billion government bailout of the nation's financial institutions.[97]

Most leaders want to take credit and responsibility for good news but pawn off bad news. It's a way of protecting the ego. When Bank of America CEO Kenneth Lewis led a takeover of Wall Street giant Merrill Lynch at the height of the U.S. financial crisis in 2008, it was celebrated by Lewis as a daring takeover. But soon shareholders began questioning whether Lewis paid too much for Merrill, whose losses were substantial. When Bank of America received a second $45 billion bailout by the federal government, share value evaporated and the board stripped Lewis of his chairmanship. He resigned in 2009.[98]

Accountability is the implicit or explicit expectation that one may be called on to justify one's beliefs, feelings, and actions to others.[99] Accountability implies that people who do not provide a satisfactory justification for their actions will suffer negative consequences. However, there are multiple forms and types of accountability, each with their own beneficial as well as detrimental effects on decision making. The following are considerations regarding accountability in organizational decision making.[100]

- *Accountability to an audience with known versus unknown views:* People who know what conclusion the ultimate audience wants to hear often conform. For example, financial-aid agents who do not know their audience's preferences match awards to needs effectively; agents who know their audience's preferences tell them what they want to hear (not what will actually meet their needs).[101]

[95]McNeal, A. (2009, August 1). Unethical deeds or outright fraud? *Internal Auditor, 66*(4), 71–75.

[96]Gino, F., Gu, J., & Zhong, C. (2009). Contagion or restitution? When bad apples can motivate ethical behavior. *Journal of Experimental Social Psychology, 45*, 1299–1302.

[97]Kroft, S. (2008, October 6). As Lehman collapsed, execs were rewarded. *Cbsnews.com*

[98]Story, L., & Dash, E. (2009, October 1). Bank of America chief to depart at year's end. *New York Times*, p. B1.

[99]Lerner, J. S., & Tetlock, P. E. (1999). Accounting for the effects of accountability. *Psychological Bulletin, 125*(2), 255–275.

[100]Ibid.

[101]Adelberg, S., & Batson, C. D. (1978). Accountability and helping: When needs exceed resources. *Journal of Personality and Social Psychology, 36*, 343–350.

- *Pre-versus post-decision accountability:* After people irrevocably commit themselves to a decision, they will attempt to justify their decisions. For example, people form less complex thoughts and hold more rigid and defensive views when they are accountable and express their attitudes.[102]
- *Outcome accountability versus process accountability:* Accountability for *outcomes* leads to greater escalation behavior, whereas accountability for *process* increases decision-making effectiveness.[103]
- *Legitimate versus illegitimate accountability:* If accountability is perceived as illegitimate—for example, intrusive and insulting—any beneficial effects of accountability may fail or backfire.[104]

REWARD MODEL   Hand in hand with accountability is the system for reward and promotion. As we noted in Chapter 3, reward systems shape behavior in organizations. French bank Societe Generale suffered a $7.2 billion trading loss when low-level trader, Jerome Kerviel, began making independent decisions presumably to fuel his insatiable greed. Jerome began making high-level, surreptitious moves as a result of unchecked ambition and overconfidence while he simultaneously lost touch with the goals and behaviors of his team members.[105]

APPROPRIATE ROLE MODELS   According to the trickle-down model of ethical decision making, leaders play a prominent role in influencing employees' propensity to be ethical and helpful.[106] Indeed, there is a direct, negative relationship between leadership and ethical behavior: The more ethical the leadership, the less unethical and less deviant the team's behavior.[107] Countrywide Financial was accused of a lack of oversight in the years leading up to the 2008 market collapse. Prior to that, the value of the company's portfolio rose more than $400 billion in six years. Former CEO Stanford Kurland advocated for the type of higher-risk loans that, in large numbers, went into default. Lawsuits against Countrywide accuse Kurland of instigating a culture shift that started in 2003, as the company popularized a type of loan that often came with low "teaser" interest rates and that, for some, became unaffordable when the low rate expired.[108]

ELIMINATE CONFLICTS OF INTEREST   Former Illinois Governor Rod Blagojevich essentially ran his public office like a professional criminal organization. Months of FBI surveillance of phone calls revealed stunning accounts of how he used his power for personal gain. This chief executive saw virtually every decision as another pay-for-play opportunity; "If I don't get what I want and I'm not satisfied with it, then I'll just take the Senate seat myself," said Blagojevich

---

[102]Tetlock, P. E., Skitka, L., & Boettger, R. (1989). Social and cognitive strategies for coping with accountability: Conformity, complexity and bolstering. *Journal of Personality and Social Psychology, 57*, 632–640.

[103]Doney, P. M., & Armstrong, G. M. (1996). Effects of accountability on symbolic information search and information analysis by organizational buyers. *Journal of the Academy of Marketing Science, 24*, 57–65.

[104]Lerner & Tetlock, "Accounting for the effects of accountability."

[105]Palfini, J. (2008, February 4). Societe Generale debacle: Losing touch could mean losing it all [Web log post]. blogs.bnet.com

[106]Brown, M. E., Trevino, L. K., & Harrison, D. A. (2005). Ethical leadership: A social learning perspective for construct development and testing. *Organizational Behavior and Human Decision Processes, 97*, 117-134.

[107]Mayer, D. M., Kuenzi, M., Greenbaum, R., Bardes, M., & Salvador, R. (2009). How low does ethical leadership flow? Test of a trickle-down model. *Organizational Behavior and Human Decision Processes, 108*(1), 1–13.

[108]Lipton, E. (2009, March 4). Ex-leaders of Countrywide profit from bad loans. *New York Times*, p. A1.

referring to his attempted sale of the vacated Obama Senate seat.[109] In addition to trying to scam the Senate seat, Blagojevich was charged with threatening to extort the Tribune Company.

CREATE CULTURES OF INTEGRITY   As we noted in Chapter 2, the culture of a team and organization is not under the direct control of upper management. Rather, it emerges as a result of design factors in the organization and the team. Even in the most tightly controlled, bureaucratic organizations, it is impossible to monitor the actions of every employee. This is where the cultural code is supposed to guide every team member to make the right decisions without supervision. The failure to discipline transgressions can be just as damaging as the failure to reward excellent behavior in teams. For example, when James DiBiasio of Ski.com got drunk for 3 days and hacked into the computers of his company, the CEO of Ski.Com decided not to pursue charges.[110]

Business cultures that lack the ability to take swift and decisive action run the risk of unethical behavior by default. In the steroid investigations in Major League Baseball, executives were accused of being slow to act when home run records were being shattered at a dizzying pace in the late 1990s and early 2000s and whispers began about illegal performance-enhancing drugs. When all-star New York Yankees infielder Alex Rodriguez acknowledged in 2009 that he used performance-enhancing drugs while playing for the Texas Rangers from 2001 to 2003, it cast doubt on the achievements of the player widely considered to be the best in baseball, as well as on the game itself reeling from numerous steroid controversies among its current or former stars. "I couldn't feel more regret and feel more sorry, because I have so much respect for this game and the people that follow us. And I have millions of fans out there who won't ever look at me the same," Rodriguez said. Rodriguez faced boos and taunts from visiting crowds throughout the 2009 baseball season.[111]

Conclusion

Teams make important decisions and some of them will not be good ones, despite the very best of intentions. It is unrealistic to suggest that poor decision making, or for that matter even disastrous decision making, is avoidable. The key message hearkens back to a point we made early in Chapter 1, which is to create an organization that can optimally learn from failure. Learning from failure is difficult when people suffer—especially innocent ones. The key for decision-making teams within organizations is to develop and use decision-making procedures, such as veto policies and preestablished criteria to guide decision making. All these decisions involve a certain level of risk, but that risk can be minimized. There is a clear difference between principled risk taking and unethical risk taking. Creating cultures of integrity involves ethical leadership from the top down and making sure that incentives for behavior do not encourage or reward unethical behavior.

---

[109]Saltonstall, D. (2008, December 10). *Illinois gov. Rod Blagojevich arrested in conspiracy to benefit from Obama's senate replacement.* nydailynews.com
[110]Kostigen, T. (2009, January 15). *The 10 most unethical people in business.* marketwatch.com
[111]Kepner, T. (2009, February 9). Rodriguez admits to use of performance enhancers. *New York Times*, p. A1.

CHAPTER

8

Conflict in Teams
Leveraging Differences to Create Opportunity

In 2008, Sarah Palin (then Governor of Alaska) was chosen to be the vice presidential candidate on the John McCain presidential ticket. On stage, the two projected an image of unity and collaboration. However, behind the scenes, there was tension. Several different issues contributed to the latent conflict that eventually became outright controversy. Resentment started to brew within the campaign early. Palin resisted coaching before her catastrophic Katie Couric interview. When Palin arrived at the Arizona Biltmore planning to deliver a speech before McCain's concession speech, she was told by senior McCain aides that it was not appropriate. Aides to John McCain disclosed details about having to dispatch Republican Party lawyers to retrieve Palin's expensive wardrobe purchases still in her possession after the election defeat. The volume and method of wardrobe purchases appear to have been hidden from McCain, and aides were "flabbergasted by the magnitude of spending" as the receipts for Neiman Marcus ($75K), Saks Fifth Avenue ($49K), and Bloomingdales ($5K) began trickling in. Palin aides tell a different story. She was "outraged" by the amount of money spent on her clothing and was "naïve" about what clothes cost. Palin was not pleased about what the aides had selected for her and did not wear many items. She was also not comfortable with the team that managed her appearances, and the strain worsened. When she was recorded talking to a Canadian comedian who pretended to be French president Nicolas Sarkozy, McCain aides were irate.[1]

The conflict within the Republican camp may have contributed to the defeat of the McCain–Palin ticket. Not surprisingly, team conflict is one of the top concerns of team management.[2] Many teams either actively avoid conflict and risk making "trips to Abilene" (as discussed in Chapter 7) or engage in personal, rather than principled, conflict. Some team leaders pride themselves on

---

[1]Reston, M., & Mehta, S. (2008, November 6). Election 2008: The republicans; *Palin, McCain* camps at odds. *Los Angeles Times*, p. A12.
[2]Thompson, L. (2010). Leading high impact teams: Tools for teams. Kellogg Executive program.

the fact that they never have conflict in their teams. We think these leaders do their teams a great disservice.

Differences in interests, perceptions, information, and preferences cannot be avoided, especially in teams that work together closely for extended periods of time. Conflict that is improperly managed may lead to hostility, performance deficits, and, in extreme cases, the dissolution of the team. Under some circumstances, conflict can benefit teamwork. At Google, team conflict is an accepted part of the creative process. "Organizations that exist for a long time almost always have strong cultures. "Google lives out loud . . . ," says Douglas Merrill, Google's CIO and VP of Engineering. "We argue about strategy and whether our products are good or bad. We argue about everything. But you want conflict to thrive in a supportive way. At heart, I'm an introvert, but I've learned to enjoy the give and take of ideas here. We work hard to protect people who argue."[3] Conflict can have positive consequences, such as enhancing creativity or fostering integrative solutions that reflect many points of view. Alternatively, conflict can thwart a team's effectiveness at all the levels of performance we identified in Chapter 2.

We distinguish different types of conflict in teams. We describe different styles and methods of conflict resolution. We discuss minority versus majority conflict in teams. We focus on specific interventions that teams and their leaders can take to proactively manage conflict.

TYPES OF CONFLICT

Before a team leader launches into conflict management mode, it is important to accurately diagnose the type of conflict that plagues the team. There are three distinct types of conflict: **relationship** conflict, **task** conflict, and **process** conflict (see Exhibit 8-1).[4]

Relationship conflict is personal, defensive, and resentful. Also known as **A-type conflict**, **emotional conflict**, or **affective conflict**,[5] it is rooted in anger, personal friction, personality clashes, ego, and tension. This is the type of conflict that most team leaders and team members try to avoid. Sometimes, however, they are not successful. Often, people deal with this conflict through escape or termination. For example, Milton Bradley, former outfielder for the Chicago Cubs, was under a 3-year contract, but officials of the team traded him to the Seattle Mariners because he threw temper tantrums. Bradley blamed team officials for the Cubs' failure in the World Series games. Jim Hendry, general manager of the team, wanted Bradley replaced so as to not further destroy the morale of the team.[6] Relationship conflict is not always expressed via open shouting matches. In fact, some people go to great lengths to avoid the overt expression of conflict. For example, Argyris describes a case in which lower-level managers identified a number of serious production and marketing problems in their company.[7] They told the middle

---

[3]Salter, C. (2008, March). Google: The faces and voices of the world's most innovative company. *Fast Company, 123*, 74–91.

[4]Jehn, K. A. (1995). A multimethod examination of the benefits and detriments of intragroup conflict. *Administrative Science Quarterly, 40*, 256–282; Jehn, K. A., & Mannix, E. A. (2001). The dynamic nature of conflict: A longitudinal study of intragroup conflict and group performance. *Academy of Management Journal, 44*(2), 238–251; Behfar, K. J., Peterson, R. S., Mannix, E. A., & Trochim, W. M. K. (2008). The critical role of conflict resolution in teams: A close look at the links between conflict type, conflict management strategies, and team outcomes. *Journal of Applied Psychology, 93*(1), 170–188; Peterson, R. (1997). A directive leadership style in group decision making can be both virtue and vice: Evidence from elite and experimental groups. *Journal of Personality and Social Psychology, 72*(5), 1107–1121.

[5]Guetzkow, H., & Gyr, J. (1954). An analysis of conflict in decision-making groups. *Human Relations, 7*, 367–381.

[6]Kar, M. (2009, December 19). Milton Bradley is now a Seattle Mariners. *Thaindian News*. thaindian.com

[7]Argyris, C. (1977b). Organizational learning and management information systems. *Harvard Business Review, 55*(5), 115–125.

EXHIBIT 8-1 Three Types of Conflict

Type of Conflict	Definition	Example of Items Used to Assess/Measure This Type of Conflict
Relationship conflict (also known as emotional conflict, A-type conflict, or affective conflict)	Involves disagreements based on personal and social issues that are not related to work	How often do people get angry while working in your team? How much relationship tension is there in your team?
Task conflict (also known as cognitive conflict or C-type conflict)	Involves disagreements about the work that is being done in a group	To what extent are there differences of opinion in your team? How much conflict is there about the work you do in your team? How often do people in your team disagree about opinions regarding the work to be done? How frequently are there conflicts about ideas in your team?
Process conflict	Centers on task strategy and delegation of duties and resources	How often do members of your team disagree about who should do what? How frequently do members of your team disagree about the way to complete a team task? How much disagreement about the delegation of tasks exists within your team?

Source: Jehn, K. A. (1995). A multimethod examination of the benefits and detriments of intragroup conflict. *Administrative Science Quarterly, 40,* 256–282; Jehn, K. A., & Mannix, E. A. (2001). The dynamic nature of conflict: A longitudinal study of intragroup conflict and group performance. *Academy of Management Journal, 44*(2), 238–251; Behfar, K. J., Peterson, R. S., Mannix, E. A., & Trochim, W. M. K. (2008). The critical role of conflict resolution in teams: A close look at the links between conflict type, conflict management strategies, and team outcomes. *Journal of Applied Psychology*, *93*(1), 170–188; Peterson, R. (1997). A directive leadership style in group decision making can be both virtue and vice: Evidence from elite and experimental groups. *Journal of Personality and Social Psychology, 72*(5), 1107–1121.

managers, and once the middle managers were convinced that the situation described by the lower managers was actually true, they began to release some of the bad news, but they did so carefully, in measured doses. They managed their communications carefully to make certain they were "covered" if upper management became upset. The result was that top management was never fully apprised of the problems—rather, they received a strangely edited view of the problem. Top management, therefore, continued to speak glowingly about the product, partially to ensure that it would get the financial backing it needed from within the company. Lower-level managers became confused and eventually depressed because they could not understand why top management continued to support the product. Their reaction was to reduce the frequency of their memos and the intensity of the alarm they expressed, while simultaneously turning the problem over to middle management.

   Task conflict, or **cognitive conflict**, is largely depersonalized; also known as **C-type conflict**, it consists of argumentation about the merits of ideas, plans, and projects. In some situations, task conflict can be effective in stimulating creativity because it forces people to rethink problems and arrive at outcomes that everyone can live with. When the majority is confronted by the differing opinions of minorities, it is forced to think about why the minority disagrees. This thought process can instigate novel ideas.[8]

Process conflict centers on disagreements that team members have about how to approach a task and, specifically, who should do what. Process conflict often involves disagreements among team members as to how to achieve a goal. For example, teams of negotiators often must present a united front, even when they are not in agreement on their strategy. Conflict between subgroups in negotiation teams negatively affects their performance at the negotiation table.[9]

Conflict and Culture

Differences exist among different cultures about the effects of conflict on team effectiveness. Linguistic-related challenges in multicultural teams increase the likelihood of relationship conflict.[10] Consequently, talking about the conflict might actually do more harm than good. With regard to cultural beliefs, Americans are considered to be largely individualistic as compared to Asians who are considered to be collectivistic.[11] When a norm of collectivism is manipulated (imposed on a group), members with concordant attitudes are evaluated more positively than those with dissenting attitudes; but when a norm of individualism is imposed, dissenters are more highly valued.[12] Compared to East Asians, Americans exhibit an optimistic bias about relationship conflict.[13] When it comes to task conflict, both Americans and East Asians believe in addressing conflict proactively, but when it comes to relationship conflict, European Americans don't think it is necessary to address relationship conflict to get good performance. Americans are more likely than East Asians to join a talented group that is known to have high relationship conflict.

Procter & Gamble (P&G) faced a cultural challenge at its research facility in Beijing. In China, and across much of Asia, people typically do not share challenging ideas with coworkers, certainly not with higher-ranking colleagues. Asian workers are taught to say little—especially anything that might be perceived as questioning authority—no matter how right they might be. As a result, they keep to themselves. "In Chinese culture, we don't speak in front of superiors," says Jennifer Zhu, an associate director in the research and development (R&D) division. But P&G's culture, especially in R&D, demands that researchers talk openly about their ideas and disagree with and challenge one another to make ideas stronger. Diversity of thought, emanating from cultural perspectives, fuels creativity. So in 2006, P&G executives began experimenting with a program intended to help Asian researchers develop the confidence

[8]Levine, J. M., & Moreland, R. L. (1985). Innovation and socialization in small groups. In S. Moscovici, G. Mugny, & E. van Avermaet (Eds.), *Perspectives on minority influence* (pp. 143–169). Cambridge, UK: Cambridge University Press; Nemeth, C. J. (1995). Dissent as driving cognition, attitudes, and judgments. *Social Cognition, 13*, 273–291.

[9]Halevy, N. (2008). Team negotiation: Social, epistemic, economic, and psychological consequences of subgroup conflict. *Personality and Social Psychology Bulletin, 34*(12), 1687–1702.

[10]Von Glinow, M. A., Shapiro, D. L., & Brett, J. M. (2004). Can we talk, and should we? Managing emotional conflict in multicultural teams. *Academy of Management Review, 29*(4): 578–592.

[11]Brett, J. M. (2007). *Negotiating globally: How to negotiate deals, resolve disputes, and make decisions across cultural boundaries.* San Francisco, CA: Jossey-Bass.

[12]Hornsey, M. J., Jetten, J., McAuliffe, B. J., & Hogg, M. A. (2006). The impact of individualist and collectivist group norms on evaluations of dissenting group members. *Journal of Experimental Social Psychology, 42*, 57–68.

[13]Sanchez-Burks, J., Neuman, E., Ybarra, O., Kopelman, S., Goh, K., & Park, H. (2008). Cultural folk wisdom about relationship conflict. *Negotiation and Conflict Management Research, 1*(1), 55–78.

to speak their minds. Called "gas station" because it's where workers go to recharge and fuel their skill set, newly hired researchers and scientists are immersed into a 3-day residential program. Company veterans attempt to retrain reticent employees and help them learn to thrive in the extroverted environment at P&G. In 2006, a female hire came to P&G from Tsinghua University in Beijing, where she was a top microbiology student. But at P&G she rarely spoke up. The gas station allowed her to observe successful P&G managers like Zhu and learn how they advanced in the organization. She was repeatedly told by mentors in the program: "If you don't speak, you won't have a point of view." Eventually she learned that having a point of view did not always come with bad consequences, and she soon developed the confidence to contribute to the discussion.[14]

Types of Conflict and Work Team Effectiveness

How does each type of conflict affect team performance? To answer this question, De Dreu and Weingart conducted a meta-analysis of several investigations in which different types of conflict were measured as well as performance in teams (such as task completion and team satisfaction).[15] Results indicated highly negative correlations between relationship conflict and team performance: Greater amounts of relationship conflict in a team were associated with lower levels of performance. Moreover, there was a strong negative relationship between task conflict and team performance and task conflict and team satisfaction. Teams that displayed higher levels of conflict about the task tended to perform less well and were less satisfied than were teams that did not have as much task conflict. Why? Relationship conflict interferes with the effort people put into a task because members are preoccupied with reducing threats, increasing power, and attempting to build cohesion rather than working on the task. The anxiety produced by interpersonal animosity may inhibit cognitive functioning[16] and also distract team members from the task, causing them to work less effectively and produce suboptimal products.[17] According to Jehn, who investigated everyday conflicts in six organizational work teams, relationship conflict is detrimental to performance and satisfaction (two major indices of team productivity) because emotionality reduces team effectiveness.[18] In addition, relationship conflict negatively interferes with a team's ability to process information.[19]

   The question of why task conflict also hinders performance is more puzzling. Some investigations have found that task conflict improves team performance.[20] Yet, on balance, task conflict does not help (and may hurt) team effectiveness. Teams experiencing task conflict have a hard time moving forward in terms of reaching their goal because they become preoccupied with

[14]Crockett, R. O. (2009, October 2). P&G gets reticent researchers to speak up. *Business Week.* Businessweek.com

[15]De Dreu, C. K. W., & Weingart, L. R. (2003a). Task versus relationship conflict, team effectiveness, and team member satisfaction: A meta-analysis. *Journal of Applied Psychology, 88,* 741–749.

[16]Roseman, I., Wiest, C., & Swartz, T. (1994). Phenomenology, behaviors, and goals differentiate emotions. *Journal of Personality and Social Psychology, 67,* 206–221.

[17]Wilson, D. C., Butler, R. J., Cray, D., Hickson, D. J., & Mallory, G. R. (1986). Breaking the bounds of organization in strategic decision making. *Human Relations, 39,* 309–332.

[18]Jehn, K. A. (1997). A qualitative analysis of conflict types and dimensions in organizational groups. *Administrative Science Quarterly, 42,* 530–557.

[19]De Dreu & Weingart, "Task versus relationship conflict, team effectiveness, and team member satisfaction."

[20]Jehn, "Multimethod examination of intragroup conflict," p. 202; Shah, P. P., & Jehn, K. A. (1993). Do friends perform better than acquaintances? The interaction of friendship, conflict, and task. *Group Decision and Negotiation, 2*(2), 149–165; Amabile, T. M., Nasco, C. P., Mueller, J., Wojcik, T., Odomirok, P. W., Marsh, M., & Kramer, S. J. (2001). Academic-practitioner collaboration in management research: A case of cross-profession collaboration. *Academy of Management Journal, 44*(2), 418–431.

and distracted by conflict. In short, the ability of a team to process information relevant to a task is hindered.[21] A small amount of task conflict may be beneficial, but it can quickly backfire as conflict becomes more intense, thereby increasing cognitive load and information processing demands among team members. Task conflict is less disruptive for teams when relationship conflict is lower. As might be expected, teams perform worst when task and relationship conflict is high. The more complex a team's task is, the more disruptive conflict is.

When it comes to team satisfaction, relationship conflict is more disruptive for teams than is task conflict.[22] Indeed, relationship conflict is more interpersonal and emotional and is likely to be directed at others.

Some investigations have studied the time course of conflict in teams. Groups that have high levels of trust among their members during the early stages of group development are buffered from experiencing future relationship conflict (see Exhibit 8-2). When groups receive negative performance feedback early on, both relationship and task conflict increase.[23] Increased team conflict also leads teams to unintentionally restructure themselves inefficiently. When teams experience conflict, they have lower trust, which leads them to reduce individual autonomy and loosen task interdependencies in the team.[24]

EXHIBIT 8-2 Trust Tempers Negative Conflict

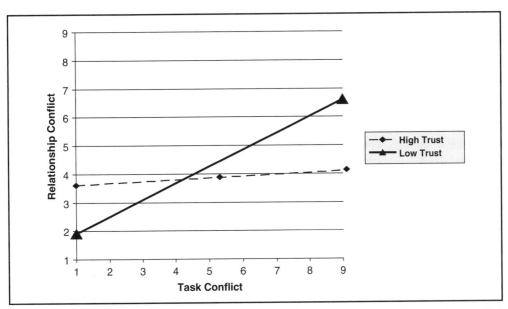

Source: Peterson, R., & Behfar, K. (2003). The dynamic relationship between performance feedback, trust, and conflict in groups: A longitudinal study. *Organizational Behavior and Human Decision Processes, 92,* 102–112.

---

[21]De Dreu & Weingart, "Task versus relationship conflict, team effectiveness, and team member satisfaction."
[22]Ibid.
[23]Peterson, R., & Behfar, K. (2003). The dynamic relationship between performance feedback, trust, and conflict in groups: A longitudinal study. *Organizational Behavior and Human Decision Processes, 92,* 102–112.
[24]Langfred, C. W. (2007). The downside of self-management: A longitudinal study of the effects of conflict on trust, autonomy, and task interdependence in self-managing teams. *Academy of Management Journal, 50,* 885–900.

Proportional and Perceptual Conflict

PROPORTIONAL CONFLICT   Team members often have different ideas about the amount and type of conflict that exists in their group. In any team, for example, there may be differing actual levels of relationship, task, and process conflicts, and the relative levels of such conflicts are crucial aspects for team leaders to understand as they affect task performance.[25] **Proportional conflict composition** describes the relationship among the three types of conflict (task, relationship, and process) as the level of each type of conflict proportional to the other two and to the overall level of conflict within the group, rather than as an absolute level or amount of any one type. Consider the following example offered by Jehn and Chatman: A team that experiences a moderate amount of constructive task conflict and no other conflict (no relationship or process conflict) will have a different experience than will members of another group with not only the same amount of task conflict but also a high proportional level of relationship conflict.[26] In the former group, members should experience less stress, less distraction, and less anger, which are frequent consequences of relationship conflict[27] as compared to members of the group containing more moderate levels of task and relationship conflicts. Indeed, teams with a high proportion of task conflict experience a higher level of team member commitment, cohesiveness, individual performance, group performance, and member satisfaction. In contrast, a high proportion of relationship conflict is negatively related to member commitment, cohesiveness, individual performance, group performance, and member satisfaction.

PERCEPTUAL CONFLICT   If proportional conflict refers to the relative amounts of task, relationship, and process conflict within a team, perceptual conflict refers to the extent to which there is agreement or a lack thereof, in terms of whether team members perceive conflict. **Perceptual conflict composition** is the degree to which each person in a team perceives levels of conflict differently compared to other team members.[28] Specifically, each member's perceptions of conflict are compared to all other members' perceptions of the group. Jehn and Chatman give the following example: Two team members in an eight-person team perceive arguments in the group pertaining to the task while the other six members do not detect such conflict.[29] These two members have a larger perceptual conflict composition score than those members who believe that there is no task conflict. Disagreements as to whether and how much conflict exists in a team negatively influence team effectiveness.

BEST PRACTICES FOR MANAGING CONFLICT IN TEAM

The most effective teams share several common practices when it comes to conflict and conflict management. They realize that conflict is an inevitable aspect of high performance teamwork. Second, they deal with conflict proactively, meaning that they develop procedures and practices to

---

[25]Jehn, K., & Chatman, J. A. (2000). Reconceptualizing conflict: Proportional and relational conflict. *International Journal of Conflict Management, 11*(1), 51–69.
[26]Ibid.
[27]Amason, A. (1996). Distinguishing the effects of functional and dysfunctional conflict on strategic decision making: Resolving a paradox for top management teams. *Academy of Management Journal, 39*(1), 123–148; Jehn, K. (1994). Enhancing effectiveness: An investigation of advantages and disadvantages of value based intragroup conflict. *The International Journal of Conflict Management, 5*, 223–238; Jehn, "Multimethod examination of intragroup conflict," p. 202.
[28]Jehn & Chatman, "Reconceptualizing conflict."
[29]Ibid.

deal with it before it emerges. And, they focus on behaviors rather than traits. Groups that improve or maintain top performance over time share three conflict resolution best practices: (1) they focus on the content of their interactions, rather than the delivery style (i.e., tone); (2) they explicitly discuss reasons behind work assignment decisions; and (3) they assign work to members who have the task expertise rather than by other means, such as volunteerism or convenience.[30]

REAL CONFLICT VERSUS SYMBOLIC CONFLICT

Some conflicts in teams center upon real, economic issues, such as pay and remuneration, and the size of office space and staff. Other conflicts center upon symbolic issues, such as differing beliefs (e.g., quality versus quantity; meritocracy versus equal opportunity).

Egocentric Bias and Scarce Resource Competition

Teams experiencing economic conflicts are competing over scarce resources. Most people feel entitled to more resources than others believe they merit. Oftentimes, this is driven by egocentric valuations of one's own contributions to a joint task. For example, in one investigation, team members were asked to complete several questionnaires.[31] These took either 45 or 90 minutes. The questionnaires were constructed so that, for each duration, some participants completed six questionnaires, whereas others completed only three. When asked to allocate monetary rewards, participants emphasized the dimension that favored them in the allocation procedure (those who worked longer emphasized time; questionnaire completion was emphasized by those who worked on more questionnaires). Most people are not aware that their own perceptions of fairness are egocentrically biased.

CONFLICT MANAGEMENT APPROACHES

According to Blake and Mouton, people can take at least five courses of action when they find themselves involved in conflict.[32] The five choices differ depending upon the extent to which people are concerned for themselves and the other party (see Exhibit 8-3).

Let's use the model to analyze a conflict that occurred at Columbia Sportswear company (see Exhibit 8-4). Before Neal Boyle (father and husband) passed away, the mother and son were engaged in a long-standing stalemate in which they did not engage or interact very much. When Neal passed away, Tim and his mother, Gert, competed, both intimidating the other. When they focused on a higher-order goal and cut their salaries and built the company up again, they were engaged in collaboration. When the question of off-shoring came up, Gert capitulated to Tim and accommodated his desires. It is fortunate for the company that Tim and Gert moved from avoidance to collaboration at a critical stage in their company's life.

A Contingency Theory of Task Conflict and Performance in Teams

De Dreu and Weingart developed a contingency perspective that views team performance as a function of the type of task conflict, the conflict management style, and the nature of the task

---

[30]Behfar, Peterson, Mannix, & Trochim, "The critical role of conflict resolution in teams."
[31]van Avermaet, E. (1974). *Equity: A theoretical and experimental analysis.* Unpublished doctoral dissertation, University of California, Santa Barbara.
[32]Blake, R. R., & Mouton, J. S. (1964). *The managerial grid.* Houston, TX: Gulf.

EXHIBIT 8-3 Managerial Grid

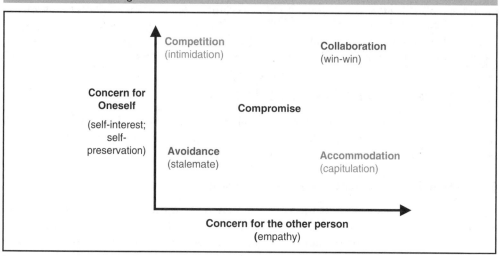

EXHIBIT 8-4 Columbia Sportswear Company: An Illustration of the Managerial Grid

In 2005, Tim Boyle and his mother, Gert, had spent 35 years arguing about how to run Columbia Sportswear Inc. After the sudden death in 1970 of Neal Boyle, Tim's father and Gert's husband, the two had to scramble in an attempt to save the small company. During their first year running the company, sales shrank 25 percent and many vital employees quit. Tensions mounted between mother and son, but by collaborating, working long hours, and agreeing to cut their salaries significantly, they pulled through and slowly began to build the company up again. However, as Columbia grew, Tim and Gert continued to butt heads. When Tim pushed to expand beyond Columbia's origins as a specialty outfitter and lined up mass-market sales channels like J.C. Penney Co., Gert opposed him. Having been a part of the company from its beginnings, and even hand-stitching some of Columbia's first fishing vests, Gert feared that big retailers would pressure the company in undesirable ways. Tim, however, was never good at explaining the reasoning behind his decision making to his mother. According to Tim, "I was always the one who would say, 'The company needs to go in this direction.' I wasn't good at articulating why." Tim now admits that this attitude probably added to the friction between him and his mother. In the 1980s, when Tim argued to move manufacturing offshore to dramatically cut assembly costs, his mother winced. She knew many of the company's seamstresses and didn't want to see them lose their jobs. The two finally compromised and agreed to enlist the help of advisers to mediate the dispute (something they continued to do with many other disputes thereafter). Gert eventually accommodated Tim's wishes and agreed to move production to Asia. The mother and son team have now carved out separate areas of authority, avoiding frequent contact and opportunities to butt heads. While Tim focuses on driving Columbia's strategy, expanding the company globally, and building up the footwear business, Gert has become the company's ambassador to the world, hosting tour groups and starring in Columbia's marketing ads as "one tough mother." Their differing responsibilities, and the fact that they moved their offices to opposite sides of Columbia's headquarters, reduce the number of potential squabbles on any given day. The two have learned how to work together, and separately, for the benefit of the company.

performed by the group.[33] As can be seen in Exhibit 8-5, the amount of conflict is a direct determinant of team performance and individual well-being (i.e., individual satisfaction). Individual well-being exerts a powerful effect on how people deal with conflict. For example, people who endure levels of high stress activate hormones that result in a number of negative, physiological outcomes including headaches and increased cardiovascular response.[34] Several investigations—one involving over 3,000 employees—reveal a positive and significant correlation between conflict at work and physical health problems.[35]

Another determinant of team performance is the approach that team members use to manage conflict. According to the model, team members may either collaborate (similar to Blake and Mouton's high concern for self and other party mode) or "contend" with one another (using either rights- or power-based styles). A **rights-based argument** focuses on applying some standard of fairness, precedent, contract, or law. A **power-based approach** is characterized by the use of force, intimidation, rank, or power. Avoidance is yet another option for team members. Collaborative styles of conflict management, such as "constructive controversy" are more beneficial for team performance (for a review, see De Dreu and Weingart).[36] An **interest-based approach** focuses on satisfying both parties' core interests; when people set aside questions of right and wrong, they can sometimes craft terms that meet their most important interests, but usually not all of them.

EXHIBIT 8-5 Conflict and Team Performance

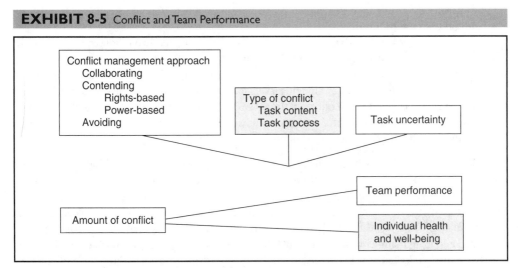

Source: De Dreu, C., & Weingart, L. (2003b). A contingency theory of task conflict and performance in groups and organizational teams. In M. A. West, D. Tjosvold, & K. G. Smith (Eds.), *International handbook of organizational teamwork and cooperative working.* Chichester: John Wiley & Sons.

---

[33]De Dreu, C., & Weingart, L. (2003). A contingency theory of task conflict and performance in groups and organizational teams. In M. A. West, D. Tjosvold, & K. G. Smith (Eds.), *International handbook of organizational teamwork and cooperative working.* New York: John Wiley & Sons.

[34]Pennebaker, J. W. (1982). *The psychology of physical symptoms.* New York: Springer-Verlag.

[35]Spector, P. E., & Jex, S. M. (1998). Development of four self-report measures of job stressors and strain: Interpersonal conflict at work scale, organizational constraints scale, quantitative workload inventory, and physical symptoms inventory. *Journal of Occupational Health Psychology, 3,* 356–367.

[36]De Dreu & Weingart, "A contingency theory of task conflict and performance in groups and organizational teams."

As an example of the difference between collaborating (interests) and contending (i.e., rights- or power-based approaches) in teams, consider a team in which there has been a serious, long-standing conflict concerning the nature of the assignments given to team members. Some assignments are clearly regarded as more attractive and career-enhancing than others. However, for the organization to be successful, all assignments must be covered by the team. One of the members, Larry, begins a meeting by stating, "I am not at all happy with how the assignments for the project are handled. I consistently have to do the least attractive part of the project and it is a lot of work. I want to be excused from that part of the project in the future." Three team members might respond in the following ways, depending on which approach they take to the conflict at hand:

1. *Collaborative (interests-based) response:* "Larry, I've sensed that this is of great concern to you. We'd all like to hear more about your own views on this and what your proposals are. I will be honest in saying that I am not sure anything can change, at least for now, but I think that it is important that we all have a chance to understand exactly how each one of us perceives the workload and assignments on the project at this point."

2. *Contending (rights-based) response:* "Look, Larry, you agreed to cover that part of the project when we first took on the challenge 4 years ago. As a matter of fact, I believe that I have an e-mail from you indicating that you would agree to do that part of the work. As far as I am concerned, this is strictly a matter of precedent and what people have agreed to do. I am sure that our supervisor would reach the same conclusion as I would if she saw the e-mail I am referring to."

3. *Contending (power-based) response:* "I think you are completely out of line, Larry. It is not helping our team effort to have people like yourself acting like prima donnas and demanding special treatment. We all have important things to do to meet the project goals. I am tired of having to walk on eggshells around this issue and I don't think that discussing unrealistic and selfish goals is a good use of our team time. We could simply follow a principle of rank in our team, but that would be bad for you. I am ready to continue our democratic process, but only on the condition that you start working with us as a team!"

The power-based team member in this example is using several techniques designed to threaten and intimidate. First, there are numerous unflattering character attacks—Larry is labeled as "out of line," "demanding," a "prima donna," and "unrealistic and selfish." This comment also contains some thinly disguised threats: If Larry does not shut up, this team member intends to pull rank. The rights-based team member, by focusing on the past, effectively says, "We cannot have this discussion." The interests-based team member clearly states that there may not be any room for movement, but she is open to discussion. In this way, the interests-based response models the double-loop style of communication.[37] Most people, when faced with sensitive and important issues, find it far easier to launch into rights- or power-based arguments. However, nearly any rights- or power-based argument can be converted into an interests-based response without forcing team members to capitulate to others.

In the model, the type of conflict may be either the content of the task or the process of the task (similar to task conflict and process conflict, described earlier). **Task-content conflicts** are disagreements among team members' ideas and opinions about the task being performed, including debates over facts or opinions. In contrast, **task-process conflicts** are conflicts about logistical and delegation issues, such as how to proceed and allocate work.

---

[37]Argyris, C. (1977a). Double loop learning. *Harvard Business Review, 55*(5), 115–125.

When groups perform highly uncertain tasks, they need to integrate large amounts of information, form multiple perspectives, and collaborate closely. In such situations, collaboration is essential.[38]

WAGEMAN AND DONNENFELDS' CONFLICT INTERVENTION MODEL

Wageman and Donnenfeld distinguish four kinds of interventions that team leaders and managers can use to improve the quality of conflict resolution processes.[39]

- *Team (re)Design:* Deliberate changes in the structure (e.g., environment, tasks) in which teams do their work. Interventions might include increasing the amount of task interdependence that a team has in accomplishing a given work product. Team design usually involves very specific, structural changes to a group, which may include how the goal is defined, who is on the team, the nature and amount of resources allocated to the team, team rewards, and norms of conduct.
- *Task process coaching:* Coaching that helps the team perform better via changes in effort, strategy, and talent. Task process coaching is different from conflict process coaching in that task process coaching is aimed exclusively at improving motivation, strategy, and talent but not conflict per se. Task process coaching might include developing team member's skills, improving the communication system, and so on.
- *Conflict process coaching:* Direct intervention in a team to improve the quality of conflict the team is having.[40] Interventions might include trust-building exercises, structured debate, and appointing a devil's advocate.
- *Changing the individual:* Individual-level training with the goal of making specific team members more tolerant, thoughtful, and capable when they disagree with others.[41] This might include behavioral training in negotiation.

Wageman and Donnenfeld propose four guiding principles for enhancing teams with respect to conflict.[42]

Principle 1: Of all the strategies listed above, Team (re)Design has the largest effects. For this reason Wageman and Donnenfeld suggest starting at this point of intervention.[43] An effective team design addresses the root causes of most team conflicts. One important aspect of team design is the stated goal of the team.

Teams that agree on a common goal or shared vision are more successful than those that don't or can't.[44] When Great Britain won seven of the 10 track cycling gold medals at the 2008

---

[38]De Dreu, & Weingart, "A contingency theory of task conflict and performance in groups and organizational teams."

[39]Wageman, R., & Donnenfeld, A. (2007) Intervening in intra-team conflict. In K. M. Behfar & L. L. Thompson (Eds.), *Conflict in organizational groups: New directions in theory and practice.* Evanston, IL: Northwestern University Press.

[40]Hackman, J. R., & Wageman, R. (2005). A theory of team coaching. *Academy of Management Review, 30,* 269–287.

[41]Lewicki, R. J., Weiss, S. E., & Lewin, D. (1992). Models of conflict, negotiation, and third party intervention: A review and synthesis. *Journal of Organizational Behavior, 13*(2), 209–252.

[42]Wageman & Donnenfeld, "Intervening in intra-team conflict."

[43]Ibid.

[44]Kramer, R. M., & Brewer, M. B. (1984). Effects of group identity on resource use in a simulated commons dilemma. *Journal of Personality and Social Psychology, 46,* 1044–1057; Sherif, M., Harvey, O. J., White, B. J., Hood, W. R., & Sherif, C. W. (1961). *Intergroup conflict and cooperation: The Robbers Cave experiment.* Norman, OK: Institute of Group Relations, University of Oklahoma.

Beijing Summer Olympics, it was an amazing turnaround for a program that didn't win a single cycling medal in an Olympic Games as recently as 1996. And it was made possible by a commitment to winning—and little else. Twenty fewer athletes were chosen to train for the national team, and a "management team" of technical and psychological managers kept the athletes on track in varying ways. "We never stop asking the question: 'Will this get us a gold medal?'" said Chris Boardman, a former gold medal Olympian who manages the technical aspects of the program in Beijing.[45]

Common goals do not imply homogeneous thinking, but they do require everyone to share a vision. At Van Meter Industrial, Inc. in Cedar Rapids, Iowa, employees receive the equivalent of several weeks pay in company stock accounts each year. But management got a wake-up call when at a company meeting a few years ago an employee stood up and said he didn't care at all about the stock fund, asking, "Why don't you just give me a couple hundred bucks for beer and cigarettes?" As it turned out, many employees at the 100 percent employee-owned company, didn't know what stock was, didn't know what an (employee) owner was. CFO Mick Slinger admitted, "I made the mistake of thinking that everyone thinks like me." Now, Instead of continuing to simply pass out stock statements once a year, company executives educate workers about ownership; an employee committee was established to make sure workers knew the ins and outs of the program. The employee committee has also rolled out a series of campaigns, with catchy slogans and giveaways, to raise awareness of stock ownership and get workers thinking about what each of them as owners can do to raise the price of company stock—and how it affects their own net worth. Company stock rose 78 percent in the first 5 years of the program, and turnover fell by an annual rate of 10 percent—an improvement that executives correlated to employee engagement and commitment.[46]

Principle 2: After the team is well designed, the team leader should use the strategy of coaching the team. Coaching the team can work only if the team is well designed. Coaching that focuses on the key performance drivers reinforces the team design. For example, coaching helped well-designed teams at Xerox exploit their talents but did not help poorly designed teams.[47]

Principle 3: Coaching about conflict might engender resistance relative to discussions about motivation, strategy, or leveraging talent in the team. In some cases, coaching about conflict and relationships may even backfire.[48] Yet, if a team proactively develops strategies for dealing with potential, future conflicts, this can often be effective. Indeed, groups who develop norms regarding how they will manage conflict are more effective than those that do not develop norms.[49] And, groups that develop collaborative (interest-based) conflict norms make more effective group decisions than do groups who use contending (e.g., rights and power) or avoidance styles. Conflict norms also carry over to affect other team activities, such as decision making, that don't necessarily involve conflict. Furthermore, friends are better at applying

---

[45]Barnes, S. (2008, December 29). One-track minds that put team on way to gold rush: Team of the year Great Britain cycling team. *The Times*, pp. 16–17.

[46]Covel, S. (2008, February 7). How to get workers to think and act like owners. *Wall Street Journal*, p. B6.

[47]Wageman, R. (2001). How leaders foster self-managing team effectiveness: Design choices versus hands-on coaching. *Organization Science, 12*(5), 559–577.

[48]Kaplan, R. E. (1979). The conspicuous absence of evidence that process consultation enhances task performance. *The Journal of Applied Behavioral Science, 15*, 346–360.

[49]Kuhn, T., & Poole, M. S. (2000). Do conflict management styles affect group decision making? Evidence from a longitudinal field study. *Human Communication Research, 26*(4), 558–590.

EXHIBIT 8-6 Shared Goals Despite Conflict

> At the Mayo Clinic in Rochester, Minnesota, concern for the patient leads to a culture where every-thing, including conflict, keeps that concern in mind. In its 100-year-plus history, the clinic has never had a CEO with a business degree or background. Doctors' salaries are capped after 5 years, and employees work toward shared goals beyond their own individual needs. All employees are on salary, and no one is measured by productivity or given a financial incentive. "Everyone is working together for the same thing," says Kent Selman, a marketing manager at Mayo. "There are 43,000 employees. You could walk up to any of them and ask: 'What's the mission?' 'The needs of the patient come first' is on the lips of virtually every employee."

Source: Based on Lee, A. (2008, September 8). How to build a brand. *Fast Company.* Fastcompany.com

effective conflict management strategies to suit the task at hand than are teams of strangers whose conflict management approaches are less sophisticated.[50]

One type of intervention is structured debate. Most people, even seasoned managers and executives, feel uncomfortable about conflict. However, it is much easier to deal with conflict by creating a time and place for it to occur, rather than expecting it to naturally erupt. Furthermore, discussing the potential for conflict before it erupts is a lot more effective than trying to deal with it after the fact. As an example of how organizations create a forum for conflict, consider the Mayo Clinic teams described in Exhibit 8-6.

With regard to conflict coaching, it is important to focus on content rather than style. In other words, focus on the substance, not the delivery. The most successful project teams are those that rise above style issues and focus on content.[51] The focus on content, rather than style, is similar to the prescriptive advice of "separating the people from the problem."[52]

Principle 4: Changing individuals will have its greatest impact only after the team design and team processes are addressed. People have a better chance of changing when the team design is optimal and the core team processes are positive, thereby serving to reinforce individual behavior.

NORMS OF FAIRNESS

Many conflicts in teams emerge because people feel misunderstood or ignored. Think about how many times you have heard people complain that they were not listened to or were ignored. People in teams want to be understood and heard. Letting another person express himself or herself does not mean you agree with them. You are simply listening. Indeed, many people feel more satisfied with their teams and organizations only because they were heard.[53] Moreover, people who are aware of their status in their team are more concerned about having a voice.[54] When group members know where they stand, they are more concerned about justice.

---

[50]Shah & Jehn, "Do friends perform better than acquaintances?" p. 205.
[51]Behfar, Peterson, Mannix, & Trochim, "The critical role of conflict resolution in teams," p. 202.
[52]Fisher, R., & Ury, W. (1981). *Getting to yes: Negotiating agreement without giving in.* Boston, MA: Houghton Mifflin.
[53]Lind, E. A., & Tyler, T. R. (1988). *The social psychology of procedural justice.* New York: Plenum.
[54]Van Prooijen, J.-W., Van den Bos, K., & Wilke, H. A. M. (2005). Procedural justice and intragroup status: Knowing where we stand in a group enhances reactions to procedures. *Journal of Experimental Social Psychology, 41,* 664–676.

Another problem that causes conflict among team members is that there are several different "norms" or "methods" of fair allocation. Consider the following:

- *Equity* method (or contribution-based distribution) prescribes that benefits (and costs) should be proportional to team members' contributions.[55]
- *Equality* method (or blind justice) prescribes that all team members should suffer or benefit equally, regardless of input.[56]
- *Need* method (or welfare-based justice) prescribes that benefits (and costs) should be proportional to members' needs.[57]

Egocentric judgments influence which norm of fairness is preferred: Members who contribute less prefer to divide resources equally, whereas those who contribute more prefer the equity rule.[58] In groups containing members who have different power or status levels, those with low power want equality, whereas those with high power desire equity.[59]

There is no one objectively correct method of justice. In fact, teams often have several different methods in operation at any one time. For example, consider a study group in a semester-long course. They might assign work on a joint project on the basis of equity, such that people with greater experience and skills in a certain subject area are expected to bring more knowledge to the task (e.g., the finance major may be expected to read the financial report individually, perform all the calculations, and develop a spreadsheet by himself or herself). In terms of booking study group rooms and bringing snacks for group meetings, the group might use an equality method, such that each week a different group member is expected to supply drinks and cookies and book a room. This group may occasionally invoke a need-based justice system when, for example, a study group member misses three group meetings in preparation for a wedding. The rest of the group may agree to cover his or her work so that the teammate can prepare for the wedding. The question of how to reduce self-serving, or egoistic, judgments of entitlements in teams is vexing. Whereas it would seem that perspective taking might minimize egocentric judgments, people who are encouraged to consider the perspectives of others increase their egoistic (selfish) behavior, such that they actually take more available resources.[60]

MINORITY AND MAJORITY CONFLICT IN GROUPS

Thus far, we have focused on conflict between individual team members. Sometimes, conflicts involve subgroups within a given team. Often, these subgroups represent a statistical minority. When we refer to a minority in a team, we are not referring to a demographic minority; rather, we are referring to a statistical minority. People in the statistical minority exert a considerable influence in teams.[61]

---

[55]Adams, S. (1965). Inequity in social exchange. In L. Berkowitz (Ed.), *Advances in experimental social psychology* (Vol. 2, pp. 267–299). New York: Academic Press.

[56]Messick, D. (1993). Equality as a decision heuristic. In B. A. Mellers & J. Baron (Eds.), *Psychological perspectives on justice* (pp. 11–31). New York: Cambridge University Press.

[57]Deutsch, M. (1975). Equity, equality, and need: What determines which value will be used as the basis of distributive justice? *Journal of Social Issues, 31,* 137–149.

[58]Allison, S., & Messick, D. (1990). Social decision heuristics and the use of shared resources. *Journal of Behavioral Decision Making, 3,* 195–204.

[59]Komorita, S., & Chertkoff, J. (1973). A bargaining theory of coalition formation. *Psychological Review, 80,* 149–162; Shaw, M. E. (1981). *Group dynamics: The psychology of small group behavior* (3rd ed.). New York: McGraw-Hill.

[60]Epley, N., Caruso, E. M., & Bazerman, M. (2006). When perspective taking increases taking: Reactive egoism in social interaction. *Journal of Personality and Social Psychology, 91*(5), 872–889.

[61]Nemeth, C. (2003). Minority dissent and its "hidden" benefits. *New Review of Social Psychology, 2,* 20–28; Wood, W., Lundgren, S., Ouellette, J. A., Busceme, S., & Blackstone, T. (1994). Minority influence: A meta-analytical review of social influence processes. *Psychological Bulletin, 115,* 323–345.

Minority and Majority Influence

There are two ways in which majorities and minorities influence their teams. One method is through **direct influence**, such as when they entice other team members to adopt their position. Another method is via **indirect influence** in which people in the majority privately agree with the minority.[62] When people change their attitudes and behavior as a result of direct influence or pressure, this is referred to as **compliance** (early and direct adoption of a position); in contrast, when people change their attitudes and behavior as a result of their own thinking about a subject, this is known as **conversion** (private acceptance). Conversion can occur at a latent level and have a delayed impact, such as when change occurs later, known as the **sleeper effect**.[63] Obviously, conversion is a more stable form of attitude change because a person changes inwardly, not just outwardly, to please others. Minorities induce conversion, whereas majorities induce compliance.

However, minorities are certainly not always successful in terms of stimulating conversion. Indeed, people in groups may want to actively dissociate from the minority subgroup so as to avoid ridicule and rejection.[64] When group members actively avoid minority members, their attitudes on related topics may change.[65]

Benefits of Minority Influence

In general, minorities in groups are believed to be beneficial because they stimulate greater thought about issues.[66] In short, when minorities in a group express a differing opinion, the general level of cognitive activity in the group increases and group members engage in more message scrutiny.[67]

Minority opinions do not simply get groups to focus on a given message; they stimulate much broader thinking about the issue in general and open the doors to considering multiple perspectives, perhaps only one of which might represent the minority's view.[68] Indeed, people who have been exposed to minority dissent search for more information on all sides of an issue,[69] remember more information,[70] deploy more effective performance strategies,[71] detect solutions that are elusive to others,[72] think in more complex ways,[73] and are more

---

[62]Mugny, G. (1982). *The power of minorities*. London: Academic Press; Nemeth, C., & Wachtler, J. (1974). Creating perceptions of consistency and confidence: A necessary condition for minority influence. *Sociometry, 37*, 529–540.

[63]Moscovici, S., Mugny, G., & Papastamou, S. (1981). Sleeper effect and/or minority effect? *Cahiers de Psychologie Cognitive, 1*, 199–221.

[64]Perez, J. A., & Mugny, G. (1987). Paradoxical effects of categorization in minority influence: When being an out-group is an advantage. *European Journal of Social Psychology, 17*, 157–169.

[65]Mugny, *Power of minorities*, p. 216; Crano, W. D. (2000). Social influence: Effects of leniency on majority and minority-induced focal and indirect attitude change. *Revue Internationale de Psychologie Sociale, 15*, 89–121.

[66]Nemeth, C. J. (1986). Differential contributions of majority and minority influence. *Psychological Review, 93*, 23–32; Perez, J. A., & Mugny, G. (1996). The conflict elaboration theory of social influence. In E. H. Witte and J. H. Davis (Eds.), *Understanding group behavior: Small group processes and interpersonal relations* (Vol. 2, pp. 191–210). Mahwah, NJ: Erlbaum.

[67]Moscovici, S. (1980). Towards a theory of conversion behavior. In L. Berkowitz (Ed.), *Advances in Experimental Social Psychology* (Vol. 13, pp. 209–239). San Diego, CA: Academic Press.

[68]Nemeth, "Differential contributions," p. 217; Nemeth, C. J. (1997). Managing innovation: When less is more. *California Management Review, 40*, 59–74.

[69]Nemeth, C., & Rogers, J. (1996). Dissent and the search for information. *British Journal of Social Psychology, 35*, 67–76.

[70]Nemeth, C., Mayseless, O., Sherman, J., & Brown, Y. (1990). Improving recall by exposure to consistent dissent. *Journal of Personality and Social Psychology, 58*, 429–437.

[71]Butera, F., Mugny, G., Legrenzi, P., & Perez, J. A. (1996). Majority and minority influence: Task representation and inductive reasoning. *British Journal of Social Psychology, 67*, 123–136.

[72]Nemeth, C., & Wachtler, J. (1983). Creating problem solving as a result of majority vs. minority influence. *European Journal of Social Psychology, 13*, 45–55.

[73]Gruenfeld, D. H. (1995). Status, ideology, and integrative complexity on the U.S. Supreme Court: Rethinking the politics of political decision making. *Journal of Personality & Social Psychology, 68*, 5–20.

creative.[74] The authors of U.S. Supreme Court majority opinions tend to concern themselves with specifying all imaginable contingencies under which the law should and should not apply to ensure the longevity of their precedent. In contrast, the authors of minority U.S. Supreme Court opinions often focus on arguments that could eventually facilitate the precedent's over-ruling. People who are exposed to members who hold a minority view experience an increase in their own levels of integrative thought; in contrast, people exposed to majority opinions or unanimous groups actually experience a decrease in integrative thinking.[75] Teams make better decisions when there is a minority viewpoint present and expressed.[76]

In addition to instigating greater message scrutiny and cognitive activity, statistical minorities stimulate divergent thinking.[77] Whereas majorities induce thoughts that are convergent, in the sense of focusing on one solution to the exclusion of all others, minorities induce divergent thinking, by considering several perspectives.[78] In this sense, minorities are more likely than majorities to have more original thoughts. For example, their associations to words under dispute are more original than majority groups.[79]

One important implication of this research is that even when a minority are wrong about a given issue, their presence adds value to a group by stimulating divergent thinking, increasing creative ideas, generating more ideas, and arriving at better solutions.

However, minorities might be harassed or pressured by the majority. In fact, a "harassed" minority is actually more persuasive than a nonharassed minority on both direct and indirect measures of influence.[80] The reason why harassed minorities are viewed more positively is rooted in the **courage hypothesis**—people who persist in the face of hardship and ridicule are viewed as particularly sincere, confident, and courageous, given that they are willing to risk social censure. The braver the minority appears to be, the greater the impact they have. And, if harassed minorities persist in public (rather than in private), they are even more admired and persuasive.[81]

CROSS-FUNCTIONAL TEAMS AND CONFLICT

In Chapter 2, we identified two types of diversity: one based on social categories, easily visible on the surface, and another based on deeper levels of diversity, such as expertise and training. Here we focus on conflict at the deeper, functional level.

Cross-functional teams are deliberately constructed to be diverse at the deeper level. Cross-functional teams are composed of people from multiple disciplines, functions, and divisions (e.g., engineers, sales, marketing, and manufacturing) who have relevant but different

---

[74]Nemeth, C., & Kwan, J. (1985). Originality of word associations as a function or majority vs. minority influence processes. *Social Psychology Quarterly, 48,* 277–282; Nemeth, C., Rogers, J., & Brown, K. (2001). Improving decision making by means of dissent. *Journal of Applied Social Psychology, 31,* 48–58.

[75]Gruenfeld, D. H., Thomas-Hunt, M. C., & Kim, P. (1998). Cognitive flexibility, communication strategy, and integrative complexity in groups: Public versus private reactions to majority and minority status. *Journal of Experimental Social Psychology, 34,* 202–226.

[76]Van Dyne, L., & Saavedra, R. (1996). A naturalistic minority influence experiment: Effects on divergent thinking, conflict and originality in work groups. *British Journal of Social Psychology, 35,* 151–167.

[77]Nemeth, C. (1976). A comparison between majority and minority influence. Invited Address. International Congress for Psychology. Joint Meeting of SESP and EAESP, Paris; Nemeth, "Differential contributions," p. 217.

[78]Nemeth & Rogers, "Dissent and the search for information."

[79]Nemeth & Kwan, "Originality of word associations," p. 217.

[80]Baron, R., & Bellman, S. (2007). No guts, no glory: Courage, harassment and minority influence. *European Journal of Social Psychology, 37,* 101–124.

[81]McLeod, P., Baron, R., Marti, M., & Yoon, K. (1997). The eyes have it: Minority influence in face to face and computer mediated group discussion. *Journal of Applied Psychology, 82,* 706–718.

expertise. Their diversity can be a benefit, as we saw in a discussion of communication and collective intelligence in Chapter 6, but their diversity can also be a source of conflict. The advantages of functional diversity are often not realized because these teams experience conflict.[82]

When LEGO was near bankruptcy in 2004, the company divided their innovation team into eight distinct groups, dubbed the Executive Innovation Goverance Group. Responsibility for the groups was divided across four groups: functional groups; the Concept Lab; Product and Marketing Development; and a unit named Community, Education and Direct. The groups were given license, to determine strategy, define new products, delegate authority, coordinate mutual efforts, and evaluate results. Moreover, team goals were tied to company strategy, and responsibility for innovation was shared. Following this cross-functional restructuring, profits rose 30 percent in the 4 years following.[83] One model of cross-functional team conflict focuses on the role of **representational gaps**, or the way people think about a task in these teams[84] (see Exhibit 8-7). A team that has a large representational gap has inconsistent views about the definition of the team's problem or task. In this sense, team members have different mental models about the task. In one investigation, a large cross-functional project team at a U.S. automobile manufacturer was studied. The vehicle design team was composed of more than 200 members responsible for all aspects of auto design, engineering, and production of future models. The vehicle team was subdivided into small teams, each responsible for a specific component or system of the car (e.g., body and chassis). Intensive study of these teams and how they work on

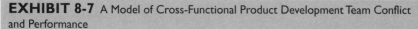

EXHIBIT 8-7 A Model of Cross-Functional Product Development Team Conflict and Performance

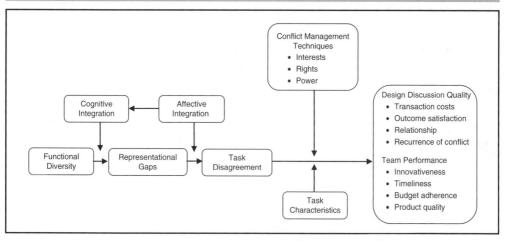

Source: Weingart, L., Cronin, M., Houser, C., Cagan, J., & Vogel, C. (2005). Functional diversity and conflict in cross-functional product development teams: Considering representational gaps and task characteristics. In L. Neider & C. Schriesheim (Eds.), *Understanding teams* (pp. 89–100). Greenwich, CT: IAP.

---

[82]Williams, K. Y., & O'Reilly, C. A. (1998). Demography and diversity in organizations. In L. L. Cummings & B. M. Staw (Eds.), *Research in organizational behavior* (Vol. 20, pp. 77–140). Greenwich, CT: JAI Press.
[83]Robertson, D., & Hjuler, P. (2009, September). Innovating a turnaround at LEGO. *Harvard Business Review, 87*(9), 20–21.
[84]Weingart, L., Cronin, M., Houser, C., Cagan, J., & Vogel, C. (2005). Functional diversity and conflict in cross-functional product development teams: Considering representational gaps and task characteristics. In L. Neider & C. Schriesheim (Eds.), *Understanding teams* (pp. 89–100). Greenwich, CT: IAP.

a day-to-day basis revealed that task disagreement was a necessary part of team functioning. The greater the representational gap, the more teams disagreed about a task.

To effectively close representational gaps in cross-functional teams, teams should share some degree of collective understanding about a problem so that they can "translate" their own knowledge bases.[85] This may be achieved through education or experience. Team members who are motivated to learn about others' perspectives are more successful than those who are less motivated.

Conclusion

Conflict in teams is unavoidable. However, it does not have to result in decreased productivity. Managed effectively, conflict can be key to leveraging differences of interest to arrive at creative solutions. However, many people intuitively respond to conflict in a defensive fashion, and this emotional type of conflict can threaten productivity. To the greatest extent possible, team members should depersonalize conflict. We have presented a variety of ways to achieve this.

---

[85]Cronin, M., & Weingart, L. (2007). Representational gaps, information processing, and conflict in functionally diverse teams. *Academy of Management Review, 32*(3), 761–773.

9 Creativity

Mastering Strategies for High Performance

The Aflac Duck is a rock star in Japan. The year that Aflac introduced the duck in Japan, Aflac became the leading insurance company, with sales increasing by 12 percent and Aflac insuring one out of every four households in Japan. How the duck became the marketing symbol for Aflac was a rather strange set of circumstances. In the late 1990s, American Family Life Assurance Company wanted some new TV advertisements and invited several agencies to pitch a creative "shoot-out." The top two agencies were invited to submit five ads for actual testing. One of the agencies was New York Kaplan Thaler Group, who came up with the duck concept because of a short-term memory problem. Seriously. They'd had a hard time remembering the clumsy name of their client's company, and one day, one of them tiredly asked a colleague, "What's the name of the account we're pitching?" The smart-aleck colleague replied, "It's Aflac— Aflac—Aflac—Aflac!" Someone then said, "You sound like a duck," and the rest is history. Kind of. Kaplan Thaler took a risk in pitching the duck because they were concerned that they would offend the client (after all they were mocking their name). The company allowed the Aflac duck to be pitched in a test commercial (after an "Everybody loves Raymond" episode), and the rating scores went through the roof! However, company execs were not pleased. Fortunately, the CEO was the biggest advocate for the duck and took a risk in spending $1 million for an initial campaign and promised to drop the duck if the numbers were not good. Success was immediate and overwhelming. On the first day, Aflac had more visits to their website than in the entire year before. Within weeks, they started getting requests for a stuffed-animal version of the duck. Aflac decided that all proceeds should go the Atlanta Cancer Care facility. When the duck went global, however, his abrasive, interrupting style did not work with the soft-spoken Japanese culture. So, the duck became a mixture of a duck and a good-luck white cat and had a softer voice. Also, the Japanese duck interacts with people.[1]

---

[1]Amos, D. (2010). CEO explains how he fell for the duck. *Harvard Business Review, 88*(1), 131–134.

Creativity requires departure from tradition and the appropriate way of conducting business. Creativity pays off. For example, in the area of "green technology" a dollar spent on research and development into cleaner energy generates $11 of economic good. Research and development accounts for nearly half of U.S. economic growth, and the rate of return in the United States is as high as 30 percent.[2]

Just because the task facing a team calls for creativity, there is no guarantee that the team members will be creative. In fact, many factors inhibit idea exchange in groups. Common wisdom holds that creativity in teams is lurking below the surface and that, with the proper intervention or team design, it can be unleashed. This view of creativity as a latent or dormant force is not accurate. Common wisdom also holds that teams are more creative than individuals. However, there is no empirical support for this; in fact, the opposite is true!

In this chapter, we explore factors that enhance creativity in teams. Team creativity is one of the least understood aspects of teamwork: Everyone wants it, but very few people know where to look for it or how to set up the conditions to make it happen.

First, we discuss creative realism and describe how creativity can be measured. Next, we explain the differences between individual creativity and team creativity. We describe several types of reasoning, including analogical reasoning and convergent and divergent thinking. Finally, we examine brainstorming techniques and discuss the advantages and disadvantages of each technique.

CREATIVE REALISM

Most people think that creative ideas are wild ideas; on the contrary, **creativity** or **ideation** is the production of *novel* and *useful* ideas—the ability to form new concepts using existing knowledge. A creative act is original and valuable. **Innovation** is the realization of novel and useful ideas in the form of products and services.

In Finke's model of creativity, there are two dimensions: creativity and structural connectedness (usefulness, Exhibit 9-1).[3] With regard to creativity, ideas can either be conservative or creative. Teams should strive to achieve creative ideas (i.e., highly original and novel ideas) as opposed to conservative, traditional ideas.

The other dimension is **structural connectedness**. Ideas that work with existing products and services are high in structural connectedness; ideas that cannot work with existing products and services are low in structural connectedness. Structural connectedness distinguishes ideas that are realistic (connected to current ideas and knowledge) from ideas that are idealistic (disconnected from current knowledge). If ideas are not connected to current ideas and knowledge, they probably are not implementable.

The most desirable ideas are those in the upper left quadrant. This domain is called **creative realism**, because these ideas are highly imaginative and highly connected to current structures and ideas. An excellent example of creative realism was Thomas Edison's development of the electric light system. Many of Edison's inventions developed through continuity with earlier inventions (see Exhibit 9-2).[4]

---

[2]Atkinson, R., & Wial, H. (2008). Creating a national innovation foundation: In this blueprint, the foundation would build on the few federal programs that already promote innovation and borrow the best public policy ideas from other nations. *Issues in Science and Technology, 25*(1), 75–84.
[3]Finke, R. A. (1995). Creative realism. In S. M. Smith, T. B. Ward, & R. A. Finke (Eds.), *The creative cognition approach* (pp. 303–326). Cambridge, MA: MIT Press.
[4]Weisberg, R. W. (1993). *Creativity: Beyond the myth of genius.* San Francisco, CA: Freeman.

EXHIBIT 9-1 Four General, Conceptual Domains Into Which New Ideas Can Be Classified

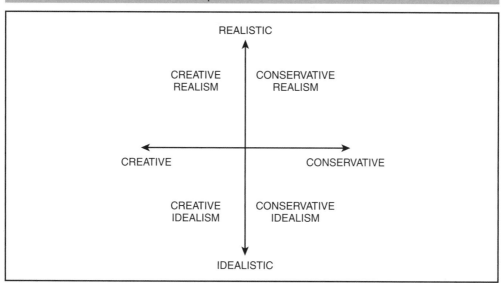

Source: Finke, R. A. (1995). Creative realism. In S. M. Smith, T. B. Ward, & R. A. Finke (Eds.), *The creative cognition approach* (pp. 303–326). Cambridge, MA: MIT Press. Copyright © 1995 Massachusetts Institute of Technology, published by The MIT Press.

EXHIBIT 9-2 Analogy in Edison's Development of an Electric Lighting System

After Thomas Edison invented the incandescent light, his next project was to develop an entire system whereby the invention could be made commercially successful. At the time, there were two in-place lighting systems (neither developed by Edison): gas lights and electrical arc lights. Gas lights could be directly controlled for brightness; gas fuel was produced offsite and sent through buried gas mains. Arc lighting was produced by an electrical spark between carbon rods, was very hot, and produced fumes. The generating plant was located directly by the user. Edison's electric lighting system was based on the principles of gas lighting. Edison wrote in his workbooks that he completely imitated the gas system, replacing the gas with electricity. In Edison's electric system, the source of power was remote from the user, and the wires that brought the power were underground. Furthermore, the individual lights were turned on and off by the user. The light bulb in Edison's system was called a burner and was designed to produce the same amount of light as a gas burner.

Source: Basalla, G. (1988). *The evolution of technology.* New York: Cambridge University Press; Weisberg, R. W. (1997). Case studies of creative thinking. In S. M. Smith, T. B. Ward, & R. A. Finke (Eds.), *The creative cognition approach.* Cambridge, MA: MIT Press.

As for the other quadrants, **conservative realism** represents ideas that are highly traditional and highly connected to current knowledge and practices. This creates little ambiguity and little uncertainty. **Conservative idealism** is an extension of a common idea that is unrealistic to begin with. These ideas exhibit little or no imagination and are not connected to existing knowledge. **Creative idealism** represents highly original, yet highly unrealistic, ideas.

How can teams maximize the probability of generating ideas that will eventually lead to novel and useful products and services? The key is to actively encourage team members to generate ideas in all of the quadrants. This way, it is possible for a great idea to emerge from a silly one. David Kelley of IDEO design believes that *enlightened trial and error beats the planning of the lone genius.*[5] According to IDEO, people *should fail early and fail often.*[6] That is why suggesting silly or ridiculous ideas (creative idealism) actually helps pave the way toward truly innovative ideas.

MEASURING CREATIVITY

Creative ideas are highly original and useful. The last part is the challenge—many people can come up with totally bizarre but useless ideas. One common way of evaluating the creativity of a team's ideas is via three indices: fluency, flexibility, and originality.[7]

- *Fluency*   is a simple measure of how many ideas a person (or team) generates. Alex Osborn, the creator of modern brainstorming, was right: Quantity often does breed quality.[8]
- *Flexibility*   is a measure of how many types of ideas a person (or team) generates.
- *Originality*   is the ability to generate unusual solutions and unique answers to problems.[9]

As a way of thinking about these three indices of creativity, do the following exercise: See how many uses you can think of for a cardboard box. (Give yourself about 10 minutes to do this.)

Now let's score your creativity (or your team's creativity) on the cardboard box challenge. Suppose one person who completed this exercise, Geoff, generated three ideas: using the box as a cage for a hamster, a container for a turtle, and a kennel for a dog. Geoff receives three points for fluency of ideas because these are three different ideas, but only one point for flexibility because the ideas are of the same category (i.e., a home for animals). It seems likely that creative people would generate more novel and unusual ways to use a cardboard box.

Suppose that another person, Avi, generates these unusual ideas for a cardboard box: placing it on an altar, using it as a telephone (e.g., two boxes and some string), and trading it as currency.[10] Avi would get a score of three points for fluency (the same as Geoff) and three points for flexibility, because there are three separate categories of ideas for use, one involving religion, another communication, and yet another entirely different idea concerning economics. Think of flexibility as a kind of mental gymnastics—the ability to entertain different types of ideas, all in a short amount of time. Most people, and in particular, most teams, tend to get stuck in one of two types of categories of thought. This is a kind of cognitive arthritis. However, some

---

[5]Kelley, T., & Littman, J. (2001). The art of innovation: Lessons in creativity from IDEO, America's leading design firm. New York: Currency Books.

[6]Brown, T. (2009). *Change by design: How design thinking transforms organizations and inspires innovation.* New York: Harper Collins.

[7]Guilford, J. P. (1959). *Personality.* New York: McGraw-Hill; Guilford, J. P. (1967). *The nature of human intelligence.* New York: McGraw-Hill.

[8]Dennis, A. R., Valacich, J. S., Connolly, T., & Wynne, B. E. (1996). Process structuring in electronic brainstorming. *Information Systems Research, 7,* 268–277.

[9]Ibid.

[10]Kurtzberg, T. (2000). *Creative styles and teamwork: Effects of coordination and conflict on group outcomes* (Doctoral dissertation). Retrieved from Proquest Dissertations & Theses: Full Text (AAT 9974311).

of Avi's ideas clearly do not meet the requirements for structural connectedness, but as we will see, Avi and his team are in a much better position to set the stage for creative realism than is Geoff.

It is easy to see how flexibility, or thinking about different categories of use—influences originality. Thus, one simple key for enhancing creativity is to simply think of different categories, which can act as "primes" or "stimulants" for more ideas. By listing different categories of use for a cardboard box (containers, shelter, building material, therapy, religion, politics, weaponry, communication, etc.), a person's score on these three dimensions could increase dramatically. Thus, a key strategy is to think in terms of categories of ideas, not just number of ideas. This can often help teams escape from a narrow perspective on a problem and open up new opportunities for creative solutions. For example, teams generate more diverse ideas when they are exposed to ideas from a wide range of categories.[11]

Originality refers to creativity on the conservative-creative continuum in Exhibit 9-1. Statistically, for an idea to be considered "original," less than 5 percent of a given population thinks of it. Thus, if there are 100 people in a company, an originality point is given to a given idea only if five or fewer people think of it.

There is a strong correlation among the three measures of fluency, flexibility, and originality. The people who get the highest scores on originality also get high scores on flexibility and fluency. And creative teams know that quantity is the best predictor of quality. There is a strong relationship between quantity, diversity, and novelty of ideas. According to Guilford, flexibility is the most important.[12] This seems to contradict most business notions of creativity, in which diversity of ideas is often not rewarded and quantity is interpreted as poor quality. Rather, in most companies and in most teams, quality is regarded as the most important objective. If flexibility is indeed the most important, how do we set the stage for it?

Convergent and Divergent Thinking

There are two key skills involved in creative thinking: **divergent thinking** and **convergent thinking**.[13] Convergent thinking is thinking that proceeds toward a single answer. For example, the expected value of a 70 percent chance of earning $1,000 is obtained by multiplying $1,000 by 0.7 to reach $700. Conversely, divergent thinking does not require a single, correct answer; rather, divergent thinking moves outward from the problem in many directions and involves thinking without boundaries.

Once a team generates ideas in a divergent fashion, eventually, they need to select an idea to develop. This is where convergent thinking is necessary. In convergent thinking, a team or person evaluates the various ideas presented as to their feasibility, practicality, and overall merit. For example, at the Tata Consultancy Services (TCS) 50 senior managers are sent every year to its 4-day "Technovator" workshop, at which its programmers are taught to think creatively. Five hours of an employee's 45-hour week can be used for personal projects, such as learning a skill or developing an idea. To better capture ideas, the company launched IdeaMax, a social network that lets any employee submit, comment, and vote on ideas. Since it was

[11]Nijstad, B. A., Stroebe, W., & Lodewijkx, H. F. M. (2003). Production blocking and idea generation: Does blocking interfere with cognitive processes? *Journal of Experimental Social Psychology, 39*, 531–548.
[12]Guilford, J. P. (1950). Creativity. *American Psychologist, 5*, 444–454.
[13]Guilford, *Personality*; Guilford, *The nature of human intelligence*.

launched in 2008, IdeaMax has collected tens of thousands of ideas, several hundred of which have become projects. As much as 10 percent of company revenues are now directly traceable to innovation activity.[14]

Task conflict stimulates divergent thinking in teams.[15] For example, teams in which a single member proposes unusual or even incorrect solutions outperform teams in which no such "deviance" occurs. Teams instructed to "debate" are more creative than teams instructed to "brainstorm."[16] Furthermore, once a team has experienced this type of activity, these performance advantages generalize to subsequent, unrelated tasks, even when the vocal, cognitively deviant member is not present.[17]

People working independently excel at divergent thinking because there are no cognitive or social pressures to constrain their thought. In short, there are no conformity pressures. In contrast, teams are much less proficient at divergent thinking. To avoid social censure, people conform to the norms of the team. Teams excel compared with individuals in convergent thinking. Teams are better at judging the quality of ideas. This suggests that an effective team design for promoting creativity involves separating the generation of ideas—leaving this to individual team members—and then evaluating and discussing the ideas as a team.

Divergent thinking is somewhat like **Janusian thinking**. Janusian thinking refers to the Roman deity Janus, who had two faces looking in opposite directions. Janusian thinking refers to the ability to cope with (and even welcome) conflicting ideas, paradoxes, ambiguity, and doubt. Teams stimulate Janusian thinking in different ways. To stimulate Janusian thinking, Tom Verberne suggests asking, "What if the world turned into your worst nightmare or your nicest dream?"[18] Open-ended questions stimulate divergent thinking. Divergent thinking is important so that people do not prematurely settle upon a suboptimal solution. At Mackay Mitchell Envelope Co. in Arizona, brainstorming meetings draw from sales, customer service, and production teams to capture divergent views and create contradiction. "If you truly want to brainstorm a problem, you can't have everyone from the same department in the room," says chairman Harvey McKay.[19]

Impossibilities can also stimulate divergent thinking. For example, challenging participants to think of ideas that are impossible to execute (e.g., living on the moon traveling by satellite) and then identifying conditions that might lead to the idea's fruition.

Many of the factors that facilitate creative problem solving are related to divergent thinking. However, teams also need to engage in convergent thinking. The common problem is that teams often focus on convergent thinking at the expense of divergent thinking. Teams are better than groups at convergent thinking, but they are worse than them at divergent thinking. Even though the scientific evidence is clear, most people strongly believe that teams are more creative than individuals when, in fact, they aren't.

[14]Scanlon, J. (2009, August 19). How to build a culture of innovation. *Business Week.* businessweek.com

[15]Nemeth, C. J., & Ormiston, M. (2007). Creative idea generation: Harmony versus stimulation. *European Journal of Social Psychology, 37*(3), 524–535; Nemeth, C. J., Personnaz, M., Personnaz, B., & Goncalo, J. A. (2004). The liberating role of conflict in group creativity: A study in two countries. *European Journal of Social Psychology, 34*, 365–374; Nemeth, C. J., & Nemeth-Brown, B. (2003). Better than individuals? The potential benefits of dissent and diversity for group creativity. In P. B. Paulus & B. A. Nijstad (Eds.), *Group creativity: Innovation through collaboration* (pp. 63–84). New York: Oxford University Press.

[16]Nemeth & Ormiston, "Creative idea generation," p. 227.

[17]Smith, C. M., Tindale, R. S., & Dugoni, B. L. (1996). Minority and majority influence in freely interacting groups: Qualitative vs. quantitative differences. *British Journal of Social Psychology, 35*, 137–149.

[18]Verberne, T. (1997). Creative fitness. *Training and Development, 51*(8), 68–71.

[19]Mackay, H. (2008, October 12). Employers should encourage employee brainstorming. *The Arizona Republic.* Azcentral.com

Exploration and Exploitation

James March distinguished two types of processes that companies pursue: exploration and exploitation.[20] **Exploration** refers to activities such as search, variation, risk taking, experimentation, play, flexibility, discovery, and innovation. According to Tim Brown, CEO of IDEO, you can't have an organization that says it's OK to innovate but punishes people every time they fail.[21] When IDEO designers take a break from working with particular clients such as Kraft and Samsung to experiment in "pure future gazing," they start to explore.[22] Even in difficult economic times, exploration is a vital part of business strategy. "Innovation has a bad name in down times, but bad times focus the mind and the best-focused minds in the down times are looking for the opportunities," says David Thompson, chief executive and cofounder of Genius.com Inc. "You do have to batten down the hatches and reduce expenses, but you can't do it at the expense of the big picture. You always have to keep in mind the bigger picture that's coming down the road in two or three years."[23] An examination of leader behaviors in seven companies that stimulate creativity revealed that leaders who provide their teams a great deal of autonomy are more creative.[24] When Amazon introduced the Kindle, an electronic reader, in 2008, the company made a calculated risk of *making* an electronic instead of merely *selling* electronics. For Amazon CEO Jeff Bezos, it was a risk worth taking. "There are two ways to extend a business," Bezos said. "Take inventory of what you're good at and extend out from your skills. Or determine what your customers need and work backward, even if it requires learning new skills. Kindle is an example of working backward." The Kindle sold more units than the iPod in its first year, more than justifying the risk to Amazon. "We want to plant seeds that grow into big trees, and that may take five to seven years," Bezos said. "You also have to be willing to repeatedly fail—and to be misunderstood for long periods of time."[25]

In contrast, **exploitation** refers to refinement, choice, production, efficiency, selection, implementation, and execution of an idea. There is a balance between the two activities. Teams that engage in exploration to the exclusion of exploitation are likely to find that they suffer the costs of experimentation without gaining many of its benefits, and they will exhibit too many underdeveloped new ideas and too little distinctive competence. For example, when Swiss watchmaker Victorinox acquired Swiss Army Brand, the leading manufacturer of Swiss Army knives, it was obvious that a blade couldn't be integrated into a watch. So, it was contingent upon designers to create a watch in the spirit of Swiss Army's outdoor theme. Eighteen months later, the Night Vision watch was created, which features a button on the side that turns on a white ray of light, a handy feature for campers or anybody needing a quick light in the dark. The same button, if pushed for 5 seconds, activates an emergency signal: The light flashes regularly for 7 days, a potential lifesaver that can be seen at night from a distance of more than a mile.[26] Teams and organizations that engage in exploitation to the exclusion of exploration may find themselves trapped in old ways of thinking. For individuals that are high in learning orientation (dispositionally inclined to learn), team learning behavior and exploration bolsters

---

[20]March, J. G. (1991). Exploration and exploitation in organizational learning. *Organization Science, 2*(1), 71–87.

[21]Budman, M. (2009, Fall). Grand designs. *The Conference Board Review*, pp. 25–33.

[22]McKeough, T. (2009, December). Blowing hot and cold. *Fast Company*, p. 66.

[23]Rae-Dupree, J. (2008, November 2). It's no time to forget about innovation. *New York Times*, p. 4.

[24]Amabile, T. M., Schatzel, E. A., Moneta, G. B., & Kramer, S. J. (2004). Leader behaviors and the work environment for creativity: Perceived leader support. *Leadership Quarterly, 15*, 5–32.

[25]Salter, C. (2009, February 11). #9 Amazon. *Fast Company*. fastcompany.com

[26]Gelnar, M. (2008, June 23). No time for nonsense. *Wall Street Journal*, p. R6.

creativity.[27] Despite the seemingly contradictory tasks of exploration (creativity) and exploitation (standardization), they can be complementary. For example, 90 service technician teams of a large multinational corporation found that standardization leads to greater customer satisfaction, but greater creativity leads to better team performance.[28]

Creativity and Context Dependence

Creative acts take place within a particular context and a particular domain, given a set of certain resources.[29] Consider the *Mona Lisa*, Stephen Hawking's theory of the universe, and the development of the microcomputer. All these are tremendously creative acts that seem to go above and beyond the simple measures of fluency, flexibility, and originality. These achievements are not only unique but also impressive because they were invented with limited resources and in the face of numerous obstacles. If an artist painted the *Mona Lisa* today—even if it had not already been done by Leonardo da Vinci—it probably would not be regarded as an especially creative act. A more sobering example is the tattoo artists in Russia's prison system.[30] The inmates use ink made from soot from shoes mixed with urine, injected via guitar strings attached to electric shavers. The tattoos are murals covering entire chests and backs that are coded biographies of life stories. Such behavior might seem ghoulish or even barbarian, but in the context of the Russian prison, the tattoos are a mark of resourcefulness, self-expression, and industriousness.

CREATIVE PEOPLE OR CREATIVE TEAMS?

Is creativity a characteristic of individuals or groups? The answer is both. There is little doubt that some people are more creative than others. Creativity is highly correlated with intelligence, motivation, ambition, persistence, commitment, determination, education, and success in general. Creative people are passionate about specific things. Perhaps this is why when former professor Joseph Campbell selected postdoctoral students for his laboratory at Sarah Lawrence College, he did not want people who earned straight As or Bs. He searched for the student who made both As and Fs, because he believed these people are not just smart—they let their passions rule them.[31] According to Amabile, the most important aspect of creativity is loving what you do.[32] Creative people are also in tune with their creativity, and they know how to reinvigorate themselves. As a case in point, Michael Jordan, who, by the mid-1990s, was the most financially successful basketball player in history, had a "love of the game" clause in his contract, which secured him the right to play in "pick-up games" whenever he wished. Jordan did not always play because it was contracted for him to do so; rather his love of the game guided him. Amabile's experimental evidence also reveals that evaluation, surveillance, and even offering rewards to people can undermine creativity.[33]

---

[27]Hirst, G., Knippenberg, D. V., & Zhou, J. (2009). A cross-level perspective on employee creativity: Goal orientation, team learning behavior, and individual creativity. *The Academy of Management Journal, 52*(2), 280–293.

[28]Gilson, L. L., Mathieu, J. E., Shalley, C. E., & Ruddy, T. M. (2005). Creativity and standardization: Complementary or conflicting drivers of team effectiveness. *Academy of Management Journal, 48*(3), 521–531.

[29]Csikszentmihalyi, M. (1988). Society, culture and person: A systems view of creativity. In R. Sternberg (Ed.), *The nature of productivity: Contemporary psychological perspectives.* New York: Cambridge University Press.

[30]Flora, C. (2009, November 1). Every day creativity. *Psychology Today, 42*(6), 62–43.

[31]Muoio, A. (1997, August). They have a better idea . . . do you? *Fast Company, 10*, 73–79.

[32]Amabile, T. M. (1997). Motivating creativity in organizations: On doing what you love and loving what you do. *California Management Review, 40*(1), 39–58.

[33]Ibid.

An extended period of preparation is involved in most creative products and ideas. Creative people work very hard. For example, creative scientists typically work 70 to 80 hours a week. It typically takes people at least 10 years to develop expertise in their domain, no matter what it is— chess, tennis, astrophysics, or management. Skilled chess players undergo years of study before they become "masters."[34] And, no one composes outstanding music without at least 10 years of intensive musical preparation.[35] This all adds up to about 10,000 hours of focused practice. Basically, if you have been working hard for years at something, think in terms of decades before you become truly great! Ideally companies should select people who are passionate and skilled in what they do, and then bring those people together with others who are similar (in the sense of being passionate) but different (in terms of ways of thinking). Individualistic groups who are instructed to be creative are more creative than collectivistic groups, given the same instructions.[36] Creative combinations of people can be more effective than trying to select creative people because creativity is much more a function of the right idea at the right time than a chronic disposition. Jacques Heim, who founded Diavolo Dance Theater, was in Aspen, Colorado, with his dance company, using an elementary classroom as a dressing room. The classroom was full of toys. Heim saw a box of blocks, including identical five-sided pyramids that created a cube. "I was inspired by the geometry behind it," Heim said, "and played with it for months."' Ultimately those cubes led to a performance piece called "Foreign Bodies," set to music by Esa-Pekka Salonen, music director of the Los Angeles Philharmonic. Members of Diavolo—gymnasts, actors, and dancers—use everyday objects like doors, stairs, and chairs for dramatic movement, as well as the three mobile pyramids for Foreign Bodies. "I believe that if you have the child inside you and you walk down the streets, things happen to you," Heim said. "Intuition. That's how I operate."[37]

Brainstorming

Alex Osborn, an advertising executive in the 1950s, believed that one of the main hindrances to organizational creativity was the premature evaluation of ideas. Osborn was convinced that two heads were better than one when it came to generating ideas, but only if people could be trained to defer judgment of their own and others' ideas during the idea generation process. Therefore, Osborn developed the most widespread strategy used by organizations to encourage creative thought in teams: **brainstorming**.

In an influential book, *Applied Imagination*, Osborn suggested that brainstorming could dramatically increase the quality and quantity of ideas produced by group members.[38] In short, Osborn believed that the group product could be greater than the sum of the individual parts if certain conditions were met. Hence, Osborn developed rules to govern the conduct of brainstorming. Contrary to corporate lore that brainstorming sessions are wild and crazy free-for-alls where anything goes, Osborn's rules were specific and simple: (1) criticism is ruled out, (2) free-wheeling is welcome, (3) quantity is desired, and (4) combination and improvement of ideas are encouraged (see Exhibit 9-3).

---

[34]DeGroot, A. (1966). Perception and memory versus thought: Some old ideas and recent findings. In B. Kleinmuntz (Ed.), *Problem solving: Research, method, and theory* (pp. 19–50). New York: John Wiley & Sons.
[35]Weisberg, R. W. (1986). *Creativity, genius and other myths.* New York: Freeman.
[36]Goncalo, J. A., & Staw, B. M. (2006). Individualism-collectivism and group creativity. *Organizational Behavior and Human Decision Processes, 100*, 96–109.
[37]Meece, M. (2008, October 23). Inspiration can be found in many places, but you need to be looking. *New York Times*, p. B9.
[38]Osborn, A. F. (1957). *Applied imagination* (rev. ed.). New York: Scribner; Osborn, A. F. (1963). *Applied imagination* (3rd ed.). New York: Scribner.

EXHIBIT 9-3 Rules for Brainstorming

Expressiveness:	Group members should express any idea that comes to mind, no matter how strange, weird, or fanciful. Group members are encouraged not to be constrained or timid. They should freewheel whenever possible.
Nonevaluation:	Do not criticize ideas. Group members should not evaluate any of the ideas in any way during the generation phase; all ideas should be considered valuable.
Quantity:	Group members should generate as many ideas as possible. Groups should strive for quantity, as the more ideas, the better. Quantity of ideas increases the probability of finding excellent solutions.
Building:	Because all of the ideas belong to the group, members should try to modify and extend the ideas suggested by other members whenever possible.

Source: Adapted from Osborn, A. F. (1957). *Applied imagination* (rev. ed.). New York: Scribner.

Brainstorming caught on like wildfire in corporations and is a technique that has remained very popular.[39] The goal of brainstorming is to maximize the quantity and quality of ideas. Osborn aptly noted that quantity is a good predictor of quality. A team is more likely to discover a really good idea if it has a lot of ideas to choose from. But there is more to brainstorming than mere quantity. Osborn believed that the ideas generated by one person in a team could stimulate ideas in other people in a synergistic fashion, also known as **cognitive stimulation**.

Osborn believed, as did others, that the four rules enhanced motivation among team members by stimulating them to higher levels of productivity via establishment of a benchmark or via competitive rivalry to see who could generate the most ideas. Osborn also thought that the social reinforcement of fellow members increased motivation. Finally, Osborn believed in a **priming effect**, namely, that members would make mutual associations upon hearing the ideas presented by others.

Brainstorming on Trial

Osborn claimed that a team who adopted these four rules could generate twice as many ideas as a similar number of people working independently. But he did not provide any scientific evidence. Consequently, the question that organizational psychologists and management theorists asked of the brainstorming technique was, "Is it effective?" Controlled, scientific studies supported Osborn's intuition. Brainstorming instructions enhance the generation of ideas within a team, in comparison to teams working without those instructions.[40] Thus, following the four brainstorming guidelines increases team creativity as compared to no rules.

However, Osborn's most controversial claim was that group brainstorming would be more effective—"twice as productive," in his words—than **individual brainstorming**, in

---

[39]Kayser, T. A. (1995). *Mining group gold: How to cash in on the collaborative genius of work teams.* Chicago, IL: Irwin.
[40]Parnes, S. J., & Meadow, A. (1959). Effect of "brain-storming" instructions on creative problem-solving by trained and untrained subjects. *Journal of Educational Psychology, 50,* 171–176.

which group members work independently.[41] The research evidence testing this assertion has found that the opposite is true (see Exhibit 9-4). In a typical investigation, the performance of a real group is compared to a control group, the same number of people who work alone and never interact. The control group is called a **nominal group** because they are a group in number only.

Nearly all controlled investigations have found that *group brainstorming is less efficient than solitary brainstorming in both laboratory and organizational settings.*[42] *Solitary brainstorming is much more productive than group brainstorming, in terms of quality and quantity of ideas.*[43] In fact, virtually all of the empirical studies on group brainstorming are strongly (not just mildly) negative in regard to its effectiveness compared with solitary brainstorming.[44] Thus, over 50 years of research on brainstorming has found that brainstorming is significantly worse in terms of fostering creativity than having the same number of people work independently on a given task.

These results have been replicated several hundred times with a variety of teams brainstorming about all kinds of things. "It appears particularly difficult to justify brainstorming

EXHIBIT 9-4 Performance Data of Brainstorming and Solitary Groups

	Face-to-Face Brainstorming Group	Same Number of People Working Independently (Solitary Brainstorming)
Quantity: The number of ideas generated	28	74.5
Quality: Percentage of "Good ideas" as judged by independent experts who did not know whose ideas they were evaluating	8.9%	12.7%

Source: Based on Diehl, M., & Stroebe, W. (1987). Productivity loss in brainstorming groups: Toward a solution of a riddle. *Journal of Personality and Social Psychology, 53*, 497–509.

[41]Osborn, *Applied imagination* (rev. ed.), p. 230.
[42]Diehl, M., & Stroebe, W. (1987). Productivity loss in brainstorming groups: Toward a solution of a riddle. *Journal of Personality and Social Psychology, 53*(3), 497–509; Jablin, F. M. (1981). Cultivating imagination: Factors that enhance and inhibit creativity in brainstorming groups. *Human Communication Research, 7*(3), 245–258; Mullen, B., Johnson, C., & Salas, E. (1991). Productivity loss in brainstorming groups: A meta-analytic integration. *Basic and Applied Social Psychology, 12*, 3–23; Paulus, P. B., & Dzindolet, M. T. (1993). Social influence processes in group brainstorming. *Journal of Personality and Social Psychology, 64*, 575–586; Paulus, P. B., Larey, T. S., & Ortega, A. H. (1995). Performance and perceptions of brainstormers in an organizational setting. *Basic and Applied Social Psychology, 17*, 249–265; Taylor, D. W., Berry, P. C., & Block, C. H. (1958). Does group participation when using brainstorming facilitate or inhibit creative thinking? *Administrative Science Quarterly, 3*, 23–47.
[43]Rietzschel, E. F., Nijstad, B. A. & Stroebe, W. (2006). Productivity is not enough: A comparison of interactive and nominal groups on idea generation and selection. *Journal of Experimental Social Psychology, 42*(2), 244–251; McGlynn, R. P., McGurk, D., Effland, V. S., Johll, N. L., & Harding, D. J. (2004). Brainstorming and task performance in groups constrained by evidence. *Organizational Behavior and Human Decision Processes, 93*, 1, 75–90; Diehl & Stroebe, "Productivity loss in brainstorming groups," p. 232; Mullen, Johnson, & Salas, "Productivity loss in brainstorming groups," p. 232.
[44]Diehl & Stroebe, "Productivity loss in brainstorming groups," p. 232; Mullen, Johnson, & Salas, "Productivity loss in brainstorming groups," p. 232.

techniques in terms of any performance outcomes, and the long-lived popularity of brainstorming techniques is unequivocally and substantially misguided."[45] Whereas nominal groups outperform real groups when it comes to idea generation, nominal groups do not outperform real groups when it comes to idea selection.[46]

Thus, official rules of brainstorming, when followed, enhance team performance, but brainstorming teams still generate fewer ideas than similar numbers of solitary brainstormers (nominal groups). Despite the empirical evidence attesting to the ineffectiveness of brainstorming, teams engaged in brainstorming suffer from an illusion of productivity.[47] In short, they believe they are more creative, when in fact they aren't.

THREATS TO TEAM CREATIVITY

Why are individuals more creative than teams? Four major problems stifle the effectiveness of team brainstorming. The problem is not teamwork itself, but rather the social and cognitive processes that operate in teams and how teams are managed. We refer to these problems as social loafing, conformity, production blocking, and performance matching.

Social Loafing

Social loafing is the tendency for people to slack off—for example, not work as hard (either mentally or physically) in a group as they would alone. Indeed, as the number of team members increases, each person is more likely to free ride.[48] It is as if members say to themselves, "I don't need to work really hard when thinking of ideas, because everyone else is working too." This free-riding tendency may be especially true when members' outcomes cannot be individually identified or evaluated. Moreover, when team members perceive their own contributions to be unidentifiable and dispensable, they are likely to loaf.[49] Contrary to intuition, the degree to which a brainstorming topic is regarded as "enjoyable" does not affect persistence.[50]

Conformity

A basic human principle is the desire to be liked and accepted by others (in particular, groups). People identify with groups and will sometimes engage in bizarre behaviors to gain acceptance by the group.[51] People on a team may be somewhat apprehensive about expressing their ideas

---

[45]Mullen, Johnson, & Salas, "Productivity loss in brainstorming groups," p. 232.

[46]Rietzschel, Nijstad, & Stroebe, "Productivity is not enough," p. 232.

[47]Paulus, P. B., Dzindolet, M. T., Poletes, G., & Camacho, L. M. (1993, February). Perception of performance in group brainstorming: The illusion of group productivity. *Personality and Social Psychology Bulletin, 19*(1), 78–89; McGlynn, McGurk, Effland, Johll, & Harding, "Brainstorming and task performance," p. 232.

[48]Karau, S. J., & Williams, K. D. (1993). Social loafing: A meta-analytic review and theoretical integration. *Journal of Personality and Social Psychology, 65,* 681–706; Shepperd, J. A. (1993). Productivity loss in performance groups: A motivation analysis. *Psychological Bulletin, 113,* 67–81.

[49]Bouchard, T. J. (1972). Training, motivation, and personality as determinants of the effectiveness of brainstorming groups and individuals. *Journal of Applied Psychology, 56*(4), 324–331; Diehl & Stroebe, "Productivity loss in brainstorming groups," p. 232; Harkins, S. G., & Petty, R. E. (1982). Effects of task difficulty and task uniqueness on social loafing. *Journal of Personality and Social Psychology, 43*(6), 1214–1229; Shepperd, "Productivity loss in performance groups," p. 233.

[50]Nijstad, B. A., Stroebe, W., & Lodewijkx, H. F. M. (1999). Persistence of brainstorming groups: How do people know when to stop? *Journal of Experimental Social Psychology, 35,* 165–185.

[51]Tajfel, H. (Ed.). (1978). *Differentiation between social groups: Studies in the social psychology of intergroup relations.* New York: Academic Press.

because they are concerned about others judging and evaluating them.[52] This is the need to be liked, which we discussed in Chapter 7 (decision making). Most people desire to be viewed positively by others.[53] This concern for "what others will think of me" may inhibit idea generation in teams.[54] **Conformity** can occur even when group members are concerned that others in the group will be critical of their suggestions, despite instructions designed to minimize such concerns.[55] In particular, team members may suggest "appropriate," traditional, conservative, and highly similar ideas—exactly the kind of behavior that most teams want to avoid. Many social conventions, even those in companies, suggest that in most settings, people should stay "on topic" and not present ideas that diverge greatly from the ones being discussed. Indeed, in interactive teams, there is much more of a tendency to stay on topic than with individual brainstorming. This convergent pattern limits the exchange of ideas that are relatively novel to the team and possibly have the most stimulation value. For example, people make more conventional and clichéd responses to word associations when they are in a group than when they are alone.

Production Blocking

Production blocking occurs when group members cannot express their ideas because others are presenting their ideas. Essentially, research on multitasking unambiguously reveals that trying to do two or more things makes people less productive.[56] Production blocking is an example of a coordination problem. A person who is working alone on a problem can enjoy an uninterrupted flow of thought. Participants in a face-to-face brainstorming group must not only think of ideas but also listen to others' ideas, and they have to wait for their turn to speak and remember to use conventional floor-taking and floor-yielding signals. It is cognitively difficult to maintain a train of thought or remember ideas generated while others are talking.[57] Members of teams may be prevented from generating new ideas during a team discussion because they are distracted by hearing the contributions of other members while waiting for their turn to participate. During the waiting period, members may listen to others' contributions and, in the process, forget to rehearse the ideas they want to mention. Consequently, people may forget their ideas or decide not to present them during the waiting period.[58] Furthermore, the inability to express ideas or get floor time may be frustrating and depress motivation. Whereas Osborn theorized that groups could "build on" the ideas suggested by others, there is no evidence for any stimulating impact of unique or rare ideas in brainstorming.[59] Production blocking

[52]Mullen, Johnson, & Salas, "Productivity loss in brainstorming groups," p. 232.
[53]Leary, M. (1995). *Self-presentation: Impression management and behavior.* Dubuque, IA: Brown & Benchmark.
[54]Camacho, L. M., & Paulus, P. B. (1995). The role of social anxiousness in group brainstorming. *Journal of Personality and Social Psychology, 68,* 1071–1080.
[55]Collaros, P. A., & Anderson, L. R. (1969). Effect of perceived expertness upon creativity of members of brainstorming groups. *Journal of Applied Psychology, 53*(2, Pt. 1), 159–163; Diehl & Stroebe, "Productivity loss in brainstorming groups," p. 232; Harari, O., & Graham, W. K. (1975). Tasks and task consequences as factors in individual and group brainstorming. *Journal of Social Psychology, 95*(1), 61–65.
[56]Pashler, H. (2000). Task switching and multitask performance. In S. Monsell & J. Driver (Eds.), *Attention and performance XVIII: Control of mental processes* (pp. 227–308). Cambridge, MA: MIT Press.
[57]Diehl & Stroebe, "Productivity loss in brainstorming groups," p. 232.
[58]Diehl & Stroebe, "Productivity loss in brainstorming groups," p. 232; Diehl, M., & Stroebe, W. (1991). Productivity loss in idea-generating groups: Tracking down the blocking effect. *Journal of Personality and Social Psychology, 61*(3), 392–403; Stroebe, W., & Diehl, M. (1994). Why are groups less effective than their members? On productivity losses in idea generating groups. *European Review of Social Psychology, 5,* 271–301.
[59]Connolly, T., Routhieaux, R. L., & Schneider, S. K. (1993). On the effectiveness of group brainstorming: Test of one underlying cognitive mechanism. *Small Group Research, 24,* 490–503.

interferes with idea generation in two distinct ways: (1) it disrupts the organization of idea generation when delays are relatively long and (2) it reduces the flexibility of idea generation when delays are unpredictable.[60]

Performance Matching

It is commonly observed that the performance of people working within a group tends to converge over time. Social comparison processes may lead team members to converge their performance levels into one another.[61] For example, at CDW, salespeople working in the same physical location in the building report monthly sales figures more similar to one another than those working in other buildings and areas.[62] There is a pervasive tendency for the lowest performers in a group to dampen the team average. Indeed, people working in brainstorming groups tend to match their performance to that of the least productive members, also known as **downward norm setting.**[63] Performance matching is most likely to occur when there are no strong internal or external incentives for high performance in teams.[64] For example, the initial performance level of the two lowest-performing members predicts the performance of a group of four toward the end of the session.[65] This performance level may set the benchmark for a team, in that it is seen as an appropriate or typical level of performance. Because groups start their brainstorming by performing at a relatively low level, high performers may feel like "deviants." As a result, they may move their performance in the direction of the low group standard. For example, participants in interactive dyads or groups of four tend to be more similar in their rate of idea generation than non-interacting groups.[66] Unfortunately, the least productive members of the team are often more influential in determining overall team performance than the high performers. When teams are competing against another team, however, they do not fall victim to performance matching.[67]

What Goes on During a Typical Group Brainstorming Session?

What exactly could we expect to observe in a typical team brainstorming session? Video and audio recordings reveal an interesting set of events. The four problems noted above conspire to cause people in most brainstorming groups to:

- Fail to follow, or abide by, the rules of brainstorming
- Experience inhibitions, anxiety, and self-presentational concerns
- Slack off production

---

[60]Nijstad, Stroebe, & Lodewijkx, "Production blocking and idea generation."
[61]Jackson, J. M., & Harkins, S. G. (1985). Equity in effort: An explanation of the social loafing effect. *Journal of Personality and Social Psychology, 49,* 1199–1206.
[62]This observation was shared by a manager in the company.
[63]Camacho & Paulus, "Role of social anxiousness," p. 234; Paulus & Dzindolet, "Social influence processes," p. 232.
[64]Shepperd, "Productivity loss in performance groups," p. 233.
[65]Paulus & Dzindolet, "Social influence processes," p. 232.
[66]Camacho & Paulus, "Role of social anxiousness," p. 234; Paulus & Dzindolet, "Social influence processes," p. 232.
[67]Munkes, J., & Diehl, M. (2003). Matching or competition? Performance comparison processes in an idea generation task. *Group Processes and Intergroup Relations, 6,* 305–320.

- Participate in nonproductive social rituals, such as telling stories, repeating ideas, and giving positive feedback (a natural pattern of conversation that works well at cocktail parties, but that kills creativity)
- Set their performance benchmarks too low
- Conform in terms of ideas
- Conform in terms of rate of idea generation

Most disturbing is that most people on brainstorming teams have no idea that this is occurring, such that their performance is suffering; paradoxically, interactive brainstorming teams feel quite confident about their productivity. Thus, the group suffers from a faulty performance illusion. Brainstorming teams and the companies who use them are their own worst enemy. They fall prey to the illusion that they function very effectively. They suffer from illusions of invulnerability, collective rationalization, belief in the morality of the group, and stereotyping of outgroups. In fact, the illusion of performance is so self-serving that people often take credit for the ideas generated by others.[68]

Brainstorming is simply not as effective as it was hoped to be. What can be done to restructure the design of brainstorming groups?

ENHANCING TEAM CREATIVITY

Fortunately, there are actions that team leaders can take to ward off the typical problems that brainstorming produces.[69] We organize our best practices into three areas: cognitive-goal instructions, social-organizational suggestions, and structural-environmental suggestions (see Exhibit 9-5). The best practices outlined in Exhibit 9-5 all have a strong scientific research basis, yet they are practical as well.[70]

EXHIBIT 9-5 Best Practices for Improving Creative Teamwork

Cognitive-Goal Instructions	Social-Organizational Methods	Structural-Environmental Methods
• Set high-quantity goals	• Trained facilitators	• Diversify the team
• Explicit set of rules	• Brainwriting	• Fluid membership
• Paulus's new rules	• Brief breaks	• Organizational networking
• Positive mood	• Nominal group	• Traverse industries
• Increase individual accountability	technique	• Build a creative space and environment
• Analogical reasoning	• Delphi technique	
	• Stepladder technique	

[68]Stroebe, W., Diehl, M., & Abakoumkin, G. (1992). The illusion of group effectivity. *Personality and Social Psychology Bulletin, 18*(5), 643–650.

[69]Thompson, L. (2003). Improving the creativity of organizational work groups. *Academy of Management Executive, 17*(1), 96–109.

[70]Paulus, P. B., & Nakui, T. (2005). Facilitation of group brainstorming. In S. Schuman (Ed.), *The IAF handbook of group facilitation* (pp. 103–114). San Francisco, CA: Jossey-Bass; Paulus, P. B., & Brown, V. R. (2003). Enhancing ideational creativity in groups: Lesson from research on brainstorming. In P. B. Paulus & B. A. Nijstad (Eds.), *Group creativity: Innovation through collaboration* (pp. 110–136). New York: Oxford University Press.

Cognitive-Goal Instructions

Cognitive-goal instructions focus on how to change the mind-set and accompanying cognitions of team members.

SET HIGH-QUANTITY GOALS   Brainstorming groups often underperform because they don't have relevant goals or benchmarks. Information about other members' activity levels may increase performance as long as the benchmark is not too discrepant.[71] Providing brainstormers with high performance standards greatly increases the number of ideas generated.[72] Even when members work independently and announce how many ideas they are generating every 5 minutes, the number of ideas generated by the team is enhanced.[73] Similarly, a facilitator can periodically call brainstormers' attention to a graph on a computer screen indicating how the team's performance compares with that of other teams—this significantly enhances the number of ideas generated by the group.[74] Forewarning teams that they will see a display of all ideas at the end of the session increases the number of unique ideas generated.[75] Exposure to a high number of ideas increases creativity.[76] It is desirable to set goals for quantity, but it is undesirable to set actual production goals. Goal-setting for production goals (such as when Ford came out with the Pinto, a veritable death machine) can lead to short-cuts and disasters.[77]

At Memorial Hospital in South Bend, CEO Phillip Newbold created the Innovation Cafe, which encourages staff to have fun by making cardboard prototypes of their planned projects and rewards those who come up with even "good tries." Newbold holds regular brainstorming sessions and often makes everyone stand for the entire 21-minute exercise so they will think fast on their feet.[78]

Another way of setting high benchmarks is through internal competition. For example, people working on a task perform better when they are paired with a partner who is slightly better (versus slightly worse or the same).[79] In late 2007, Cisco systems announced the *I Prize* competition, with a goal of building a new billion-dollar Cisco business around the winning idea to emerge from among many outside contributions. The contest called for an idea that would align with Cisco's strategy and take advantage of its leadership position in Internet technology. More than 2,500 people from 104 countries registered on the *I Prize* Web site and submitted more than 1,200 ideas. After a nearly yearlong process of winnowing and evaluation, an in-house judging panel chose an idea for creating a "smart" electricity grid—a natural fit with Cisco's competencies and long-term strategy.[80]

---

[71]Seta, J. J. (1982). The impact of comparison processes on coactors' task performance. *Journal of Personality and Social Psychology, 42*, 281–291.

[72]Paulus & Dzindolet, "Social influence processes," p. 232.

[73]Paulus, P. B., Larey, T. S., Putman, V. L., Leggett, K. L., & Roland, E. J. (1996). Social influence process in computer brainstorming. *Basic and Applied Social Psychology, 18*, 3–14.

[74]Shepherd, M. M., Briggs, R. O., Reinig, B. A., Yen, J., & Nunamaker, J. F., Jr. (1995–1996). Invoking social comparison to improve electronic brainstorming: Beyond anonymity. *Journal of Management Information Systems, 12*, 155–170.

[75]Roy, M. C., Gauvin, S., & Limayem, M. (1996). Electronic group brainstorming: The role of feedback on productivity. *Small Group Research, 27*, 215–247.

[76]Dugosh, K. L., & Paulus, P. B. (2005). Cognitive and social comparison processes in brainstorming. *Journal of Experimental Social Psychology, 41*, 313–320.

[77]Ordóñez, L. D., Schweitzer, M. E., Galinsky, A. D., & Bazerman, M. H. (2009, February). Goals gone wild: The systematic side effects of overprescribing goal setting. *Academy of Management Perspectives, 23*(1), 6–16.

[78]Lublin, J. S. (2008, September 2). A CEO's recipe for fresh ideas. *Wall Street Journal*, p. D4.

[79]Seta, "The impact of comparison processes on coactors' task performance."

[80]Jouret, G. (2009, September 1). Inside Cisco's search for the next big idea. *Harvard Business Review, 87*(9), 43–45.

EXPLICIT SET OF RULES   Any rules are better than no rules. Teams that follow Osborn's four rules of brainstorming are more effective than those that don't.[81] And companies that develop and use rules for the creative process report greater gains. Many companies use the original brainstorming rules suggested by Osborn 50 years ago. At IDEO, seven rules govern every brainstorming session: defer judgment, encourage wild ideas, build on the ideas of others, stay focused on the topic, one conversation at a time, be visual, and go for quantity.[82] Cambridge Technology Partners made up three rules to govern their teamwork: (1) a 2-minute rule for seeking advice (don't wait more than 2 minutes to ask for help from the team when stuck); (2) learn as you go (group spends half day assessing its work); (3) fast has to be fun (e.g., going on team outings once a week and having a database of the team's favorite ice-cream flavors).[83] At W.L. Gore & Associates, there are no titles on business cards and 10 percent "dabble time."[84]

PAULUS'S NEW RULES   Paulus and his colleagues examined the effects of four new brainstorming rules:[85]

- Stay focused on the task.
- Do not tell stories or explain ideas.
- When no one is suggesting ideas, restate the problem and encourage each other to generate ideas.
- Encourage those who are not talking to make a contribution.

In one investigation, either a trained experimenter or someone selected from the group enforced the rules.[86] There was a 40 percent increase in the number of ideas generated using the new rules. These groups generated ideas at a level comparable to that of nominal groups. Other research found clear benefits of the additional rules under a variety of conditions. The benefits of the additional rules also increase the efficiency of ideas, meaning that members are more parsimonious (i.e., use fewer words) to express a given idea.

INCREASE INDIVIDUAL ACCOUNTABILITY   Team members who feel individually accountable for their idea are more productive than teams in which it is not possible to discern who contributed what. Individual accountability decreases the free-rider (social loafing) effect discussed in Chapter 2.

POSITIVE MOOD   Positive affect—whether it comes from reading a funny cartoon or seeing puppies play—increases creativity.[87] In a complementary fashion, negative mood decreases

[81]Parnes & Meadow, "Effect of 'brain-storming' instructions on creative problem-solving by trained and untrained subjects."

[82]Dominguez, P. (2008, June 16). IDEO's 7 rules of brainstorming. *Green Business Innovators.* Greenbusinessinnovators.com

[83]Matson, E. (1996). Four rules for fast teams. *Fast Company*, vol.4. Retreived from www.fastcompany.com/magazine/04/speed3.html

[84]Glader, P. (2009, October 7). Cultivate the creative class within your companies . . . or else [Web log post]. blogs.wsj.com

[85]Paulus, P. B., Nakui, T., Putman, V. L., & Brown, V. R. (2006). Effects of task instructions and brief breaks on brainstorming. *Group Dynamics: Theory, Research, and Practice, 10*(3), pp. 206–219.

[86]Oxley, N. L., Dzindolet, M. T., & Paulus, P. B. (1996). The effects of facilitators on the performance of brainstorming groups. *Journal of Social Behavior and Personality, 11*(4), 633–646.

[87]Isen, A. M., Daubman, K. A., & Nowicki, G. P. (1987). Positive affect facilitates creative problem solving. *Journal of Personality and Social Psychology, 47*, 1206–1217.

productivity. The creativity of a large high-technology firm was studied before, during, and after a major downsizing.[88] Obviously, downsizings engender negative mood and, in this case, were accompanied by decreases in project team creativity. In an investigation of 222 employees in seven companies, positive affect is associated with greater creativity.[89] With regard to stress, there is a curvilinear relationship between evaluative stress and creativity, such that low evaluative contexts increase creativity, but highly evaluative contexts decrease creativity.[90]

ANALOGICAL REASONING   Analogical reasoning is the act of applying one concept or idea from a particular domain to another domain. The simplest analogy might be something like this: Green is to go as red is to stop. A much more complex analogy that indicates creative genius is Kepler's application of concepts from light to develop a theory of the orbital motion of planets.[91] Similarly, chemist Friedrich Kekulé discovered the closed hexagonal structure of the benzene ring by imagining a snake biting its own tail. Teams at Apple visited a candy factory to study the nuances of jelly bean making and used the jelly bean idea as an analogy for the Apple iMac contained in a translucent blue shell.[92]

Creative teams often apply a concept, idea, or process from one domain to a new domain. To the extent that teams can recognize when a particular concept might be useful for solving a new problem, creativity can be enhanced. The problem is that it is not easy to transfer relevant information from one domain to another—humans tend to solve problems based upon their surface similarity to other situations, rather than their deep, structural similarity.

Surface Versus Structural Analogies   To see the difference between surface-level similarity and deep-level similarity, consider the problem presented in Exhibit 9-6. The problem is how to use a ray to destroy a patient's tumor given that the ray at full strength will destroy the healthy tissue en route to the tumor. An elegant (but not obvious) solution involves using a series of

---

EXHIBIT 9-6 The Tumor Problem

Suppose you are a doctor faced with a patient who has a malignant tumor in his stomach. It is impossible to operate on the patient, but unless the tumor is destroyed, the patient will die. There is a kind of ray that can be used to destroy the tumor. If the rays reach the tumor all at once at a sufficiently high intensity, the tumor will be destroyed. Unfortunately, at this intensity, the healthy tissue that the rays pass through on the way to the tumor will also be destroyed. At lower intensities, the rays are harmless to healthy tissue, but they will not affect the tumor either. What type of procedure might be used to destroy the tumor with the rays and, at the same time, avoid destroying the healthy tissue?

Source: Gick, M. L., & Holyoak, K. J. (1980). Analogical problem-solving. *Cognitive Psychology, 12*, 306–355. Adapted from Duncker, K. (1945). On problem solving. *Psychological Monographs, 58*(5), Whole no. 270.

---

[88]Amabile, T. M., & Conti, R. (1999). Changes in the work environment for creativity during downsizing. *Academy of Management Journal, 42*(6), 630–640.

[89]Amabile, T. M., Barsade, S. G., Mueller, J. S., & Staw, B. M. (2005). Affect and creativity at work. *Administrative Science Quarterly, 50*, 367–403.

[90]Byron, K., Khazanchi, S., & Nazarian, D. (2010). The relationship between stressors and creativity: A meta-analysis examining competing theoretical models. *Journal of Applied Psychology, 95*(1), 201–212.

[91]Gentner, D., Brem, S., Ferguson, R., & Wolff, P. (1997). Analogy and creativity in the works of Johannes Kepler. In T. B. Ward, S. M. Smith, & J. Vaid (Eds.), *Creative thought: An investigation of conceptual structures and processes* (pp. 403–459). Washington, DC: American Psychological Association.

[92]Burrows, P. (2006, September 25). The man behind Apple's design magic. *Business Week, 4002*, 26–33.

low-intensity rays from different angles that all converge on the tumor site as their destination.[93] Only about 10 percent of people solve this problem. It would stand to reason that performance might improve if people were given an analogous problem beforehand. Consider the problem in Exhibit 9-7. In this problem, a general needs to capture a fortress but is prevented from making a frontal attack by the entire army. An elegant (and analogous) solution is to divide the army into small troops that approach the fortress from a different road at the same time. At a surface level, the problems seem to have little or nothing in common—one from the medical world and the other from a military context. However, at a deeper level, the problems are highly analogous, as can be seen in Exhibit 9-8. What do you think happens when people are given the tumor problem prior to reading the fortress problem?

Even when given the tumor problem, only 41 percent of people spontaneously apply the convergence solution to the radiation problem. Yet when simply told to "think about the earlier problem," solution rates rise to around 85 percent. If people are given a story about a doctor treating a brain tumor in a similar fashion, solution rates rise to 90 percent.[94] This points up an important aspect of creativity and knowledge: *People usually have the knowledge they need to solve problems, but they fail to access it because it comes from a different context.* Thus, a key limitation of managers is not that they are lacking information and knowledge, but that they do not have access to relevant aspects of their own experience when they need it. Thus, applying previously learned knowledge to new situations is surprisingly difficult for most managers.

Inert Knowledge Problem   How many of us have experienced the frustration of seeing a connection only after it was pointed out to us? This is known as the **inert knowledge problem**—it

EXHIBIT 9-7 The Fortress Problem

A small country fell under the iron rule of a dictator. The dictator ruled the country from a strong fortress. The fortress was situated in the middle of the country, surrounded by farms and villages. Many roads radiated outward from the fortress like spokes on a wheel. A great general arose, who raised a large army at the border and vowed to capture the fortress and free the country of the dictator. The general knew that if his entire army could attack the fortress at once, it could be captured. His troops were poised at the head of one of the roads leading to the fortress, ready to attack. However, a spy brought the general a disturbing report. The ruthless dictator had planted mines on each of the roads. The mines were set so that small bodies of men could pass over them safely, since the dictator needed to be able to move troops and workers to and from the fortress. However, any large force would detonate the mines. Not only would this blow up the road and render it impassable, but the dictator would destroy many villages in retaliation. A full-scale direct attack on the fortress therefore appeared impossible.

The general, however, was undaunted. He divided his army up into small groups and dispatched each group to the head of a different road. When all was ready, he gave the signal, and each group charged down a different road. All of the small groups passed safely over the mines, and the army then attacked the fortress in full strength. In this way, the general was able to capture the fortress and overthrow the dictator.

Source: Gick, M. L., & Holyoak, K. J. (1983). Schema induction and analogical transfer. *Cognitive Psychology, 15,* 1–38. Reprinted in Holyoak, K. J., & Thagard, P. (1995). *Mental leaps: Analogy in creative thought.* Cambridge, MA: MIT Press.

---

[93]Gick, M. L., & Holyoak, K. J. (1980). Analogical problem-solving. *Cognitive Psychology, 12,* 306–355.
[94]Ibid.

EXHIBIT 9-8 A Visual Analog of the Tumor Problem

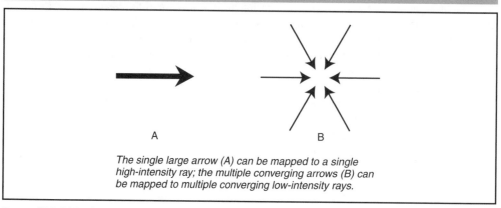

A   B

The single large arrow (A) can be mapped to a single high-intensity ray; the multiple converging arrows (B) can be mapped to multiple converging low-intensity rays.

Source: Gick, M. L., & Holyoak, K. J. (1983). Schema induction and analogical transfer. *Cognitive Psychology, 15,* 1–38. Reprinted in Holyoak, K. J., & Thagard, P. (1995). *Mental leaps: Analogy in creative thought.* Cambridge, MA: MIT Press.

means that people's ability to take full advantage of their prior experience is highly limited.[95] Even when they possess the relevant experience necessary to deal with a novel problem, they often fail to do so when their previous experience comes from a different context.

When people encounter a new situation or problem, they are reminded not of prior problems with the same underlying deep structure (such as how the tumor problem is similar to the fortress problem), but of problems with the same surface features.[96] In fact, they recall problems that have surface similarity about 55 percent of the time and problems that are deeply relevant about 12 percent of the time. This points to an important fact about managerial information processing: The knowledge people gain from their daily experience is often not accessed, despite the fact that once it is called to their attention they regard it to be helpful.[97]

How Companies Use Analogy for Creative Thinking   New ideas are often old ideas wrapped in new clothing. Finding innovation solutions by analogy requires: (1) in-depth understanding of the problem and (2) searching for something else that has already solved the

[95]Loewenstein, J., & Thompson, L. (2000). The challenge of learning. *Negotiation Journal, October,* 399–408; Thompson, L., Loewenstein, J., & Gentner, D. (2000). Avoiding missed opportunities in managerial life: Analogical training more powerful than individual case training. *Organizational Behavior and Human Decision Processes, 82*(1), 60–75.

[96]Gentner, D., Rattermann, M. J., & Forbus, K. D. (1993). The roles of similarity in transfer: Separating retrievability from inferential soundness. *Cognitive Psychology, 25*(4), 524–575.

[97]Gentner, D., Loewenstein, J., Thompson, L., & Forbus, K. (2009). Reviving inert knowledge: Analogical encoding supports relational retrieval of past events. *Cognitive Science, 33,* 1343–1382; Forbus, K. D., Gentner, D., & Law, K. (1995). MAC/FAC: A model of similarity-based retrieval. *Cognitive Science, 19*(2), 141–205; Gentner, D., & Landers, R. (1985). Analogical reminding: A good match is hard to find. *Proceedings of the International Conference on Cybernetics and Society* (pp. 607–613), Tucson, AZ, and New York: Institute of Electrical and Electronics Engineers; Gentner, Rattermann, & Forbus, "Roles of similarity in transfer," p. 242; Gick & Holyoak, "Analogical problem-solving," p. 240; Gick, M. L., & Holyoak, K. J. (1983). Schema induction and analogical transfer. *Cognitive Psychology, 15,* 1–38. Reprinted in Holyoak, K. J., & Thagard, P. (1995). *Mental leaps: Analogy in creative thought.* Cambridge, MA: MIT Press; Holyoak, K. J., & Koh, K. (1987). Surface and structural similarity in analogical transfer. *Memory and Cognition, 15*(4), 332–340; Reeves, L., & Weisberg, R. W. (1994). The role of content and abstract information in analogical transfer. *Psychological Bulletin, 115*(3), 381–400; Ross, B. H. (1987). This is like that: The use of earlier problems and the separation of similarity effects. *Journal of Experimental Psychology: Learning, Memory and Cognition, 13*(4), 629–639.

problem.[98] In one demo, business executives are challenged to think about how to engage in their weight-training program while on business travel. It is not practical to travel with 50 pound dumbbells, but Markman suggests thinking about how water contains weight, such as a water mattress. Water weights are small and compact, and they can be filled with tap water from hotel bathrooms. Following is another analogy: When a team of NASA scientists needed to fix the distorted lenses in the Hubble telescope in orbit, one of the experts mentioned that small inversely distorted mirrors would adjust the images. However, they were impossible to fit into the hard-to-reach space inside the telescope. Engineer Jim Crocker noticed the European-style showerhead mounted on adjustable rods in a German hotel and thought to extend the mirrors into the telescope by mounting them on similar folding arms. Following is another use of analogy: A manufacturer of potato chips faced a frequently encountered problem—potato chips took up too much shelf space when they were packed loosely, but they crumbled when packed in smaller packages. The manufacturer found a solution by using a direct analogy: Dried leaves are highly similar to potato chips. They crumble very easily, and they are bulky. Pressed leaves are flat. Could potato chips be shipped flat? As it turned out, they could not. However, the team realized that leaves are not pressed when they are dry, but when they are moist. So they packed potato chips in stacks, moist enough not to crumble, but dry enough to be nearly flat. The result was Pringles.[99]

Analogical reasoning involves the application of diverse categories to a company's present problem or challenge. IDEO designers used the analogy of how people use their mouths for heat and cooling. "Blow" is a minimalist thermostat that you control with your own lungs; if your room is too cold, you breathe at the device with your mouth open, as if you were warming your hands in the winter, and heat comes on. Blow with a pursed mouth, as if you were cooling a bowl of soup turns on the air conditioning.[100] Hargadon calls the use of analogy in companies "knowledge brokering" and notes that the best innovators use old ideas as the raw material for new ideas.[101] Moreover, the most dramatic impacts of new technologies often come from industries other than the ones in which they first emerged. For example, the steam engine, developed in the mining industry, revolutionized the railroad and shipping industries. Hargadon and Sutton outline four critical steps in the knowledge brokering cycle: (1) capturing good ideas, (2) keeping ideas alive, (3) imagining new uses for old ideas, and (4) putting promising concepts to the test.[102]

Social-Organizational Methods

Social-organizational suggestions focus on how to alter the relationships among team members and alter the way in which they interact, often by introducing new norms and strategies.

TRAINED FACILITATORS   A trained facilitator can better follow rules of brainstorming (which are often unwittingly violated), help create an organizational memory, and keep teams on track. Indeed, trained facilitators can bring the level of team performance up to that of

[98]Markman, A. B., & Wood, K. L. (Eds.). (2009). *Tools for innovation: The science behind the practical methods that drive innovation.* New York: Oxford University Press.

[99]Russo, F. (2006, January 16). The hidden secrets of the creative mind. *Time, 167*(3), pp. 89–90.

[100]Bone, M., & Johnson, K. (2009). *I miss my pencil.* San Francisco, CA: Chronicle Books.

[101]Hargadon, A. B. (1998). Firms as knowledge brokers: Lessons in pursuing continuous innovation. *California Management Review, 40*(3), 209–227.

[102]Hargadon, A. B., & Sutton, R. I. (2000, May/June). Building an innovation factory. *Harvard Business Review, 78*(3), 157–166.

nominal groups.[103] Furthermore, there are long-term benefits to this investment. Teams that are given several sessions in which they are guided by facilitators into productive idea generation patterns demonstrate high levels of productivity in subsequent sessions without the facilitators.[104] Apparently, teams can become accustomed to sharing ideas without extensive social interaction or "filler" talk. For example, at IDEO design firm, group leaders are used to facilitate all brainstorming sessions. According to IDEO managers, the key qualification of the facilitators is that they are "good with groups," not because they are experts in the particular product area.[105] Another skill trained facilitators have is the ability to eliminate filler talk; indeed, the highest levels of productivity are obtained when the most ideas are allowed to be shared.[106]

BRAINWRITING   **Brainwriting** is not brainstorming. Brainwriting is the simultaneous generation of written ideas. Brainwriting works like this: At key intervals during a brainstorming session, group members cease all talking and all interaction and write their ideas silently and independently.[107]

Writing ideas instead of speaking them eliminates the problem of production blocking because group members do not have to "wait their turn" to generate ideas. It may also reduce conformity because the written format eliminates the need for public speaking and is typically more anonymous than verbal brainstorming. The written ideas can subsequently be shared by the group in a round-robin fashion and summarized on a blackboard or flip chart. Investigations of brainstorming groups of four people revealed that brainwriting, followed by round-robin exchange, eliminated production blocking and social loafing as compared with standard brainwriting.[108]

Many groups may not welcome the idea of brainwriting, claiming that it ruins the flow of the group process. But the proof is incontrovertible: Brainwriting groups consistently generate more and better ideas than groups that follow their instincts. Alternating between team ideation and individual ideation is desirable because it allows teams to circumvent production blocking (coordination problems), and it also sets the stage for divergent thinking. This two-step technique requires a considerable number of conditions to be in place for optimal productivity in group brainstorming. Each member needs to take time out for solitary meditations. Similar benefits can be accomplished through preliminary writing sessions, quotas or deadlines, brief breaks, and the use of specific, simple, and subdivided problems. Thus, by working together, then alone, and then together, teams are more likely to achieve the best in creative thinking.[109]

---

[103]Oxley, Dzindolet, & Paulus, "The effects of facilitators on the performance of brainstorming groups."

[104]Paulus, P. B., Putman, V. L., Coskun, H., Leggett, K. L., & Roland, E. J. (1996). Training groups for effective brainstorming. Presented at the Fourth Annual Advanced Concepts Conference on Work Teams–Team Implementation Issues, Dallas.

[105]Brown, *Change by design.*

[106]Dugosh, K. L., Paulus, P. B., Roland, E. J., & Yang, H.-C. (2000). Cognitive stimulation in brainstorming. *Journal of Personality and Social Psychology, 79*(5), 722–735.

[107]Geschka, H., Schaude, G. R., & Schlicksupp, H. (1973, August). Modern techniques for solving problems. *Chemical Engineering,* 91–97; Paulus, P. B. (1998). Developing consensus about groupthink after all these years. *Organizational Behavior and Human Decision Processes, 73*(2–3), 362–374; Paulus, P. B., & Yang, H. (2000). Idea generation in groups: A basis for creativity in organizations. *Organizational Behavior and Human Decision Processes, 82*(1), 76–87.

[108]Paulus & Yang, "Idea generation in groups," p. 244.

[109]Osborn, *Applied imagination* (3rd ed.), p. 230.

Even if brainwriting is not used, at the very least, all talking should be stopped periodically to allow members to think silently; the more pauses and silences that occur during brainstorming, the higher the quality of the ideas. Giving members brief breaks, even if they don't write anything down, can help.[110] Indeed, periods of "incubation" in which group members reflect on ideas can generate additional ideas.[111]

BRIEF BREAKS   Teams that take a short break (2 to 5 minutes in length) halfway through a 20- or 30-minute brainstorming session increase their productivity following the break compared to teams that brainstorm continuously without a break.[112] The specific mental activity that the brainstorming person is engaged in during the break is important. If the break activity does not allow task-relevant ideas and concept to remain active in memory, then the categories will have to be reactivated following the break, and productivity will suffer. Breaks also allow brainstorming groups to overcome mental blocks. Breaks can stimulate a different approach to a problem.

NOMINAL GROUP TECHNIQUE   A much better method of group brainstorming is to prepare by having a prior session of solitary writing, known as the **nominal group technique**.[113] The nominal group technique, or NGT, is a variation of the standard brainwriting technique[114] and involves an initial session of brainwriting prior to interactive teamwork. Thus, NGT separates the idea generation phase from the idea evaluation phase. To use the NGT, it is useful to have a facilitator, but it is not necessary. The facilitator introduces a problem on the board or on a flip chart. Once members understand the topic or issue, they silently write ideas for 10 to 15 minutes. Members state their ideas in a round-robin fashion, and each idea is given an identification number. Once ideas are all listed, the team discusses each item, focusing on clarification. Following this, members privately rank the five solutions or ideas they most prefer. The leader-facilitator collects the cards and averages the rating to yield a group decision.

It is worth noting that the NGT was compared with an interactive brainstorming process and overwhelmingly outperformed the standard brainstorming group.[115] Also, nominal groups that perform in the same room generate more ideas than those in separate rooms.[116] The advantage of the NGT is that it maximizes information gain, ensures a democratic representation of all members' ideas (i.e., avoids the lumpy participation effect), and avoids production blocking. Yet members still have an opportunity for face-to-face discussion of issues. Although it might seem that the NGT would run the risk of generating redundant ideas, they are no more common per number of total ideas than in real face-to-face groups. There are some disadvantages of the NGT; it is less spontaneous and may require a separate meeting for each topic.

---

[110]Horn, E. M. (1993). *The influence of modality order and break period on a brainstorming task.* Unpublished honors thesis, University of Texas at Arlington.

[111]Dugosh, Paulus, Roland, & Yang, "Cognitive stimulation in brainstorming."

[112]Mitchell, C. K. (1998). *The effects of break task on performance during the second session of brainstorming.* Unpublished manuscript, University of Texas at Arlington; Horn, *Influence of modality order,* p. 244.

[113]Delbecq, A. L., & Van de Ven, A. H. (1971). A group process model for identification and program planning. *Journal of Applied Behavioral Sciences, 7,* 466–492.

[114]Geschka, Schaude, & Schlicksupp, "Modern techniques for solving problems," p. 244; Van de Ven, A. H., & Delbecq, A. L. (1974). The effectiveness of nominal, Delphi, and interacting group decision making processes. *Academy of Management Journal, 17*(4), 605–621.

[115]Gustafson, D. H., Shukla, R. K., Delbecq, A. L., & Walster, G. W. (1973). A comparative study of differences in subjective likelihood estimates made by individuals, interacting groups, Delphi groups, and nominal groups. *Organizational Behavior and Human Performance, 9,* 280–291.

[116]Mullen, Johnson, & Salas, "Productivity loss in brainstorming groups," p. 232.

One variant of the NGT is the **anonymous nominal group technique**. In the anonymous NGT, members write down their ideas on individual sheets of paper or note cards. The meeting facilitator (or a group member) collects the note cards, shuffles them, and redistributes them randomly to members, who read the cards aloud or discuss their contents in small groups. This variation creates greater acceptance of others' ideas because the ideas are semi-anonymous; it also prevents individual members from championing only their own ideas.

Another variation, the **rotating nominal group technique**, requires members to write their ideas on individual sheets of paper or note cards. The meeting facilitator collects the note cards, shuffles them, and distributes them to individual group members, who read the cards aloud or discuss them in small groups. This variation creates greater acceptance of others' ideas and prevents individual members from championing their own ideas.

DELPHI TECHNIQUE   Another variant of the NGT is the **Delphi technique**.[117] In this technique, group members do not interact face to face at any point. This technique is ideally suited for groups whose members are geographically dispersed (making meetings difficult to attend) and for teams whose members experience such great conflict that it is difficult to meet about sensitive issues. This technique requires a leader or facilitator who is trusted by the team members. The entire process proceeds through questionnaires, followed by feedback that can be computerized. The leader distributes a topic or question to members and asks for responses from each team member. The leader then aggregates the responses, sends them back to the team, and solicits feedback. The process is repeated until there is resolution on the issue in question. The Delphi technique avoids production blocking. The technique is a good alternative for teams who are physically separated but nevertheless need to make decisions. Because members respond independently, conformity pressures and evaluation apprehension are limited. One problem associated with this technique, which is not associated with regular brainstorming or nominal brainstorming, is that it can be quite time consuming. Sessions can last several days, even weeks.

STEPLADDER TECHNIQUE   The **stepladder technique**, a variant of the membership change technique, is a decision-making approach in which members are added one by one to a team.[118] The first step involves the creation of a two-person subgroup (the core), which begins preliminary discussion of the group's task. After a fixed interval, another member joins the core group and presents his or her ideas concerning the task. The three-person group then discusses the task in a preliminary manner. The process continues until all members have systematically joined the core group. When this occurs, the group arrives at a final solution. Each member must have sufficient time to think about the problem before entering into the core group. More important, the entering members must present their preliminary solutions before hearing the core group's preliminary solutions. A final decision cannot be reached until the group has formed in its entirety. Self-pacing stepladder groups (which proceed through the paces at a self-determined pace) produce significantly higher-quality group decisions than conventional groups.[119] Members with the best individual decisions exert more influence in stepladder groups than in free interaction groups.

---

[117]Helmer, O. (1966). *Social technology*. New York: Basic Books; Helmer, O. (1967). *Analysis of the future: The Delphi method*. Santa Monica, CA: The Rand Corporation.
[118]Rogelberg, S. G., Barnes-Farrell, J. L., & Lowe, C. A. (1992). The stepladder technique: An alternative group structure facilitating effective group decision making. *Journal of Applied Psychology, 77*(5), 730–737.
[119]Rogelberg, S. G., & O'Connor, M. S. (1998). Extending the stepladder technique: An examination of self-paced stepladder groups. *Group Dynamics: Theory, Research, and Practice, 2*(2), 82–91.

Structural-Environmental Methods

Structural-environmental methods focus on how to change the environment to improve creativity.

DIVERSIFY THE TEAM   The benefits of diversity outlined in Chapter 5 extend to creativity. Indeed, teams in which members are diverse with regard to background and perspective outperform teams with homogeneous members on tasks requiring creative problem solving and innovation.[120] This occurs when coworkers experience cognitive conflict (i.e., task conflict) in the absence of conformity pressures and respond by revising fundamental assumptions and generating novel insights.[121] As a result, teams with heterogeneous members generate more arguments,[122] apply a greater number of strategies,[123] detect more novel solutions,[124] and are better at integrating multiple perspectives[125] than teams without conflicting perspectives. A field study of 39 research teams within a global Fortune 100 Science & Technology company reveals that diverse teams, containing a breadth of research and business unit experience, were more effective when there was a knowledge-sharing climate in the team and when the leader also had breadth.[126] Walt Disney's Toy Division created a systematic brainstorming and prototyping process that supports the continuous innovation necessary to overhaul toy lineups every 6 months. People assemble 20 to 30 times a year for 3- or 3-day brainstorming sessions at hotels around the world. The group of up to 50 people is always diverse: Disney designers, engineers, artists, salespersons, animators, video game designers, marketers, and theme park employees are split into teams that partner with licensee companies that design and eventually manufacture the products.[127]

FLUID MEMBERSHIP   As we saw in Chapter 2, members enter and exit groups. Although maintaining consistent membership increases comfort and the perception of creativity, it does not lead to better creativity.[128] Teams that experience membership change (i.e., an entry of a new member and an exit of an old member) generate not only more ideas (high fluency) but also more diverse ones (higher flexibility) than do groups who remain intact.[129] Teams that stay together, without any change in membership, develop a sort of cognitive arthritis—they get stuck in a rut when it comes

---

[120]Jackson, S. E. (1992). Team composition in organizational settings: Issues in managing an increasingly diverse work force. In S. Worchel, W. Wood, & J. A. Simpson (Eds.), *Group Process and Productivity* (pp. 138–173). Newbury Park, CA: Sage.
[121]Levine, J. M., Resnick, L. B., & Higgins, E. T. (1993). Social foundations of cognition. *Annual Review of Psychology, 44*, 585–612; Nemeth, C. J. (1994). The value of minority dissent. In S. Moscovici, A. Mucchi-Faina, & A. Maass (Eds.), *Minority influence: Nelson-Hall series in psychology* (pp. 3–15). Chicago, IL: Nelson-Hall Publishers.
[122]Smith, Tindale, & Dugoni, "Minority and majority influence in freely interacting groups."
[123]Nemeth, C. J., & Wachtler, J. (1983). Creative problem solving as a result of majority vs. minority influence. *European Journal of Social Psychology, 13*(1), 45–55.
[124]Nemeth, C. J., & Kwan, J. L. (1987). Minority influence, divergent thinking and detection of correct solutions. *Journal of Applied Social Psychology, 17*(9), 788–799.
[125]Gruenfeld, D. H. (1994). Status and integrative complexity in decision-making groups: Evidence from the United States Supreme Court and a laboratory experiment. *Dissertation Abstracts International, Section B: The Sciences & Engineering, 55*(2-B), 630; Gruenfeld, D. H. (1995). Status, ideology and integrative complexity on the U.S. Supreme Court: Rethinking the politics of political decision making. *Journal of Personality and Social Psychology, 68*(1), 5–20; Peterson, R. S., & Nemeth, C. J. (1996). Focus versus flexibility: Majority and minority influence can both improve performance. *Personality and Social Psychology Bulletin, 22*(1), 14–23.
[126]Griffith, T. L., & Sawyer, J. E. (2009). Multilevel knowledge and team performance. *Journal of Organizational Behavior. Advance online publication.* Doi: 10.1002/job.660.
[127]Joseph. D. (2009, July 1). Inside disney's toy factory. *Business Week.* businessweek.com
[128]Nemeth & Ormiston, "Creative idea generation," p. 227.
[129]Choi, H. S., & Thompson, L. (2005). Old wine in a new bottle: Impact of membership change on group creativity. *Organizational Behavior and Human Decision Processes, 98*(2), 121–132.

to idea generation. There is a negative relationship between repeat collaboration and creativity.[130] In contrast, teams that experience a change in membership are naturally exposed to more ideas due to a greater diversity in task-relevant skills and information. When a group experiences a membership change, they are in a unique position to look at themselves more thoughtfully. The presence of a newcomer can motivate old-timers to revisit their task strategy and develop improved methods for performing group tasks.[131] This effect is known as creative abrasion: wherein people who lack a previous collaboration are more likely to generate ideas.[132] Successful new product development (NPD) teams have (1) higher project complexity; (2) cross-functionality; (3) temporary membership; (4) fluid team boundaries; and (5) embeddedness in organizational structures.[133]

ORGANIZATIONAL NETWORKING   The extent to which teams and their leaders have weak ties across organizational units and boundaries can positively promote creativity.[134] In an investigation of product development in project teams, teams that have fluid team boundaries, allowing cross-team networking, are more creative than those with tight boundaries.[135] When teams have fluid group boundaries, team members are forced to make new connections across traditional boundaries. In this way, team members trade the depth and intensity of "strong ties" for a larger number of "weak ties." For example, after Procter & Gamble reviewed its research and development process, it transformed the process into a new strategy called "connect and develop," in which open-source innovation allows people to team up across organizational boundaries.[136] Networking also means spending time with customers and clients. A large meta-analysis of team-level antecedents of creativity revealed that organizational support for innovation, vision, task orientation, and external communication were associated with the highest levels of creativity.[137]

TRAVERSE INDUSTRIES   One method for reviving products and services within a given industry is to leverage other industries and domains.[138] For example, Samsung wanted to expand the market for flat LCD screens larger than 10 inches and move 600,000 units or more. They struggled with reaching maximum capacity for televisions, monitors, and digital cameras, and so they looked outside the tried-and-true and thought about vending machines as large, dynamic touch-screen displays. Vending machines are a stagnant industry, but a wireless connection could give vendors access to an entire network of machines, monitoring inventory and product information. Coca-Cola licensed uVending first at the 2008 Beijing Olympics, and a completely new revenue stream for flat panels was launched.[139]

---

[130]Guimerá, R., Uzzi, B., Spiro J., & Amaral. (2005). L. A. N. Team assembly mechanisms determine collaboration network structure and team performance. *Science, 308*, 697—702.

[131]Choi & Thompson, "Old wine in a new bottle," p. 248; Ziller, R. C. (1965). Toward a theory of open and closed groups. *Psychological Bulletin, 64*, 164–182.

[132]Skilton, P. F., & Dooley, K. J. (2010). The effects of repeat collaboration on creative abrasion. *Academy of Management Review, 35*(1), 118–134.

[133]Edmondson, A. C., & Nembhard, I. M. (2009). Product development and learning in project teams: The challenges are the benefits. *Journal of Product Innovation Management, 26*(2), 123–138.

[134]Perry-Smith, J. E., & Shalley, C. E. (2003). The social side of creativity: A static and dynamic social network perspective. *Academy of Management Review, 28*(1), 89–107.

[135]Edmondson & Nembhard, "Product development and learning in teams."

[136]McGregor, J., Arndt, M., Berner, R., Rowley, I., & Hall, K. (2006, April 24). The world's most innovative companies. *BusinessWeek, 3981*, 62.

[137]Hulsheger, U. R., Anderson, N., & Salgado, J. F. (2009). Team-level predictors of innovation at work: A comprehensive meta-analysis spanning three decades of research. *Journal of Applied Psychology, 94*(5), 1128–1145.

[138]Hargadon, A. (2003). *How breakthroughs happen: The surprising truth about how companies innovate.* Boston, MA: Harvard Business School Publishing.

[139]Hira, N. (2009, December 16). Fahrenheit 212—The innovator's paradise. *CnnMoney.* money.cnn.com

BUILD A CREATIVE SPACE AND ENVIRONMENT   Space and distance define how people interact. Work environments clearly affect creativity. The {e}house studio office space in Charleston, South Carolina, specializes in Web design and marketing—a highly creative environment. Although the studio benefits from wood flooring, French doors, lots of windows, and original brick fireplaces, owners Rick, Aaron, and Chris Quinns's additions have turned it into a work area that's ideal for themselves, other employees and their clients. The working space includes eco-friendly beanbag chairs, art from local artists, and paint colors that match the company's Web site and printed material. Chalkboard walls cut down on paper and provide a place where an idea can be jotted down instantly. Employees of {e}house studio use laptops so they're not tethered to their desks. "We didn't want people to have separate offices, so our entire team works in an open space where we can all see each other and communicate when needed—dogs included," says Chris Quinn.[140]

Spaces that are designed to foster creativity involve a lot of nontraditional elements. Learning Sciences International eschewed traditional cubicles and instead divided areas with chin-height screen panels. Desks were arranged in zig-zag patterns or honeycomb clusters. The furniture is ultramodern. "If a worker enters an atmosphere that is too serious-looking, it can be intimidating and keep him or her from volunteering ideas," Chief Learning Officer (CLO) Toth says.[141] Some companies have taken the concept of creative space to a much grander scale. "New century cities" and "science parks" have emerged in the downtowns of several large cities. The idea goes way beyond the Research Triangle Park in North Carolina. For example, a high-tech business incubator at 22@Barcelona hosts 55 start-ups nestled within a sprawling science park. The goal of new century cities is to kick-start high-priority industries with new spaces where companies and universities can work together. According to Don Tapscott, coauthor of *Wikinomics: How mass collaboration changes everything*, "the innovation bandwidth in a cafeteria is significantly greater than the bandwidth for innovation over the internet." To do this requires good food, wine, aesthetics, hiking, biking trails, and more. For example, *Fusionopolis* in Singapore is a soaring 24-story home for media, communications, and IT companies. To draw creative talent, *Fusionopolis* has trendy restaurants, athletic facilities, and apartments equipped with networked appliances.[142]

ELECTRONIC BRAINSTORMING

Electronic brainstorming (EBS) has recently been introduced into organizations as a means of generating ideas; it uses computers to allow members to interact and exchange ideas. In a typical EBS session, members are seated at a table that contains computer stations. A large screen projects all ideas generated by members. The ideas that are generated using EBS are anonymous and, thus, tend to be expressed more freely and in greater quantity.

EBS is used as part of a regular organizational meeting process. It gives organizations the opportunity to gather ideas efficiently, organize those ideas, and subsequently make decisions. It speeds up the meeting at which it is used, increases productivity, and allows the focus to remain on the ideas rather than on the people who spawned them. When members run out of ideas, they access the ideas produced by the team.

---

[140]Wang, J. (2008, January 8). Why you (yes you!) need a cool office. *Entrepreneur.* Entrepreneur.com
[141]Veronikis, E. (2008, August 21). Not your average office. *Central Penn Business Journal, 24*(35), 2–4.
[142]Engardio, P. (2009, November 19). Innovation Goes Downtown. *Business Week, 4157,* 50–52.

In EBS, people are usually not identified by their contributions. Typically, participants can view subsets of ideas generated by other team members on part of the screen at any time by using a keystroke. Ideas are projected on a large screen, and people are asked to evaluate them. The team may eventually vote on the most preferred ideas. A facilitator guides both the idea generation and the decision processes.[143]

EBS sessions at IBM area called Innovation Jams.[144] In July 2008, IBM held a 5-day, open-source global jam and invited nearly 100,000 clients, consultants, partners, and even journalists to brainstorm new ideas. To channel discussion, jam designers segmented it into four topic threads: adapting to survive, customers as partners, globally integrated organizations, and environmental and social sustainability.[145]

Advantages of Electronic Brainstorming

The key advantages of EBS are that it addresses all the blocks to productivity that occur in traditional brainstorming—that is, the threats to performance that occur because people have to compete for floor time; only one person can talk at one time while others listen; members may feel inhibited making suggestions, especially if there are status differences among the team members; people have a difficult time staying focused on idea generation, as opposed to repeating or evaluating someone else's idea; and the organizational memory for ideas can be cumbersome or incomplete. EBS elegantly circumvents most of these problems.

PARALLEL ENTRY OF IDEAS   Parallel entry of ideas, like brainwriting, means that all members of the team can generate ideas simultaneously. Although it might seem desirable to have members listen attentively to others' ideas, this in fact is highly inefficient. To be sure, EBS does not mean that members disregard or tune out the ideas of others; rather, it means that they can both contribute and listen in a much more interactive and efficient fashion. The result is that most members regard the entire process to be more egalitarian and satisfying than a traditional brainstorming session, which can be dominated by one person or a subset of members and consequently highly frustrating for others.

ANONYMITY   In addition to finessing the floor competition that can take place in traditional brainstorming sessions, EBS also has the attractive feature of reducing many people's inhibitions and concerns about what others think of them. As we saw in Chapter 2 (performance and productivity), performance pressure can lead to choking, and as we saw in Chapter 7 (decision making), conformity pressures are extremely strong in teams, even those whose members value independent thought. Because the ideas that are generated in EBS are anonymous, people can express themselves without having to worry about criticism, and the team, therefore, will be less conforming. This is especially true when teams are composed of members of differing status levels. K. C. Guinn, the CEO of Southwest Gas, said about EBS, "Because the process is anonymous, the sky's the limit in terms of what you can say, and as a result it is more thought-provoking. As a CEO, you'll probably discover things you might not want to hear but need to be aware of."[146] In this sense, EBS can be a venue for the type of

---

[143]Jessup, L. M., & Valacich, J. S., (Eds.). (1993). *Group support systems.* New York: Macmillan; Nunamaker, J. F., Jr., Briggs, R. O., & Mittleman, D. D. (1995). Electronic meeting systems: Ten years of lessons learned. In D. Coleman & R. Khanna (Eds.), *Groupware: Technology and applications* (pp. 149–193). Upper Saddle River, NJ: Prentice Hall.

[144]Hempel, J. (2006, August 7). Big blue brainstorm. *BusinessWeek*, p. 70.

[145]Hamm, S. (2009, October). IBM's innovation jam brainstorming wingding. blogs.businessweek.com

[146]Dennis, A. R., Nunamaker, J. F., Jr., Paranka, D., & Vogel, D. R. A. (1990). A new role for computers in strategic management. *Journal of Business Strategy, 11*(5), 38–42.

evaluations that we discussed in Chapter 3 (rewarding teamwork). That is, managers can get feedback on what others think of their ideas.

SIZE   Traditional brainstorming groups suffer greatly from coordination and communication problems as the team grows. In contrast, EBS can easily handle large teams. This can be an advantage for the organization, putting more minds to work on the problem and involving several people in the creative process. It also has the potential for improving organizational memory.

PROXIMITY   An important way that EBS clearly dominates traditional brainstorming is that EBS groups can meet synchronously while being physically dispersed. The members do not have to be in the same place, or even in the same country, to interact. IBM's Innovation Jam generated nearly 90,000 log-ins from five continents and produced more than 32,000 posts. Independent authorities from a variety of fields guided jam discussions, resulting in tens of thousands of new ideas.[147]

MEMORY   As noted, the creation and use of organizational memory is greatly facilitated with EBS. The members, whether or not they attended the EBS, have the option of viewing the session via computer disk. The concept of the idea boneyard is to create a repository for all ideas that are brainstormed. At HTC, the Taiwanese company that manufactured the first Google phone and has built itself into one of the world's leading manufacturers of mobile phones, strong ideas generated from brainstorming sessions do not fade away, regardless of their immediacy to the moment. According to John Wang, HTC chief marketing officer, some ideas among the hundreds generated each day are promising enough to be filed away in a database, where people will use them as seeds for other brainstorming sessions. Among those, a few live on. After prototypes are made, if the concept proves to be excellent and gets a lot of positive feedback, it's developed further. Eventually a few ideas become innovations.[148]

REFINEMENT AND EVALUATION OF IDEAS   EBS allows the use of specialized software to help refine, organize, and evaluate ideas. Some software manufacturers have three types of components in their software: presession planning, in-session management, and postsession organization. Collectively, these tools finesse much of the task-management skills that are needed in meetings. Instead of a person being delegated to perform these activities, they are automated.

EQUALITY   EBS places every participant on a level-playing field. Practically, this means that no individual can dominate the meeting through rank, status, or raised voice. Thus, EBS ensures equality of input. Equality has many virtues in this type of teamwork. When members feel more equal, there is often more participation, which can increase productivity. For example, one company used traditional brainstorming to develop 1-year and 5-year plans.[149] The committee, composed of five members, spent 2 days trying to develop a mission statement. In the end, the statement was unacceptable to several key people in the company. When the same team used EBS, they developed a mission statement in 2 hours. Then they developed further objectives, goals, and strategies. This plan was accepted by the board, with no changes. The EBS session was more effective because each member of the team had input into the process.

---

[147]IBM (2010). Innovation jam 2008 executive report. ibm.com
[148]Pattison, K. (2008, September). How innovation led HTC to the dream. *Fast Company.* Fastcompany.com
[149]Dennis, Nunamaker, Paranka, & Vogel, "A new role for computers in strategic management."

Disadvantages of Electronic Brainstorming

EBS does have disadvantages. As with most new technologies, the unrealistic expectation is that it will solve all known problems and not create any new ones. Technology cannot replace thinking: Members must generate ideas and then evaluate them. In one investigation, meetings held by 11 groups who used group decision support systems had lower fluency.[150]

SMALL TEAMS   Smaller EBS groups do not generate as many ideas as do larger groups. For example, an 18-person EBS group generated more ideas than a 3-person EBS group.[151] This is not really a disadvantage, but rather an admonition to EBS managers that larger teams are more productive—something that is not true in traditional brainstorming. However, this in no way implies that EBS with small teams is less effective than face-to-face brainstorming. Quite the contrary!

LOSS OF SOCIAL INTERACTION   Probably the most notable disadvantage is that EBS prevents members from interacting socially. Although we have seen that natural social interaction leads to inefficiencies in performance, social interaction does do other (positive) things for teams. Nonverbal communication, such as facial expressions, laughing, and intonation, is important for building feelings of rapport and trust between members. Furthermore, when people do not interact directly, greater misunderstanding and miscommunication can result. EBS may actually promote antisocial behavior, with people being more judgmental, pointed, and abrupt in their communications—something we discuss more in Chapter 13 on virtual teamwork. These drawbacks may leave team members less satisfied than when traditional brainstorming is used. There may be a dissociation between two measures of productivity: actual productivity (quantity and quality of ideas produced) and team satisfaction. The manager (and team) may have to make some hard choices about which objective to prioritize.

LOSS OF POWER   Paralleling the greater equality that EBS creates in the organizations that use it is a resultant loss of power for individuals higher in status. Anonymity and equality of input may very well be regarded to be a disadvantage for managers accustomed to having their own ideas implemented. Thus, there could be a backlash, with organizational members accustomed to greater power attempting to return to traditional status hierarchies.

NO CREDIT   The downside of the anonymity aspect of EBS is that members who generate ideas don't receive credit for them. As we saw in Chapter 3, recognition is often the most powerful form of reward. Because EBS is anonymous, this means that members are not accountable for generating and evaluating ideas. This means that some members may work hard, and others may do nothing or free ride on the efforts of others.[152] Furthermore, EBS participants may feel that their contribution to the team will not make a difference. In contrast, people in traditional brainstorming groups are keenly aware of the contributions of others, which may promote high levels of participation.

It is important to note that EBS has not proven to be more successful than the NGT. In summary, EBS is extraordinarily useful for managing the discussions of large, physically separated teams. EBS limits the demands of social synchronization—that is, coordination loss—and

---

[150]Jackson, M. H., & Poole, M. S. (2003). Idea generation in naturally-occurring contexts: Complex appropriation of a simple procedure. *Human Communication Research, 29*, 560–591.
[151]Gallupe, R. B. (1992). Electronic brainstorming and group size. *Academy of Management Journal, 35*, 351–353.
[152]Diehl & Stroebe, "Productivity loss in brainstorming groups," p. 232.

allows flexibility in accessing one's own, or others', ideas. It also creates a transactive memory system by using an external storage system that may limit the potentially debilitating effects of keeping track of ideas generated during the exchange of ideas.[153]

Capstone on Brainstorming

There is no evidence that conventional brainstorming teams can exceed the performance of people working alone. The various inhibitory social and cognitive factors in teams simply outweigh the potential positive effects of social and cognitive stimulation.[154]

Why then, with all of its faults, is face-to-face group brainstorming so pervasive in companies? Part of the reason is that people falsely believe it is effective. Most managers severely underestimate the process loss in teams—that is, the inhibitory cognitive and social factors such as social loafing, production blocking, coordination loss, task irrelevant behaviors, and filler talk—because they lack a relevant benchmark.

It is not uncommon for teams to cite advantages of brainstorming, such as increasing cohesion and building morale. They may suggest that productivity is a rather narrow basis for evaluating the effectiveness of idea-generating techniques such as group brainstorming. They suggest that group brainstorming can have a number of positive side benefits, such as increased morale and a generally more effective work environment.

We don't suggest that companies and teams abandon brainstorming. Rather, we suggest they develop hybrid methods for creative work that capitalize on individuals' strengths and combine those with team strengths. For example, one manager told us that the simple act of asking team members to submit items before their weekly group meeting resulted in a tenfold increase in volume of ideas and higher quality of those ideas. With some simple changes, the productivity of teams can increase dramatically. The positive perspective on brainstorming stems from the validation that people receive when interacting in teams, especially those with cooperative goals, such as in brainstorming. For this reason, it is not at all surprising that brainstorming maintains a high degree of popularity in organizations.[155] The key is to use brainstorming at the right time and in the right way.

Conclusion

Many of our intuitions about creativity are incorrect. We see this most clearly in the case of face-to-face brainstorming. The process of generating novel and useful ideas is often blocked in teams. Most creative ideas are applications or transfers of concepts, ideas, and processes from one domain to another. This may sound easy or straightforward, but most people under most conditions do not transfer ideas across domains, even when it would be useful. Johannes Kepler's analogy of the Sun and planets as magnets, conceiving the heart as a pump, or even comparing potato chips to dried leaves may seem obvious in hindsight, but it is the getting there that is the hard part. The techniques described in this chapter are the keys to promoting creative teamwork.

---

[153]Nagasundaram, M., & Dennis, A. R. (1993). When a group is not a group: The cognitive foundation of group idea generation. *Small Group Research, 24*, 463–489.

[154]Paulus, P. B., Larey, T. S., Brown, V., Dzindolet, M. T., Roland, E. J., Leggett, K. L., Putman, V. L., & Coskun, H. (1998, June). *Group and electronic brainstorming: Understanding production losses and gains in idea generating groups.* Paper presented at Learning in Organizations Conference, Carnegie-Mellon University, Pittsburgh, PA.

[155]Grossman, S. R., Rodgers, B. E., & Moore, B. R. (1989, December). Turn group input into stellar output. *Working Woman*, pp. 36–38; Rickards, T. (1993). Creative leadership: Messages from the front line and the back room. *Journal of Creative Behavior, 27*, 46–56.

External Dynamics

10 Networking, Social Capital, and Integrating across Teams

After the terrorist attacks on September 11, 2001, Valdis Krebs, a consultant who produces social network "maps" for corporate and nonprofit clients, decided to map the networks of the hijackers. Krebs started with two of the plotters, Khalid al-Midhar and Nawaf Alhazmi, and produced a chart of interconnections based on shared addresses, telephone numbers, and frequent-flyer numbers in the group. Only a few links separated the 19 hijackers from one another, and a disproportionate number of links converged on the leader, Mohammed Atta. Even before 9/11, an Army project called Able Danger mapped al Qaeda by looking for patterns and identifying linkages. Analysts produced link charts identifying suspected al Qaeda figures, some of which were over 20 feet long when printed. To make sense of such maps, analysts look for hubs, or certain "connector" people. All 19 hijackers were within two steps of the two original suspects uncovered in 2000. Social network metrics reveal Mohammed Atta emerging as the local leader. Disruption and attack by counterterrorist agencies often focus on the isolation and capture of highly connected individuals. However, transnational terrorist networks are extremely resilient against attack; strategies to disrupt them actually strengthen their ability to attain balance at remaining secret while being operationally effective.[1]

In the opening example, network analysis is used to examine (and predict) the behavior of terrorists. In this chapter, we examine how network analysis can be used to examine the behavior and performance of teams. Teams are dependent on their leaders and members to plug them into the right people in the organization for their needed resources, contacts, and opportunities.

Team members interact with one another in the context of a broader organization. A team's environment includes the organization to which the team belongs and the clients they serve. This chapter focuses on the team's relationship to people outside of the team, who nevertheless affect the team's ability to achieve its goals. Organizations call upon teams to span traditional boundaries

---

[1]Krebs, V. (2008). Connecting the dots: Tracking two identified terrorists. orgnet.com; Lindelauf, R., Borm, P., & Hamers, H. (2009). The influence of secrecy on the communication structure of covert networks. *Social Networks, 31*, 126–137.

both inside companies, where they might provide a closer coupling between functional units, and outside companies, where they might provide links to customers, suppliers, or competitors.[2]

In this chapter, we discuss team boundaries. We describe five prototypical teams in organizations in terms of how they manage their team boundaries and the trade-offs associated with each. Next, we focus on the external roles that team members play. We then discuss networking within the organization and contrast clique networks to entrepreneurial networks and strategies for increasing team effectiveness.

TEAM BOUNDARIES

An identifiable boundary exists between the team and the other parts of the organization. This is one of the key defining characteristics of a team, as indicated in Chapter 1. In this chapter, we examine the in- and outflow of information, resources, and people across this border.

Team boundaries differentiate one work group from another and affect knowledge transfer and distribution of resources. In some cases, boundaries are well defined, but in other cases, boundaries are ambiguous. If the boundary becomes too open or indistinct, the team risks becoming overwhelmed and losing its identity. If its boundary is too exclusive, the team might become isolated and lose touch with suppliers, managers, peers, or customers.[3] Thus, teams can be **underbounded**—having many external ties but an inability to coalesce and motivate members to pull together—or **overbounded**—having high internal loyalty and a complex set of internal dynamics but an inability to integrate with others when needed. There is a trade-off between internal cohesion and external ties—more cohesive teams are less likely to engage in external initiatives.[4] Although there is no clear solution for how to deal with the tension between internal cohesion and the external environment, we raise key issues and suggest strategies for arranging the team environment so as to be maximally productive.

Leaders play an integral role in connecting a team with their external environment. Some leaders focus all their energies on the internal functioning of the team through classic coaching; other leaders spend most of their efforts on promoting the team within the organization. These two extremes are equally ineffective. In this section, we point to the choices leaders have in managing the interface between their team and the broader environment. The choices that a leader has, in terms of managing the interface, parallel the choices for control outlined in Chapter 1. Recall our analysis of manager-led, self-managing, self-designing, and self-governing teams. In the case of the leader managing the team within its environment, the relationship of interest is between the team and the environment. Exhibit 10-1 outlines five types of teams in terms of their relationship to the environment: insulating teams, broadcasting teams, marketing teams, surveying teams, and X-teams.[5] Of course, these are five pure strategies, and blends may exist. It is useful to try to identify which style best characterizes a particular team.

---

[2]Clark, K. B., & Fujimoto, T. (1989a). Overlapping problem solving in product development. In K. Ferdows (Ed.), *Managing international manufacturing* (pp. 127–152). North Holland: Amsterdam; von Hippel, E. A. (2005). *Democratizing innovation.* Cambridge, MA: MIT Press.

[3]Alderfer, C. P. (1977). Group and intergroup relations. In J. R. Hackman & J. L. Suttle (Eds.), *Improving life at work* (pp. 227–296). Palisades, CA: Goodyear.

[4]Alderfer, C. P. (1976). Boundary relations and organizational diagnosis. In M. Meltzer & F. Wickert (Eds.), *Humanizing organizational behavior* (pp. 142–175). Springfield, IL: Charles C. Thomas; Sherif, M. (1966). *In common predicament: Social psychology of intergroup conflict and cooperation.* Boston, MA: Addison-Wesley.

[5]Ancona, D. G. (1990). Outward bound: Strategies for team survival in an organization. *Academy of Management Journal, 33*(2), 334–365.

EXHIBIT 10-1 Relationships Teams May Have with Their Environment

Team's Relationship with Environment	Key Focus and Activities	Advantages	Disadvantages
Insulating	Team is isolated from other parts of organization or its customers; team concentrates solely on internal functioning; usually highly goal driven	• Less likely to compromise ideals and objectives • Especially conducive for creative teams	• Disconnected from rest of organization • May develop groupthink or overconfidence
Broadcasting	Team concentrates on internal team processes until the team is ready to inform outsiders of its intentions	• Control over negative information • Broadcasting is relatively inexpensive	• May fail to sense true needs of customers • May fail to develop customer support
Marketing	Team concentrates on getting buy-in from outsiders through advertising, self-promotion, lobbying	• High visibility often is helpful for team	• May fail to meet true needs of customers • Marketing costs can be high
Surveying	Team concentrates on diagnosing needs of customers, experimenting with solutions, revising their knowledge, initiating programs, and collecting data	• Greatest potential customer satisfaction • Understand outsiders' demands • Rated by outsiders as higher performers	• Often extremely costly and time consuming • May surface latent conflict within the organization • Possible low cohesion (due to divergent views created by surveying) • Possible dissatisfaction
X-Teams	Exploration, exploitation, exportation	• Rapid execution, • Rapid prototyping	• Need top management support, setting appropriate milestones so that exploitation does not dwarf exploration

Source: Based on Ancona, D. G. (1990). Outward bound: Strategies for team survival in an organization. *Academy of Management Journal, 33*(2), 334–365; Ancona, D., & Bresman, H. (2007). *X-teams: How to build teams that lead, innovate and succeed.* Boston, MA: Harvard Business School Publishing; Ancona, D., Backman, E., & Bresman, H. (2009, September 1). X-Teams break new ground. *Financial Post,* p. FP9; Ancona, D., Bresman, H., & Caldwell, D. (2009). Six steps to leading high-performing x-teams. *Organizational Dynamics, 38*(3), 217–224.

Insulating Teams

Insulating teams are, for the most part, sequestered from the environment. This may be a deliberate choice by the manager or leader; other times, the team may be ostracized by the organization. Managers often want to isolate their teams for security reasons (e.g., the Los Alamos team that developed the atomic bomb) or intellectual reasons (e.g., the Xerox PARC team, which developed the computer). The greatest threat to the effectiveness of insulating teams is dissociation from the organization. Insulating teams may fail to develop a viable product or service because they are out of touch with the rest of the organization and industry, or they may have a great product but lack the support they need for success.

Insulating teams not only have to insulate themselves from others in the company so that they can focus on the work that needs to be done, they also need to insulate themselves from outsiders, who have strategic reasons to learn their secrets. Competitors often want access to information so that they can decipher long-range business plans. Information technology has made insulation much more challenging. One company went to extreme lengths to preserve their project plans.[6] They scheduled a particularly important strategic planning conference and had checked into the hotel. The conference room number and the name of their company were listed on the hotel's daily agenda sign, but no one showed up. At the appointed hour, without fanfare, they boarded a chartered bus designated for a nonexistent "tour group." From there, they travelled to an unannounced locale and began their meeting far from the eyes of outsiders who wanted to infiltrate the meeting.

Broadcasting Teams

Broadcasting teams concentrate on their internal processes and simply inform others what they are doing. More often than not, the broadcasting team has little outside contact; it makes decisions about how to serve its customers from within. The team members let others outside the team know what they are doing after they have already made decisions.

Marketing Teams

Marketing teams promote their objectives, products, services, and culture actively within their organization. Their objective is to get buy-in from above and receive recognition. They differ from broadcasting teams in that they actively tailor their communication to suit the needs, interests, and objectives of the organization.

Surveying Teams

Surveying teams have their finger on the pulse of the organization, their clients, and customers. In 2007, Asish Shah, general manager for GE Healthcare's Technology Organization in India, and his team tried to figure out the average Indian customer's propensity to pay for an ECG. "That was the wake-up call for a company like ours—the answer was only $1," said Shah. Then they looked at the same question from another angle: What can the person providing the service afford to pay for the device? The answer: $700. At the time, the average price of ECG machines in the market was $2,000. So the team started from scratch and built a product for Indian conditions. For example, some villages didn't have power, so the device had to be battery operated and take at least 100 ECGs once charged. Taking costs out was another challenge. The printer accounts for a big portion of the cost of an ECG machine, so the printer in the machine was replaced with a simpler version. Fifteen months and half a million dollars later, the MAC 400 was born.[7]

The downside of surveying, of course, is that the team may spend an undue amount of time and resources surveying clients and customers instead of engaging in the task at hand. In this sense, a surveying team is really a task force. At some point, the surveying team has to make critical decisions about when to stop collecting and probing for information and develop a product or service.

---

[6]Kaltenheuser, S. (2002, July 1). Working the crowd. *Across the Board*, pp. 50–55.
[7]Mahajan-Bansal, N., & Goyal, M. (2009, December 9). Finger on the pulse, at last. *Forbes*. forbes.com

It is rare for teams to be self-sufficient. Their dependence on others for economic, social, and political support drives many of the strategies for interacting with the environment. Xerox PARC is an example wherein a team used its insulation to advantage in developing essentially all the technology used in today's computer age. However, the team members were unsuccessful in selling their ideas to their own management (because virtually no broadcasting or marketing had been done). Therefore, Xerox did not obtain the benefits of its own special research group.

X-Teams

X-teams are highly externally oriented, and their members reach out across the organization to forge dense networks.[8] X-teams enable rapid execution, using a three-phase process: exploration, exploitation, and exportation.[9] During **exploration**, X-team members try to understand their task from a novel vantage point, generating as many insights and ideas as possible. During **exploitation**, X-teams settle upon one product they wish to create, using rapid prototyping to move from possibilities to reality. Finally, during **exportation**, they find ways to move their product and their knowledge and excitement into the broader organization and market. One example is British Petroleum, whose senior project leaders had the goal of improving the company's product-management capabilities. Leaders are configured into X-teams of 30 people and spend 1 year moving through "explore, exploit, and export."[10] The six steps of X-team behavior are as follows:[11]

1. Choosing team members for their networks
2. Making external outreach the modus operandi
3. Help the team focus on scouting, ambassadorship, and task coordination
4. Set milestones and deliverables for exploration, exploitation, and exportation
5. Use internal process to facilitate external work
6. Work with top management for commitment, resources, and support

The relationship a team has with its environment evolves, sometimes from direct managerial intervention, but more often from organizational norms, culture, and situational constraints. For example, consider how "founding teams" in organizations influence organizational development.[12] The development of all organizations begins with a single (founding) team. Founding teams have a profound impact on the organization as well as the community, by creating new populations. When these organizations disband, they create a large amount of employment volatility through job creation and destruction. In one investigation of 830 entrepreneurs of founding teams, two factors strongly affected the composition of these entrepreneurs' founding teams: homophily and network constraints based on "strong ties." Specifically, homophily or similarity was a key determinant of team composition. The existence of strong ties (marriage and long-term friendship) was also key.

Our discussion of team management vis-à-vis the external environment may seem to be overly politicized. There is a trade-off between the team members actually doing their work and

---

[8]Ancona, D., & Bresman, H. (2007). *X-teams: How to build teams that lead, innovate and succeed.* Boston, MA: Harvard Business School Publishing.

[9]Ancona, D., Backman, E., & Bresman, H. (2009, September 1). X-Teams break new ground. *Financial Post,* p. FP9.

[10]Ibid.

[11]Ancona, D., Bresman, H., & Caldwell, D. (2009). Six steps to leading high-performing x-teams. *Organizational Dynamics, 38*(3), 217–224.

[12]Ruef, M., Aldrich, H. E., & Carter, N. M. (2003). The structure of organizational founding teams: Homophily, strong ties, and isolation among U.S. entrepreneurs. *American Sociological Review, 68*, 195–222.

their efforts at influencing management and other relevant external entities. If leaders fail to effectively manage the relationship between the team and the external environment, the team may be regarded as ineffective, regardless of its actual productivity. However, by placing constraints and barriers upon the team's ability to control and gain access to resources, such as education, knowledge, and economic resources, team effectiveness may be hindered.

The interaction between a team and the organization is similar to the interaction between the members and the team itself in that there are struggles for power, status, and roles.[13] Just as members spend time during the formation of a team to determine what role they will play and which members will have power, teams play out these same issues with other organizational entities. For example, top management may set constraints and provide direction. Teams may react in a variety of ways: some welcome the direction, some try to shape the new directives, and others reject direction.

Just as people develop reputations and make impressions on others in the organization within the first few months of their arrival, so do teams. On the basis of this initial impression, a negative or positive escalating cycle of team reputation and team performance begins. Reputations may persist over time, despite efforts to change them. Teams that do not overcome a negative initial evaluation may be perceived as failures—even if they eventually achieve their goals. "The inability to influence top management early on can be devastating to a team. In short, labeling creates self-fulfilling prophecies."[14] Often, teams want to get down to work and not waste time navigating their external relationships. However, these very issues—if ignored early on—can haunt the team in the future. Therefore, even though teams must fulfill both internal and external activities, the point in time at which they undertake those activities is not trivial. Obtaining support from the environment is critical if a team is to enter a positive escalation cycle.[15]

EXTERNAL ROLES OF TEAM MEMBERS

Members develop roles for the internal functioning as well as the external functioning of a team. Identifying and understanding the roles that team members play vis-à-vis the inflow and outflow of information to the team is an important predictor of team productivity and performance. Often, roles are not formally assigned; rather, through an implicit process of team negotiation, roles are taken on by members of the group. Members quickly size up others' abilities, and tasks are often delegated on the basis of demonstrated performance in these areas.

Although it would be impossible to list an exhaustive set of roles, Exhibit 10-2 lists some of the most common and important roles in work groups.[16]

Not all of these roles are identifiable in all teams. An important role is that of external customer relations. An investigation of 403 senior leaders from 42 facilities operating in 16 countries revealed that there was a positive relationship between the senior leadership team's customer

---

[13]Ancona, D. G. (1990). Outward bound: Strategies for team survival in an organization. *Academy of Management Journal, 33*(2), 334–365.

[14]Ancona, D. G. (1993). The classics and the contemporary: A new blend of small group theory. In J. K. Murnighan (Ed.), *Social psychology in organizations: Advances in theory and research* (p. 233). Upper Saddle River, NJ: Prentice Hall.

[15]Ibid.

[16]Ancona, "Outward bound," p. 261; Ancona, D. G., & Caldwell, D. F. (1987). Management issues facing new-product teams in high technology companies. In D. Lewin, D. Lipsky, & D. Sokel (Eds.), *Advances in industrial and labor relations* (Vol. 4, pp. 199–221). Greenwich, CT: JAI Press; Ancona, D. G., & Caldwell, D. F. (1988). Beyond task and maintenance: Defining external functions in groups. *Groups and Organizational Studies, 13*, 468–494; Ancona, D. G., & Caldwell, D. F. (1992b). Bridging the boundary: External process and performance in organizational teams. *Administrative Science Quarterly, 37*, 634–665; Ancona, D. G., & Caldwell, D. F. (1992). Demography and design: Predictors of new product team performance. *Organization Science, 3*(3), 321–341.

EXHIBIT 10-2 Common Roles in Work Groups

- The **boundary spanner** acts as a bridge between units or people in an organization who would not otherwise interact. Boundary spanners are exposed to more ideas than members who do not interact with other groups. Indeed, boundary spanners who spend time with different groups exhibit greater integrative complexity in their thinking (a form of creativity) than people who don't boundary span.*
- The **bufferer** protects the team from bad or disappointing news that might cause morale to suffer and volunteers to absorb pressure or criticism from others.
- The **interpreter** shapes the collective understanding of the team. This is important because in many cases the messages that teams receive from others are ambiguous and open to interpretation.
- The **advisor** informs the team about which options they should consider and what approach they should take in dealing with changing events.
- The **gatekeeper** controls the flow of information to and from a team.
- The **lobbyist** is an extremely critical role, especially for new-product groups. By providing meanings about what the team is doing and how successful it is to people outside the team, the lobbyist controls the interpretation of what the team is perceived to be doing. For example, Tom West, the leader of a team at IBM designing a computer, presented his computer differently to various groups (from Kidder, 1981). By presenting it as "insurance" (i.e., we will have it in case the other one designed by another team in the company does not work) to top management, he was allowed to set up a team that competed with another team in the company. By presenting it as a "technical challenge" to engineers, he was able to attract the best ones. By not saying anything at all to external competitors, he protected his company.**
- The **negotiator or mediator** is empowered by the team to negotiate on behalf of the group. This person has extraordinary power in terms of garnering resources, defining options, and so on. This person may act as a mediator in cases where the team is in conflict with others.
- The **spokesperson** is the voice of the team. This position is determined in two ways: by the group members themselves (e.g., "Talk to Bob if you want to find out what happened in Lois's promotion decision") and by the members of the external environment who have their choice in terms of contacting group members.
- The **strategist**, like the negotiator, plans how to approach management for resources and deal with threats and other negative information.
- The **coordinator** arranges formal or informal communication with other people or units outside the team.

Sources: *Gruenfeld, D. H., & Fan, E. T. (1999). What newcomers see and what oldtimers say: Discontinuities in knowledge exchange. In L. Thompson, J. Levine, & D. Messick (Eds.), *Shared cognition in organizations: The management of knowledge.* Mahwah, NJ: Lawrence Erlbaum & Associates.

**Ancona, D. G. (1987). Groups in organizations: Extending laboratory models. In C. Hendrick (Ed.), *Annual review of personality and social psychology: Group and intergroup processes* (pp. 207–231). Beverly Hills, CA: Sage.

orientation and employee customer orientation.[17] Because the boundary-spanning role has been studied in detail and can significantly affect the course of individuals' career paths within the organization,[18] we discuss it in more detail.

One concern when it comes to roles is role overload. Despite the benefits of boundary spanning for teams, boundary spanning can be stressful and challenging, requiring significant effort

[17]Liao, H., & Subramony, M. (2008). Employee customer orientation in manufacturing organizations: Joint influences of customer proximity and senior leadership team. *Journal of Applied Psychology, 93*, 317–328.
[18]Burt, R. S. (1999). Entrepreneurs, distrust, and third parties: A strategic look at the dark side of dense networks. In L. Thompson, J. Levine, & D. Messick (Eds.), *Shared cognition in organizations: The management of knowledge.* Mahwah, NJ: Lawrence Erlbaum & Associates.

and time.[19] **Role overload** occurs when a person has too much work to do in the time available.[20] A study of the impact of individual boundary spanning on role overload and team viability revealed that carrying out boundary-spanning efforts is taxing for team members, but high levels of boundary spanning within the team can mitigate personal costs and improve team viability.[21]

NETWORKING: A KEY TO SUCCESSFUL TEAMWORK

The shift away from top-down management and bureaucratic structures means that more than ever team members are in control of their own movement within the organization. This can bring opportunity for the team, the organization, and its members, but only if this task is handled optimally. The heart of this task involves management of relationships. In this section, we describe the key issues that managers should know when building the relationship between their team and the organization.

Communication

In an ideal organizational environment, there is clear and consistent communication among the different functional and geographic units. Communication quickly disperses innovation, reduces unnecessary duplication of effort, and facilitates the implementation of best practices.

However, the reality of organizational communication may be a far cry from the ideal. Communication among different functional and geographically dispersed units does not occur as frequently as it should. Who talks to whom is much more a function of informal, social networks than a bureaucrat's organizational chart might lead one to believe.

Most organizations are composed of informal communication networks, in which communication is incomplete and information is not ubiquitously dispersed throughout the company. Information may be controlled or held only by certain people, as opposed to being directly accessible to everyone in the organization.

Human Capital and Social Capital

Why is it that some teams are singled out and win more approval from senior management than other teams? The typical explanation centers upon **human capital**: Inequalities result from differences in individual ability. People who are more intelligent, educated, and experienced rise to the top of their organization; those who are less qualified do not.

However, there is another explanation that accounts for the existence of inequality. **Social capital** is the value managers add to their teams and organizations through their ties to other people.[22] Social capital refers to the resources available through social networks and elite institutional ties—such as club memberships—that a person can use to enhance his or her position. Social capital is the value that comes from knowing who, when, and how to coordinate through various contacts. Whereas human capital refers to individual ability, social capital refers to opportunity created through relationships. Managers with more social capital get higher returns on their human capital because they are positioned to identify and develop more

---

[19]Aldrich, H., & Herker, D. (1977). Boundary spanning roles and organization Structure. *Academy of Management Review, 2*(2), 217–230.

[20]Beehr, T. A., Walsh, J., & Taber, B. (1976), Relationship of stress to individually and organizationally valued states—Higher order needs as a moderator. *Journal of Applied Psychology, 61*(1), 41–49.

[21]Marrone, J. A., Tesluk, P. E., & Carson, J. B. (2007). A multilevel investigation of the antecedents and consequences to team member boundary spanning. *Academy of Management Journal, 50*, 1423–1439.

[22]Coleman, J. S. (1988). Social capital in the creation of human capital. *American Journal of Sociology, 94*, S95–S120.

rewarding opportunities.[23] Certain managers are connected to certain others, trust certain others, feel obligated to support certain others, and are dependent on exchange and reciprocity with certain others, above and beyond those in their immediate functional unit.

To understand the value of social capital within the organization and how it affects team performance, it is necessary to consider the broader organizational environment. Organizational charts are rather crude depictions that reveal the chain of command and report relationships. However, as many managers can attest, the way that work gets done and information gets spread within an organization is a far cry from published organizational charts. Instead, informal systems of connections and relationships, developed over time, guide the flow of information between people and teams. Let's explore these informal networks in detail.

Exhibit 10-3 is a somewhat crude depiction of two social networks in an organization. The dots represent people. The lines that connect the dots are the communication networks between

EXHIBIT 10-3 Social Networks of Two Managers within the Same Company

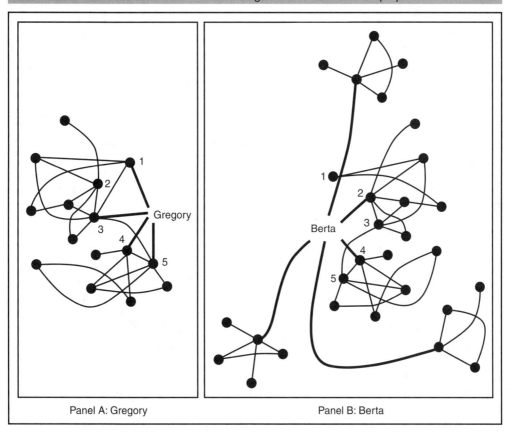

Panel A: Gregory   Panel B: Berta

Source: Burt, R. S. (1999). Entrepreneurs, distrust, and third parties: A strategic look at the dark side of dense networks. In L. Thompson, J. Levine, & D. Messick (Eds.), *Shared cognition in organizations: The management of knowledge.* Mahwah, NJ: Lawrence Erlbaum & Associates.

---

[23]Burt, R. S. (1992). *The social structure of competition.* Cambridge, MA: Harvard University Press.

people in the organization—simply, who trusts whom. To be sure, members of a given department or functional unit are more interconnected than are members of completely different functional units. However, even within particular departments, there is a high variation in communication. Moreover, there is high variation among organizational members in terms of who reaches beyond the walls of the functional teams and communicates with others.

Perceived networks may predict performance more than actual networks.[24] The accuracy of perceived advice networks is related to increased power in organizations.[25] People who have an astute knowledge of where the network links are in a position of power. First, this information provides a good assessment of who is powerful in the organization. Second, this information can be used to identify where the coalitions are in an organization, their size, and their sources of support. Third, an accurate assessment of the network can expose the weaknesses in other groups by exposing holes, gaps, and lack of support.

Consider the two different panels in Exhibit 10-3. Panel A depicts the network (or communication) structure of a manager, Gregory, who has a network of relatively close colleagues—most likely from the same functional unit. This type of close-knit, self-contained network is a **clique network** and is reminiscent of the traditional family unit. In the clique network, groups of people, all of whom know one another quite well, share largely redundant communication structures. At the extreme, members of clique networks are only aware of others with whom they have direct contact.

When we contrast Gregory's communication network to Berta's in Panel B, we notice some striking differences. First, Berta's network is much less tightly knit than is Gregory's network. Second, Berta's network spans what appears to be more functional units than does Gregory's network. In a sense, Berta knows more people who don't know each other. Third, Berta's network is structurally more unique than is Gregory's network. Simply stated, Gregory's network is highly identical to all the other people in his clique. In contrast, Berta's network does not look like anyone else's, in terms of the connections she has. Before reading further, how do you think these differing network structures affect the performance of the team, the individuals involved, and the larger organization?

Boundary Spanning

Individuals (and teams) who span organizational divides and integrate the knowledge and best practices from different areas of the organization (who otherwise have little incentive to do so) are extremely valuable for the organization. These people are known as **boundary spanners**. Boundary spanners bridge the functional gaps, or the **structural holes**, that exist in organizations. Structural holes separate nonredundant social contacts in the organization. A person who bridges or spans a structural hole fills a unique spot in the organizational network: bringing together people, knowledge, and information that would otherwise not be connected. This, of course, is critical for maximizing diversity of ideas and setting the stage for creative thinking in the organization—not to mention avoiding duplication of effort and speeding along organizational innovations to relevant units. Teams whose members have access to different social networks, independent of their individual knowledge and skills, may be more likely to learn through relationships than teams whose members' social ties are redundant.[26] The value of a boundary spanner is the ability to capitalize on the social structure of the organization that, as we have seen, is structurally imperfect.

---

[24]Kilduff, M., & Krackhardt, D. (1994). Bringing the individual back in: A structural analysis of the internal market for reputation in organizations. *Academy of Management Journal, 37*(1), 87–108.

[25]Krackhardt, D. (1990). Assessing the political landscape: Structure, cognition, and power in organizations. *Administrative Science Quarterly, 35*(2), 342–369.

[26]Granovetter, M. (1973). The strength of weak ties. *American Journal of Sociology, 78*, 1360–1379.

When we again compare the networks of Gregory and Berta, we see that Gregory has a network that spans one structural hole (i.e., the relatively weak connection between a cluster reached through contacts 1, 2, and 3 versus the other cluster that is reached through contacts 4 and 5). In contrast, Berta preserves the connections with both clusters in Gregory's network but expands the network to a more diverse set of contacts. Berta's network, adding three new clusters of people, spans 10 structural holes.

The structural holes that exist between people, functional units, and teams represent opportunities for teams and their leaders. Boundary spanners broker the flow of information between people on opposite ends of a structural hole and control the nature of projects that bring people together on opposite ends of the structural hole. In interlocking teams, the functional teams are networked to other teams in different functions via a supervisor who coordinates activities. In this way, the structure of a network is a competitive advantage for certain people and certain teams in the organization.

Managers with contact networks rich in structural holes are the people who know about, have a hand in, and exercise more control over rewarding opportunities. They have broader access to information because of their diverse contacts. They are more aware of new opportunities and have easier access to these opportunities than do their peers—even their peers of equivalent or greater human capital! For this reason, they are also more likely to be discussed as suitable candidates for inclusion in new opportunities. They are also likely to have sharpened and displayed their capabilities because they have more control over the substance of their work defined by relationships with subordinates, superiors, and colleagues. A study of 64 software development teams revealed that boundary spanning, buffering, and boundary reinforcement were positively related to team performance and psychological safety.[27]

Cliques Versus Boundary-Spanning Networks

In Exhibit 10-3, Gregory is in a tightly constructed, dense clique network. In contrast, Berta's network is much less dense, more unique, and more varied. Members of clique networks consider one another to be their closest contacts, and because they focus their efforts at primarily internal communications, they are often sequestered from the larger organization (see Exhibit 10-4).

EXHIBIT 10-4 Understanding Dense Networks

Stumbling into a dense network can be a little alarming. Take the case of Thomas Tamm. In the spring of 2004, Tamm had just finished a yearlong assignment at a sensitive Justice Department unit handling wiretaps of suspected terrorists and spies. While there, Tamm learned of a highly classified National Security Agency (NSA) Program that seemed to be eavesdropping on U.S. citizens. When Tamm began asking questions, his supervisors told him to drop the subject. One volunteered that "the program" (as it was commonly called within the office) was "probably illegal." The program Tamm unknowingly worked for was in fact a wide range of covert surveillance activities authorized by President George W. Bush in the aftermath of 9/11. Through secret orders, Bush authorized the NSA for the first time to eavesdrop on phone calls and e-mails between the United States and a foreign country without any court review. Not able to get information from his superiors, Tamm one afternoon called *The New York Times* with the story. The newspaper soon reported that President George W. Bush had secretly authorized the NSA to intercept phone calls and e-mails of individuals inside the United States without judicial warrants.

Source: Based on Isikoff, M. (2008, December 22). The fed who blew the whistle. *Newsweek, 152*(25), 40–48.

---

[27]Faraj, S., & Yan, A. (2009). Boundary work in knowledge teams. *Journal of Applied Psychology, 94*(3), 604–617.

The loyalty and cohesiveness of inner circles can be both comforting to those situated securely in them and intimidating to those who stumble into them without a real ally.

Berta's **entrepreneur network** is a less tightly knit group, with contacts in a variety of disparate organizational areas. In fact, Berta does not appear to be housed in any particular network. On the surface it might seem that Gregory would feel more secure, nestled in his cohesive group, and, hence, be more successful. Berta is a boundary spanner, a link between different subgroups and functional units that without her would not be connected. Berta occupies a unique position in her network as she single-handedly bridges these separate groups. In this sense, Berta is an **information broker**, because she alone is at the critical junction between these networks and serves the important role of brokering information. The people in Berta's functional group are more dependent on Berta than on Gregory for information. In a very crude sense, Gregory is an organizational clone—expendable—at least on a sociostructural level. In contrast, Berta is a critical player; remove her and the organization may suffer serious consequences and lost opportunities. Berta serves an important team and organizational function by garnering information that would otherwise be unavailable to the team or the organization.

Gregory is in a highly cohesive group, which can be advantageous when it comes to managing the internal team environment. The problem is that Gregory does not really learn anything new by interacting with the members of his group. In contrast, because Berta's contacts do not know one another and, therefore, cannot apply social pressure on each other—as they can in clique networks—Berta is potentially privy to a greater amount of accurate and nonredundant information. Berta's position as a structural hole is an indicator that people on either side of the hole circulate in different flows of information. The structural hole between two clusters (or teams) does not mean that people in the two clusters are unaware of one another. Rather, people are so focused on their own activities that they have little time to attend to the activities of people in the other cluster.

In comparing Gregory's and Berta's networks, the information benefits in Berta's network are enhanced in several important ways that go a long way toward furthering individual, team, and organizational goals—the very things that we outlined in Chapter 2 to be critical measures of performance. From Berta's view, there is more benefit reaped because more contacts are included in the network. The diversity of contacts enhances the quality of benefits, because each cluster of contacts is an independent source of information. One cluster (e.g., a team), no matter how numerous its members, is only one source of information because people connected to one another know about the same things at approximately the same time. Because nonredundant contacts are linked only through the leader at the center of the network, the leader is assured of being the first to see new opportunities created by the need of one team that could be served by skills in another team. Berta has the opportunity of bringing together otherwise disconnected individuals where it will be rewarding. Furthermore, having more diverse contacts means that the manager is more likely to be among the people discussed as suitable candidates for inclusion in new opportunities. Because people communicate through Berta, she can adjust her image with each contact. Berta is able to monitor information more effectively than is possible with typical bureaucratic control; she is highly mobile relative to bureaucracy.

For a summary of the advantages and disadvantages of cliques and boundary-spanning networks, see Exhibits 10-5 and 10-6.

In comparison with others who are equal in human capital, boundary spanners enjoy more organizational success. Managers with larger networks of disconnected contacts get promoted earlier than comparable managers with smaller networks of more interconnected

EXHIBIT 10-5 Advantages and Disadvantages of Clique and Boundary-Spanning Networks

	Clique Network	**Boundary-Spanning Network**
Advantages	High cohesion Loyalty and support Increased efficiency of decision making	Leverages diversity Capitalizes on opportunity Greater innovation Earlier promotions Higher salaries
Disadvantages	Redundant communication Biased communication Groupthink Dispensable members	Greater conflict, both task and relationship Power struggles

EXHIBIT 10-6 Minority Managers

"Fast-track" minority managers develop networks that are well connected to both minority and white informal circles. In contrast, high-potential whites and non-fast-track minorities have few, if any, network ties with minorities. Ironically, many non-fast-track minorities feel that networking with members of their racial group is detrimental to their careers. Yet the more successful minorities consistently stress the value of same-race contacts in helping them to develop and implement strategies for career success. Minority fast-trackers develop networks that span a much broader set of social and corporate circles than the non-fast-trackers.

Source: Ibarra, H. (1995). Race, opportunity, and diversity of social circles in managerial networks. *Academy of Management Journal, 38*(3), 673–703.

contacts.[28] In an investigation of 3,000 senior managers in a high-technology firm with over 100,000 employees, those promoted early had more social capital—as determined by their social network analysis.[29] CEOs' compensation is positively predicted by the social capital of the chair of the compensation committee and the CEO's social capital relative to the chair.[30] The success of Broadway musical teams from 1945 through 1989 revealed that the "small world" (connected quality) of creative artists directly affected the financial and artistic success of the show as well as the percentage of hits and flops and raves.[31] Similarly, the success of scientific teams in social psychology, ecology, and astronomy is also directly predicted by the structure of the creative collaboration network of the scientists in these communities.[32]

---

[28]Burt, *Social structure of competition,* p. 267; Podolny, J. M., & Baron, J. N. (1997). Resources and relationships: Social networks and mobility in the workplace. *American Sociological Review, 62*(5), 673–693; Sparrowe, R. T., & Popielarz, P. A. (1995). *Weak ties and structural holes: The effects of network structure on careers.* Paper presented at the annual meetings of the Academy of Management, Vancouver, BC.

[29]Burt, *The social structure of competition.*

[30]Belliveau, M. A., O'Reilly, III, C. A., & Wade, J. B. (1996). Social capital: The effects of social similarity and status on CEO compensation. *Academy of Management Journal, 39,* 1568–1593.

[31]Uzzi, B., & Spiro, J. (2005). Collaboration and creativity: The small world problem. *American Journal of Sociology, 111,* 447–504.

[32]Guimerà, R., Uzzi, B., Spiro, J., & Nunes Amaral, L. A. (2005). Team assembly mechanisms determine collaboration network structure and team performance. *Science, 308*(5722), 697–702.

However, a study of 525 companies that recently went public reveals that their boards are best comprised of a majority of the original top management team (TMT) members, rather than independent outsiders.[33] Board members possess valuable tacit knowledge of the company; outsiders should provide resources for the TMTs to execute strategies, rather than monitor them.

The network structure of team members affects how much information they share in common with others in a team. For this reason, boundary spanners are more cognitively central (i.e., aware of what other people know) than are non–boundary spanners. This affects their ability to influence the team. The more information team members share with others, the more cognitively central they are in the team. Also, cognitively central members acquire pivotal power in a team and exert more influence on consensus than members who are not cognitively central.[34] Thus, those who are connected are more influential.

Group Social Capital

Group social capital is the configuration of team members' social relationships within a group and in the social structure of the broader organization.[35] Although boundary-spanning activities can benefit team performance, pursuing social relationships outside one's team might decrease the group's internal cohesiveness,[36] which can, in turn, negatively affect performance.[37] Some teams have greater social group capital "liquidity" because their members have positions in the overall social structure of the organization. For example, rapid access to information and political support is greater for teams whose members socialize during their free time with organization's upper management. In an investigation of work-related ties that extend into social realms outside of work, the optimal configuration was a moderate level of internal closure within the group and a large number of "bridging" relationships to other groups' leaders.[38] It is actually counterproductive for a team when all of the members socialize informally outside of the organization. It is better for the team members to socialize outside of the team *and* outside of work. Such ties are particularly critical because the shift in focus from work to social interaction invites a shift in the types of resources that are transferred among members. A meta-analysis of 37 studies of teams in real organizations indicated that teams with densely configured interpersonal ties attain their goals better and are more committed to staying together.[39] In another investigation involving 51 teams working in two wood composite plants, external coordination (extra-team relationships) had a significant, positive impact on team performance.[40]

---

[33]Kroll, M., Walters, B. A., & Le, S. A. (2007). The impact of board composition and top management team ownership structure on post-IPO performance in young entrepreneurial firms. *Academy of Management Journal, 50,* 1198–1216.
[34]Kameda, T., Ohtsubo, Y., & Takezawa, M. (1997). Centrality in sociocognitive networks and social influence: An illustration in a group decision-making context. *Journal of Personality and Social Psychology, 73*(2), 296–309.
[35]Oh, H., Chung, M.-H., & Labianca, G. (2004). Group social capital and group effectiveness: The role of informal socializing ties. *Academy of Management Journal, 47,* 860–875.
[36]Keller, R. T. (1978). Dimensions of management systems and performance in continuous process organizations. *Human Relations, 31,* 119–129.
[37]Beal, D. J., Cohen, R. R., Burke, M. J., & McLendon, C. L. (2003). Cohesion and performance in groups: A meta-analytic clarification of construct relations. *Journal of Applied Psychology, 88,* 989–1004.
[38]Oh, Chung, & Labianca, "Group social capital and group effectiveness."
[39]Balkundi, P., & Harrison, D. A. (2006). Ties, leaders, and time in teams: Strong inference and network structure's effects on team viability and performance. *Academy of Management Journal, 49*(1), 305–325.
[40]Michael, J. H., Barsness, Z., Lawson, L., & Balkundi, P. (2004). Focus please: Team coordination and performance at wood manufacturers. *Forest Products Journal, 54*(12), 250–255.

Leadership Ties

The network structure of team leaders is important for team performance. Teams with leaders who are central in teams' intragroup networks and teams that are central in their intergroup network perform better.[41] According to the **leader centrality–performance hypothesis**, team leaders from whom subordinates seek advice or friendship tend to have relatively comprehensive views of the social structures of their teams. Such a perspective helps them make better decisions. Central leaders occupy structurally advantageous positions in their social networks and often act as gatekeepers and regulators of resource flow.[42] In a study of 300 self-managing teams at a large manufacturing plant of a Fortune 500 corporation, leaders who contributed most to their team's success excelled at managing the boundary between the team and the larger organization.[43] This boundary-management behavior involved four key skills: relating, scouting, persuading, and empowering (see Exhibit 10-7).[44] Teams with more prestigious formal leaders (i.e., leaders whom a high proportion of subordinate sought out for advice) experienced lower levels of conflict and had higher levels of team viability.[45] In contrast, leaders who had advice ties with subordinates (who did not have advice ties with each other) had elevated levels of team

EXHIBIT 10-7 Team Effectiveness

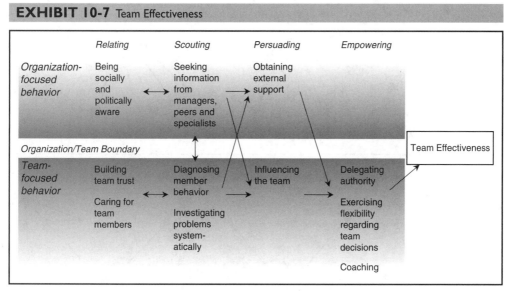

Source: Druskat, V., & Wheeler, J. (2003). Managing from the boundary: The effective leadership of self-managing work teams. *Academy of Management Journal, 46*(4), 435–457. Copyright 2003 by Academy of Management (NY). Reproduced with permission of Academy of Management (NY) in the format of Textbook via Copyright Clearance Center.

---

[41]Balkundi & Harrison, "Ties, leaders, and time in teams."

[42]Krackhardt, D. (1996). Social networks and the liability of newness for managers. In C. L. Cooper & D. M. Rousseau (Eds.), *Trends in organizational behavior* (pp. 159–173). New York: Wiley.

[43]Druskat, V. U., & Wheeler, J. V. (2004). How to lead a self-managing team. *MIT Sloan Management Review, 45*(4), 65–71.

[44]Druskat, V., & Wheeler, J. (2003). Managing from the boundary: The effective leadership of self-managing work teams. *Academy of Management Journal, 46*(4), 435–457.

[45]Balkundi, P., Barsness, Z., & Michael, J. (2009). Unlocking the influence of leadership network structures on team conflict and viability. *Small Group Research, 40*(3), 301–322.

conflict and lower levels of team viability. Coworkers tend to place more trust in fellow coworkers who are trusted by the team's formal leaders than in those who are less trusted by the leader.[46]

INCREASING YOUR SOCIAL CAPITAL

How can managers best expand their network and link their team within the organization? Strategic network expansion involves connecting to people and teams in such a way that the manager (and the team) is filling a structural hole. To see the difference between typical network expansion and strategic network expansion, see Exhibit 10-8.

EXHIBIT 10-8 Strategic Network Expansion

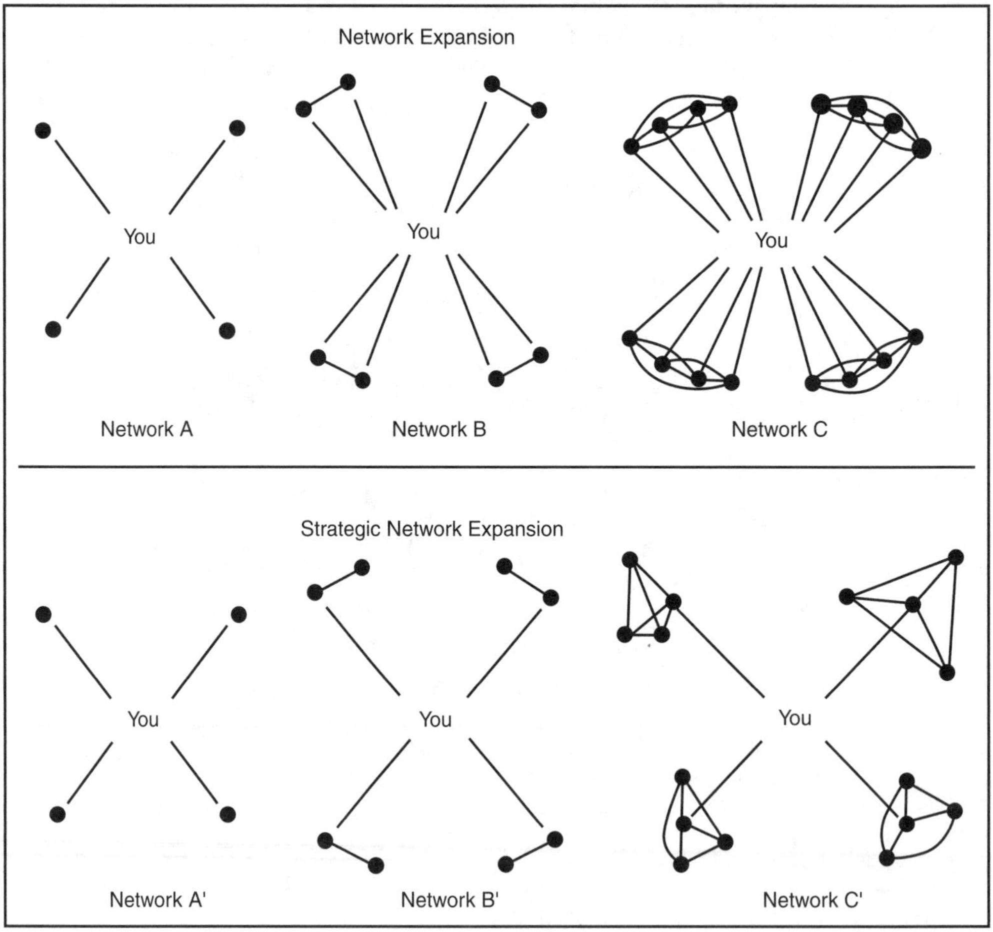

Source: Burt, R. S. (1992). *Structural holes: The social structure of competition.* Cambridge, MA: Harvard University Press. Composite of two figures reprinted by permission of the publisher. Copyright © 1992 by the President and Fellows of Harvard College.

[46]Lau, D. C., & Liden, R. C. (2008). Antecedents of coworker trust: Leaders' blessings. *Journal of Applied Psychology, 93*, 1130–1138.

We advocate a team-based view of structural positioning within the organization. That is, teams are more likely to achieve their goals and stay in touch with the needs of the organization if they have connections with others within the organization. Thus, the structural positioning of an entrepreneurial, as opposed to clique, network has benefits for individual team members, the team, and the organization.

From the point of view of the employee, organizational benefits are maximized in a large network of nonredundant contacts. It is better to know a lot of people who don't know one another. The opportunity is there because most people are too busy to keep in touch directly. Furthermore, people in organizations display a type of functional ethnocentrism, believing that their own functional area is of key importance and that the other units do not matter as much. Entrepreneurs, such as Berta, take advantage of functional ethnocentrism and act as critical go-betweens to bring individuals, teams, and units together in ways that are profitable to themselves and the organization.

Consider the following strategies as practical steps that individuals, teams, and organizations can take to build more connections across functional groups:

Analyze Your Social Network

Organizational actors who hold an accurate perception of their own social network are more effective than those who hold inaccurate perceptions.[47]

Determine the Brokers in Your Social Network

Everyone cannot be a boundary spanner or information broker. Managers who are aware of who their information brokers are, are more effective in using their own networks. (As an exercise, follow the three-step guide in Exhibit 10-9.) Just because you know who the brokers are in your

EXHIBIT 10-9 Six Degrees of Separation Worksheet

(Step 1)	(Step 2)	(Step 3)
Your circle of key business contacts	Who introduced you to the contact in column B? (These are the brokers in your network)	Who did you introduce the contact in column B to? (You are a broker in their network)
1.		
2.		
3.		
4.		
5.		
6.		
7.		
8.		
9.		
10.		

Source: Adapted from Uzzi, B., & Dunlap, S. (2005). How to build your network. *Harvard Business Review, 83*(12), 53–60. Copyright © 2005 by HBS Publishing.

---

[47]Krackhardt, "Assessing the political landscape."

network does not automatically entitle you to rely on them. For example, when Liz Ryan, a syndicated workplace advice columnist, received a phone call from a young woman who announced that she found her on LinkedIn (a network site), the caller requested that Liz use her own large network to help the caller launch a new show to a TV producer. There was no benefit offered and so Liz Ryan politely refused.[48]

Identify "Structural Holes" in Your Organization

Structural holes are the gaps that are created when members of cliques (closed networks) do not connect. Identify those gaps and find a way to bridge those gaps. When a manager identifies structural holes, he or she recognizes and overcomes the clique network system. Clique networks contain a number of disadvantages for the organization and the team. People in clique networks fall prey to the homogeneity bias. For example, men in clique networks include significantly fewer women among their contacts.[49] This can stifle creativity, propagate prejudice, and hinder the benefits of diversity.

Expand the Size of the Network

Expanding the size of the network does not mean increasing the size of the team but, rather, increasing the number of people that the manager and the team come into contact with. Speed interviewing is an example of maximizing contacts. Companies can't slowly evaluate finance candidates over weeks or months because others will hire them first. One recruiting director explains "companies take four or five candidates and interview them for 30 or 40 minutes. If a candidate fits the bill, they bring them back for a long interview." Interviewers make up their minds within the first 12 minutes of the discussion, so much of the traditional interview can be a waste of time.[50]

Understand Gender Scripts in Networks

Quite often, business opportunities are conducted in the context of social relationships.[51] Many social relationships are common and therefore highly scripted or routinized, such as conducting a business meeting on the golf course. These scripts are significant because they define the conditions under which networks are most effective.[52] For this reason, it is difficult to form close relationships across gender lines if they are built through socializing activities such as playing golf, going to the theater, or evening dinner gatherings because these practices often have a different meaning between men and women than they do between persons of the same gender.[53] (See Exhibit 10-10 for an examination of women's and men's networks.)

---

[48]Ryan, L. (2006, June 5). The really heinous networking stories are instructive too. *NewsWest.net*.

[49]Burt, *The social structure of competition*.

[50]Silverman, C. (2008, April 7). The traditional interview: That's so yesterday; Employers are realizing candidates who rock the interview prove they're mastered the process, but not necessarily the job itself. *The Globe and Mail*, p. L3.

[51]Uzzi, B. (1997). Social structure and competition in interfirm networks: The paradox of embeddedness. *Administrative Science Quarterly, 42*, 35–67.

[52]Uzzi, B., & Gillespie, J. J. (1999). Access and governance benefits of social relationships and networks: The case of collateral, availability, and bank spreads. In H. Rosenblum (Ed.), *Business access to capital and credit*. Washington, DC: Federal Reserve Bank.

[53]Etzkowitz, H., Kemelgor, C., & Uzzi, B. (1999). *Social capital and career dynamics in hard science: Gender, networks, and advancement*. New York: Cambridge University Press.

EXHIBIT 10-10 Social Capital and Gender

Etzkowitz, Kemelgor, and Uzzi investigated why women scientists with human capital equal to, or better than, their male counterparts do poorer in graduate school and are thereafter disadvantaged by a lack of contacts to the resources and tacit information important for identifying, developing, and following through on leading-edge research projects. The differential performance of women follows from their disadvantaged position in a social structure of relations, not their human capital endowments. By actively managing social networks, key barriers to the advancement of women in science can be overcome.

Source: Based on Etzkowitz, H., Kemelgor, C., & Uzzi, B. (2000). *Athena unbound: The advancement of women in science and technology.* New York: Cambridge University Press.

Diversify Networks

The homogeneity bias pulls people toward developing cliques of like-minded people—which is exactly the wrong type of network to foster. It may be more comfortable in the short run, but it will have negative, long-term consequences for the individual, the team, and the organization. A better alternative is to develop a diversified network, which means crossing organizational boundaries and functional areas. Uzzi distinguished embedded ties (social ties) from arm's length (nonsocial, purely business) ties.[54] According to Uzzi, at the network level, the optimal composition of ties is achieved when a network has an integrated mix of embedded and arm's length ties.[55] This is because embedded ties and arm's length ties can offer complementary benefits when combined, just as the overall value of a portfolio increases when it is composed of complementary assets that offset each other's inherent weaknesses and strengths. Networks dominated by one type of tie produce fewer benefits, which partly accounts for the negative effects of overly embedded (e.g., "old-boy") networks, or overly disembedded exchange networks (e.g., whipsawing of suppliers by large manufacturers).[56]

Consider Joshi's model for understanding the networking of teams based on their organizational demography (see Exhibit 10-11).[57] Organizational demography refers to the composition of teams in terms of the proportion of majority and minority members on the team.[58] The majority is an identity group that has typically enjoyed access to power and authority in the organization. The minority represents an identity group that has been marginalized from a position of power and authority. The model distinguishes three types of team demographics: homogeneous majority teams, homogeneous minority teams, and diverse teams. Homogeneous majority teams are predominantly composed of people belonging to a high-status majority identity group. Homogeneous minority teams are composed of members belonging to a single identity group that is not that of the larger organization. Diverse or heterogeneous teams represent both majority and minority members equally. According to the model, homophilous ties may limit the extent to which team members have access to diverse

---

[54]Uzzi, B. (1997). Social structure and competition in interfirm networks: The paradox of embeddedness. *Administrative Science Quarterly, 42,* 35–67.
[55]Ibid.
[56]Ibid.
[57]Joshi, A. (2006). The influence of organizational demography on the external networking behavior of teams. *Academy of Management Review, 31*(3), 583–595.
[58]Ibid.

EXHIBIT 10-11 External Team Networking in the Context of Organizational Demography

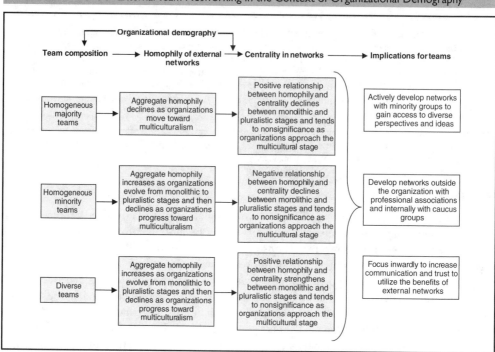

Source: Joshi, A. (2006). The influence of organizational demography on the external networking behavior of teams. *Academy of Management Review, 31*(3), 583–595. Copyright 2006 by Academy of Management (NY). Reproduced with permission of Academy of Management (NY) in the format Textbook via Copyright Clearance Center.

perspectives in homogeneous majority teams. As organizations move toward pluralistic settings, these teams may lose support and information from minority peers. In terms of homogenous minority teams, lack of networking opportunities with peers and upper management can be detrimental; such teams need to devise strategies to compensate for the numerical scarcity of minority members. Diverse teams can gain centrality in external networks through homophilous interactions of its majority team members. To maximally use the benefits of their external networks, diverse teams may need to focus on building trust and cooperation internally in monolithic and pluralistic settings.

Build Hierarchical Networks

In bureaucratic organizations, boundary spanners need to network not only laterally but also hierarchically. An improvisational theater group in Denver, Colorado, Playback Theatre West, takes this idea literally. The group's tool, called **sociometry**, which they introduce at company retreats, asks each employee to line up behind the supervisor they trust the most (other than the boss). Thus the "real" hierarchical network, a map of the informal networks inside the company, appears.[59]

---

[59]Palmer, L. (1996, April 30). There's no meetings like business meetings. *Fast Company*, 2.

Multiteam Systems

Multiteam systems (MTS) are two or more teams that interface directly and interdependently in response to environmental contingencies toward the accomplishment of shared goals.[60] Although the teams pursue different proximal goals, they share at least one goal. In MTS, the effectiveness of cross-team processes is important for MTS effectiveness.[61]

Teams can introduce structural strategies for integrating with other teams. Exhibit 10-12 reviews seven structural solutions for integrating across teams within an organization. Three of

EXHIBIT 10-12 Integrating Across Teams: Formal Structural Solutions

Integration between Teams			Integration Across Multiple Teams and Components of a Business Unit (Tighter Integration)			
Liaison roles	Overlapping membership	Cross-team integrating teams	Management teams	Representative integrating teams	Individual integrating teams	Improvement teams
Liaison roles			One boundary spanner is formally a member of one team but sits in on meetings of another team to share and gather information (e.g., a day-shift worker sits in on the night shift).			
Overlapping membership			Several employees are members of two groups simultaneously or in sequence.			
Cross-team integrating teams			Team composed of several members from other teams with integration needs, responsible for documenting and communicating changes in a timely manner.			
Management teams			Forge strategy and direction for multiple teams in business unit; make resource trade-offs among teams that are consistent with strategy, manage team performance.			
Representative integrating teams			Nonmanagement team with authority to make decisions that affect system or context in which embedded teams are composed of peers of team members.			
Individual integrating roles			Individuals in specific function provide integration with more flexibility than a team (e.g., a salesperson pulls together team for specific customer or project).			
Improvement teams			Teams that initiate changes in how parts of business unit work together to improve business unit performance; must have legitimacy from the level of the organization at which their changes will be enacted; often not a full-time assignment but must be managed as an official project team.			

Sources: Gruenfeld, D. H. (1997, May). Integrating across teams: Formal structural solutions. Presentation at Kellogg School of Management, Evanston, IL; also based on Mohrman, S. A., Cohen, S. G., & Mohrman, A. M. (1995). *Designing team-based organizations.* San Francisco, CA: Jossey-Bass.

---

[60]Mathieu, J. E., Marks, M. A., & Zaccaro, S. J. (2001). Multi-team systems. In N. Anderson, D. S. Ones, H. K. Sinangil, & C. Viswesvaran (Eds.), *Handbook of industrial, work and organizational psychology* (Vol. 2, pp. 289–313). London: Sage.
[61]Marks, M. A., DeChurch, L. A., Mathieu, J. E., Panzer, F. J., & Alonso, A. (2005). Teamwork in multiteam systems. *Journal of Applied Psychology, 90*(5), 964–971.

the strategies focus on integrating between teams. Four of the strategies focus on integrating across multiple teams and components of a business unit.

None of these strategies is flawless. In fact, even though boundary spanning often increases cognitive growth, teams usually exhibit a cognitive territoriality in response to the presence of others. For example, old-timers in teams use a greater number of their own ideas after newcomers arrive than before (for more details, see Exhibit 10-13).[62]

Greater integration is important to achieving the four major goals of productivity outlined in Chapter 2: achieving team goals, fostering team spirit, enhancing individual development, and furthering organizational objectives. In many cases, though, integration is not a choice—it is an absolute necessity for organizations to keep up with the industry demands. For example, Rory Granros, director of process industries at Infor, a relationship management software company, argues that integration among teams reduces the time to get a product to market from 3 years to for months. "You need collaboration between formulating and packaging," says Granros. "The formula people don't have to know all about the packaging, but they do have to know if the acid is too hot for the bottle." There are many steps involved in a product going to market, and team integration can help the shared goal of the company to be reached faster.[63]

TYPES OF TIES IN TEAMS

People in teams bond along three specific types of ties: friendship, trust, and advice.[64] **Friendship ties** are close interpersonal ties between people, characterized by positive, amicable relationships.[65] Friendship ties are voluntary and often communal in nature, such that people provide for one

---

EXHIBIT 10-13 An Investigation of Itinerant and Indigenous Team Members

Gruenfeld, Martorana, and Fan ingeniously investigated the consequences of temporary membership changes for itinerant members (i.e., members who leave their core group to visit a foreign work team and then, subsequently, return) and indigenous members of those foreign and origin groups. Although it would seem that itinerant members would learn new ideas that would transfer back to their core group once they returned, this was not always the case. In fact, members of all groups produced more unique ideas after itinerant members returned to their core group than before they left or during the temporary change period, but the ideas produced by the itinerant members were significantly less likely to be included in a group project designed to draw on knowledge of the work team than the ideas of indigenous members. After their return, itinerant members were perceived as highly involved in the group activity, but they were also perceived as more argumentative than they were before leaving, and although they produced more unique ideas than indigenous members, their contributions to the team project were perceived as less valuable. As a result, itinerant group members had less direct influence after their boundary-spanning stint than they did prior to it!

Source: Gruenfeld, D. H., Martorana, P. V., & Fan, E. T. (2000). What do groups learn from their worldliest members? Direct and indirect influence in dynamic teams. *Organizational Behavior and Human Decision Processes, 82*(1), 45–59.

---

[62]Gruenfeld, D. H., & Fan, E. T. (1999). What newcomers see and what oldtimers say: Discontinuities in knowledge exchange. In L. Thompson, J. Levine, & D. Messick (Eds.), *Shared cognition in organizations: The management of knowledge.* Mahwah, NJ: Lawrence Erlbaum & Associates.
[63]Spiegel, R. (2007, December). Collaboration proliferates as companies go global. *Automation World*, p. 34.
[64]Shah, P. P., & Dirks, K. T. (2003). The social structure of diverse groups: Integrating social categorization and network perspectives. *Research on Managing Groups and Teams, 5*, 113–133.
[65]Jehn, K., & Shah, P. (1997). Interpersonal relationships and task performance: An examination of mediating processes in friendship and acquaintance groups. *Journal of Personality and Social Psychology, 72*, 775–790; Rawlins, W. K. (1983). Negotiating close friendship: The dialectic of conjunctive freedoms. *Human Communication Research, 9*, 255–266.

another without exception of reciprocation of benefits.[66] Friendship facilitates performance due to consensus and information sharing, but hinders performance when people focus more on social aspects than getting the work done. **Idiosyncratic deals (i-deals)** are personalized employment arrangements negotiated between individual workers and employees and intended to be of mutual benefit.[67] In a study of 20 R&D groups, acceptance of i-deals was greater for group members who were personal friends. The friendship network is critical for acceptance of i-deals, but the advice network is negatively related.[68] **Trust ties** involve both an affective (emotional) and a cognitive (task) perspective. The affective aspect is based on principles of social exchange. The cognitive perspective is based on reliability. Trust does not have a direct effect on performance.[69]

Advice ties represent instrumental rather than expressive relationships. Advice ties represent the exchange of expertise and information necessary to complete one's task. Unlike the voluntary nature of friendship and trust ties, advice ties may be dictated by the demands of the team task. Although both friendship and advice ties are severely decimated in the aftermath of a layoff, advice networks regenerate more quickly than friendship networks.[70] Advice seekers on teams will weigh the costs of obtaining knowledge with the expected value of the knowledge itself.[71] Offering advice (even unsolicited) is one way of expanding your network. Julie Isaac joined Twitter and realized she needed to give people a reason to start following her. So, she started tweeting daily creativity tips for writers and soon attracted 15,000 followers that eventually blossomed into an e-book, and a live weekly writing salon.[72]

How personality affects network ties, education, and "neuroticism" (i.e., how much people worry) predicts their centrality in their social networks: People who are highly educated and do not worry (i.e., are low in neuroticism) are high in advice and friendship centrality.[73] Team members who have similar values to their teammates also have more central advice and friendship networks.

Advice, friendship, and trust ties are not mutually exclusive. For example, friends can be trusted and approached for advice. An investigation of 35 groups of MBA students revealed that high-performing strong-relationship groups (groups with numerous, intense internal friendship ties) engaged in greater constructive controversy than low-performing strong-relationship groups.[74] These results suggest that successful, strong-relationship teams use processes that capitalize on the positive, affective interchanges among members and minimize the negative consequences of group cohesion.

Whereas much research has focused on the relationship between positive relations among group members (e.g., friendship and trust), the question of how negative ties affect performance is equally intriguing. Just as a financial ledger records financial assets and liabilities, the social ledger is a theoretical account of social assets, derived from positive relationships and social

[66]Clark, M. S., & Mills, J. R. (1979). Interpersonal attraction in exchange and communal relationships. *Journal of Personality and Social Psychology, 37*, 12–24.

[67]Rousseau, D. M. (2005). *I-deals: idiosyncratic deals employees bargain for themselves*. New York: M.E. Sharpe.

[68]Lai, L., Rousseau, D. M., & Chang, K. T. T. (2009). Idiosyncratic deals: Coworkers as interested third parties. *Journal of Applied Psychology, 94*(2), 547–556.

[69]Dirks, K. T. (1999). The effects of interpersonal trust on work group performance. *Journal of Applied Psychology, 84*, 445–455.

[70]Shah, P. P. (2000). Network destruction: The structural implications of downsizing. *Academy of Management Journal, 43*(1), 101–112.

[71]Nebus, J. (2006). Building collegial information networks: A theory of advice network generation. *Academy of Management Review, 31*(3), 615–637.

[72]Spark, D. (2009, April 28). 12 inspiring stories of successful social networks. *Business Week*. businessweek.com

[73]Klein, K. J., Lim, B., Saltz, J. L., & Mayer, D. M. (2004). How do they get there? An examination of the antecedents of centrality in team networks. *Academy of Management Journal, 47*(6), 952–963.

[74]Shah, P. P., Dirks, K. T., & Chervany, N. (2006). The multiple pathways of high performing groups: The interaction of social networks and group processes. *Journal of Organizational Behavior, 27*(3), 299–317.

liabilities derived from negative relationships.[75] Whereas all relationships have some negative attributes, a negative relationship represents an enduring, recurring set of negative judgments, feelings, and behavioral intensions toward another person.[76] Typically, negative relationships make up only 1 to 8 percent of the total number of relationships in an organization.[77] Four inter-playing characteristics determine the extent to which negative relationships hurt team and organizational effectiveness: relationship strength, reciprocity, cognition, and social distance.[78]

> **Relationship strength** refers to the intensity of dislike. As intensity increases, people may find it increasingly difficult to focus on interdependent goals.
>
> **Reciprocity** refers to whether an individual is the object or source of dislike or if dislike is reciprocated. Negative outcomes exist when dislike is reciprocal and even unreciprocated.
>
> **Cognition** refers to whether the person knows the other person dislikes him or her. Awareness of the negative relationship will cause more discomfort and may exacerbate reciprocation.
>
> **Social distance** refers to whether the negative tie is direct or indirect. If someone is directly involved in a negative relationship, the social liabilities are larger than when someone is indirectly involved in a negative relationship (e.g., a friend of someone who is intensely disliked by their superior).

KNOWLEDGE VALUATION

We've been working under assumption that people value the advice and knowledge offered by people in their teams and networks. In this sense, we've assumed that information and knowledge is valued for its intrinsic quality, not as a function of who it is offered by.

Rationally, managers should use knowledge that is of high quality, rather than focusing on apparently irrelevant considerations such as whether it comes from within the team or organization or from the outside. However, intuition and experience tell us that managers do not operate with this level of objectivity. One line of research, drawing from psychological theories of ingroup favoritism, determined that members of research groups are often subject to the **not-invented-here (NIH) syndrome,** in which they overvalue knowledge that comes from ingroup members.[79] However, whereas the NIH syndrome applies in some organizations, consider how managers in other organizations confer enormous authority to consultants and carefully monitor the ideas put forth by their competitors in the marketplace—all the while ignoring insiders and their ideas. Managers, particularly those in competitive situations, place greater value on knowledge that comes from the outside (e.g., competitors and consultants), versus the same knowledge that might come from inside (e.g., colleagues and an internal task force).[80] As a case in point, Menon and

[75]Labianca, G., & Brass, D. J. (2006). Exploring the social ledger: Negative relationships and negative asymmetry in social networks in organizations. *Academy of Management Review, 31*(3), 596–614.

[76]Fiske, S. T., & Taylor, S. E. (1991). *Social cognition.* New York: McGraw-Hill.

[77]Kane, G., & Labianca, G. (2005). *Accounting for clergy's social ledgers: Mixed blessings associated with direct and in-direct negative ties in a religious organization.* Paper presented at the Intra-Organizational Network (ION) Conference, Atlanta.

[78]Labianca & Brass, "Exploring the social ledger."

[79]Brewer, M. (1979). Ingroup bias in the minimal intergroup situation: A cognitive-motivational analysis. *Psychological Bulletin, 86*, 307–324; Katz, R., & Allen, T. J. (1982). Investigating the not invented here (NIH) syndrome: A look at the performance, tenure, and communication patterns of 50 R&D project groups. *R&D Management, 121*, 7–19.

[80]Menon, T., & Pfeffer, J. (2003). Valuing internal vs. external knowledge: Explaining the preference for outsiders. *Management Science, 49*, 497–513.

Pfeffer describe the curious acquisition of Zoopa by Fresh Choice. Fresh Choice and Zoopa, at least up until 1997, were competitors, both offering quick, cafeteria-style salad buffets and soups. Prior to and during its acquisition of Zoopa, Fresh Choice scrupulously benchmarked and investigated Zoopa's best practices. However, after the acquisition, the value of the knowledge and information about Zoopa's best practices, which would now be quite easy to obtain, were seemingly not as valued. Similarly, managers at Xerox displayed very little interest in a new Internet technology that internal scientists at Xerox PARC had developed. However, several years later when an external firm developed a similar technology, Xerox responded favorably to the idea and even sent their executives to investigate it as they contemplated acquiring the company.

Strategic alliances are one way that companies can gain external knowledge. Google and Procter & Gamble experimented with another strategy: Namely, swapping employees to share expertise. In "federation" arrangements, companies exchange much more than their knowledge, profits, or workers. They share access to parts of their information and tech systems. Accenture gave Microsoft employees access to its collaboration software. This allowed Microsoft staff to find, chat with, instant message, or videoconference with any employee at the other company. Accenture CIO Frank Modruson received eight requests from clients in the following month to set up a similar structure with Accenture.[81]

In an empirical investigation of knowledge valuation, people are more likely to value knowledge that comes from an external rival or external network and devalue knowledge that comes from an internal member of the team.[82] Even when the knowledge is identical, the source makes a big difference in whether a teammate feels threatened or intrigued by the information. People often hesitate to embrace the knowledge of network "insiders" because they fear that they will lose personal status if they use that knowledge. To minimize the potential loss of status and to save face, team members can attempt to self-affirm, by reminding themselves of their personal accomplishments. When they do this, they are more likely to learn from and incorporate knowledge from insiders.[83]

Menon and Pfeffer offer two explanations for outsider bias in knowledge valuation.[84] They contend that the availability or scarcity of internal versus external knowledge affects how it is valued. Internal knowledge is more readily available and hence subject to greater scrutiny, whereas external knowledge is unique. Thus, managers venerate competitors, whose ideas they see from a distance, while they reject internal ideas that are visible close up, warts and all. They value external ideas, which are seen as final products, while they are critical about internal ideas that they see in their earliest most unpolished state. And, finally, they value scarce, external ideas that are protected by patents and are nearly impossible to acquire, while they reject the internal knowledge that is so easily accessible to them.

Second, organizational incentives often punish managers by reducing their status when they learn from insiders[85] and reward them when they learn from outsiders. Managers conducting a performance evaluation rewarded external learners more than they rewarded internal learners.[86] Specifically, executives participated in a simulation in which they were a manager of a large hotel chain and were asked to evaluate the performance of two individuals

[81]McGregor, J. (2009, March 23). Can companies share one nervous system? *Business Week, 4124*, (40).
[82]Menon, T., Thompson, L., & Choi, H. S. (2006). Tainted knowledge vs. tempting knowledge: People avoid knowledge from internal rivals and seek knowledge from external rivals. *Management Science, 52*(8), 1129–1144.
[83]Ibid.
[84]Ibid.
[85]Blau, P. M. (1955). *The dynamics of bureaucracy.* Chicago, IL: University of Chicago Press.
[86]Menon, Thompson, & Choi, "Tainted knowledge vs. tempting knowledge."

who were described as hotel managers within their chain. The two managers had achieved identical performance, but one manager had learned from insiders within the chain while the other manager had learned from a competitor chain. The executives rated the external learner as more creative and competent, giving him more status, and they were more likely to promote him and reward him with a higher bonus, compared with the internal learner.

Menon and Blount developed a broader framework to explain how relationships between knowledge messengers and receivers affect knowledge valuation.[87] Rather than a rational perspective in which managers are expected to cull the best knowledge from their environments, or a random process in which receivers accept knowledge in the more arbitrary "garbage can model,"[88] they propose a relational perspective in which social relationships between knowledge messengers and receivers affect how a piece of knowledge comes to be evaluated. They identify several relational schemas that represent the ways in which a receiver might perceive the messenger who delivers them knowledge.[89] By determining the degree to which the messenger threatens the receiver's self or group, they generate six relational types, including colleagues, deviants, rivals, advisors, enemies, and intruders. Relationships evoke a variety of social psychological forces—including social comparison, status threats, and ingroup identification and favoritism—that shape the processes by which managers decide whether a piece of knowledge is valuable.

Conclusion

Teams are not independent entities within the organization. There is a critical tension between the internal relations among team members and the relationship the team shares with the rest of the organization. Both are necessary; neither is sufficient to ensure long-term survival of the team. Depending on the nature of the task that the team is working on, structural solutions should be put into place to ensure that the team is integrated with other individuals and teams within the organization. This activity itself requires that some members of the team act as boundary spanners and gate-keepers to bring needed information to the team, as well as distributing knowledge outside the team.

Managing the internal and external dynamics in a team is a difficult task, requiring constantly changing focus. The frequency of external communication may come at the expense of attention to internal processes (the ability to set goals, coordinate members' strategies, maintain cohesion, etc.).[90] Given that managing the internal team process and the external environment are somewhat opposing processes, how can leaders optimize the probability of successful teamwork? An important first step is to talk with team members about the importance of both internal functioning and external relationships. A second step is to assign roles or talk about how to manage the dual processes of internal dynamics and external relations. This can go a long way toward minimizing the diffusion of responsibility problem that often haunts teams. A third step is to identify goals and indices of team success at the outset; this largely avoids rationalizing behavior after the fact. A final step is to develop a team charter—a document written by all members that focuses on internal and external management issues.

[87]Menon, T., & Blount, S. (2003). The Messenger bias: A relational model of knowledge valuation. *Research in Organizational Behavior, 25,* 137–186.
[88]Cohen, M. D., March, J. P., & Olsen, J. P. (1972). A garbage can model of organizational choice. *Administrative Science Quarterly, 17,* 1–25.
[89]Baldwin, M. W. (1992). Relational schemas and the processing of social information. *Psychological Bulletin, 112*(3), 461–484.
[90]Ancona & Caldwell, "Bridging the boundary," p. 265.

11 Leadership

Managing the Paradox

"Prepare for impact!" was the only thing that 155 passengers remember hearing pilot Chesley B. "Sully" Sullenberger III announce before the plane made an emergency landing on the Hudson River on January 15, 2009. The Airbus A320 bound for Charlotte, North Carolina, struck a flock of birds during takeoff minutes earlier at LaGuardia airport and both engines immediately failed. Moments before the crash, the plane was flying impossibly low but steady over the bank of the Hudson, as if the pilot were approaching a runway in a controlled descent. Upon landing in the icy waters, the plane remained afloat, but was sinking slowly downriver. The water temperature was 36 degrees, and Coast Guard Lieutenant Commander Moore estimates that passengers had only 5 to 8 minutes to live in water at that temperature. Sully's bravery and clearheadedness saved the lives of all 155 people, including an infant, from death. As it turns out, Sully spent practically his whole life preparing for the 5-minute ultimate test on U.S. Airways Flight 1549. Sully earned his pilot's license at age 14, flew fighter jets in the Air Force, investigated air disasters, mastered glider flying, and studied the psychology of how cockpit crews behave under crisis. Sully trained as an airline safety expert, consulted with NASA, and amassed 40 years of experience and also holds master's degrees in public administration and industrial psychology.[1]

Leadership saved the lives of 155 people in the U.S. Airways flight. This chapter addresses how people can be trained to become leaders and the techniques that enable leaders to be more effective. We first address the **leadership paradox**: the fact that teams usually need leaders, but the very presence of a leader threatens the autonomy of the team. We describe two theories of leadership—the Great Person theory and the Great Opportunity theory—and explain why the Great Opportunity theory better describes how leadership develops. We then describe several leadership styles and present a model to help determine how much participation is appropriate for a leader to use in various situations.

---

[1]Associated Press. (2009, January 16). Pilot's life prepared him for miracle flight. *msnbc.com*. msnbc.msn.com; Clancy, M. (2009, January 16). Miracle on the Hudson. *nbcnewyork.com*. nbcnewyork.com; N.Y. jet crash called "miracle on the Hudson." (2009, January 15). *msnbc.com*. msnbc.msn.com

THE LEADERSHIP PARADOX

The presence of a leader does not always ensure that teams will be effective and may even hinder a team. Leadership—or one person taking the helm of the group's efforts—seems antithetical to teamwork. Yet, leaders are often necessary for effective teamwork—to shape goals, coordinate effort, and motivate members. Traditional notions of leadership—that is, top-down, command-and-control approaches—may be ineffective in the team-based organization. Indeed, one investigation found that employees in highly participative work climates provided 14 percent better customer service, committed 26 percent fewer clinical errors, demonstrated 79 percent lower burnout, and were 61 percent less likely to leave the organization than employees in more authoritarian work climates.[2]

Few people understand how to transform into leaders. For example, in one plant, resistance to participative management programs took the form of supervisors keeping "hands off" as newly formed semiautonomous work teams attempted to solve problems. When questions arose that teams were unable to handle, supervisors replied, "That's not my job; it's the team's problem." In essence, the supervisors were undermining the teams so they could resume their traditional position of authority.

Leaders who have successfully empowered their teams comment that they learned something that they did not realize at the outset. In the best of circumstances, teams are empowered groups of people who collaborate in a mutually beneficial fashion to enact positive change. The question of how one leads others who are supposed to lead themselves is the essence of the team paradox encountered by leaders of self-managing and self-directing teams.[3] Attempts to cope with this new leadership challenge often result in negative supervisor reactions, including resistance to change,[4] role conflict,[5] unwillingness to relinquish power,[6] fear of appearing incompetent,[7] and fear of job termination.[8] These responses may cause leaders to engage in actions that thwart, rather than facilitate, team effectiveness.

Leadership is perhaps easier to reconcile with effective teamwork when we realize that leadership comes in many forms. For example, a team may have a manager, administrator, supervisor, facilitator, director, coordinator, spokesperson, or chairperson. Leaders can also serve a vital role coordinating team members, resolving disputes or disagreements, motivating individuals, monitoring performance, and maintaining the goals and focus of the group.

LEADERSHIP AND MANAGEMENT

Leadership is not the same as management. People don't want to be managed; they want to be led. Management is a function that must be exercised in any business or team, whereas leadership is a relationship between the leader and the led that can energize a team or organization (see

[2]Angermeier, I., Dunford, B. D., Boss, A. D., & Boss, R. W. (2009, March/April). The impact of participative management perceptions on customer service, medical errors, burnout, and turnover intentions. *Journal of Healthcare Management, 54*(2), 127–141.

[3]Stewart, G. L., & Manz, C. C. (1995). Leadership and self-managing work teams: A typology and integrative model. *Human Relations, 48*(7), 747–770.

[4]Manz, C. C., Keating, D. E., & Donnellon, A. (1990). Preparing for an organizational change to employee self-management: The management transition. *Organizational Dynamics, 19*(2), 15–26.

[5]Letize, L., & Donovan, M. (1990, March). The supervisor's changing role in high involvement organizations. *The Journal for Quality and Participation, 13*(2), 62–65.

[6]Verespej, M. A. (1990, December 3). When you put the team in charge. *Industry Week*, pp. 30–31.

[7]Manz, Keating, & Donnellon, "Preparing for an organizational change to employee self-management."

[8]Verespej, "When you put the team in charge."

EXHIBIT 11-1 Management Versus Leadership

Management	Leadership
A function	A relationship
Planning	Selecting talent
Budgeting	Motivating
Evaluating	Coaching
Facilitating	Building trust

Source: Maccoby, M. (2000). Understanding the difference between management and leadership. *Research & Technology Management*, January–February, 57–59. Reprinted with permission.

Exhibit 11-1 for the difference between management and leadership).[9] Leadership is the ability to influence people to achieve the goals of a team. A leader is able to influence people to achieve a group's or organization's goal.

One defining characteristic of leadership is the point of view that the leader of the team adopts. The leader of the team has a point of view that allows him or her to: (1) see what needs to be done; (2) understand the underlying forces that are working in the organization; and (3) initiate action to make things better.[10] Exhibit 11-2 reveals that the leader's point of view is different from that of the followers' point of view, and different still from those who are bureaucrats, administrators, and contrarians.

LEADERS AND THE NATURE–NURTURE DEBATE

Are leaders born or self-made? With regard to the nature versus nurture debate, there are two theories about what makes a leader effective. The Great Person theory asserts that leaders are born, not made; whereas the Great Opportunity theory claims that leadership skills can be learned. We review the evidence for both sides of this debate.

Leadership and Nature

The trait theory of leadership is sometimes referred to as the "Great Man theory of leadership."[11] In fact, there is not just a single trait theory of leadership. Several theories share a belief that leadership is largely an inborn characteristic of a person and therefore is largely inflexible or at least not something that can be easily developed, learned, or acquired. Strict proponents of the Great Person theory claim that people are either born leaders or born followers: They either have it or don't. If they do have it, they dictate, command, and control. If they don't have it, they follow those who do have it. "The Great Person" theory of leadership is unidirectional—from the top down, with leaders imparting truth, wisdom, and directives to those beneath them.

---

[9]Maccoby, M. (2000, January/February). Understanding the difference between management and leadership. *Research–Technology Management, 43*(1), 57–59.
[10]Clawson, D. (2003). *The next upsurge: Labor and the new social movements*. Ithaca, NY: Cornell University Press.
[11]Bass, B. M. (1990). *Bass & Stogdill's handbook of leadership: Theory, research, & management applications* (3rd ed.). New York: Free Press.

EXHIBIT 11-2 The Leader's Point of View

Point of View	Examples of What This Person Would Say
Follower	"What do you want me to do?"
	"Will you give me more authority?"
	"I need you to clear the obstacles for me."
Bureaucrat	"That's not my job."
	"I'll pass that on to so-and-so."
	"Our procedures don't allow that."
	"We've never done it that way."
	"This hasn't been approved."
	"I can't do that without my supervisor's permission."
Administrator	"What did they do last time?"
	"We've never done it that way."
	"Let's see, what was the rule on that?"
Contrarian	"That will never work!"
	"We tried that before".
	"That's a terrible idea."
	"You won't be able to fund it."
	"You will never be able to do it on time."
Leader	"Do you see what needs to be done?"
	"Do you understand the underlying forces at play?"
	"Are you willing to initiate action to make things better?"

Source: Clawson, J. C. (2003). *Level 3 leadership: Getting below the surface* (2nd ed.). Upper Saddle River, NJ: Prentice Hall. Electronically reproduced by permission of Pearson Education, Inc., Upper Saddle River, New Jersey.

INTELLIGENCE AND LEADERSHIP   One trait theory of leadership is based on innate intelligence. Many organizations, including the armed forces, have relied on intelligence testing to select leaders. For example, 96 percent of the officer corps of the armed forces has a college degree.[12] The Armed Services Vocational Aptitude Battery (ASVAB) is administered to all persons who wish to enlist in the U.S. military. And, results of large national samples of general mental ability (GMA) indicate that intelligence is linked to career success, such as income and occupational prestige.[13]

PERSONALITY AND LEADERSHIP   Another set of theories of trait leadership focuses on personality and temperament. If the Great Person theory is true, we should be able to identify personality traits that make someone a great leader or, at least, characteristics that predict the emergence of leadership. Psychologists, political scientists, and historians have studied the

---

[12]Office of the Under Secretary of Defense. (2004). Personnel and readiness. Population representation in the military services. prhome.defense.gov
[13]Judge, T. A., Klinger, R. L., & Simon, L. S. (2010). Time is on my side: Time, general mental ability, human capital, and extrinsic career success. *Journal of Applied Psychology, 95*(1), 92–107.

personalities of leaders in governmental, business, and educational organizations to identify the common threads. However, decades of research have failed to yield an agreed-upon list of key traits shared by all leaders.[14] There is little or no evidence to support connections between personality and leadership. Simonton gathered information about 100 personal attributes of all U.S. presidents, such as their family backgrounds, educational experiences, occupations, and personalities.[15] Only three of these variables—height, family size, and number of books published before taking office—correlated with how effective the presidents were in office. The 97 other characteristics, including personality traits, were not related to leadership effectiveness at all. By chance, 5 percent—5 out of the 100—would be significant!

The leader personality traits of agreeableness and conscientiousness are positively related to perceptions of ethical leadership.[16] Some research finds a link between personality traits and who *emerges* as a leader in a group. For example, people who are narcissists are more likely to *emerge* as a leader in a group, but they are no more *skilled* than nonnarcissistic people.[17] Similarly, people high in "trait dominance" emerge as leaders because they behave in ways that make them *appear* competent, even when they actually lack competence.[18]

BIRTH ORDER AND LEADERSHIP   Yet another theory of leadership as nature is based on birth order. Cross-sectional data show some indication that first-born children may be more intelligent, but longitudinal data don't support this.[19]

GENDER AND LEADERSHIP   There is much debate about whether men are more or less effective leaders than women. The stereotypical belief is that men are rational, independent, and assertive, whereas women are emotional, relationship focused, and accommodating. Alice Eagly examined this question using a meta-analysis of hundreds of studies. Contrary to stereotypical beliefs about male and female differences, men do not engage in more task-oriented behavior, nor do women behave in a more relational (considerate) fashion. Women lead in a more democratic style and men use a more autocratic style.[20]

However, the most important gender difference is not the leader's actual behavior; it is how followers *react* to the leader. Female leaders are judged more harshly than male leaders.[21] For example, women are regarded as less competent than men, and in group interaction, people give men more opportunities to speak than women.[22] People respond more favorably to men who

---

[14]Yukl, G. A. (1981). *Leadership in organizations.* London: Prentice-Hall International.

[15]Simonton, D. K. (1987). *Why presidents succeed: A political psychology of leadership.* New Haven, CT: Yale University Press.

[16]Walumbwa, F. O., & Schaubroeck, J. (2009). Leader personality traits and employee voice behavior: Mediating roles of ethical leadership and work group psychological safety. *Journal of Applied Psychology, 94*, 1275–1286.

[17]Brunell, A. B., Gentry, W. A., Campbell, W. K., Hoffman, B. J., Kuhnert, K. W., & DeMarree, K. G. (2008). Leader emergence: The case of the narcissistic leader. *Personality and Social Psychology Bulletin, 34*(12), 1663–1676.

[18]Anderson, C., & Kilduff, G. J. (2009). Why do dominant personalities attain influence in face-to-face groups? The competence-signaling effects of trait dominance. *Journal of Personality and Social Psychology, 96*(2), 491–503.

[19]Andeweg, R. B., & van den Berg, S. B. (2003). Linking birth order to political leadership: The impact of parents or sibling interaction? *Political Psychology, 24*(3), 605–623.

[20]Eagly, A. H., & Johnson, B. (1990). Gender and leadership style: A meta-analysis. *Psychological Bulletin, 108*, 233–256.

[21]Eagly, A. H., Makhijani, M. G., & Klonsky, B. G. (1992). Gender and the evaluation of leaders: A meta-analysis. *Psychological Bulletin, 111*, 3–22.

[22]Berger, J., Fisek, M. H., Norman, R. Z., & Zelditch, M. (1977). *Status characteristics and social interaction.* New York: Elsevier.

self-promote (boast) than to men who are modest; however, the opposite is true for women.[23] In fact, female leaders are devalued when they act in a masculine manner,[24] and overt displays of competence and confidence by women can result in rejection, especially from men.[25] In a simulated job interview and hiring task, both men and women prefer to hire a man over a woman if the two are equally qualified,[26] and men prefer to hire a man even when he is clearly less qualified.[27] Even more disconcerting is the credit that people accord females. When people are asked to evaluate male and female members' contributions to a joint outcome, unless they are given feedback about people's actual contributions, they devalue the work of females and rate them as less competent, less influential, and less likely to have played a leadership role, even when the contributions were identical for men and women.[28]

A meta-analysis review of 75 studies of mixed-gender groups revealed that women are less likely to become leaders than men in laboratory and naturally occurring groups.[29] Yet, the meta-analysis reveals that women display more of the desirable transformational leadership behaviors positively related to team performance than do men.[30] In sum, there are two forms of prejudice when it comes to female leaders: People perceive women less favorably when they are in leadership, and they evaluate women's behavior less favorably.[31]

When women are exposed to the gender stereotype of women (vulnerable and accommodating), they avoid leadership roles in favor of nonthreatening subordinate roles.[32] And, their aspirations for leadership positions decline. Some evidence suggests that to the extent female group leaders engage in self-monitoring (reflecting and thinking about their behaviors and how they are viewed by others), they are considered to be more influential and valuable for their groups.[33]

Great Opportunity Theory of Leadership

There is overwhelming evidence that *situational factors* can often make the leader. In fact, a great deal of evidence indicates that leadership has more to do with the environment than one's own personality.

SEATING ARRANGEMENTS Seemingly trivial situational factors, such as seating arrangements, can affect the emergence of leadership in groups. When a group sits at a table, the person at the head of the table has a greater probability of emerging as the leader, even when the seating

---

[23]Giacolone, R. A., & Riordan, C. A. (1990). Effect of self-presentation on perceptions and recognition in an organization. *The Journal of Psychology, 124*, 25–38.

[24]Eagly, Makhijani, & Klonsky, "Gender and the evaluation of leaders."

[25]Rudman, L. A. (1998). Self-promotion as a risk factor for women: The costs and benefits of counter-stereotypical impression management. *Journal of Personality and Social Psychology, 74*, 629–645.

[26]Foschi, M., Lai, L., & Sigerson, K. (1994). Gender and double standards in the assessment of job applicants. *Social Psychology Quarterly, 57*, 326–339.

[27]Foschi, M., Sigerson, K., & Lembesis, M. (1995). Assessing job applicants: The relative effects of gender, academic record, and decision type. *Small Group Research, 26*(3), 328–352.

[28]Heilman, M. E., & Haynes, M. C. (2005). No credit where credit is due: Attributional rationalization of women's success in male-female teams. *Journal of Applied Psychology, 90*(5), 905–916.

[29]Eagly, A. H., & Karau, S. J. (1991). Gender and the emergence of leaders: A meta-analysis. *Journal of Personality and Social Psychology, 60*, 685–710.

[30]Eagly, A. H., Johannesen-Schmidt, M. C., & van Engen, M. L. (2003). Transformational, transactional, and laissez-faire leadership styles: A meta-analysis comparing men and women. *Psychological Bulletin, 129*, 569–591.

[31]Eagly, A. H., & Karau, S. J. (2002). Role congruity theory of prejudice toward female leaders. *Psychological Review, 190*(3), 573–598.

[32]Davies, P. G., Spencer, S. J., & Steele, C. M. (2005). Clearing the air: Identity safety moderates the effects of stereotype threat on women's leadership aspirations. *Journal of Personality and Social Psychology, 88*, 276–287.

[33]Flynn, F. J., & Ames, D. R. (2006). What's good for the goose may not be as good for the gander: The benefits of self-monitoring for men and women in task groups and dyadic conflicts. *Journal of Applied Psychology, 91*(2), 272–281.

is randomly determined.[34] Consider the implications of seating arrangements at a five-member rectangular table.[35] Two people sat on one side of the table and three sat on the other side. Although no one sat in the end seat, specific predictions were made about who should emerge as the leader if eye contact and control of communication were important causal factors. Whereas those seated on the two-person side of the table could maintain easy eye contact with three of the group members, those on the three-person side could best focus their attention on only two members. Therefore, it was predicted that those on the two-person side would be able to influence others more, and, hence, were more likely to become leaders. Indeed, 70 percent of the leaders came from the two-person side. Judgments of leaders' power are often based on how they look on an organization chart: holding constant everything else, if there is a long vertical line by a leader's name, that leader is judged to have more power than leaders with a short vertical line.[36]

RANDOM SELECTION OF LEADERS   Probably the most damning evidence to the Great Person theory is the studies of random selection of leaders. Organizations spend millions of dollars each year carefully selecting leaders, often using psychological tests to do so. However, evidence indicates that selected leaders may hinder effective team performance. In an investigation of team performance, teams with randomly selected leaders performed better on all organizational decision-making tasks than did teams whose leaders were systematically selected.[37] Moreover, teams with a random leader adhered more strongly to the team's decision. Systematically accepted leaders often undermine group goals because they assert their personal superiority at the expense of developing a sense of shared team identity.

Nature Versus Nurture Summary

The Great Person theory is still used as a basis for recruitment and selection, and many companies and institutions routinely assess leadership potential with paper-and-pencil tests. Yet, the conclusion of decades of research is that no single test can measure leadership. Even when leadership is measured, its relationship to the kinds of performance measures we would expect to see is largely inconclusive. It is rather fruitless to attempt to identify stable characteristics that predict leadership. Even if it were possible (which we highly doubt), this kind of knowledge does not provide organizations or managers with much control over their own or another's behavior. Therefore, in a practical sense, trying to identify stable characteristics of leaders may be ill-fated.

If the Great Person theory of leadership is flawed, why do so many people believe that personality can predict leadership? There are two reasons. One has to do with the "romance" of leadership.[38] In short, the romanticized conception of leadership is that leaders have the ability to

[34]Nemeth, C. J., & Wachtler, J. (1974). Creating the perceptions of consistency and confidence: A necessary condition for minority influence. *Sociometry, 37*(4), 529–540; Riess, M. (1982). Seating preferences as impression management: A literature review and theoretical integration. *Communication, 11*, 85–113; Riess, M., & Rosenfeld, P. (1980). Seating preferences as nonverbal communication: A self-presentational analysis. *Journal of Applied Communications Research, 8*, 22–30.

[35]Howells, L. T., & Becker, S. W. (1962). Seating arrangements and leadership emergence. *Journal of Abnormal and Social Psychology, 64*, 148–150.

[36]Giessner, S. R., & Schubert, T. W. (2007). High in the hierarchy: How vertical location and judgments of leaders' power are interrelated. *Organizational Behavior and Human Decision Processes, 104*(1), 30–44.

[37]Haslam, S. A., McGarty, C., Brown, P. M., Eggins, R. A., Morrison, B. E., & Reynolds, K. J. (1998). Inspecting the emperor's clothes: Evidence that random selection of leaders can enhance group performance. *Group Dynamics: Theory, Research, and Practice, 2*(3), 168–184.

[38]Meindl, J. R., Ehrlich, S. B., & Dukerich, J. M. (1985). The romance of leadership. *Administrative Science Quarterly, 30*, 78–102.

control and influence the fates of their organizations and people. Second, the **fundamental attribution error** is the tendency to overemphasize the impact of stable personality and dispositional traits and underemphasize the impact of the situation on people's behavior.[39] In fact, more temporary, situational characteristics can usually explain a great deal of human behavior.

Why do people err on the side of attributing behavior to dispositions instead of more transient (and controllable) factors? A key reason is associated with our human need to predict and control. To the extent that people can predict the behavior of others, their chances for survival increase. For example, the ability to predict whether someone is trustworthy is highly adaptive. When people's behavior can be attributed to stable, dispositional characteristics, it is possible to more accurately predict their actions in various situations. Conversely, when people's behavior is attributed to temporary, environmental factors, it is more difficult to predict their behavior. Thus, the bias toward dispositional explanation is driven by our human need for control.

Just because we cannot "select" leaders does not mean we cannot "develop" leaders. The Great Opportunity approach focuses on how leaders do two things vis-à-vis teamwork in their organizations. First, it focuses on how leaders directly interact with their teams. The second thing these leaders do is to structure the external environment so the team can best achieve its goals. In both of these tasks, leadership is bidirectional, with leaders learning from their team just as often as they provide direction for their team. These leaders maintain the relationship between the group and organization to ensure that organizational objectives are being pursued. Leaders also coordinate team members, resolve disputes or disagreements, motivate individuals, monitor performance, and establish the goals and focus of the group.

As we have seen in Chapters 4 and 10, leadership in a team-based organization requires leaders not just to lead the team but also to interface between the organization and the team. In this sense, the leader is an important boundary spanner. No manager has all of the skills required for effective leadership, but the effective manager knows where to go to get these skills and resources.

LEADERSHIP STYLES

One trip to the bookstore, or one online search in the academic literature, can produce a dizzying array of enticing (yet poorly understood) leadership approaches. Often, these approaches are presented in the form of metaphor—leader as coach, leader as servant, leader as guide, leader as conductor, and so on.[40] In a recent literature review of academic journals, we found more than 20 variations of leadership styles spanning a wide range, including visionary, charismatic, participatory, servant, contingent, transformational, and transactional. The corporate world and popular business press have coined even more varieties of leadership—often branding them with a particularly influential individual's name, such as the "Jack Welch lexicon of leadership"[41] or the "Warren Buffet CEO."[42] Here, we consider a few of these styles. Our list is not exhaustive and does not include all the latest fads in leadership. The key point is that we don't want leaders to put themselves in the position of "diagnosing" themselves or, worse, "pigeonholing" themselves or others. Rather, the styles are presented as choices that the leader can make, or as skills to put in his or her repertoire.

---

[39]Ross, L. (1977). The intuitive psychologist and his shortcomings: Distortions in the attribution process. In L. Berkowitz (Ed.), *Advances in Experimental Social Psychology* (Vol. 10, p. 173–220). Orlando, FL: Academic Press.

[40]Thompson, L., & Rosette, A. (2004). Leading by analogy. In S. Chowdhury (Ed.), *Financial Times Next Generation Business Series*. London: Prentice Hall.

[41]Krames, J. A. (2001). *The Jack Welch lexicon of leadership: Over 250 terms, concepts, strategies & initiatives of the legendary leader*. New York: McGraw-Hill.

[42]Miles, R. P., & Osborne, T. (2001). *The Warren Buffett CEO: Secrets of the Berkshire Hathaway managers*. New York: Wiley.

Task Versus Person Leadership

As we noted in Chapter 4, the task-oriented leader focuses on accomplishing the objectives of the team; the relationship-oriented leader focuses on the process of getting there. (For an example of how leaders can examine their task–person approach, see Exhibit 11-3.)

EXHIBIT 11-3 Task–Person Leadership Questionnaire

Directions: The following items describe aspects of leadership behavior. Respond to each item according to the way you would most likely act if you were the leader of a work group. Circle whether you would most likely behave in the described way: always (A), frequently (F), occasionally (O), seldom (S), or never (N).

A F O S N   1. I would most likely act as the spokesperson of the group.
A F O S N   2. I would encourage overtime work.
A F O S N   3. I would allow members complete freedom in their work.
A F O S N   4. I would encourage the use of uniform procedures.
A F O S N   5. I would permit the members to use their own judgment in solving problems.
A F O S N   6. I would stress being ahead of competing groups.
A F O S N   7. I would speak as a representative of the group.
A F O S N   8. I would needle members for greater effort.
A F O S N   9. I would try out my ideas in the group.
A F O S N   10. I would let the members do their work the way they think best.
A F O S N   11. I would be working hard for a promotion.
A F O S N   12. I would tolerate postponement and uncertainty.
A F O S N   13. I would speak for the group if there were visitors present.
A F O S N   14. I would keep the work moving at a rapid pace.
A F O S N   15. I would turn the members loose on a job and let them go to it.
A F O S N   16. I would settle conflicts when they occur in the group.
A F O S N   17. I would get swamped by details.
A F O S N   18. I would represent the group at outside meetings.
A F O S N   19. I would be reluctant to allow the members any freedom of action.
A F O S N   20. I would decide what should be done and how it should be done.
A F O S N   21. I would push for increased production.
A F O S N   22. I would let some members have authority that I could keep.
A F O S N   23. Things would usually turn out as I had predicted.
A F O S N   24. I would allow the group a high degree of initiative.
A F O S N   25. I would assign group members to particular tasks.
A F O S N   26. I would be willing to make changes.
A F O S N   27. I would ask the members to work harder.

(*cont. on p. 270*)

A	F	O	S	N	28. I would trust the group members to exercise good judgment.
A	F	O	S	N	29. I would schedule the work to be done.
A	F	O	S	N	30. I would refuse to explain my actions.
A	F	O	S	N	31. I would persuade others that my ideas are to their advantage.
A	F	O	S	N	32. I would permit the group to set its own pace.
A	F	O	S	N	33. I would urge the group to beat its previous record.
A	F	O	S	N	34. I would act without consulting the group.
A	F	O	S	N	35. I would ask that group members follow standard rules and regulations.

T–P Leadership Style Scoring

Circle the item number for items 8, 12, 17, 18, 19, 30, 34, and 35.

Write the number 1 in front of a *circled item* number if you responded S (seldom) or N (never) to that item.

Also write a number 1 in front of *item numbers not circled* if you responded A (always) or F (frequently).

Circle the number 1s that you have written in front of the following items: 3, 5, 8, 10, 15, 18, 19, 22, 24, 26, 28, 30, 32, 34, and 35.

Count the circled number 1s. This is your score for concern for *people*.

Count the uncircled number 1s. This is your score for concern for *task*.

Source: Sergiovanni, T. J., Metzcus, R., & Burden, L. (1969). Toward a particularistic approach to leadership style: Some finds. *American Educational Research Journal, 6*, 62–79.

Transactional Versus Transformational Leadership

The transactional versus transformational paradigm views leadership as either a matter of contingent reinforcement of followers or the moving of followers beyond their self-interests for the good of the team, organization, or society.[43] **Transformational leadership** is developmental and usually begins with a transactional approach. At a basic level, leaders and their teams are in an exchange relationship that involves negotiation to establish outcomes and rewards.[44] A **psychological contract** is a person's belief in mutual obligations between that person and another party, such as an employer or leader.[45]

In contrast, **transactional leadership** depends on the leader's power to reinforce subordinates (team members) for their successful completion of the bargain (task). However, this type of leadership sets up a competitive relationship: "If you limit yourself to transactional leadership of a follower with rewards of carrots for compliance, or punishments with a stick for failure to comply with agreed-on work to be done by the follower, the follower will continue to feel like a jackass."[46]

---

[43]Bass, B. M. (1985). *Leadership and performance beyond expectations.* New York: Free Press; Burns, J. M. (1978). *Leadership.* New York: Harper & Row; Hollander, E. P. (1964). *Leaders, groups, and influence.* New York: Oxford University Press.

[44]Hollander, E. P. (1986). On the central role of leadership processes. *International Review of Applied Psychology, 35*, 39–52.

[45]Rousseau, D. M., & Tijoriwala, S. A. (1998). Assessing psychological contracts: Issues, alternatives, and measures. *Journal of Organizational Behavior, 19*, 679–695.

[46]Levinson, H. (1980). Power, leadership, and the management of stress. *Professional Psychology, 11*, 497–508.

Transformational leaders, in contrast, motivate their teams to work toward goals that go beyond immediate self-interest. Transformational leaders motivate their teams to do more than they originally expected to do as they strive for higher-order outcomes.[47] In an investigation of the performance of 118 R&D project teams from five companies, transformational leadership predicted technical quality, schedule performance, and cost performance 1 year later and profitability and speed-to-market 5 years later.[48] Because members of teams are interested in intrinsic aspects of their work, they expect their leader to be as well. Moreover, this affects performance. People who are taught skills by an extrinsically motivated leader are less interested in learning and enjoy what they are doing less than people taught by an intrinsically motivated leader, even when the lessons and the learning are identical.[49] Perhaps it is for this reason that leaders who are regarded to be most like team members are evaluated to be more effective than leaders who are seen as not very similar to their teams.[50] Transformational CEOs are more likely to have goal congruence within their team, which is related to better organizational performance.[51]

Transformational leaders rely on three behaviors—charisma, intellectual stimulation, and individualized consideration—to produce change.[52] Leaders who demonstrate vision develop employees that are adaptive and proactive in response to change.[53] Another characteristic of the transformational leader is self-sacrifice. Leaders who self-sacrifice (put aside their own self-interest in the service of the larger organization) generate higher productivity and higher effectiveness and are seen as more group-oriented.[54] In the early 1960s, when Warren Buffett was recruiting backers for one of his first investment partnerships, he deposited more than 90 percent of his personal savings into the fund. When Hewlett-Packard hit a downturn in 1970, cofounder Bill Hewlett took the same 10 percent pay cut as the rest of his employees. During the early years at Charles Schwab, whenever the customer-service phone lines got really busy, founder Chuck Schwab answered calls along with everyone else at the company who held a broker's license.[55] Transformational leaders have more satisfied subordinates.[56] Transformational leaders also predict the collective personality of the team, and, in turn, this affects team performance.[57] Specifically, transformational leaders create teams that are characterized by collective openness to experience, agreeableness, extraversion, and greater conscientiousness.

---

[47]Burns, J. M. (1978). *Leadership*. New York: Harper & Row.

[48]Keller, R. T. (2006). Transformational leadership, initiating structure, and substitutes for leadership: A longitudinal study of research and development project team performance. *Journal of Applied Psychology, 91*(1), 202–210.

[49]Wild, T. C., Enzle, M. E., Nix, G., & Deci, E. L. (1997). Perceiving others as intrinsically or extrinsically motivated: Effects on expectancy formation and task engagement. *Personality and Social Psychology Bulletin, 23*(8), 837–848.

[50]Hains, S. C., Hogg, M. A., & Duck, J. M. (1997). Self-categorization and leadership: Effects of group prototypicality and leader stereotypicality. *Personality and Social Psychology Bulletin, 23*(10), 1087–1099.

[51]Colbert, A. E., Kristof-Brown, A. L. Bradley, B. H., & Barrick, M. R. (2008). CEO transformational leadership: The role of goal importance congruence in top management teams. *The Academy of Management Journal, 51*(1), 81–96.

[52]Bass, *Leadership and performance*, p. 297. Bass, *Leadership and performance beyond expectations.*

[53]Griffin, M. A., Parker, S. K., & Mason, C. M. (2010). Leader vision and the development of adaptive and proactive performance: A longitudinal study. *Journal of Applied Psychology, 95*(1), 174–182.

[54]van Knippenberg, B., & van Knippenberg, D. (2005). Leader self-sacrifice and leadership effectiveness: The moderating role of leader prototypicality. *Journal of Applied Psychology, 90*(1), 25–37.

[55]Deutschman, A. (2009, September 21). How authentic leaders "walk the walk." *Business Week*, p. 9.

[56]Hater, J. J., & Bass, B. M. (1988). Supervisors' evaluations and subordinates' perceptions of transformational and transactional leadership. *Journal of Applied Psychology, 73*, 695–702; Ross, S. M., & Offermann, L. R. (1997). Transformational leaders: Measurement of personality attributes and work group performance. *Personality and Social Psychology Bulletin, 23*(10), 1078–1086.

[57]Hofmann, D. A., & Jones, L. M. (2005). Leadership, collective personality, and performance. *Journal of Applied Psychology, 90*(3), 509–522.

Transformational leadership can have a dark side, such as when a charismatic leader like Jim Jones motivates people to do something that is lethal.[58] Leaders who exhibit antinormative behaviors are judged more positively and given more credit relative to antinorm team members, ex-leaders, and established leaders.[59] (For an example of the "dark side" of transformational leadership, see Exhibit 11-4.) Moreover, under some conditions, charismatic leaders promote disenchantment among team members. The **hypocrisy attribution dynamic** refers to the tendency for team members to draw sinister conclusions about leader's behavior.[60] This can happen when employees are prompted to engage in sense making in strong values-driven organizations.

Active Versus Passive Leadership

Leader activity can range from highly involved and active to laissez-faire.[61] An active leader is highly involved in team activities and is highly visible to team members. In contrast, a passive leader is one who is usually not involved in the day-to-day activities of the team, and his or her influence is seldom directly felt by the team. Active leaders focus keenly on goals. For leaders who are representative of their group's identity, failure to reach a maximal goal is judged to be more effective than failure to reach a minimal goal.[62]

By all measures, Jamie Dimon, CEO of J.P. Morgan Chase, is an example of an active leader. In October 2006, William King, then J.P. Morgan's chief of securitized products, was vacationing in Rwanda, visiting the remote coffee plantations he was helping to finance. Dimon tracked him down to fire off a red alert. "Billy, I really want you to watch out for subprime!" Dimon yelled over the phone. "We need to sell a lot of our positions. I've seen it before. This stuff could go up in smoke!"[63] Conversely, Commodore Builders CEO Joe Albanese transitioned from being an active to a passive leader when he went on a 6-month tour of duty as a naval officer in Kuwait. Albanese prepared his group to function without him, and he watched with not only pride but also a trace of melancholy as it did just that. "I knew one measure of my success was that I'd feel as irrelevant as could be," says Albanese. "And I feel pretty irrelevant." When project issues emerged—problems with schedules, budgets, or materials—Albanese reined himself in.[64]

Autocratic Versus Democratic Leadership

Another view of leadership focuses on a continuum of behavior ranging from entirely autocratic to purely democratic.[65] Also known as vertical leadership (emanating from the top down), this type of leadership stems from an appointed or formal leader of a team, whereas shared leadership is a group process in which leadership is distributed among, and stems from, team members. Autocratic leadership is displayed by leaders who seek sole possession of

---

[58]Hogan, R., Raskin, R., & Fazzini, D. (1990). The dark side of charisma. In K. E. Clark & M. B. Clark (Eds.), *Measures of leadership* (pp. 343–354). West Orange, NJ: Leadership Library of America.

[59]Abrams, D., De Moura, G. R., Marques, J. G., & Hutchison, P. (2008). Innovation credit: When can leaders oppose their group's norms? *Journal of Personality and Social Psychology, 95*(3), 662–678.

[60]Cha, S. E., & Edmondson, A. C. (2006). When values backfire: Leadership, attribution, and disenchantment in a values-driven organization. *Leadership Quarterly, 17*, 57–78.

[61]Bass, *Bass & Stogdill's handbook of leadership.*

[62]Giessner, S. R., & Knippenberg, D. (2008). "License to Fail": Goal definition, leader group prototypicality, and perceptions of leadership effectiveness after leader failure. *Organizational Behavior and Human Decision Processes, 105*(1), 14–35.

[63]Tully, S. (2008, September 15). Jamie Dimon's swat team. *Fortune, 158*(5), 64–78.

[64]Buchanan, L. (2008). When absence makes the team grow stronger. *Inc., 30*(6), 40–43.

[65]Bass, *Bass & Stogdill's handbook of leadership.*

EXHIBIT 11-4 The Dark Side of Transformational Leadership

The People's Temple was a cultlike organization based in San Francisco that primarily attracted poor residents. In 1977, the Reverend Jim Jones, who was the group's political, social, and spiritual leader, moved the group with him to Jonestown, a jungle settlement in Guyana, South America. On November 18, 1978, Congressman Leo R. Ryan of California (who traveled to Guyana to investigate the cult), three members of Ryan's task force, and a cult defector were murdered as they tried to leave Jonestown by plane. Convinced that he would be arrested and implicated in the murder, which would inevitably lead to the demise of the People's Temple, Jones gathered the entire community around him and issued a call for each person's death, to be achieved in a unified act of self-destruction. In November 1978, 910 people compliantly drank, and died from, a vat of poison-laced Kool-Aid.

Source: Hogan, R., Raskin, R., & Fazzini, D. (1990). The dark side of charisma. In K. E. Clark & M. B. Clark (Eds.), *Measures of leadership* (pp. 343–354). West Orange, NJ: Leadership Library of America.

authority, power, and control, whereas democratic leadership is displayed by leaders who share authority, power, and control with their team. In one investigation, the effectiveness of 71 change management teams in companies was examined as a function of vertical versus shared leadership.[66] Team effectiveness was measured six months after leadership was assessed and was also measured from the viewpoints of managers, internal customers, and team members. Shared leadership significantly predicted team effectiveness. For a summary of several different leadership styles and their representative behaviors, see Exhibit 11-5. A study of 59 consulting teams revealed that shared leadership emanates from shared purpose, social support, voice, and external coaching. Moreover, shared leadership predicts team performance, as rated by clients.[67]

EXHIBIT 11-5 Representative Behavior of Five Types of Leaders

Leader Type	Representative Behaviors
Aversive leadership	Engaging in intimidation
	Dispensing reprimands
Directive leadership	Issuing instructions and commands
	Assigning goals
Transactional leadership	Providing personal rewards
	Providing material rewards
	Managing by exception (active)
	Managing by exception (passive)
Transformational leadership	Providing vision
	Expressing idealism
	Using inspirational communication
	Having high-performance expectations
Empowering leadership	Encouraging independent action
	Encouraging opportunity thinking
	Encouraging teamwork
	Encouraging self-development
	Participative goal setting
	Encouraging self-reward

Source: Pearce, C. L., & Sims, H. P. (2002). Vertical versus shared leadership as predictors of the effectiveness of change management teams: An examination of aversive, directive, transactional, transformational, and empowering leader behaviors. *Group Dynamics: Theory, Research and Practice, 6*(2), 172–197.

---

[66]Pearce, C. L., & Sims, Jr., H. P. (2002). Vertical versus shared leadership as predictors of the effectiveness of change management teams: An examination of aversive, directive, transactional, transformational and empowering leader behaviors. *Group Dynamics: Theory, Research, and Practice, 6*(2), 172–197.
[67]Carson, J. B., Tesluk, P. E., & Marrone, J. A.(2007). Shared leadership in teams: An investigation of antecedent conditions and performance. *Academy of Management Journal, 50*, 1217–1234.

Leader Mood

Leaders, like anyone, experience moods. And, over time, moods can belie a chronic style of leadership. Moods manifest themselves through a leader's facial, vocal, and postural cues, and team members can accurately ascertain leaders' moods on the basis of nonverbal cues. Leaders' moods influence the collective mood of the team and the performance of the team. According to the **Mood Contagion model**, leaders transmit their own moods to team members, just as a person with a cold might infect others.[68] When leaders are in a positive mood, in comparison to a negative mood, team members experience more positive moods, and groups as a whole are characterized by a more positive affective tone. Moreover, groups with leaders in a positive mood show more coordination and expend less effort than those in a negative mood. For example, the previous chairman and CEO of General Electric, Jack Welch, said, "An upbeat manager with a positive outlook somehow ends up running a team or organization filled with . . . well, upbeat people with positive outlooks. A sourpuss somehow ends up with an unhappy tribe all his own. Unhappy tribes have a tough time winning. Work can be hard. But your job as leader is to fight the gravitational pull of negativism. That doesn't mean you sugarcoat the challenges. It does mean you display an energizing, can-do attitude about overcoming them."[69]

Like other people, leaders can get angry. What is the effect of leader anger on teamwork? It depends on the team's epistemic motivation, or the team's desire to develop a thorough understanding of a situation. Teams with higher epistemic motivation (i.e., a desire to understand) perform better when their leaders display anger, but teams with lower epistemic motivation perform better when the leaders express happiness.[70] **Leader–team perceptual distance** is the difference between a leader and a team and how they perceive things.[71] The more disconnect between what the leader sees and what the team sees, the worse the team performance. And, this effect is stronger when the team's perceptions are more positive than that of the leader.[72]

LEADER–MEMBER EXCHANGE

The Leader–Member Exchange (LMX) model focuses on the relationships that leaders develop with particular subordinates and what leaders and subordinates offer and receive in such relationships. LMX theory operates on the premise that leaders give different team members (subordinates) differential amounts of attention and treatment.[73] Leaders do not treat all of their team members in the same way and may develop different types of relationships with different members. According to LMX theory, team leaders make initial decision early on about whether a given team member will be part of the in-group. Some of the key determinants that lead to close, trusting relationships are the subordinates' similarity to the leader, their demonstrated competence, and being extraverted. This may even create an "ingroup" among those with whom the leader invests.

---

[68]Sy, T., Cote, S., & Saavedra, R. (2005). The contagious leader: Impact of the leader's mood on the mood of group members, group affective tone, and group processes. *Journal of Applied Psychology, 90*, 295–305.

[69]Welch, J., & Welch, S. (2005, April 4). How to be a good leader. *Newsweek*, p. 45.

[70]Van Kleef, G. A., Homan, A. C., Beersma, B., van Knippenberg, D., van Knippenberg, B., & Damen, F. (2009). Searing sentiment or cold calculation? The effects of leader emotional displays on team performance depend on follower epistemic motivation. *Academy of Management Journal, 52*, 562–580.

[71]Gibson, C. B., Cooper, C. D., & Conger, J. A. (2009). Do you see what we see? The complex effects of perceptual distance between leaders and teams. *Journal of Applied Psychology, 94*(1), 62–76.

[72]Ibid.

[73]Graen, G. (1976). Role making processes within complex organizations. In M. D. Dunnette (ed.), *Handbook of industrial and organizational psychology*. Chicago, IL: Rand McNally.

Inner-circle members (i.e., those who are close to the leader) feel safer in their group and participate more in group discussions; leaders recognize them and give them larger bonuses.[74] Unfortunately, leaders call upon inner-circle members more even when they do not possess the expert knowledge. Consequently, team members may grow resentful and view the leader and that subordinate as a subteam or coalition, particularly when other team members do not have a close, trusting relationship with the leader. When leaders treat a certain subordinate in a more distant, impersonal fashion, that subordinate may not be as involved in her task and not perform as well. Differentiated leadership (leaders treating individuals in a group differently) diminish their group's effectiveness by lowering members' self-efficacy and group efficacy; group-focused leadership facilitates group identification and collective efficacy, which increases effectiveness.[75]

Early on in a group, team member extraversion and leader agreeableness predict relationship quality, but as the relationship develops, performance is the key predictor.[76] Leaders who are treated in a close, connected fashion to their own superiors often develop close relationships with their own subordinates. And, the closer employers believe their own leader's profile to be to their view of leadership, the better the quality of their LMX.[77] That is, the more leaders embody the leadership behaviors that their employees and teams expect of them, the better their relationships. Inclusive leaders reduce turnover in groups, especially diverse groups.[78] Leaders who invest in their members and empower them instill better individual performance and better team performance.[79] In an investigation of organizations in the People's Republic of China, the quality of LMX was a key link between transformational leadership and task performance as well as organizational citizenship behaviors.[80]

TEAM COACHING

Team coaching is "direct interaction with a team intended to help members make coordinated and task-appropriate use of their collective resources in accomplishing the team's work."[81] According to Hackman and Wageman's theory of team coaching, coaching involves three distinct features:[82]

The *functions* that coaching serves for a team

The specific *times* in the task performance process when coaching intervention are most likely to have their intended effects

The *conditions* under which team-focused coaching is likely to facilitate performance

---

[74]Burris, E. R., Rodgers, M. S., Mannix, E. A., Hendron, M. G., & Oldroyd, J. B. (2009). Playing favorites: The influence of leaders' inner circle on group processes and performance. *Personality and Social Psychology Bulletin, 35*(9), 1244–1257.
[75]Wu, J., Tsui, A., & Kinicki, A. (2010). Leading groups: Consequences of differentiated leadership in groups. *Academy of Management Journal, 53*(1), 90–106.
[76]Nahrgang, J. D., Frederick, P., Morgeson, F. P., & Ilies, L. (2009). The development of leader–member exchanges: Exploring how personality and performance influence leader and member relationships over time. *Organizational Behavior and Human Decision Processes, 108*(2), 256–266.
[77]Epitropaki, O., & Martin, R. (2005). From ideal to real: A longitudinal study of the role of implicit leadership theories on leader-member exchanges and employee outcomes. *Journal of Applied Psychology, 90*(4), 659–676.
[78]Nishii, L. H., & Mayer, D. (2009). Do inclusive leaders help the performance of diverse groups? The moderating role of leader-member exchange in the diversity to group performance. *Journal of Applied Psychology, 94*(6), 1412–1426.
[79]Gilad, C., Kirkman, B. L., Kanfer, R., Allen, D., & Rosen, B. (2007). A multilevel study of leadership, empowerment, and performance in teams. *Journal of Applied Psychology, 92*(2), 331–346.
[80]Wang, H., Law, K. S., Hackett, R. D., Wang, D., & Chen, Z. X. (2005). Leader-member exchange as a mediator of the relationship between transformational leadership and followers' performance and organizational citizenship behavior. *Academy of Management Journal, 48*, 420–432.
[81]Hackman, J. R., & Wageman, R. (2005). A theory of team coaching. *Academy of Management Review, 30*(2), 269–287.
[82]Ibid.

The impact of team coaching, whether provided by a formal team leader or by fellow group members, depends directly on the degree to which the proper coaching functions are fulfilled competently at appropriate times and circumstances.

Examples of coaching include a "press" meeting before a new product is announced, giving the team feedback on their performance or asking the team thoughtful questions about their recommendations for a new strategy. By contrast, a leader who personally coordinates the work of a team or negotiates resources is, on the surface, doing things that are quite useful for the team, but that is not coaching.[83] According to Hackman, "coaching is about building teamwork, not about doing the team's work."[84] As important as coaching is for team success, leaders focus their behavior less on team coaching than on other aspects of the team leadership portfolio.[85]

Types of Coaching

The integrated model of teamwork, as laid out in Chapter 2, provides insight into three types of coaching. Recall that essential conditions for team performance include ability (knowledge, skills, education, and information), motivation, and strategy. Coaching can be educational, motivational, or strategic (see Exhibit 11-6).[86] Coaching that focuses on ability, knowledge, and skill is **educational** in nature. For example, a coach might either provide or suggest that a person get training on particular skills, such as marketing or emotional intelligence. Coaching that focuses on how to enhance involvement is **motivational** in nature. For example, a coach might suggest that team members enhance their commitment to the team by outlining their goals and target dates for completing those goals. Finally, coaching that focuses on how to best integrate

EXHIBIT 11-6 Structural, Contextual, and Coaching Contributions to Team Performance Processes

Performance Process	Contribution from			
	Direction	Structure	Context	Coaching
Effort (motivation)	Challenging	Task design	Reward system	Minimize social loafing
				Build team commitment
Performance strategy (coordination)	Clear	Team norms	Information system	Minimize habitual behavior
				Invent uniquely appropriate strategies
Knowledge and Skill (ability)	Consequential	Team composition	Educational system	Minimize poor weighting
				Build pool of talent

Source: Hackman, J. R., & Wageman, R. (2005). When and how team leaders matter. *Research in Organizational Behavior, 26,* 37–74.

[83]Hackman, J. R. (2002). *Leading teams: Setting the stage for great performances.* Boston: Harvard Business School Press.
[84]Ibid.
[85]Wageman, R., Hackman, J. R., & Lehman, E. V. (2005). The team diagnostic survey: Development of an instrument. *The Journal of Applied Behavioral Science, 41*(4), 373–398.
[86]Hackman & Wageman, "Theory of team coaching," p. 304; Hackman, *Leading teams.*

members' strengths and abilities is **consultative** in nature. For example, a coach might suggest that the team members practice performing a particular task with one another.

According to Hackman and Wageman, the three coaching functions, education, motivation, and consultation, address a team's task performance processes, not members' interpersonal relationships. Thus, coaching functions are those interventions that inhibit threats to performance and enhance synergetic gains for each of these three performance processes. For team coaching to be effective, four conditions have to be present:[87]

First, the team performance processes that are essential for success (i.e., knowledge and skill, motivation, and coordination) must be relatively unconstrained by task or organizational requirements.

Second, the team must be well designed and the organizational context supportive. Well-designed teams respond better to good coaching and are undermined less by ineffective coaching than poorly designed teams.[88]

Third, coaching behaviors should focus on salient task performance processes, rather than interpersonal relationships or processes not under a team's control. For example, in one investigation, leaders trained in two specific forms of process facilitation, strategy development and coordinating, were better able to lead their teams through a specific battle simulation operation.[89]

Finally, coaching interventions should be introduced when the team is ready and able to incorporate them. For motivational interventions, the beginning of the task cycle is ideal. For consultative-strategy interventions, the midpoint is ideal, and for educational interventions, the end of the task cycle is ideal.

According to Hackman and Wageman, team leaders' decisions about coaching are often made implicitly, without much thought, rather than deliberately, and the interventions are often suboptimal.[90] Moreover, team satisfaction may not always go hand in hand with team effectiveness. For example, leaders who use active coaching are evaluated less positively in terms of team member satisfaction with leadership, yet their teams are more effective, particularly under change and disruption.[91]

LEADERSHIP AND POWER

As noted earlier, leadership, at its heart, involves a relationship between people. In any relationship, power operates as a key dynamic. **Power** is the ability of a person to control the outcomes of another person in a relationship.[92] Control over others' outcomes can be direct or indirect. And control can be unilateral or bilateral. Leadership always involves power; even if a person is not a leader, he or she can still exercise power. Anyone in a leadership position needs to know about the use of power and how it affects others as well as themselves.

---

[87]Hackman, J. R., & Wageman, R. (2005). A theory of team coaching. *Academy of Management Review, 30*(2), 269–287.

[88]Wageman, R. (2001). How leaders foster self-managing team effectiveness: Design choices versus hands-on coaching. *Organization Science, 12*(5), 559–577.

[89]DeChurch, L. A., & Marks, M. A. (2006). Leadership in multiteam systems. *Journal of Applied Psychology, 91*(2), 311–329.

[90]Wageman, R., & Hackman, J. R. (2005). When and how team leaders matter. *Research in Organizational Behavior, 26*, 37–74.

[91]Morgeson, F. P. (2005). The external leadership of self-managing teams: Intervening in the context of novel and disruptive events. *Journal of Applied Psychology, 90*, 497–508.

[92]Kelley, H. H., & Thibaut, J. (1978). *Interpersonal relations: A theory of interdependence.* New York: Wiley.

EXHIBIT 11-7 Sources of Power

Source of Power	Definition
Legitimate power	Based on a person's holding of a formal position; other person complies because of belief in legitimacy of power holder.
Reward power	Based on a person's access to rewards; other person complies because of desire to receive rewards.
Coercive power	Based on a person's ability to punish; other person complies because of fear of punishment.
Expert power	Based on personal expertise in a certain area; other person complies because of belief in power holder's knowledge.
Referent power	Based on a person's attractiveness to others; other person complies because of respect and liking for power holder.

Source: French, J. R. P., Jr., & Raven, B. H. (1968). The bases of social power. In D. Cartwright & A. F. Zander (Eds.), *Group dynamics* (pp. 259–270). New York: Harper & Row.

Sources of Power

Power is the capacity to influence; influence is the actual use of power by specific behaviors.[93] French and Raven identified five key sources of power that people use in organizations and teams: expert, legitimate, reward, coercive, and referent power (see Exhibit 11-7).[94] In one investigation, one member of a group was given power over others based on either higher expertise (expert power) or position (legitimate power). They then used either harsh or soft tactics with their team. Power holders who influence using harsh tactics have greater self-evaluations (feelings of superiority), but do not appreciate their team.[95] Leaders who use expert power are more liked, more influential, and engender more confidence when they express themselves in a manner congruent with their status, such as using powerful speech.[96]

Using Power

Wageman and Mannix identify three patterns of power use by team members:[97]

> **Overuse:** The team member uses his or her power (e.g., special status) to exert influence over most aspects of group functioning and to dominate the team. For example, when leaders make an explicit command, team members are more likely to make a deviant

---

[93]Klocke, U. (2009). "I Am the Best": Effects of influence tactics and power bases on powerholders' self-evaluation and target evaluation. *Group Processes & Intergroup Relations, 12*(5), 619–637.

[94]French, J. R. P., & Raven, B. (1968). The bases of social power. In D. Cartwright & A.F. Zander (Eds.), *Group dynamics* (pp. 259–270). New York: Harper & Row.

[95]Klocke, "I Am the Best."

[96]Loyd, D. L., Phillips, K. W., Whitson, J., & Thomas-Hunt, M. C. (2010). How congruence between status speech style affects reactions to unique knowledge. *Group Process and Intergroup Relations, 13*(3), 379–395.

[97]Wageman, R., & Mannix, E. A. (Eds.). (1998). *Uses and misuses of power in task-performing teams. Power and influence in organizations*. Thousand Oaks, CA: Sage.

decision.[98] Similarly, the powerful team member who uses his or her special status to exert influence hinders the group's effectiveness.[99]

Abdication: The team member with power exerts no special influence over the task. This pattern is also dysfunctional, and such teams tend toward mediocre to poor performance because they fail to use the resources that the powerful team member has access to.

Managing the resource: The powerful team member influences other members only in the specific domain of his or her special resources. This is the most effective use of power. For example, in an investigation of 16 team operating rooms learning to use a new technology for cardiac surgery, a key question is whether team leaders could work together under pressure (i.e., real life and death situations) and successfully use new technology.[100] The most effective leaders communicated a motivating rationale and minimized their status differences. This allowed other team members to speak up.

Implications of Using Power

Research evidence reveals some surprising findings about the effects of power on those who use it.

First, using power feels good; the use of power itself is rewarding and stimulating. Thus, people are attracted to power. Second, people who are in a position of power often have an egocentrically biased view of themselves, believing themselves to be more fair, generous, and trustworthy than others evaluate them to be. In a complementary fashion, those who lack power are highly distrustful of those who have power.[101] People regard power-seeking individuals to be unethical and question the motives of those who seek to enhance their control. Third, people who are dependent on leaders not only tend to evaluate and judge them quite often but also have particular expectations of leaders, or **implicit leadership theories** (ILTs), about whether a leader is worthy of influence (or LWI).[102] ILTs are preconceived ideas that specify what teams expect of their leaders.[103] Consequently, if a leader is judged to be an LWI, teams are more willing to be influenced by that leader. Thus, the degree of LWI respect accorded by teams in large part determines the effectiveness of the leader. Given that ILTs drive LWI, it behooves leaders to understand the ILTs that teams hold. The behaviors that people expect of leaders (the ILTs that drive LWI) are somewhat different for appointed versus elected leaders.[104] For appointed leaders, being sympathetic (i.e., humorous, caring, interested, truthful, and open to ideas) and taking charge (i.e., responsible, active, determined, influential, aggressive, and in command) are key. For elected leaders, being well dressed (i.e., clean cut), kind, and authoritative are most important. (For a specific list of the characteristics, see Exhibit 11-8.)

It would seem that leaders would be hypervigilant about their styles, seeking constant feedback as to the effectiveness of their approach. However, the opposite is true. People in positions of

---

[98]Conway, L. G., & Schaller, M. (2005). When authorities' commands backfire: Attributions about consensus effects on deviant decision making. *Journal of Personality and Social Psychology, 89*(3), 311–326.

[99]Wageman & Mannix, *Uses and misuses of power in task-performing teams.*

[100]Edmonson, A. (2003). Speaking up in the operating room: How team leaders promote learning in interdisciplinary action teams. *Journal of Management Studies, 40*(6), 1419–1452.

[101]Lind, E. A., & Tyler, T. R. (1988). *The social psychology of procedural justice.* New York: Plenum.

[102]Kenney, R. A., Schwartz-Kenney, B. M., & Blascovich, J. (1996). Implicit leadership theories: Defining leaders described as worthy of influence. *Personality and Social Psychology Bulletin, 22*(11), 1128–1143.

[103]Lord, R. G., & Maher, K. J. (1993). *Leadership and information processing: Linking perceptions and performance.* New York: Routledge.

[104]Kenney, Schwartz-Kenney, & Blascovich, "Implicit leadership theories."

EXHIBIT 11-8 Leader Behaviors That Determine Whether People Accord Influence to a Leader

Appointed Leaders Are Expected to Have These Characteristics and Skills	Elected Leaders Are Expected to Have These Characteristics and Skills
Caring	Tall
Interested	Clean-cut
Sense of humor	Open to others' ideas
Truthful	Respect for team
Open to others' ideas	Friendly
Imaginative	Caring
Knowledgeable	Honest
Responsible	Enthusiastic
Speak well	Sense of humor
Active	Popular
Determined	Knowledgeable
Influential	Responsible
Aggressive	Speak well
In command	Independent
	Influential
	Determined
	Risk taker
	Aggressive
	In command

Source: Kenney, R. A., Schwartz-Kenney, B. M., & Blascovich, J. (1996). Implicit leadership theories: Defining leaders described as worthy of influence. *Personality and Social Psychology Bulletin, 22*(11), 1128–1143.

power are less motivated to scan their environment or process information. From a rational point of view, they are less dependent on others and, therefore, less motivated to pay attention to the actions of others. In contrast, people who are powerless (i.e., resource dependent on others) have an incentive to carefully attend to those who are in power. Graduate students (who are dependent on professors to obtain their degree) spend an inordinate amount of time recalling and processing behaviors and activities engaged in by faculty members.[105] Similarly, those who have more power show more variability in their behaviors—in short, they engage in a broader array of behaviors.[106]

Power also makes people see the world with "rose-colored glasses"—that is, it makes people focus on more positive, rewarding information and less on negative, threatening information. Powerful people make more optimistic judgments regarding the risks they face in their lives (e.g., health risks) compared with powerless individuals.[107] When powerful people interact with others, they are more likely to focus on how much others like them and less likely to focus on

[105]Kramer, R. M. (1996). Divergent realities, convergent disappointments in the hierarchic relation: Trust and the intuitive auditor at work. In R. M. Kramer & T. R. Tyler (Eds.), *Trust in organizations* (pp. 216–245). Thousand Oaks, CA: Sage.
[106]Guinote, A., Judd, C. M., & Brauer, M. (2002). Effects of power on perceived and objective group variability: Evidence that more powerful groups are more variable. *Journal of Personality and Social Psychology, 82*(5), 708–721.
[107]Anderson, C., & Galinsky, A. D. (2006). Power, optimism, and risk-taking. *European Journal of Social Psychology, 36*, 511–536.

others' negative feelings toward them.[108] This tendency to focus on rewards might help explain why powerful people sometimes choose risky strategies in the pursuit of their goals. When contemplating a potential high-risk merger, for example, powerful organizational leaders might focus more on the potential payoffs of the merger and less on the inherent dangers.

DECISION ANALYSIS MODEL: HOW PARTICIPATIVE DO YOU WANT TO BE?

Leaders are more effective when they understand that not every decision requires the input of their entire team. Similarly, leaders are more effective when they realize that they cannot be a demagogue. Thus, all leaders face decisions concerning how participative they want to be. The amount of team participation varies along a continuum from zero to total involvement. How much participation is ideal? It is simply not practical to consult the team on every organizational issue, but where to draw the line is unclear. The decision analysis model of Vroom and Yetton provides a way to balance authority and delegate.[109]

As can be seen in Exhibit 11-9, the key questions facing the leader concern the quality of the decision to be made (e.g., is it necessary to find the best outcome, given time and budget constraints, or are most outcomes basically sufficient?), the acceptance needed for the decision (e.g., how much does the ultimate outcome need to be accepted by the organization?), the length of time required to make the decision (efficiency), and the amount of growth or development of the team. The model prompts leaders to be more deliberate in the decision-making process. This has the effect of increasing the consistency of their behavior, and consistency is the key principle by which leaders are evaluated. This model of leadership focuses on matching the leader and the situational requirements.[110]

Decision Styles

Vroom and Jago considered five decision methods available to the leader (see top of Exhibit 11-9).[111] The first is **autocratic**, in which the leader makes the decision with little or no involvement of other team members. The second method, **inquiry**, has the leader asking for information from the team but ultimately making the decision independently. The third method, the **consultative approach**, involves different degrees of consultation with team members; however, the leader is still the final decision maker. The fourth method, **consensus building**, involves extensive consultation and consensus building with the team. Here, the leader shares a problem with team members, and together they try to reach consensus. The leader essentially is another member of the team and has no more or less influence than any other member. The final method involves total **delegation** of decision making to the team. The team makes the decision without the leader. The leader gives the problem to the team and lets the team determine the best course of action with virtually no additional input.

Problem Identification

The leader must also determine the right questions and the right order in which to ask them. This also influences the best decision style in a particular context. For example, consider a situation in

---

[108]Anderson, C., & Berdahl, J. L. (2002). The experience of power: Examining the effects of power on approach and inhibition tendencies. *Journal of Personality and Social Psychology, 83,* 1362–1377.

[109]Vroom, V. H., & Yetton, P. W. (1973). *Leadership and decision-making.* Pittsburgh, PA: University of Pittsburgh Press.

[110]Ibid., p. 310; Vroom, V. H., & Jago, A. G. (1988). *The new leadership: Managing participation in organizations.* Upper Saddle River, NJ: Prentice Hall.

[111]Vroom & Jago, *New leadership,* p. 310.

EXHIBIT 11-9 Decision Analysis Model

AI	Leader makes the decision alone.
AII	Leader asks for information from the team but makes the decision alone. The team may or may not be told what the problem is.
CI	Leader shares the problem with the team and asks for information and evaluations from them. Meetings take place with each member separately, not as a group, and the leader makes the decision.
CII	Leader and team meet as a group to discuss the problem, but the leader makes the decision.
GII	Leader and team meet as a group to discuss the problem, and the team as a whole makes the decision.

Note: A = alone, C = consultation, G = group.

QR	Quality requirement:	How important is the technical quality of this decision?
CR	Commitment requirement:	How important is subordinate commitment to this decision?
LI	Leader's information:	Do you have sufficient information to make a high-quality decision?
ST	Problem structure:	Is the problem well structured?
CP	Commitment probability:	If you were to make a decision by yourself, is it reasonably certain that your subordinate(s) would be committed to the decision?
GC	Goal congruence:	Do subordinates share the organizational goals to be attained in solving this problem?
CO	Subordinate conflict:	Is conflict among subordinates over preferred solution likely?
SI	Subordinate information:	Do subordinates have sufficient information to make a high-quality decision?

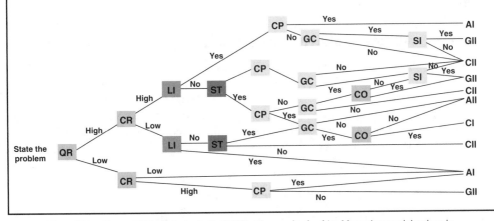

Source: Adapted from Vroom, V. H., & Jago, A. G. (1988). *The new leadership: Managing participations in organizations.* Englewood Cliffs, NJ: Prentice Hall.

which a high-quality decision is crucial (the stakes are high), the leader has enough information or expertise to make the decision alone, and acceptance by the team is not crucial—that is, the decision will work even without their support. In this case, a relatively autocratic style of decision making is ideal. It is efficient, and getting the decision implemented will cost very little. In contrast, consider a situation in which a high-quality decision is necessary and the leader has enough information to make the decision alone, but acceptance by subordinates is crucial—that is, the decision will not work without their active support. Here, a more participative style would be preferable. Indeed, leaders who adapt their style of decision making to existing conditions are generally more successful than those who are either uniformly autocratic or participative.[112] However, most team members prefer a participative approach by their leader, even under conditions in which the decision model recommends an autocratic style.[113] This means, of course, that the perceived effectiveness of decisions among leaders may very well differ from how the team feels.[114] Teams have strong aversion to autocratic decision-making strategies, even when these are predicted by the model to be most effective. Thus, the decision-making model is a useful device for helping the leader to be a consistent decision maker, but team members generally prefer participation.

Decision Tree Model

The decision tree model is one in which all of these questions and alternatives are put together to formulate a sound decision, as illustrated in Exhibit 11-9. A fundamental assumption in this model is that consultation with teams and individuals is inefficient because it requires time; therefore, the model is conservative in that it tends to push the leader toward autocratic or independent decision making. However, in cases where the model recommends a relatively autocratic or individual control strategy, the leader must not let people think that they have control when they actually do not.

One question is whether the Vroom–Yetton model actually leads to better decisions. Many investigations have compared the effects of decisions made according to the model's prescriptions with effects of decisions made in a way inconsistent with the model (for a review, see Yukl).[115] In general, results support the model. For example, Vroom and Jago computed the mean rate of success across five investigations and found that for decisions made in accordance with the model, the mean success rate was 62 percent, versus 37 percent for decisions made using a decision procedure outside of the feasible set.[116]

ENCOURAGING PARTICIPATIVE MANAGEMENT

Some managers believe that power and control should remain in the hands of a few high-level executives. This model of leadership assumes that the leader has all of the answers, knowledge, and ideas in the organization. This view, however, is being challenged by a model of leadership that delegates authority downward, toward individuals and groups. In this model, leadership is more equally shared by members as teams develop over time. Empowering leadership is positively related to knowledge sharing and team efficacy, which in turn are positively related to better team

[112]Vroom, V. H., & Jago, A. G. (1978). The validity of the Vroom-Yetton model. *Journal of Applied Psychology, 63*(2), 151–162.
[113]Heilman, M. E., Hornstein, H. A., Cage, J. H., & Herschlag, J. K. (1984). Reactions to prescribed leader behavior as a function of role perspective: The case of the Vroom-Yetton model. *Journal of Applied Psychology, 69*(1), 50–60.
[114]Field, R. H. G., & House, R. J. (1990). A test of the Vroom-Yetton Model using manager and subordinate reports. *Journal of Applied Psychology, 75*(3), 362–366.
[115]Yukl, G. A. (2002). *Leadership in organizations* (5th ed.). Upper Saddle River, NJ: Prentice Hall.
[116]Vroom & Jago, *New leadership*, p. 310.

EXHIBIT 11-10 Team Empowerment Continuum

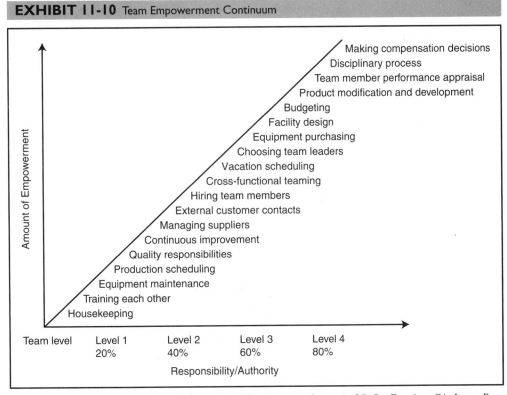

Source: Wellins, R. S., Byham, W. C., & Wilson, J. M. (1991). *Empowered teams* (p. 26). San Francisco, CA: Jossey-Bass.

performance.[117] When teams have to learn a new task requiring coordination, leadership style (participative versus authoritative) makes a difference in the development and implementation of effective tactics. Teams led by a "coordinator," in which all team members share equal responsibility for determining the team strategy and directing its activities, implement better tactics than commander-led teams.[118]

Many managers claim that their team is empowered when, in fact, it is not. Just what does an "empowered" team do? Exhibit 11-10 depicts a continuum of team empowerment. Level 1 teams have the least power; they are often new teams, perhaps lacking the skills, experience, or training to implement more control. Perhaps this is why many successful self-directed organizations intentionally devote 20 percent of the team members' and leaders' time to training in the first year.[119] Job skill training is necessary to give team members the depth and breadth they need to effectively carry out the broadened range of activities that self-directed teams perform.

Understanding existing social and structural factors is critical to successfully forming empowered work teams. Probably the most regrettable state of affairs in the organization is when employees feel powerless. Feelings of powerlessness lead to depression and organizational decline.

---

[117]Srivastave, A., Bartol, K. M., & Locke, E. A. (2006). Empowering leadership in management teams: Effects on knowledge sharing, efficacy, and performance. *Academy of Management Journal, 49*(6), 1239–1251.

[118]Durham, C., Knight, D., & Locke, E. A. (1997). Effects of leader role, team-set goal difficulty, efficacy, and tactics on team effectiveness. *Organizational Behavior and Human Decision Processes, 72*(2), 203–231.

[119]Wellins, R. S. (1992). Building a self-directed work team. *Training and Development, 46*(12), 24–28.

EXHIBIT 11-11   Factors That Lead to a Potential State of Powerlessness

Context Factor Leading to State of Powerlessness	Condition
Organizational factors	• Significant organizational change/transitions
	• Start-up ventures
	• Excessive, competitive pressures
	• Impersonal, bureaucratic climate
	• Poor communications and limited network-forming systems
	• Highly centralized organizational resources
Supervisory style	• Authoritarian (high control)
	• Negativism (emphasis on failures)
	• Lack of reason for actions/consequences
Reward systems	• Noncontingency (arbitrary reward allocations)
	• Low incentive value of rewards
	• Lack of competence-based work
	• Lack of innovation-based rewards
Job design	• Lack of role clarity
	• Lack of training and technical support
	• Unrealistic goals
	• Lack of appropriate authority/discretion
	• Low task variety
	• Limited participation in programs, meetings, and decisions that have a direct impact on job performance
	• Lack of appropriate/necessary resources
	• Lack of network-forming opportunities
	• Highly established work routines
	• Too many rules and guidelines
	• Low advancement opportunities
	• Lack of meaningful goals/tasks
	• Limited contact with senior management

Source: Conger, J. (1989). The art of empowering others. *Academy of Management Executive, 3*(1), 17–24. Reprinted with permission. Copyright 1989 by Academy of Management (NY). Reproduced with permission of Academy of Management (NY) in the format Textbook via Copyright Clearance Center.

Part of effective team leadership should include a check on four factors, listed in Exhibit 11-11, that can lead to a state of powerlessness in the organization: organizational factors, the leader's supervisory style, the organizational reward system, and job design. Furthermore, instead of the leader performing this check, the team members should do it themselves.

Once management has considered the potential benefits of a more employee-empowering leadership style, management must determine how to best implement this new structure. Next, we provide several strategies to make a smooth transition from a bureaucratic to a commitment organization. *Empowerment*, *participative management*, and *self-managing teams* are popular buzzwords. However, they don't happen overnight—even when upper management has made a public commitment to creating an empowered workforce. Many companies that want to become more participatory in their management styles don't know how to begin. What are some down-to-earth, concrete steps for moving power downward in the organization into the hands of team members?

The variety of approaches to inviting participation in the workforce can be clustered into four types of approaches: task delegation, parallel suggestion involvement, job involvement, and organizational involvement.[120]

Task Delegation

Delegation is the handing over of the responsibility and authority required to accomplish a task without relinquishing final accountability. The spirit of task delegation is multifold: to invite others to have a share in the performance of work; to have leaders do other, more important things; and to mentor. This not only serves the interests of the employees, who presumably want to have a greater hand in the work and operations of the company, but also serves the interests of the leader and the organization in creating more efficient uses of time. Many people have a somewhat old-fashioned view of leadership that holds that a leader is responsible not only for creating and defining the vision of the organization but also for handling all of the details, managing all of the personal relationships, and determining the process. Many managers mistakenly think that every task requires their constant attention from beginning to end.

If it is to be effective, leadership requires delegation, and leaders are still accountable for their delegates, as well as for themselves. Delegation is much easier said than done: There are right and wrong ways to delegate that depend on things such as team members' skill levels and the nature of the work. Exhibit 11-12 outlines guidelines for successful delegation.

The inability to delegate effectively creates two negative consequences for the organization: overloaded executives and underused subordinates. Each of these conditions is associated with work-related stress and burnout—not to mention many forms of underperformance. By giving meaningful responsibility to subordinates, managers give them the opportunity to perform their jobs well, demonstrate ability, experience success, be visible within the organization, develop skills, and experience new challenges.

Parallel Suggestion Involvement

The idea behind parallel suggestion involvement is to invite employees and team members to make suggestions about organizational procedures and processes. Thus, employees are given opportunities and are actively encouraged to recommend tactics for increasing sales, minimizing production costs, increasing customer satisfaction, and so on. The classic example of parallel suggestion involvement is the suggestion box, which is not even limited to employees—customers can be asked to make recommendations as well. Quality circles also invite workers to share ideas about improving production and products. The parallel suggestion strategy is cost effective; providing a venue to solicit suggestions can be relatively inexpensive, but it can potentially have huge payoffs in terms of improving organizational functioning. What's more, parallel suggestion involvement can significantly reduce turnover and absenteeism because employees who feel that their interests, concerns, and ideas are valued are more motivated. An examination of 23 neonatal intensive care units showed that the extent to which team leaders are inclusive (i.e., minimize status differences and allow members to collaborate in process improvement), teams are more engaged in their work

[120]Lawler, E. E. (1988). Choosing an involvement strategy. *Academy of Management Executive, 11*(3), 197–204.

EXHIBIT 11-12 Key Guidelines for Successful Delegation

Use delegation to develop, not dump. As people become more concerned about time management, there has been a tendency to think that this means getting rid of unwanted tasks. Be sure that you and your subordinates discuss the task in terms of what is in it for them. Don't just pass the buck. Pass on challenge, responsibility, and a chance to learn new skills or aspects of the organization.

Set specific goals with subordinates. This includes a review of the task, especially the results expected, and a timetable for getting things done and reviewing progress. Don't assume that they understand what you expect and/or need. Be specific and check for understanding.

Discuss the meaning of the assignment in terms of its value within the larger organizational picture.

Provide for autonomy. Make it clear that subordinates have the authority and resources

and are free to "run with the ball," but reassure them that you will be there to provide support.

Elicit questions from the subordinate. Test for understanding of the talk.

Get additional ideas or other inputs from the subordinate.

Provide feedback. Your subordinates need to know how they are doing. This is helpful for taking corrective action before a deadline. It is especially reinforcing after a goal is accomplished.

Provide times for follow-up. Don't just delegate and expect the results to just happen. Plan to meet, review preliminary results, discuss problems, and so forth.

Select the most motivated person.

Delegate only once, and to only one person, group, or team. Nothing is more demoralizing for subordinates than to find out that other people are working on a project that they thought had been delegated solely to them.

Source: Hall, F. (1997). Effective delegation. In D. D. Brown, R. J. Lewicki, D. T. Hall, & F. S. Hall (Eds.), *Experiences in management and organizational behavior* (4th ed.). New York: John Wiley & Sons. Reprinted with permission.

and learn from one another to improve their performance.[121] For example, AO Precision LL of Daytona Beach, Florida, a maker of internal parts for M16s used by the United States military, involves each of their 186 employees in the entire manufacturing process. Awards are given for suggestions that are put into place, ranging from company hats to several hundred dollars, depending on the value of the suggestion. The factory is arranged into cells, or teams, which manufacture a piece from start to finish; each cell has a spokesperson who communicates their ideas to management on ways to improve quality, cut costs, or work more efficiently.[122]

When using parallel suggestion involvement, it is important to differentially and accurately weigh staff input. Simply stated, team members differ in their ability to contribute to solving a problem. Distributed expertise refers to the fact that team members differ in the amount of knowledge and information that each bring to the problem.[123] Until leaders have had an opportunity to gather information they feel is relevant to their determination of each team member's ability to contribute, they may weight each person's input equally. Leaders have difficulty differentially weighting their staff as much as they should and tend to use an equal-weighting strategy.[124] Once

[121]Nembhard, I. M., & Edmondson, A. (2006). Making it safe: The effects of leader inclusiveness and professional status on psychological safety and improvement efforts in health care teams. *Journal of Organizational Behavior, 27*(7), 941–966.
[122]Grant, W. (2010, January 14). Employee involvement boosts quality. *Hometown News.* myhometownnews.net
[123]Hollenbeck, J. R., Ilgen, D. R., Sego, D. J., Hedlund, J., Major, D. A., & Phillips, J. (1995). Multilevel theory of team decision making: Decision performance in teams incorporating distributed expertise. *Journal of Applied Psychology, 80,* 292–316.
[124]Brehmer, B., & Hagafors, R. (1986). Use of experts in complex decision making: A paradigm for the study of staff work. *Organizational Behavior and Human Decision Processes, 38,* 181–195.

leaders have had experience with their team, some may have greater influence on the basis of their competence, ability, and willingness to accept extra-role responsibilities.[125] In one investigation, 84 leaders of four-person decision-making teams made 63 decisions. Both experience and providing leaders with accurate information about particular members led to greater differentiation and better accuracy in differentiation.[126]

Job Involvement

Job involvement entails restructuring the tasks performed by employees to make them more rewarding, enriching, and, in the case of teams, more autonomous. When people are challenged with interesting tasks, they perform more effectively and creatively. There are a variety of ways by which this may be achieved, such as providing employees with feedback from customers, restructuring tasks so that employees complete a whole and meaningful piece of work, and training employees with new skills and knowledge so that their job scope increases. With job involvement, employees at the lowest levels get new information, power, and skills, and they may be rewarded differently. For example, people may be rewarded for team effort and group-level productivity. Unlike parallel suggestion involvement, job involvement affects the daily work activities of employees. For this reason, job involvement is considerably more costly than parallel suggestion involvement because of the high start-up costs of reconfiguring job descriptions, training, and, in many cases, the physical reconfiguration of the workplace. At Universal Services of America, all vice presidents are required to bring forward five "up and comers" every month to interview for a management-training program. The company also picks five hourly workers every year to join its vice presidents and managers at an annual planning retreat. Workers get job training every two weeks, and they receive immediate awards for great work–including movie tickets and entry into a quarterly drawing for $200.[127]

In February of 2008, Starbucks briefly shut down all 7,100 of its stores and retrained its baristas. CEO Howard Schultz described it as a "comprehensive educational curriculum for all U.S. store partners" that provided a "renewed focus on espresso standards" and "reignited employees' enthusiasm for customer service." After completing the training, each partner signed a promise to exceed customers' expectations by delivering the perfect drink every time.[128]

Organizational Involvement

The fact that leaders want to move in the direction of participation and empowerment, however, does not mean that this can be done by merely changing their own behavior and style independent of other organizational forces. Leadership style and strategy must be integrated into the organizational context.

Consider two types of organizations: bureaucratic and commitment organizations. **Bureaucratic organizations** are the traditional, hierarchical style of leadership; information, rewards, knowledge, and power are concentrated at the top of the organization. In the classic bureaucratic organization, teams do not exist or at least are not acknowledged. Furthermore,

---

[125]Graen, G., & Scandura, T. A. (1987). Toward a psychology of dyadic organizing. In B. Staw & L. L. Cummings (Eds.), *Research in organizational behavior* (Vol. 9, pp. 175–208). Greenwich, CT: JAI Press.

[126]Phillips, J. M. (1999). Antecedents of leader utilization of staff input in decision-making teams. *Organizational Behavior and Human Decision Processes, 77*(3), 215–242.

[127]Irving, D. (2009, December 7). Security firm in O.C.'s "top workplace." The Orange County Register. ocregister.com

[128]Kranz, G. (2008, March). Has Starbucks' training brewed heightened expectations? *Workforce Management.* workforcemanagement.com

when they do emerge, they are often ignored, suppressed, contained, or neglected.[129] **Commitment organizations** are at the opposite extreme. Teams are encouraged to form, power is not hierarchical, and the organization has a deliberately flat structure.

Organizational involvement, or the commitment approach, restructures the organization so that employees at the lowest level will have a sense of involvement (commitment) not just in how they do their own jobs (as in the job involvement approach) but also in the performance of the entire organization. Organizational involvement strategies invite employees to contribute to higher-order strategy decisions. The **McGregor Method** and **Theory Y** are examples of high-involvement strategies in which employees make decisions about work activities, as well as organizational direction.[130] Organizational involvement is based on the belief that if employees are going to care about the performance of their organization, they need to know about it, be able to influence it, be rewarded for it, and have the knowledge and skills to contribute to it.

A key difference between parallel suggestion involvement and organizational involvement is that employees not only make recommendations about how to improve organizational functioning but also implement their suggestions. Thus, employees and team members have **implementation power**. The disadvantage of the organizational involvement strategy is that it is very difficult to know which employee-suggested strategies are, in fact, worthwhile to implement. The Broken Arrow (Oklahoma) Police Department includes a leadership team that operates at the policy level and whose members serve irrespective of rank. The team makes binding decisions on a array of organizational issues. Members are elected by peers, appointed by the chief, or appointed by the police union to act as representatives for their coworkers. Team members have equal voting rights, and decisions require a two-thirds majority. The leadership team's bylaws make it an independent body with authority to effect change and make binding decisions on policy issues, working conditions, and strategic matters.[131]

Another type of organizational involvement involves **top-management teams** (TMTs). TMTs, as opposed to individuals, are more likely to represent the wide range of interests of the people and groups in the organization and provide valuable development experiences for its members.[132] Leadership via TMTs challenges the traditional view of leadership because it moves away from the image of the leader as autonomous, prophetic, and omniscient and toward the idea that leadership is a team process. Leaders of TMTs need to consider several process choices (see Exhibit 11-13).[133] The model addresses each of three basic failures, including self-interested behavior that threatens group viability, failure to surface relevant information, and self-serving behavior. The TMT leader must make three process choices: (1) how to reach closure on a decision (outcome control), (2) how to facilitate a group discussion (process intervention), and (3) how to structure a debate (process design).

It would seem that empowerment and greater employee participation would be the preferred mode in most companies—certainly, at least, from the view of the employees. However, humans have a fundamental need for structure, and new employees are often uncomfortable in the absence of clear structures, guidelines, and constraints. For example, newly matriculated MBA students

[129]Walton, R. E., & Hackman, J. R. (1986). Groups under contrasting management strategies. In P. S. Goodman and associates (Eds.), *Designing effective workgroups.* San Francisco, CA: Jossey-Bass.
[130]McGregor, D. (1960). *The human side of enterprise.* New York: McGraw-Hill.
[131]Wuestewald, T. (2010, January). The changing face of police leadership. *Police Chief Magazine.* policechiefmagazine.org
[132]Beer, M., Eisenstat, R. A., & Spector, B. (1990). *The critical path to corporate renewal.* Boston, MA: Harvard Business School Press.
[133]Edmondson, A., Roberto, M. A., & Watkins, M. D. (2003). A dynamic model of top management team effectiveness: Managing unstructured task streams. *The Leadership Quarterly, 14*(3) 297–325.

EXHIBIT 11-13 Leader's Process Choice in Top Management Teams

Team-situation	Process Failure	Leader's Process Choice	Behavioral Attributes of High Level of Process Choice	Outcome of Process Choice for Team Effectiveness
Interest Asymmetry	Value-claiming behavior reduces the potential for group value creation or joint gains; emotional conflict	Outcome control (high or low)	Leader decides the final outcome and imposes decision on group after deliberations are complete	Decision outcome is likely to create most value for organization as a whole and emotional conflict is reduced
Information Asymmetry	Relevant information fails to surface in group discussion; silos emerge and remain	Process intervention (high or low)	Leader intervenes actively and frequently in the discussion to: facilitate sharing of information; clarify others' contributions; inquire about views of silent members	Situation-specific information is revealed and discussed in the group
Interaction Effect	Self-serving behavior exaggerates information-sharing failures; people withhold information to enhance their power	Process design (high or low)	Leader imposes a structured process to ensure debate and thorough discussion of alternatives (e.g., devil's advocacy)	Healthy debate between more than one alternative

Source: Edmondson, A., Roberto, M. A., & Watkins, M. D. (2003). A dynamic model of top management team effectiveness: Managing unstructured task streams. *The Leadership Quarterly, 14*(3), 297–325.

frequently lobby for instructor-assigned, rather than free-forming, study groups. What is the effect of empowerment and the ambiguity it brings to the individual, the team, and the organization?

When an organization removes existing structures to provide empowerment in a more democratic fashion, it may find the ambiguity associated with the new structure uncomfortable and respond by imposing a more controlling and bureaucratic structure than the one it sought to replace. This

EXHIBIT 11-14 Tightening the Iron Cage

ISE Communications is a small manufacturing company in a mountain state, located in a metropolitan area. ISE manufactures voice and data transmission circuit boards for the telecommunications industry. It employs a total of 150 employees, 90 of whom are in manufacturing. Originally, ISE was a division of a large telecommunications firm. The ISE management team bought it outright in 1984, although the large firm still remains ISE's largest customer. ISE has traditional manufacturing, engineering, sales, marketing, human resources, and executive staffs. ISE converted from traditional manufacturing into self-managing teams in 1988.

In 1988, the CEO of ISE made a commitment to restructure the organization into self-managing teams. Literally overnight he reconfigured the physical workspace and created several work teams called Red, Blue, Green, Orange, and so on. Before the change, the structure of ISE was such that three levels of managerial hierarchy existed between the vice president and the manufacturing workers. Line and shift supervisors formed the first managerial link. The assembly line in manufacturing organized the plant, with workers manufacturing circuit boards according to their place on the line. Workers had little input into work-related decisions (i.e., not even parallel suggestion involvement). Management disciplined all workers and interviewed and hired all new workers.

(cont.on p.293)

After the change, the managerial hierarchy extended directly from the new manufacturing teams to the vice president. Team work areas replaced the old assembly lines. Teams were responsible for all aspects of the product: complete fabrication, testing, packaging, and so on. Team members took on management issues within each team, electing someone to coordinate information, and to discipline, interview, hire, and terminate members. When workers reported to the plant on the next business day, there was mass confusion and chaos. What happened in the ensuing months was surprising.

ISE is an example of a company in which upper management moved from bureaucratic control to participative management. However, many of the effects were not intended. Three distinct phases were observed over a 4-year period of change.

In the first phase, the challenge for the teams was to learn how to work together and supervise themselves functionally, that is, how to get a customer's order manufactured and out the door.

In the second phase, the teams had to deal with the socialization processes that had shaped the norms of the group. The company prospered, and a large number of new workers had to be integrated into the teams; workers were unfamiliar with the existing teams' value consensus, and they posed an immediate challenge to the power relationships that the older employees had formed.

In the third phase, the company began to stabilize and turn a profit; teams' normative rules became more and more rationalized; and simple norms (e.g., we all need to be at work on time) became highly objective rules similar to ISE's old bureaucratic structure (e.g., if you are more than 5 minutes late, you're docked a day's pay). The social rules were more rigid. The senior group members took on the role of leader within each team. Not surprisingly, many employees were frustrated and confused. It is a bitter irony that some looked back fondly on the days in which there was greater bureaucratic control.

Source: Barker, J. R. (1993). Tightening the iron cage: Concertive control in self-managing teams. *Administrative Science Quarterly, 38*, 408–437.

highly rational but powerfully oppressive bureaucracy is known as the **iron cage**.[134] Out of a desire for order, people continually rationalize their bureaucratic relationships, making them less negotiated (i.e., less based upon commitment) and more structural.[135] As a case in point, see Exhibit 11-14.

Conclusion

In bureaucratic organizations, participative management of the sort we have described seems like antimanagement or an admission of failure at one's own job. One senior-level banker from an international banking firm put it this way: "If I do the kind of things you are describing here—inviting other people who are supposed to be under me to make suggestions about how to accomplish my division's objectives—I am going to work myself out of a job."[136] This investment banker was worried about others doing his job better than he could. This is perhaps the most often-cited reason against participative management. The irony of this example is that the company would probably be better off if all of its employees invited participation. Traditional leadership may no longer be the right image of leadership in a corporate world that is placing an ever-heavier emphasis on team-based work units. A new image of leadership is necessary, one that is associated with being a leader among equals, rather than a leader of followers. Teams (or at least some teams) are often composed of talented individuals selected for their specific knowledge or skills to fit a particular role; in this case, the leader as director is not the right image. The leader as coordinator or assembler may be a better image. When this is true, the leader functions better, activities are performed better, teams work better, and the organization is more successful.

---

[134]Weber, M. (1958). *The protestant ethic and the spirit of capitalism.* Translated by T. Parsons. New York: Scribner's.
[135]Weber, M. (1978). *Economy and society: An outline of interpretive sociology* (G. Roth & C. Wittich, Trans.). Berkeley, CA: University of California Press.
[136]Personal communication from an investment banker in 1998.

12 Interteam Relations
Competition and Cooperation

Teams, not individuals, are invited to race in the prestigious Tour de France. When Lance Armstrong returned to pro cycling in 2009, he joined the Astana team, along with eight other riders, including 2007 tour champion Spaniard Alberto Contador. Shortly into the 3-week tour, problems emerged in the team. Lance Armstrong said that Contador did not "go by the plan" when he surged in the mountains at the end of the seventh stage and put seven-time tour champion Armstrong behind him by 2 seconds. One of pro cycling's unwritten team rules is that you don't chase down a teammate. So when Contador "attacked" (sped ahead in the mountains), Armstrong hung back, gritting his teeth. Another of pro cycling's unwritten rules is that everybody on the team helps their best teammate maintain their lead. Deep into the stage race, Astana team manager Johann Bruyneel had positioned his team to attempt an unprecedented 1-2-3 victory (Contador first, Lance second, and Kloeden third). To pull this off would require intense teamwork. However, when Contador attacked during stage 17—the final climb of the race—the hopes of a 1-2-3 Astana podium were dashed. The Contador attack occurred 3 kilometers from the summit and less than 20 kilometers from the finish. Until then, the team was in a perfect position to help German teammate Andreas Kloeden move into the top three, as Contador and Kloeden had broken free from the pack along with two members of a rival team, Andy and Frank Schleck of Saxo Bank. But when Contador attacked, his own teammate (Kloeden) was the only one who could not follow, and thus, lost his position and any chance of an all-Astana podium. Instead, two members of another team, Andy and Frank Schleck (Saxo Bank), accelerated to take further time out of Kloeden. By the finish, Kloeden had lost 2 minutes and 27 seconds to the lead trio.[1]

---

[1]Lance calls Contador's late surge "a surprise." (2009, July 10). *Nbcsports.com.* nbcsports.msnbc.com; Murphy, A. (2009, July 13). As tour rests, rivalry between Armstrong and Contador heats up. *Sports Illustrated.* sportsillustrated.cnn.com

In a parallel fashion to cycling, NASCAR is another venue that requires competitors to cooperate in order to win.[2] First, NASCAR imposes engineering restrictions that prevent any driver from attaining a major equipment advantage over rivals. Second, as in cycling, drafting (following the car in front very closely) allows cooperating cars to go faster because there is a remarkable drop in air resistance. As long as two car racers stay in partnership, they can take turns drafting one another and catch up or pass other cars who are not drafting. However, such a partnership does not allow one to win. So, just as Contador pulled out and surged on his own, NASCAR racers are tempted to do the same thing.

Most people are part of teams that work together to achieve a shared goal. In most companies, members need to set aside self-interest to work for their teams. Moreover, teams need to work collaboratively with other groups inside the organization. However, people often do not act in a way that enhances their own team. Teams often view other teams with disdain, making cross-team collaboration difficult. In this chapter, we examine not only how teams get work done but also how they act as important sources of identity for people in organizations. People feel protective of their teams and at the same time feel threatened by the mere presence of other teams in the company. Often, unwitting managers can magnify these processes by fostering competition between teams. In this chapter, we examine individual and team identity, interteam relationships, and biases associated with intergroup conflict. We conclude by outlining strategies for reducing the negative effects of intergroup conflict.

PERSONAL AND TEAM IDENTITY

People define themselves in many ways by the organizations they belong to and the teams they are a member of. For this reason, people naturally seek group affiliations; consequently, the reputation and accomplishments of their teams are a critical source of their self-identity and self-esteem. Indeed, feeling good about ourselves is often dependent upon feeling that our groups are adequate or superior to other groups.[3] Moreover, teams provide people with a buffer against threats and setbacks: When our self-esteem is shaken by personal setbacks, our groups provide us with reassurance and identity.[4] There is a potentially infinite number of group distinctions that people can use to define their identity. The following types of teams and groups are common to many people's identities:

- Gender groups
- Position, level, and class (e.g., rank and how many people supervised)
- Functional unit (e.g., marketing and sales)
- Regional unit (e.g., Midwestern and Northeastern)
- Ethnicity and race

The extent to which a given person identifies with a group occurs on three distinct levels: cognitive, emotional, and behavioral.[5] In other words, people's affiliation with their team affects

---

[2]Ronfeldt, D. (2000). Social science at 190 MPH on NASCAR's biggest superspeedways. *First Monday.* firstmonday.org; Duhigg, C. (2003, February 17). Fortune 500, meet Daytona 500. *Slate Magazine.* slate.com

[3]Tajfel, H., & Turner, J. C. (1986). The social identity theory of intergroup behavior. In S. Worchel & W. G. Austin (Eds.), *Psychology of intergroup relations* (pp. 7–24). Chicago, IL: Nelson-Hall.

[4]Meindl, J. R., & Lerner, M. O. (1984). Exacerbation of extreme responses to an out-group. *Journal of Personality and Social Psychology, 47*(1), 71–84.

[5]Henry, K. B., Arrow, H., & Carini, B. (1999). A tripartite model of group identification: Theory and measurement. *Small Group Research, 30*(5), 558–581.

EXHIBIT 12-1 Three Sources of Group Identity: Emotional, Behavioral, and Cognitive

Source of Identity	Items
Emotional (Affective)	I would prefer to be in a different group. (R)
	Members of this group like one another.
	I enjoy interacting with the members of this group.
	I don't like many of the other people in this group. (R)
Behavioral	In this group, members don't have to rely on one another. (R)
	All members need to contribute to achieve the group's goals.
	This group accomplishes things that no single member could achieve.
	In this group, members do not need to cooperate to complete group tasks. (R)
Cognitive	I think of this group as a part of who I am.
	I see myself as quite different from other members of this group. (R)
	I don't think of this group as part of who I am. (R)
	I see myself as quite similar to other members of this group.

Note: Items with an (R) are reverse scored.
Source: Henry, K. B., Arrow, H., & Carini, B. (1999). A tripartite model of group identification: Theory and measurement. *Small Group Research, 30*(5), 558–581.

how they think, feel, and act. To see how these three aspects of group identity can be measured, see Exhibit 12-1.

Individual, Relational, and Collective Selves

People's self-concepts consist of three fundamental self-representations: the individual self, the relational self, and the collective self. Specifically, people define themselves in terms of their unique traits (individual self), dyadic relationships (relational self), and group and team memberships (collective self).[6]

The **individual self** is realized by differentiating ourselves from others and relies on interpersonal comparison processes and is associated with the motive of protecting or enhancing the person psychologically.[7] The **relational self** is achieved by assimilating with significant others (i.e., relationship partners, parents, friends, siblings, et al.) and is based on personalized bonds of attachment. The **collective self** is achieved by inclusion in large, social groups and contrasting the group to which one belongs with relevant outgroups. These three self-representations coexist within the same person. However, at any given time, one or more of these self-identities may seem relevant. (Exhibit 12-2 is one example of how personal, social, and collective identities are measured.)

---

[6]Brewer, M. B., & Gardner, W. (1996). Who is this "we"? Levels of collective identity and self representations. *Journal of Personality and Social Psychology, 71*, 83–93.
[7]Ibid., p. 324; Markus, H. (1977). Self-schemata and processing information about the self. *Journal of Personality and Social; Psychology, 35*, 63–78.

EXHIBIT 12-2 Aspects of Identity Questionnaire

Instructions: For each of the statements below, indicate how characteristic or true it is for yourself.

1—Not important to my sense of who I am.
2—Slightly important to my sense of who I am.
3—Somewhat important to my sense of who I am.
4—Very important to my sense of who I am.
5—Extremely important to my sense of who I am.

_____   1. My moral standards and personal values.
_____   2. Being popular.
_____   3. Being a part of the many generations of my family.
_____   4. My imagination and dreams.
_____   5. The ways other people react to what I say and do.
_____   6. My race and ethnic background.
_____   7. My personal goals and hopes for the future.
_____   8. My physical appearance.
_____   9. My religion or faith.
_____   10. My feelings and emotions.
_____   11. The reputation I have.
_____   12. Places where I live or where I was raised.
_____   13. My thoughts and ideas.
_____   14. My attractiveness to other people.
_____   15. How I deal with fears and anxieties.
_____   16. Being a unique person, distinct from others.
_____   17. Knowing that I continue to be essentially the same person even though life involves many changes.
_____   18. My gestures and mannerisms, the impression I make on others.
_____   19. My feeling of belonging to my community.
_____   20. My self-knowledge, such as knowing what kind of person I really am.
_____   21. My social behavior, such as the way I act when meeting people.
_____   22. My feeling of pride in my country, being proud to be a citizen.
_____   23. My personal self-evaluation, the private opinion I have of myself.
_____   24. My allegiance on political issues or my political activities.
_____   25. My language, such as my regional accent and a second language that I know.

Note: To score your personal identity, average items: 1, 4, 7, 10, 13, 15, 16, 17, 20, 23
      To score your social identity, average items: 2, 5, 8, 11, 14, 18, 21
      To score your collective identity: average items: 3, 6, 9, 12, 19, 22, 24, 25

Source: Adapted from Cheek, J. M., Tropp, L. R., Chen, L. C., & Underwood, M. K. (1994). *Identity orientations: Personal, social, and collective aspects of identity.* Paper presented at the meeting of the American Psychological Association, Los Angeles, CA.

Independent Versus Interdependent Self-Orientation

We noted in Chapter 1 that a defining characteristic of teamwork is interdependence. Gardner, Gabriel, and Lee distinguish two types of **relational focus** when it comes to teamwork: **independent** and **interdependent**.[8] This distinction is also known as egocentric versus

---

[8]Gardner, W. L., Gabriel, S., & Lee, A. Y. (1999). "I" value freedom, but "we" value relationships: Self-construal priming mirrors cultural differences in judgment. *Psychological Science, 10*(4), 321–326.

sociocentric[9] or individualism versus collectivism.[10] People with an independent outlook focus on the extent to which they are autonomous and unique; in contrast, people with an interdependent outlook focus on the extent to which they are embedded within a larger social network.

In one simple task, people were given a sheet of paper and asked to write 20 statements about themselves, each beginning with "I am."[11] People who are independent in their relational orientation tend to write statements that describe their inner values, attributes, and appearance (e.g., ambitious, creative, and muscular). People who are interdependent tend to write statements that describe themselves in relation to others and their social roles (e.g., father, son, and community member).

Whether a team member views herself as independent or interdependent influences the motivations she has and how she achieves her goals.[12] Our cultural values influence our world outlook. Most North Americans value independence and autonomy, show a great disdain for conformity, and seek to be unique. In contrast, Asians value interdependence and collectivity, show a disdain for uniqueness, and seek conformity.[13] However, even within a culture, there is variation in individualism versus collectivism. For example, within the United States, people in the Deep South are more collectivistic and those in the Mountain West and Great Plains are most individualistic.[14]

Perhaps even more striking is the fact that interdependence and independence can be activated within one person at any given time. For example, in one investigation, some people were instructed to read a paragraph containing primarily independent pronouns (e.g., *I*, *me*, and *mine*); in contrast, other people read identical paragraphs that contained collective pronouns (e.g., *we*, *us*, and *ours*); then, motivations and behaviors were examined.[15] European Americans who read collectivist pronouns (*we*, *us*, and *ours*) shifted toward collectivist values and judgments.

Self-Interest Versus Group Interest

One of the most important challenges of effective teamwork is the fact that people often focus only on self-interest rather than team interests. In many groups, self- and team-interests are at odds. One deterrent of self-interest is the extent to which a person feels "identified" with his team. Strengthening group identity (rather than personal identity) increases the value that people attach to their team's welfare versus their personal welfare.[16] When groups receive performance

---

[9]Schweder, R. A., & Bourne, E. J. (1984). Does the concept of the person vary cross-culturally? In R. A. Schweder & R. A. LeVine (Eds.), *Culture theory: Essays on mind, self and emotion* (pp. 158–199). New York/Cambridge, MA: Cambridge University Press.

[10]Triandis, H. C. (1989). Cross-cultural studies of individualism and collectivism. In J. J. Berman (Ed.), *Cross-cultural perspectives: Nebraska symposium on motivation* (Vol. 37, pp. 41–133). Lincoln, NE: University of Nebraska Press.

[11]Gabriel, S., & Gardner, W. L. (1999). Are there his and hers types of interdependence? The implications of gender differences in collective versus relational interdependence for affect, behavior, and cognition. *Journal of Personality and Social Psychology, 77*, 642–655.

[12]Markus, H. R., & Kitayama, S. (1991, April). Culture and the self: Implications for cognition, emotion, and motivation. *Psychological Review, 98*(2), 224–253; Morris, M. W., Podolny, J. M., & Ariel, S. (2000). Missing relations: Incorporating relational constructs into models of culture. In P. C. Earley & H. Singh (Eds.), *Innovations in international and cross-cultural management* (pp. 52–90). Thousand Oaks, CA: Sage Publications.

[13]Kim, H., & Markus, H. R. (1999). Deviance or uniqueness, harmony or conformity? A cultural analysis. *Journal of Personality and Social Psychology, 77*(4), 785–800.

[14]Vandello, J. A., & Cohen, D. (1999). Patterns of individualism and collectivism across the United States. *Journal of Personality and Social Psychology, 77*(2), 279–292.

[15]Gardner, Gabriel, & Lee, " 'I' value freedom, but 'we' value relationships."

[16]De Cremer, D., & Van Vugt, M. (1999). Social identification effects in social dilemmas: A transformation of motives. *Journal of Experimental Social Psychology, 29*, 871–893.

feedback, teams that have strong group identities show an increase in group-level interest.[17] However, if personal identity, rather than team identity, is salient, members will act in a more self-interested fashion.

Ingroups and Outgroups

Team members categorize themselves and others in terms of ingroups and outgroups. In short: "Are you one of us or one of them?" People consider ingroups to be people who are like themselves or who belong to the same groups; outgroups are people who are not in their group or who are members of competitor groups. However, the distinction between ingroups and outgroups is subjective. Consider Exhibit 12-3, in which one sees progressively more and more inclusive ways to categorize oneself. At the very basic level, a person might see himself or herself as an individual. At another level, a person might see himself or herself as a member of a particular team. At still another level, a person might see himself or herself as a member of a unit or functional area. One's chronic way of perceiving ingroups and outgroups affects one's behavior. Simply stated: A person who identifies with the company is going to engage in more cooperative behavior when interacting with a person from a different group because his or her self-identity is defined at the company level. In contrast is a person who sees oneself primarily in terms of one's team membership or individual identity. In one investigation, some people were told to think of themselves as individuals and others to think of themselves as group members. The group

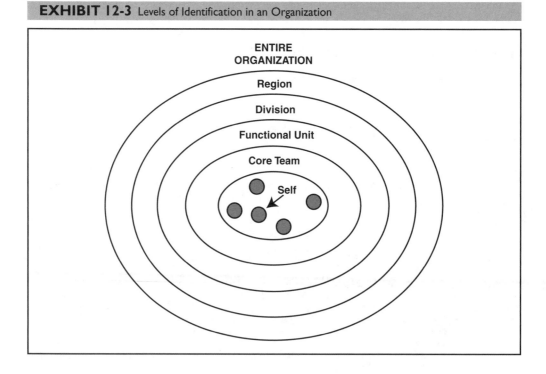

EXHIBIT 12-3 Levels of Identification in an Organization

orientation led to more generous, voluntary contributions of resources in a resource dilemma situation.[18] People are more satisfied when conflict occurs at a superordinate level (i.e., involving the entire group) rather than at the intragroup level (involving competition between different subgroups within the team).[19]

People's perceptions of themselves and their groups can expand and contract. The more narrowly we define our groups, the more competitive and self-serving our behavior. Conversely, when we focus on the larger collective, we are more cooperative. The challenge for the team leader is to carefully balance "team spirit" with the competition that will naturally arise when the team sets itself apart from the rest of the company.

Optimal Distinctiveness Theory

The theory of optimal distinctiveness is a theory of collective social identity.[20] The theory was developed to explain why people seek and maintain conceptualizations of the self that extend to the collective level.[21] A person's collective identity derives from the interplay of two opposing social motives: inclusion and differentiation. On the one hand, people desire to be included in larger social collectives and teams. However, people also want to feel distinct or different from others. The two motives act as opposing drives. For example, as a person becomes immersed in their project team, the need for inclusion decreases (e.g., when they find themselves eating all meals with their team as they furiously attempt to meet a client deadline). However, the motive to differentiate himself or herself increases. Conversely, as a person moves toward disconnection from a team (perhaps after the engagement ends), the need for inclusion increases. The optimal collective social identity meets a person's need for inclusion by assimilating with groups and teams and serves a need for differentiation by distinguishing oneself from others.

Balancing the Need to Belong and the Need to Be Distinct

Most people seek an **optimal distinctiveness** to their self-identities, such that they want to be neither too different nor too similar to others.[22] Personal identity is the individuated self—those characteristics that differentiate one person from others in a given team. Social identities are categorizations of the self into more inclusive social units that effectively depersonalize the self-concept, where *I* becomes *we*. For most people, the self-concept is expandable and contractible, such that some of the time, we want to be distinct from our team; other times, we want to be part of the group. Within an organization, the need to belong is often fulfilled through our primary team affiliations. The need for distinctiveness is often met through intergroup comparisons—in other words, teams may compare themselves with other teams within

---

[18]Brewer, M. B., & Kramer, R. M. (1986). Choice behavior in social dilemmas: Effects of social identity, group size, and decision framing. *Journal of Personality and Social Psychology, 50*(3), 543–549.

[19]Duck, J. M., & Fielding, K. S. (1999). Leaders and subgroups: One of us or one of them? *Group Processes and Intergroup Relations, 2*(3), 203–230.

[20]Brewer, M. (1991). The social self: On being the same and different at the same time. *Personality and Social Psychology Bulletin, 17*(5), 475–482; Brewer, M. (1993). The role of distinctiveness in social identity and group behavior. In M. A. Hogg & D. Abrams (Eds.), *Group motivation: Social psychological perspectives*. New York: Harvester Wheatsheaf.

[21]Turner, J. C. (1987). A self-categorization theory. In J. C. Turner, M. A. Hogg, P. J. Oakes, S. D. Reicher, & M. Witherell (Eds.), *Rediscovering the social group: A self-categorization theory* (pp. 42–67). Oxford, UK: Basil Blackwell; Brewer, M. B., & Roccas, S. (2001). Individual values, social identity, and optimal distinctiveness. In C. Sedikidess   & M. B. Brewer (Eds.), *Individual self, relational self, collective self* (pp. 219–237). Philadelphia, PA: Psychology Press.

[22]Brewer, "The social self."

a company. One implication of the optimal distinctiveness model is that to secure loyalty, teams must not only satisfy members' needs for affiliation and belonging within a group but must also maintain clear boundaries that differentiate them from other groups. The balance of individual versus social identities also affects people's behavior. For example, when faced with a conflict between making a profit for themselves and helping to preserve a collective resource, people who feel a need to belong are more likely to contribute to the greater good, whereas those who need to feel distinct act in a self-interested fashion.[23]

Although there is not a perfect negative correlation between group size and distinctiveness, if the vast majority of people in an organization are not sufficiently differentiated, they will often mobilize into minority groups to meet their distinctiveness needs. Members of low-status groups are faced with a double conflict between positive social identity and distinctiveness in a way that is more difficult for them to resolve than in the case of high-status majority members.[24] On the one hand, members of minority groups can dissociate themselves from their group membership and seek positive identity elsewhere, but this threatens their distinctiveness. On the other hand, they can embrace their distinctive group identity but may not enjoy the positive evaluations that come from the majority.[25]

Intrateam and Interteam Respect

Because teams are so important for one's identity, it is important for the members to feel respected and accepted by their teams. The implications of respect extend far beyond the self-esteem of the members; people who don't feel respected by their team are not as loyal to their team and not as committed.[26] Conversely, respected members of "devalued" groups (organizational groups that have low status and prestige) are the most likely to donate their time to their team and work to improve its image, rather than their personal image.[27] In contrast, disrespected members of prestigious groups invest in group activity only if they might improve their personal image.

INTERTEAM RELATIONSHIPS

People derive a part of their identity from their teams, and identity is flexible—meaning that in some situations people see themselves as part of the team, but in others they need to distinguish themselves from their team. Given that organizations are composed of multiple teams, each with its own identity, what might we expect in the way of interteam relationships?

Social Comparison

Consider a situation in which you are a member of a team that has little organizational support within your company. Your team competes with two other groups in your organization—one is a disadvantaged group (they don't have a lot of organizational support and resources), and the

[23]Caporael, L. R., Dawes, R. M., Orbell, J. M., & van de Kragt, A. J. C. (1989). Selfishness examined: Cooperation in the absence of egoistic incentives. *Behavioral and Brain Sciences, 12*, 683–739.

[24]Brewer, "The social self."

[25]Steele, S. (1990). *The content of our character: A new vision of race in America* (pp. 111–125). New York: St. Martin's Press.

[26]Barreto, M., & Ellemers, N. (2002). The impact of respect versus neglect of self-identities on identification and group loyalty. *Personality and Social Psychology Bulletin, 28*(5), 629–639.

[27]Branscombe, N. R., Spears, R., Ellemers, N., & Doosje, B. (2002). Intragroup and intergroup evaluation effects on group behavior. *Personality and Social Psychology Bulletin, 28*(6), 744–753.

other is an advantaged group (they have much organizational support and many resources).[28] The performance of the disadvantaged team changes over time, so that it becomes either equal, worse, or better than your team's performance. How would you feel? Social comparison theory predicts that when a comparable team in your organization performs similarly to or better than your team, the identity of your team is threatened.[29] Under such conditions, your team might be most likely to discriminate against (i.e., hurt) other disadvantaged teams that perform similarly to or better than your own team. Conversely, your team is most helpful and supportive of other teams whose performance deteriorates over time—because such groups provide positive social comparison for your group (i.e., they make your team look good). In contrast, the "advantaged" outgroup is not as much of a threat to your team (because it is not easily comparable). Thus, teams are more likely to harm and discriminate against disadvantaged groups when their performance increases—thus threatening one's own team's performance.[30]

Social comparison also occurs when people act on behalf of their team. For example, people work harder when they are being outperformed by an outgroup instead of ingroup member.[31] Similarly, when peoples' individual performance is compared to a lower-status outgroup member than a higher-status one, they work harder.[32] Low-status outgroup members are especially threatening for peoples' self-esteem.

Team Discontinuity Effect

The team discontinuity effect refers to the fact that people in teams behave more competitively toward one another than do individuals, holding constant the task and stake involved.[33] Further, the size of the group does not matter; both small and large groups are demonstrably more competitive with one another than are individuals.[34] For example, when people play against each other in prisoner's-dilemma-type games, they are not particularly competitive, averaging only 6.6 percent competitive responses over the course of the game. However, when a group plays against another group, competition rises to 53.5 percent over all the moves.[35] This suggests that even though most people may prefer to cooperate when they are in teams, a competitive orientation takes over.

---

[28]Rothgerber, H., & Worchel, S. (1997). The view from below: Intergroup relations from the perspective of the disadvantaged group. *Journal of Personality and Social Psychology, 73*(6), 1191–1205.

[29]Crocker, J., & Major, B. (1989). Social stigma and self-esteem: The self-protective properties of stigma. *Psychological Review, 96*, 608–630.

[30]Rothgerber & Worchel, "The view from below."

[31]Lount, R. B., & Phillips, K. W. (2007). Working harder with the out-group: The impact of social category diversity on motivation gains. *Organizational Behavior and Human Decision Processes, 103*(2), 214–224.

[32]Pettit, N. C., & Lount, R. B., Jr. (2010). Looking down and ramping up: The impact of status differences on effort in intergroup settings. *Journal of Experimental Social Psychology, 46*(1), 9–20.

[33]Sedikides, C., Insko, C. A., & Schopler J. (Eds.). (1998). *Intergroup cognition and intergroup behavior.* New Jersey: Erlbaum; Carnevale, P. J., Pruitt, D., & Seilheimmer, S. (1981). Looking and competing: Accountability and visual access in integrative bargaining. *Journal of Personality and Social Psychology, 40*, 111–120; Insko, C., Pinkley, R., Hoyle, R., Dalton, B., Hong, G., Slim, R., Landry, P., Holton, B., Ruffin, P., & Thibaut, J. (1987). Individual versus group discontinuity: The role of a consensus rule. *Journal of Experimental Social Psychology, 23*, 250–267; McCallum, D., Harring, K., Gilmore, R., Drenan, S., Chase, J., Insko, C., & Thibaut, J. (1985). Competition and cooperation between groups and between individuals. *Journal of Experimental Social Psychology, 21*, 301–320; van Oostrum, J., & Rabbie, J. M. (1995). Intergroup competition and cooperation within autocratic and democratic management regimes. *Small Group Research, 26*(2), 269–295.

[34]McGlynn, R. P., Harding, D. J., & Cottle, J. L. (2009). Individual–group discontinuity in group–individual interactions: Does size matter? *Group Processes & Intergroup Relations, 12*(1), 129–143.

[35]Insko et al. "Individual versus group discontinuity."

Team Rivalry

Companies often try to create (healthy) rivalry between different groups and departments within the organization. Sometimes, there are substantial economic and status-based rewards. What is the effect of competition on team rivalry? First, the degree of competition between rival teams depends on how close they are in terms of competitiveness on the key dimension. For example, people become more competitive and less willing to maximize overall company gains when they and their rivals are highly ranked (e.g., number 2 or number 3) than when they are not (e.g., number 202 or number 203).[36] The degree of competition between rivals also increases when other meaningful standards are introduced, such as the bottom of a ranking scale or a qualitative threshold in the middle of a scale. Millions of viewers watch a classic model of team rivalry on the NBC television show *The Apprentice*. Each week contestants are placed into teams and given a task. The winning team receives an exclusive reward, while Donald Trump decides which team member from the losing team will be fired.

Vicarious Retribution occurs when people who are not directly harmed by a rival group nonetheless seek retribution against members of that outgroup, who were not the original perpetrators of the initial attack on the ingroup.[37] The more highly identified people are with their ingroup, the more they engage in vicarious retribution. The desire to talk about power is greater among members of disadvantaged rather than advantaged group.[38] And, highly identified members of disadvantaged groups want to talk about power more; whereas members of advantaged groups generally prefer to talk about commonalities between groups.

Postmerger Behavior

In most organizations, groups cannot always choose to maintain their distinct identity. For better or for worse, they must undergo mergers and reorganizations. Some mergers occur internally and some occur through external means (e.g., acquisitions). Although mergers between groups are quite common, more than half result in negative consequences, such as stress, turnover, and productivity loss.[39] Moreover, the negative effects of ingroup bias may be heightened when companies merge (see Exhibit 12-4). Anticipated mergers between groups can be viewed as the ultimate threat to group distinctiveness in that premerger boundaries are undermined and group members must lose their premerger identity.[40] In 2000, America Online (AOL) merged with Time Warner in the largest merger in American history. But what was hailed then as a historic moment in new media dissolved a decade later when Time Warner finally spun off AOL— leaving the companies at about one-seventh of their worth on the day of the merger. Besides massive job losses, decimation of retirement accounts, and investigations by the Securities and

---

[36]Garcia, S. M., Tor, A., & Gonzales, R. (2006). Ranks and rivals: A theory of competition. *Personality and Social Psychology Bulletin, 32*(7), 970–982.

[37]Stenstrom, D. M., Lickel, B., Denson, T. F., & Miller, N. (2008). The Roles of ingroup identification and outgroup entitativity in intergroup retribution. *Personality and Social Psychology Bulletin, 34*(11), 1570–1582.

[38]Saguy, T., Dovidio, J. F., & Pratto, F. (2008). Beyond contact: Intergroup contact in the context of power relations. *Personality and Social Psychology Bulletin, 34*, 432–445.

[39]Mottola, G. R., Bachman, B. A., Gaertner, S. L., & Dovidio, J. F. (1997). How groups merge: The effects of merger integration patterns on anticipated commitment to the merged organization. *Journal of Applied Social Psychology, 27*, 1335–1358; Schweiger, D. M., & Walsh, J. P. (1990). Mergers and acquisitions: An interdisciplinary view. In K. M. Rowland & G. R. Ferris (Eds.), *Research in personnel and human resource management* (Vol. 8, pp. 41–107). Greenwich, CT: JAI Press.

[40]Terry, D. J., Carey, C. J., & Callan, V. J. (2001). Employee adjustment to an organizational merger. *Personality and Social Psychology Bulletin, 27*(3), 267–280.

EXHIBIT 12-4 Ingroup Bias in Response to an Organizational Merger

Employees from two hospitals were studied during the period of planning for a merger. One hospital was higher in status than the other hospital—a common issue that occurs when firms merge. How did the proposed merger affect intergroup relations between the two hospitals? A merger between two previously independent organizations made employees' premerger group membership more salient, and the unequal status issues meant an accentuation of intergroup status differences. There was clear evidence of an ingroup ("we are better than they are") bias, particularly among the low-status employees. Why? Employees of the lower-status organization may have been particularly threatened by the merger situation and, therefore, more likely to engage in a high level of ingroup bias—a form of identity protection. High-status employees rated the ingroup far better than the low-status hospital on status-relevant dimensions (high prestige in the community, challenging job opportunities, and high variety in patient type). In contrast, the low-status employees engaged in greater ingroup bias on the status-irrelevant dimensions (degree of industrial unrest, good relations between staff, good communication by management, relaxed work environment, and modern patient accommodations). The question is: Why? High-status employees were motivated to acknowledge their position of relatively high status. In contrast, the low-status employees, motivated by a desire to attain positive social identity, focused on dimensions that did not highlight the status differential that existed between the hospitals. Indeed, low-status employees recognized the superior status of the high-status hospital, and high-status employees were especially generous when evaluating the low-status group on dimensions that are irrelevant to status. Yet the amount of ingroup bias that the low-status employees exhibited on the status-irrelevant dimensions exceeded the extent to which the high-status employees were willing to acknowledge the strengths of the low-status employees on these dimensions.

Source: Terry, D. J., & Callan, V. J. (1998). In-group bias in response to an organizational merger. *Group Dynamics: Theory, Research, and Practice, 2*(2), 67–81.

Exchange Commission and Justice Department, the postmerger sides just didn't seem to like one another. A division president at Time Warner said, " . . . if we're the crown jewel, why are all our best and most important people leaving here and going to New York?"

Timothy Boggs, head of government relations at Time, who learned of the deal at 8 a.m. on the morning of the merger, said, " . . . I saw AOL in a much less favorable light, much more opportunistic, made up of folks who were really trying to merely exploit the market they were in as opposed to developing something that was enduring, and I was very leery about this deal."[41]

The threat of a merger depends on the status of the group. For low-status organizational groups, a merger with a high-status group might provide opportunities to obtain higher status.[42] And, indeed, members of low-status groups are motivated to undermine boundaries with the high-status outgroup to improve the status of their group.[43] On the other hand, low-status groups resist mergers when the status differences remain salient between groups or when they expect not to be adequately represented in the merged group.[44] High-status groups are accepting of mergers, except when they fear that mergers will undermine their group's superior

[41]Arango, T. (2010, January 11). How the AOL—Time Warner merger went so wrong. *New York Times*, p. B1.

[42]Hornsey, M. J., & Hogg, M. A. (2002). The effects of status on subgroup relations. *British Journal of Social Psychology, 41*, 203–218.

[43]Jetten, J., Spears, R., Hogg, M. A., & Manstead, A. S. R. (2000). Discrimination constrained and justified: The variable effects of group variability and ingroup identification. *Journal of Experimental Social Psychology, 36*, 329–356.

[44]Van Knippenberg, D., Van Knippenberg, B., Monden, L., & De Lima, F. (2002). Organizational identification after a merger: A social identity perspective. *British Journal of Social Psychology, 44*, 233–262.

position.[45] During an organizational merger, high-status groups may feel less threatened than low-status groups.[46] Low-status groups feel most negative about mergers—as based on studies of airline companies and scientific organizations.[47]

Not surprisingly, leaders play an important role in defining the relationship between the pre-merger groups. And, as might be expected, group members prefer an ingroup leader over an outgroup one, and the ingroup leader will favor the ingroup.[48] However, members of high-status groups do not show preference for an ingroup leader.[49] Leaders have four choices when it comes to balancing ingroups and outgroups: They can treat both groups equally, favor the ingroup, favor the outgroup, or behave in a complementary fashion, by favoring one group over the other on particular dimensions.[50] Ingroup leaders are evaluated more favorably and are more likely to engender a common identity in the merged group when they behave in an ingroup-favoring fashion or in a complementary fashion.[51]

Intergroup Conflict

Just as there can be conflict among members within a team, there can be conflict and competition between teams. As noted in Chapter 8, there are two types of conflict between teams: realistic and symbolic.[52] We explain these concepts in more detail here.

REALISTIC CONFLICT   This type of conflict erupts when teams compete over scarce resources. For example, teams in one company might compete over assignments, clients, space (i.e., real estate), or ability to hire new personnel. Realistic group conflict involves competition between groups for the same resources (e.g., teams that compete over new hires, office space, assignments, territory, information, contacts, and, of course, remuneration). Groups in organizations prefer to be the "haves" rather than the "have nots," so they take steps to achieve two interrelated outcomes: (1) attaining the desired resources and (2) preventing other groups from reaching their goals.[53] As competition persists, teams perceive one another in increasingly negative ways, and competition often leads to direct and open conflict.

As another example, consider the conflict between Andersen Consulting (now Accenture) and Arthur Andersen. Prior to the schism between the companies, each group felt justified in claiming a greater share of the profit stream. Andersen Consulting, the smaller of the two groups, was highly profitable and felt justified in demanding more resources. Arthur Andersen, the

[45]Terry, Carey, & Callan, "Employee adjustment to an organizational merger."

[46]Terry, D. J., & O'Brien, A. T. (2001). Status, legitimacy, and ingroup bias in the context of an organizational merger. *Group Processes and Intergroup Relations, 4*, 271–289.

[47]Terry, Carey, & Callan, "Employee adjustment to an organizational merger," p. 333; Terry & O'Brien, "Status, legitimacy, and ingroup bias in the context of an organizational merger," p. 333.

[48]Duck & Fielding, "Leaders and subgroups."

[49]Jetten, J., Duck, J., Terry, D. J., & O'Brien, A. (2001). When groups merge: Low- and high-status groups' responses to aligned leaders. Unpublished raw data, University of Exeter.

[50]Jetten, J., Duck, J., Terry, D. J., & O'Brien, A. (2002). Being attuned to intergroup differences in mergers: The role of aligned leaders for low-status groups. *Personality and Social Psychology Bulletin, 28*(9), 1194–1201.

[51]Ibid.

[52]Bobo, L. (1983). Whites' opposition to busing: Symbolic racism or realistic group conflict? *Journal of Personality and Social Psychology, 45*(6), 1196–1210.

[53]Campbell, D. T. (1965). Ethnocentric and other altruistic motives. In D. Levine (Ed.), *Nebraska symposium on motivation* (pp. 283–311). Lincoln, NE: University of Nebraska Press; LeVine, R. A., & Campbell, D. T. (1972). *Ethnocentrism: Theories of conflict, ethnic attitudes and group behavior.* New York: John Wiley & Sons.

founding company, saw the situation quite differently, arguing that the opportunities Arthur Andersen provided (e.g., clients and infrastructure) entitled it to a greater share of profits. The two firms split after a bitter court case.

One disadvantage of realistic group conflict is that group members often must be extremely vigilant about possible threats to the protected resource. Teams that are involved in realistic conflict with other groups must divide valuable material and psychological resources between foraging activity and risk-monitoring activity. For example, at a well-known research institution, laboratories competed viciously for parking space for their research participants. Several laboratory groups became convinced that other groups were "stealing" their parking spaces. This led some groups to hire full-time assistants to monitor the parking lot and even to install outdoor cameras. In many groups, only a subset of members engage in risk-monitoring, whereas others are able to fully focus on enjoying the resource.[54]

SYMBOLIC CONFLICT   This conflict exists independent of resource scarcity; it reflects fundamental differences in values. Such conflict in organizations does not seem to have its roots in resource scarcity; rather, it stems from fundamental differences in values or beliefs (e.g., team members in sales think marketing is dumb). Symbolic conflict involves differences of beliefs. (For an example of symbolic conflict and its independence from economic interests, see Exhibit 12-5.)

It is often the presence of an outside threat that can lead to greater feelings of cohesion and homogeneity within a group. For example, when group members believed that a team from a rival institution was biased against them, the members of the group saw themselves as being more similar than different—an important ingredient for cohesion.[55] Indeed, when a person's social identity is threatened, people try to reduce the threat and restore a positive and distinct social identity.[56] This cuts both ways, in terms of internal threat decreasing cohesion. For example, when group members believe that other team members think negatively of the team, they see the group members as dissimilar from one another.[57] Even thinking negative thoughts about one's own team leads to feelings of dissimilarity from the team. For example, when German team members were asked to list negative (compared with positive) attributes of their group, they described themselves as being less similar to the team as a whole.[58]

MIXED-MOTIVE CONFLICT   Most conflicts, whether they are realistic or symbolic, represent mixed-motive conflicts, particularly when they occur between groups in an organization. Mixed-motive conflicts involve a combination of cooperation and competition. Simply said, teams have a desire to cooperate because they all work for the same company but simultaneously feel they are in competition with other teams.

---

[54]Kameda, T., & Tamura, R. (2007). "To eat or not to be eaten?" Collective risk-monitoring in groups. *Journal of Experimental Social Psychology, 43*(2), 168–179.

[55]Rothgerber, H. (1997). External intergroup threat as an antecedent to perceptions of in-group and out-group homogeneity. *Journal of Personality and Social Psychology, 73*(6), 1206–1212.

[56]Tajfel & Turner, "The social identity theory of intergroup behavior."

[57]Doosje, B., Spears, R., & Koomen, W. (1995). When bad isn't all bad: Strategic use of sample information in generalization and stereotyping. *Journal of Personality and Social Psychology, 69*, 642–655.

[58]Simon, B., Pantaleo, G., & Mummendey, A. (1995). Unique individual or interchangeable group member? The accentuation of intragroup differences versus similarities as an indicator of the individual self versus the collective self. *Journal of Personality and Social Psychology, 69*, 106–119.

EXHIBIT 12-5 Symbolic Conflict and Busing

Sears and Allen examined a controversial issue—busing. *Busing* is a shorthand term meant to refer to the transportation of children in a city to different schools so as to achieve racial balance. Whereas traditionally, children attend schools based on their housing district, busing attempts to even out the racial mix. Obviously, parents of children who are being bused could claim to have economic interests—their children's welfare is clearly affected in their eyes. People who don't have children, however, would most likely not have any economic interest in busing. However, Sears and Allen found that people whose lives were not affected by busing made strong protests against it. Thus, they concluded that busing does not represent an economic issue but rather a symbolic issue.

Source: Sears, D. O., & Allen, H. M., Jr. (1984). The trajectory of local desegregation controversies and whites' opposition to busing. In N. Miller & M. Brewer (Eds.), *Groups in contact: The psychology of desegregation* (pp. 123–151). New York: Academic Press.

EXTREMISM   Inevitably, conflicts occur between groups, teams, and factions. Groups on opposite sides of a conflict tend to see the other side as being extremist. Members of teams exaggerate the degree of conflict they actually have with other teams and groups—opposing groups typically assume that the difference between the two sides' attitudes is 1.5 to 4 times greater than the actual difference. This means, of course, that escalation of interteam conflict is often more illusion than reality. As an example, consider the Western Canon debate—a dispute over the choice of books in introductory civilization and literature courses that has divided faculty and students within many universities, such as Stanford, Michigan, and the University of California, Berkeley. There are two sides in the debate: traditionalists and revisionists. Traditionalists advocate preserving the prominence of the traditional canon; revisionists advocate teaching more works by female and minority authors.

To measure the degree of conflict between traditionalists and revisionists, English teachers in California were asked to select 15 books from a list of 50 for their own course and to indicate which books they believed the "other side" would want. Traditionalists predicted that they would have no books in common. In actuality, traditionalists and revisionists had almost 50 percent—or seven books—in common![59]

Careful inspection of group members' perceptions, however, reveals a striking asymmetry in the accuracy of misperception: The status quo, or the group in power, is much less accurate than a group that is not in power. Traditionalists predicted no overlap in book choices, whereas revisionists predicted a six-book overlap. Why is this?

Majority group members typically enjoy benefits of greater power. They are prone to exaggerate the views of their own and the other side. Minority group members are perceived by both sides to be more extremist than majority group members. For example, high-status social group members judge the personality and emotions of other members less accurately than do low-status group members.[60] In contrast, high-status members' emotions are more accurately judged by both low- and high-status members.

BIASES ASSOCIATED WITH INTERGROUP CONFLICT

Groups that are embroiled in interteam conflict do not always look at their situations objectively. In fact, they sometimes suffer from serious biases or misassumptions. Bias and prejudice are common in organizations and adversely affect the ability of teams and their organizations to accomplish their goals. Below are biases that should be identified and dealt with.

Stereotyping

Stereotyping occurs when people categorize others on the basis of superficial information. When we stereotype someone, we don't consider their individuality; rather, we make assumptions about them on the basis of their similarity to a social group. Several negative stereotypes exist about social groups, such as racial groups and functional groups in companies. Stereotypes are detrimental for understanding people as individuals. A longitudinal investigation of architecture, engineering, and construction management teams engaged in designing and planning a $5 million construction project revealed that team members relied on early impressions of others.[61] Specifically, team members tended to make snap judgments about how trustworthy a given team member was and then they used that information to make a judgment as to whether that team member delivered on his or her commitments. Further, judgments of trustworthiness were relatively stable over time.

Categorization: Us Versus Them

Even when natural categories and teams don't exist in an organization, people will create them. The tendency to create ingroups and outgroups is known as the "need for categorization." In fact, from the first few microseconds of perception, people begin the categorization process. When we

---

[59]Robinson, R. J., & Keltner, D. (1996). Much ado about nothing? Revisionists and traditionalists choose an introductory English syllabus. *Psychological Science, 7*(1), 18–24.

[60]Gruenfeld, D. H., Keltner, D. J., & Anderson, C. (2003). The effects of power on those who possess it: An interpersonal perspective on social cognition. In G. Bodenhausen & A. Lambert (Eds.), *Foundations of social cognition: A festschrift in honor of Robert S. Wyer, Jr.* Mahwah, NJ: Erlbaum.

[61]Zolin, R., Hinds, P. J., Fruchter, R., & Levitt, R. E. (2004). Interpersonal trust in cross-functional, geographically distributed work: A longitudinal study. *Information and Organization, 14*(1), 1–26.

meet a person for the first time, we immediately (and unconsciously) classify them according to gender, race, age, and so forth. Whereas this may seem harmless (as well as natural), it essentially means that we rely on stereotypes to guide our impression of someone. Consequently, we see others as conforming more to stereotypes than is warranted. Furthermore, even when given an opportunity to consider stereotypical and nonstereotypical information about someone, we preferentially attend to stereotype-confirming, rather than disconfirming, information. Additionally, when we can question a person directly, we usually seek to confirm our stereotypical beliefs.[62]

To see how readily people categorize others, consider the following investigations:

• *Case 1:*   In a room of adults who do not know one another, a box containing two kinds of cards is passed around. One kind of cards is labeled "alphas" and the other "betas." Each person randomly draws a card from the box. Two groups are formed on the basis of an obviously arbitrary procedure. Members of each do not speak or communicate in any form with the members of the other group, nor do they talk among themselves. They are a group in name only. Nevertheless, in a subsequent evaluation period, members of each group rate the members of their own group as superior on a number of dimensions relative to members of the other group.[63]

• *Case 2:*   In a room of adults who do not know one another, each person is presented with a page containing several dots and then asked to estimate the total number of dots on the page. Two groups are then formed: those who allegedly underestimate the actual number of dots on the page and those who overestimate the dots.[64] When group members are subsequently asked to evaluate the competence, intelligence, creativity, and personal qualities of both groups, they favor their own group—even though they have not communicated with the other members of their group and dot estimation is nondiagnostic.

• *Case 3:*   In simulated negotiations between Stanford and Cornell MBA students, each group awards the other significantly fewer stock options when given the opportunity.[65] Furthermore, group members reject options that would pay both teams extremely well; instead, team members seemed more intent on creating large payment differences, rather than maximizing their own welfare.

In all the preceding examples, when people categorize the world into two or more groups and then face the task of evaluating or judging these groups, they uniformly favor their own group. Ingroup bias, or the favorable treatment of one's own group and the subsequent harming of other groups, is rooted in feelings of threat. Specifically, when people or teams feel threatened by the presence or performance of another group, they are likely to show bias.[66]

There are a number of consequences of categorization. First, the benefits: Categorization can clearly help groups achieve their goals and protect their interests. For example, in the competitive business of new product development, teams need to know who they are talking to.

---

[62]Snyder, M. (1984). When belief creates reality. In L. Berkowitz (Ed.), *Advances in experimental social psychology* (Vol. 18, pp. 248–306). New York: Academic Press.

[63]Brewer, M. (1979). Ingroup bias in the minimal intergroup situation: A cognitive-motivational analysis. *Psychological Bulletin, 86,* 307–324; Tajfel, H. (1982). Social psychology of intergroup relations. *Annual Review of Psychology, 33,* 1–39; Tajfel & Turner, "The social identity theory of intergroup behavior," p. 324.

[64]Bettencourt, B. A., Brewer, M. B., Croak, M. R., & Miller, N. (1992). Cooperation and the reduction of intergroup bias: The role of reward structure and social orientation. *Journal of Experimental Social Psychology, 28*(4), 301–319.

[65]Thompson, L., Valley, K. L., & Kramer, R. M. (1995). The bittersweet feeling of success: An examination of social perception in negotiation. *Journal of Experimental Social Psychology, 31*(6), 467–492.

[66]Flippen, A. R., Hornstein, H. A., Siegal, W. E., & Weitzman, E. A. (1996). A comparison of similarity and interdependence as triggers for in-group formation. *Personality and Social Psychology Bulletin, 22*(9), 882–893.

Second, categorizing people simply makes life easier because we can take their point of view. Thus, there are some clear benefits of categorization. However, there are some downsides that teams need to know about: First, we evaluate members of outgroups much more extremely. Second, we use stereotypes to predict people's behavior.

Ingroup Bias (or "We Are Better Than Them")

People don't just segment the world into ingroup and outgroup members. Once they categorize others, they view members of their own group more favorably than those of the outgroup. The **ingroup bias** effect is so strong that members of groups systematically judge their group members to be better than the group average and above the median on a variety of social traits, even when all the members are judged consecutively![67] When this occurs at a group level, it is called ingroup bias; when it occurs at the level of nations, regions, or ethic categories, it is called **ethnocentrism**.[68] Ingroup bias—the universal strong liking for one's own group and the simultaneous negative evaluation of outgroups—generates a set of stereotypes in which each group sees itself as good and the outgroup as bad, even when both groups engage in the same behaviors.[69] For example, the beliefs that "we are loyal; they are clannish" or "we are brave and willing to defend our rights; they are hostile and arrogant" are examples of the double standards. **Collective narcissism** refers to an emotional investment in an unrealistic belief about one's own group's greatness; the greater the groups' collective narcissism, the more aggressive they are toward outgroups.[70] Ingroup and outgroup distinctions have implications for leadership as well. For example, when a leader is aligned with a perceived outgroup, people expect that leader to favor the outgroup (even if she actually does not).[71]

In one investigation, teams were involved in an engaging task (making art posters).[72] The teams then underwent reorganizations in which new members were added or deleted from either the same source group (ingroup exchange) or a different source group (outgroup exchange). Posters were then evaluated for quality. Posters were evaluated much more generously when ingroup, rather than outgroup, reorganizations occurred, especially when team members identified strongly with their source group. When every group received an (bogus) identical negative evaluation of its poster, the bogus criticism was more upsetting when ingroup rather than outgroup exchanges were made.

Ingroup bias also effects the selection and evaluation of team members. Despite a verbal preference for people who behave in an "egalitarian" way, people actually prefer others to display ingroup bias.[73] **Implicit ingroup metafavoritism** refers to the fact that we prefer ingroup members to display ingroup bias. And, we also prefer that authorities in our organizations to be ingroup members. We expect ingroup authorities to favor our groups; people react more angrily

---

[67]Klar, Y. (2002). Way beyond compare: Nonselective superiority and inferiority biases in judging randomly assigned group members relative to their peers. *Journal of Experimental Social Psychology, 38*, 331–351.

[68]Sumner, W. (1906). *Folkways.* New York: Ginn.

[69]Hastorf, A. H., & Cantril, H. (1954). They saw a game: A case study. *Journal of Abnormal Social Psychology, 49*, 129–134.

[70]de Zavala, A. G., Cichocka, A., Eidelson, R., & Jayawickreme, N. (2009). Collective narcissism and its social consequences. *Journal of Personality and Social Psychology, 97*(6), 1074–1096.

[71]Duck & Fielding, "Leaders and subgroups."

[72]Moreland, R. L., & McMinn, J. G. (1999). Gone but not forgotten: Loyalty and betrayal among ex members of small groups. *Personality and Social Psychology Bulletin, 25*(12), 1476–1486.

[73]Castelli, L., Tomelleri, S., & Zogmaister, C. (2008). Implicit ingroup metafavoritism: Subtle preference for ingroup members displaying ingroup bias. *Personality and Social Psychology Bulletin, 34*(6), 807–818.

when ingroup authorities show procedural discrimination.[74] Members of high-status groups favor social inequality, and this is particularly true when high-status groups are threatened and identify highly with their groups.[75]

Racism and Racial Discrimination

In his dissenting opinion in the *Wards Cove Packing Company v. Atonio* Supreme Court decision, Justice Harry Blackmun stated, "[O]ne wonders whether the majority still believes that race discrimination—or more accurately, race discrimination against nonwhites—is a problem in our society, or even remembers that it ever was."[76] To investigate the extent of race-based discrimination in hiring, the Urban Institute in Washington, D.C., selected and trained minority and majority group testers. Testers, matched on age, gender, physical strength and size, appearance, education, experience, demeanor, openness, observed energy level, and articulateness—all possible characteristics except for race—applied for the same advertised low-skill, entry-level jobs.[77] Four hundred and seventy-six audits conducted by 10 pairs of testers (each pair comprising one African American man and one Caucasian man) revealed clear differences in the treatment of minority and majority job seekers. In 20 percent of the audits, Caucasians progressed further in the hiring process than their equally qualified African American testing partners; in 15 percent of the audits, the Caucasian received a job offer but his African American counterpart did not. Caucasian men received favorable treatment in the hiring process three times more frequently than equally qualified African American men.[78] Government data agree with these field results. In fiscal year 2008 alone, the Office of Federal Contract Compliance Program obtained settlements worth $67.5 million. Ninety-nine percent of funds were collected in cases of "systemic discrimination" involving substantial numbers of applicants or employees subjected to allegedly discriminatory practices or policies.[79] Full-time working men in the United States earn 19 percent more than women, and the earnings of all Caucasians exceed that of all African Americans by 18 percent.[80]

Obviously, these statistics suggest that gender and racial discrimination continues to be a problem and should be addressed.

Denial

"In 1956, if a male coworker offered a female colleague a 'courtly' compliment on her appearance ('you sure look pretty today'), it would have been unlikely to be viewed as a demeaning or a discriminating action, and indeed, may well have been received with pleasure."[81] However, 50 years later, this same comment would not only be perceived as offensive and condescending but

---

[74]Cheng, G. H. L., Fielding, K. S., Hogg, M. A., & Terry, D. J. (2009). Reactions to procedural discrimination in an intergroup context: The role of group membership of the authority. *Group Processes & Intergroup Relations, 12*(4), 463–478.

[75]Morrison, K. R., Fast, N. J., & Ybarra, O. (2009). Group status, perceptions of threat, and support for social inequality. *Journal of Experimental Social Psychology, 45*, 204–210.

[76]*Wards Cove Packing Company, Inc. v. Atonio*, 109 S. Ct. 2115 (1989).

[77]Turner, M. A., Fix, M., & Struyk, R. J. (1991). *Opportunities denied, opportunities diminished: Racial discrimination in hiring.* Washington, DC: The Urban Institute Press.

[78]Ibid.

[79]Ogletree Deakins. (2009, January/February). "Higher and higher": OFCCP obtains record $67.5 million from contractors. *The employment law authority*, p. 2.

[80]United States Department of Labor. (2010, January 21). Usual weekly earnings summary. *Bureau of labor statistics.* bls.gov

[81]Inman, M. L., & Baron, R. S. (1996). Influence of prototypes on perceptions of prejudice. *Journal of Personality and Social Psychology, 70*(4), 727–739.

also might well put the perpetrator out of a job. In short, as our norms and awareness of roles and power change, so do our definitions of prejudice and discrimination. Noticing and correctly categorizing prejudice and discrimination is key in changing behavior.

Although evidence clearly indicates that the problems of racism, stereotyping, and discrimination are neither small, isolated, or problems of the past, many people do not believe they exist. Victims (and likely targets) of prejudice are more likely to perceive it. For example, women are more likely than men to perceive sexism and racism; moreover, African-Americans are more likely than Caucasians to perceive racism.[82] This denial—the belief that "I have not seen it"—is an act of discrimination itself. One reason that people often don't see it is that the opposite of discrimination—privilege—is invisible.[83] **Unearned privilege** refers to advantages that accrue to people simply on the basis of their membership in a group.[84] These advantages are unearned because they are based on ascribed characteristics, such as race, gender, age, class, and religion, as opposed to achieved characteristics, such as individual merit, effort, and ability. In one investigation, group situations were examined in which some groups clearly had unearned privilege that other groups did not. This distinction was more noticeable by groups without the unearned privilege as opposed to those with the unearned privilege.[85]

Yet the perception of discrimination is different from blaming one's lot on discrimination. Members of high-status groups are more likely than members of low-status groups to blame their failure on discrimination and less likely to blame it on themselves.[86] Caucasians perceive less of a threat in the face of failure if they blame discrimination processes.

Ingroup Prototypicality

Ingroup members judge themselves as more prototypical of the superordinate groups than other subgroups.[87] But, groups who believe their ingroup interests to be undermined by remaining part of the superordinate group will downplay their ingroup's prototypicality as a way to sustain their separatist position. For example, Scottish people who support Scottish independence judge Scots to be less prototypical of Britain than the English.[88]

Outgroup Homogeneity Bias

Suppose that white managers watch a videotape of a discussion among members of a mixed-race group of three African-American men and three Caucasian men. After watching the videotape, the managers are presented with the actual text of the conversation and asked to indicate

[82]Ibid.

[83]Rosette, A. S., & Thompson, L. (2005). The camouflage effect: Separating achieved status and unearned privilege in organizations. In M. Neale, E. Mannix, & M. Thomas-Hunt (Eds.), *Research on managing teams and groups* (Vol. 7, pp. 259–281). San Diego, CA: Elsevier.

[84]Rosette, A. S. (2006). Unearned privilege: Race, gender, and social inequality in US organizations. In M. Karsten (Ed.), *Gender, ethnicity, and race in the workplace* (pp. 253–268). Westport, CT: Praeger.

[85]Rosette, A. (2004). Unacknowledged privilege: Setting the stage for discrimination in organizational settings. In D. Nagao (Ed.), *Best paper proceedings of the 64th annual meeting of the Academy of Management (CD)*, ISSN 1543–8643. New Orleans, LA.

[86]Ruggiero, K. M., & Marx, D. M. (1999). Less pain and more to gain: Why high-status group members blame their failure on discrimination. *Journal of Personality and Social Psychology, 77*(4), 774–784.

[87]Waldzus, S., Mummendey, A., Wenzel, M., & Boettcher, F. (2004). Of bikers, teachers and Germans: Groups' diverging views about their prototypicality. *British Journal of Social Psychology, 43*, 385–400.

[88]Sindic, D., & Reicher, D. (2008). The instrumental use of group prototypicality judgments. *Journal of Experimental Social Psychology, 44*, 1425–1435.

who said what. They are told they will be evaluated based upon the accuracy of their memory. They are accurate at remembering whether a black or white person made a particular comment, and they are fairly accurate in distinguishing among the three white men's comments, but their accuracy in terms of differentiating which African-American man said what is abysmal.[89] Thus, within-race errors are more prevalent than between-race errors, because people categorize members of outgroups not as individuals but simply as "black men." The faulty memory of the manager illustrates a pervasive tendency for people to assume much greater homogeneity of opinion, belief, expression, and interest among members of the outgroup than those of their own group.[90]

The managerial implications of the "they all look alike" effect are detrimental and very serious. Consider, for example, a police lineup in which a victim is asked to identify an assailant. A white victim is more likely to falsely identify a black perpetrator than a white perpetrator.[91] Consider, also, the implications of a mixed-sex task force in a corporation. Moreover, when we fail to individuate members of other groups, we are more likely to behave in a punitive fashion.

Outgroup Approach Bias

When people anticipate interacting with an ingroup member, they show approach-like behavior; however, when interacting with outgroup members, they show avoidance-like behavior. For example, people are faster in engaging in approach-like motor movements (such as moving their arms forward) toward ingroup members of the same race, nationality, age, and political persuasion than toward outgroup members.[92] Ingroup favoritism also shows up nonverbally and preconsciously: Facial expressions of joy elicit fear in outgroup perceivers relative to ingroup perceivers.[93]

STRATEGIES FOR REDUCING NEGATIVE EFFECTS OF INTERGROUP CONFLICT

Intergroup conflict seriously hinders individual, group, and organizational effectiveness. It is a leader's job to deal effectively with these issues. Once intergroup hostility becomes established, it is no simple matter to reduce it. This section considers a number of strategies to effectively deal with the negative component of intergroup competition.

---

[89]Linville, P. W., Fischer, G. W., & Salovey, P. (1989). Perceived distributions of the characteristics of in-group and out-group members: Empirical evidence and a computer simulation. *Journal of Personality and Social Psychology, 57*, 165–188.

[90]Judd, C. M., & Park, B. (1988). Out-group homogeneity: Judgments of variability at the individual and group levels. *Journal of Personality and Social Psychology, 54*(5), 778–788; Katz, D., & Braly, K. (1933). Racial stereotypes of 100 college students. *Journal of Abnormal and Social Psychology, 28*, 280–290; Park, B., & Rothbart, M. (1982). Perception of outgroup homogeneity and levels of social categorization: Memory for subordinate attitudes of ingroup and outgroup members. *Journal of Personality and Social Psychology, 42*, 1050–1068.

[91]Knight-Ridder Newspapers. (1991, October 13). Whites' IDs of blacks in crime cases often wrong, studies show. *Columbus Dispatch.*

[92]Paladino, M., & Castelli, L. (2008). On the immediate consequences of intergroup categorization: Activation of approach and avoidance motor behavior toward ingroup and outgroup members. *Personality and Social Psychology Bulletin, 34*(6), 755–768.

[93]Weisbuch, M., & Ambady, N. (2008). Affective divergence: Automatic responses to others' emotions dependent on group membership. *Journal of Personality and Social Psychology, 95*, 1063–1079.

Superordinate Goals

Groups that focus on superordinate goals—those that represent the greater good—are much more likely to cooperate with one another than when they focus on local goals.[94] People show less intergroup bias and greater willingness for contact when they categorize others using a superordinate identity.[95] When groups share a common identity, they are more likely to forgive outgroups for transgressions.[96]

Contact

The "mere contact" strategy is based on the principle that greater contact among members of different groups increases cooperation between members. In a study of ethnic students in several different countries, contact reduced prejudice and prejudice also reduced contact.[97] Unfortunately, contact in and of itself does not lead to better intergroup relations, and, in some cases, it may even exacerbate negative relations between groups. For example, contact between African-Americans and Caucasians in desegregated schools does not reduce racial prejudice;[98] there is little relationship between interdepartmental contact and conflict in organizations;[99] and college students studying in foreign countries become increasingly negative toward their host countries the longer they remain in them.[100]

Several conditions need to be in place before contact can have its desired effects of reducing prejudice:

• *Social and institutional support:* For contact to work, there should be a framework of social and institutional support. That is, people in positions of authority should be unambiguous in their endorsement of the goals of the integration policies. This fosters the development of a new social climate in which more tolerant norms can emerge.

• *Acquaintance potential:* A second condition for successful contact is that it be of sufficient frequency, duration, and closeness to permit the development of meaningful relationships between members of the groups concerned. Infrequent, short, and casual interaction will do little to foster more favorable attitudes and may even make them worse.[101] One of

[94]Kramer, R. M., & Brewer, M. B. (1984). Effects of group identity on resource use in a simulated commons dilemma. *Journal of Personality and Social Psychology, 46,* 1044–1057.

[95]Gomez, A., Dovidio, J. F., Huici, C., Gaertner, S. L., & Cuadrado, I. (2008). The other side of we: When outgroup members express common identity. *Personality and Social Psychology Bulletin, 34*(12), 1613–1626.

[96]Noor, M., Brown, R., González, R., Manzi, J., & Lewis, C. A. (2008). On positive psychological outcomes: What helps groups with a history of conflict to forgive and reconcile with each other? *Personality and Social Psychology Bulletin, 34,* 819–832.

[97]Binder, J., Zagefka, H., Brown, R., Funke, F., Kessler, T., Mummendey, A., Maquil, A., Demoulin, S., Leyens, J. P. (2009). Does contact reduce prejudice or does prejudice reduce contact? A longitudinal test of the contact hypothesis among majority and minority groups in three European countries. *Journal of Personality and Social Psychology, 96,* 843–856.

[98]Gerard, H. (1983). School desegregation: The social science role. *American Psychologist, 38,* 869–878; Schofield, J. W. (1986). Black and white contact in desegregated schools. In M. Hewstone & R. J. Brown (Eds.), *Contact and conflict in intergroup encounters* (pp. 79–92). Oxford, UK: Blackwell.

[99]Brown, R. J., Condor, F., Mathew, A., Wade, G., & Williams, J. A. (1986). Explaining intergroup differentiation in an industrial organization. *Journal of Occupational Psychology, 59,* 273–286.

[100]Stroebe, W., Lenkert, A., & Jonas, K. (1988). Familiarity may breed contempt: The impact of student exchange on national stereotypes and attitudes. In W. Stroebe, A. W. Kruglanski, D. Bar-Tal, & M. Hewstone (Eds.), *The social psychology of intergroup conflict* (pp. 167–187). New York: Springer-Verlag.

[101]Brewer, M. B., & Brown, R. J. (1998). Intergroup relations. In D. T. Gilbert, S. T. Fiske, & G. Lindzey (Eds.), *The handbook of social psychology* (4th ed., Vol. 2, pp. 554–594). New York: McGraw-Hill.

the keys to successful contact is self-disclosure, or the revealing of information about oneself.[102] This type of close interaction will lead to the discovery of similarities and disconfirm negative stereotypes.

• *Equal status:*   The third condition necessary for contact to be successful is that participants have equal status. Many stereotypes of outgroups comprise beliefs about the inferior ability of outgroup members to perform various tasks. If the contact situation involves an unequal-status relationship between men and women, for example, with women in the subordinate role (e.g., taking notes and acting as secretaries), stereotypes are likely to be reinforced rather than weakened.[103] If, however, the group members work on equal footing, prejudiced beliefs become hard to sustain in the face of repeated experience of task competence by the outgroup member.

• *Shared goal:*   When members of different groups depend on one another for the achievement of a jointly desired objective, they have instrumental reasons to develop better relationships. The importance of an overriding, clear, shared group goal is a key determinant of intergroup relations. In 2009, American and Chinese coal companies realized that they had a shared goal and began sharing technologies for burning cleaner coal and capturing and storing CO_2 emissions. "China is leading the world in investing in clean energy, and we can make greater progress working together," said Duke Energy CEO Jim Rogers.[104] Sometimes a common enemy is a catalyst for bonding among diverse people and groups. For example, by "waging a war against cancer," members of different medical groups and laboratories can work together.

• *Cross-group friendships:*   Sometimes it is not necessary for groups to have real contact with one another to improve intergroup relations. If group members know that another member of their own group has a friendship or relationship with a member of the outgroup, or a cross-group friendship, ingroup members have less negative attitudes toward the outgroup.[105] It is not necessary that all members have cross-group friendships; merely knowing that one member of the group has such a relationship can go a long way toward reducing negative outgroup attitudes. For example, when team members are given crosscut role assignments to other groups, this decreases bias not only of dominant, ingroup members but also of the minority, outgroup members.[106] Moreover, members of groups don't even have to have prior interaction. Cross-group friendships not only lead to more intergroup interactions but also have the added benefit of reducing stress (as measured by cortisol levels).[107]

A meta-analytic test of intergroup contact theory, including 713 independent samples from 515 studies, reveals that intergroup contact reduces prejudice.[108] The contact hypothesis

---

[102]Ensari, N., & Miller, N. (2002). The out-group must not be so bad after all: The effects of disclosure, typicality, and salience on intergroup bias. *Journal of Personality of Social Psychology, 82*(2), 313–329.

[103]Bradford, D. L., & Cohen, A. R. (1984). *Managing for excellence.* New York: John Wiley & Sons.

[104]Aston, A. (2009, November 17). China and U.S. energy giants team up for "clean coal." *Business Week.* businessweek.com

[105]Wright, S. C., Aron, A., McLaughlin-Volpe, T., & Ropp, S. A. (1997). The extended contact effect: Knowledge of cross-group friendships and prejudice. *Journal of Personality and Social Psychology, 73*(1), 73–90.

[106]Bettencourt, B. A., & Dorr, N. (1998). Cooperative interaction and intergroup bias: Effects of numerical representation and cross-cut role assignment. *Personality and Social Psychology Bulletin, 24*(12), 1276–1293.

[107]Page-Gould, E., Mendoza-Denton, R., & Tropp, L. (2008). With a little help from my cross-group friend: Reducing anxiety in intergroup contexts through crossgroup friendship. *Journal of Personality and Social Psychology, 95*, 1080–1094.

[108]Pettigrew, T. F., & Tropp, L. (2006, May). A meta-analytic test of intergroup contact theory. *Journal of Personality and Social Psychology, 90*(5), 751–783.

has received support in groups ranging from students at a multiethnic high school to banking executives involved in corporate mergers.[109] Contact helps people develop a common shared identity. For example, when groups composed of Democratic and Republican Party supporters are brought into a situation that involves a common fate and intergroup interaction, bias is reduced, even when measured in terms of the pleasantness of nonverbal facial reactions.[110] It also helps for people to focus on their emotions rather than their thoughts when they think about interteam relations. People who focus on their emotions are more willing to interact with other groups.[111]

Crosscut Role Assignments

When numerical representations of groups are markedly different, cooperation alone is not sufficient for intergroup interaction.[112] In fact, being in a numerical minority prevents members' attitudes from benefiting from cooperative interaction.[113] Crosscut role assignments are situations in which people are simultaneously members of more than one task group or team. Crosscut role assignments decrease ingroup bias of both minority and majority groups.[114]

Communal-Sharing Norms

Communal-sharing norms can often help groups share common resources.[115] The **communal-sharing norm** is about social exchange, designating uncertain resources as common properties to be shared with other members of a social group. Uncertainty involved in resource acquisition is a key factor that triggers the psychology of communal sharing. Communal-sharing norms are sustainable, even in organizations in which there are possible free riders (i.e., people who want to consume the resource without contributing).[116] There are two types of reactions to free riders: intolerance (free riders are sanctioned and blocked access to the resource) and tolerance (free riders are identified but not blocked). In an investigation of Japanese and American participants who were given a windfall (expected monetary resources), the groups opted for egalitarianism in resource sharing.[117]

---

[109]Gaertner, S. L., Dovidio, J. F., & Bachman, B. A. (1996). Revisiting the contact hypothesis: The induction of a common ingroup identity. *International Journal of Intercultural Relations, 20*(3 & 4), 271–290.

[110]Gaertner, S. L., Dovidio, J. F., Rust, M. C., Nier, J. A., Banker, B. S., Ward, C. M., Mottola, G. R., & Houlette, M. (1999). Reducing intergroup bias: Elements of intergroup cooperation. *Journal of Personality and Social Psychology, 76*(3), 388–402.

[111]Esses, V. M., & Dovidio, J. F. (2002). The role of emotions in determining willingness to engage in intergroup contact. *Personality and Social Psychology Bulletin, 28*(9), 1202–1214.

[112]Rogers, M., Hennigan, K., Bowman, C., & Miller, N. (1984). Intergroup acceptance in classroom and playground settings. In N. Miller & M. B. Brewer (Eds.), *Groups in contact: The psychology of desegregation* (pp. 187–212). Orlando, FL: Academic Press.

[113]Bettencourt, B. A., Charlton, K., & Kernahan, C. (1997). Cooperative interaction and intergroup bias: The interaction between numerical representation and social orientation. *Journal of Experimental Social Psychology, 33*, 630–659.

[114]Bettencourt & Dorr, "Cooperative interaction and intergroup bias."

[115]Kameda, T., Takezawa, M., & Hastie, R. (2003). The logic of social sharing: An evolutionary game analysis of adaptive norm development. *Personality and Social Psychology Review, 7*, 2–19.

[116]Ibid.

[117]Kameda, T., Takezawa, M., Tindale, R. S., & Smith, C. (2002). Social sharing and risk reduction: Exploring a computational algorithm for the psychology of windfall gains. *Evolution and Human Behavior, 23*, 11–33.

Group Affirmation

Self-affirmation is the process of thinking about one's values, accomplishments, and attributes.[118] If outgroups threaten ingroup members, then reducing the threat through a positive affirmation of the group might lead to more accepting behavior toward outgroups. In one investigation, athletes exhibited a group-serving bias, which was subsequently eliminated with a group affirmation.[119] The affirmation technique works for fans too: the most highly identified sports fans tend to exhibit the greatest outgroup bias, which is eliminated when they make a group affirmation.

Conclusion

People identify with their teams. Conflict and competition between groups is a natural consequence of the process of establishing our social identity. We examined the positive consequences of interteam conflict in terms of enhancing cohesion and stimulating creativity. We also looked at the dark side of interteam competition and the biased perceptions that can prevail. Leaders who see their teams engaging in interteam competition should congratulate themselves—as this is an indication that the individuals in the team have identified strongly with their team. On the other hand, effective team leaders need to address the potential negative aspects of interteam conflict.

---

[118]Sherman, D. K., & Cohen, G. L. (2006). The psychology of self-defense: Self-affirmation theory. In M. P. Zanna (Ed.), *Advances in Experimental Social Psychology* (Vol. 38, pp. 183–242). San Diego, CA: Academic Press.
[119]Sherman, D. K., Kinias, Z., Major, B., Kim, H. S., & Prenovost, M. (2007). The group as a resource: Reducing biased attributions for group success and failure via group affirmation. *Personality and Social Psychology Bulletin, 33,* 1100–1112.

13 Teamwork via Information Technology

Teaming Across Distance and Culture

Wi-Fi, laptops, cell phones, and meeting software have made it possible to work from anywhere but the office. However, an increasing number of people miss something that they had in the office: community. Christine Durst, author of Work at Home Now, says that people who decide to work at home often experience an initial sense of euphoria: no boss looking over their shoulder, no dress code, and no rush hour commute, but then they discover that the solitude can be stifling. Some people crave human contact, and so they work from Starbucks just to be in the presence of others. But these people don't want to be seen as the loner in the corner with the laptop. So, they have formed communities. For example, New Work City—a rented office space in Manhattan where people can drop in, hook up their laptops, and work alongside others. Membership is run like that in a gym: The plans range from a monthly fee for two visits per week up to getting your own key. Inside, New Work City looks like a typical startup: a couple of conference rooms, main rooms with tables pushed together, a kitchen where you put a $1 in a jar for a bag of chips, and supplies shelf. There are silly contests that take place, and, of course, friendship and business relationships develop there. There is no janitor, and everyone takes turns cleaning up. Public libraries have gotten in on the act, too, by offering conferencing and other business services. Office Nomads in Seattle, Sandbox Suites in San Francisco, and Beehive Baltimore offer similar options for the community-craving worker.[1]

The opening example of workers who need community suggests that the virtual workplace is still being shaped. Teams of managers armed with laptop computers, fax modems, e-mail, voice mail, videoconferencing, interactive databases, and frequent-flyer memberships are charged with conducting business in the global arena. Virtual teams are expected to efficiently harness the knowledge of company employees regardless of their location, thereby enabling organizations to respond

---

[1]Goetz, K. (writer). (2009, January 6). Co-Working offers community to solo workers [Radio broadcast episode]. *Morning Edition.* Washington, DC: National Public Radio; Blake, J. (2010, January 7). *Working in 'Wi-Fi' limbo.* Cnn.com

faster to increased competition. Information technology brings together teams of people who would otherwise not be able to interact. Information technology offers the potential for improving information access and information-processing capability. Information technology offers the potential for members to participate without regard to temporal and spatial impediments.

However, as the Mars Climate Orbiter example in Exhibit 13-1 illustrates, not all virtual teamwork proceeds seamlessly. Distance is a formidable obstacle, despite electronic media and jet travel. A decision made in one country is interpreted with reference to one's own cultural norms and standards or perhaps elicits an unexpected reaction from team members in another country. Remote offices fight for influence with the head office. Telephone conferences find distant members struggling to get onto the same page, literally and figuratively. Group members at sites separated by even a few kilometers begin to talk in the language of "us" and "them."[2] Thus, there is considerable debate among managers as to whether technology fosters or hinders teamwork in the workplace at the global, and even local, level.

This chapter examines the impact of information technology on teamwork. We first describe a simple model of social interaction called the place–time model. Using this framework we evaluate various modes of information technology and how they affect team interaction. The model focuses on where teams work (same or different physical location) and the time they work (synchronously or asynchronously). Then, we move to a discussion of virtual teams, making the point that whenever teams must work together in a non-face-to-face fashion, this constitutes a virtual team. We describe strategies to help virtual teams do their work better. We describe what transnational teams do and what it takes to get there. Obviously, transnational teams and global teamwork

---

EXHIBIT 13-1 English-Metric Faulty Communication Meets with Disaster

On September 23, 1999, the Mars Climate Orbiter fired its main engine to go into orbit around the planet. All the information coming from the spacecraft leading up to that point looked normal. The engine burn began as planned, 5 minutes before the spacecraft passed behind the planet as seen from the Earth. However, flight controllers did not detect a signal when the spacecraft was expected to come out from behind the planet. "We had planned to approach the planet at an altitude of about 150 kilometers (93 miles)," said Richard Cook, a project manager for the Mars Surveyor Operations Project at NASA's Jet Propulsion Laboratory. "We thought we were doing that, but upon review of the last 6 to 8 hours of data leading up to arrival, we saw indications that the actual approach altitude had been much lower. It appears that the actual altitude was about 60 kilometers (37 miles)" (Media Relations Office, NASA Jet Propulsion Laboratory, 1999). The spacecraft was over 56 miles off course and was ultimately lost in space—an avoidable human error that cost hundreds of millions of dollars. The key problem concerned a "failed translation of English units into metric units"—one team used English units (e.g., inches, feet, and pounds); the other used metric units for a key spacecraft operation. The failure investigation board concluded the following: There were inconsistent communications, the operational navigation team was not fully informed on details, the communication channels were too informal, and the verification and validation process was inadequate.

Sources: Isbell, D., Hardin, M., & Underwood, J. (1999, September 30). *Mars climate orbiter team finds likely cause of loss.* Washington, DC: Jet Propulsion Laboratory for NASA's Office of Space Science. Release No. 99–113; Isbell, D., & Savage, D. (1999, November 10). *Mars climate orbiter failure board releases report, numerous NASA actions underway in response.* Washington, DC: Jet Propulsion Laboratory for NASA's Office of Space Science. Release No. 99–134.

---

[2]Armstrong, D. J., & Cole, P. (1995). Managing distances and differences in geographically distributed work groups. In S. E. Jackson & M. N. Ruderman (Eds.), *Diversity in work teams: Research paradigms for a changing workplace* (pp. 187–215). Washington, DC: American Psychological Association.

involve the diversity issues that we dealt with in Chapter 4. We follow this discussion with a section on how information technology affects human behavior. We do not provide a state-of-the-art
review on types of information technology (which would be foolish to do in a book); our purpose
is to identify considerations that managers must wrestle with when attempting to bring together
groups of people who are not in the same place.

PLACE–TIME MODEL OF SOCIAL INTERACTION

The Place–Time model considers teams in terms of their geographic location (together versus
separated) and temporal relationship (interacting in real time versus asynchronously). For any
team meeting, there are four possibilities as depicted in the place–time model in Exhibit 13-2. As
might be suspected, communication and teamwork unfold differently face-to-face than they do
via electronic media.

Richness is the potential information-carrying capacity of the communication medium.
Face-to-face communication is relatively "rich," and formal written messages, such as
memos, are relatively "lean"[3] (see Exhibit 13-3). Face-to-face communication conveys the
richest information because it allows the simultaneous observation of several cues, including
body language, facial expression, and tone of voice, providing people with a greater
awareness of context. In contrast, formal, numerical documentation conveys the least rich
information, providing few clues about the context. Groups are often constrained in their
choice of communication medium.

Face-to-Face Communication

Face-to-face contact is crucial in the initiation of relationships and collaborations. People are more
cooperative when interacting face-to-face than via other forms of communication. Without face-to-face
communication, relationships between businesspersons are often strained and contentious.

Face-to-face meetings are ideal when teams must wrestle with complex problems. For
example, researchers need regular face-to-face contact to be confident that they accurately

EXHIBIT 13-2 Place–Time Model of Interaction

	Same Place	**Different Place**
Same Time	Face-to-face	Telephone
		Videoconference
Different Time	Single text editing	E-mail
	Shift work	Voice mail

Source: Thompson, L. (2008). *The mind and heart of the negotiator* (4th ed.).
Electronically reproduced by permission of Pearson Education, Inc., Upper Saddle
River, New Jersey.

---

[3]Daft, R. L., & Lengel, R. H. (1984). Information richness: A new approach to managerial behavior and organization
design. *Research in Organization Behavior, 6,* 191–223; Daft, R. L., Lengel, R. H., & Trevino, L. K. (1987). Message
equivocality, media selection, and manager performance: Implications for information systems. *MIS Quarterly, 11*(3),
355–366.

EXHIBIT 13-3 Psychological Distancing Model

FACE-TO-FACE	TWO-WAY T.V.	TELEPHONE	COMPUTER MESSAGING
(Kinetic, visual, paralinguistic, linguistic)	(Visual, paralinguistic, linguistic)	(Paralinguistic, linguistic)	(Linguistic)

CLOSE ⸻ PSYCHOLOGICAL DISTANCE ⸻ REMOTE

Source: Adapted from Wellens, A. R. (1989, September). Effects of telecommunication media upon information sharing and team performance: Some theoretical and empirical findings. *IEEE AES Magazine,* p. 14.

understand each other's work, particularly if it involves innovative ideas. Confidence decays over time as researchers communicate through telephone and computer conferences; face-to-face contact is required to renew trust in their mutual comprehension.[4] Face-to-face team meetings are particularly important when a group forms, when commitments to key decisions are needed, and when major conflicts must be resolved.[5] Work groups form more slowly, and perhaps never fully, when they don't have face-to-face contact.[6]

In most companies, the incidence and frequency of face-to-face communication are almost perfectly predicted by how closely people are located to one another: Employees who work in the same office or on the same floor communicate much more frequently than those on different floors or in different buildings. The likelihood of communication literally comes down to feet—even a few steps can have a huge impact. For example, communication frequency between R&D researchers drops off logarithmically after only 5 to 10 meters of distance between offices.[7] In a study of molecular biologists, critical techniques for producing monoclonal antibodies were not reported in journals, but were passed from scientist to scientist at the lab bench.[8] People in adjacent offices communicate twice as often as those in offices on the same floor, including via e-mail and telephone.[9] A study of 207 U.S. firms in

---

[4]DeMeyer, A. (1991). Tech talk: How managers are stimulating global R&D communication. *Sloan Management Review, 32*(3), 49–58; DeMeyer, A. (1993). Internationalizing R&D improves a firm's technical learning. *Research-Technical Management, 36*(4), 42–49.

[5]DeMeyer, "Tech talk," p. 350; Galegher, J., Kraut, R. E., & Egido, C. (Eds.). (1990). *Intellectual teamwork: Social and technological foundations of cooperative work.* Hillsdale, NJ: Erlbaum; Sproull, L., & Keisler, S. (1991). *Connections: New ways of working in the networked organization.* Cambridge, MA: MIT Press.

[6]DeMeyer, "Tech talk," p. 350; Galegher, Kraut, & Egido, *Intellectual teamwork,* p. 350.

[7]Allen, T. J. (1977). *Managing the flow of technology: Technology transfer and the dissemination of technological information within the R&D organization.* Cambridge, MA: MIT Press.

[8]MacKenzie, M., Cambrosio, A., & Keating, P. (1988). The commercial application of a scientific discovery: The case of the hybridoma technique. *Research and Policy, 17*(3), 155–170.

[9]Galegher, Kraut, & Egido, *Intellectual teamwork,* p. 350.

11 industries revealed that firm performance increased as the proportion of top management teams with offices in the same location increased.[10] Physical distance affects how members feel about their teams: People are more likely to assume that the behavior of a group is driven by common goals for physically distant groups, presumably because common goals would be the only means by which they are united.[11]

Just what cues do people get out of face-to-face contact that makes it so important for interaction and productivity? Primarily, two things: First, face-to-face communication is easier and, therefore, more likely to occur than other forms of communication. Simply stated, most people need a reason to walk up the stairs or make a phone call. They underestimate how much information they get from chance encounters, which never happen in any mode but face-to-face. Second, people primarily rely on nonverbal signals to help them conduct social interactions. One estimate is that 93 percent of the meaning of messages is contained in the nonverbal part of communication, such as voice intonation.[12] For example, it is possible to predict which executives will win a business competition solely on the basis of the nonverbal social signals that they send (e.g., tone of voice, gesticulation, and proximity to others).[13] Perhaps this is why business executives endure the inconveniences of travel across thousands of miles and several time zones so that they can have face-to-face contact with others, even if it is only for a short period. The emphasis on the human factor is not just old-fashioned business superstition. Important behavioral, cognitive, and emotional processes are set into motion when people meet face-to-face. However, unless people are specially trained, they don't know what exactly it is about face-to-face interaction that facilitates teamwork—they just know that things go smoother.

Face-to-face interaction allows people to develop rapport—the feeling of being "in sync" or "on the same wavelength" with another person. Rapport is a powerful determinant of trust. The degree of rapport determines the efficiency and the quality of progress toward goal achievement, and whether the goal is ever achieved.[14]

Nonverbal (body orientation, gesture, eye contact, and nodding) and paraverbal behavior (speech fluency, use of "uh-huhs," etc.) is key to building rapport. When our conversation partner sits at a greater distance, with an indirect body orientation, backward lean, crossed arms, and low eye contact, we feel less rapport than when the same person sits with a forward lean, an open body posture, nods, and maintains steady eye contact. Nonverbal and paraverbal cues affect the way people work and the quality of their work as a team.

However, face-to-face communication is not the best modality for all teamwork. As a clear case in point, we saw in our discussion of creativity and brainstorming (see Chapter 9) that face-to-face brainstorming is less productive compared with other, less rich forms of interaction.

---

[10]Cannella, A. A., Park, J. H., & Lee, H. O. (2008). Top management team functional background diversity and firm performance examining the roles of team member collocation and environmental uncertainty. *Academy of Management Journal, 51*, 768–784.

[11]Henderson, M. D. (2009). Psychological distance and group judgments: The effect of physical distance on beliefs about common goals. *Personality and Social Psychology Bulletin, 35*(10), 1330–1341.

[12]Mehrabian, A. (1971). *Silent messages*. Belmont, CA: Wadsworth.

[13]Pentland, A. (2010, January–February). We can measure the power of charisma. *Harvard Business Review, 88*(1), 34–35.

[14]Tickle-Degnen, L., & Rosenthal, R. (1987). Group rapport and nonverbal behavior. In *Review of Personality and Social Psychology* (Vol. 9, pp. 113–136). Beverly Hills, CA: Sage.

Same Time, Different Place

In the same-time, different-place mode, people communicate in real time but are not physically in the same place. The most common means is via cell phone. In a 2008 study, 75 percent of workers used a mobile phone for work purposes.[15] In telephone conversations, people lack facial cues; in videoconferencing, they lack social cues, such as pauses, mutual gaze, and posture. Yet at the same time, electronic interaction, such as brainstorming in groups, increases team productivity.

Experienced team leaders like Billie Williamson of Ernst and Young offer some important guidelines for managing virtually.[16] The key one is to *get dressed*. Don't work in your pajamas; getting dressed helps you focus. Also, decorate your homespace with pictures and profiles of your team members, a discussion board, and a calendar. Keeping photos by the phone is a tool used by other leaders, as well, such as Karen Sorensen, CIO of J&J.[17] Atlanta-based Accenture consultant, Keyur Patel, keeps three clocks on this desk; one set for Manila, another for Bangalore, and yet another for San Francisco.[18] This practice helps him identify with his team. In a direct comparison of FTF (face-to-face) versus computer-mediated (CM) groups, group identity (i.e., cohesion and "we-feeling") was consistently lower in CM groups, especially when they underwent membership change (i.e., reorganization).[19] Similarly, in a comparison of FTF, desktop videoconference, and text-based chat teamwork, the constructive interaction score (e.g., supportive and instructive communication versus aggressive behavior) was higher in FTF groups than in videoconference and chat teams.[20] However, teams working in richer communication media did not achieve higher task performance than those communicating through less rich media.

What are the major ways in which group members who are physically distant from one another suffer because of their physical separation? There are several effects of physical separation of the team, some of which might not be immediately obvious.

LOSS OF INFORMAL COMMUNICATION   **Virtual distance** is a term that refers to the feelings of separation engendered by communicating by e-mail, text, audioconferencing, etc.[21] Probably the effect felt most is the inability to chat informally in the hall, inside offices, and by the watercooler. The impromptu and casual conversations that employees have by the watercooler and the coffee machine are often where the most difficult problems are solved and important interpersonal issues are addressed. Beyond a very short distance, people miss the spontaneous exchanges that occur outside of formal meetings. Remote group members feel cut off from key conversations that occur over lunch and in the hall. Spontaneous communication plays a pivotal role in mitigating conflict in distributed teams.[22] Distributed teams experience more relationship and

[15]Wajcman, J., Bittman, M., Johnstone, L., Brown, J., & Jones, P. (2008, March). *The impact of the mobile phone on work/life balance.* Australian Mobile Telecommunications Association. amta.org.au

[16]Williamson, B. (2009, June 17). Managing virtually; First get dressed. *Business Week.* businessweek.com

[17]Lojeski, K. S., & Reilly, R. R. (2008). *Transforming leadership and innovation in the globally integrated enterprise.* New Jersey: John Wiley & Sons Inc.

[18]Marquez, J. (2008, September 22). Connecting a virtual workforce. *Workforce Management, 87*(15), 1, 23–25.

[19]Bouas, K. S., & Arrow, H. (1996). The development of group identity in computer and face to face groups with membership change. *Computer Supported Cooperative Work, 4,* 153–178.

[20]Hambley, L. A., O'Neil, T. A., & Kline, T. J. B. (2007). Virtual team leadership: The effects of leadership style and communication medium on team interaction styles and outcomes. *Organizational Behavior and Human Decision Process, 103*(1), 1–20.

[21]Lojeski & Reilly, *"Transforming leadership and innovation in the globally integrated enterprise."*

[22]Hinds, P. J., & Mortensen, M. (2005). Understanding conflict in geographically distributed teams: The moderating effects of shared identity, shared context, and spontaneous communication. *Organizational Science, 16*(3), 290–307.

task conflict than do collocated teams. Because employees don't get to attend industry trade shows, company executives at Qualcomm developed an "internal tradeshow" to bring people together from different departments.[23]

DISCONNECTED FEEDBACK   Another negative impact of physical separation is feedback; greater distance tends to block the corrective feedback loops provided by chance encounters. One manager contrasted how employees who worked in his home office related to his decisions, compared with employees 15 kilometers away.[24] Engineers in the home office would drop by and catch him in the hall or at lunch. "I heard you were planning to change project X," they would say. "Let me tell you why that would be stupid." The manager would listen to their points, clarify some details, and all would part better informed. In contrast, employees at the remote site would greet his weekly visits with formally prepared objections, which took much longer to discuss and were rarely resolved as completely as the more informal hallway discussions. In short, groups working remotely do not get the coincidental chances to detect and correct problems on a casual basis. Geographic sites promote an informal, spontaneous group identity, reinforced by close physical proximity and the dense communication it promotes. Those working in an office all tend to have friends in nearby companies or groups, hear the same industry rumors, and share similar beliefs about technological trends. Thus, any distance—whether it be 12 miles or 12,000 miles—is problematic in this regard.

LOSS OF INFORMAL MODELING   Another impact of information technology is the loss of informal modeling and observational learning. Casual observation is invaluable for monitoring and mentoring performance, especially for one-on-one team coaching. The inability of remote employees to observe successful project managers is a barrier to effective coaching of task and interpersonal-related skills.

OUT-OF-THE-LOOP EMPLOYEES   Distant employees tend to be left out of discussions or forgotten altogether. In a sense, they are out of sight, out of mind. The default behavior is to ignore the person on the speakerphone. This is especially magnified when the person or group with less status is on the phone.

Time differences amplify the effects of physical distance. Distributed group members face the challenge of finding each other at the same time while they are living in different time zones. Time differences sometimes highlight cultural differences. However, teams can try to overcome these cultural barriers. One group based in the United States and Italy celebrated a project milestone in their weekly videoconference by sharing foods on the video screen and fax. The East Coast team, at 9 A.M., sent images of bagels and coffee. The Italian team, at 3 P.M. in their time zone, sent images of champagne and cookies.

Conflicts are expressed, recognized, and addressed more quickly if group members work in close proximity. A manager can spot a problem, nip it in the bud, and solve the problem quickly. In geographically separated groups, the issues are more likely to just get dropped and go unresolved, contributing to a slow buildup in aggravation. People complain to their coworkers, reinforcing local perceptions of events, but do not complain to the distant leaders until feelings reach extremely high levels.

---

[23]Kranz, G. (2009, November). Tricks of the trade show: Innovation and informal learning. *Workforce Management.* workforce.com
[24]Armstrong & Cole, "Managing distances and differences in geographically distributed workgroups."

Although there are many disadvantages of distance, it is not always a liability for teams. The formality of a scheduled phone meeting compels each party to prepare for the meeting and to address the issues more efficiently. In addition, distance can reduce micromanagement. Some managers hinder their employees' performance by monitoring them too closely and demanding frequent updates. Edmondson provides four tactics to help people reframe their purpose on their team:[25]

1. Tell yourself that the project is different from anything you've done before and presents a challenging and exciting opportunity to try out a new approach and learn.
2. See yourself as vitally important to a successful outcome, and to achieve the goal, you need the willing participation of others.
3. Tell yourself that others are vitally important to a successful outcome and may bring key pieces of the puzzle that you don't anticipate.
4. Communicate with others on the team as you would if the above three statements were true.

Different Time, Same Place

In the different-time, same-place mode, team members interact asynchronously but share the same work space. An example might be shift workers who pick up the task left for them by the previous shift or collaborators working on the same electronic document. After one partner finishes working on the document, it goes to the other partner, who further edits and develops it.

Although people may not realize it, they rely a lot on their physical environment for important information and cues. Remember the concept of transactive memory systems that we introduced in Chapter 6: People often supplement their own memories and information-processing systems—which are fallible—with environmental storage. We discussed at length in Chapter 6 how people use other team members as information storage, retrieval, and processing devices. The same is true for the physical environment. A Post-it note on the back of a chair or a report placed in a certain bin can symbolize an entire procedural system (e.g., how to make a three-way conference call). Just as people become information dependent on other people, they can also become information dependent upon aspects of the physical environment in order to do their work. At the extreme, this type of dependence can be a limitation for groups that find it impossible to work outside the idiosyncratic confines of their work space. Information and work space dependence can negatively affect the productivity and motivation of a team. For example, during site visits, software development teams observed and interacted with their distant colleagues in their colleagues' context, thus gaining a deeper understanding of their behavior within the physical context of the work.[26] As they interacted, teams reviewed their collaborative practices, which further facilitated trust. After team members returned to their home site, some of the new collaborative practices carried over to their work with other distant colleagues.

The productivity of any team, and organizational effectiveness in general, is a joint function of the technical and the social system.[27] The structure of a group, both internally and externally, and the technology the group works with are products of an active adaptation

---

[25]Edmondson, A. (2003). Framing for learning: Lessons in successful technology implementation. *California Management Review, 45*(2), 34–54.

[26]Hinds, P. (2010, January). Situated knowing who: Why site visits matter in global work. Technology and Social Behavior colloquium, Northwestern University, Evanston, IL.

[27]Emery, F. E., & Trist, E. L. (1973). *Towards a social ecology: Contextual appreciation of the future in the present.* New York: Plenum Press.

process, in which the technology is shaped by the organization or its subunits, as well as being a factor in shaping the organization. For example, consider the introduction of a new technology, CT scanners, in two hospitals.[28] The introduction of the CT scanners increased uncertainty and upset the distribution of expertise and the division of labor in the hospital units. Both hospital units became more decentralized with the introduction of the CT scanners and the associated increase in uncertainty.

Different Place, Different Time

In the different-place, different-time mode, people communicate asynchronously in different places. The most pervasive means is e-mail. The Internet has only been around since 1983, but as of September 2009, more than 1.7 billion people use it.[29]

Yet e-mail changes the nature of behavior and team dynamics. When asked to communicate tones such as sarcasm and sincerity via e-mail, people believe they convey the correct tone, when in fact their messages are often misunderstood. Communicating via e-mail strips the message "of the paralinguistic and nonverbal cues that enable us to communicate these sorts of subtle emotions and tones."[30]

The problem of conveying mood and tone via e-mail communication is a challenge for teams. Because it is easy to send a message and social norms are not present when sending e-mail, people often take more risks. Furthermore, there is virtually no competition to attain and hold the floor, so people are at liberty to send frequent and long messages. Some people receive several hundred electronic messages each day.

Employees at U.S. Cellular try to go without e-mail every Friday under a policy implemented that gives workers a break from the e-mail avalanche. The idea was for employees to talk to one another and collaborate more. One Friday, executive John Coyle was about to send an e-mail to a colleague in the finance department whom he had never met. But he called him instead. That's when the two realized they had similar phone numbers—meaning that they were not only in the same town, but in the same building. "I'm like, 'Oh, really, where?' He said, 'On the fourth floor,'" Coyle remembers. "And I said, 'I'm on the fourth floor.'" After more details were exchanged, "I literally got up, walked around the corner, and there he was. I had no idea."[31] There is etiquette to sending e-mail. You can check your e-mail acuity by reviewing Exhibit 13-4.

Is e-mail effective for learning? In the fall of 1996, an experiment was carried out in which 33 students enrolled in a social statistics course at California State University at Northridge. The students were randomly divided into two groups—one taught in a traditional classroom and the other taught virtually on the Web.[32] Text, lectures, and exams were standardized for both classes;

---

[28]Barley, S. R. (1996). Technicians in the workplace: Ethnographic evidence for bringing work into organization studies. *Administrative Science Quarterly, 41*(3), 404–441.

[29]Internet World Stats. Usage and Population Statistics. (2009, September 30). *Internet usage statistics: The internet big picture.* internetworldstats.com

[30]Gomes, L. (2006, June 27). Talking tech: How email can set the stage for big misunderstandings. *Wall Street Journal,* p. B3.

[31]Schaper, D (writer). (2008, June 20). An e-mail vacation: Taking Fridays off [Radio broadcast episode]. *Morning Edition.* Washington, DC: National Public Radio.

[32]Schutte, J. G. (1996). Virtual teaching in higher education: The new intellectual superhighway or just another traffic jam? Working paper, California State University, Northridge, CA.

EXHIBIT 13-4 E-Communication Assessment and Etiquette

The following questions are important to consider when using e-communication in business

- Will e-mail be used for routine communication, while voice mail is the standard for more urgent communication?
- When is it appropriate to page people?
- What constitutes an acceptable use of cell phones?
- What is the appropriate use of PDAs and other wireless devices during meetings?
- How should instant messaging be utilized, and what limits should be placed on its use?
- What types of information should be communicated by voice mail?
- What are the standards for length of voice mail and e-mail messages and for distribution (who should/should not be copied)?
- Are there size limits on documents attached to e-mail?
- When should spreadsheets, slide presentations, and multimedia resources be used to share information?
- When should the intranet, shared drives, or file transfer sites be used?
- What are appropriate methods for filtering information and messages?
- How often are associates expected to access various message and information sources?

Source: Dinnocenzo, D. (2006). *How to lead from a distance: Building bridges in the virtual workplace* (p. 35). Dallas: Walk the Talk. Used by permission of Debra A. Dinnocenzo. www.virtualworkswell.com

the virtual class scored an average of 20 percent higher than the traditional class on examinations. Furthermore, the virtual class had significantly higher peer contact, more time spent on class work, a perception of more flexibility, better understanding of the material, and a greater liking for math than the traditional class. The virtual students seemed more frustrated, but not from the technology. Instead, their inability to ask questions of the professor in a face-to-face environment led paradoxically to greater involvement among classmates, who formed study groups to "pick up the slack of not having a real classroom." Thus, the performance differences are most likely attributable to the collaboration among students instigated by the technology. The lack of rich communication in the virtual class led to the improved performance of students, who were sparked by the inadequacies of the virtual medium.

Information technology leads to the formation of virtual groups and communities. It might seem that this type of community interaction is a far cry from the business world of information technology, but that is just the point. It is becoming harder to separate the personal lives of people and the communities to which they belong from their professional or business lives.

Information Technology and Social Behavior

Information technology has extremely powerful effects on social behavior.[33] Many people are surprised at how they behave when communicating via e-mail. What are the key things to expect when interacting with teammates via information technology?

---

[33]Keisler, S., & Sproull, L. (1992). Group decision making and communication technology. *Organizational Behavior and Human Decision Processes, 52,* 96–123.

Reduced Status Differences: The "Weak Get Strong" Effect

In face-to-face interactions, people do not contribute to conversation equally. One person or one clique usually dominates the discussion. People with higher status tend to talk more, even if they are not experts on the subject. Not surprisingly, managers speak more than subordinates and men speak more than women.

However, an odd thing happens on the way to the information technology forum: The traditional static cues are missing, and the dynamic cues are distinctly less impactful. This has a dramatic effect on social behavior: Power and status cues are weakened, and status differences are reduced. This means that high-status members (e.g., leaders) are less likely to dominate discussions in CM groups than in FTF groups;[34] and a dominant member is less likely to emerge in CM groups than in FTF groups.[35]

Decision making occurs on the basis of task expertise, rather than status.[36] People who are in weak positions in face-to-face encounters become more powerful because status cues are harder to discern in non–face-to-face interaction.[37] Traditional, static cues, like position and title, are not as obvious on e-mail. It is often impossible to tell whether you are communicating with a president or clerk. In most networks, when people send e-mail, the only signs of position and personal attributes are names and addresses. Addresses are often shortened and may be difficult to comprehend. Even when they can be deciphered, addresses identify the organization, but not the subunit, job title, social importance, or level in the organization of the sender. Dynamic status cues, such as dress, mannerisms, age, and gender, are also missing in e-mail. In this sense, e-mail acts as an equalizer because it is difficult for high-status people to dominate discussions. When a group of executives meet face-to-face, the men in these groups are five times more likely than the women to make the first decision proposal. When the same groups meet via computer, women make the first proposal as often as do men.[38]

Equalization of Participation

The greater anonymity associated with virtual interaction reduces inhibitions and increases the likelihood that all members will contribute to the discussion.[39]

When interacting via e-mail, people respond more openly and conform less to social norms and other people. They focus more on the content of the task and less on the direction of high-status opinion leaders. Computer-mediated communication (CMC) is more democratic and less hierarchical, with bad news conveyed upward to superiors with less delay.[40] However, CMC does not appear to reduce gender differences. The question of whether disguising individual and gender identity during group interaction would lead to more equal participation of men and women and the

[34]Dubrovsky, V. J., Keisler, S., & Sethna, B. N. (1991). The equalization phenomenon: Status effects in computer-mediated and face-to-face decision-making groups. *Human-Computer Interaction, 6*(2), 119–146.

[35]Hiltz, S. R., Johnson, K., & Turoff, M. (1986). Experiments in group decision making: Communication process and outcome in face-to-face versus computerized conferences. *Human Communication Research, 13*(2), 225–252.

[36]Eveland, J. D., & Bikson, T. K. (1989). *Workgroup structures and computer support: A field experiment.* Santa Monica, CA: RAND Corp.

[37]Sproull & Kiesler, *Connections.*

[38]McGuire, T. W., Keisler, S., & Siegel, J. (1987). Group and computer-mediated discussion effects in risk decision making. *Journal of Personality and Social Psychology, 52*(5), 917–930.

[39]Ibid.; Siegel, Dubrovsky, Keisler, & McGuire, "Group processes in computer-mediated communication."; Weisband, S. P. (1992). Group discussion and first advocacy effects in computer-mediated and face-to-face decision making groups. *Organizational Behavior and Human Decision Processes, 53*, 352–380.

[40]Sproull & Kiesler, *Connections.*

disappearance of gender differences (compared with face-to-face groups) was examined.[41] Surprisingly, gender differences in dominance were greatest when people were unable to individuate each other! At the same time, there is less awareness of the needs of the group or its members.[42] With more rudeness and less inhibition, conflicts in CMC are sharper and escalate more quickly. Consensus on complex, nontechnical issues is more difficult to reach.[43]

Technology Can Lead to Face-to-Face Meetings

An important value of information technology may come from the ability to generate face-to-face meetings that simply would not have occurred otherwise. Harold Sirkin, the global leader of Boston Consulting's operations practice, stays up past midnight e-mailing to employees in 38 countries. "I'm very responsive to e-mail, but you can't lead a global organization without meeting the people you're working with. They need to have a chance to ask questions and be part of the management decision-making process. And you have to be there and be listening. You can't do this by e-mail or phone alone." So, for the past 10+years, Sirkin and his 15-person leadership team meet twice a year, in Chicago and Paris, to talk business and build personal relationships.[44]

Increased Time to Make Decisions

CM groups have more difficulty reaching consensus than FTF groups.[45] The difficulty may be attributable in part to the diversity of opinions generated in CM interaction. CM groups take 4 to 10 times longer to reach a decision than face-to-face groups, with the greater differential occurring under no time constraints.[46] It takes longer to write than it does to speak; hence, communicating via information technology is slower. It takes four times as long for a three-person group to make a decision in a real-time computer conference as in a face-to-face meeting.[47] It takes as much as 10 times as long in a four-person computer-conference group that lacks time restrictions.[48] This is especially true when the technology is new.

Communication

Members of FTF teams engage in more communication than CM teams.[49] The lower frequency of communication in CM groups is known as **information suppression**.[50] CM groups may compensate for information suppression by sending more task-oriented messages as a proportion of their

[41]Postmes, T., & Spears, R. (2002). Behavior online: Does anonymous computer communication reduce gender inequality? *Personality and Social Psychology Bulletin, 28*(8), 1073–1083.

[42]McGrath, J. E. (1990). Time matters in groups. In J. Galegher, R. E. Kraut, & C. Egido (Eds.), *Intellectual teamwork: Social and technological foundations of cooperative work.* Mahwah, NJ: Lawrence Erlbaum & Associates.

[43]Hiltz, Johnson, & Turoff, "Experiments in group decision making."

[44]Ginsburg, M. (2009, January). Overseeing overseas. *Workforce Management.* workforce.com

[45]Dubrovsky, Keisler, & Sethna, "The equalization phenomenon."; Hiltz, S. R., Johnson, K., & Turoff, M. (1986). Experiments in group decision making: Communication process and outcome in face-to-face versus computerized conferences. *Human Communication Research, 13*(2), 225–252; Siegel, Dubrovsky, Kiesler, & McGuire, "Group processes in computer-mediated communication."

[46]Dubrovsky, Keisler, & Sethna, "The equalization phenomenon."; Siegel, Dubrovsky, Kiesler, & McGuire, "Group processes in computer-mediated communication."

[47]Siegel, Dubrovsky, Keisler, & McGuire, "Group processes," p. 358.

[48]Dubrovsky, Keisler, & Sethna, "The equalization phenomenon."

[49]For a review, see Hedlund, J., Ilgen, D. R., & Hollenbeck, J. R. (1998). Decision accuracy in computer-mediated versus face-to-face decision making teams. *Organizational Behavior and Human Decision Processes, 76*(1), 30–47.

[50]Hollingshead, A. B. (1996a). Information suppression and status persistence in group decision making: The effects of communication media. *Human Communication Research, 23*, 193–219; Hollingshead, A. B. (1996b). The rank-order effect in group decision making. *Organizational Behavior and Human Decision Processes, 68*(3), 181–193.

total messages,[51] generating more diverse opinions or decision recommendations,[52] and having information more readily accessible. CM lowers inhibition and thus leads to greater expression of personal opinions, including the use of personal insults and profanity—the "flaming effect."[53] In one investigation, 64 four-person teams worked for 3 hours on a computer simulation interacting either face-to-face or via a computer-mediated network. Members of FTF teams were better informed and made recommendations that were more predictive of the correct team decision, but leaders of CM teams were better at differentiating team members on the quality of their decisions (i.e., greater accountability).

Risk Taking

People intuitively perform cost-benefit analyses when considering different courses of action and, consequently, do not treat gains commensurately with losses. However, electronic interaction affects risk-taking behavior. Consider the following choices:

A. Return of $20,000 over 2 years
B. Fifty percent chance of gaining $40,000; 50 percent of gaining nothing

Option A is the safer investment; option B is riskier. However, these two options are mathematically identical, meaning that in an objective sense, people should not favor one option over the other. When posed with these choices, most managers are risk averse, meaning that they select the option that has the sure payoff as opposed to holding out for the chance to win big (or, equally as likely, not win at all). However, consider what happens when the following choice is proposed:

C. Sure loss of $20,000 over 2 years
D. Fifty-fifty percent chance of losing $40,000; 50 percent of losing nothing

Most managers are risk seeking and choose option D. Why? According to the framing effect, people are risk averse for gains and risk seeking for losses.[54] This can lead to self-contradictory, quirky behavior. By manipulating the reference point, a person's fiscal policy choices can change.

We saw in Chapter 7 that groups tend to make riskier decisions than do individuals in the same situation. Paradoxically, groups that make decisions via electronic communication are risk seeking for both gains and losses.[55] CM groups make riskier decisions and exhibit greater polarization of judgment than FTF groups.[56] For example, in FTF groups, members' decision recommendations tended to conform to the prior recommendations of other members. In CM groups, the last decision recommendations were as divergent from the group's final decision as were the first.[57] Furthermore, executives are just as confident of their decisions whether they are made through electronic communication or FTF communication.

---

[51]Hiltz, Johnson, & Turoff, "Experiments in group decision making," p. 358; Siegel, Dubrovsky, Keisler, & McGuire, "Group processes," p. 358.

[52]Dubrovsky, Keisler, & Sethna, "Equalization phenomenon," p. 358; Weisband, "Group discussion," p. 358.

[53]Dubrovsky, Keisler, & Sethna, "Equalization phenomenon," p. 358; Siegel, Dubrovsky, Keisler, & McGuire, "Group processes," p. 358; Weisband, "Group discussion," p. 358.

[54]Kahneman, D., & Tversky, A. (1979). Prospect theory: An analysis of decision under risk. *Econometrica, 47*, 263–291.

[55]McGuire, Keisler, & Siegel, "Group and computer-mediated discussion," p. 358.

[56]McGuire, Keisler, & Siegel, "Group and computer-mediated discussion," p. 358; Siegel, Dubrovsky, Keisler, & McGuire, "Group processes," p. 358; Weisband, "Group discussion," p. 358.

[57]Weisband, "Group discussion," p. 358.

Social Norms

When social context cues are missing or weak, people feel distant from others and somewhat anonymous. They are less concerned about making a good appearance, and humor tends to fall apart or to be misinterpreted. Additionally, the expression of negative emotion is no longer minimized because factors that keep people from acting out negative emotions are not in place when they communicate via information technology. Simply, in the absence of social norms that prescribe the expression of positive emotion, people are more likely to express negative emotion. When people communicate via e-mail, they are more likely to negatively confront others. Conventional behavior, such as politeness rituals and acknowledgment of others' views, decreases; rude, impulsive behavior, such as flaming, increases. People are eight times more likely to flame in electronic discussions than in face-to-face discussions.[58]

Task Performance and Quality of Group Decisions

Are people more effective when they communicate via information technology? The jury is still out. Studies analyzing the quality of group decisions have either found no differences between the two communication modes or differences in favor of FTF groups.[59] When the decision outcomes depend heavily on information exchange, FTF groups have an advantage over CM groups, but when other factors contribute to decision quality, CM groups may be better able to compensate for less information exchange.[60]

All the team configurations discussed in this chapter, with the exception of the same-time, same-place teams, are virtual teams, and, as such, face special challenges. In the sections that follow, we consider strategies for enhancing rapport and teamwork in local teams and remotely distributed teams.

ENHANCING LOCAL TEAMWORK: REDESIGNING THE WORKPLACE

Telecommuting often calls to mind a "bathrobe-clad knowledge worker" throwing in her contribution from the comfort of a home office.[61] In 2008, approximately 17.2 million Americans worked from home or remotely at least 1 day per month.[62] Managing virtual teams, making people accountable, and establishing clear goals are major challenges to telecommuting.

Teams that must work together don't necessarily confine themselves to traditional space and time. The trend seems to be work anywhere, anytime—in your car, home, office, and even your client's office. It means a radical disaggregation of work, going beyond the walls and confines of the traditional office.[63] By redesigning the environment that they work in, teams work more efficiently and effectively. Indeed, technology that can boost employee efficiency and mobility is surpassing facilities and real estate as the second biggest corporate operating

---

[58]Dubrovsky, Keisler, & Sethna, "Equalization phenomenon."

[59]For a review, see Hedlund, Ilgen, & Hollenbeck, "Decision accuracy in computer mediated versus face-to-face decision making teams."

[60]For a review, see Hedlund, Ilgen, & Hollenbeck, "Decision accuracy in computer mediated versus face-to-face decision making teams."

[61]Radigan, J. (2001, December 1). Remote possibilities: Companies are more interested than ever in a far-flung workforce. *CFO*, p. S5.

[62]The Dieringer Research Group Inc. (2009, February). *Telework trendlines 2009 World at work.* worldatwork.com

[63]O'Hamilton, J., Baker, S., & Vlasic, B. (1996, April). The new workplace. *Business Week, 3473*, 106–117.

expense, after salaries and benefits.[64] Increasingly, architects, interior designers, facilities managers, and furniture companies are assuming the new role of strategic design consultants not only with blueprints but also with human behavior in the organization. Many of the old perks, such as paneled offices and private lunchrooms, are disappearing. Instead, employees of every rank are out in the open.

The headquarters of the Danish audio and electronics company, Bang Olufsen, known as "The Farm" consists of glass boxes with wood floors perched on columns in the same rural meadow where the firm was founded in 1925.[65] When executives at Unilever noticed that much of their office space was either unused or unoccupied as workers traveled, they took away 36 percent of their employees' personal space. The company's offices in Leatherhead, England, now feature "agile" space: an open office where workers rearrange themselves throughout the day depending upon their tasks. They collaborate with one another while sitting at a table, take a break in a curvy "vitality" space, or concentrate alone in a small individual work area.[66] At IT and consulting company G.1440, exposed brickwork and strategically placed windows frame a small stream running through the building. And, when they're not hard at work, employees can chill out at the campus' snazzy pool, relax on comfy couches in the meeting room, or stroll the campus's walking trails. "It's not uncommon to see employees show up in flip-flops and jeans at 10 A.M. and stay well into the evening. People enjoy coming to work but, at the same time, they work really hard."[67]

Virtual or Flexible Space

Virtual or flexible space is physical space that is used on a temporary and changing basis to meet different needs. Instead of physical space setting limits on managerial behavior, such as how many people can be in a meeting at any one time and what information technology is or is not available, virtual space means that people determine their needs first and design the space to fit those needs. It is an entirely different way of thinking about space. Most important, virtual or flexible space does not mean open, fixed cubicles.

A prime example of virtual or flexible space is the "cave and commons" design. The idea is to balance individual work and teamwork, as well as privacy and community. A 2008 study by global architecture and consulting firm Gensler found a direct correlation between office design and performance, using space as a business tool. The study looked at four key work modes—focus, collaboration, learning, and social interaction—and found that organizations that support all four through their work space design perform better than organizations that do not.[68]

Coworking Communities

Coworking is a new way that people can be near others, but those other people are not on their team. In a coworking community, people drive to an office, and there are people in the office, but they are not working together, rather they are sharing a space, much like the way that people

---

[64]Ibid.

[65]Keeps, D. A. (2009, September 1). Out-of-the-box offices. *Cnn Money.* Money.cnn.com

[66]Reed, S. E. (2009, December 24). On the death of the cubicle. *Global Post.* globalpost.com

[67]Antoniades, C. B. (2009, February). 25 best places to work. *Baltimore Magazine.*

[68]*Can a well-designed office pay off* [Audio podcast]? (2008, October 21). businessweek.com.

EXHIBIT 13-5 Before Implementing Alternative Forms of Office Space . . .

1. The presence or absence of a strong champion is very important to the success/failure of the project.
2. Many issues that management may feel are barriers to implementing innovative ideas are perceived barriers.
3. A richer, more varied set of work settings that truly support the range of work activities must be provided.
4. A business approach to implementing innovations must be used instead of a cost approach.
5. User involvement is very critical to the success of the project.
6. Reinvesting a portion of the innovation cost savings is likely to result in a far higher level of employee satisfaction.
7. Using a pilot project to apply a standardized solution is ineffective.
8. The reassessment and data collection phase must not be eliminated.
9. Employees must be given time to adjust to the new work patterns.

Source: Becker, F., Quinn, K. L., Rappaport, A. J., & Sims, W. R. (1994). *Implementing innovative workplaces.* Ithaca, NY: New York State College of Human Ecology, Department of Design and Environmental Analysis, Cornell University.

---

work out a gym in the presence of others. The new design of offices and furniture indicates that most managers and executives regard FTF communication to be the ideal—and the more of it the better. However, it is not always possible to bring team members together, especially those who are spread across the globe. The answer is the virtual team.

Implementing these types of alternative office spaces should be considered carefully (consider the lessons in Exhibit 13-5).

VIRTUAL TEAMS

A **virtual team** is a task-focused group that meets without all members necessarily being physically present or even working at the same time. In the United States alone, as many as 8.4 million people are members of one or more virtual teams.[69] The years 2003 to 2008 saw an 800 percent jump in the number of virtual employees.[70] On the days that they worked, 21 percent of employed persons in 2008 did some or all of their work at home, and 86 percent did some or all of their work at their workplace.[71] But only 8.5 percent of workers worked in their company's headquarters.[72] Virtual teams work closely together even though they may be separated by many miles or even continents. Virtual teams may meet through conference calls, videoconferences, e-mail, or other communications tools, such as application sharing. Teams may include employees only, or they may include outsiders, such as a customer's employees. Virtual teams work well for global companies, but they can also benefit small companies operating from a single location, especially if decision makers are often at job sites or on the

---

[69]Ahuja, M., & Galvin, J. (2003). Socialization in virtual groups. *Journal of Management, 29,* 161–185.
[70]Fisher, A. (2009, November 19). How to build a (strong) virtual team. *CNNmoney.com.* money.cnn.com
[71]United States Department of Labor, Bureau of Labor Statistics. (2009, June 24). *American time survey—2008 results.* bls.gov.com
[72]Nemertes Research. (2008). *Nemertes benchmark: Building a successful virtual workplace.* nemertes.com

road. They can be short lived or permanent, such as operational teams that run their companies virtually.

Virtual teams are not just a necessity for companies that have multiple sites; they offer some distinct advantages over traditional teams.[73] First, virtual teams combine the best talents of people in companies, thereby allowing better use of human resources. And because of their virtual nature, they can provide team members with a level of empowerment that more traditional teams do not enjoy.

A 2009 internal study by Cisco found that approximately 69 percent of 2,000 employees surveyed cited higher productivity when working remotely, and 75 percent of those surveyed said the timeliness of their work improved. "A properly executed program for telecommuting can be extremely effective at unlocking employee potential by increasing work-life balance, productivity and overall satisfaction," said Rami Mazid, vice president for Global Client Services and Operations.[74]

If a company needs virtual teams, the biggest challenge for productivity is coordination of effort: how to get people to work together compatibly and productively, even though face-to-face contact is limited and communication is confined to phone, fax, and e-mail. Virtual teams need to consider three factors for their ultimate success: (1) their locations relative to one another, (2) the percentage of time they spend FTF, and (3) their level of technical support.[75] Conflict is just as important for virtual teams as it is for colocated teams (see Exhibit 13-6). An investigation of a large software firm revealed that virtual teams have greater "process conflict" than do colocated teams.[76]

Threats to Effective Processes in Virtual Teams

According to Wageman, process loss or threats to performance can take different forms for virtual teams than traditional teams.[77] Following the basic model of teamwork, introduced in Chapter 2, consider Wageman's analysis of threats to performance and synergistic gains in virtual teams.

First, in terms of effort or motivation, the physical distance and asynchronous aspect of communication may both act to dampen effort. Withdrawal of effort by one member of the team, however unintentional, may well lead to the withdrawal of effort by other members. Team members might make "untested attributions" about the level of commitment others have to the team. Members may assume that a given member's (apparently) low effort reflects a low level of motivation. This withdrawal can spread to other members and thus affect the motivational norms of the group. Further, the asynchronic method of communication may contribute to this pattern.

With respect to knowledge and skill, teams may not make the best use of the actual talents of its members. In fact, members of virtual teams may have considerably less knowledge about members' task-relevant knowledge and skill than do traditional teams. Leaders might know why

[73]Wageman, R. (2003). Virtual processes: Implications for coaching the virtual team. In R. Peterson & E. A. Mannix (Eds.), *Leading and managing people in the dynamic organization* (pp. 65–86). Mahwah, NJ: Lawrence Erlbaum Associates.

[74]Cisco study finds telecommuting significantly increases employee productivity, work-life flexibility and job satisfaction. (2009, June 26). Marketwire.com

[75]Griffith, T. L., Mannix, E. A., & Neale, M. A. (2002). Conflict and virtual teams. In S. G. Cohen & C. B. Gibson (Eds.), *Creating conditions for effective virtual teams*. San Francisco, CA: Jossey-Bass.

[76]Ibid.

[77]Wageman, "Virtual processes."

EXHIBIT 13-6 Traditional, Hybrid, and Virtual Teams

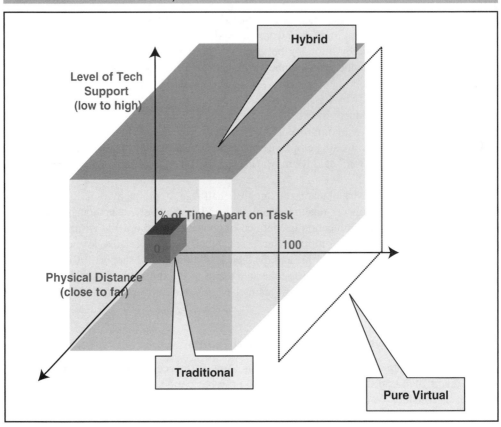

Source: Griffith, T. L., Mannix, E. A., & Neale, M. A. (2002). Conflict and virtual teams. In S. G. Cohen & C. B. Gibson (Eds.), *Creating conditions for effective virtual teams.* San Francisco, CA: Jossey-Bass.

certain members were selected for the virtual team, but members may not. Consider two types of information in teams: **tacit knowledge** and **codified knowledge**.[78] Tacit knowledge is hard to articulate and acquired through experience.[79] In contrast, codified knowledge refers to knowledge that is transmittable in formal, symbolic language. Data from multiple hospitals learning to use a new technology revealed that when team performance relies on tacit knowledge, performance was more varied. Team members were unable to describe to other hospital sites precisely what they did to get the technology to work.

With regard to communication and strategy, virtual teams have steep challenges to surmount. Simple decisions, such as scheduling a conference call can often lead to confusion about time zones.

---

[78]Edmondson, A., Winslow, A., Bohmer, R., & Pisano, G. (2003). Learning how and learning what: Effects of tacit and codified knowledge on performance improvement following technology adoption. *Decision Sciences, 34*(2), 197–223.
[79]Polanyi, M. (1966). *The tacit dimension.* London: Routledge & Kegan Paul.

EXHIBIT 13-7 Managerial Interventions During Virtual Project Team Life Cycle

Forming	Storming	Norming	Performing
• Realistic virtual project team previews	• Face-to-face team-building sessions	• Create customized templates or team charters specifying task requirements	• Ensure departmental and company culture supports virtual teamwork
• Coaching from experienced team members	• Training on conflict resolution	• Set individual accountabilities, completion dates, and schedules	• Provide sponsor support and resources for team to perform
• Develop a shared understanding and sense of team identity	• Encourage conflicting employees to work together to find common ground	• Establish procedures for sharing information	
• Develop a clear mission	• Shuttle diplomacy and mediation to create compromise solutions	• Distinguish task, social, and contextual information; design procedures appropriate for each	
• Acquire senior management support		• Assign a team coach with skills for managing virtually	

Source: Furst, S., Reeves, M., Rosen, B., & Blackburn, R. (2004). Managing the life cycle of virtual teams. *Academy of Management Executive, 18*(2), 6–20. Copyright 2004 by Academy of Management (NY). Reproduced with permission of Academy of Management (NY) in the format Textbook via Copyright Clearance Center.

Strategies for Enhancing the Virtual Team

There are a variety of methods for enhancing the performance of virtual teamwork. Some of the strategies involve structural interventions and support. Other strategies involve specific behaviors of the people involved (see also Exhibit 13-7 for a description of the interventions managers can make in virtual teams during the four stages of forming, storming, norming, and performing). We first explore structural solutions and then focus on interpersonal solutions.

STRUCTURAL SOLUTIONS FOR VIRTUAL TEAMWORK   The following methods are used by various companies to address the rapport and trust problem that virtual teams encounter. Few of these methods have been tested in rigorous controlled research. We begin by discussing the most elaborate (and most expensive).

Group Support Systems   A group support system (GSS), or electronic meeting system, combines communication, computer, and decision technologies to support decision making and related group activities.[80] Examples of GSS include electronic messaging and chat, teleconferencing, document management, and calendaring.

Poole identifies four types of GSS depending upon group size and location (see Exhibit 13-8).[81] The "decision room" is the electronic equivalent to traditional face-to-face meeting and is similar to electronic brainstorming. One feature of decision rooms is a "topic

---

[80]Poole, S. (2003). Group support systems. *Encyclopedia of Information Systems, 2,* 501–507.
[81]Ibid.

EXHIBIT 13-8 Possible Configurations for Group Support Systems (GSS)

	Small Group	Large Group
Colocated	Decision room	Legislative session
Dispersed	Local area decision network	Computer-mediated conference

Source: Poole, S. (2003). Group support systems. *Encyclopedia of Information Systems, 2,* 501–507.

commenter," in which team members enter their idea about a topic and then view and comment on others' entries as they are presented on their computer screen. This creates a "running conversation" that occurs via text. GSS is not intended to replace group communication but rather to provide additional channels for communication. A group might use GSS only at certain points during a meeting.

One example of a GSS is a collaboratory. A **collaboratory** is the combination of technology, tools, and infrastructure that allows scientists to work with remote facilities and each other as if they were collocated.[82] It is a center without walls in which scientists and technicians can perform research without regard to geographic location. For example, the University of Colorado, Colorado State University, the Colorado School of Mines, and the U.S. Department of Energy's National Renewable Energy Laboratory (NREL) formed a collaboration where scientists and academic researchers work with each other and with private companies to develop new energy technologies and transfer them to the marketplace. Instead of marketing individual programs and research, the organizations present themselves as one entity.[83] Parallels in the business world include virtual corporations in the place of physical corporations and a global workplace instead of national or local workplaces.[84] Although the collaboratory requires no face-to-face contact, teams often need some degree of face-to-face contact to establish rapport. There are several types of interaction that will help develop rapport among team members and force them to work in a single geographic location. The length of the face-to-face interaction varies by method. Among them are initial face-to-face experience, temporary engagement, and the 1-day videoconference.

Virtual Team Technology A surge of collaborative Web technology solutions for teaming have appeared in recent years. Some companies, like IBM, use 3D technology that runs virtual worlds such as Second Life.[85] IBM builds virtual work spaces that allow employees scattered all over the globe use avatars to negotiate such tasks as rehearsing presentations or learning about employee benefits. Similarly, at Sun Microsystems, nearly 50 percent of employees may work outside traditional office spaces on a given day and use virtual world technology to build a global corporate culture.

---

[82]Finholt, T. A., & Olson, G. M. (1997). From laboratories to collaboratories: A new organizational form for scientific collaboration. *Psychological Science, 8*(1), 28–36.
[83]Department of Public Relations Colorado State University. (2008, June 4). *Collaboratory receives economic development honor, major progress after 18 months.* news.colostate.edu
[84]Davidow, W. H., & Malone, M. S. (1992). *The virtual corporation: Structuring and revitalizing the corporation for the 21st century.* New York: HarperCollins; O'Hara-Devereaux, M., & Johansen, R. (1994). *Global work: Bridging distance, culture and time.* San Francisco, CA: Jossey-Bass.
[85]The (virtual) global office. (2008, May 5). *Business Week.* businessweek.com

Another type of technology is a combination of Facebook and Twitter within a company,[86] online tools in which salespeople can record their prospects and completed deals so that other employees can be in the loop about who's doing what. Employees post their corporate activities and choose whose activities they want to follow. Known as a "walled garden," you only follow or broadcast to colleagues. Informal, online networks of virtual employees share ideas that blur the margins between personal life and work. Of course one concern is that these tools carry risks. Employees encouraged to tap social networking sites can fritter away hours, or, worse, they may compromise confidential information or malign the company. For this reason, consultants are often called in to help companies work out their strategies for blogs and micro blogging. In one case, a consultant for FedEx had an ugly encounter with a racist at the Memphis airport, and he twittered that "he would die if he had to live" in the city. The tweet produced a hailstorm of blogged fury from FedEx employees.[87]

Some companies that have a highly virtual workforce have introduced "clubs" that bring people together. For example, approximately 40 percent of IBM's 400,000 employees are virtual.[88] IBM clubs are an old company tradition that was long ago discarded until executives resurrected them. The clubs bring employees (and sometimes their families) together for trips, such as to the zoo, as well as work-related coaching and mentoring sessions.

Group technologies may be classified into four major categories based on the functional role that the technology plays in the work of a group (see Exhibit 13-9).[89]

Initial Face-to-Face Experience   Bringing together team members for a short, face-to-face experience is often used by companies who want to lay a groundwork of trust and communication for later teamwork that will be conducted strictly electronically. It is much easier for people to work together if they have met face-to-face. Face-to-face contact humanizes people and creates expectations for team members to use in their subsequent long-distance work together. A study of 208 senior business students revealed that as compared to those who met face to face for an introductory meeting, those who met electronically lagged significantly behind in terms of trust and collaboration.[90] The introductory face-to-face meeting plays a large role in the development of trust and collaboration, especially when the context is competitive.

Temporary Engagement   In a temporary engagement, team members work face-to-face before they are separated for distance work. When Boeing built the Dreamliner passenger jet, it sought to expand its longtime outsourcing efforts, in which the suppliers would also be Boeing's partners. Design teams met in face-to-face settings, but most of the work was performed in separate locations.[91]

One-Day Videoconference   When forklift manufacturer Clark Material Handling was bought out by Youn-An Hat, a Korean company, sales engineers like Clark Simpson had a hard time communicating with their new colleagues, given that they were physically not able to talk to one another face to face. So, the company engineers started using video conferencing to

---

[86]Lashinsky, A. (2009, December 3). Salesforce.com gets social [Web log post]. brainstormtech.blogs.fortune.cnn.com
[87]Baker, S. (2009, December 14). Beware social media snake oil. *Business Week*, *4159*, 48–51.
[88]Fisher, "How to build a (strong) virtual team."
[89]McGrath, J. E., & Hollingshead, A. B. (1994). *Groups interacting with technology*. Newbury Park, CA: Sage.
[90]Hill, N. S., Bartol, K. M., Tesluk, P. E., & Langa, G. A. (2009). Organizational context and face-to-face interaction: Influence on the development of trust and collaborative behaviors in computer-mediated groups. *Organizational Behavior & Human Decision Process*, *109*, 187–201.
[91]Wash, W. (2009, September 6). A Dream Interrupted at Boeing. *The New York Times*, p. BU1.

EXHIBIT 13-9 Technologies that Support Groups		
Technology	**Functional Role**	**Example**
GCSS (Group Communication Support Systems)	Providing or modifying within-group communication	Video conference Phone conference Computer conference Voice mail E-mail Fax Homepages Web sites
GISS (Group Information Support Systems)	Supplementing information available to the group or its members by information drawn from databases	Quantitative databases (e.g., sales records and production and cost data) Qualitative databases or archives (e.g., libraries and newspaper files)
GXSS (Group eXternal Support Systems)	Providing or modifying external communication with those outside the group	Extranets (e.g., for obtaining upgrades)
GPSS (Group Performance Support Systems)	Channeling or modifying the group's task performance processes and task products	Tools for electronic brain-storming, evaluation and voting tools, etc.

Source: Hollingshead, A. B. (2001). Communication technologies, the internet, and group research. In M. Hogg and R. S. Tindale (Eds.), *Blackwell handbook of social psychology, Vol. 3: Group Processes* (pp. 557–573). Oxford, UK: Blackwell.

develop better relationships. "It's a major improvement over teleconferencing. Somehow, because we can see one another's facial expressions and hand gestures, we can understand one another better. There's something about being able to see one another that makes us relate more informally, too. We joke back and forth, which we never did over the telephone. It changes the tone of the meeting."[92] Thus, if an initial face-to-face meeting is out of the question, an alternative may be to at least get everyone online so that people can attach a name to a face. Depending on the size of the team and locations of members, this alternative may be more feasible than a face-to-face meeting.

Touching Base   If teams do not have an opportunity to work together at the outset of a project, then providing an opportunity for them to touch base at some later point can be helpful. This method is most useful for teams in which one or two members are remotely located. There are often special problems when just one member of the team is remotely located from the rest of the local team. Because much teamwork is done informally at the watercooler or at lunch, the remote person often feels lonely and disconnected from the rest of the team, and the rest of the team may leave that person out of the loop—if not deliberately, then just because it is cumbersome to bring the outsider up to date on all team actions.

---

[92]Olsen, P. (2008, April 20). An ocean apart, bridged by forklift. *The New York Times*, p. BU17.

INTERPERSONAL SOLUTIONS FOR VIRTUAL TEAMWORK   We now focus on interpersonal solutions for enhancing virtual teamwork.

Schmoozing   **Schmoozing** (as described in Chapter 5) is our name for contact between people that has the psychological effect of having established a relationship with someone. Also referred to as the **virtual handshake,**[93] the exchange of some basic personal information significantly expedites the operation of virtual teams. There are a variety of non–face-to-face schmoozing strategies, such as exchanging pictures or biographical information or engaging in a simple get-acquainted e-mail exchange. Schmoozing increases liking and rapport and results in more profitable business deals than when people just get down to business.[94] Perhaps the most attractive aspect of schmoozing is that it is relatively low cost and efficient. Merely exchanging a few short e-mails describing yourself can lead to better business relations. However, you should not expect people to naturally schmooze—at least at the outset of a business relationship. Team members working remotely have a tendency to get down to business. A field study of 43 teams, 22 colocated and 21 distributed from a large multinational company revealed that virtual teams reported more task and interpersonal conflict than did co-located teams. However, the teams that engaged in "spontaneous communication" developed a stronger sense of shared group identity and mitigated conflict.[95] In this study, spontaneous communication, like schmoozing, referred to informal, unplanned interactions among team members.

Master Virtual Communication Etiquette   Unless people have had special training, they are likely to commit blunders when communicating virtually. Think of virtual teamwork as requiring an intensified state of communication. Consider five key best practices for improving your own virtual communication etiquette (see also Exhibit 13-10, the virtual meeting checklist).[96]

• *Establish the purpose and importance of the team up front:*   The goal of the team and of each meeting of the team needs to be clear. This means writing it down and making sure everyone receives the goal before the communication commences. Ask for feedback about the relevance of the goal. Invite people to critique whether a meeting at this time is mission critical for achieving the goal.

• *Listen actively:*   In a face-to-face meeting, we can often decipher meaning from the context of the participants and their nonverbal behavior. However, none of these nonverbal cues are readily available in a virtual team meeting. Most people listen passively; in virtual teams, it is important to actively listen. This means asking questions.

• *Avoid monologues:*   The tendency to "show and tell" can be overpowering in a virtual team meeting. Avoid the monologue trap by inviting interaction and input from others. Ask particular people for input, rather than just saying, "What do you all think?" One investigation of 47 technical and administration work teams in a multinational energy company revealed that larger teams were more likely to use technology to dominate one another rather than to collaborate.[97] Moreover, such "appropriation" was negatively related to team

[93]Teten, D., & Allen, S. (2005). *The virtual handshake.* New York: AMACOM.

[94]Moore, D., Kurtzberg, T., Thompson, L., & Morris, M. (1999). Long and short routes to success in electronically-mediated negotiations: Group affiliations and good vibrations. *Organizational Behavior and Human Decision Processes, 77*(1), 22–43.

[95]Hinds & Mortensen, "Understanding conflict in geographically distributed teams."

[96]Dinnocenzo, D. (2006). *How to lead from a distance: Building bridges in the virtual workplace.* Dallas, TX: Walk the Talk.

[97]DeSanctis, G., Poole, M. S., & Dickson, G. W. (2000). Teams and technology: Interactions over time. *Research on Managing Groups and Teams, 3*, 1–27.

EXHIBIT 13-10 The Virtual Meeting Checklist

Before the Meeting	During the Meeting	After the Meeting
• Plan the agenda • Distribute the agenda • Clarify responsibilities • Identify the technology to be used • Arrange for required equipment, information, and people • Test the technology	• Encourage all participants to introduce themselves and identify themselves when they speak • Establish expectations for involvement • Distribute visual or graphic resources ahead of time • Remind everyone to speak slowly, clearly, and in direction of microphones • Suggest using mute button to eliminate background noise	• Distribute the meeting summary • Schedule follow-up • Implement action steps • Solicit feedback from participants as to how the meeting could be improved

Source: Dinnocenzo, D. (2006). *How to lead from a distance: Building bridges in the virtual workplace* (pp. 32–33). Dallas, TX: Walk the Talk. Used by permission of Debra A. Dinnocenzo. www.virtualworkswell.com

outcomes. And, teams with more sophisticated knowledge of technology were the most likely to dominate via appropriation.

   • *Summarize often and confirm understanding:*   Throughout the conversation, summarize the progress and decisions. Refer back to the goal of the meeting. A study of 115 teams in 20 subsidiaries of a multinational organization revealed that responsiveness and knowledge management increased learning within the team and led to better performance and interpersonal relations.[98]

   • *Agree on actions and next steps:*   Never conclude a virtual meeting without discussing the future. Think at least 3 months out and get commitments on what every team member will do and when they will deliver. Summarize the plan and then follow up with an e-mail or posting that people can refer to.

Undercommit and Overdeliver   On virtual teams, reputations are formed quickly and often create a self-fulfilling prophecy. The first 30 days are very important. One of the best ways to get a reputation for being a "good virtual team" member is to be reliable. To be thought of as reliable, you need to deliver what you promise. Many people overpromise and underdeliver. A far better approach is to undercommit and overdeliver. Dinnocenzo suggests three steps for building your own **reliability capital:** (1) Keep a written list of all the agreements, promises, and commitments you make. Check it frequently. (2) Ask your team to tell you one thing you can do to be more reliable in their eyes, and then do it. (3) Be available to support and respond to team members. When you are not available, follow up as soon as possible.

Show Integrity   Virtual teamwork creates situations ripe for taking advantage, hidden agendas, and confusion. Without daily face-to-face opportunities to discuss situations and share concerns, people may start to question the integrity of some team members. It is

---

[98]Zellmer-Bruhn, M., & Gibson, C. (2006). Multinational organizational context: Implications for team learning and performance. *Academy of Management Journal, 49*(3), 501–518.

important to demonstrate your integrity in your virtual team interactions. Dinnocenzo suggests four steps to demonstrate your integrity to your virtual team: (1) Be truthful and forthright without being obnoxious about it. This means providing others with honest feedback. (2) Avoid sarcasm, joking, and teasing in your distance interactions. Jokes can be misinterpreted and set the stage for evasive conversations. (3) Maintain confidences; don't spread gossip or share confidential information. Tell people your standards. (4) Handle sensitive material appropriately.[99]

Increase your Familiarity   Distributed (virtual) teams experienced higher levels of conflict than colocated teams.[100] Being distant from one's team and relying on technology to interact can breed conflict because team members do not feel that they have a shared sense of identity and do not know one another. Thus, it is important to become familiar to your team. The **mere-exposure effect** refers to the tendency of people to like those whom they are exposed to more often. In other words, if you are familiar to people, they like you more! However, virtual teams can severely inhibit familiarity. Therefore, it is important to take every opportunity to talk with your team by phone and schedule face-to-face meetings (even if they are only 10 minutes long) whenever you can.[101]

Coach the Virtual Team   Wageman's model of coaching the virtual team focuses on interventions at team launch, natural breakpoints, and at the end of a performance period.[102] The launch of a virtual team should outline a goal and motivating purpose that will shape virtual team members' motivation. In addition, the team should have a set of clear boundaries, such that all members know who is on the team and why. This is a good point to apprise members of the skills of others. Another opportunity for coaching occurs at natural breakpoints, such as when a milestone has occurred.

CROSS-CULTURAL TEAMWORK

In most virtual teams, people must work closely and competently with people from different geographic and national cultures. As if distance were not challenging enough, cross-cultural teamwork can also create misunderstanding and conflict, thereby threatening performance.

Cultural Intelligence

Cultural Intelligence is a person's capability to adapt effectively to new cultural contexts.[103] Cultural intelligence is believed to enhance the likelihood that teams on global assignments will actively engage in four key states of learning: experience, reflection, conceptualization, and experimentation.[104] (See Exhibit 13-11 for Earley's Cultural Intelligence scale.)

---

[99]Dinnocenzo, *How to lead from a distance.*
[100]Armstrong & Cole, "Managing distances and differences," p. 348; Hinds, P. J., & Bailey, D. E. (2003). Out of sight, out of sync: Understanding conflict in distributed teams. *Organization Science, 14*(6), 615–632.
[101]Dinnocenzo, *How to lead from a distance.*
[102]Wageman, "Virtual processes."
[103]Earley, C. P. (2002). Redefining interactions across cultures and organizations: Moving forward with cultural intelligence. In B. M. Staw & R. M. Kramer (Eds.), *Research in organizational behavior* (Vol. 24, pp. 271–299). Oxford, UK: Elsevier.
[104]Ng, K., Van Dyne, L., & Ang, S. (2009). From experience to experiential learning: Cultural intelligence as a learning capability for global leader development. *Academy of Management Learning & Education, 8*(4), 511–526.

EXHIBIT 13-11 Assessing Cultural Intelligence

Rate the extent to which you agree with each statement, using the following scale:
1 = strongly disagree, 2 = disagree, 3 = neutral, 4 = agree, 5 = strongly agree.

_____ Before I interact with people from a new culture, I ask myself what I hope to achieve.

_____ If I encounter something unexpected while working in a new culture, I use this experience to figure out new ways to approach other cultures in the future.

_____ I plan how I'm going to relate to people from a different culture before I meet them.

_____ When I come into a new cultural situation, I can immediately sense whether something is going well or something is wrong.

Total _____ ÷ 4 = _____ **Cognitive CQ**

_____ It's easy for me to change my body language (e.g., eye contact and posture) to suit people from a different culture.

_____ I can alter my expression when a cultural encounter requires it.

_____ I modify my speech style (e.g., accent and tone) to suit people from a different culture.

_____ I easily change the way I act when a cross-cultural encounter seems to require it.

Total _____ ÷ 4 = _____ **Physical CQ**

_____ I have confidence that I can deal well with people from a different culture.

_____ I am certain that I can befriend people whose cultural backgrounds are different from mine.

_____ I can adapt to the lifestyle of a different culture with relative ease.

_____ I am confident that I can deal with a cultural situation that's unfamiliar.

Total _____ ÷ 4 = _____ **Emotional/motivational CQ**

Source: Earley, C., & Mosakowski, E. (2004). Cultural intelligence. *Harvard Business Review, 82*(10), 139–146. Reprinted by permission of Harvard Business Review. Copyright © 2004 by the Harvard Business School Publishing Corporation, all rights reserved.

Work Ways

Work ways describe a culture's signature pattern of workplace beliefs, mental models, and practices that embody that culture's ideas about what is good, true, and efficient within the domain of work.[105] Cultural differences are amplified rather than diminished in work contexts.[106]

The fusion principle of coexistence facilitates the ability of global teams to extract information and make decisions as compared to letting the dominant culture dictate the work ways or compromising.[107]

Cultural Values

People from various cultures can differ in many ways. We focus on the "big three" cultural differences[108] (see Exhibit 13-12):

- Individualism versus collectivism

---

[105]Sanchez-Burks, J., & Lee, F. (2007). Cultural psychology of workways. In S. Kitayama & D. Cohen (Eds.), *Handbook of cultural psychology.* New York: Guilford Press.

[106]Sanchez-Burks, J. (2002). Protestant relational ideology and (in) attention to relational cues in work settings. *Journal of Personality and Social Psychology, 83*, 919–929.

[107]Janssens, M., & Brett, J. M. (2006). Cultural intelligence in global teams: A fusion model of collaboration. *Group & Organization Management, 31*, 124–153.

[108]Brett, J. M. (2007). *Negotiating globally: How to negotiate deals, resolve disputes, and make decisions, across cultural boundaries.* San Francisco, CA: Jossey-Bass.

EXHIBIT 13-12 Dimensions of Culture

Goal: individual versus collective orientation	*Individualists/Competitors:* Key goal is to maximize self-interest; source of identity is the self; people regard themselves as free agents and independent actors.	*Collectivists/Cooperators:* Key goal is to maximize the welfare of the group or collective; source of identity is the group; individuals regard themselves as group members; focus is on social interaction.
Influence: egalitarianism versus hierarchy	*Egalitarians:* Do not perceive many social obligations; believe that status differences are permeable.	*Hierarchists:* Regard social order to be important in determining influence; subordinates are expected to defer to superiors; superiors are expected to look out for subordinates.
Communication: direct versus indirect	*Direct Communicators:* Engage in explicit, direct information exchange; ask direct questions.	*Indirect Communicators:* Engage in tacit information exchange such as storytelling, inference making; situational norms.

Source: Brett, J. M. (2007). *Negotiating globally: How to negotiate deals, resolve disputes, and make decisions, across cultural boundaries* (2nd ed.). San Francisco, CA: Jossey-Bass.

- Egalitarianism versus hierarchy
- Direct versus indirect communication

INDIVIDUALISM VERSUS COLLECTIVISM   For people from individualistic cultures, the pursuit of happiness and regard for personal welfare is paramount. The focus is on the individual as a distinctive level of analysis. For people in collectivist cultures, the focus is on the social group or unit. The fundamental unit of analysis is not the individual, in possession of his or her unalienable rights; rather, the focus is on the social group. People from individualistic cultures are more likely to use *I*, *me*, and *mine* pronouns; people from collectivistic cultures are more likely to use plural pronouns, such as *we*, *us*, and *ours*. Most modern Western and democratic societies and their organizations place ultimate value on the individual person; this creates an intrinsic and inherently irresolvable tension between the individual and the group and the individual and the organization.[109] In contrast, Eastern and Asian societies have a synergistic view of the person and the group. Perhaps it is for this reason that when publishing giant Wolters Kluwer needed to penetrate in China, they used a team model. Pairs of salespeople worked together and were compensated as a team.[110]

EGALITARIANISM VERSUS HIERARCHY   Egalitarianism versus hierarchy refers to how the different status layers in a society or organization relate to one another. In egalitarian cultures, members of high- and low-status groups communicate frequently and do not go to great lengths to perpetuate differences. Further, the status levels in egalitarian cultures are inherently permeable—meaning that if a person works hard enough, he or she can advance in an organization.

---

[109]Drechsler, W. (1995). Collectivism. In H. Drechsler, W. Hillinge, & F. Neumann (Eds.), *Society and state: The lexicon of politics* (9th ed., pp. 458–459). Munich, Germany: Franz Vahlen.

[110]Mehta, S. (2008, December 18). How to sell in China. *CNNmoney.com.* money.cnn.com

In hierarchical cultures and organizations, status differences are not easily permeated. As a consequence, members of different classes or status levels do not communicate frequently, and there is a deep sense of obligation among those at the highest levels to provide for and protect those at the lowest-status levels who, in turn, put their trust in the high-status members of their organization.

DIRECT VERSUS INDIRECT COMMUNICATION   A key difference among cultures is in terms of how people communicate. Some cultures are characterized by direct communication between organizational actors. In other cultures, communication, particularly that between members of different status levels, is indirect and highly nuanced.

Conclusion

Teams have been dealing with place and time issues for several decades. The traditional approach was to relocate employees; newer solutions are more varied, creative, (often) cheaper, and less permanent. There is a strong intuition in the business world that face-to-face communication is necessary for trust, understanding, and enjoyment. However, face-to-face communication in no way ensures higher team productivity—especially in the case of creative teams. Information technology can increase productivity of teams. The skilled manager knows when to use it, and knows which obstacles are likely to crop up when using it, and how to address those obstacles.

Appendixes

APPENDIX 1

Managing Meetings

A Toolkit

"A meeting is a gathering where people speak up, say nothing, and then all disagree."

—Kayser, 1990

The work of teams largely proceeds through meetings. Whether they are regularly scheduled or called out of need, effective meeting management is a key to success. Furthermore, people spend a lot of time in meetings. Senior managers attend nearly 23 hours of meetings every week;[1] middle managers spend 35 percent of their work week in meetings, and top managers spend 50 to 80 percent of their time in meetings.[2] In addition to scheduled meetings, managers are involved in unscheduled and non-job-related meetings.

Perhaps meetings would not be a bad thing if they were economical and effective. At least 28 percent of professionals believe meetings are unproductive, and almost half (45 percent) think employees would be more productive if meetings were banned 1 day a week.[3] As one senior executive put it, "To waste your own time is unfortunate, but to waste the time of others is unforgivable." Companies are so overburdened with meetings that experts say it's a wonder any work gets done. Meetings also trigger stress. John Murray, president of the Buffalo Niagara YMCA, often travels to meet with YMCA leaders in places such as Greece, Albania, and Kosovo. Though he usually has a translator to help him during the meetings, it sometimes doesn't work out as planned. At a recent meeting in Greece, the board had a heated 40-minute discussion, during which his translator said nothing. "I just sat there, had some coffee and tried to stay engaged," he said. "The difficulty is how do you stay engaged when you have no idea what's being said?! I've been to meetings where someone really insulted someone, and it got really heated, and you don't know what to say."[4] Not surprisingly, managers have resorted to using various tactics, which vary from the radical (removing all chairs to make people stand, locking the doors, requiring people to pay 25 cents before speaking, etc.) to the more tame. Dixon Schwabl Advertising arms its 82 employees with water guns, which employees are instructed to bring to all meetings[5] (see example in Exhibit A1–1).

[1]Rogelberg, S. G., Scott, C., & Kello, J. (2007, Winter). The Science and fiction of meetings. *MIT Sloan Management Review, 48*(2), 18–21.

[2]Boiney, L. G. (2009). Knowledge is power. *Pepperdine University.* Retrieved from http://gbr.pepperdine.edu

[3]Van der Pool, L. (2009, May 7). Survey: Office meetings often a waste of time. *Boston Business Journal.* boston.bizjournals.com

[4]Drury, T. (2008, August 1). A bad meeting is just that. *Business First.* buffalo.bizjournals.com

[5]Maltby, E. (2010, January 7). Boring meetings? Get out the water guns. *Wall Street Journal*, p. B5.

EXHIBIT A1-1 Meeting Tactics

Frustrated by workers so plugged in to technology that they tuned out in the middle of business meetings, some Silicon Valley companies have put a ban on laptops in meetings, along with BlackBerrys and iPhones. While some companies have spent years coming up with novel ways to keep meetings from sucking up time—for example, removing chairs and forcing people to stand and having everyone drink a glass of water beforehand—the omnipresence of small laptops and smart phones created a new diversion for bored meeting participants. Adaptive Path encourages everyone to leave their laptops at their desks. Mobile and smart phones are stowed on a counter or in a box during meetings.

Photo-sharing site SmugMug Inc. in Mountain View, California, is a self-described "anti-meeting" company, according to founder Don MacAskill. "We have a single all-hands meeting once per week, and the emphasis is on getting it over fast. Each person is expected to answer the question 'What am I working on this week?' and is expressly forbidden to talk about what they did the week before, make announcements, ask questions, etc."

Heather Logrippo, owner and publisher of *Distinctive Homes* magazine once handed out construction paper and crayons and told her employees to find a quiet place for 30 minutes. Workers were asked to use the crayons and paper to brainstorm a customer-incentive program, part of an effort to make staff meetings more efficient. "This was a situation where you couldn't just Google the answer," Logrippo said.

Managers at Russell Construction introduced a device at a quarterly meeting that calculated the average salary of those in attendance and determined how much the meeting was costing the company. When it was discovered that the initial 90-minute meeting cost the firm roughly $5,000, employees began calculating the cost of many other meetings and have saved as much as $100 per meeting.

AscendWorks LLC, in Austin, Texas, uses a program called Mindjet Catalyst that allows employees to write out the talking points of a meeting during the meeting itself. "It's like thinking out loud, except it's on a screen," said company President Don Dalrymple.

Source: Guynn, J. (2008, March 31). The state. *Los Angeles Times.* latimes.com; Maltby, E. (2010, January 7). Boring meetings? Get out the water guns. *Wall Street Journal*, p. B5.

THE 4P MEETING MANAGEMENT MODEL

The 4P model is a method for designing and implementing effective meetings.[6] It has four key steps (see Exhibit A1–2): (1) specify the purpose of the meeting, (2) invite the right people, (3) carefully plan the meeting content and format, and (4) effectively manage the meeting's process.

Skilled meeting managers do not just sit at the head of the table and call upon people to speak in a round-robin fashion. Nor do they run a "talk show" by simply airing ideas, conflicts, and concerns. Skilled meeting managers do not write down everything that is said; rather, they call out and punctuate key themes. Skilled meeting managers do not orally paraphrase members' ideas; rather, they record them visually. Skilled meeting managers do not try to induce dominant members to yield the floor by saying, "keep it short" or "we need to hear from everyone"; rather, they use brainwriting at select times. They do not organize the meeting by who is there; rather, by what is to be done. According to Tropman, it is better to organize meeting by content: Announcements should come first, then decisions, followed by discussion time, in that order.[7]

---

[6]Whetton, D. A., & Cameron, K. S. (1991). *Developing management skills* (2nd ed.). New York: HarperCollins.
[7]Tropman, J. E. (2003). *Making meetings work: Achieving high quality group decisions* (2nd ed.). Thousand Oaks, CA: Sage.

EXHIBIT A1-2 4P Meeting Management Model

Key Skills	Questions to Ask
Purpose • A complex problem needs to be resolved using the expertise of several people. • Team members' commitment to a decision or to each other needs to be enhanced. • Information needs to be shared simultaneously among several key people.	• What is the purpose of the meeting? • Is the purpose clear to participants? • Is a meeting the most appropriate means of accomplishing the goal? • Are key people available to attend the meeting? • Is the cost of the meeting in proportion to what will be accomplished?
Participants • The size of the team should be compatible with the task. • A balance between people with strong task orientations and those with strong interpersonal skills is desirable.	• Is the size of the meeting appropriate given the problem of coordination costs? • What diversity of skills and backgrounds is important to have in the meeting?
Plan • Provide for adequate physical space, etc. • Establish priorities by sequencing agenda items and allotting time limits to each item. • Prepare and distribute the agenda before or at the beginning of the meeting. • Organize the agenda by content, not by who is there. Use a three-step approach: announcements, decisions, and discussion. • Think about your visual aids: Visual aids are 43 percent more persuasive than no visuals. • Choose the most appropriate decision-making structure (e.g., brainstorming and normal group technique).	• Has an agenda been created? • Has the agenda for the meeting been distributed to members prior to the meeting? • Have members been forewarned if they will be asked to report? • Has the physical arrangement been considered (e.g., whiteboards, overheads and flipcharts)? • Has key information been put into proper information displays? • Has a note taker been assigned?
Process • At the beginning, restate the overall purpose of the meeting and review the agenda and time constraints. • Make note of the ground rules, such as how decisions will be made (e.g., raised hands and secret ballot). • Use techniques to ensure equal participation from members. • Conclude the meeting by summarizing key decisions, reviewing assignments, and determining objectives for the next meeting.	• If this is the first meeting of a team, has an icebreaker been included? • Does the icebreaker get people involved in a behavioral or emotional way (at a minimum, a handshake or high-five)? • Have the ground rules been determined and shared with members in advance of the meeting?

Sources: Adapted from Whetton, D. A., & Cameron, K. S. (1991). *Developing management skills* (2nd ed.). New York: HarperCollins; Armour, S. (1997, December 8). Business' black hole. *USA Today,* p. 1A; Tropman, J. E. (2003). *Making meetings work: Achieving high quality group decisions* (2nd ed.). Thousand Oaks, CA: Sage.

EXHIBIT A1-3 Typical Group Members

Thelma Talk-a-Lot	("I just have to say this")
Sam Stall	("Let's not rush into this")
Don Domineering	(talks 75 percent of the time about his own ideas)
Nick Negative	(explains that someone has to be the devil's advocate)
Ted Theorizer	("It's really complex")
Nancy Nuts-'n'-Bolts	(always comes up with an impossible example to deal with)
Jim Just-a-Little-Bit-More-Information-on-This-Topic-Please	("I don't feel we should decide until we know more")
Herman Hypochondriacal	(is convinced that any path makes vulnerabilities increase)
Yolanda You're-Not-Going-to-Believe-What-Happened-to-Me	(uses immediate, personal events rather than overarching views to analyze problems)

Source: Tropman, J. E. (2003). *Making meetings work: Achieving high quality group decisions* (2nd ed.). Thousand Oaks, CA: Sage.

Munter and Netzley provide a full checklist for the meeting organizer and organize discussions around five key planning questions:[8]

1. Why meet? (Define your purpose and choose your channel.)
2. Who to include? (Select and analyze the participants.)
3. What to discuss? (Orchestrate roles and set the agenda.)
4. How to record ideas? (Plan for graphic facilitation.)
5. Where to meet? (Plan for technology and logistics.)

Recording the comments in the meeting is a critical aspect of successful meeting management and presents a variety of different ways to organize information on flip charts, and so on.

DEALING WITH PROBLEM PEOPLE IN MEETINGS

There is no surefire way to deal with "problem people." As a general principle, having structure helps. It can also be helpful to give group members a list of desirable and undesirable role descriptions prior to the meeting. Exhibit A1–3 is a list of typical group members. Although stated in jest, each description has a ring of truth to it.

ADVICE FOR MEETING ATTENDEES

The burden of effective meeting management does not rest solely on the shoulders of the leader. Group members need to engage in the following proactive strategies:[9]

---

[8]Munt.er, M., & Netzley, M. (2002). *Guide to meetings.* Upper Saddle River, NJ: Prentice Hall.
[9]Whetton, D. A., & Cameron, K. S. (1991). *Developing management skills* (2nd ed.). New York: HarperCollins.

- *Determine whether you need to attend the meeting.* Don't attend merely because you have been invited. If you have doubts about whether the meeting's agenda applies to you, discuss with the leader why he or she feels your presence is important.
- *Prepare.* Acquaint yourself with the agenda, and prepare any reports or information that will facilitate others' understanding of the issues. Come prepared with questions that will help you understand the issues.
- *Be on time.* Stragglers not only waste the time of other participants by delaying the meeting or requiring summaries of what has happened but also hinder effective team building and hurt morale.
- *Ask for clarification on points that are unclear or ambiguous.* Most of the time, you will find that others in the room have the same question but are too timid to speak out.
- *When giving information, be precise and to the point.* Don't bore everyone with anecdotes and details that add little to your point.
- *Listen.* Keep eye contact with whoever is speaking, and try to ascertain the underlying ideas behind the comments. Be sensitive to the effect of your nonverbal behavior on speakers, such as slouching, doodling, or reading.
- *Be supportive of other group members.* Acknowledge and build on the comments of others (e.g., "As Jane was saying . . .").
- *Ensure equitable participation.* Take the lead in involving others so that everyone's talents are used. This is especially important if you know that some participants' points of view are not being included in the discussion. This can be accomplished by encouraging those who rarely participate (e.g., "Jim, your unit worked on something like this last year. What was your experience like?").
- *Make disagreements principle based.* If it is necessary to disagree with, or challenge, the comments of others, follow the guidelines for collaborative conflict management (e.g., base your comments on commonly held principles or values; for instance: "That's an interesting idea, Bill, but how does it square with the president's emphasis on cost-cutting?").
- *Act and react in a way that will enhance the group performance.* In other words, leave your personal agendas at the door and work toward the goals of the group.

COMMON MEETING DISEASES AND FALLACIES

It is almost impossible to predict where most meetings will go awry. The following is a description of the most common meeting diseases and some ideas on how to combat them.

The Overcommitment Phenomenon

Symptoms: Many people agree to perform tasks and accomplish goals that they cannot possibly do in the time allowed. In some cases, this problem is attributable to the pressures placed on managers to accomplish goals and say "yes." However, in many more instances, the overcommitment problem stems from a fundamental inability to estimate how long it will take to accomplish a task.[10] In addition, people tend to make commitments in advance because their confidence in

---

[10]Lovallo, D., & Kahneman, D. (July, 2003). Delusions of success: How optimism undermines executives' decisions. *Harvard Business Review*, pp. 56–63.

their ability to finish is higher when they are further away from the task.[11] Most people make subjective mental estimates of how long it will take to accomplish a task, such as writing a report, collecting information, or interviewing a recruit, by imagining the scenario and then estimating a time line based upon the running of the scenario. However, peoples' mental simulations fail to take into account the process losses that will inevitably thwart their efforts. For example, when they expect to spend 2 weeks writing a report, they fail to anticipate that their printer will break down and that they will have to spend a day offsite. Consequently, most managers are consistently behind schedule.

In many cases, managers and executives are asked to commit themselves to perform tasks and events at some time in the distant future. For example, a team leader might be asked to enroll in a 3-day course next year, travel abroad to interview other team members, or attend a conference. Many people agree to these future invitations, but when the time approaches, regret that they have to do what they promised.[12] People fail to adequately weigh the importance of their future opportunities and time constraints, so they commit to things in the future that they would most likely decline to do in the present.

Treatment: The easiest way to deal with the overcommitment problem is to simply double (or triple) the amount of time projected to accomplish a task. For example, publishers typically add 6 months to an author's projected completion time for a manuscript. Another way of combating the bias is to break the task down into its different elements and then estimate the time necessary to complete each part—people are more accurate at estimating the time necessary to accomplish smaller tasks. When someone asks you to do something, such as write a report, travel, or make a presentation, imagine that you are being asked to do this the next week, or even the next day. If you are disinclined, it may not be a good idea to take it on.

Calls for More Information

Symptoms: Often, teams are uncomfortable making decisions. This is particularly true when the decision matter is complex and value laden. Under such conditions, teams will do nearly anything to avoid making decisions. The manager faces an avoidance-avoidance conflict: Making a decision is difficult, but not making a decision makes one appear indecisive. Managers often respond to this avoidance-avoidance conflict by requesting more information. In theory, the amount of information relevant to any decision situation is boundless; however, at some point, decisions must be made. One way of avoiding decision making, but not appearing to be indecisive, is to request additional information. This makes people feel as though they are making progress, but actually, the additional information may not be diagnostic or useful. It is merely gathered so that the team members can better cognitively justify their decision. Decision avoidance is a particular concern when teams make negative decisions, such as downsizing.

Consider, for example, the following scenario:

A businessman contemplates buying a certain piece of property. He considers the outcome of the next presidential election relevant to the attractiveness of the purchase. So, to clarify the matter for himself, he asks whether he would buy if he knew that the Republican candidate were going to win, and decides that he would do so. Similarly, he considers whether he would buy if he knew that the

---

[11]Gilovich, T., Kerr, M., & Medvec, V. H. (1993). The effect of temporal perspective on subjective confidence. *Journal of Personality and Social Psychology, 64*(4), 552–560.

[12]Loewenstein, J., & Prelic, D. (1991). Negative time preference. *AEA Papers and Proceedings, 81*(2), 347–352.

Democratic candidate were going to win, and again, finds that he would do so. Seeing that he would buy in either event, he decides that he should buy, even though he does not know which event occurs.[13]

The preceding rationale is known as the **sure-thing principle**. It would seem irrational, or somewhat silly, if the businessperson in this case were to delay purchase until after the election or to pay money to find out the election results ahead of time. Yet in organizations, decision makers often pursue noninstrumental information—information that appears relevant, but if available, would have no impact on choice. The problem does not end there. Once they pursue such information, people then use it to make their decision. Consequently, the pursuit of information that would have had no impact on choice leads people to make choices they otherwise would not have made.[14]

Treatment: The decision trap of calling for more information can best be dealt with by keeping a clear log that details the history of the decision. For example, a team member might say something like, "You know, this issue was first brought up two years ago, and it was agreed that a competitive analysis was necessary. This competitive analysis was performed and I brought you the results the following spring. Then, it was suggested that a task force be formed. We did this and came to some conclusions in a report circulated last fall. We agreed at that time that we would make a decision at this meeting. I realize that more information is always better, but I am beginning to wonder whether the costs of continuing to search for information are a way of avoiding a decision." This strategy is especially important in teams where membership changes (and, hence, organizational memory is lost) and in teams that must make tough decisions (e.g., employment terminations).

Failed Memory and Reinventing the Wheel

Symptoms: Many teams face decisions that they make on a repeated basis. For example, merit review decisions, hiring decisions, admission decisions, funding decisions, and so on are all decisions that must be made repeatedly. However, teams often exhibit a memory loss of sorts, in terms of how they made previous decisions. As a result, they spend precious time arguing with one another as to how they made the decision in the past, and memories prove to be fallible. The failed memory problem is most likely to afflict teams that have not created a sufficient organizational memory. The failed memory problem also haunts teams that experience turnover. Under these situations, team members who take notes, or have some kind of record, have an enormous advantage.

Treatment: The key here is to make the process explicit and then to have it recorded in some fashion so that it can be later retrieved. The problem is that most people trust their memories at the time they are discussing the issue or making the decision; consequently, they don't bother to write down what they believe will be burned into their memory.

[13]Savage, L. J. (1954). *The foundations of statistics*. New York: John Wiley & Sons.
[14]Bastardi, A., & Shafir, E. (1998). On the pursuit and misuse of useless information. *Journal of Personality and Social Psychology, 75*(1), 19–32.

APPENDIX 2

Tips For Meeting Facilitators

One of the most challenging tasks is to facilitate a meeting for a company. Many companies think this is easy work to do and, consequently, expect miracles to happen. When the meeting does not accomplish what was hoped for, it is easy to blame the consultant or facilitator. There is also an information asymmetry. The consultant/facilitator is not privy to group norms and interpersonal dynamics. Many companies expect facilitators to immediately dissect the motives of each member. Many mistakes are made prior to the beginning of the meeting. Often, teams that need outside facilitators are besieged by thorny political and personnel issues. Even the issue of who hires the facilitator can be a political one. Others may see the facilitator as a hired gun.

What can an outside facilitator do to make the most out of meetings?

DO YOUR HOMEWORK

Find out as much as you can about the group, the company, and the individual members before the meeting. Ideally, interview the members of the group individually, either by phone, in person, or via a short questionnaire to determine their views of the issues to be addressed in the meeting and their major concerns about the ability of the meeting to accomplish these objectives. Of course, you should guarantee each person that you will not reveal the particulars of what they have said. If you plan to provide a summary overview, tell each person that. This is your first meeting with each team member, and trust is a key issue in getting the information that you need and securing your future relationship with the group. At the very least, get biographies of the group members and ask them how long they've been with the organization, their role in the team, and so on. I find it useful to ask them to map out the team's reporting relationships—it reveals how they think about the group.

PLAN THE PHYSICAL ENVIRONMENT

Most people seriously underestimate the effect that the physical environment can have on the nature of interaction. It is useful to ask for floor plans and diagrams. Send the desired diagram to the meeting coordinator several weeks in advance and create explicit diagrams of where chairs and tables should be. It is usually too late to move furniture by the time you arrive for the meeting; people will want to talk to you, not rearrange the room. Your key materials for the meeting should include a room large enough for people to sit comfortably; movable chairs; conference table seating for small groups; half-rounds, or full-rounds for larger groups; a Post-it pad of paper or note cards for each member and a pencil or pen; two or three flip charts; and a whiteboard or a chalkboard. It is useful to also have an overhead projector. If you don't know the group, ask for name badges or nameplates that are computer printed. Usually, it is impossible to read handwriting on nametags unless you are standing only 2 feet away, and you will probably be about 15 to 20 feet away.

EXPLAIN WHO YOU ARE AND WHY YOU ARE THERE

Your host should introduce you. Begin the meeting by stating in your own words why you are there and what the goals of the meeting are. You will be viewed as an outsider, or interloper, to the group. This creates tension. People will often feel defensive, paranoid, and suspicious of what is to come. You should immediately state that you are there to facilitate the process and to help the group make the best use of their time, and that you do not have a particular stake in the substantive issues. In most cases, you should be clear about who asked you to come in. Above all, don't assume that the reasons for hiring a meeting facilitator have been accurately communicated to the group. Even if a memo was sent out, it may not have been read. Some people may feel strongly opposed to an outside facilitator. Tell the group who you are, but don't try to impress them. You can also "normalize" the situation by giving them statistics that support the idea that making the best use of meetings is of quintessential importance and that even the best organizations are not experts at meeting management. The objective is to give them confidence that you are qualified to do this job. Often, the group will feel somewhat defensive that they need to hire someone to manage their meetings.

FIND OUT WHO THE GROUP IS

You know who the individual members are, but the group will have its own personality. This is extremely tricky. The group members, in most cases, will know one another intimately, but you will not know them.

If the group members do not know one another well, it is useful for everyone to introduce themselves. If the group members do know one another well, having members talk about themselves is boring for other people. In this case, a useful technique is the **next-in-line strategy**, in which members introduce others in the group. For example, each person introduces the person to their left. This is more interesting for group members because they hear, perhaps for the first time, how they are viewed by others. This also serves as an icebreaker, because members are often flattered at the admiration given to them by others. (Often, people sit by others whom they like, so having someone introduce the person sitting next to them ensures a favorable introduction.)

ESTABLISH GROUND RULES

It is imperative to let the group know that you will be using and enforcing meeting ground rules. You may want to acknowledge that the ground rules may seem somewhat silly or reminiscent of their school days, but that companies that use these ground rules are more effective. If you have the time, it is best to have the group suggest some ground rules, so that they "own" them. If you don't have the time, you can write some rules quickly on a flip chart and briefly walk through it with the members. An example list of ground rules is presented in Exhibit A2–1. You may not want to use all of these, but they give you a starting point from which members can add their own rules (or modify the ones on the list).

The most difficult challenge facing the facilitator is enforcing the ground rules. They will get broken, and the temptation will be to excuse or ignore rule-breaking behavior. However, it is imperative to demonstrate that you will enforce these ground rules. You should actually do this early on in the meeting (e.g., "Pat, I need to remind you that we agreed to not mention personal names when talking about the peer review," or "Stan, your five minutes are up"). Enlist group members to enforce ground rules too.

EXHIBIT A2-1 Meeting Ground Rules

- Everyone stays for duration of meeting.
- Form an agenda and stick to it.
- Form a time line and stick to it.
- No "new business."
- No semantic/philosophical discussions.
- No "let's call for more information" (decision avoidance).
- No evaluation of ideas until evaluation period.
- No more reports.

CREATE AN AGENDA

You should ideally have an agenda that is distributed to members in advance of the meeting. Expect to be challenged on the agenda either directly (e.g., "If you don't mind, I want to bring up x, y, and z") or indirectly (e.g., "Don't you think we should talk about x, y, and z before we do this?"). The best way of handling this is to create a postdiscussion agenda and explain that there may be time for these issues after the scheduled meeting.

CLOSING THE MEETING

It is important to bring the meeting to a close in a way that gives the members a sense of what has been accomplished and decided, what steps need to be taken before the next meeting, and what the goal of the next meeting will be (which should be scheduled with everyone present). Finally, you should close in a way that allows each member to "briefly and deeply" reflect on the meeting. Each one of the agenda items should be recapped, and homework or follow-up should be assigned to individual members. A summary of decision and action items should be distributed as soon as possible to the group. I like to spend the last 5 to 10 minutes going around and having each person say the one thing that happened today that they "did not expect" (otherwise everyone will state the obvious, like "we got a lot done" or "the time passed quickly").

SOLICIT FEEDBACK FOR YOURSELF AND THE GROUP

This step is important, especially if you have not worked with the group in the past. Distribute to each participant a short questionnaire that asks the following questions: (1) What in this meeting went well and should be kept? (2) What in this meeting did not go so well and should be eliminated? (3) What in this meeting did not happen and should be included?[1] If you will be working with the group again, aggregate the list of responses and circulate it among group members.

---

[1]Tropman, J. E. (2003). *Making meetings work: Achieving high quality group decisions* (2nd ed.). Thousand Oaks, CA: Sage.

APPENDIX 3

A Guide For Creating Effective Study Groups

Most students enrolled in MBA programs must work in groups to complete important projects and requirements en route to obtaining their degrees. Some students work with the same group throughout their program; other students work with several groups each semester. This is a guide for helping these groups to be as effective as possible.

VERY EARLY ON

In the beginning, when the group is forming, it is helpful to do some kind of structured exercise that moves beyond chitchat. For this reason, it is helpful to have a somewhat structured but fun exercise that moves people beyond superficial pleasantries and encourages them to talk about their expectations for the team, work styles, and so on. For great resources on team exercises, the following resources and books are very useful:

- The Kellogg Teams and Groups (KTAG) Center's cases on the Dispute Resolution Research Center's CD-ROM of cases and exercises[1]
- *Experiences in Management and Organizational Behavior* (4th edition)[2]
- *Leadership Games;*[3] *Principles of Human Relations*[4]
- *The Role-Play Technique: A Handbook for Management and Leadership Practice*[5]
- *A Handbook of Structured Experiences for Human Relations Training*[6]
- *A Handbook of Structured Experiences*[7]
- *The Big Book of Team Building Games*[8]
- *More Team Games for Trainers*[9]
- Hay Group[10]
- Human Synergistics[11]

---

[1]The Kellogg Teams and Groups (KTAG) center cases and exercises cited in this appendix are available through the Dispute Resolution Research Center (DRRC), Kellogg School of Management, Northwestern University, 2001 Sheridan Road, Evanston, IL 60208. Phone: (847) 491–8068; e-mail: drrc@kellogg.northwestern.edu; order form is available online at www.kellogg.northchwestern.edu/research/drrc/documents/cd_orderform.pdf

[2]Bowen, D. D., Lewicki, R. J., Hall, D. T., & Hall, F. S. (1997). *Experiences in management and organizational behavior* (4th ed.). New York: John Wiley & Sons.

[3]Kaagan, S. S. (1999). *Leadership games: Experiential learning for organizational development.* Thousand Oaks, CA: Sage.

[4]Maier, N. R. F. (1952). *Principles of human relations, applications to management.* New York: John Wiley & Sons.

[5]Maier, N. R. F., Solem, A. R., & Maier A. A. (1975). *The role-play technique: A handbook for management and leadership practice.* LaJolla, CA: University Associates.

[6]Pfeiffer, J. W. (1974). *A handbook of structured experiences for human relations training* (Vol. 1–10). LaJolla, CA: University Associates.

[7]Pfeiffer, J. W., & Jones, J. E. (1994). *A handbook of structured experiences* (Vol. 1–10). San Diego, CA: Pfeiffer & Company.

[8]Newstrom, J., & Scannell, E. (1997). *The big book of team building games.* New York: McGraw-Hill.

[9]Nilson, C. D. (2004). *More team games for trainers.* New York: McGraw Hill.

[10]Available at haygroup.com

[11]Available at humansyn.com

SOMETIME DURING THE FIRST WEEK OR TWO

A host of tensions and dilemmas can threaten the effectiveness of any study group. We suggest the team meet and complete a "team charter."

We also suggest that groups that will work together for long periods discuss the following issues in the first week or two:

Team Goals

- *Learning:* "Are we here to learn and to help others learn or are we here to get a good grade?" There is not a right answer to this question, but differing goals in the group can hurt performance.
- *Standards:* "Is perfectionism more important than being on time, or vice versa?"
- *Performance:* "Are we a high-pass (dean's list) group or a pass (survival) group?"

Thought Questions

- What happens if the project leader has lower standards than some other members about writing a paper or report?
- What happens if one group member is not very skilled at some topic area (i.e., how do you use that member's input on group projects and incorporate ideas that do not appear to be adding value)?

Person-Task Mapping

- Is it best to capitalize on the existing strengths of team members or to play to people's weaknesses?
- Suppose your team has a quantitative guru. Do you want to assign the "quant jock" to do all the math and econometrics problems, or use this as an opportunity to let other team members learn?

Additional Questions

- *Member skills:* Do you want to use your study group meeting time to bring all group members up to speed, or should those who need help get it on their own time?
- *Person-task focus:* Are people the group's first priority, or is working the first priority?
- *Structure:* Should the team meeting be structured (e.g., agenda, timekeeper, and assigned roles) or should it be free form?
- *Interloper:* Are other people (outside the group) allowed to attend group meetings and have access to group notes, outlines, homework, and so on, or is group work considered confidential?
- *Communication standards:* Are group members expected to adapt to the most advanced methods of communication, or does group work happen at the lowest common denominator?
- *Project leader pacing:* There would seem to be an advantage for group members who volunteer early on for group projects because commitments and pressures build up later in the semester. How will the group meeting process adapt to increasing workloads?

AFTER THE GROUP IS WELL UNDER WAY

After the group is well under way, it is a good idea to take stock of how the group is working together. We suggest the "team assessment," ideally administered by a coach, facilitator, or instructor acquainted with the study group (see the KTAG cases and exercises).

Another useful idea is to do some version of a peer-feedback performance review, wherein individuals receive confidential feedback and ratings about how they are viewed by other team members. This can often be completely computerized (see Appendix 4).

ON A REGULAR BASIS

It is important that study groups revisit the team charter. Are the expectations being met? What issues and topics that are not in the charter should be talked about? What issues in the charter do not seem relevant?

SPECIAL TIPS FOR LONG-TERM STUDY GROUPS

Consider the actual advice from MBA students who were enrolled in an intensive 2-year program. Their study groups were assigned to them and maintained throughout the 2-year program. During the time they worked together, members were asked for their input on what did and did not work in their study groups in regard to maximizing learning and using time effectively. Exhibit A3–1 summarizes the students' responses.

EXHIBIT A3-1 Advice for Long-Term Study Groups

- An agenda should be distributed before each group meeting date so everyone can prepare properly. Decide upon the agenda for the next meeting before adjourning the current meeting.
- Define who is expected to do what for each project.
- A written outline or "straw man" is needed to focus the group discussion on any particular project. Several alternatives should be evaluated during the outline stage before selecting which alternative will be taken for any project.
- Each major group project has a project leader responsible for doing most of the writing (in some cases, all of the writing). Other group members provide input early in the project and after a draft has been written. Assignments can be done in parallel by using this method, which helps to meet deadlines.
- Some groups summarize class readings for the project leader during the weeks that they are busy completing the project.

- The workload is not divided equally on every project. Over a 2-year period, everyone will get the chance to contribute.
- Rotate responsibilities with each module or semester. For example, one person in the group may be the agenda captain for an entire module. The agenda captain organizes the meeting agendas and runs the meetings for that entire module. Rotating responsibilities every week wastes time deciding who does what.
- Try to meet on the same day and time each week. This makes it easier to plan travel schedules in advance.
- At the end of each major assignment, review the effectiveness of the process used to fulfill requirements. Adjust the process to improve effectiveness.
- Improve communication within the group by using e-mail and standardized software.
- Focus on the goals of the meeting first, then socialize.
- Maintain a sense of humor!

Source: Taken from compiled lists from the Executive Masters Program, Kellogg School of Management, Northwestern University, Evanston, IL. Lists compiled by R. Weeks (1996) and K. Murnighan (1998). Reprinted with the permission of the author.

APPENDIX 4

Example Items from Peer Evaluations and 360-Degree Performance Evaluations

Chapter 3 went into detail about the purpose and implementation of 360-degree evaluations. Some people, however, may be unfamiliar with 360-degree evaluations. In this appendix, we present examples of two 360-degree evaluation tools. The first one is a peer evaluation system; it is brief and designed for students enrolled in MBA programs. The second one is much more extensive and designed to provide senior managers with confidential feedback about their leadership abilities and potential.

LEADNET

LeadNet is the Kellogg School of Management's Web-based peer evaluation system; it was developed by students, faculty, and staff to enable students to give one another anonymous feedback on their team skills. The method is simple and completely automated. At the end of each academic quarter, students sign on to a Web page and provide anonymous feedback to their teammates by rating each other on 12 key criteria related to improving team-based outcomes. The computer then compiles mean and standard deviation scores for each student. After all responses are compiled, students automatically receive a private e-mail with their personal scores from each of their teams. To enable them to track their progress in building their team skills over time, students also receive their scores from prior terms.

The system allows students to get direct and timely feedback on their team skills. They can track their skill development in particular areas (e.g., leadership) over time and across different teams and projects to focus on skill development. What's more, students learn how to use peer-based reviews. The automated process means that the information is collected and disseminated efficiently. The feedback is intended for personal growth and does not impact a student's grades nor is it transmitted to employers, and so on. LeadNet also enables managers-in-training to practice giving feedback to team members.

Exhibit A4–1 illustrates how students using the LeadNet Web site can select the specific team and teammates they want to evaluate; Exhibit A4–2 illustrates a sample matrix for evaluating a teammate and lists all 12 items on the LeadNet questionnaire; and Exhibit A4–3 illustrates a sample of an output feedback that a student might receive from the LeadNet system.

EXHIBIT A4-1 Selecting a Team to Evaluate Using LeadNet

Note: The values for this demonstration have been selected below and are reflected in subsequent figures.

Please select the course for the team you will be evaluating, and complete the related information:

Course/Section: ACCT D30 Section 62 Tue–Fri 9:00–10:40 ▼

Number of Teammates (Do not count yourself) 4 ▼

Hours/week of Team Meeting (avg.) 3 ▼

Team Selection Method Assigned ▼

Did you use a team consultant? ○ Yes ⦿ No

Please select the names of your teammates.

Have you been this person's teammate before?

		Yes	No
Teammate 1:	Joe Smith ▼	○	⦿
Teammate 2:	Jan Smith ▼	○	⦿
Teammate 3:	John Doe ▼	○	⦿
Teammate 4:	Jane Doe ▼	○	⦿

Source: Uzzi, B. (2010). *LeadNet Demo*. Kellogg School of Management.

EXHIBIT A4-2 LeadNet Questionnaire Items and Rating System

Each teammate receives feedback in the matrix below (one matrix per question; one question per website frame):

Teammate	Needs Improvement (bottom 10% of all students with whom you've worked in a group)	Does not meet your expectations	Meets your expectations	Exceeds your expectations	Exceptional contributor (top 10% of all students with whom you've worked in a group)
	1	2	3	4	5
Jane Doe	O	O	O	O	O
John Doe	O	O	O	O	O
Jan Smith	O	O	O	O	O
John Smith	O	O	O	O	O

Comments:

Jane Doe ☐
John Doe ☐
Jan Smith ☐
Joe Smith ☐

Items Rated:
Reconciles differences among teammates to keep team functioning optimally
Encouraged innovation among teammates by introducing new perspectives and information
Evenly contributed to the work load by coming to meetings prepared and consistently producing high quality output
Maintained appropriate balance between talking and attentive listening
Changed his/her opinion when appropriate, considering entire range of factors
Communicated ideas effectively and confidently
Helped develop team goals and maintain focus on them
Collaboratively developed team norms and values with teammates
Consistently adhered to high ethical work practices
Effective in team's time management: flexible in scheduling, on time to meetings, and used team time efficiently
Provided feedback effectively
Productively responded to feedback

Source: Uzzi, B. (2010). *LeadNet Demo*. Kellogg School of Management.

INDUSTRIAL EXAMPLE OF 360-DEGREE EVALUATIONS

The questionnaire in Exhibit A4–4 from RHR International Company is designed to assess leadership behavior among senior employees. These behaviors encompass critical success factors in the company. The leaders choose at least nine people (one or two line managers, four or five peers, and four or five subordinates) to complete the questionnaire, which is processed confidentially.

EXHIBIT A4-3 Sample LeadNet Output Feedback Sheet

Note: The values for this demonstration do not reflect any student's actual scores.

The *mean* and *standard deviation* of the evaluations you received for each class are listed below.

The aggregate statistics combine all of the peer evaluations you received for all your classes last term, including classes that lacked sufficient respondents to report individually; however, stats for sections in which you did not complete a TeamNet evaluation are not included and are omitted in the aggregate stats.

John Doe — Scale: 1-needs serious improvement 5-exceptional	Team: Reconcile differences	Strategic: Encourage innovation	Individual: Contribution and preparation	Individual: Balanced talking and listening	Operational: Changed own opinion as needed	Individual: Communicated effectively	Team: Focused on team goals	Team: Collaborated on norms/values	Strategic: Ethical work practices	Individual: Time management	Individual: Gave effective feedback	Individual: Receptive of feedback
Winter 03-04												
Accounting	4.7 0.6	3.9 2.3	4.7 0.6	4.9 0.6	4.9 0.6	4.9 0.6	4.7 0.6	4.7 0.6	4.9 0.6	5.0 0	4.9 0.6	5.0 0
Economics	*Sorry. Since you did not complete a TeamNet evaluation for this section, you are unable to receive scores for this section.*											
Management & Strategy	.5 1.7	4.4 2.3	4.5 1.7	4.4 2.3	4.5 1.7	4.7 1.2	4.5 1.7	4.7 1.2	4.5 1	4.7 1.2	4.5 1	4.7 1.2
Marketing	*Fewer than 3 responses; insufficient number to report for this section.*											
Org. Behavior	.5 1.7	4.2 2.1	4.4 2.3	4.4 2.3	4.7 1.2	4.7 1.2	4.5 1.7	4.7 1.2	4.7 1.2	4.7 1.2	4.7 1.2	4.7 1.2
Aggregate	4.6 1.3	4.6 1.3	4.1 2	4.5 1.5	4.5 1.7	4.7 1.1	4.7 0.9	4.6 1.3	4.7 0.9	4.7 0.9	4.8 0.9	4.7 0.9

Comments for this term: Great team player! Strong listening and communication skills; responsible and creative.

Source: Uzzi, B. (2010). *LeadNet Demo.* Kellogg School of Management.

EXHIBIT A4-4 360-Degree Leadership

Key Leadership Quality	Questions
Provide Vision: "Developing vision and demonstrating commitment to the company's strategies, and inspiring a sense of direction"	• Establishes initiatives that promote a global mind-set in the organization • Creates a compelling scenario of the future involvement with the team and inspires buy-in • Identifies and applies models and processes that will stimulate behaviors in support of the company's vision • Puts the vision in practice by adopting desired behaviors and corresponding values • Actively gains information concerning markets and environment factors that can have an impact on strategies • Ensures that team and individual objectives support the company's vision • Creates a sense of team purpose according to vision and strategies • Shares insights and facilitates understanding and open communication around vision • Is able to imagine scenarios that are in discontinuity with the existing processes or products
Show Entrepreneurship: "Thinking ahead, seizing opportunities to develop new markets, products, or services and taking calculated risks to achieve growth"	• Demonstrates passion and energy to move forward • Invents strategies using various sources of data and individual experiences • Encourages proactive behaviors resulting in business growth • Takes calculated risks, then decides • Supports and rewards self-starting behaviors of collaborators • Seeks solutions beyond current practices • Demonstrates an action-oriented attitude • Explores and optimizes the use of resources and expertise available within the team • Communicates information and personal perceptions on new business opportunities for the company
Influence and Convince: "Persuading others to share a point of view, to adopt a specific position, or to take a course of action"	• Determines appropriate strategies to influence people • Builds networks and uses the authority or power of view, to adopt a specific position, others to convince • Develops propositions tailored to the interest of the different parties involved • Builds a climate of trust

	• Expresses perspective with courage and integrity • Listens to others' viewpoints or objections and tests their ideas • Seeks to convince by underlining potential benefits of proposed solutions • Negotiates proposals to determine common course of action • Gains team adherence through effective communication
Achieve Results: "Directing the activity of others by setting challenging goals for personal and team accomplishment and by controlling their achievements"	• Sets the example by showing high performance • Sets challenging goals that require a "step change" • Develops strategies and facilitates actions to overcome barriers • Initiates corrective actions to address performance • Supports and works alongside others to help improve performance and results • Introduces and applies new methods within the company • Communicates performance expectations to others • Creates a performance-oriented spirit within the team • Provides regular feedback on achieved performance • Puts in place performance measurement tools
Focus on Customer: "Managing proactively the various customer demands while maintaining a consistent level of effectiveness"	• Demonstrates a "customer first" attitude and meets with customers regularly • Is involved in the customer's decision-making process • Identifies customer needs and communicates relevant customer-related information • Acts as an advocate by influencing the company on the customer's behalf • Initiates actions that add value to the customer • Ensures team priorities and cooperation are in line with customer service requirements • Asks customers for feedback on service quality • Ensures that performance matches the customer's needs • Keeps close to customers' business evaluations • Is responsive to customer complaints and keeps word

(cont.on p.366)

Enhance Cooperation and Adaptation: "Managing people and teams across businesses and cultures"	• Creates an environment that fosters and rewards cooperation among diverse work teams • Identifies interdependencies and understands the dynamics of bringing different cultures together • Has gained credibility in managing outside home country • Challenges self and others to consider issues from a wider and more global perspective • Is sensitive and adaptable to other cultures • Understands the challenges and opportunities of doing business globally • Shares best practices, solutions, and a wide array of management processes across businesses • Explores diverse methods of learning and acting • Encourages relationships between people to enhance trust and communication across distances and differences
Empower: "Allocating decision-making authority and creating sense of ownership of the job, missions, or project assignments"	• Sets the example in creating a collaborative team spirit to stimulate initiative • Facilitates the free expression of ideas by showing tolerance such that others are willing to act • Approves and facilitates decision-making among collaborators and is supportive in times of crisis

Note: All questions answered on 4-point scale: 1 = almost never; 2 = sometimes; 3 = usually; 4 = almost always; CS = can't say.
Source: 360 Degree Leadership. RHR International Co., © 1998. Reprinted with permission from RHR International Co., Wood Dale, IL.

REFERENCES

Aarts, H., Gollwitzer, P. M., & Hassin, R. R. (2004). Goal contagion: Perceiving is for pursuing. *Journal of Personality and Social Psychology, 87*, 23–37.

Abele, S., & Diehl, M. (2008). Finding teammates who are not prone to sucker and free-rider effects: The Protestant Work Ethic as a moderator of motivation losses in group performance. *Group Processes and Intergroup Relations, 11*, 39–54.

Abrams, D. A., De Moura, G. R., Marques, J. M., & Hutchison, P. (2008). Innovation credit: When can leaders oppose their group's norms? *Journal of Personality and Social Psychology, 95*(3), 662–678.

Adams, S. (1965). Inequity in social exchange. In L. Berkowitz (Ed.), *Advances in experimental social psychology* (Vol. 2, pp. 267–299). New York: Academic Press.

Adelberg, S., & Batson, C. D. (1978). Accountability and helping: When needs exceed resources. *Journal of Personality and Social Psychology, 36*, 343–350.

Ahuja, M., & Galvin, J. (2003). Socialization in virtual groups. *Journal of Management, 29*, 161–185.

Albright, M. (2010, February 23). Man vs. Walmart in blueberry battle; Fight for cheap berries brings clarity on policy from HQ. *St. Petersburg Times*, p. A1

Alderfer, C. P. (1976). Boundary relations and organizational diagnosis. In M. Meltzer & F. Wickert (Eds.), *Humanizing organizational behavior* (pp. 142–175). Springfield, IL: Charles C. Thomas.

Alderfer, C. P. (1977). Group and intergroup relations. In J. R. Hackman & J. L. Suttle (Eds.), *Improving life at work* (pp. 227–296). Palisades, CA: Goodyear.

Aldrich, H., & Herker, D. (1977). Boundary spanning roles and organization Structure. *Academy of Management Review, 2*(2), 217–230.

Allen, T. J. (1977). *Managing the flow of technology: Technology transfer and the dissemination of technological information within the R&D organization.* Cambridge, MA: MIT Press.

Allen, V. L. (1965). Situational factors in conformity. In L. Berkowitz (Ed.), *Advances in experimental social psychology* (Vol. 2, pp. 267–299). New York: Academic Press.

Allison, S., & Messick, D. (1990). Social decision heuristics and the use of shared resources. *Journal of Behavioral Decision Making, 3*, 195–204.

Alter, M. (2008, January 1). Performance based pay. *Inc Magazine.* inc.com.

Amabile, T. M. (1997). Motivating creativity in organizations: On doing what you love and loving what you do. *California Management Review, 40*(1), 39–58.

Amabile, T. M., Barsade, S. G., Mueller, J. S., & Staw, B. M. (2005). Affect and creativity at work. *Administrative Science Quarterly, 50*, 367–403.

Amabile, T. M., & Conti, R. (1999). Changes in the work environment for creativity during downsizing. *Academy of Management Journal, 42*(6), 630–640.

Amabile, T. M., Nasco, C. P., Mueller, J., Wojcik, T., Odomirok, P. W., Marsh, M., & Kramer, S. J. (2001). Academic-practitioner collaboration in management research: A case of cross-profession collaboration. *Academy of Management Journal, 44*(2), 418–431.

Amabile, T. M., Schatzel, E. A., Moneta, G. B., & Kramer, S. J. (2004). Leader behaviors and the work environment for creativity: Perceived leader support. *Leadership Quarterly, 15*, 5–32.

Amason, A. (1996). Distinguishing the effects of functional and dysfunctional conflict on strategic decision making: Resolving a paradox for top management teams. *Academy of Management Journal, 39*(1), 123–148.

Amos, D. (2010). CEO explains how he fell for the duck. *Harvard Business Review, 88*(1), 131–134.

Ancona, D. G. (1987). Groups in organizations: Extending laboratory models. In C. Hendrick (Ed.), *Annual review of personality and social psychology: Group and intergroup processes* (pp. 207–231). Beverly Hills, CA: Sage.

Ancona, D. G. (1990). Outward bound: Strategies for team survival in an organization. *Academy of Management Journal, 33*(2), 334–365.

Ancona, D. G. (1993). The classics and the contemporary: A new blend of small group theory. In J. K. Murnighan (Ed.), *Social psychology in organizations:*

Advances in theory and research (p. 233). Upper Saddle River, NJ: Prentice Hall.

Ancona, D., Backman, E., & Bresman, H. (2009, September 1). X-Teams break new ground. *Financial Post*, p. FP9.

Ancona, D., & Bresman, H. (2007). *X-teams: How to build teams that lead, innovate and succeed.* Boston, MA: Harvard Business School Publishing.

Ancona, D., Bresman, H., & Caldwell, D. (2009). Six steps to leading high-performing x-teams. *Organizational Dynamics, 38*(3), 217–224.

Ancona, D. G., & Caldwell, D. F. (1987). Management issues facing new-product teams in high technology companies. In D. Lewin, D. Lipsky, & D. Sokel (Eds.), *Advances in industrial and labor relations* (Vol. 4, pp. 199–221). Greenwich, CT: JAI Press.

Ancona, D. G., & Caldwell, D. F. (1988). Beyond task and maintenance: Defining external functions in groups. *Groups and Organizational Studies, 13*, 468–494.

Ancona, D. G., & Caldwell, D. F. (1992a). Demography and design: Predictors of new product team performance. *Organization Science, 3*(3), 321–341.

Ancona, D. G., & Caldwell, D. F. (1992b). Bridging the boundary: External process and performance in organizational teams. *Administrative Science Quarterly, 37*, 634–665

Ancona, D. G., & Nadler, D. A. (1989). Top hats and executive tales: Designing the senior team. *Senior Management Review, 31*(1), 19–28.

Ancona, D. G., Okhuysen, G. A., & Perlow, L. A. (2001). Taking time to integrate temporal research. *Academy of Management Review, 26*, 512–529.

Anders, G. (2005, October 10). When mom is chairwoman and son is CEO, tension reigns. *Wall Street Journal*, p. B1.

Anderson, C., Ames, D., & Gosling, S. (2008). Punishing hubris: The perils of overestimating one's status in a group. *Personality and Social Psychology Bulletin, 34*(1), 90–101.

Anderson, C., & Berdahl, J. L. (2002). The experience of power: Examining the effects of power on approach and inhibition tendencies. *Journal of Personality and Social Psychology, 83*, 1362–1377.

Anderson, C., & Galinsky, A. D. (2006). Power, optimism, and risk-taking. *European Journal of Social Psychology, 36*, 511–536.

Anderson, C., & Kilduff, G. J. (2009). Why do dominant personalities attain influence in face-to-face groups? The competence-signaling effects of trait dominance. *Journal of Personality and Social Psychology, 96*(2), 491–503.

Andeweg, R. B., & van den Berg, S. B. (2003). Linking birth order to political leadership: The impact of parents or sibling interaction? *Political Psychology, 24*(3), 605–623.

Angermeier, I., Dunford, B. D., Boss, A. D., & Boss, R. W. (2009, March/April). The impact of participative management perceptions on customer service, medical errors, burnout, and turnover intentions. *Journal of Healthcare Management, 54*(2), 127–141.

Anonymous. (1996). Microsoft teamwork. *Executive Excellence, 13*(7), 6–7.

Antoniades, C. B. (2009, February). 25 best places to work. *Baltimore Magazine*. Retrevied from http://www.baltimoremagazine.net/

Antonioni, D. (1994). The effects of feedback accountability on upward appraisal ratings. *Personnel Psychology, 47*, 349–356.

Arango, T. (2010, January 11). How the AOL—Time Warner merger went so wrong. *New York Times*, p. B1.

Argote, L. (1989). Agreement about norms and work-unit effectiveness: Evidence from the field. *Basic and Applied Social Psychology, 10*(2), 131–140.

Argote, L., Insko, C. A., Yovetich, N., & Romero, A. A. (1995). Group learning curves: The effects of turnover and task complexity on group performance. *Journal of Applied Social Psychology, 25*, 512–529.

Argote, L., & Kane, A. (2003). Learning from direct and indirect organizations: The effects of experience content, timing, and distribution. In P. Paulus & B. Nijstad (Eds.), *Group creativity*. New York: Oxford University Press.

Argote, L., McEvily, B., & Reagans, R. (2003). Managing knowledge in organization: An integrative framework and review of emerging themes. *Management Science, 49*(4), 571–582.

Argyris, C. (1977a). Double loop learning. *Harvard Business Review, 55*(5), 115–125.

Argyris, C. (1977b). Organizational learning and management information systems. *Harvard Business Review, 55*(5), 115–125.

Ariley, D. (2008). *Predictably irrational: The hidden forces that shape our decisions.* New York: HarperCollins.

Ariely, D. (2009, March 4). Massive bonuses might actually cause poor performance. *New York Times.* nytimes.com

Arkes, H. R., & Blumer, C. (1985). The psychology of sunk cost. *Organizational Behavior and Human Decision Process, 35* 1, 124–129.

Armstrong, D. J., & Cole, P. (1995). Managing distances and differences in geographically distributed work groups. In S. E. Jackson & M. N. Ruderman (Eds.), *Diversity in work teams: Research paradigms for a changing workplace* (pp. 187–215). Washington, DC: American Psychological Association.

Armour, S. (1997, December 8). Business' black hole. *USA Today*, p. 1A.

Arnold, D. W., & Greenberg, C. I. (1980). Deviate rejection within differentially manned groups. *Social Psychology Quarterly, 43*(4), 419–424.

Arrow, H. (1998). Standing out and fitting in: Composition effects on newcomer socialization. *Research on Managing Groups and Teams, 1,* 59–80.

Arrow, H., & Burns, K. (2004). Self-organizing culture: How norms emerge in small groups. In M. Schaller & C. S. Crandall (Eds.), *The psychological foundations of culture.* Mahwah, NJ: Lawrence Erlbaum Associates.

Arrow, H., & Crosson, S. (2003). Musical chairs: Membership dynamics in self-organized group formation. *Small Group Research, 34*(5), 523–556.

Arrow, H., & McGrath, J. E. (1995). Membership dynamics in groups at work: A theoretical framework. *Research in organizational behavior, 17,* 373–411.

Arrow, H., Poole, M. S., Henry, K. B., Wheelan, S., & Mooreland, R. L. (2004). Time, change, and development: The temporal perspective on groups. *Small Group Research, 35*(1), 73–105.

Asch, S. E. (1956). Studies of independence and conformity: A minority of one against a unanimous majority. *Psychological Monographs, 70*(9), Whole No. 416.

Ashford, S. J., & Cummings, L. L. (1983). Feedback as an individual resource: Personal strategies of creating information. *Organizational Behavior and Human Decision Processes, 32,* 370–398.

Associated Press. (2003, February 14). Before Columbia, NASA Mulled Space Repairs.

Associated Press. (2009, January 16). Pilot's life prepared him for miracle flight. *msnbc.com.* msnbc.msn.com.

Aston, A. (2009, November 17). China and U.S. energy giants team up for "clean coal." *Business Week.* businessweek.com

Atkinson, R., & Wial, H. (2008). Creating a national innovation foundation: In this blueprint, the foundation would build on the few federal programs that already promote innovation and borrow the best public policy ideas from other nations. *Issues in Science and Technology, 25*(1), 75–84.

Back, K. W. (1951). Influence through social communication. *Journal of Abnormal Social Psychology, 46,* 9–23.

Baily, J. (2008, December). The education of an educated CEO. *Inc., 30*(12), 100–106.

Baker, S. (2009, December 14). Beware social media snake oil. *Business Week, 4159,* 48–51.

Baldwin, M. W. (1992). Relational schemas and the processing of social information. *Psychological Bulletin, 112*(3), 461–484.

Bales, R. F. (1955). *How people interact in conferences.* New York: Scientific American.

Bales, T. (1958). Task roles and social roles in problem-solving groups. In E. E. Maccoby, T. M. Newcomb, & E. I. Hartley (Eds.), *Readings in Social Psychology.* New York: Holt, Rinehart & Winston.

Balkundi, P., Barsness, Z., & Michael, J. (2009). Unlocking the influence of leadership network structures on team conflict and viability. *Small Group Research, 40*(3), 301–322.

Balkundi, P., & Harrison, D. A. (2006). Ties, leaders, and time in teams: Strong inference and network structure's effects on team viability and performance. *Academy of Management Journal, 49*(1), 305–325.

Bamberger, P., & Biron, M. (2007). Group norms and excessive absenteeism: The role of peer referent others. *Organizational Behavior and Human Decision Processes, 103*, 179–196.

Barboza, D. (1998, September 20). Loving a stock, not wisely, but too well. *New York Times,* Section 3, p. 1.

Barchas, P. R., & Fisek, M. H. (1984). Hierarchical differentiation in newly formed groups of Rhesus and humans. In P. R. Barchas (Ed.), *Essays toward a sociophysiological perspective* (pp. 23–33). Westport, CT: Greenwood Press.

Barker, J. R. (1993). Tightening the iron cage: Concertive control in self-managing teams. *Administrative Science Quarterly, 38*, 408–437.

Barley, S. R. (1996). Technicians in the workplace: Ethnographic evidence for bringing work into organization studies. *Administrative Science Quarterly, 41*(3), 404–441.

Barnes, C., Hollenbeck, J., Wagner, D., DeRue, S., Nahrgang, J., & Schwind, K. (2008). Harmful help: The costs of backing-up behavior in teams. *Journal of Applied Psychology, 93*(3), 529–539.

Barnes, S. (2008, December 29). One-track minds that put team on way to gold rush: Team of the year Great Britain cycling team. *The Times*, pp. 16–17.

Baron, R. (2006). So right it's wrong: Groupthink and the ubiquitous nature of polarized group decision making. University of Iowa, manuscript.

Baron, R., & Bellman, S. (2007). No guts, no glory: Courage, harassment and minority influence. *European Journal of Social Psychology, 37*, 101–124.

Barreto, M., & Ellemers, N. (2002). The impact of respect versus neglect of self-identities on indentification and group loyalty. *Personality and Social Psychology Bulletin, 28*(5), 629–639.

Barrick, M. R., Bradley, B. H., Kristof-Brown, A. L., & Colbert, A. E. (2007). The moderating role of top management team interdependence: Implications for real teams and working groups. *Academy of Management Journal, 50*, 544–577.

Barrick, M. R., Stewart, G. L., Neubert, M. J., & Mount, M. K. (1998). Relating member ability and personality to work-team processes and team effectiveness. *Journal of Applied Psychology, 83*, 377–391.

Barsade, S. G. (2000). *The ripple effect: Emotional contagion in groups.* New Haven, CT: Yale University School of Management.

Barsade, S., & Gibson, D. E. (1998). Group emotion: A view from the top and bottom. In D. Gruenfeld, B. Mannix, & M. Neale (Eds.), *Research on managing groups and teams.* Greenwich, CT: JAI Press.

Barsness, Z., Tenbrunsel, A., Michael, J., & Lawson, L. (2002). Why am I here? The influence of group and relational attributes on member-initiated team selection. In M. A. Neale, E. Mannix, & H. Sondak (Eds.), *Toward phenomenology of groups and group membership* (Vol. 4, pp. 141–171). **Greenwich, CT: JAI Press.**

Bartel, C., & Saavedra, R. (2000). The collective construction of work group moods. *Administrative Science Quarterly, 45*, 197–231.

Basalla, G. (1988). *The evolution of technology.* New York: Cambridge University Press; Weisberg, R. W. (1997). Case studies of creative thinking. In S. M. Smith, T. B. Ward, & R. A. Finke (Eds.), *The creative cognition approach.* Cambridge, MA: MIT Press.

Bass, B. M. (1985). *Leadership and performance beyond expectations.* New York: Free Press.

Bass, B. M. (1990). *Bass & Stogdill's handbook of leadership: Theory, research, & management applications* (3rd ed.). New York: Free Press.

Bastardi, A., & Shafir, E. (1998). On the pursuit and misuse of useless information. *Journal of Personality and Social Psychology, 75*(1), 19–32.

Baumeister, R. F., & Scher, S. J. (1988). Self-defeating behavior patterns among normal individuals. *Psychological Bulletin, 104*, 3–22.

Baumeister, R. F., & Steinhilber, A. (1984). Paradoxical effects of supportive audiences on performance under pressure: The home field disadvantage in sports championships. *Journal of Personality and Social Psychology, 47*(1), 85–93.

Bavelas, J. B., Black, A., Lemery, C. R., & Mullett, J. (1987). Motor mimicry as primitive empathy.

In N. Eisenberg & J. Strayer (Eds.), *Empathy and its development* (pp. 317–338). Cambridge, UK: Cambridge University Press.

Bazerman, M. H. (2009). *Judgment in managerial decision making* (7th ed.). Hoboken, NJ: John Wiley & Sons.

Beal, D. J., Cohen, R. R., Burke, M. J., & McLendon, C. L. (2003). Cohesion and performance in groups: A meta-analytic clarification of construct relations. *Journal of Applied Psychology, 88*, 989–1004.

Becker, F., Quinn, K. L., Rappaport, A. J., & Sims, W. R. (1994). *Implementing innovative workplaces.* Ithaca, NY: New York State College of Human Ecology, Department of Design and Environmental Analysis, Cornell University.

Beehr, T. A., Walsh, J., & Taber, B. (1976), Relationship of stress to individually and organizationally valued states—Higher order needs as a moderator. *Journal of Applied Psychology, 61*(1), 41–49.

Beer, M., Eisenstat, R. A., & Spector, B. (1990). *The critical path to corporate renewal.* Boston, MA: Harvard Business School Press.

Beersma, B., Hollenbeck, J. R., Conlon, D. E., Humphrey, S. E., & Moon, h. (2009). Cutthroat cooperation: The effects of team role decisions on adaption to alternative reward structures. *Organizational Behavior and Human Decision Process, 108*, 131–142.

Behfar, K. J., Peterson, R. S., Mannix, E. A., & Trochim, W. M. K. (2008). The critical role of conflict resolution in teams: A close look at the links between conflict type, conflict management strategies, and team outcomes. *Journal of Applied Psychology, 93*(1), 170–188

Belliveau, M. A., O'Reilly, C. A., III, & Wade, J. B. (1996). Social capital: The effects of social similarity and status on CEO compensation. *Academy of Management Journal, 39*, 1568–1593.

Benne, K. D., & Sheats, P. (1948). Functional roles of group members. *Journal of Social Issues, 4*, 41–49.

Bennis, W., & Nanus, B. (1985). *Leaders.* New York: Harper & Row.

Berger, J., Fisek, M. H., Norman, R. Z., & Zelditch, M. (1977). *Status characteristics and social interaction.* New York: Elsevier.

Berger, J., Rosenholtz, S. J., & Zelditch, M. (1980). Status organizing processes. *Annual Review of Sociology, 6*, 479–508.

Berman, S. L., Down, J., & Hill, C. W. H. (2002). Tacit knowledge as a source of competitive advantage in the National Basketball Association. *Academy of Management Journal, 45*, 13–31.

Bernardin, H. J., & Cascio, W. F. (1988). Performance appraisal and the law. In R. S. Schuler, S. A. Youngblood, & V. L. Huber (Eds.), *Readings in personnel and human resource management* (3rd ed., p. 239). St. Paul, MN: West.

Bernieri, F., Reznick, J. S., & Rosenthal, R. (1988). Synchrony, pseudosynchrony, and dissynchrony: Measuring the entrainment process in mother-infant dyads. *Journal of Personality and Social Psychology, 54*, 243–253.

Bettencourt, B. A., Brewer, M. B., Croak, M. R., & Miller, N. (1992). Cooperation and the reduction of intergroup bias: The role of reward structure and social orientation. *Journal of Experimental Social Psychology, 28*(4), 301–319.

Bettencourt, B. A., Charlton, K., & Kernahan, C. (1997). Cooperative interaction and intergroup bias: The interaction between numerical representation and social orientation. *Journal of Experimental Social Psychology, 33*, 630–659.

Bettencourt, B. A., & Dorr, N. (1998). Cooperative interaction and intergroup bias: Effects of numerical representation and cross-cut role assignment. *Personality and Social Psychology Bulletin, 24*(12), 1276–1293.

Bettenhausen, K., & Murnighan, J. K. (1985). The emergence of norms in competitive decision-making groups. *Administrative Science Quarterly, 30*, 350–372.

Binder, J., Zagefka, H., Brown, R., Funke, F., Kessler, T., Mummendey, A., et al. (2009). Does contact reduce prejudice or does prejudice reduce contact? A longitudinal test of the contact hypothesis among majority and minority groups in three European countries. *Journal of Personality and Social Psychology, 96*, 843–856.

Blake, J. (2010, January 7). *Working in 'Wi-Fi' limbo.* Cnn.com.

Blake, R. R., & Mouton, J. S. (1964). *The managerial grid.* Houston, TX: Gulf.

Blascovich, J., Mendes, W. B., Hunter, S. B., & Salomon, K. (1999). Social "facilitation" as challenge and threat. *Journal of Personality and Social Psychology, 77*(1), 68–77.

Blau, P. M. (1955). *The dynamics of bureaucracy.* Chicago, IL: University of Chicago Press.

Blinder, A. S. (1990). Pay, participation, and productivity. *Brookings Review, 8*(1), 33–38.

Bloomfield, R., Libby, R., & Nelson, M. W. (1996). Communication of confidence as a determinant of group judgment accuracy. *Organizational Behavior and Human Decision Processes, 68*(3), 287–300.

Bobo, L. (1983). Whites' opposition to busing: Symbolic racism or realistic group conflict? *Journal of Personality and Social Psychology, 45*(6), 1196–1210.

Bohrnstedt, G. W., & Fisher, G. A. (1986). The effects of recalled childhood and adolescent relationships compared to current role performances on young adults' affective functioning. *Social Psychology Quarterly, 49*(1), 19–32.

Boiney, L. G. (2009). Knowledge is power. *Pepperdine University.* Retrieved from www.gbr.pepperdine.edu

Boisjoly, R. M. (1987, December 13–18). *Ethical decisions—Morton Thiokol and the space shuttle Challenger disaster* (p. 7). Speech presented at the American Society of Mechanical Engineers, Winter Annual Meeting, Boston, MA.

Bond, C. F., & Anderson, E. L. (1987). The reluctance to transmit bad news: Private discomfort or public display? *Journal of Experimental Psychology, 23,* 176–187.

Bond, R. (2005). Group size and conformity. *Group Processes and Intergroup Relations, 8*(4), 331–354.

Bone, M., & Johnson, K. (2009). *I miss my pencil.* San Francisco, CA: Chronicle Books.

Bonner, B., Sillito, S., & Baumann, M. (2007). Collective estimation: Accuracy, expertise, and extroversion as sources of intra-group influence. *Organizational Behavior and Human Decision Processes, 103*(1), 121–133.

Boone, C., Olffen, W., Van Witteloostuijn, A., & Brabander, B. (2004). The genesis of top management team diversity: Selective turnover among top management teams in Dutch newspaper publishing, 1970–1994. *Academy of Management Journal, 47*(5), 633–656.

Bouas, K. S., & Arrow, H. (1996). The development of group identity in computer and face to face groups with membership change. *Computer Supported Cooperative Work, 4,* 153–178.

Bouchard, T. J. (1972). Training, motivation, and personality as determinants of the effectiveness of brainstorming groups and individuals. *Journal of Applied Psychology, 56*(4), 324–331.

Bowen, D. D., Lewicki, R. J., Hall, D. T., & Hall, F. S. (1997). *Experiences in management and organizational behavior* (4th ed.). New York: John Wiley Sons.

Bradford, D. L., & Cohen, A. R. (1984). *Managing for excellence.* New York: John Wiley & Sons.

Branscombe, N. R., Spears, R., Ellemers, N., & Doosje, B. (2002). Intragroup and intergroup evaluation effects on group behavior. *Personality and Social Psychology Bulletin, 28*(6), 744–753.

Brawley, L. R., Carron, A. V., & Widmeyer, W. N. (1988). Exploring the relationship between cohesion and group resistance to disruption. *Journal of Sport and Exercise Psychology, 10*(2), 199–213.

Brehmer, B., & Hagafors, R. (1986). Use of experts in complex decision making: A paradigm for the study of staff work. *Organizational Behavior and Human Decision Processes, 38,* 181–195.

Brenner E. (2009, November 1). Agents find benefits in teaming up. *New York Times,* p. RE5

Brett, J. M. (2001). *Negotiating globally: How to negotiate deals, resolve disputes, and make decisions, across cultural boundaries.* San Francisco, CA: Jossey-Bass.

Brett, J. M. (2007). *Negotiating globally: How to negotiate deals, resolve disputes, and make decisions across cultural boundaries.* San Francisco, CA: Jossey-Bass.

Brewer, M. (1979). Ingroup bias in the minimal intergroup situation: A cognitive-motivational analysis. *Psychological Bulletin, 86,* 307–324.

Brewer, M. (1991). The social self: On being the same and different at the same time. *Personality and Social Psychology Bulletin, 17*(5), 475–482.

Brewer, M. (1993). The role of distinctiveness in social identity and group behavior. In M. A. Hogg & D. Abrams (Eds.), *Group motivation: Social psychological perspectives.* New York: Harvester Wheatsheaf.

Brewer, M. B., & Brown, R. J. (1998). Intergroup relations. In D. T. Gilbert, S. T. Fiske, & G. Lindzey (Eds.), *The handbook of social psychology* (4th ed., Vol. 2, pp. 554–594). New York: McGraw-Hill.

Brewer, M. B., & Gardner, W. (1996). Who is this "we"? Levels of collective identity and self representations. *Journal of Personality and Social Psychology, 71,* 83–93.

Brewer, M. B., & Kramer, R. M. (1986). Choice behavior in social dilemmas: Effects of social identity, group size, and decision framing. *Journal of Personality and Social Psychology, 50*(3), 543–549.

Brewer, M. B., & Roccas, S. (2001). Individual values, social identity, and optimal distinctiveness. In C. Sedikidess & M. B. Brewer (Eds.), *Individual self, relational self, collective self* (pp. 219–237). Philadelphia, PA: Psychology Press.

Brickner, M. A., Harkins, S. G., & Ostrom, T. M. (1986). Effects of personal involvement: Thought-provoking implications for social loafing. *Journal of Personality and Social Psychology, 51*(4), 763–770.

Brooks, D. (2009, October 27). The fatal conceit. *New York Times*, p. A31.

Brown, M. E., Trevino, L. K., & Harrison, D. A. (2005). Ethical leadership: A social learning perspective for construct development and testing. *Organizational Behavior and Human Decision Processes, 97,* 117-134.

Brown, P., & Levinson, S. (1987). *Politeness: Some universals in language use.* Cambridge, UK: Cambridge University Press.

Brown, R. (1986). *Social psychology* (2nd ed.). New York: Free Press.

Brown, R. J., Condor, F., Mathew, A., Wade, G., & Williams, J. A. (1986). Explaining intergroup differentiation in an industrial organization. *Journal of Occupational Psychology, 59,* 273–286.

Brown, T. (2009). *Change by design: How design thinking transforms organizations and inspires innovation.* New York: Harper Collins.

Brunell, A. B., Gentry, W. A., Campbell, W. K., Hoffman, B. J., Kuhnert, K. W., & DeMarree, K. G. (2008). Leader emergence: The case of the narcissistic leader. *Personality and Social Psychology Bulletin, 34*(12), 1663–1676.

Buchanan, L. (2008). When absence makes the team grow stronger. *Inc., 30*(6), 40–43.

Budman, M. (2009, Fall). Grand designs. *The Conference Board Review*, 25–33.

Burke, P. J. (1967). The development of task and social-emotional role differentiation. *Sociometry, 30,* 379–392.

Burns, J. M. (1978). *Leadership.* New York: Harper & Row.

Burris, E. R., Rodgers, M. S., Mannix, E. A., Hendron, M. G., & Oldroyd, J. B. (2009). Playing favorites: The influence of leaders inner circle on group processes and performance. *Personality and Social Psychology Bulletin, 35*(9), 1244–1257.

Burrows, P. (2006, September 25). The man behind Apple's design magic. *Business Week, 4002,* 26–33.

Burt, R. S. (1992a). *Structural holes: The social structure of competition.* Cambridge, MA: Harvard University Press.

Burt, R. S. (1992b). *The social structure of competition.* Cambridge, MA: Harvard University Press.

Burt, R. S. (1999). Entrepreneurs, distrust, and third parties: A strategic look at the dark side of dense networks. In L. Thompson, J. Levine, & D. Messick (Eds.), *Shared cognition in organizations: The management of knowledge.* Mahwah, NJ: Lawrence Erlbaum & Associates.

Bushe, G. R. (1984). Quality circles in quality of work life projects: Problems and prospects for increasing employee participation. *Canadian Journal of Community Mental Health, 3*(2), 101–113.

Butera, F., Mugny, G., Legrenzi, P., & Perez, J. A. (1996). Majority and minority influence: Task representation and inductive reasoning. *British Journal of Social Psychology, 67,* 123–136.

Buzanowski, J. G. (2009, February 5). Generals reflect on importance of diversity. Secretary of the Air Force Public Affairs. .af.mil

BW 50 Interactive Scoreboard. (2008). *Business Week.* bwnt.businessweek.com

Byron, K., Khazanchi, S., & Nazarian, D. (2010). The relationship between stressors and creativity: A meta-analysis examining competing theoretical models. *Journal of Applied Psychology, 95*(1), 201–212.

Cadiz, D., Sawyer, J. E., & Griffith, T. L. (2009). Developing and validating field measurement scales for absorptive capacity and experienced community of practice. *Educational and psychological measurement, 20*(1), 1–23.

Cain, D., Loewenstein, G., & Moore, D. (2005). The dirt on coming clean: Perverse effects of disclosing conflicts of interest. *Journal of Legal Studies, 34,* 1–25.

Camacho, L. M., & Paulus, P. B. (1995). The role of social anxiousness in group brainstorming. *Journal of Personality and Social Psychology, 68,* 1071–1080.

Camerer, C. F., Loewenstein, G., & Weber, M. (1989). The curse of knowledge in economic settings: An experimental analysis. *Journal of Political Economy, 97,* 1232–1254.

Campbell, D. T. (1958). Common fate, similarity, and other indices of the status of aggregates of persons as social entities. *Behavioral Science, 3,* 14–25.

Campbell, D. T. (1965). Ethnocentric and other altruistic motives. In D. Levine (Ed.), *Nebraska symposium on motivation* (pp. 283–311). Lincoln, NE: University of Nebraska Press.

Can a well-designed office pay off [Audio podcast]? (2008, October 21). businessweek.com

Cannella, A. A., Park, J. H., & Lee, H. O. (2008). Top management team functional background diversity and firm performance examining the roles of team member collocation and environmental uncertainty. *Academy of Management Journal, 51,* 768–784.

Cannon-Bowers, J. A., Salas, E., & Converse, S. A. (1993). Shared mental models in expert team decision making. In N. J. Castellan (Ed.), *Individual and group decision making* (pp. 221–246). Mahwah, NJ: Lawrence Erlbaum & Associates.

Cannon-Bowers, J. A., Tannenbaum, S. I., Salas, E., & Converse, S. A. (1991). Toward an integration of training theory and technique. *Human Factors, 33*(3), 281–292.

Caporael, L. R., Dawes, R. M., Orbell, J. M., & van de Kragt, A. J. C. (1989). Selfishness examined: Cooperation in the absence of egoistic incentives. *Behavioral and Brain Sciences, 12,* 683–739.

Carmichael, M. (2009, July 1). Case study Wyeth consumer healthcare an all-round appraisal success. *Human Resources,* 74.

Carnevale, P. J., Pruitt, D., & Seilheimmer, S. (1981). Looking and competing: Accountability and visual access in integrative bargaining. *Journal of Personality and Social Psychology, 40,* 111–120.

Carron, A. V., Widmeyer, W. N., & Brawley, L. R. (1988). Group cohesion and individual adherence to physical activity. *Journal of Sport and Exercise Psychology, 10*(2), 127–138.

Carson, J. B., Tesluk, P. E., & Marrone, J. A.(2007). Shared leadership in teams: An investigation of antecedent conditions and performance. *Academy of Management Journal, 50,* 1217–1234.

Caruso, E., Epley, N., & Bazerman, M. (2006). *The costs and benefits of undoing egocentric responsibility assessments in groups. Journal of Personality and Social Psychology, 91*(5), 857–871.

Castelli, L., Tomelleri, S., & Zogmaister, C. (2008). Implicit ingroup metafavoritism: Subtle preference for ingroup members displaying ingroup bias. *Personality and Social Psychology Bulletin, 34*(6), 807–818.

Castore, C. H., & Murnighan, J. K. (1978). Determinants of support for group decisions. *Organizational Behavior and Human Performance, 22,* 75–92.

Cf. Kraiger, K., & Ford, J. K. (1985, February). A meta-analysis of ratee race effects in performance ratings. *Journal of Applied Psychology, 70*(1), 56–65.

Cha, S. E., & Edmondson, A. C. (2006). When values backfire: Leadership, attribution, and disenchantment in a values-driven organization. *Leadership Quarterly, 17,* 57–78.

Charan, R., & Useem, J. (2002, May 27). Why companies fail. *Fortune, 145*(11), 50–62.

Chatman, J. A., Polzer, J. T., Barsade, S. G., & Neale, M. A. (1998). Being different yet feeling similar: The influence of demographic composition and organizational culture on work processes and outcomes. *Administrative Science Quarterly, 43*, 749–80.

Chatman, J., Boisnier, A., Spataro, S., Anderson, C., & Berdahl, J. (2008). Being distinctive versus being conspicuous: The effects of numeric status and sex-stereotyped tasks on individual performance in groups. *Organizational Behavior and Human Decision Processes, 107*(2), 141–160.

Cheek, J. M., Tropp, L. R., Chen, L. C., & Underwood, M. K. (1994). *Identity orientations: Personal, social, and collective aspects of identity.* Paper presented at the meeting of the American Psychological Association, Los Angeles, CA.

Chen, G. (2005). Newcomer adaptation in teams: Multilevel antecedents and outcomes. *Academy of Management Journal, 48*(1), 101–116.

Chen, G., Donahue, L. M., & Klimoski, R. J. (2004). Training undergraduates to work in organizational teams. *Academy of Management: Learning and Education, 3*(1), 27–40.

Chen, G., & Klimoksi, R. J. (2003). The impact of expectations on newcomer performance in teams as mediated by work characteristics, social exchanges, and empowerment. *Academy of Management Journal, 46*(5), 591–607.

Cheng, G. H. L., Fielding, K. S., Hogg, M. A., & Terry, D. J. (2009). Reactions to procedural discrimination in an intergroup context: The role of group membership of the authority. *Group Processes & Intergroup Relations, 12*(4), 463–478.

Choi, H. S., & Thompson, L. (2005). Old wine in a new bottle: Impact of membership change on group creativity. *Organization Behavior and Human Decision Processes, 98*(2), 121–132.

Christensen, C., Larson, J. R., Jr., Abbott, A., Ardolino, A., Franz, T., & Pfeiffer, C. (2000). Decision-making of clinical teams: Communication patterns and diagnostic error. *Medical Decision Making, 20*, 45–50.

Cialdini, R. B. (1989). *Indirect tactics of image management: Beyond basking.* Mahwah, NJ: Lawrence Erlbaum & Associates.

Cini, M., Moreland, R. L., & Levine, J. M. (1993). Group staffing levels and responses to prospective and new members. *Journal of Personality and Social Psychology, 65*, 723–734.

Cisco study finds telecommuting significantly increases employee productivity, work-life flexibility and job satisfaction. (2009, June 26). Marketwire.com.

Citrin, J. M. (2009, October 2). Performance lessons from Olympians. *Wall Street.*

Clancy, M. (2009, January 16). Miracle on the Hudson. *nbcnewyork.com.* nbcnewyork.com

Clark, K. B., & Fujimoto, T. (1989). Overlapping problem solving in product development. In K. Ferdows (Ed.), *Managing international manufacturing* (pp. 127–152). North Holland: Amsterdam

Clark, M. S., & Mills, J. R. (1979). Interpersonal attraction in exchange and communal relationships. *Journal of Personality and Social Psychology, 37*, 12–24.

Clawson, D. (2003). *The next upsurge: Labor and the new social movements.* Ithaca, NY: Cornell University Press.

Clawson, J. C. (2003). *Level 3 leadership: Getting below the surface* (2nd ed.). Upper Saddle River, NJ: Prentice Hall.

Coen, J., Pearson, R., Chase, J., & Kidwell, D. (2008, December 10). Feds arrest Gov. Blagojevich to stop … —A political "crime spree"—Governor faces shocking array of charges—topped by accusations he tried to auction a U.S. Senate seat. *Chicago Tribune*, p. 1.

Cohen, G. L., Steele, C. M., & Ross, L. D. (1999). The mentor's dilemma: Providing critical feedback across the racial divide. *Personality and Social Psychology Bulletin, 25*(10), 1302–1318.

Cohen, M. D., March, J. P., & Olsen, J. P. (1972). A garbage can model of organizational choice. *Administrative Science Quarterly, 17*, 1–25.

Cohen, T. R., Gunia, B. C., Kim-Jun, S. Y., & Murnighan, J. K. (2009). Do groups lie more than individuals? Honesty & deception as a function of strategic self-interest. *Journal of Experimental Social Psychology, 45*, 1321–1324.

Colbert, A. E., Kristof-Brown, A. L. Bradley, B. H., & Barrick, M. R. (2008). CEO transformational leadership: The role of goal importance congruence in top management teams. *Academy of Management Journal, 51*(1), 81–96.

Cole, M., Walter, F., & Bruch, H. (2008). Affective mechanisms linking dysfunctional behavior to performance in work teams: A moderated mediation study. *Journal of Applied Psychology, 93*(5), 945–958.

Cole, R. E. (1982). Diffusion of participating work structures in Japan, Sweden and the United States. In P. S. Goodman (Ed.), *Change in organizations* (pp. 166–225). San Francisco, CA: Jossey-Bass.

Coleman, J. S. (1988). Social capital in the creation of human capital. *American Journal of Sociology, 94*, S95–S120.

Collaros, P. A., & Anderson, L. R. (1969). Effect of perceived expertness upon creativity of members of brainstorming groups. *Journal of Applied Psychology, 53*(2, Pt. 1), 159–163.

Collins, E. G., & Guetzkow, H. (1964). *A social psychology of group processes for decision making.* New York: John Wiley Sons.

Conger, J. (1989). The art of empowering others. *Academy of Management Executive, 3*(1), 17–24.

Connolly, T., Routhieaux, R. L., & Schneider, S. K. (1993). On the effectiveness of group brainstorming: Test of one underlying cognitive mechanism. *Small Group Research, 24*, 490–503.

Conway, L. G., Schaller, M. (2005). When authorities' commands backfire: Attributions about consensus effects on deviant decision making. *Journal of Personality and Social Psychology, 89*(3), 311–326.

Cottrell, C., Neuberg, S., & Li, N. (2007). What do people desire in others? A sociofunctional perspective on the importance of different valued characteristics. *Journal of Personality and Social Psychology, 92*(2), 208–231.

Covel, S. (2008, February 7). How to get workers to think and act like owners. *Wall Street Journal*, p. B6.

Crano, W. D. (2000). Social influence: Effects of leniency on majority and minority-induced focal and indirect attitude change. *Revue Internationale de Psychologie Sociale, 15*, 89–121.

Crocker, J., & Major, B. (1989). Social stigma and self-esteem: The self-protective properties of stigma. *Psychological Review, 96*, 608–630.

Crocker, J., Voelkl, K., Testa, M., & Major, B. (1991). Social stigma: The affective consequences of attributional ambiguity. *Journal of Personality and Social Psychology, 60*, 218–228.

Crockett, R. O. (2009, October 2). P&G gets reticent researchers to speak up. *Business Week.* Business week.com

Cronin, M. A. (2004). The effect of respect on interdependent work. *Unpublished doctoral dissertation*, Pittsburgh, PA: Carnegie Mellon University.

Cronin, M., & Weingart, L. (2007a). The differential effects of trust and respect on team conflict. In K. Behfar & L. Thompson (Eds.), *Conflict in organizational groups: New directions in theory and practice.* Chicago, IL: NU Press.

Cronin, M., & Weingart, L. (2007b). Representational gaps, information processing, and conflict in functionally diverse teams. *Academy of Management Review, 32*(3), 761–773.

Cross, S. E., Bacon, P. L., & Morris, M. L. (2000). The relational-interdependent self-construal and relationships. *Journal of Personality and Social Psychology, 78*(4), 791–808.

Csikszentmihalyi, M. (1988). Society, culture and person: A systems view of creativity. In R. Sternberg (Ed.), *The nature of productivity: Contemporary psychological perspectives.* New York: Cambridge University Press.

Csikszentmihalyi, M. (1990). *Flow: The psychology of optimal experience* (p. 74). New York: HarperCollins.

Csikszentmihalyi, M. (2003). *Good business: Leadership, flow, and the making of meaning.* New York: Viking Press.

Cummings, T. G., & Mohrman, S. A. (1987). Self-designing organizations: Towards implementing quality-of-work-life innovations. In R. W. Woodman & W. A. Pasmore (Eds.), *Research in organizational change and development* (Vol. 1, pp. 275–310). Greenwich, CT: JAI Press.

Daft, R. L., & Lengel, R. H. (1984). Information richness: A new approach to managerial behavior and organization design. *Research in Organization Behavior, 6*, 191–223.

Daft, R. L., Lengel, R. H., & Trevino, L. K. (1987). Message equivocality, media selection, and manager performance: Implications for information systems. *MIS Quarterly, 11*(3), 355–366.

Dahlin, K., Weingart, L., & Hinds, P. (2005). Team diversity and information use. *Academy of Management Journal, 48*(6), 1107–1123.

Dash, E., & Glater, J. (2009, March 26). Paid handsomely to stay. *New York Times*, p. B1.

David, B., & Turner, J. C. (1996). Studies in self-categorization and minority conversion: Is being a member of the out-group an advantage? *British Journal of Social Psychology, 35*, 179–199.

Davidow, W. H., & Malone, M. S. (1992). *The virtual corporation: Structuring and revitalizing the corporation for the 21st century.* New York: HarperCollins.

Davies, P. G., Spencer, S. J., & Steele, C. M. (2005). Clearing the air: Identity safety moderates the effects of stereotype threat on women's leadership aspirations. *Journal of Personality and Social Psychology, 88*, 276–287.

Davis, J. (1969). *Group performance.* Reading, MA: Addison-Wesley.

Dawes, R., Orbell, J., & van de Kragt, A. (1988). Not me or thee but we: The importance of group identity in eliciting cooperation in dilemma situations. *Acta Psychologica, 68*, 83–97.

DeChurch, L. A., & Marks, M. A. (2006). Leadership in multiteam systems. *Journal of Applied Psychology, 91*(2), 311–329.

DeChurch, L. A., & Mesmer-Magnus, J. R. (2010). The cognitive underpinnings of effective teamwork: A meta-analysis. *Journal of Applied Psychology, 95*(1), 32–53.

De Cremer, D. (2002). Respect and cooperation in social dilemmas: The importance of feeling included. *Personality and Social Psychology Bulletin, 28*(10), 1335–1341.

De Cremer, D., & van Dijk, E. (2002). Reactions to group success and failure as a function of identification levels: A test of the goal-transformation hypothesis in social dilemmas. *Journal of Experimental Social Psychology, 38*, 435–442.

De Cremer, D., & Van Vugt, M. (1999). Social identification effects in social dilemmas: A transformation of motives. *Journal of Experimental Social Psychology, 29*, 871–893.

De Dreu, C. K. W. (2007). Cooperative outcome interdependence, task reflexivity, and team effectiveness: A motivated information processing perspective. *Journal of Applied Psychology, 92*(3), 628–638.

De Dreu, C. K. W., & Weingart, L. R. (2003a). Task versus relationship conflict, team effectiveness, and team member satisfaction: A meta-analysis. *Journal of Applied Psychology, 88*, 741–749.

De Dreu, C., & Weingart, L. (2003b). A contingency theory of task conflict and performance in groups and organizational teams. In M. A. West, D. Tjosvold, & K. G. Smith (Eds.), *International handbook of organizational teamwork and cooperative working.* New York: John Wiley & Sons.

DeGroot, A. (1966). Perception and memory versus thought: Some old ideas and recent findings. In B. Kleinmuntz (Ed.), *Problem solving: Research, method, and theory* (pp. 19–50). New York: John Wiley & Sons.

Delbecq, A. L., & Van de Ven, A. H. (1971). A group process model for identification and program planning. *Journal of Applied Behavioral Sciences, 7*, 466–492.

DeMeyer, A. (1991). Tech talk: How managers are stimulating global R&D communication. *Sloan Management Review, 32*(3), 49–58.

DeMeyer, A. (1993). Internationalizing R&D improves a firm's technical learning. *Research-Technical Management, 36*(4), 42–49.

Dennis, A. R., Nunamaker, J. F., Jr., Paranka, D., & Vogel, D. R. A. (1990). A New role for computers in strategic management. *Journal of Business Strategy, 11*(5), 38–42.

Dennis, A. R., Valacich, J. S., Connolly, T., & Wynne, B. E. (1996). Process structuring in electronic brainstorming. *Information Systems Research, 7*, 268–277.

Department of Public Relations Colorado State University. (2008, June 4). *Collaboratory receives economic development honor, major progress after 18 months.* news.colostate.edu

DerGurahian, J. (2009, November 2). Changing course. A few well-publicized cases of medical errors have led the hospitals involved to transform how they approach patient safety. *Modern Healthcare*, p. 6.

DeRue, D. S., Hollenbeck, J. R., Johnson, M. D., Ilgen, D. R., & Jundt, D. K. (2008). How different team downsizing approaches influence team-level adaptation and performance. *Academy of Management Journal, 51*, 182–196.

DeSanctis, G., Poole, M. S., & Dickson, G. W. (2000). Teams and technology: Interactions over time. *Research on Managing Groups and Teams, 3*, 1–27.

Deutsch, M. (1975). Equity, equality, and need: What determines which value will be used as the basis of distributive justice? *Journal of Social Issues, 31*, 137–149.

Deutsch, M., & Gerard, H. B. (1955). A study of normative and informational social influence upon individual judgment. *Journal of Abnormal and Social Psychology, 51*, 629–636.

Deutschman, A. (2009, September 21). How authentic leaders "walk the walk." *Business Week*, 9.

Devadas, R., & Argote, L. (1995). *Organizational learning curves: The effects of turnover and work group structure*. Invited paper presented at the annual meeting of the Midwestern Psychological Association, Chicago, IL.

Devadas, R., & Argote, L. (1995, May). *Collective learning and forgetting: The effects of turnover and group structure*. Paper presented at the meeting of the Midwestern Psychological Association, Chicago, IL.

DeVoe, S. E., & Iyengar, S. S. (2010). Medium of exchange matters: What's fair for goods is unfair for money. *Psychological Science*.

De Zavala, A. G., Cichocka, A., Eidelson, R., & **Jayawickreme, N.** (2009). Collective narcissism and its social consequences. *Journal of Personality and Social Psychology, 97*(6), 1074–1096.

Diehl, M., & Stroebe, W. (1987). Productivity loss in brainstorming groups: Toward a solution of a riddle. *Journal of Personality and Social Psychology, 53*(3), 497–509.

Diehl, M., & Stroebe, W. (1991). Productivity loss in idea-generating groups: Tracking down the blocking effect. *Journal of Personality and Social Psychology, 61*(3), 392–403.

Dietz-Uhler, B. (1996). The escalation of commitment in political decision making groups: A social identity approach. *European Journal of Social Psychology, 26*, 611–629.

Dinnocenzo, D. (2006). *How to lead from a distance: Building bridges in the virtual workplace*. Walk the Talk: Dallas.

Dion, K. (2000). Group cohesion: From "field of forces" to multidimensional construct. *Group Dynamics: Theory, Research, and Practice, 4*(1), 7–26.

Dion, K. L., & Evans, C. R. (1992). On cohesiveness: Reply to Keyton and other critics of the construct. *Small Group Research, 23*(2), 242–250.

Dirks, K. T. (1999). The effects of interpersonal trust on work group performance. *Journal of Applied Psychology, 84*, 445–455.

Dominguez, P. (2008, June 16). IDEO's 7 rules of brainstorming. *Green Business Innovators*. Green businessinnovators.com

Doney, P. M., & Armstrong, G. M. (1996). Effects of accountability on symbolic information search and information analysis by organizational buyers. *Journal of the Academy of Marketing Science, 24*, 57–65.

Doosje, B., Spears, R., & Koomen, W. (1995). When bad isn't all bad: Strategic use of sample information in generalization and stereotyping. *Journal of Personality and Social Psychology, 69*, 642–655.

Dorit, N., Izak, B., & Yair, W. (2009, October 29). Who Knows What? *The Wall Street Journal*, p. R4.

Drach-Zahavy, A., & Erez, M. (2002). Challenge versus threat effects on the goal-performance relationship. *Organizational Behavior and Human Decision Processes, 88*, 667–682.

Drechsler, W. (1995). Collectivism. In H. Drechsler, W. Hillinge, & F. Neumann (Eds.), *Society and state: The lexicon of politics* (9th ed., pp. 458–459). Munich, Germany: Franz Vahlen.

Drolet, A., Larrick, R., & Morris, M. W. (1998). Thinking of others: How perspective-taking changes negotiators' aspirations and fairness perceptions as a function of negotiator relationships. *Basic and Applied Social Psychology, 20*(1), 23–31.

Drury, T. (2008, August 1). A bad meeting is just that. *Business First*. buffalo.bizjournals.com

Druskat, V. U., & Wheeler, J. V. (2004). How to lead a self-managing team. *MIT Sloan Management Review, 45*(4), 65–71.

Druskat, V., & Wheeler, J. (2003). Managing from the boundary: The effective leadership of self-managing work teams. *Academy of Management Journal, 46*(4), 435–457.

Dubrovsky, V. J., Keisler, S., & Sethna, B. N. (1991). The equalization phenomenon: Status effects in computer-mediated and face-to-face decision-making groups. *Human-Computer Interaction, 6*(2), 119–146.

Duck, J. M., & Fielding, K. S. (1999). Leaders and subgroups: One of us or one of them? *Group Processes and Intergroup Relations, 2*(3), 203–230.

Duclos, S. E., Laird, J. D., Schneider, E., Sexter, M., Stern, L., & Van Lighten, O. (1989). Categorical vs. dimensional effects of facial expressions on emotional experience. *Journal of Personality and Social Psychology, 57,* 100–108.

Dugosh, K. L., & Paulus, P. B. (2005). Cognitive and social comparison processes in brainstorming. *Journal of Experimental Social Psychology, 41,* 313–320.

Dugosh, K. L., Paulus, P. B., Roland, E. J., & Yang, H.-C. (2000). Cognitive stimulation in brainstorming. *Journal of Personality of Social Psychology, 79*(5), 722–735.

Duguid, M., Loyd, D. L., & Tolbert, P. S. Dimensions of status: How categorical, numeric, and work group status interact to affect preference for demographically similar others. Under review at Organization Science.

Duhigg, C. (2003, February 17). Fortune 500, meet Daytona 500. *Slate Magazine.* slate.com

Duncker, K. (1945). On Problem Solving. *Psychological Monographs, 58*(5), Whole No. 270.

Durham, C., Knight, D., & Locke, E. A. (1997). Effects of leader role, team-set goal difficulty, efficacy, and tactics on team effectiveness. *Organizational Behavior and Human Decision Processes, 72*(2), 203–231.

Eagly, A. H., Johannesen-Schmidt, M. C., & van Engen, M. L. (2003). Transformational, transactional, and laissez-faire leadership styles: A meta-analysis comparing men and women. *Psychological Bulletin, 129,* 569–591.

Eagly, A. H., & Johnson, B. (1990). Gender and leadership style: A meta-analysis. *Psychological Bulletin, 108,* 233–256.

Eagly, A. H., & Karau, S. J. (1991). Gender and the emergence of leaders: A metaanalysis. *Journal of Personality and Social Psychology, 60,* 685–710.

Eagly, A. H., & Karau, S. J. (2002). Role congruity theory of prejudice toward female leaders. *Psychological Review, 190*(3), 573–598.

Eagly, A. H., Makhijani, M. G., & Klonsky, B. G. (1992). Gender and the evaluation of leaders: A meta-analysis. *Psychological Bulletin, 111,* 3–22.

Earley, C., & Mosakowski, E. (2004). Cultural intelligence. *Harvard Business Review, 82*(10), 139–146.

Earley, C. P. (2002). Redefining interactions across cultures and organizations: Moving forward with cultural intelligence. In B. M. Staw & R. M. Kramer (Eds.), *Research in organizational behavior* (Vol. 24, pp. 271–299). Oxford, UK: Elsevier.

Edgar, K. (2008, June 18). 210th Fires conducts convoy training. *United States Army.* army.mil

Edmondson, A. (1999). Psychological safety and learning behavior in work teams. *Administrative Science Quarterly, 44,* 350–383.

Edmondson, A. (2003). Framing for learning: Lessons in successful technology implementation. *California Management Review, 45*(2), 34–54.

Edmondson, A., Roberto, M. A., & Watkins, M. D. (2003). A dynamic model of top management team effectiveness: Managing unstructured task streams. *Leadership Quarterly, 14*(3), 297–325.

Edmondson, A. C., & Nembhard, I. M. (2009). Product development and learning in project teams: The challenges are the benefits. *Journal of Product Innovation Management, 26*(2), 123–138.

Edmondson, A., Winslow, A., Bohmer, R., & Pisano, G. (2003). Learning how and learning what: Effects of tacit and codified knowledge on performance improvement following technology adoption. *Decision Sciences, 34*(2), 197–223.

Edmonson, A. (2003). Speaking up in the operating room: How team leaders promote learning in interdisciplinary action teams. *Journal of Management Studies, 40*(6), 1419–1452.

Edwards, B., Day, E., Arthur, W., & Bell, S. (2006). Relationships among team ability composition, team mental models, and team performance. *Journal of Applied Psychology, 91*(3), 727–736.

Eggen, D., DeYoung, K., & Hsu, S. (2009, December 27). Plane suspect was listed in terror database after father alerted US officials. *The Washington Post*, p. AO1.

Eisenberger, R., & Selbst, M. (1994). Does reward increase or decrease creativity? *Journal of Personality and Social Psychology, 49,* 520–528.

Ellis, A. (2006). System breakdown: The role of mental models and transactive memory in the relationships between acute stress and team performance. *Academy of Management Journal, 49*(3), 576–589.

Emery, F. E., & Trist, E. L. (1973). *Towards a social ecology: Contextual appreciation of the future in the present.* New York: Plenum Press.

Employee job satisfaction & retention survey 2007/2008. (2008). Salary.com Employers Resource Council. (2008). *Variable pay plans.* www.ercnet.org.

Engardio, P. (2009, November 19). Innovation Goes Downtown. *Business Week, 4157*, pp. 50–52.

Ensari, N., & Miller, N. (2002). The out-group must not be so bad after all: The effects of disclosure, typicality, and salience on intergroup bias. *Journal of Personality of Social Psychology, 82*(2), 313–329.

Epitropaki, O., & Martin, R. (2005). From ideal to real: A longitudinal study of the role of implicit leadership theories on leader-member exchanges and employee outcomes. *Journal of Applied Psychology, 90*(4), 659–676.

Epley, N., Caruso, E. M., & Bazerman, M. (2006). When perspective taking increases taking: Reactive egoism in social interaction. *Journal of Personality and Social Psychology, 91*(5), 872–889.

Esses, V. M., & Dovidio, J. F. (2002). The role of emotions in determining willingness to engage in intergroup contact. *Personality and Social Psychology Bulletin, 28*(9), 1202–1214.

Etzkowitz, H., Kemelgor, C., & Uzzi, B. (1999). *Social capital and career dynamics in hard science: Gender, networks, and advancement.* New York: Cambridge University Press.

Etzkowitz, H., Kemelgor, C., & Uzzi, B. (2000). *Athena unbound: The advancement of women in science and technology.* New York: Cambridge University Press.

Evans, T. (2009, December 21). Entrepreneurs seek ways to draw out workers ideas. *Wall Street Journal*, p. 22.

Eveland, J. D., & Bikson, T. K. (1989). *Workgroup structures and computer support: A field experiment.* Santa Monica, CA: RAND Corp.

Fan, E. T., & Gruenfeld, D. H. (1998). When needs outweigh desires: The effects of resource interdependence and reward interdependence on group problem solving. *Basic and Applied Social Psychology, 20*(1), 45–56.

Faraj, S., & Sproull, L. (2000). Coordinating expertise in software development teams. *Management Science, 46*(12), 1554–1568.

Faraj, S., & Yan, A. (2009). Boundary work in knowledge teams. *Journal of Applied Psychology, 94*(3), 604–617.

Feldman, D. C. (1977). The role of initiation activities in socialization. *Human Relations, 30,* 977–990.

Field, R. H. G., & House, R. J. (1990). A test of the Vroom-Yetton model using manager and subordinate reports. *Journal of Applied Psychology, 75*(3), 362–366.

Finholt, T. A., & Olson, G. M. (1997). From laboratories to collaboratories: A new organizational form for scientific collaboration. *Psychological Science, 8*(1), 28–36.

Finke, R. A. (1995). Creative realism. In S. M. Smith, T. B. Ward, & R. A. Finke (Eds.), *The creative cognition approach* (pp. 303–326). Cambridge, MA: MIT Press.

Fischhoff, B. (1975). Hindsight does not equal foresight: The effect of outcome knowledge on judgment under uncertainty. *Journal of Experimental Psychology: Human Perception and Performance, 1,* 288–299.

Fischhoff, B., Slovic, P., & Lichtenstein, S. (1977). Knowing with certainty: The appropriateness of extreme confidence. *Journal of Experimental Psychology: Human Perception and Performance, 3*(4), 552–564.

Fisher, A. (2009, November 19). How to build a (strong) virtual team. *CNNmoney.com.* money.cnn.com

Fisher, K., & Fisher, M. D. (1998). *The distributed mind: Achieving high performance through the collective intelligence of knowledge work teams.* Chicago, IL: AMACOM American Management Association.

Fisher, R., & Ury, W. (1981). *Getting to yes: Negotiating agreement without giving in.* Boston, MA: Houghton Mifflin.

Fisher Gale, S. (2008, December). Virtual training with real results. *Workforce Management.* workforce.com

Fiske, S. T., & Taylor, S. E. (1991). *Social cognition.* New York: McGraw-Hill.

Flandez, R. (2009, July 7). Rewards Help Soothe Hard Times. *Wall Street Journal,* p. B4.

Flippen, A. R., Hornstein, H. A., Siegal, W. E., & Weitzman, E. A. (1996). A comparison of similarity and interdependence as triggers for in-group formation. *Personality and Social Psychology Bulletin, 22*(9), 882–893.

Flora, C. (2009, November 1). Every day creativity. *Psychology Today, 42*(6), 62–43.

Flynn, F. J., & Ames, D. R. (2006). What's good for the goose may not be as good for the gander: The benefits of self-monitoring for men and women in task groups and dyadic conflicts. *Journal of Applied Psychology, 91*(2), 272–281.

Forbus, K. D., Gentner, D., & Law, K. (1995). MAC/FAC: A model of similarity-based retrieval. *Cognitive Science, 19*(2), 141–205.

Forsyth, D. (1990). *Group dynamics* (2nd ed., p. 286). Pacific Grove, CA: Brooks/Cole.

Forsyth, D. R. (1983). *Group dynamics* (2nd ed.). Pacific Grove, CA: Brooks/Cole.

Foschi, M., Lai, L., & Sigerson, K. (1994). Gender and double standards in the assessment of job applicants. *Social Psychology Quarterly, 57,* 326–339.

Foschi, M., Sigerson, K., & Lembesis, M. (1995). Assessing job applicants: The relative effects of gender, academic record, and decision type. *Small Group Research, 26*(3), 328–352.

Foushee, H. C., Lauber, J. K., Baetge, M. M., & Comb, D. B. (1986). *Crew factors in flight operations: III. The operational significance of exposure to short-haul air transport operations* (NASA TM 88322). Moffett Field, CA: NASA Ames Research Center.

Frank, R. H., & Cook, P. J. (1995). *The winner-take-all society.* New York: Penguin.

Frank, R. H., Gilovich, T., & Regan, D. T. (1993). Does studying economics prohibit cooperation? *Journal of Economic Perspectives, 7*(2), 159–171.

Frauenheim, E. (2006, April 24). On the clock but off on their own: Pet-project programs set to gain wider acceptance. *Workforce Management,* 40–41.

Frauenheim, E. (2008, October 20). Kaiser permanente: Optimas award winner for ethical practice. *Workforce Management,* 35.

Frauenheim, E. (2009a, April 20). Talent tools still essential. *Workforce Management,* 20.

Frauenheim, E. (2009b, November 16). Commitment issues—restoring employee. *Workforce Management,* 20–25.

Freedman, J. L., Cunningham, J. A., & Krismer, K. (1992). Inferred values and the reverse incentive effect in induced compliance. *Journal of Personality and Social Psychology, 62,* 357–368.

French, J. R. P., & Raven, B. (1968). The bases of social power. In D. Cartwright & A. F. Zander (Eds.), *Group dynamics* (pp. 259–270). New York: Harper & Row.

Friedlander, F. (1987). The design of work teams. In J. W. Lorsch (Ed.), *Handbook of organizational behavior.* Upper Saddle River, NJ: Prentice Hall.

Fuegen, K., & Biernat, M. (2002). Reexamining the effects of solo status for women and men. *Personality and Social Psychology Bulletin, 28*(7), 913–925.

Furnham, A. (1990a). *The Protestant work ethic.* New York: Routledge.

Furst, S., Reeves, M., Rosen, B., & Blackburn, R. (2004). Managing the life cycle of virtual teams. *Academy of Management Executive, 18*(2), 6–20.

Gabrenya, W. K., Latané, B., & Wang, Y. (1983). Social loafing in cross-cultural perspective: Chinese on Taiwan. *Journal of Cross-Cultural Psychology, 14*(3), 368–384.

Gabriel, S., & Gardner, W. L. (1999). Are there "his" and "hers" types of interdependence? The implications of gender differences in collective versus relational interdependence for affect, behavior, and cognition. *Journal of Personality and Social Psychology, 77,* 642–655.

Gaertner, S. L., Dovidio, J. F., & Bachman, B. A. (1996). Revisiting the contact hypothesis: The induction of a common ingroup identity. *International Journal of Intercultural Relations, 20*(3 & 4), 271–290.

Gaertner, S. L., Dovidio, J. F., Rust, M. C., Nier, J. A., Banker, B. S., Ward, C. M., Mottola, G. R., & Houlette, M. (1999). Reducing intergroup bias: Elements of intergroup cooperation. *Journal of Personality and Social Psychology, 76*(3), 388–402.

Galegher, J., Kraut, R. E., & Egido, C. (Eds.). (1990). *Intellectual teamwork: Social and technological foundations of cooperative work.* Hillsdale, NJ: Erlbaum.

Gallupe, R. B. (1992). Electronic Brainstorming and Group Size. *Academy of Management Journal, 35,* 351–353.

Garcia, S. M., Tor, A., & Gonzales, R. (2006). Ranks and rivals: A theory of competition. *Personality and Social Psychology Bulletin, 32*(7), 970–982.

Gardner, W. L. (1992). Lessons in organizational dramaturgy: The art of impression management. *Organizational Dynamics, 21*(1), 33–46.

Gardner, W. L., Gabriel, S., & Lee, A. Y. (1999). "I" value freedom, but "we" value relationships: Self-construal priming mirrors cultural differences in judgment. *Psychological Science, 10*(4), 321–326.

Garvin, D., & Collins, E. (2009, November 30). RL Wolfe: Implementing self-directed teams. *The Harvard Business Review.* Boston, MA: Harvard Business Publishing.

Gauron, E. F., & Rawlings, E. I. (1975). A procedure for orienting new members to group psychotherapy. *Small Group Behavior, 6,* 293–307.

Gearino, D. (2009, November 5). Beat the clock. *The Columbus Dispatch.* dispatch.com

Gelnar, M. (2008, June 23). No time for nonsense. *Wall Street Journal,* p. R6.

Gentner, D., Brem, S., Ferguson, R., & Wolff, P. (1997). Analogy and creativity in the works of Johannes Kepler. In T. B. Ward, S. M. Smith, & J. Vaid (Eds.), *Creative thought: An investigation of conceptual structures and processes* (pp. 403–459). Washington, DC: American Psychological Association.

Gentner, D., & Gentner, D. R. (1983). Flowing waters or teeming crowds: Mental models of electricity. In D. Gentner & A. Stevens (Eds.), *Mental models.* Mahwah, NJ: Lawrence Erlbaum & Associates.

Gentner, D., & Landers, R. (1985). Analogical reminding: A good match is hard to find. *Proceedings of the International Conference on Cybernetics and Society* (pp. 607–613), Tucson, AZ, and New York: Institute of Electrical and Electronics Engineers.

Gentner, D., Loewenstein, J., & Thompson, L. (2003). Learning and transfer: A general role for analogical encoding. *Journal of Educational Psychology, 95,* 393–408.

Gentner, D., Loewenstein, J., Thompson, L., & Forbus, K. (2009). Reviving inert knowledge: Analogical encoding supports relational retrieval of past events. *Cognitive Science, 33,* 1343–1382

Gentner, D., Rattermann, M. J., & Forbus, K. D. (1993). The roles of similarity in transfer: Separating retrievability from inferential soundness. *Cognitive Psychology, 25*(4), 524–575.

George, J. M. (1990). Personality, affect, and behavior in groups. *Journal of Applied Psychology, 75,* 107–116.

George, J. M. (1996). Group affective tone. In: M. A. West (Ed.), *Handbook of work group psychology* (pp. 77–93). Chichester, UK: Wiley.

Gerard, H. (1983). School desegregation: The social science role. *American Psychologist, 38,* 869–878.

Gersick, C. J. C. (1988). Time and transition in work teams: Toward a new model of group development. *Academy of Management Journal, 31,* 9–41.

Geschka, H., Schaude, G. R., & Schlicksupp, H. (1973, August). Modern techniques for solving problems. *Chemical Engineering,* 91–97.

Giacolone, R. A., & Riordan, C. A. (1990). Effect of self-presentation on perceptions and recognition in an organization. *Journal of Psychology, 124,* 25–38.

Gibb, J. R. (1951). *Dynamics of participative groups.* Boulder, CO: University of Colorado.

Gibson, C., & Vermuelen, F. (2003). A healthy divide: Subgroups as a stimulus for team learning behavior. *Administrative Science Quarterly, 48,* 202–239.

Gibson, C. B., Cooper, C. D., & Conger, J. A. (2009). Do you see what we see? The complex effects of perceptual distance between leaders and teams. *Journal of Applied Psychology, 94*(1), 62–76.

Gick, M. L., & Holyoak, K. J. (1980). Analogical problem-solving. *Cognitive Psychology, 12,* 306–355.

Gick, M. L., & Holyoak, K. J. (1983). Schema induction and analogical transfer. *Cognitive Psychology, 15,* 1–38.

Giessner, S. R., & Knippenberg, D. (2008). "License to Fail": Goal definition, leader group prototypicality, and perceptions of leadership effectiveness after leader failure. *Organizational Behavior and Human Decision Processes, 105*(1), 14–35.

Giessner, S. R., & Schubert, T. W. (2007). High in the hierarchy: How vertical location and judgments of leaders' power are interrelated. *Organizational Behavior and Human Decision Processes, 104*(1), 30–44.

Gigone, D., & Hastie, R. (1993). The common knowledge effect: Information sharing and group judgment. *Journal of Personality and Social Psychology, 65*(5), 959–974.

Gigone, D., & Hastie, R. (1997). The impact of information on small group choice. *Journal of Personality and Social Psychology, 72*(1), 132–140.

Gilad, C., Kirkman, B. L., Kanfer, R., Allen, D., & Rosen, B. (2007). A multilevel study of leadership, empowerment, and performance in teams. *Journal of Applied Psychology, 92*(2), 331–346.

Gillespie, D. F., & Birnbaum-More, P. H. (1980). Status concordance, coordination and success in interdisciplinary research teams. *Human Relations, 33*(1), 41–56.

Gilovich, T. (1987). Second hand information and social judgment. *Journal of Experimental Social Psychology, 23*(1), 59–74.

Gilovich, T., Kerr, M., & Medvec, V. H. (1993). The effect of temporal perspective on subjective confidence. *Journal of Personality and Social Psychology, 64*(4), 552–560.

Gilovich, T., Savitsky, K., & Medvec, V. H. (1998). The illusion of transparency: Biased assessments of others' ability to read one's emotional states. *Journal of Personality and Social Psychology, 75*(2), 332–346.

Gilson, L. L., Mathieu, J. E., Shalley, C. E., & Ruddy, T. M. (2005). Creativity and standardization: Complementary or conflicting drivers of team effectiveness. *Academy of Management Journal, 48*(3), 521–531.

Gino, F., Gu, J., & Zhong, C. (2009). Contagion or restitution? When bad apples can motivate ethical behavior. *Journal of Experimental Social Psychology, 45,* 1299–1302.

Gino, F., & Moore, D. (2007). Effects of task difficulty on use of advice. *Journal of Behavioral Decision Making, 20*(1), 21–35.

Ginsburg, M. (2009, January). Overseeing overseas. *Workforce Management.* workforce.com

Glader, P. (2009, October 7). Cultivate the creative class within your companies... or else [Web log post]. blogs.wsj.com

Glasford, D., Dovidio, J., & Pratto, F. (2009). I continue to feel so good about us: In-group identification and the use of social identity—enhancing strategies to reduce intragroup dissonance. *Personality and Social Psychology Bulletin, 35*(4), 415–427.

Glickman, A. S., Zimmer, S., Montero, R. C., Guerette, P. J., Campbell, W. J., Morgan, B. B., Jr., & Salas, E. (1987). *The evolution of teamwork skills: An empirical assessment with implications for training* (US Naval Training Systems Center Technical Reports, No. 87-016). Orlando, FL: Naval Training Systems Center.

Goetz, K. (writer). (2009, January 6). Co-Working offers community to solo workers [Radio broadcast episode]. *Morning Edition.* Washington, DC.: National Public Radio.

Gold, M., & Yanof, D. S. (1985). Mothers, daughters, and girlfriends. *Journal of Personality and Social Psychology, 49*(3), 654–659.

Gomes, L. (2006, June 27). Talking tech: How email can set the stage for big misunderstandings. *Wall Street Journal,* p. B3.

Gomez, A., Dovidio, J. F., Huici, C., Gaertner, S. L., & Cuadrado, I. (2008). The other side of we: When outgroup members express common identity. *Personality and Social Psychology Bulletin, 34*(12), 1613–1626.

Goncalo, G. A., & Duguid, M. D. (2008). Hidden consequences of the group-serving bias: Casual attributions and the quality of group decision making. *Organizational Behavior and Human Decision Processes, 107*, 219–233.

Goncalo, J. A., & Staw, B. M. (2006). Individualism-collectivism and group creativity. *Organizational Behavior and Human Decision Processes, 100*, 96–109.

Goodman, P. S., & Garber, S. (1988). Absenteeism and accidents in a dangerous environment: Empirical analysis of underground coal mines. *Journal of Applied Psychology, 73*(1), 81–86.

Goodman, P. S., & Leyden, D. P. (1991). Familiarity and group productivity. *Journal of Applied Psychology, 76*(4), 578–586.

Graen, G. (1976). Role making processes within complex organizations. In M. D. Dunnette (Ed.), *Handbook of industrial and organizational psychology*. Chicago, IL: Rand McNally.

Graen, G., & Scandura, T. A. (1987). Toward a psychology of dyadic organizing. In B. Staw & L. L. Cummings (Eds.), *Research in organizational behavior* (Vol. 9, pp. 175–208). Greenwich, CT: JAI Press.

Graffin, S. D., Wade, J. B., Porac, J. F., & McNamee, R. C. (2008). The impact of CEO status diffusion on the economic outcomes of other senior managers. *Organization Science, 19*(3), 457–474.

Granovetter, M. (1973). The strength of weak ties. *American Journal of Sociology, 78*, 1360–1379.

Grant, A. M., Campbell, E. M., Chen, G., Cottone, K., Lapedis, D., & Lee, K. (2007). Impact and the art of motivation maintenance: The effects of contact with beneficiaries on persistence behavior. *Organizational Behavior and Human Decision Processes, 103*, 53–67.

Grant, W. (2010, January 14). Employee involvement boosts quality. *Hometown News*. myhometownnews.net

Greenberg, J. (1988). Equity and workplace status: A field experiment. *Journal of Applied Psychology, 75*, 561–568.

Greenberg, J. (1996). *Managing behavior in organizations* (p. 189). Upper Saddle River, NJ: Prentice Hall.

Greenberg, J., & Baron, R. A. (2008). *Behavior in Organizations* (9th ed.). Upper Saddle River, NJ: Pearson Education.

Greene, C. N. (1989). Cohesion and productivity in work groups. *Small Group Behavior, 20*, 70–86.

Greenhouse, S. (2008, April 20). Working Life (High and Low). *New York Times*, p. BU, p. 1.

Greenwald, A. G., & Banaji, M. (1995). Implicit social cognition: Attitudes, self-esteem, and stereotypes. *Psychological Review, 102*(1), 4–27.

Griffin, D. W., & Ross, L. (1991). Subjective construal, social inference, and human misunderstanding. In M. P. Zanna (Ed.), *Advances in experimental social psychology* (Vol. 24, pp. 319–359). San Diego, CA: Academic Press.

Griffin, M. A., Parker, S. K., & Mason, C. M. (2010). Leader vision and the development of adaptive and proactive performance: A longitudinal study. *Journal of Applied Psychology, 95*(1), 174–182.

Griffith, T. L., Mannix, E. A., & Neale, M. A. (2002). Conflict and virtual teams. In S. G. Cohen & C. B. Gibson (Eds.), *Creating conditions for effective virtual teams*. San Francisco, CA: Jossey-Bass.

Griffith, T., & Sawyer, J. (2009). Multilevel knowledge and team performance. *Journal of Organizational Behavior. Advance online publication. doi:* 10.1002/job.660.

Gross, S. E. (1995). *Compensation for teams: How to design and implement team-based reward programs* (pp. 129). New York: AMACOM.

Gross, S. E. (2000). Team-based pay. In L. A. Berger & D. R. Berger (Eds.), *The compensation handbook: A state-of-the-art guide to compensation strategy and design* (4th ed., pp. 261–273). New York: McGraw-Hill.

Grossman, S. R., Rodgers, B. E., & Moore, B. R. (1989, December). Turn group input into stellar output. *Working Woman*, 36–38.

Gruenfeld, D. H. (1994). Status and integrative complexity in decision-making groups: Evidence from the united states supreme court and a laboratory experiment. *Dissertation Abstracts International, Section B: The Sciences & Engineering, 55*(2-B), 630.

Gruenfeld, D. H. (1995). Status, ideology and integrative complexity on the U.S. supreme court: Rethinking the politics of political decision making. *Journal of Personality and Social Psychology, 68*(1), 5–20.

Gruenfeld, D. H. (1997, May). Integrating across teams: Formal structural solutions. Presentation at Kellogg School of Management, Evanston, IL.

Gruenfeld, D. H. (1998a). Personal communication.

Gruenfeld, D. H. (Ed.). (1998b). *Composition.* Stamford, CT: JAI Press.

Gruenfeld, D. H., & Fan, E. T. (1999). What newcomers see and what oldtimers say: Discontinuities in knowledge exchange. In L. Thompson, J. Levine, & D. Messick (Eds.), *Shared cognition in organizations: The management of knowledge.* Mahwah, NJ: Lawrence Erlbaum & Associates.

Gruenfeld, D. H., Keltner, D. J., & Anderson, C. (2003). The effects of power on those who possess it: An interpersonal perspective on social cognition. In G. Bodenhausen & A. Lambert (Eds.), *Foundations of social cognition: A festschrift in honor of Robert S. Wyer, Jr.* Mahwah, NJ: Lawrence Erlbaum Associates.

Gruenfeld, D. H., Mannix, E. A., Williams, K. Y., & Neale, M. A. (1996). Group composition and decision making: How member familiarity and information distribution affect process and performance. *Organizational Behavior and Human Decision Processes, 67*(1), 1–15.

Gruenfeld, D. H., Martorana, P., & Fan, E. T. (2000). What do groups learn from their worldliest members? Direct and indirect influence in dynamic teams. *Organizational Behavior and Human Decision Processes, 82*(1), 45–59.

Gruenfeld, D. H., Thomas-Hunt, M. C., & Kim, P. (1998). Cognitive flexibility, communication strategy, and integrative complexity in groups: Public versus private reactions to majority and minority status. *Journal of Experimental Social Psychology, 34*, 202–226.

Guetzkow, H., & Gyr, J. (1954). An analysis of conflict in decision-making groups. *Human Relations, 7,* 367–381.

Guilford, J. P. (1950). Creativity. *American Psychologist, 5,* 444–454.

Guilford, J. P. (1959). *Personality.* New York: McGraw-Hill.

Guilford, J. P. (1967). *The nature of human intelligence.* New York: McGraw-Hill.

Guimerá, R., Uzzi, B., Spiro J., & Amaral. (2005). L. A. N. Team assembly mechanisms determine collaboration network structure and team performance. *Science, 308,* 697—702.

Guimerà, R., Uzzi, B., Spiro, J., & Nunes Amaral, L. A. (2005). Team assembly mechanisms determine collaboration network structure and team performance. *Science, 308*(5722), 697–702.

Guinote, A., Judd, C. M., & Brauer, M. (2002). Effects of power on perceived and objective group variability: Evidence that more powerful groups are more variable. *Journal of Personality and Social Psychology, 82*(5), 708–721.

Gustafson, D. H., Shukla, R. K., Delbecq, A. L., & Walster, G. W. (1973). A comparative study of differences in subjective likelihood estimates made by individuals, interacting groups, Delphi groups, and nominal groups. *Organizational Behavior and Human Performance, 9,* 280–291.

Guynn, J. (2008, March 31). The state. *Los Angeles Times.* latimes.com

Guzzo, R. A., Salas, E., & Associates. (1995). *Team effectiveness and decision making in organizations.* San Francisco, CA: Jossey-Bass.

Guzzo, R. A., Yost. P. R., Campbell, R. J., & Shea, G. P. (1993). Potency in groups: Articulating a construct. *British Journal of Social Psychology, 32,* 87–106.

Hackman, J. R. (1983). Designing work for individuals and for groups. In J. R. Hackman (Ed.), *Perspectives on behavior in organizations* (pp. 242–256). McGraw-Hill, New York.

Hackman, J. R. (1987). The design of work teams. In J. W. Lorsch (Ed.), *Handbook of organizational behavior.* Upper Saddle River, NJ: Prentice Hall.

Hackman, J. R. (1990). Introduction: Work teams in organizations: An oriented framework. In J. Hackman (Ed.), *Groups that work and those that don't.* San Francisco, CA: Jossey-Bass.

Hackman, J. R. (2002). *Leading teams: Setting the stage for great performances.* Boston, MA: Harvard Business School Press.

Hackman, J. R., Brousseau, K. R., & Weiss, J. A. (1976). The interaction of task design and group performance strategies in determining group effectiveness. *Organizational Behavior and Human Performance, 16,* 350–365.

Hackman, J. R., & Morris, C. G. (1975). Group tasks, group interaction process and group performance effectiveness. A review and proposed integration. In L. Berkowitz (Ed.), *Advances in experimental social psychology* (Vol. 8, pp. 45–99). New York: Academic Press.

Hackman, J. R., & Oldham, G. R. (1980). *Work redesign.* Menlo Park, CA: Addison-Wesley.

Hackman, J. R., & Wageman, R. (2005). A theory of team coaching. *Academy of Management Review, 30,* 269–287.

Hains, S. C., Hogg, M. A., & Duck, J. M. (1997). Self-categorization and leadership: Effects of group prototypicality and leader stereotypicality. *Personality and Social Psychology Bulletin, 23*(10), 1087–1099.

Halevy, N. (2008). Team negotiation: Social, epistemic, economic, and psychological consequences of subgroup conflict. *Personality and Social Psychology Bulletin, 34*(12), 1687–1702.

Hall, F. (1997). Effective delegation. In D. D. Brown, R. J. Lewicki, D. T. Hall, & F. S. Hall (Eds.), *Experiences in management and organizational behavior* (4th ed.). New York: John Wiley & Sons.

Hambley, L. A., O'Neil, T. A., & Kline, T. J. B. (2007). Virtual team leadership: The effects of leadership style and communication medium on team interaction styles and outcomes. *Organizational Behavior and Human Decision Process, 103*(1), 1–20.

Hamm, S. (2009, December 7). Obama's big gov swat SWAT team. *Business Week, 4158,* 44–46.

Hanks, M., & Eckland, B. K. (1978). Adult voluntary association and adolescent socialization. *Sociological Quarterly, 19*(3), 481–490.

Harber, K. D. (1998). Feedback to minorities: Evidence of a positive bias. *Journal of Personality and Social Psychology, 74*(3), 622–628.

Hargadon, A. (2003). *How breakthroughs happen: The surprising truth about how companies innovate.* Boston, MA: Harvard Business School Publishing.

Hargadon, A. B. (1998). Firms as knowledge brokers: Lessons in pursuing continuous innovation. *California Management Review, 40*(3), 209–227.

Hargadon, A. B., & Sutton, R. I. (2000, May/June). Building an innovation factory. *Harvard Business Review, 78*(3), 157–166.

Harkins, S. G., & Jackson, J. M. (1985). The role of evaluation in eliminating social loafing. *Personality and Social Psychology Bulletin, 11,* 457–465.

Harkins, S. G., & Petty, R. E. (1982). Effects of task difficulty and task uniqueness on social loafing. *Journal of Personality and Social Psychology, 43*(6), 1214–1229.

Harkins, S. G., & Szymanski, K. (1987). *Social loafing and social facilitation: New wine in old bottles.* Beverly Hills, CA: Sage.

Harvey, J. (1974). The Abilene paradox: The management of agreement. *Organizational Dynamics, 3*(1), 63–80. © American Management Association International. Reprinted with permission.

Harvey, O. J., & Consalvi, C. (1960). Status and conformity to pressure in informal groups. *Journal of Abnormal and Social Psychology, 60,* 182–187.

Haslam, S. A., McGarty, C., Brown, P. M., Eggins, R. A., Morrison, B. E., & Reynolds, K. J. (1998). Inspecting the emperor's clothes: Evidence that random selection of leaders can enhance group performance. *Group Dynamics: Theory, Research, and Practice, 2*(3), 168–184.

Hastie, R., & Kameda, T. (2005). The robust beauty of majority rules in group decisions. *Psychological Review, 112*(2), 494–508.

Hastie, R., Penrod, S., & Pennington, N. (1983). *Inside the jury.* Cambridge, MA: Harvard University Press.

Hastorf, A. H., & Cantril, H. (1954). They saw a game: A case study. *Journal of Abnormal Social Psychology, 49,* 129–134.

Hastorf, A. H., Northcraft, G. B., & Picciotto, S. R. (1979). Helping the handicapped: How realistic is the performance feedback received by the physically handicapped? *Personality and Social Psychology Bulletin, 5,* 373–376.

Hater, J. J., & Bass, B. M. (1988). Supervisors' evaluations and subordinates' perceptions of transformational and transactional leadership. *Journal of Applied Psychology, 73,* 695–702.

Hatfield, E., Cacioppo, J. T., & Rapson, R. (1994). *Emotional contagion.* New York: Cambridge University Press.

Hausmann, L., Levine, J., & Higgins, E. (2008). Communication and group perception: Extending the "saying is believing" effect. *Group Processes and Intergroup Relations, 11*(4), 539–554.

Heath, C. (1999). On the social psychology of agency relationships: Lay theories of motivation overemphasize extrinsic rewards. *Organizational Behavior and Human Decision Processes, 78*(1), 25–62.

Heath, D., & Heath, C. (2009, February). The curse of incentives. *Fast Company, 132,* 48–49.

Hecht, T. D., Allen, N. J., Klammer, J. D., & Kelly, E. C. (2002). Group beliefs, ability and performance: The potency of group potency. *Group Dynamics: Theory, Research and Practice, 6*(2), 143–152.

Hedlund, J., Ilgen, D. R., & Hollenbeck, J. R. (1998). Decision accuracy in computer-mediated versus face-to-face decision making teams. *Organizational Behavior and Human Decision Processes, 76*(1), 30–47.

Heilman, M. E., Hornstein, H. A., Cage, J. H., & Herschlag, J. K. (1984). Reactions to prescribed leader behavior as a function of role perspective: The case of the Vroom-Yetton model. *Journal of Applied Psychology, 69*(1), 50–60.

Heilman, M. E., & Haynes, M. C. (2005). No credit where credit is due: Attributional rationalization of women's success in male-female teams. *Journal of Applied Psychology, 90*(5), 905–916.

Helmer, O. (1966). *Social technology.* New York: Basic Books.

Helmer, O. (1967). *Analysis of the future: The Delphi method.* Santa Monica, CA: The RAND Corporation.

Hempel, J. (2006, August 7). Big Blue Brainstorm. *Business Week,* 70.

Henderson, M. D. (2009). Psychological distance and group judgments: The effect of physical distance on beliefs about common goals. *Personality and Social Psychology Bulletin, 35*(10), 1330–1341.

Henry, K. B., Arrow, H., & Carini, B. (1999). A tripartite model of group identification: Theory and measurement. *Small Group Research, 30*(5), 558–581.

Hertel, G., Kerr, N. L., & Messe, L. A. (2000). Motivation gains in performance groups: paradigmatic and theoretical developments on the köhler effect. *Journal of Personality and Social Psychology, 79*(4), 580–601.

Higgins, E. T. (1999). "Saying is believing" effects: When sharing reality about something biases knowledge and evaluations. In L. Thompson, J. M. Levine, & D. M. Messick (Eds.), *Shared cognition in organizations: The management of knowledge.* Mahwah, NJ: Lawrence Erlbaum & Associates.

Higgins, T., & McCann, D. (1984). Social encoding and subsequent attitudes, impressions, and memory: "Context-driven" and motivational aspects of processing. *Journal of Personality and Social Psychology, 47*(1), 26–39.

Hill, M. (1982). Group versus individual performance: Are n11 heads better than one? *Psychological Bulletin, 91,* 517–539.

Hill, N. S., Bartol, K. M., Tesluk, P. E., & Langa, G. A. (2009). Organizational context and face-to-face interaction: Influence on the development of trust and collaborative behaviors in computer-mediated groups. *Organizational Behavior & Human Decision Process, 109,* 187–201.

Hill, S. (1995). The social organization of boards of directors. *British Journal of Sociology, 46*(2), 245–278.

Hiltz, S. R., Johnson, K., & Turoff, M. (1986). Experiments in group decision making: Communication process and outcome in face-to-face versus computerized conferences. *Human Communication Research, 13*(2), 225–252.

Hinds, P. (2010, January). Situated knowing who: Why site visits matter in global work. Technology and

Social Behavior colloquium, Northwestern University, Evanston, IL.

Hinds, P., Carley, K. M., Krackhardt, D., & Wholey, D. (2000). Choosing workgroup members: The balance of similarity, competence, and familiarity. *Organizational Behavior and Human Decision Making Processes, 81*(2), 226–251.

Hinds, P. J., & Bailey, D. E. (2003). Out of sight, out of sync: Understanding conflict in distributed teams. *Organization Science, 14*(6), 615–632.

Hinds, P. J., & Mortensen, M. (2005). Understanding conflict in geographically distributed teams: The moderating effects of shared identity, shared context, and spontaneous communication. *Organization Science, 16*(3), 290–307.

Hinsz, V. B., Tindale, R. S., & Nagao, D. H. (2008). Accentuation of information processes and biases in group judgments integrating base-rate and case specific information. *Journal of Experimental Social Psychology, 44*(1), 116–126.

Hira, N. (2009, December 16). Fahrenheit 212—The innovator's paradise. *CnnMoney.* money.cnn.com

Hirschfeld, R., Jordan, M., Field, H., Giles, W., & Armenakis, A. (2006). Becoming team players: Team members' mastery of teamwork knowledge as a predictor of team task proficiency and observed teamwork effectiveness. *Journal of Applied Psychology, 91*(2), 467–474.

Hirst, G., Knippenberg, D. V., & Zhou, J. (2009). A cross-level perspective on employee creativity: Goal orientation, team learning behavior, and individual creativity. *Academy of Management Journal, 52*(2), 280–293.

Hoffman, L. R., & Maier, N. R. F. (1966). An experimental reexamination of the similarity-attraction hypothesis. *Journal of Personality and Social Psychology, 3,* 145–152.

Hoffman, R. (1995, April). Ten reasons you should be using 360-degree feedback. *HR Magazine, 40*(4), 82–85.

Hofmann, D. A., & Jones, L. M. (2005). Leadership, collective personality, and performance. *Journal of Applied Psychology, 90*(3), 509–522.

Hogan, R., Raskin, R., & Fazzini, D. (1990). The dark side of charisma. In K. E. Clark & M. B. Clark (Eds.), *Measures of leadership* (pp. 343–354). West Orange, NJ: Leadership Library of America.

Hogg, M. A. (1987). Social identity and group cohesiveness. In J. C. Turner, M. A. Hogg, P. J. Oakes, S. D. Reicher, & M. Wetherell (Eds.), *Rediscovering the social group: A self-categorization theory* (pp. 89–116). Oxford, UK: Basil Blackwell.

Hogg, M. A. (1992). *The social psychology of group cohesiveness: From attraction to social identity.* London/New York: Harvester Wheatsheaf/New York University Press.

Hollander, E. P. (1964). *Leaders, groups, and influence.* New York: Oxford University Press.

Hollander, E. P. (1986). On the central role of leadership processes. *International Review of Applied Psychology, 35,* 39–52.

Hollenbeck, J. R., Ilgen, D. R., LePine, J. A., Colquitt, J. A., & Hedlund, J. (1998). Extending the multilevel theory of team decision making: Effects of feedback and experience in hierarchical teams. *Academy of Management Journal, 41,* 269–282.

Hollenbeck, J. R., Ilgen, D. R., Sego, D. J., Hedlund, J., Major, D. A., & Phillips, J. (1995). Multilevel theory of team decision making: Decision performance in teams incorporating distributed expertise. *Journal of Applied Psychology, 80,* 292–316.

Hollingshead, A. B. (1996a). Information suppression and status persistence in group decision making: The effects of communication media. *Human Communication Research, 23,* 193–219.

Hollingshead, A. B. (1996b). The rank-order effect in group decision making. *Organizational Behavior and Human Decision Processes, 68*(3), 181–193.

Hollingshead, A. B. (1998). Group and individual training. *Small Group Research, 29*(2), 254–280.

Hollingshead, A. B. (2000). Perceptions of expertise and transactive memory in work relationships. *Group Processes and Intergroup Relations, 3*(3), 257–267.

Hollingshead, A. B. (2001). Communication technologies, the internet, and group research. In M. Hogg and R. S. Tindale (Eds.), *Blackwell handbook of social psychology, Vol. 3: Group Processes* (pp. 557–573). Oxford, UK: Blackwell.

Holyoak, K. J., & Koh, K. (1987). Surface and structural similarity in analogical transfer. *Memory and Cognition, 15*(4), 332–340.

Holyoak, K. J., & Thagard, P. (1995). *Mental Leaps: Analogy in Creative Thought.* Cambridge, MA: MIT Press.

Homan, A., van Knippenberg, D., Van Kleef, G., & De Dreu, C. (2007). Bridging faultlines by valuing diversity: Diversity beliefs, information elaboration, and performance in diverse work groups. *Journal of Applied Psychology, 92*(5), 1189–1199.

Homan, A. C., Hollenbeck, J. R., Humphrey, S., van Knippenberg, D., Ilgen, D. R., & van Kleef, G. A. (2008). Facing differences with an open mind: Openness to experience, salience of intragroup differences, and performance of diverse work groups. *Academy of Management Journal, 51*, 1204–1222.

Homans, G. (1950). *The human group.* New York: Harcourt Brace.

Horn, E. M. (1993). *The influence of modality order and break period on a brainstorming task.* Unpublished honors thesis, University of Texas at Arlington.

Hornsey, M. J., & Hogg, M. A. (2002). The effects of status on subgroup relations. *British Journal of Social Psychology, 41*, 203–218.

Hornsey, M. J., Jetten, J., McAuliffe, B. J., & Hogg, M. A. (2006). The impact of individualist and collectivist group norms on evaluations of dissenting group members. *Journal of Experimental Social Psychology, 42*, 57–68.

Hornsey, T., Grice, J., Jetten, N., Paulsen, V., & Callan, V. (2007). Group-directed criticisms and recommendations for change: Why newcomers arouse more resistance than old-timers. *Personality and Social Psychology Bulletin, 33*(7), 1036–1048.

How failure breeds success. (2006, July 10). *Business Week.*

Howells, L. T., & Becker, S. W. (1962). Seating arrangements and leadership emergence. *Journal of Abnormal and Social Psychology, 64,* 148–150.

Huber, V. L., Neale, M. A., & Northcraft, G. B. (1987). Judgment by heuristics: Effects of ratee and rater characteristics and performance standards on performance-related judgments. *Organizational Behavior and Human Decision Processes, 40,* 149–169.

Hudepohl, D. (2001, March 1). Face your fears. *Sports Illustrated for Women,* p. 53.

Huff, C. (2006, September 11). Recognition that resonates. *Workforce Management,* 25–27.

Huguet, P., Charbonnier, E., & Monteil, J. (1999). Productivity loss in performance groups: People who see themselves as average do not engage in social loafing. *Group Dynamics: Theory, Research, and Practice, 3*(2), 118–131.

Hulsheger, U. R., Anderson, N., & Salgado, J. F. (2009). Team-level predictors of innovation at work: A comprehensive meta-analysis spanning three decades of research. *Journal of Applied Psychology, 94*(5), 1128–1145.

Humphrey, S., Morgeson, F., & Mannor, M. (2009). Developing a theory of the strategic core of teams: A role composition model of team performance. *Journal of Applied Psychology, 94*(1), 48–61.

Hunt, T. (2008, November). Triumphant Obama turns to sobering challenges. *WSBT (Weather, Sport, West Bend).* Wsbt.com

Ibarra, H. (1995). Race, opportunity, and diversity of social circles in managerial networks. *Academy of Management Journal, 38*(3), 673–703.

IBM. (2010). Innovation jam 2008 executive report. .ibm.com

IBM professional marketplace matches consultants with clients. (n.d.). In IBM.com.

Ickes, W. (1983). A basic paradigm for the study of unstructured dyadic interaction. *New Directions for Methodology of Social and Behavioral Science, 15,* 5–21.

Ickes, W., & Turner, M. (1983). On the social advantages of having an older, opposite-sex sibling: Birth order influences in mixed-sex dyads. *Journal of Personality and Social Psychology, 45*(1), 210–222.

Ilgen, D. R., & Feldman, J. M. (1983). Performance appraisal: A process focus. In L. L. Cummings & B. M. Staw (Eds.), *Research in organizational behavior* (Vol. 5, pp. 141–197). Greenwich, CT: JAI Press.

Ilies, R., Wagner, D., & Morgeson, F. (2007). Explaining affective linkages in teams: Individual differences in susceptibility to contagion and individualism-collectivism. *Journal of Applied Psychology, 92*(4), 1140–1148.

Inman, M. L., & Baron, R. S. (1996). Influence of prototypes on perceptions of prejudice. *Journal of Personality and Social Psychology, 70*(4), 727–739.

Insko, C., Pinkley, R., Hoyle, R., Dalton, B., Hong, G., Slim, R., Landry, P., Holton, B., Ruffin, P., & Thibaut, J. (1987). Individual versus group discontinuity: The role of a consensus rule. *Journal of Experimental Social Psychology, 23,* 250–267.

Internet World Stats. Usage and Population Statistics. (2009, September 30). *Internet usage statistics: The internet big picture.* internetworldstats.com

Irving, D. (2009, December 7). Security firm in O.C.'s "top workplace". *The Orange County Register.* ocregister.com.

Isbell, D., Hardin, M., & Underwood. J. (1999, September 30). *Mars climate orbiter team finds likely cause of loss.* Washington, DC: Jet Propulsion Laboratory for NASA's Office of Space Science. Release No. 99–113.

Isbell, D., & Savage, D. (1999, November 10). *Mars climate orbiter failure board releases report, numerous NASA actions underway in response.* Washington, DC: Jet Propulsion Laboratory for NASA's Office of Space Science. Release No. 99–134.

Isen, A. M., Daubman, K. A., & Nowicki, G. P. (1987). Positive affect facilitates creative problem solving. *Journal of Personality and Social Psychology, 47,* 1206–1217.

Isikoff, M. (2008, December 22). The fed who blew the whistle. *Newsweek, 152*(25), 40–48.

Jablin, F. M. (1981). Cultivating imagination: Factors that enhance and inhibit creativity in brainstorming groups. *Human Communication Research, 7*(3), 245–258.

Jackson, J. M., & Harkins, S. G. (1985). Equity in effort: An explanation of the social loafing effect. *Journal of Personality and Social Psychology, 49,* 1199–1206.

Jackson, M. H., & Poole, M. S. (2003). Idea generation in naturally-occurring contexts: Complex appropriation of a simple procedure. *Human Communication Research, 29,* 560–591.

Jackson, S. E. (1992). Team composition in organizational settings: Issues in managing an increasingly diverse work force. In S. Worchel, W. Wood, & J. A. Simpson (Eds.), *Group process and productivity* (pp. 138–173). Newbury Park: Sage.

Jackson, S. E., Brett, J. F., Sessa, V. I., Cooper, D. M., Julin, J. A., & Peyronnin, K. (1991). Some differences make a difference: Individual dissimilarities and group heterogeneity as correlates of recruitment, promotions, and turnover. *Journal of Applied Psychology, 76*(5), 675–689.

Jacobs, R. C., & Campbell, D. T. (1961). The perpetuation of an arbitrary tradition through several generations of a laboratory microculture. *Journal of Abnormal and Social Psychology, 62,* 649–658.

Janis, I. L. (1972). *Victims of groupthink.* Boston, MA: Houghton Mifflin.

Janssens, M., & Brett, J. M. (2006). Cultural intelligence in global teams: A fusion model of collaboration. *Group & Organization Management, 31,* 124–153.

Jehn, K. (1994). Enhancing effectiveness: An investigation of advantages and disadvantages of value-based intragroup conflict. *International Journal of Conflict Management, 5,* 223–238.

Jehn, K., & Chatman, J. A. (2000). Reconceptualizing conflict: Proportional and relational conflict. *International Journal of Conflict Management, 11*(1), 51–69.

Jehn, K. A. (1995). A multimethod examination of the benefits and detriments of intragroup conflict. *Administrative Science Quarterly, 40,* 256–282.

Jehn, K. A. (1997). A qualitative analysis of conflict types and dimensions in organizational groups. *Administrative Science Quarterly, 42,* 530–557.

Jehn, K. A., & Mannix, E. A. (2001). The dynamic nature of conflict: a longitudinal study of intragroup conflict and group performance. *Academy of Management Journal, 44*(2), 238–251.

Jehn, K. A., Northcraft, G. B., & Neale, M. A. (1999). Why differences make a difference: A field study of diversity, conflict and performance in workgroups. *Administrative Science Quarterly, 44*(4), 741–763.

Jehn, K., & Shah, P. (1997). Interpersonal relationships and task performance: An examination of mediating processes in friendship and acquaintance groups. *Journal of Personality and Social Psychology, 72,* 775–790.

Jessup, L. M., & Valacich, J. S., (Eds.). (1993). *Group support systems.* New York: Macmillan.

Jetten, J., Duck, J., Terry, D. J., & O'Brien, A. (2001). When groups merge: Low- and high-status groups' responses to aligned leaders. Unpublished raw data, University of Exeter.

Jetten, J., Duck, J., Terry, D. J., & O'Brien, A. (2002). Being attuned to intergroup differences in mergers: The role of aligned leaders for low-status groups. *Personality and Social Psychology Bulletin, 28*(9), 1194–1201.

Jetten, J., Spears, R., Hogg, M. A., & Manstead, A. S. R. (2000). Discrimination constrained and justified: The variable effects of group variability and ingroup identification. *Journal of Experimental Social Psychology, 36,* 329–356.

Johnson, A., & Winslow, R. (2008, June 30). Drug makers say FDAfda safety focus is slowing new-medicine pipeline. *Wall Street Journal,* p. A1.

Johnson, M., Hollenbeck, J., Humphrey, S., Ilgen, D., Jundt, D., & Meyer, C. (2006). Cutthroat cooperation: Asymmetrical adaptation to changes in team reward structures. *Academy of Management Journal, 49*(1), 103–119.

Johnson-Laird, P. N. (1980). Mental models in cognitive science. *Cognitive Science, 4*(1), 71–115.

Jones, E. E., Carter-Sowell, A. R., Kelly, J. R., & Williams, K. D. (2009). "I'm out of the loop": Ostracism through information exclusion. *Group Processes & Intergroup Relations, 12*(2), 157–174.

Jones, E. E., Farina, A., Hastorf, A. H., Markus, H., Miller, D. T., & Scott, R. A. (1984). *Social stigma: The psychology of marked relationships.* New York: W. H. Freeman.

Jones, E. E., Stires, L. K., Shaver, K. G., & Harris, V. A. (1968). Evaluation of an ingratiator by target persons and bystanders. *Journal of Personality, 36*(3), 349–385.

Jordan, M. H., Field, H. S., & Armenakis, A. A. (2002). The relationship of group process variables and team performance: A team-level analysis in a field setting. *Small Group Research, 33*(1), 121–150.

Jordan, P. J., & Lawrence, S. A. (2009). Emotional intelligence in teams: Development and initial validation of the short version of the Workgroup Emotional Intelligence Profile (WEIP-S). *Journal of Management & Organization, 15,* 452–469.

Jordan, P. J., & Troth, A. C. (2002). Emotional intelligence and conflict resolution: Implications for human resource development. *Advances in Developing Human Resources, 4*(1), 62–79.

Jordan, P. J., & Troth, A. C. (2004). Managing emotions during team problem solving: Emotional intelligence and conflict resolution. *Human Performance, 17,* 195–218.

Joseph. D. (2009, July 1). Inside Disney's Toy Factory. *Business Week.* businessweek.com

Joshi, A. (2006). The influence of organizational demography on the external networking behavior of teams. *Academy of Management Review, 31*(3), 583–595.

Jouret, G. (2009, September 1). Inside Cisco's search for the next big idea. *Harvard Business Review, 87*(9), p43–45.

Judd, C. M., & Park, B. (1988). Out-group homogeneity: Judgments of variability at the individual and group levels. *Journal of Personality and Social Psychology, 54*(5), 778–788.

Judge, T. A., Klinger, R. L., & Simon, L. S. (2010). Time is on my side: Time, general mental ability, human capital, and extrinsic career success. *Journal of Applied Psychology, 95*(1), 92–107.

Jung, D. I., & Sosik, J. J. (2003). Group potency and collective efficacy: Examining their predictive validity, level of analysis, and effects of performance feedback on future group performance. *Group & Organization Management, 28,* 366–391.

Kaagan, S. S. (1999). *Leadership games: Experiential learning for organizational development.* Thousand Oaks, CA: Sage.

Kahneman, D., & Tversky, A. (1979). Prospect theory: An analysis of decision under risk. *Econometrica, 47,* 263–291.

Kaltenheuser, S. (2002, July 1). Working the crowd. *Across the Board*, pp. 50–55.

Kameda, T., Ohtsubo, Y., & Takezawa, M. (1997). Centrality in sociocognitive networks and social influence: An illustration in a group decision-making context. *Journal of Personality and Social Psychology, 73*(2), 296–309.

Kameda, T., Takezawa, M., & Hastie, R. (2003). The logic of social sharing: An evolutionary game analysis of adaptive norm development. *Personality and Social Psychology Review, 7,* 2–19.

Kameda, T., Takezawa, M., Tindale, R. S., & Smith, C. (2002). Social sharing and risk reduction: Exploring a computational algorithm for the psychology of windfall gains. *Evolution and Human Behavior, 23,* 11–33.

Kameda, T., & Tamura, R. (2007). "To eat or not to be eaten?" Collective risk-monitoring in groups. *Journal of Experimental Social Psychology, 43*(2), 168–179.

Kanaracus, C. (2009, July 20). Success factors aims for small business with new HR app. *PCWorld*. pcworld.com

Kane, A., & Argote, L. (2002). *Social identity and knowledge transfer between groups*. Paper presented at the Annual Meeting of the Academy of Management, Denver, CO.

Kane, A., Argote, L., & Levine, J. (2005). Knowledge transfer between groups via personnel rotation: Effects of social identity and knowledge quality. *Organizational Behavior and Human Decision Processes, 96,* 56–71.

Kane, G., & Labianca, G. (2005). *Accounting for clergy's social ledgers: Mixed blessings associated with direct and in- direct negative ties in a religious organization*. Paper presented at the Intra-Organizational Network (ION) Conference, Atlanta, GA.

Kanter, R. M. (1977). Some effects of proportions on group life: Skewed sex ratios and responses to token women. *American Journal of Sociology, 82,* 465–490.

Kaplan, R. E. (1979). The conspicuous absence of evidence that process consultation enhances task performance. *Journal of Applied Behavioral Science, 15,* 346–360.

Kar, M. (2009, December 19). Milton Bradley is now a Seattle Mariners. *Thaindian News*. thaindian.com

Karau, S., & Kelly, J. (1992). The effects of time scarcity and time abundance on group performance quality and interaction process. *Journal of Experimental Social Psychology, 28,* 542–571.

Karau, S., Markus, M., & Williams, K. (2000). On the elusive search for motivation gains in groups: Insights from the collective effort model. *Zeitschrift fur Sozialpsychologie, 31*(4), 179–190.

Karau, S., Moneim, A., & Elsaid, M. (2009). Individual differences in beliefs about groups. *Group Dynamics: Theory, Research and Practice, 13*(1), 1–13.

Karau, S., & Williams, K. (1993). Social loafing: A meta-analytic review and theoretical integration. *Journal of Personality and Social Psychology, 65,* 681–706.

Katz, D., & Braly, K. (1933). Racial stereotypes of 100 college students. *Journal of Abnormal and Social Psychology, 28,* 280–290.

Katz, D., & Kahn, R. L. (1978). *The social psychology of organizations* (2nd ed.). New York: John Wiley & Sons.

Katz, R. (1982). The effects of group longevity on project communication and performance. *Administrative Science Quarterly, 27,* 81–104.

Katz, R., & Allen, T. J. (1982). Investigating the not invented here (NIH) syndrome: A look at the performance, tenure, and communication patterns of 50 R&D project groups. *R&D Management, 121,* 7–19.

Kayser, T. A. (1995). *Mining group gold: How to cash in on the collaborative genius of work teams*. Chicago, IL: Irwin.

Keeps, D. A. (2009, September 1). Out-of-the-box offices. *Cnn Money*. Money.cnn.com

Keisler, S., & Sproull, L. (1992). Group decision making and communication technology. *Organizational Behavior and Human Decision Processes, 52,* 96–123.

Keller, R. T. (1978). Dimensions of management systems and performance in continuous process organizations. *Human Relations, 31,* 119–129.

Keller, R. T. (1986). Predictors of the performance of project groups in R&D organizations. *Academy of Management Journal, 29,* 715–725.

Keller, R. T. (2006). Transformational leadership, initiating structure, and substitutes for leadership: A longitudinal study of research and development project team performance. *Journal of Applied Psychology, 91*(1), 202–210.

Kelley, H. H. (1962). *The development of cooperation in the minimal social situation.* Washington, DC: American Psychological Association.

Kelley, H. H. (1983). The situational origins of human tendencies: A further reason for the formal analysis of structures. *Personality and Social Psychology Bulletin, 9*(1), 8–36.

Kelley, H. H., & Thibaut, J. (1978). *Interpersonal relations: A theory of interdependence.* New York: John Wiley Sons.

Kelley, T., & Littman, J. (2001). The art of innovation: Lessons in creativity from IDEO, America's leading design firm. New York: Currency Books.

Kelly, J. B. (1991). Parent interaction after divorce: Comparison of mediated and adversarial divorce processes. *Behavioral Sciences and Law, 9,* 387–398.

Kelly, J. R. (1987). *Mood and interaction.* Unpublished doctoral dissertation, University of Illinois, Urbana-Champaign.

Kelly, J. R. (2001). Mood and emotion in groups. In M. Hogg & S. Tindale (Eds.), *Blackwell handbook in social psychology* (Vol. 3: Group processes, pp. 164–181). Oxford, UK: Blackwell.

Kelly, J. R., & Barsade, S. G. (2001). Mood and emotions in small groups and work teams. *Organizational Behavior and Human Decision Processes, 86,* 99–130.

Kelly, J. R., Futoran, G. C., & McGrath, J. E. (1990). Capacity and capability: Seven studies of entrainment of task performance rates. *Small Group Research, 21*(3), 283–314.

Kelly, J. R., & Karau, S. J. (1999). Group decision making: The effects of initial preferences and time pressure. *Personality and Social Psychology Bulletin, 25*(11), 1342–1354.

Kelly, J. R., & McGrath, J. E. (1985). Effects of time limits and task types on task performance and interaction of four-person groups. *Journal of Personality and Social Psychology, 49*(2), 395–407.

Kelly, J., & Loving, T. (2004). Time pressure and group performance: Exploring underlying processes in the Attentional Focus Model. *Journal of Experiental Social Psychology, 40,* 185–198.

Kempton, W. (1986). Two theories of home heat control. *Cognitive Science, 10,* 75–90.

Kempton, W. (1987). *Two theories of home heat control.* New York: Cambridge University Press.

Kenney, R. A., Schwartz-Kenney, B. M., & Blascovich, J. (1996). Implicit leadership theories: Defining leaders described as worthy of influence. *Personality and Social Psychology Bulletin, 22*(11), 1128–1143.

Kepner, T. (2009, February 9). Rodriguez admits to use of performance enhancers. *New York Times*, p. A1.

Kerr, N. L. (1983). Motivation losses in small groups: A social dilemma analysis. *Journal of Personality and Social Psychology, 45,* 819–828.

Kerr, N. L. (1989). Illusions of efficacy: The effects of group size on perceived efficacy in social dilemmas. *Journal of Experimental Social Psychology, 25,* 287–313.

Kerr, N. L., & Bruun, S. (1981). Ringelmann revisited: Alternative explanations for the social loafing effect. *Journal of Personality and Social Psychology, 37,* 224–231.

Kerr, N. L., Messé, L. M., Seok, D., Sambolec, E., Lount, R. M., & Park, E. S. (2007). Psychological mechanisms underlying the Köhler motivation gain. *Personality and Social Psychology Bulletin, 33*(6), 828–841.

Kerr, N., Messé, L., Park, E., & Sambolec, E. (2005). Identifiablility, performance feedback and the Köhler effect. *Group Processes and Intergroup Relations, 8*(4), 375–390.

Kessler, T., & Hollbach, S. (2005). Group-based emotions as determinants of ingroup identification. *Journal of Experimental Social Psychology, 41*(6), 677–685.

Keysar, B. (1998). Language users as problem solvers: Just what ambiguity problem do they solve? In S. R. Fussell & R. J. Kreuz (Eds.), *Social and cognitive approaches to interpersonal communication* (pp. 175–200). Mahwah, NJ: Lawrence Erlbaum & Associates.

Keysar, B., & Henly, A. (2002). Speakers' overestimation of their effectiveness. *Psychological Science, 13*(3), 207–212.

Kilduff, M., & Krackhardt, D. (1994). Bringing the individual back in: A structural analysis of the internal market for reputation in organizations. *The Academy of Management Journal, 37*(1), 87–108.

Kim, H., & Markus, H. R. (1999). Deviance or uniqueness, harmony or conformity? A cultural analysis. *Journal of Personality and Social Psychology, 77*(4), 785–800.

Kim, P. (1997). When what you know can hurt you: A study of experiential effects on group discussion and performance. *Organizational Behavior and Human Decision Processes, 69*(2), 165–177.

King, R. (2008, July 11). 10 web 2.0 ideas that failed. *Fast Company.* fastcompany.com

Kirsner, S. (2002, September). How to get bad news to the top. *Fast Company,* 56.

Klar, Y. (2002). Way beyond compare: Nonselective superiority and inferiority biases in judging randomly assigned group members relative to their peers. *Journal of Experimental Social Psychology, 38,* 331–351.

Klein, K. J., Lim, B., Saltz, J. L., & Mayer, D. M. (2004). How do they get there? An examination of the antecedents of centrality in team networks. *Academy of Management Journal, 47*(6), 952–963.

Klimoski, R., & Inks, L. (1990, April). Accountability forces in performance appraisal. *Organizational Behavior and Human Decision Processes, 45*(2), 194–208.

Klimoski, R., & Jones, R. G. (1995). Staffing for effective group decision making. In R. A. Guzzo & E. Salas (Eds.), *Team effectiveness and decision making* (pp. 9–45). San Francisco, CA: Jossey-Bass.

Klimoski, R., & Mohammed, S. (1997). Team mental model: Construct or metaphor? *Journal of Management, 20*(2), 403–437.

Klocke, U. (2009). "I Am the Best": Effects of influence tactics and power bases on powerholders' self-evaluation and target evaluation. *Group Processes & Intergroup Relations, 12*(5), 619–637.

Knight-Ridder Newspapers. (1991, October 13). Whites' IDs of blacks in crime cases often wrong, studies show. *Columbus Dispatch.*

Knowles, M., & Gardner, W. (2008). Benefits of membership: The activation and amplification of group identities in response to social rejection. *Personality and Social Psychology Bulletin, 34*(9), 1200–1213.

Kohn, A. (1993, September–October). Why incentive plans cannot work. *Harvard Business Review, 71,* 54–63.

Komorita, S., & Chertkoff, J. (1973). A bargaining theory of coalition formation. *Psychological Review, 80,* 149–162.

Komorita, S., & Parks, C. (1994). *Social dilemmas.* Madison, WI: Brown & Benchmark.

Konana, P. (2009, October 16). The executive compensation debate. *The Hindu.* beta.thehindu.com.

Kostigen, T. (2009, January 15). *The 10 most unethical people in business.* marketwatch.com

Krackhardt, D. (1990). Assessing the political landscape: Structure, cognition, and power in organizations. *Administrative Science Quarterly, 35,* 342–369.

Krackhardt, D. (1996a). Social networks and the liability of newness for managers. *Journal of Organizational Behavior, 3,* 159–173.

Krackhardt, D. (1996b). Social networks and the liability of newness for managers. In C. L. Cooper & D. M. Rousseau (Eds.), *Trends in organizational behavior* (pp. 159–173). New York: Wiley.

Kramer, R. M. (1996). Divergent realities, convergent disappointments in the hierarchic relation: Trust and the intuitive auditor at work. In R. M. Kramer & T. R. Tyler (Eds.), *Trust in organizations* (pp. 216–245). Thousand Oaks, CA: Sage.

Kramer, R. M. (1999). Social uncertainty and collective paranoia in knowledge communities: Thinking and acting in the shadow of doubt. In L. Thompson, J. Levine, & D. Messick (Eds.), *Social cognition in organizations: The management of knowledge.* Mahwah, NJ: Lawrence Erlbaum Associates.

Kramer, R. M., & Brewer, M. B. (1984). Effects of group identity on resource use in a simulated commons dilemma. *Journal of Personality and Social Psychology, 46,* 1044–1057.

Krames, J. A. (2001). *The Jack Welch lexicon of leadership: Over 250 terms, concepts, strategies & initiatives of the legendary leader.* New York: McGraw-Hill.

Kranz, G. (2008, March). Has Starbucks' training brewed heightened expectations? *Workforce Management.* workeforcemanagement.com

Kranz, G. (2009, November). Tricks of the trade show: Innovation and informal learning. *Workforce Management.* workforce.com

Krauss, R. M., & Fussell, S. R. (1991). Perspective-taking in communication: Representations of others' knowledge in reference. *Social Cognition, 9,* 2–24.

Krauss, R. M., & Fussell, S. R. (1996). Social psychological models of interpersonal communication. In E. T. Higgins & A. W. Kruglanski (Eds.), *Social psychology: Handbook of basic principles* (pp. 655–701). New York: Guilford.

Kravitz, D. A., Martin, B. (1986). Ringelmann rediscovered: The original article. *Journal of Personality and Social Psychology, 50*(5), 936–941.

Krebs, V. (2008). Connecting the dots: Tracking two identified terrorists. orgnet.com

Kresa, K. (1991). Aerospace leadership in a vortex of change. *Financier, 15*(1), 25–28.

Krizan, Z., & Windschitl, P. D. (2007). Team allegiance can lead to both optimistic and pessimistic predictions. *Journal of Experimental Social Psychology, 43,* 327–333.

Kroft, S. (2008, October 6). As Lehman collapsed, execs were rewarded. *Cbsnews.com*

Kroll, M., Walters, B. A., & Le, S. A. (2007). The impact of board composition and top management team ownership structure on post-IPO performance in young entrepreneurial firms. *Academy of Management Journal, 50,* 1198–1216.

Kuhn, T., & Poole, M. S. (2000). Do conflict management styles affect group decision making? Evidence from a longitudinal field study. *Human Communication Research, 26*(4), 558–590.

Kurtzber, T. (2000). *Creative styles and teamwork: Effects of coordination and conflict on group outcomes* (Doctoral dissertation). Retrieved from Proquest Dissertations & Theses: Full Text (AAT 9974311).

Labianca, G., & Brass, D. J. (2006). Exploring the social ledger: Negative relationships and negative asymmetry in social networks in organizations. *Academy of Management Review, 31*(3), 596–614.

LaFasto, F. M. J., & Larson, C. E. (2001). *When teams work best: 6,000 team members and leaders tell what it takes to succeed.* Newbury Park, CA: Sage.

Lai, L., Rousseau, D. M., & Chang, K. T. T. (2009). Idiosyncratic deals: Coworkers as interested third parties. *Journal of Applied Psychology, 94*(2), 547–556.

Lance calls Contador's late surge "a surprise." (2009, July 10). *Nbcsports.com.* nbcsports.msnbc.com

Langfred, C. W. (2004). Too much of a good thing? Negative effects of high trust and individual autonomy in self-managing teams. *Academy of Management Journal, 47*(3), 385–399.

Langfred, C. W. (2007). The downside of self-management: A longitudinal study of the effects of conflict on trust, autonomy, and task interdependence in self-managing teams. *Academy of Management Journal, 50,* 885–900.

Larson, C. E., Foster-Fishman, P. G., & Keys, C. B. (1994). Discussion of shared and unshared information in decision-making groups. *Journal of Personality and Social Psychology, 67*(3), 446–461.

Larson, C. E., & LaFasto, F. M. J. (1989). *Teamwork: What must go right/what can go wrong.* Newbury Park, CA: Sage.

Larson, J. R., Christensen, C., Franz, T. M., & Abbott, A. S. (1998). Diagnosing groups: The pooling, management, and impact of shared and unshared case information in team-based medical decision making. *Journal of Personality and Social Psychology, 75*(1), 93–108.

Larson, J. R., Foster-Fishman, P. G., & Franz, T. M. (1998). Leadership style and the discussion of shared and unshared information in decision-making groups. *Personality and Social Psychology Bulletin, 24*(5), 482–495.

Larson, J. R., & Harmon, V. M. (2007). Recalling shared vs. unshared information mentioned during group discussion: Toward understanding differential repetition rates. *Group Processes and Intergroup Relations, 10*(3), 311–322.

Lashinsky, A. (2009, December 3). Salesforce.com gets social [Web log post]. brainstormtech.blogs. fortune.cnn.com

Latané, B. (1981). The psychology of social impact. *American Psychologist, 36,* 343–356.

Latané, B., & Darley, J. M. (1968). Group inhibition of bystander intervention in emergencies. *Journal of Personality and Social Psychology, 10,* 215–221.

Latané, B., & Darley, J. M. (1970). *The unresponsive bystander: Why doesn't he help?* New York: Appleton-Century-Crofts.

Lau, D. C., & R. C. Liden, R. C. (2008). Antecedents of coworker trust: Leaders' blessings. *Journal of Applied Psychology, 93,* 1130–1138.

Lau, D., & Murnighan, K. (1998). Demographic diversity and faultlines: The compositional dynamics of organizational groups. *Academy of Management Review, 23,* 325–340.

Lau, D., & Murnighan, K. (2005). Interactions within gorups and subgroups: The effects of demographic faultlines. *Acadmy of Management Journal, 48*(4), 645–659.

Laughlin, P., Bonner, B., Miner, A., & Carnevale, P. (1999). Frames of references in quantity estimations by groups and individuals. *Organizational Behavior and Human Decision Processes, 80*(2), 103–117.

Laughlin, P., Gonzalez, C., & Sommer, D. (2003). Quantity estimations by groups and individuals: Effects of known domain boundaries. *Group Dynamics: Theory, Research and Practice, 7*(1), 55–63.

Laughlin, P., Hatch, E., Silver, J., & Boh, L. (2006). Groups perform better than the best individuals on letters-to-numbers problems: Effects of group size. *Journal of Personality and Social Psychology, 90*(4), 644–651.

Laughlin, P., Zander, M., Knievel, E., & Tan, T. (2003). Groups perform better than the best individuals on letters-to-numbers problems: Informative equations and effective strategies. *Journal of Personality and Social Psychology, 85*(4), 684–694.

Laughlin, P. R. (1980). Social combination processes of cooperative problem-solving groups on verbal interactive tasks. In M. Fishbein (Ed.), *Progress in social psychology* (Vol. 1). Mahwah, NJ: Lawrence Erlbaum & Associates.

Laughlin, P. R., Bonner, B. L., & Miner, A. G. (2002). Groups perform better than the best individuals on letters-to-numbers problems. *Organizational Behavior and Human Decision Processes, 88,* 605–620.

Laughlin, P. R., Carey, H. R., & Kerr, N. L. (2008). Group-to-individual problem-solving transfer. *Group Processes & Intergroup Relations, 11*(3), 319–330.

Lawler, E. E. (1988). Choosing an involvement strategy. *Academy of Management Executive, 11*(3), 197–204.

Lawler, E. E. (1992). *The ultimate advantage: Creating the high-involvement organization.* San Francisco, CA: Jossey-Bass.

Lawler, E. E. (2000). *Rewarding excellence: Pay strategies for the new economy.* San Francisco, CA: Jossey-Bass.

Lawler, E. E., Mohrman, S. A., & Ledford, G. E., Jr. (1995). *Creating high performance organizations: Practices and results of employee involvement and total quality management in fortune 1000 companies.* San Francisco, CA: Jossey-Bass.

Leach, C. W., Ellemers, N., & Barreto, M. (2007). Group virtue: The importance of morality (vs. competence and sociability) in the positive evaluation of ingroups. *Journal of Personality and Social Psychology, 93,* 234–249.

Leary, M. (1995). *Self-presentation: Impression management and behavior.* Dubuque, IA: Brown & Benchmark.

Lee, A. (2008, September 8). How to build a brand. *Fast Company.* fastcompany.com

Leith, K. P., & Baumeister, R. F. (1996). Why do bad moods increase self-defeating behavior? Emotion, risk-taking, and self-regulation. *Journal of Personality and Social Psychology, 71*(6), 1250–1267.

LePine, J. (2005). Adaptation of teams in response to unforeseen change: Effects of goal difficulty and team composition in terms of cognitive ability and goal orientation. *Journal of Applied Psychology, 90*(6), 1153–1167.

LePine, J., Hollenbeck, J. R., Ilgen, D. R., Colquitt, J. A., & Ellis, A. (2002). Gender composition, situational strength, and team decision-making acccuracy: A criterion decomposition approach. *Organizational Behavior and Human Decision Processes, 88*(1), 445–475.

Lerner, J. S., & Tetlock, P. E. (1999). Accounting for the effects of accountability. *Psychological Bulletin, 125*(2), 255–275.

Letize, L., & Donovan, M. (1990, March). The supervisor's changing role in high involvement organizations. *Journal for Quality and Participation,* 62–65.

Letzing, J. (2009, December 3). For battle-tested Bartz, how hard could running yahoo be? *Wall Street Journal Market Watch.* marketwatch.com

Levin, D., Kurtzberg, T., Phillips, K., & Lount, R. (2010). The role of affect in knowledge transfer. *Group Dynamics.*

Levine, J. M. (1989). Reaction to opinion deviance in small groups. In P. Paulus (Ed.), *Psychology of group influence* (2nd ed., pp. 187–231). Mahwah, NJ: Lawrence Erlbaum & Associates.

Levine, J. M., & Choi, H.-S. (2004). Impact of personnel turnover on team performance and cognition. In E. Salas & S. M. Fiore (Eds.), *Team cognition: Understanding the factors that drive process and performance* (pp. 153–176). Washington, DC: American Psychological Association.

Levine, J. M., Choi, H.-S., & Moreland, R. L. (2003). Newcomer innovation in work teams. In P. B. Paulus & B. A. Nijstad (Eds.), *Group creativity: Innovation through collaboration* (pp. 202–224). New York: Oxford University Press.

Levine, J. M., & Moreland, R. L. (1985). Innovation and socialization in small groups. In S. Moscovici, G. Mugny, & E. van Avermaet (Eds.), *Perspectives on minority influence* (pp. 143–169). Cambridge,UK: Cambridge University Press.

Levine, J. M., & Moreland, R. L. (1991). Culture and socialization in work groups. In L. B. Resnick, J. M. Levine, & S. D. Teasley (Eds.), *Perspectives on socially shared cognition* (pp. 585–634). Washington, DC: American Psychological Association.

Levine, J. M., Resnick, L. B., & Higgins, E. T. (1993). Social foundations of cognition. *Annual Review of Psychology, 44,* 585–612.

Levine, R. (2006, June 12). The new right stuff. *Fortune, 153*(11), 116.

LeVine, R. A., & Campbell, D. T. (1972). *Ethnocentrism: Theories of conflict, ethnic attitudes and group behavior.* New York: John Wiley & Sons.

Levinson, H. (1980). Power, leadership, and the management of stress. *Professional Psychology, 11,* 497–508.

Levinson, S. C. (1983). *Pragmatics* (p. 264). Cambridge, England: Cambridge University Press.

Lewicki, R. J., Weiss, S. E., & Lewin, D. (1992). Models of conflict, negotiation, and third party intervention: A review and synthesis. *Journal of Organizational Behavior, 13*(2), 209–252.

Lewis, B. P., & Linder, D. E. (1997). Thinking about choking? Attentional processes and paradoxical performance. *Personality and Social Psychology Bulletin, 23*(9), 937–944.

Lewis, K., Belliveau, M., Herndon, B., & Keller, J. (2007). Group cognition, membership change, and performance: Investigating the benefits and detriments of collective knowledge. *Organizational Behavior and Human Decision Processes, 103*(2), 159–178.

Lewis, S. A., Langan, C. J., & Hollander, E. P. (1972). Expectation of future interaction and the choice of less desirable alternatives in conformity. *Sociometry, 35,* 440–447.

Liao, H., Chuang, A., & Joshi, A. (2008). Perceived deep-level dissimilarity: Personality antecedents and impact on overall job attitude, helping, work withdrawal, and turnover. *Organizational Behavior and Human Decision Processes, 106,* 106–124.

Liao, H., & Subramony, M. (2008). Employee customer orientation in manufacturing organizations: Joint influences of customer proximity and senior leadership team. *Journal of Applied Psychology, 93,* 317–328.

Liang, D. W., Moreland, R. L., & Argote, L. (1995). Group versus individual training and group performance: The mediating role of transactive memory. *Personality and Social Psychology Bulletin, 21*(4), 384–393.

Libby, R., Trotman, K. T., & Zimmer, I. (1987). Member variation, recognition of expertise, and group performance. *Journal of Applied Psychology, 72*(1), 81–87.

Liberman, N., & Trope, Y. (1998). The role of feasibility and desirability considerations in near and distant future decisions: A test of temporal construal theory.

Journal of Personality and Social Psychology, 75(1), 5–18.

Lind, E. A., & Tyler, T. R. (1988). *The social psychology of procedural justice.* New York: Plenum.

Lindelauf, R., Borm, P., & Hamers, H. (2009). The influence of secrecy on the communication structure of covert networks., *Social Networks, 31,* 126–137.

Linville, P. W., Fischer, G. W., & Salovey, P. (1989). Perceived distributions of the characteristics of in-group and out-group members: Empirical evidence and a computer simulation. *Journal of Personality and Social Psychology, 57,* 165–188.

Lipton, E. (2009, March 4). Ex-leaders of Countrywide profit from bad loans. *New York Times,* p. A1.

Littlepage, G., Robison, W., & Reddington, K. (1997). Effects of task experience and group experience on group performance, member ability, and recognition of expertise. *Organizational Behavior and Human Decision Processes, 69*(2), 133–147.

Loersch, C., Aarts, H., Payne, B. K., & Jefferis, V. E. (2008). The influence of social groups on goal contagion. *Journal of Experimental Social Psychology, 44,* 1555–1558.

Loewenstein, J., & Prelic, D. (1991). Negative time preference. *AEA Papers and Proceedings, 81*(2), 347–352.

Loewenstein, J., & Thompson, L. (2000, October). The challenge of learning. *Negotiation Journal, 16,* 399–408.

Lojeski, K. S., & Reilly, R. R. (2008). *Transforming leadership and innovation in the globally integrated enterprise.* New Jersey: John Wiley & Sons Inc.

Longnecker, C. O., Sims, H. P., & Gioia, D. A. (1987). Behind the mask: The politics of employee appraisal. *Academy of Management Executive, 1,* 183–193.

Lord, R. G., & Maher, K. J. (1993). *Leadership and information processing: Linking perceptions and performance.* New York: Routledge.

Louis, M. R. (1980). Surprise and sense making: What newcomers experience in entering unfamiliar organizational settings. *Administrative Science Quarterly, 25,* 226–251.

Lount, R. B, & Phillips, K. W. (2007). Working harder with the out-group: The impact of social category

diversity on motivation gains. *Organizational Behavior and Human Decision Processes, 103*(2), 214–224.

Lount, R. B., Park, E. S., Kerr, N. L., Messe, L. A., & Seok, D. (2008). Evaluation concerns and the Kohler effect: The impact of physical presence on motivation gains. *Small Group Research, 39*(6), 795–809.

Lount, R. M., Kerr, N. L., Messé, L. M., Seok, D., & Park, E. S. (2008). An examination of the stability and persistence of the Köhler motivation gain effect. *Group Dynamics: Theory, Research, and Practice, 12*(4), 279–289.

Lovallo, D., & Kahneman, D. (July, 2003). Delusions of success: How optimism undermines executives' decisions. *Harvard Business Review.*

Loyd, D. L., Phillips, K. W., Whitson, J., & Thomas-Hunt, M. C. (2010). How congruence between status speech style affects reactions to unique knowledge. *Group Process and Intergroup Relations,13*(3), 379–395.

Lublin, J. S. (2008, September 2). A CEO's recipe for fresh ideas. *Wall Street Journal,* p. D4.

Lucken, M., & Simon, B. (2005). Cognitive and afective experiences of minority and majority members: The role of gorup size, status, and power. *Journal of Personality and Social Psychology, 41,* 396–413.

Maccoby, M. (2000, January/February). Understanding the difference between management and leadership. *Research Technology Management,* 57–59.

Mackay, H. (2008, October 12). Employers should encourage employee brainstorming. *The Arizona Republic.* Azcentral.com

MacKenzie, M., Cambrosio, A., & Keating, P. (1988). The commercial application of a scientific discovery: The case of the hybridoma technique. *Research and Policy, 17*(3), 155–170.

Mahajan-Bansal, N., & Goyal, M. (2009, December 9). Finger on the pulse, at last. *Forbes.* forbes.com

Maier, N. R. F. (1952). *Principles of human relations, applications to management.* New York: John Wiley & Sons.

Maier, N. R. F., Solem, A. R., & Maier A. A. (1975). *The role-play technique: A handbook for management and leadership practice.* LaJolla, CA: University Associates.

Main, E. C., & Walker, T. G. (1973). Choice shifts and extreme behavior: Judicial review in the federal courts. *Journal of Social Psychology. 91*(2), 215–221.

Makary, M., Sexton, B., Freischlag, J., Holzmueller, C. G., Millman, E. A., Rowen, L. A. & Pronovost, P. J. (2006). Operating room teamwork among physicians and nurses: Teamwork in the eye of the beholder. *Journal of the American College of Surgeons, 202*(5), 746—752.

Makiney, J. D., & Levy, P. E. (1998). The influence of self-ratings versus peer ratings on supervisors' performance judgments. *Organizational Behavior and Human Decision Processes, 74*(3), 212–228.

Maltby, E. (2010, January 7). Boring meetings? Get out the water guns. *Wall Street Journal*, p. B5.

Manning, J. F., & Fullerton, T. D. (1988). Health and well-being in highly cohesive units of the U.S. Army. *Journal of Applied Social Psychology, 18,* 503–519.

Mannix, E., Thompson, L., & Bazerman, M. H. (1989). Negotiation in small groups. *Journal of Applied Psychology, 74,* 508–517.

Manz, C. C., Keating, D. E., & Donnellon, A. (1990). Preparing for an organizational change to employee self-management: The management transition. *Organizational Dynamics, 19*(2), 15–26.

March, J. G. (1991). Exploration and exploitation in organizational learning. *Organization Science, 2*(1), 71–87.

Markham, S. E., Dansereau, F., & Alutto, J. A. (1982). Group size and absenteeism rates: A longitudinal analysis. *Academy of Management Journal, 25*(4), 921–927.

Markman, A. B., & Wood, K. L. (Eds.). (2009). *Tools for innovation: The science behind the practical methods that drive innovation.* New York: Oxford University Press.

Marks, M. A., DeChurch, L. A., Mathieu, J. E., Panzer, F. J., & Alonso, A. (2005). Teamwork in multiteam systems. *Journal of Applied Psychology, 90*(5), 964–971.

Marks, M. A., Mathieu, J. E., & Zaccaro, S. J. (2001). A temporally based framework and taxonomy of team processes. *Academy of Management Review, 26,* 356–376.

Markus, H. (1977). Self-schemata and processing information about the self. *Journal of Personality and Social Psychology, 35,* 63–78.

Markus, H. R., & Kitayama, S. (1991, April). Culture and the self: Implications for cognition, emotion, and motivation. *Psychological Review, 98*(2), 224–253.

Marquez, J. (2008, September 22). Connecting a virtual workforce. *Workforce Management, 87*(15), p1, pp. 23–25.

Marrone, J. A., Tesluk, P. E., & Carson, J. B. (2007). A multilevel investigation of the antecedents and consequences to team member boundary spanning. *Academy of Management Journal, 50,* 1423–1439.

Massey, G. C., Scott, M. V., & Dornbusch, S. M. (1975). Racism without racists: Institutional racism in urban schools. *Black Scholar, 7*(3), 2–11.

Mathieu, J. E., Marks, M. A., & Zaccaro, S. J. (2001). Multi-team systems. In N. Anderson, D. S. Ones, H. K. Sinangil, & C. Viswesvaran (Eds.), *Handbook of industrial, work and organizational psychology* (Vol. 2, pp. 289–313). London: Sage.

Mathieu, J. E., & Rapp, T. L. (2009). Laying the foundation for successful team performance trajectories: The roles of team charters and performance strategies. *Journal of Applied Psychology, 94*(1), 90–103.

Mathieu, J. E., & Schulze, W. (2006). The influence of team knowledge and formal plans on episodic team process-performance relationships. *Academy of Management Journal, 49*(3), 605–619.

Mathieu, J., Gilson, L., & Ruddy, T. (2006). Empowerment and team effectiveness: An empirical test of an integrated model. *Journal of Applied Psychology, 91*(1), 97–108.

Matson, E. (1996). Four rules for fast teams. *Fast Company*, (4).

Mayer, D. M., Kuenzi, M., Greenbaum, R., Bardes, M., & Salvador, R. (2009). How low does ethical leadership flow? Test of a trickle-down model. *Organizational Behavior and Human Decision Processes, 108*(1), 1–13.

Mayer, R. C., Davis, J. H., & Schoorman, F. D. (1995). An integrative model of organizational trust. *Academy of Management Review, 20,* 709–734.

Mazur, A. (1985). A biosocial model of status in face-to-face groups. *Social Forces, 64,* 377–402.

McCallum, D., Harring, K., Gilmore, R., Drenan, S., Chase, J., Insko, C., & Thibaut, J. (1985). Competition and cooperation between groups and between individuals. *Journal of Experimental Social Psychology, 21,* 301–320.

McCauley, C. (1998). Groupthink dynamics in Janis's theory of groupthink: Backward and forward. *Organizational Behavior and Human Decision Processes, 73*(2–3), 142–162.

McGlynn, R. P., Harding, D. J., & Cottle, J. L. (2009). Individual–group discontinuity in group–individual interactions: Does size matter? *Group Processes & Intergroup Relations, 12*(1), 129–143.

McGlynn, R. P., McGurk, D., Effland, V. S., Johll, N. L., & Harding, D. J. (2004). Brainstorming and task performance in groups constrained by evidence. *Organizational Behavior and Human Decision Processes, 93*(1), 75–90.

McGrath, J. E. (1984). *Groups: Interaction and performance.* Upper Saddle River, NJ: Prentice Hall.

McGrath, J. E. (1990). Time matters in groups. In J. Galegher, R. E. Kraut, & C. Egido (Eds.), *Intellectual teamwork: Social and technological foundations of cooperative work.* Mahwah, NJ: Lawrence Erlbaum & Associates.

McGrath, J. E., & Hollingshead, A. B. (1994). *Groups interacting with technology.* Newbury Park, CA: Sage.

McGrath, J. E., Kelly, J. R., & Machatka, D. E. (1984). The social psychology of time: Entrainment of behavior in social and organizational settings. *Applied Social Psychology Annual, 5,* 21–44.

McGregor, D. (1960). *The human side of enterprise.* New York: McGraw-Hill.

McGregor, J. (2009, March 23). Can companies share one nervous system? *Business Week, 4124,* 40.

McGregor, J., Arndt, M., Berner, R., Rowley, I., & Hall, K. (2006, April 24). The world's most innovative companies. *Business Week, 3981,* 62.

McGuire, T., Keisler, S., & Siegel, J. (1987). Group and computer-mediated discussion effect in risk decision-making. *Journal of Personality and Social Psychology, 52*(5), 917–930.

McIntosh, D. N., Druckman, D., & Zajonc, R. B. (1994). Socially induce affect. In D. Druckman & R. A. Bjork (Eds.), *Learning, remembering, believing: Enhancing human performance* (pp. 251–276). Washington, DC: National Academy Press.

McKeough, T. (2009, December). Blowing hot and cold. *Fast Company*, 66.

McLeod, P., Baron, R., Marti, M., & Yoon, K. (1997). The eyes have it: Minority influence in face to face and computer mediated group discussion. *Journal of Applied Psychology, 82,* 706–718.

McNeal, A. (2009, August 1). Unethical deeds or outright fraud? *Internal Auditor, 66*(4), 71–75.

Meece, M. (2008, October 23). Inspiration can be found in many places, but you need to be looking. *New York Times*, p. B9.

Mehrabian, A. (1971). *Silent messages.* Belmont, CA: Wadsworth.

Mehta, S. (2008, December 18). How to sell in China. *CNNmoney.com.* money.cnn.com.

Meindl, J. R., Ehrlich, S. B., & Dukerich, J. M. (1985). The romance of leadership. *Administrative Science Quarterly, 30,* 78–102.

Meindl, J. R., & Lerner, M. O. (1984). Exacerbation of extreme responses to an out-group. *Journal of Personality and Social Psychology, 47*(1), 71–84.

Menon, T., & Blount, S. (2003). The Messenger bias: A relational model of knowledge valuation. *Research in Organizational Behavior, 25,* 137–186.

Menon, T., & Pfeffer, J. (2003). Valuing internal vs. external knowledge: Explaining the preference for outsiders. *Management Science, 49,* 497–513.

Menon, T., Thompson, L., & Choi H. (2006). Tainted knowledge vs. tempting knowledge: People avoid knowledge from internal rivals and seek knowledge from external rivals. *Management Science, 52*(8), 1129–1144.

Mesmer-Magnus, J., & DeChurch, L. (2009). Information sharing and team performance: A meta-analysis. *Journal of Applied Psychology, 94*(2), 535–546.

Messick, D. (1993). Equality as a decision heuristic. In B. A. Mellers & J. Baron (Eds.), *Psychological perspectives on justice* (pp. 11–31). New York: Cambridge University Press.

Meyer, C. (1994, May–June). How the right measures help teams excel. *Harvard Business Review,* 95–103.

Michael, J. H., Barsness, Z., Lawson, L., & Balkundi, P. (2004). Focus please: Team coordination and performance at wood manufacturers. *Forest Products Journal, 54*(12), 250–255.

Michaels, S. W., Brommel, J. M., Brocato, R. M., Linkous, R. A., & Rowe, J. S. (1982). Social facilitation in a natural setting. *Replication in Social Psychology, 4*(2), 21–24.

Michaelsen, L. K., Watson, W. E., & Black, R. H. (1989). A realistic test of individual versus group consensus decision making. *Journal of Applied Psychology, 74*(5), 834–839.

Michalisin, M. D., Karau, S. J., & Tangpong, C. (2004). Top management team cohesion and superior industry returns: an empirical study of the resource-based view. *Group and Organization Management, 29,* 125–40.

Michel, J. G., & Hambrick, D. C. (1992). Diversification posture and top management team characteristics. *Academy of Management Journal, 35*(1), 9–37.

Milch, K. F., Weber, E. U., Appelt, K. C., Handgraaf, M. J., & Krantz, D. H. (2009). From individual preference construction to group decisions: Framing effects and group processes. *Organizational Behavior and Human Decision Processes, 108*(2), 242–255.

Miles, R. P., & Osborne, T. (2001). *The Warren Buffett CEO: Secrets of the berkshire hathaway managers.* New York: John Wiley Sons.

Miller, C. C. (2009, June 25). Start-up's software goes to employees for company forecasts [Web log post]. bits.blogs.nytimes.com

Miller, C. E., Jackson, P., Mueller, J., & Schersching, C. (1987). Some social psychological effects of group decision rules. *Journal of Personality and Social Psychology, 52,* 325–332.

Miller, D. T. (1999). The norm of self-interest. *American Psychologist, 54*(12), 1053–1060.

Miller, D. T., & Ratner, R. (1998). The disparity between the actual and assumed power of self-interest. *Journal of Personality and Social Psychology, 74*(1), 53–62.

Milliman, J. F., Zawacki, R. F., Norman, C., Powell, L., & Kirksey, J. (1994, November). Companies evaluate employees from all perspectives. *Personnel Journal, 73*(11), 99–103.

Mitchell, C. K. (1998). *The effects of break task on performance during the second session of brainstorming.* Unpublished manuscript, University of Texas–Arlington.

Mitchell, J. (2009, November 14). Alert on errant jet took too long, FAA says. *Wall Street Journal,* p. A3.

Mitchell, R., Boyle, B., & Nicholas, S. (2009). The impact of goal structure in team knowledge creation. *Group Processes & Intergroup Relations, 12*(5), 639–651.

Mohrman, S. A., Cohen, S. G., & Mohrman, A. M. (1995). *Designing team-based organizations.* San Francisco, CA: Jossey-Bass.

Mohrman, S. A., Lawler, E. E., & Mohrman, A. M. (1992). Applying employee involvement in schools. *Educational Evaluation and Policy Analysis, 14*(4), 347–360.

Mojzisch, A., Schulz-Hardt, S., Kerschreiter, R., & Frey, D. (2008). Combined effects of knowledge about others' opinions and anticipation of group discussion on confirmatory information search. *Small Group Research*, *39*(2), 203–223.

Moons, W. G., Leonard, D. J., Mackie, D. M., & Smith, E. R. (2009). I feel our pain: Antecedents and consequences of emotional self-stereotyping. *Journal of Experimental Social Psychology, 45*(4), 760–769.

Moore, D., Kurtzberg, T., Thompson, L., & Morris, M. (1999). Long and short routes to success in electronically-mediated negotiations: Group affiliations and good vibrations. *Organizational Behavior and Human Decision Processes, 77*(1), 22–43.

Moreland, R. L., Argote, L., & Krishnan, R. (1996). Socially shared cognition at work. In J. L. Nye & A. M. Brower (Eds.), *What's social about social cognition?* Thousand Oaks, CA: Sage.

Moreland, R. L., Argote, L., & Krishnan, R. (1998). Training people to work in groups. In R. S. Tindale

& Colleagues (Eds.), *Theory and research on small groups.* New York: Plenum Press.

Moreland, R. L., & Levine, J. M. (1982). Socialization in small groups: Temporal changes in individual-group relations. In L. Berkowitz (Ed.), *Advances in experimental social psychology* (Vol. 15, pp. 137–192). New York: Academic Press.

Moreland, R. L., & Levine, J. M. (1989). Newcomers and oldtimers in small groups. In P. Paulus (Ed.), *Psychology of group influence* (2nd ed., pp. 143–186). Hillsdale, NJ: Erlbaum.

Moreland, R. L., & Levine, J. M. (1992). The composition of small groups. In E. J. Lawler, B. Markovsky, C. Ridgeway, & H. A. Walker (Eds.), *Advances in group processes* (Vol. 9, pp. 237–280). Greenwich, CT: JAI Press.

Moreland, R. L., & Levine, J. M. (2000). Socialization in organizations and work groups. In M. Turner (Ed.), *Groups at work: Theory and research* (pp. 69–112). Mahwah, NJ: Lawrence Erlbaum Associates.

Moreland, R. L., & Levine, J. M. (2002). Socialization and trust in work groups. *Group Processes and Interpersonal Relations, 5*(3), 185–201.

Moreland, R. L., & McMinn, J. G. (1999). Gone but not forgotten: Loyalty and betrayal among ex members of small groups. *Personality and Social Psychology Bulletin, 25*(12), 1476–1486.

Morgan, B. B., & Bowers, C. A. (1995). Teamwork stress: Implications for team decision making. In R. A. Guzzo & E. Salas (Eds.), *Team effectiveness and decision making in organizations* (pp. 262–290). San Francisco, CA: Jossey-Bass.

Morgeson, F. P. (2005). The external leadership of self-managing teams: Intervening in the context of novel and disruptive events. *Journal of Applied Psychology, 90,* 497–508.

Morris, M. W., Podolny, J. M., & Ariel, S. (2000). Missing relations: Incorporating relational constructs into models of culture. In P. C. Earley & H. Singh (Eds.), *Innovations in international and cross-cultural management* (pp. 52–90). Thousand Oaks, CA: Sage.

Morrison, K. R., Fast, N. J., & Ybarra, O. (2009). Group status, perceptions of threat, and support for social inequality. *Journal of Experimental Social Psychology, 45,* 204–210.

Moscovici, S. (1980). Towards a theory of conversion behavior. In L. Berkowitz (Ed.), *Advances in Experimental Social Psychology* (Vol. 13, pp. 209–239). San Diego, CA: Academic Press.

Moscovici, S. (1985a). Innovation and minority influence. In S. Moscovici, G. Mugny, & E. Van Avermaet (Eds.), *Perspectives on minority influence* (pp. 9–52). Cambridge, England: Cambridge University Press.

Moscovici, S. (1985b). Social influence and conformity. In G. Lindzey & E. Aronson (Eds.), *Handbook of social psychology* (3rd ed., Vol. 2, pp. 347–412). New York: Random House.

Moscovici, S., Mugny, G., & Papastamou, S. (1981). Sleeper effect and/or minority effect? *Cahiers de Psychologie Cognitive, 1,* 199–221.

Mottola, G. R., Bachman, B. A., Gaertner, S. L., & Dovidio, J. F. (1997). How groups merge: The effects of merger integration patterns on anticipated commitment to the merged organization. *Journal of Applied Social Psychology, 27,* 1335–1358.

Mugny, G. (1982). *The power of minorities.* London: Academic Press.

Mullen, B., Johnson, C., & Salas, E. (1991). Productivity loss in brainstorming groups: A meta-analytic integration. *Basic and Applied Social Psychology, 12,* 3–23.

Mulvey, P. W., Veiga, J. F., & Elsass, P. M. (1996). When teammates raise a white flag. *Academy of Management Executive, 10*(1), 40–49.

Munkes, J., & Diehl, M. (2003). Matching or competition? Performance comparison processes in an idea generation task. *Group Processes and Intergroup Relations, 6,* 305–320.

Munter, M., & Netzley, M. (2002). *Guide to meetings.* Upper Saddle River, NJ: Prenctice Hall.

Muoio, A. (1997, August). They have a better idea … do you? *Fast Company, 10,* 73–79.

Murphy, A. (2009, July 13). As tour rests, rivalry between Armstrong and Contador heats up. *Sports Illustrated.* sportsillustrated.cnn.com

Nadler, J., Thompson, L., & Van Boven, L. (2003). Learning negotiation skills: Four models of knowledge creation and transfer. *Management Science, 49*(4), 529–540.

Nagasundaram, M., & Dennis, A. R. (1993). When a group is not a group: The cognitive foundation of group idea generation. *Small Group Research, 24,* 463–489.

Nagourney, A., Rutenberg, J., & Zeleny, J. (2008, October 5). Obama campaign team rarely stumbled. *New York Times.* nytimes.com

Nahavandi, A., & Aranda, E. (1994). Restructuring teams for the re-engineered organization. *Academy of Management Review, 8*(4), 58–68.

Nahrgang, J. D., Frederick, P. Morgeson, F. P., & Ilies, L.(2009). The development of leader–member exchanges: Exploring how personality and performance influence leader and member relationships over time. *Organizational Behavior and Human Decision Processes, 108*(2), 256–266.

Naylor, J. C., & Briggs, G. E. (1965). Team-training effectiveness under various conditions. *Journal of Applied Psychology, 49,* 223–229.

Nebus, J. (2006). Building collegial information networks: A theory of advice network generation *Academy of Management Review, 31*(3), 615–637.

Nelson, B. (2005). *1001 ways to reward employees* (2nd ed.). New York: Workman.

Nembhard, I. M., & Edmondson, A. (2006). Making it safe: The effects of leader inclusiveness and professional status on psychological safety and improvement efforts in health care teams. *Journal of Organizational Behavior, 27*(7), 941–966.

Nemertes Research. (2008). *Nemertes benchmark: Building a successful virtual workplace.* nemertes .com

Nemeth, C. (1976). A comparison between majority and minority influence. Invited Address. International Congress for Psychology. Joint Meeting of SESP and EAESP, Paris.

Nemeth, C. (2003). Minority dissent and its "hidden" benefits. *New Review of Social Psychology, 2,* 20–28.

Nemeth, C. J. (1986). Differential contributions of majority and minority influence. *Psychological Review, 93,* 23–32.

Nemeth, C. J. (1994). The value of minority dissent. In A. Mucchi-Faina, A. Maass, & S. Moscovici (Eds.), *Minority Influence: Nelson-Hall Series in Psychology* (pp. 3–15). Chicago: Nelson-Hall.

Nemeth, C. J. (1995). Dissent as driving cognition, attitudes, and judgments. *Social Cognition, 13,* 273–291.

Nemeth, C. J. (1997). Managing innovation: When less is more. *California Management Review, 40,* 59–74.

Nemeth, C. J., & Kwan, J. (1985). Originality of word associations as a function of majority minority influence. *Social Psychology Quarterly, 48,* 277–282.

Nemeth, C. J., & Kwan, J. L. (1987). Minority influence, divergent thinking and detection of correct solutions. *Journal of Applied Social Psychology, 17*(9), 788–799.

Nemeth, C. J., & Nemeth-Brown, B. (2003). Better than individuals? The potential benefits of dissent and diversity for group creativity. In P. B. Paulus & B. A. Nijstad (Eds.), *Group creativity: Innovation through collaboration* (pp. 63–84). New York: Oxford University Press.

Nemeth, C. J., & Ormiston, M. (2007). Creative idea generation: Harmony versus stimulation. *European Journal of Social Psychology, 37*(3), 524–535.

Nemeth, C. J., Personnaz, M., Personnaz, B., & Goncalo, J. A. (2004). The liberating role of conflict in group creativity: A study in two countries. *European Journal of Social Psychology, 34,* 365–374.

Nemeth, C. J., & Rogers, J. (1996). Dissent and the search for information. *British Journal of Social Psychology, 35,* 67–76.

Nemeth, C. J., & Wachtler, J. (1974). Creating the perceptions of consistency and confidence: A necessary condition for minority influence. *Sociometry, 37*(4), 529–540.

Nemeth, C. J., & Wachtler, J. (1983). Creative problem solving as a result of majority vs. minority influence. *European Journal of Social Psychology, 13*(1), 45–55.

Nemeth, C., Brown, K., & Rogers, J. (2001). Devil's advocate versus authentic dissent: Simulating quantity and quality. *European Journal of Social Psychology, 31,* 707–720.

Nemeth, C., Connell, J., Rogers, J., & Brown, K. (2001). Improving decision making by means of dissent. *Journal of Applied Social Psychology, 31*(1), 48–58.

Nemeth, C., Mayseless, O., Sherman, J., & Brown, Y. (1990). Improving recall by exposure to consistent dissent. *Journal of Personality and Social Psychology, 58,* 429–437.

Neuman, G. A., Wagner, S. H., & Christiansen, N. D. (1999). The relationship between work-team personality composition and the job performance of teams. *Groups and Organization Management, 24,* 28–45.

Neuman, G. A., & Wright, J. (1999). Team effectiveness: Beyond skills and cognitive ability. *Journal of Applied Psychology, 84*(3), 376–389.

Newstrom, J., & Scannell, E. (1997). *The big book of team building games.* New York: McGraw-Hill.

Ng, K., Van Dyne, L., & Ang, S. (2009). From experience to experiential learning: Cultural intelligence as a learning capability for global leader development. *Academy of Management Learning & Education, 8*(4), 511–526.

Nieva, V. F., Myers, D., & Glickman, A. S. (1979, July). An exploratory investigation of the skill qualification testing system. *U.S. Army Research Institute for the Behavioral and Social Sciences,* TR 390.

Nijstad, B. A., Stroebe, W., & Lodewijkx, H. F. M. (1999). Persistence of brainstorming groups: How do people know when to stop? *Journal of Experimental Social Psychology, 35,* 165–185.

Nijstad, B. A., Stroebe, W., & Lodewijkx, H. F. M. (2003). Production blocking and idea generation: Does blocking interfere with cognitive processes? *Journal of Experimental Social Psychology, 39,* 531–548.

Nilson, C. D. (2004). *More team games for trainers.* New York: McGraw Hill.

Nishii, L. H., & Mayer, D. (2009). Do inclusive leaders help the performance of diverse groups? The moderating role of leader-member exchange in the diversity to group performance. *Journal of Applied Psychology, 94*(6), 1412–1426.

Noor, M., Brown, R., González, R., Manzi, J., & Lewis, C. A. (2008). On positive psychological outcomes: What helps groups with a history of conflict to forgive and reconcile with each other? *Personality and Social Psychology Bulletin, 34,* 819–832.

Novak, C. J. (1997, April). Proceed with caution when paying teams. *HR Magazine, 42*(4), 73–78.

N.Y. jet crash called "miracle on the Hudson." (2009, January 15). *msnbc.com.* msnbc.msn.com

Oaksford, M., & Chater, N. (1994). A rational analysis of the selection task as optimal data selection. *Psychological Review, 101,* 608–631.

O'Brien, J. (2008, May 26). Team building in paradise. *Fortune International, 157*(10), 74–82.

O'Brien, J. M. (2009, January 22). The 10 commandments of zappos. Money.cnn.com

Office of the Under Secretary of Defense. (2004). Personnel and readiness. Population representation in the military services. prhome.defense.gov

Ogletree Deakins. (2009, January/February). "Higher and higher": OFCCP obtains record $67.5 million from contractors. *The employment law authority,* p. 2.

Oh, H., Chung, M.-H., & Labianca, G. (2004). Group social capital and group effectiveness: The role of informal socializing ties. *Academy of Management Journal, 47,* 860–875.

O'Hamilton, J., Baker, S., & Vlasic, B. (1996, April). The new workplace. *Business Week, 3473,* 106–117.

O'Hara-Devereaux, M., & Johansen, R. (1994). *Global work: Bridging distance, culture and time.* San Francisco, CA: Jossey-Bass.

Ohngren, K. (2009, May 13). Cheap ways to motivate you team. Entrepreneur.com

Ohtsubo, Y., & Miler, C. E. (2008). Test of a Level of Aspiration model of group decision making: Non-obvious group preference reversal due to an irrelevant alternative. *Journal of Experimental Social Psychology, 44*(1), 105–115.

Olsen, P. (2008, April 20). An ocean apart, bridged by forklift. *The New York Times,* p. BU17.

Olson, M. (1965). *The logic of collective action.* Cambridge, MA: Harvard University Press.

O'Reilly, C. A., & Caldwell, D. F. (1985). The impact of normative social influence and cohesiveness on task perceptions and attitudes: A social-information processing approach. *Journal of Occupational Psychology, 58,* 193–206.

Ordeshook, P. (1986). *Game theory and political theory: An introduction.* Cambridge, UK: Cambridge University Press.

Ordóñez, L. D., Schweitzer, M. E., Galinsky, A. D., & Bazerman, M. H. (2009, February). Goals gone wild: The systematic side effects of overprescribing goal setting. *Academy of Management Perspectives, 23*(1), 6–16.

Orsburn, J. D., Moran, L., Musselwhite, E., & Zenger, J. H. (2000). *The new self-directed work teams.* New York: McGraw-Hill.

Osborn, A. F. (1957). *Applied imagination* (rev. ed.). New York: Scribner

Osborn, A. F. (1963). *Applied magination* (3rd ed.). New York: Scribner.

Oudenhoven-van der Zee, K., Paulus, P., Vos, M., & Parthasarathy, N. (2009). The impact of group composition and attitudes towards diversity on anticipated outcomes of diversity in Groups. *Group Processes & Intergroup Relations, 12*(2), 257–280.

Oxley, N. L., Dzindolet, M. T., & Paulus, P. B. (1996). The effects of facilitators on the performance of brainstorming groups. *Journal of Social Behavior and Personality, 11*(4), 633–646.

Page-Gould, E., Mendoza-Denton, R., & Tropp, L. (2008). With a little help from my cross-group friend: Reducing anxiety in intergroup contexts through crossgroup friendship. *Journal of Personality and Social Psychology, 95,* 1080–1094.

Paladino, M., & Castelli, L. (2008). On the immediate consequences of intergroup categorization: Activation of approach and avoidance motor behavior toward ingroup and outgroup members. *Personality and Social Psychology Bulletin, 34*(6), 755–768.

Palfini, J. (2008, February 4). Societe Generale debacle: Losing touch could mean losing it all [Web log post]. blogs.bnet.com

Palmer, A. (2009, December 9). Global Engagement. *Incentive, 183*(11), 16–23.

Palmer, L. (1996, April 30). There's no meetings like business meetings. *Fast Company,* 2.

Park, B., & Rothbart, M. (1982). Perception of outgroup homogeneity and levels of social categorization: Memory for subordinate attitudes of ingroup and outgroup members. *Journal of Personality and Social Psychology, 42,* 1050–1068.

Parks, C. D., & Cowlin, R. A. (1996). Acceptance of uncommon information into group discussion when that information is or is not demonstrable. *Organizational Behavior and Human Decision Processes, 66*(3), 307–315.

Parnes, S. J., & Meadow, A. (1959). Effect of "brainstorming" instructions on creative problem-solving by trained and untrained subjects. *Journal of Educational Psychology, 50,* 171–176.

Parsons, T., Bales, R. F., & Shils, E. (1953). *Working paper in the theory of action.* Glencoe, IL: Free Press.

Pashler, H. (2000). Task switching and multitask performance. In S. Monsell & J. Driver (Eds.), *Attention and performance XVIII: Control of mental processes* (pp. 227–308). Cambridge, MA: MIT Press.

Pattison, K. (2008, September). How innovation led HTC to the dream. *Fast Company.* Fastcompany.com

Paulus, P. B. (1998). Developing consensus about groupthink after all these years. *Organizational Behavior and Human Decision Processes, 73*(2–3), 362–374.

Paulus, P. B., & Brown, V. R. (2003). Enhancing ideational creativity in groups: Lesson from research on brainstorming. In P. B. Paulus & B. A. Nijstad (Eds.), *Group creativity: Innovation through collaboration* (pp. 110–136). New York: Oxford University Press.

Paulus, P. B., & Dzindolet, M. T. (1993). Social influence processes in group brainstorming. *Journal of Personality and Social Psychology, 64,* 575–586.

Paulus, P. B., Dzindolet, M. T., Poletes, G., & Camacho L. M. (1993, February). Perception of performance in group brainstorming: The illusion of group productivity. *Personality and Social Psychology Bulletin, 19*(1), 78–89.

Paulus, P. B., Larey, T. S., Brown, V., Dzindolet, M. T., Roland, E. J., Leggett, K. L., Putman, V. L., &

Coskun, H. (1998, June). *Group and electronic brainstorming: understanding production losses and gains in idea generating groups.* Paper presented at Learning in Organizations Conference, Carnegie-Mellon University, Pittsburgh, PA.

Paulus, P. B., Larey, T. S., & Ortega, A. H. (1995). Performance and perceptions of brainstormers in an organizational setting. *Basic and Applied Social Psychology, 17,* 249–265.

Paulus, P. B., Larey, T. S., Putman, V. L., Leggett, K. L., & Roland, E. J. (1996). Social influence process in computer brainstorming. *Basic and Applied Social Psychology, 18,* 3–14.

Paulus, P. B., & Nakui, T. (2005). Facilitation of group brainstorming. In S. Schuman (Ed.), *The IAF handbook of group facilitation* (pp. 103–114). San Francisco, CA: Jossey-Bass.

Paulus, P. B., Nakui, T., Putman, V. L., & Brown, V. R. (2006). Effects of task instructions and brief breaks on brainstorming. *Group Dynamics: Theory, Research, and Practice, 10*(3), 206–219.

Paulus, P. B., Putman, V. L., Coskun, H., Leggett, K. L., & Roland, E. J. (1996). Training groups for effective brainstorming. Presented at the Fourth Annual Advanced Concepts Conference on Work Teams–Team Implementation Issues, Dallas.

Paulus, P. B., & Yang, H. (2000). Idea generation in groups: A basis for creativity in organizations. *Organizational Behavior and Human Decision Processes, 82*(1), 76–87.

Paumgarten, N. (2010, January 4). Food fighter. *The New Yorker*, pp. 36–47.

Pearce, C. L., & Sims, H. P., Jr. (2002). Vertical versus shared leadership as predictors of the effectiveness of change management teams: An examination of aversive, directive, transactional, transformational and empowering leader behaviors. *Group Dynamics: Theory, Research, and Practice, 6*(2), 172–197.

Pearsall, M., Ellis, A., & Stein, J. (2009). Coping with challenge and hindrance stressors in teams: Behavioral, cognitive, and affective outcomes. *Organizational Behavior and Human Decision Processes, 109*(1), 18–28.

Pearsall, M. J., Christian, M. S., & Ellis, A. P. J. (2010). Motivating interdependent teams: Individual rewards, shared rewards, or something in between? *Journal of Applied Psychology, 95*(1), 183–191.

Pearsall, M. J., Ellis, A. P. J., & Bell, B. S. (2010). Building the infrastructure: The effects of role identification behaviors on team cognition development and performance. *Journal of Applied Psychology, 95*(1), 192–200.

Pelled, L. H., Eisenhardt, K. M., & Xin, K. R. (1999). Exploring the black box: An analysis of work group diversity, conflict, and performance. *Administrative Science Quarterly, 44,* 1–28.

Pennebaker, J. W. (1982). *The psychology of physical symptoms.* New York: Springer-Verlag.

Pentland, A. (2010, January–February). We can measure the power of charisma. *Harvard Business Review, 88*(1), 34–35.

Perez, J. A., & Mugny, G. (1987). Paradoxical effects of categorization in minority influence: When being an out-group is an advantage. *European Journal of Social Psychology, 17,* 157–169.

Perez, J. A., & Mugny, G. (1996). The conflict elaboration theory of social influence. In E. H. Witte, & J. H. Davis (Eds.), *Understanding group behavior: Small group processes and interpersonal relations* (Vol. 2, pp. 191–210). Mahwah, NJ: Lawrence Erlbaum Associates.

Perkins, D. V. (1982). Individual differences and task structure in the performance of a behavior setting: An experimental evaluation of Barker's manning theory. *American Journal of Community Psychology, 10*(6), 617–634.

Perrow, C. (1984). *Normal accidents: Living with high-risk technologies* (p. 215). New York: Basic Books.

Perry-Smith, J. E., & Shalley, C. E. (2003). The social side of creativity: A static and dynamic social network perspective. *Academy of Management Review, 28*(1), 89–107.

Peterson, R. (1997). A directive leadership style in group decision making can be both virtue and vice: Evidence from elite and experimental groups. *Journal of Personality and Social Psychology, 72*(5), 1107–1121.

Peterson, R., & Behfar, K. (2003). The dynamic relationship between performance feedback, trust, and conflict in groups: A longitudinal study. *Organizational Behavior and Human Decision Processes, 92,* 102–112.

Peterson, R. S., & Nemeth, C. J. (1996). Focus versus flexibility: Majority and minority influence can both improve performance. *Personality and Social Psychology Bulletin, 22*(1), 14–23.

Peterson, R. S., Owens, P. D., Tetlock, P. E., Fan, E. T., & Martorana, P. (1998). Group dynamics in top management teams: Groupthink, vigilance, and alternative models of organizational failure and success. *Organizational Behavior and Human Decision Processes, 73,* 272–305.

Pettigrew, T. F., & Tropp, L. (2006, May). A meta-analytic test of intergroup contact theory. *Journal of Personality and Social Psychology, 90*(5), 751–783.

Pettit, N. C., & Lount, R. B., Jr. (2010). Looking down and ramping up: The impact of status differences on effort in intergroup settings. *Journal of Experimental Social Psychology, 46*(1), 9–20.

Petty, R. E., Cacioppo, J. T., & Kasmer, J. (1985). *Effects of need for cognition on social loafing.* Paper presented at the Midwestern Psychology Association Meeting, Chicago.

Petty, R. M., & Wicker, A. W. (1974). Degree of manning and degree of success of a group as determinants of members' subjective experiences and their acceptance of a new group member. *Catalog of Selected Documents in Psychology, 4,* 43.

Pfeffer, J. (1983). Organizational demography. In B. M. Staw, & L. L. Cummings (Eds.), *Research in organizational behavior* (Vol. 5, pp. 299–359). Greenwich, CT: JAI Press.

Pfeffer, J. (2009, July 23). Managers and employees alike sense the truth: Workplace appraisals aren't working. *Business Week,* p. 24.

Pfeffer, J., & Sutton, R. (2006). Evidence- based management. *Harvard Business Review, 84*(1), 62–74.

Pfeiffer, J. W. (1974). *A handbook of structured experiences for human relations training* (Vols. 1–10). LaJolla, CA: University Associates.

Pfeiffer, J. W., & Jones, J. E. (1994). *A handbook of structured experiences* (Vols. 1–10). San Diego, CA: Pfeiffer & Company.

Phelps, R. (1996, September). Cadbury trusts in teamwork. *Management Today,* p. 110.

Phillips, J. M. (1999). Antecedents of leader utilization of staff input in decision-making teams. *Organizational Behavior and Human Decision Processes, 77*(3), 215–242.

Phillips, K., Liljenquist, K., & Neale, M. (2009). Is the pain worth the gain? The advantages and liabilities of agreeing with socially distinct newcomers. *Personality and Social Psychology Bulletin, 35*(3), 336–351.

Phillips, K. W. (2003). The effects of categorically based expectations on minority influence: The importance of congruence. *Personality Sociology and Psychology Bulletin, 29,* 3–13.

Phillips, K. W., & Loyd, D. (2006). When surface and deep-level diversity collide: The effects on dissenting group members. *Organizational Behavior and Human Decision Processes, 99*(2), 143–160.

Phillips, K. W., Mannix, E. A., Neale, M. A., & Gruenfeld, D. H. (2004). Diverse groups and information sharing: The effects of congruent ties. *Journal of Experimental Social Psychology, 40*(4), 497–510.

Podolny, J. M., & Baron, J. N. (1997). Resources and relationships: Social networks and mobility in the workplace. *American Sociological Review, 62*(5), 673–693.

Polanyi, M. (1966). *The tacit dimension.* London: Routledge & Kegan Paul.

Polzer, J. T., Milton, L. P., & Swann, W. B. (2002). Capitalizing on diversity: Interpersonal congruence in small work groups. *Administrative Science Quarterly, 47,* 296–324.

Poole, S. (2003). Group support systems. *Encyclopedia of Information Systems, 2,* 501–507.

Porter, C., Hollenbeck, J., Ilgen, D., Ellis, A., West, B., & Moon, H. (2003). Backing up behaviors in teams: The role of personality and legitimacy of need. *Journal of Applied Psychology, 88*(3), 391–403.

Postmes, T., & Spears, R. (2002). Behavior online: Does anonymous comptuer communication reduce gender inequality? *Personality and Social Psychology Bulle*tin, *28*(8), 1073–1083.

Prentice, D. A., Miller, D. T., & Lightdale, J. R. (1994). Asymmetries in attachments to groups and to their members: Distinguishing between common-identity and common-bond groups. *Personality and Social Psychology Bulletin, 20,* 484–493.

PriceWaterhouseCoopers. (2010). *Reward and recognition.* pwc.com.

Price, M. (2010, January). The antidote to medical errors. *Monitor on Psychology, 41*(1), 50–53.

Quinn, A., & Schlenker, B. (2002). Can accountability produce independence? Goals as determinants of the impact of accountability and conformity. *Personality and Social Psychology Bulletin, 28*(4), 472–483.

Radigan, J. (2001, December 1). Remote possibilities: Companies are more interested than ever in a far-flung workforce. *CFO,* p. S5.

Rae-Dupree, J. (2008, November 2). It's no time to forget about innovation. *New York Times,* p. 4.

Ragins, B. R., & Sundstrom, E. (1989). Gender and power in organizations: a longitudinal perspective. *Psychological Bulletin, 105,* 51–88.

Rao, R. D., & Argote, L. (2006). Organizational learning and forgetting: The effects of turnover and structure. *European Management Review, 3,* 77–85.

Rawlins, W. K. (1983). Negotiating close friendship: The dialectic of conjunctive freedoms. *Human Communication Research, 9,* 255–266.

Reagans, R., Argote, L., & Brooks, D. (2005). Individual experience and experience working together: Predicting learning rates from knowing who knows what and knowing how to work together. *Management Science, 51*(6), 869–881.

Reed, S. E. (2009, December 24). On the death of the cubicle. *Global Post.* globalpost.com

Reeves, L., & Weisberg, R. W. (1994). The role of content and abstract information in analogical transfer. *Psychological Bulletin, 115*(3), 381–400.

Ren, Y., Carley, K., & Argote, L. (2006). The contingent effects of transactive memory: When is it more beneficial to know what others know? *Management Science, 52*(5), 671–682.

Reston, M., & Mehta, S. (2008, November 6). Election 2008: The republicans; *Palin, McCain* camps at odds. *Los Angeles Times,* p. A12.

Rickards, T. (1993). Creative leadership: Messages from the front line and the back room. *Journal of Creative Behavior, 27,* 46–56.

Riess, M. (1982). Seating preferences as impression management: A literature review and theoretical integration. *Communication, 11,* 85–113.

Riess, M., & Rosenfeld, P. (1980). Seating preferences as nonverbal communication: A self-presentational analysis. *Journal of Applied Communications Research, 8,* 22–30.

Rietzschel, E. F., Nijstad, B. A., & Stroebe, W. (2006). Productivity is not enough: A comparison of interactive and nominal groups on idea generation and selection. *Journal of Experimental Social Psychology, 42,* 244–251.

Ringelmann, M. (1913). *Aménagement des fumiers et des purins.* Paris: Librarie agricole de la Maison rustique.

Rink, F., & Ellemers, N. (2009). Temporary versus permanent group membership: How the future prospects of newcomers affect newcomer acceptance and newcomer influence. *Personality and Social Psychology Bulletin, 35*(6), 764–775.

Rivera, R. J., & Paradise, A. (2009, November 12). ASTD's 2009 state of the industry report. www.astd.org

Robertson, D., & Hjuler, P. (2009, September). Innovating a turnaround at LEGO. *Harvard Business Review, 87*(9), 20–21.

Robinson, R. J., & Keltner, D. (1996). Much ado about nothing? Revisionists and traditionalists choose an introductory English syllabus. *Psychological Science, 7*(1), 18–24.

Roch, S. R. (2007). Why convene rater teams: An investigation of the benefits of anticipated discussion, consensus, and rater motivation. *Organizational Behavior and Human Decision Processes, 104*(1), 14—29

Rogelberg, S. G., Barnes-Farrell, J. L., & Lowe, C. A. (1992). The stepladder technique: An alternative group structure facilitating effective group decision making. *Journal of Applied Psychology, 77*(5), 730–737.

Rogelberg, S. G., & O'Connor, M. S. (1998). Extending the stepladder technique: An examination of self-paced stepladder groups. *Group Dynamics: Theory, Research, and Practice, 2*(2), 82–91.

Rogelberg, S. G., Scott, C., & Kello, J. (2007, Winter). The Science and fiction of meetings. *MIT Sloan Management Review, 48*(2), 18–21.

Rogers, M., Hennigan, K., Bowman, C., & Miller, N. (1984). Intergroup acceptance in classroom and playground settings. In N. Miller & M. B. Brewer (Eds.), *Groups in contact: The psychology of desegregation* (pp. 187–212). Orlando, FL: Academic Press.

Ronfeldt, D. (2000). Social science at 190 MPH on NASCAR's biggest superspeedways,. *First Monday.* firstmonday.org

Roseman, I., Wiest, C., & Swartz, T. (1994). Phenomenology, behaviors, and goals differentiate emotions. *Journal of Personality and Social Psychology, 67,* 206–221.

Rosette, A. S. (2004). Unacknowledged privilege: Setting the stage for discrimination in organizational settings. In D. Nagao (Ed.), *Best paper proceedings of the 64th annual meeting of the academy (CD), ISSN 1543-8643.* New Orleans, LA.

Rosette, A. S. (2006). Unearned privilege: Race, gender, and social inequality in US organization. In M. Karsten (Ed.), *Gender, ethnicity, and race in the workplace* (pp. 253–268). Westport, CT: Praeger.

Rosette, A. S., & Thompson, L. (2005). The camouflage effect: Separating achieved status and unearned privildge in organizations. In M. Neale, E. Mannix, & M. Thomas-Hunt (Eds.), *Research on managing teams and groups* (Vol. 7, pp. 259–281). San Diego, CA: Elsevier.

Ross, B. H. (1987). This is like that: The use of earlier problems and the separation of similarity effects. *Journal of Experimental Psychology: Learning, Memory and Cognition, 13*(4), 629–639.

Ross, J., & Staw, B. M. (1993, August). Organizational escalation and exit: Lessons from the Shoreham Nuclear Power Plant. *Academy of Management Journal, 36*(4), 701–732.

Ross, L. (1977). The intuitive psychologist and his shortcomings: Distortions in the attribution process. In L. Berkowitz (Ed.), *Advances in experimental social psychology* (Vol. 10, pp. 173–220). Orlando, FL: Academic Press.

Ross, S. M., & Offermann, L. R. (1997). Transformational leaders: Measurement of personality attributes and work group performance. *Personality and Social Psychology Bulletin, 23*(10), 1078–1086.

Rothgerber, H. (1997). External intergroup threat as an antecendent to perceptions of in-group and out-group homogeneity. *Journal of Personality and Social Psychology, 73*(6), 1206–1212.

Rothgerber, H., & Worchel, S. (1997). The view from below: Intergroup relations from the perspective of the disadvantaged group. *Journal of Personality and Social Psychology, 73*(6), 1191–1205.

Rouse, W., & Morris, N. (1986). On looking into the black box: Prospects and limits in the search for mental models. *Psychological Bulletin, 100,* 359–363.

Rousseau, D. M. (2005). *I-deals: Idiosyncratic deals employees bargain for themselves.* New York: M.E. Sharpe.

Rousseau, D. M., Sitkin, S. B., Burt, R. S., & Camerer, C. (1998). Not so different after all: Across-discipline view of trust. *Academy of Management Review, 23*(3), 393–404.

Rousseau, D. M., & Tijoriwala, S. A. (1998). Assessing psychological contracts: Issues, alternatives, and measures. *Journal of Organizational Behavior, 19,* 679–695.

Roy, D. F. (1960). "Banana time": Job satisfaction and informal interaction. *Human Organization, 18,* 158–168.

Roy, M. C., Gauvin, S., & Limayem, M. (1996). Electronic group brainstorming: The role of feedback on productivity. *Small Group Research, 27,* 215–247.

Rubin, R. S., Munz, D. C., & Bommer, W. H. (2005). Leading from within: The effects of emotion recognition and personality on transformational leadership behavior. *Academy of Management Journal, 48*(5), 845–858.

Ruder, M. K., & Gill, D. L. (1982). Immediate effects of win-loss on perceptions of cohesion in intramural and intercollegiate volleyball teams. *Journal of Sport Psychology, 4*(3), 227–234.

Rudman, L. A. (1998). Self-promotion as a risk factor for women: The costs and benefits of counter-stereotypical impression management. *Journal of Personality and Social Psychology, 74,* 629–645.

Ruef, M., Aldrich, H. E., & Carter, N. M. (2003). The structure of organizational founding teams: Homophily, strong ties, and isolation among U.S. entrepreneurs. *American Sociological Review, 68,* 195–222.

Ruggiero, K. M., & Marx, D. M. (1999). Less pain and more to gain: Why high-status group members blame their failure on discrimination. *Journal of Personality and Social Psychology, 77*(4), 774–784.

Russo, F. (2006, January 16). The hidden secrets of the creative mind. *Time, 167*(3), 89–90.

Rutkowski, G. K., Gruder, C. L., & Romer, D. (1983). Group cohesiveness, social norms, and bystander intervention. *Journal of Personality and Social Psychology, 44*(3), 545–552.

Ryan, L. (2006, June 5). The really heinous networking stories are instructive too. *NewsWest.net.* .newswest.net

Saavedra, R., & Kwun, S. K. (1993). Peer evaluation in self-managing work groups. *Journal of Applied Psychology, 78*(3), 450–462.

Sackett, P. R., DuBois, C. I. Z., & Wiggins-Noe, A. (1991). Tokenism in performance evaluation: The effects of work group representation on male-female and white-black differences in performance ratings. *Journal of Applied Psychology, 76,* 263–267.

Saguy, T., Dovidio, J. F., & Pratto, F. (2008). Beyond contact: Intergroup contact in the context of power relations. *Personality and Social Psychology Bulletin, 34,* 432–445.

Salter, C. (2008, March). Google: The faces and voices of the world's most innovative company. *Fast Company, 123,* 74–91.

Salter, C. (2009, February 11). #9 Amazon. *Fast Company.* fastcompany.com

Saltonstall, D. (2008, December 10). *Illinois gov. Rod Blagojevich arrested in conspiracy to benefit from Obama's senate replacement.* nydailynews.com

Sanchez-Burkes, J., & Huy, Q. (2009). Emotional aperture and strategic change: The accurate recognition of collective emotions. *Organization Science, 20*(1), 22–34.

Sanchez-Burks, J. (2002). Protestant relational ideology and (in) attention to relational cues in work settings. *Journal of Personality and Social Psychology, 83,* 919–929.

Sanchez-Burks, J., & Lee, F. (2007). Cultural psychology of workways. In S. Kitayama & D. Cohen (Eds.), *Handbook of cultural psychology.* New York: Guilford Press.

Sanchez-Burks, J., Neuman, E., Ybarra, O., Kopelman, S., Goh, K., & Park, H. (2008). Cultural folk wisdom about relationship conflict. *Negotiation and Conflict Management Research, 1*(1), 55–78.

Sani, F., Todman, J., & Lunn, J. (2005). The fundamentality of group principles, and perceived group entitativity. *Journal of Experimental Social Psychology, 41*(6), 567–573.

Sarno, D. (2009, September 21). Netflix awards $1M prize to recommendation wizards, announces 2nd contest [Web log post]. latimesblogs.latimes.com

Savage, L. J. (1954). *The foundations of statistics.* New York: John Wiley & Sons.

Savitsky, K., Van Boven, L., Epley, N., & Wight, W. (2005). The unpacking effect in allocations of responsibility for group tasks. *Journal of Experimental Social Psychology, 41,* 447–457.

Sawyer, J. E., Houlette, M., & Muzzy, E. L. (2002). Decision performance in racially diverse cross-functional teams: The effect of convergent versus crosscut diversity structure. Working Paper, University of Delaware, Newark.

Scanlon, J. (2009, August 19). How to build a culture of innovation. *Business Week.* businessweek.com

Schaper, D. (writer). (2008, June 20). An e-mail vacation: taking Fridays off [Radio broadcast episode]. *Morning Edition.* Washington, D.C: National Public Radio.

Schein, E. H. (1988). *Process consultation: Its role in organization development* (Vol. 1). Reading, MA: Addison-Wesley.

Schofield, J. W. (1986). Black and white contact in desegregated schools. In M. Hewstone & R. J. Brown (Eds.), *Contact and conflict in intergroup encounters* (pp. 79–92). Oxford, UK: Blackwell.

Scholten, L., van Knippenberg, D., Nijstad, B. A., & De Dreu, C. K. W. (2007). Motivated information processing and group decision making: Effects of process accountability on information processing and decision quality. *Journal of Experimental Social Psychology, 33*, 539–552.

Schroth, R. J., & Elliott, A. L. (2002). *How companies lie: Why Enron is just the tip of the iceberg.* New York: Crown Business.

Schulz-Hardt, S., Frey, D., Lüthgens, C., & Moscovici, S. (2000). Biased information search in group decision making. *Journal of Personality and Social Psychology, 78*(4), 655–669.

Schulz-Hardt, S., Jochims, M., & Frey, D. (2002). Productive conflict in group decision making: Genuine and contrived dissent as strategies to counteract biased decision making. *Organizational Behavior and Human Decision Processes, 88*, 563–586.

Schutte, J. G. (1996). Virtual teaching in higher education: The new intellectual superhighway or just another traffic jam? Working paper, California State University, Northridge, CA.

Schwartz, B. (1986). *The battle for human nature: Science, morality, and modern life.* New York: Norton.

Schweder, R. A., & Bourne, E. J. (1984). Does the concept of the person vary cross-culturally? In R. A. Schweder & R. A. LeVine (Eds.), *Culture theory: Essays on mind, self and emotion* (pp. 158–199). New York/Cambridge, MA: Cambridge University Press.

Schweiger, D. M., & Walsh, J. P. (1990). Mergers and acquisitions: An interdisciplinary view. In K. M. Rowland & G. R. Ferris (Eds.), *Research in personnel and human resource management* (Vol. 8, pp. 41–107). Greenwich, CT: JAI Press.

Scott, D., McMullen, T., & Shields, J. (2009, May). Alignment of business strategies, organization structures and reward programs: A survey of policies, practices and effectiveness. *Worldatwork.* worldatwork.org

Sears, D. O., & Allen, H. M., Jr. (1984). The trajectory of local desegregation controversies and whites' opposition to busing. In N. Miller & M. Brewer (Eds.), *Groups in contact: The psychology of desegregation* (pp. 123–151). New York: Academic Press.

Sears, D. O., & Funk, C. L. (1990). The limited effect of economic self-interest on the political attitudes of the mass public. *Journal of Behavioral Economics, 19*(3), 247–271.

Sears, D. O., & Funk, C. L. (1991). Graduate education in political psychology. Annual meeting of International Society of Political Psychology, Washington, DC. *Political Psychology, 12*(2), 345–362.

Sedekides, C., Campbell, W. K., Reeder, G. D., & Elliot, A. J. (1998). The self-serving bias in relational context. *Journal of Personality and Social Psychology, 74*(2), 378–386.

Sedikides, C., Insko, C. A., & Schopler J. (Eds.). (1998). *Intergroup cognition and intergroup behavior.* New Jersey: Erlbaum

Seeley, E. A., Gardner, W. L., Pennington, G., & Gabriel, S. (2003). Circle of friends or members of a group? Sex differences in relational and collective attachment to groups. *Group Processes and Intergroup Relations, 6*, 251–263.

Seifter, H., & Economy, P. (2001). *Leadership Eensemble: Lessons in Ccollaborative Mmanagement from the Wworld's Oonly Cconductorless Oorchestra.* New York: Henry Holt & Company, Inc.

Sekaquaptewa, D., & Thompson, M. (2002). The differential effects of solo status on members of high- and low-status groups. *Personality and Social Psychology Bulletin, 28*(5), 694–707.

Semega, J. (2009). *Men's and women's earnings by state: 2008 American Community survey.* Washington, DC: Department of Commerce, Economics and Statistics Administration, U.S. Census Bureau.

Sergiovanni, T. J., Metzcus, R., & Burden, L. (1969). Toward a particularistic approach to leadership style: Some finds. *American Educational Research Journal, 6*, 62–79.

Seta, J. J. (1982). The impact of comparison processes on coactors' task performance. *Journal of Personality and Social Psychology, 42*, 281–291.

Shah, P. P. (2000). Network destruction: The structural implications of downsizing. *Academy of Management Journal, 43*(1), 101–112.

Shah, P. P., & Dirks, K. T. (2003). The social structure of diverse groups: Integrating social categorization and network perspectives. *Research on Managing Groups and Teams, 5,* 113–133.

Shah, P. P., Dirks, K. T., & Chervany, N. (2006). The multiple pathways of high performing groups: The interaction of social networks and group processes. *Journal of Organizational Behavior, 27*(3), 299–317.

Shah, P. P., & Jehn, K. A. (1993). Do friends perform better than acquaintances? The interaction of friendship, conflict, and task. *Group Decision and Negotiation, 2*(2), 149–165.

Shaw, M. E. (1981). *Group dynamics: The psychology of small group behavior* (3rd ed.). New York: McGraw-Hill.

Shea, G. P., & Guzzo, R. A. (1987, Spring). Group effectiveness: What really matters? *Sloan Management Review, 28*(3), 25–31.

Sheehan, N. (1971). The Pentagon papers: As published by the New York Times, based on the investigative reporting by Neil Sheehan, written by Neil Sheehan [and others] (p. 450). Articles and documents edited by G. Gold, A. M. Siegal, & S. Abt. New York, Toronto: Bantam.

Shepherd, M. M., Briggs, R. O., Reinig, B. A., Yen, J., & Nunamaker, J. F., Jr. (1995–1996). Invoking social comparison to improve electronic brainstorming: Beyond anonymity. *Journal of Management Information Systems, 12,* 155–170.

Shepperd, J. A. (1993). Productivity loss in performance groups: A motivation analysis. *Psychological Bulletin, 113,* 67–81.

Sherif, M. (1936). *The psychology of social norms* (p. 3). New York: Harper & Bros.

Sherif, M. (1966). *In common predicament: Social psychology of intergroup conflict and cooperation.* Boston, MA: Addison-Wesley.

Sherif, M., Harvey, O. J., White, B. J., Hood, W. R., & Sherif, C. W. (1961). *Intergroup conflict and cooperation: The Robbers Cave experiment.* Norman, OK: Institute of Group Relations, University of Oklahoma.

Sherman, D. K., & Cohen, G. L. (2006). The psychology of self-defense: Self-affirmation theory. In M. P. Zanna (Ed.) *Advances in Experimental Social Psychology* (Vol. 38, pp. 183–242). San Diego, CA: Academic Press.

Sherman, D. K., & Kim, H. S. (2005). Is there an "I" in "team"? The role of the self in group-serving judgments. *Journal of Personality and Social Psychology, 88,* 108–120.

Sherman, D. K., Kinias, Z., Major, B., Kim, H. S., & Prenovost, M. (2007). The group as a resource: Reducing biased attributions for group success and failure via group affirmation. *Personality and Social Psychology Bulletin, 33,* 1100–1112.

Shure, G. H., Rogers, M. S., Larsen, I. M., & Tasson, J. (1962). Group planning and task effectiveness. *Sociometry, 25,* 263–282.

Siegel, J., Dubrovsky, V., Keisler, S., & McGuire, T. (1986). Group processes in computer-mediated communication. *Organizational Behavior, 37,* 157–187.

Siegman, A. W., & Reynolds, M. (1982). Interviewer-interviewee nonverbal communications: An interactional approach. In M. A. Davis (Ed.), *Interaction rhythms: Periodicity in communication behavior* (pp. 249–278). New York: Human Sciences Press.

Silverman, C. (2008, April 7). The traditional interview: That's so yesterday; Employers are realizing candidates who rock the interview prove they're mastered the process, but not necessarily the job itself. *The Globe and Mail*, p. L3.

Simon, B., Pantaleo, G., & Mummendey, A. (1995). Unique individual or interchangeable group member? The accentuation of intragroup differences versus similarities as an indicator of the individual self versus the collective self. *Journal of Personality and Social Psychology, 69,* 106–119.

Simonton, D. K. (1987). *Why presidents succeed: A political psychology of leadership.* New Haven, CT: Yale University Press.

Sims, R. R. (1992). Linking groupthink to unethical behavior in organizations. *Journal of Business Ethics, 11*(9), 651–662.

Simsek, Z., Veiga, J. F., Lubatkin, M., & Dino, R. (2005). Modeling the multilevel determinants of top management team behavioral integration. *Academy of Management Journal, 48*(1), 69–84.

Sindic, D., & Reicher, D. (2008). The instrumental use of group prototypicality judgments. *Journal of Experimental Social Psychology, 44*, 1425–1435.

Skilton, P. F., & Dooley, K. J. (2010). The effects of repeat collaboration on creative abrasion. *Academy of Management Review, 35*(1), 118–134.

Smith, C. M., Tindale, R. S., & Dugoni, B. L. (1996). Minority and majority influence in freely interacting groups: Qualitative vs. quantitative differences. *British Journal of Social Psychology, 35,* 137–149.

Smith, E. R., Seger, C., & Mackie, D. M. (2007). Can emotions be truly group-level? Evidence regarding four conceptual criteria. *Journal of Personality and Social Psychology, 93,* 431–446.

Smith, E. R., Seger, C., & Mackie, D. M. (2009). Subtle activation of a social categorization triggers group-level emotions. *Journal of Experimental Social Psychology, 45*(3), 460–467.

Smith, K., Smith, K., Olian, J., Sims, H., O'Bannon, D., & Scully, J. (1994). Top management team demography and process: The role of social integration and communication. *Administrative Science Quarterly, 39,* 412–438.

Snyder, M. (1984). When belief creates reality. In L. Berkowitz (Ed.), *Advances in experimental social psychology* (Vol. 18, pp. 248–306). New York: Academic Press.

Sommers, N. (1982). Responding to student writing. *College Composition and Communication, 33,* 148–156.

Spark, D. (2009, April 28). 12 inspiring stories of successful social networks. *Business Week.* businessweek.com

Sparrowe, R. T., & Popielarz, P. A. (1995). *Weak ties and structural holes: The effects of network structure on careers.* Paper presented at the annual meetings of the Academy of Management, Vancouver, BC.

Spector, P. E., & Jex, S. M. (1998). Development of four self-report measures of job stressors and strain: Interpersonal conflict at work scale, organizational constraints scale, qauantitative workload inventory, and physical symptoms inventory. *Journal of Occupational Health Psychology, 3,* 356–367.

Spiegel, R. (2007, December). Collaboration proliferates as companies go global. *Automation World,* 34

Spoor, J. R., & Kelly, J. R. (2004). The evolutionary significance of affect in groups: Communication and group bonding. *Group Processes and Intergroup Relations, 7,* 398–416.

Spors, K. (2008, October 13). Top small workplaces 2008: Creating great workplaces has never been more important for small businesses; nor more difficult; here are 15 companies that do it well. *Wall Street Journal,* p. R1.

Spors, K. (2009, February 22). Top small workplaces 2008 creating great workplaces has never been more important. *Wall Street Journal,* p. R1.

Spors, K. K. (2009, September 28). Top small workplaces 2009. *Wall Street Journal,* p. R1.

Sproull, L., & Keisler, S. (1991). *Connections: New ways of working in the networked organization.* Cambridge, MA: MIT Press.

Srivastave, A., Bartol, K. M., & Locke, E. A. (2006). Empowering leadership in management teams: Effects on knowledge sharing, efficacy, and performance. *Academy of Management Journal, 49*(6), 1239–1251.

Stachowski, A., Kaplan, S. A., & Waller, M. J. (2009). The benefits of flexible team interaction during crises. *Journal of Applied Psychology, 94*(6), 1536–1543.

Stajkovic, A., Lee, D., & Nyberg, A. (2009). Collective efficacy, group potency, and group performance: Meta-analyses of their relationships, and test of a mediation model. *Journal of Applied Psychology, 94*(3), 814–828.

Stasser, G. (1988). Computer simulation as a research tool: The DISCUSS model of group decision making. *Journal of Experimental Social Psychology, 24*(5), 393–422.

Stasser, G. (1992). Information salience and the discovery of hidden profiles by decision-making groups: A "thought" experiment. *Organizational Behavior and Human Decision Processes, 52,* 156–181.

Stasser, G., & Stewart, D. D. (1992). Discovery of hidden profiles by decision-making groups: Solving a problem versus making a judgment. *Journal of Personality and Social Psychology, 63,* 426–434.

Stasser, G., Stewart, D. D., & Wittenbaum, G. M. (1995). Expert roles and information exchange during discussion: The importance of knowing who knows what. *Journal of Experimental Social Psychology, 31,* 244–265.

Stasser, G., Taylor, L. A., & Hanna, C. (1989). Information sampling in structured and unstructured discussions of three- and six-person groups. *Journal of Personality and Social Psychology, 57,* 67–78.

Stasser, G., & Titus, W. (1985). Pooling of unshared information in group decision making: Biased information sampling during discussion. *Journal of Personality and Social Psychology, 48,* 1467–1478.

Stasser, G., & Titus, W. (1987). Effects of information load and percentage of shared information on the dissemination of unshared information in group discussion. *Journal of Personality and Social Psychology, 53,* 81–93.

Staw, B. H. (1976). Knee-deep in the big muddy: A study of escalating commitment to a chosen course of action. *Organizational Behavior and Human Decision Processes, 16*(1), 27–44.

Steel, E. (2009, October 15). MySpace's Reboot, From Exec Suite to Cubicles. *Wall Street Journal.* online.wsj.com

Steele, S. (1990). *The content of our character: A new vision of race in America* (pp. 111–125). New York: St. Martin's Press.

Steiner, I. (1972). *Group process and productivity.* New York: Academic Press.

Stenstrom, D. M., Lickel, B., Denson, T. F., & Miller, N. (2008). The Roles of ingroup identification and outgroup entitativity in intergroup retribution. *Personality and Social Psychology Bulletin, 34*(11), 1570–1582.

Stevens, M. A., & Campion, M. J. (1994). The knowledge, skill, and ability requirements for teamwork: Implications for human resource management. *Journal of Management, 20,* 503–530.

Stewart, D. D., Billings, R. S., & Stasser, G. (1998). Accountability and the discussion of unshared, critical information in decision making groups. *Group Dynamics: Theory, Research, and Practice, 2*(1), 18–23.

Stewart, G. I., & Manz, C. C. (1995). Leadership and self-managing work teams: A typology and integrative model. *Human Relations, 48*(7), 747–770.

Stogdill, R. M. (1972). Group productivity, drive, and cohesiveness. *Organizational Behavior and Human Performance, 8*(1), 26–43.

Stokes, J. P. (1983). Components of group cohesion: Inter-member attraction, instrumental value, and risk taking. *Small Group Behavior, 14,* 163–173.

Stoner, J. A. F. (1961). *A comparison of individual and group decisions involving risk.* Thesis, Massachusetts Institute of Technology, Boston, MA.

Story, L., & Creswell, J. (2009, February 8). For bank of America and Merrill, love was blind. *New York Times,* p. BU1.

Story, L., & Dash, E. (2009, October 1). Bank of America chief to depart at year's end. *New York Times,* p. B1.

Stroebe, W., & Diehl, M. (1994). Why are groups less effective than their members? On productivity losses in idea generating groups. *European Review of Social Psychology, 5,* 271–301.

Stroebe, W., Diehl, M., & Abakoumkin, G. (1992). The illusion of group effectivity. *Personality and Social Psychology Bulletin, 18*(5), 643–650.

Stroebe, W., Diehl, M., & Abakoumkin, G. (1996). Social compensation and the Kohler effect: Toward a theoretcial explanation of motivation gains in group productivity. In E. H. White, & J. H. Davis (Eds.), *Understanding group behavior, vol. 2: Small group processes and interpersonal relations.* Mahwah, NJ: Lawrence Erlbaum Associates.

Stroebe, W., Lenkert, A., & Jonas, K. (1988). Familiarity may breed contempt: The impact of student exchange on national stereotypes and attitudes. In W. Stroebe, A. W. Kruglanski, D. Bar-Tal, & M. Hewstone (Eds.), *The social psychology of intergroup conflict* (pp. 167–187). New York: Springer-Verlag.

Sumner, W. (1906). *Folkways.* New York: Ginn.

Sundstrom, E. D., DeMeuse, K. P., & Futrell, D. (1990). Work teams: Applications and effectiveness. *American Psychologist, 45*(2), 120–133.

Sundstrom, E. D., Mcintyre, M., Halfhill, T., & Richards, H. (2000). Work groups: From the Hawthorne studies to work teams of the 1990s and beyond. *Group Dynamics, 4,* 44–67.

Sundstrom, E. D., & Sundstrom, M. G. (1986). *Work places: The psychology of the physical environment in offices and factories.* Cambridge, UK: Cambridge University Press.

Svenson, O. (1981). Are we all less risky and more skillful than our fellow drivers? *Acta Psychologica, 47,* 143–148.

Swann, W. B., Jr., Gomez, A., Seyle, D. C., Morales, J. F., & Huici, C. (2009). Identity fusion: The interplay of personal and social identities in extreme group behavior. *Journal of Personality and Social Psychology, 5,* 995–1011.

Swann, W. B., Milton, L. P., & Polzer, J. T. (2000). Should we create a niche or fall in line? Identity negotiation and small group effectiveness. *Journal of Personality and Social Psychology, 79*(2), 238–250.

Sy, T., Cote, S., & Saavedra, R. (2005). The contagious leader: Impact of the leader's mood on the mood of group members, group affective tone, and group processes. *Journal of Applied Psychology, 90,* 295–305.

Sycara, K., & Lewis, M. (2004). Integrating intelligent agents into human teams. In E. Salas & S. Fiore (Eds.), *Team cognition: Understanding the factors that drive process and performance.* Washington, DC: American Psychological Association.

Szalavitz, M. (2009, January 14). Study: A simple surgery checklist saves lives. *Time.* time.com

Tajfel, H. (Ed.). (1978). *Differentiation between social groups: Studies in the social psychology of intergroup relations.* New York: Academic Press.

Tajfel, H. (1982). Social psychology of intergroup relations. *Annual Review of Psychology, 33,* 1–39.

Tajfel, H., & Turner, J. C. (1986). The social identity theory of intergroup behavior. In S. Worchel & W. G. Austin (Eds.), *Psychology of intergroup relations* (pp. 7–24). Chicago, IL: Nelson-Hall.

Taylor, D. W., Berry, P. C., & Block, C. H. (1958). Does group participation when using brainstorming facilitate or inhibit creative thinking? *Administrative Science Quarterly, 3,* 23–47.

Taylor, D. W., & Faust, W. L. (1952). Twenty questions: Efficiency of problem-solving as a function of the size of the group. *Journal of Experimental Social Psychology, 44,* 360–363.

Taylor, F. W. (1911). *Shop management.* New York: Harper & Brothers.

Taylor, S. E., & Brown, J. D. (1988). Illusion of well-being: A social psychological perspective on mental health. *Psychological Bulletin, 103,* 193–210.

Teather, D. (2009, June 30). Madoff case: Damned by judge and victims, fraudster will die behind bars: 150-year prison sentence for financier who cheated investors of $65B in one of Wall Street's biggest frauds. *The Guardian,* p. 2.

Telework Revs Up as More Employers Offer Work Flexibility. (2009, February 17). World at Work press release from Dieringer Research Group's random digit dialed (RDD) telephone survey between November 6, 2008 and December 2, 2008.

Terry, D. J., Carey, C. J., & Callan, V. J. (2001). Employee adjustment to an organizational merger. *Personality and Social Psychology Bulletin, 27*(3), 267–280.

Terry, D. J., & Callan, V. J. (1998). In-group bias in response to an organizational merger. *Group Dynamics: Theory, Research, and Practice, 2*(2), 67–81.

Terry, D. J., & O'Brien, A. T. (2001). Status, legitimacy, and ingroup bias in the context of an organizational merger. *Group Processes and Intergroup Relations, 4,* 271–289.

Tesser, A., & Rosen, S. (1975). The reluctance to transmit bad news. In L. Berkowitz (Ed.), *Advances in experimental social psychology* (Vol. 8). New York: Academic Press.

Teten, D., & Allen, S. (2005). *The virtual handshake.* New York: AMACOM.

Tetlock, P., Peterson, R., McGuire, C., Chang,S., & Feld, P. (1992). Assessing political group dynamics: The test of the groupthink model. *Journal of Personality and Social Psychology, 63,* 403-425.

Tetlock, P. E., Skitka, L., & Boettger, R. (1989). Social and cognitive strategies for coping with accountability: Conformity, complexity and bolstering. *Journal of Personality and Social Psychology, 57,* 632–640.

Thatcher, S., Jehn, K., & Zanutto, E. (2003). Cracks in diversity research: The effects of diversity faultlines on conflict and performance. *Group Decision and Negotiation, 12,* 217–241.

The (virtual) global office. (2008, May 5). *Business Week.* businessweek.com

The Dieringer Research Group Inc. (2009, February). *Telework trendlines 2009 World at work.* worldat-work.com

Thomas, K. W. (1992). Conflict and conflict management: Reflections and update. *Journal of Organizational Behavior, 13,* 265–274.

Thompson, B. (2005, March). *The loyalty connection: Secrets to customer retention and increased profits.* Rightnow.com

Thompson, J. (1967). *Organizations in action.* New York: McGraw-Hill.

Thompson, L. (2003). Improving the creativity of organizational work groups. *Academy of Management Executive, 17*(1), 96–109.

Thompson, L. (2008). *The mind and heart of the negotiator* (4th ed.). Electronically reproduced by permission of Pearson Education, Inc., Upper Saddle River, New Jersey.

Thompson, L. (2010). Leading high impact teams survey. Kellogg Executive programs. Kellogg

Thompson, L., Kray, L., & Lind, A. (1998). Cohesion and respect: An examination of group decision making in social and escalation dilemmas. *Journal of Experimental Social Psychology, 34,* 289–311.

Thompson, L., Loewenstein, J., & Gentner, D. (2000). Avoiding missed opportunities in managerial life: Analogical training more powerful than individual case training. *Organizational Behavior and Human Decision Processes, 82*(1), 60–75.

Thompson, L., Mannix, E., & Bazerman, M. (1988). Group negotiation: Effects of decision rule, agenda, and aspiration. *Journal of Personality and Social Psychology, 54,* 86–95.

Thompson, L., & Rosette, A. (2004). Leading by analogy. In S. Chowdhury (Ed.), *Financial times next generation business series.* London: Prentice Hall.

Thompson, L., Valley, K. L., & Kramer, R. M. (1995). The bittersweet feeling of success: An examination

of social perception in negotiation. *Journal of Experimental Social Psychology, 31*(6), 467–492.

Tickle-Degnen, L., & Rosenthal, R. (1987). Group rapport and nonverbal behavior. In C. Hendrick (Ed.), *Review of personality and social psychology: Vol. 9. Group processes and intergroup relations* (pp. 113–136). Newbury Park, CA: Sage.

Tindale, S., & Sheffey, S. (2002). Shared information, cognitive load, and group memory. *Group Processes and Intergroup Relations, 5*(1), 5–18.

Toma, C., & Butera, F. (2009). Hidden profiles and concealed information: Strategic information sharing and use in group decision making. *Personality and Social Psychology Bulletin, 35*(6), 793–806.

Totterdell, P., Kellet, S., Teuchmann, K., & Briner, R. B. (1998). Evidence of mood linkage in work groups. *Journal of Personality and Social Psychology, 74,* 1504–1515.

Train, J. (1995, June 24). Learning from financial disaster. *Financial Times* (Weekend Money Markets), p. II.

Trends in employee recognition. (2008, April). Retrieved on January 29, 2010, worldatwork.org.

Triandis, H. C. (1989). Cross-cultural studies of individualism and collectivism. In J. J. Berman (Ed.), *Cross-cultural perspectives: Nebraska symposium on motivation* (Vol. 37, pp. 41–133). Lincoln, NE: University of Nebraska Press.

Tropman, J. E. (2003). *Making meetings work: Achieving high quality group decisions* (2nd ed.). Thousand Oaks, CA: Sage.

Tucker, A. L., Nembhard, I. M., & Edmondson, A. (2006, April). *Implementing new practices: An empirical study of organizational learning in hospital intensive care units.* Working paper, Harvard Business School Working Knowledge.

Tucker, A. T., Nembhard, I. M., & Edmondson, A. C. (2007). Implementing new practices: An empirical study of organizational learning in hospital intensive care units. *Management Science, 53*(6), 894–907

Tuckman, B. W. (1965). Developmental sequence in small groups. *Psychological Bulletin, 63*(6), 384–399.

Tully, S. (2008, September 15). Jamie Dimon's swat team. *Fortune, 158*(5), 64–78.

Turner, J. C. (1987). A self-categorization theory. In J. C. Turner, M. A. Hogg, P. J. Oakes, S. D. Reicher, & M. Witherell (Eds.), *Rediscovering the social group: A self-categorization theory* (pp. 42–67). Oxford, England: Basil Blackwell.

Turner, J. C., Hogg, M. A., Oakes, P. J., Reicher, S. D., & Wetherell, M. S. (1987). *Rediscovering the social group: A self-categorization theory.* Oxford, UK: Blackwell.

Turner, M. A., Fix, M., & Struyk, R. J. (1991). *Opportunities denied, opportunities diminished: Racial discrimination in hiring.* Washington, DC: The Urban Institute Press.

Turner, M. E., & Pratkanis, A. R. (1998). A social identity maintenance model of groupthink. *Organizational Behavior and Human Decision Processes, 73*(2–3), 210–235.

Turner, M. E., Probasco, P., Pratkanis, A. R., & Leve, C. (1992). Threat, cohesion, and group effectiveness: Testing a social identity maintenance perspective on groupthink. *Journal of Personality and Social Psychology, 63,* 781–796.

Tversky, A., & Kahneman, D. (1981). The framing of decisions and the psychology of choice. *Science, 211,* 453–458.

Tykocinski, O., Pick, D., & Kedmi, D. (2002). Retroactive pessimism: A different kind of hindsight bias. *European Journal of Social Psychology, 32,* 577–588.

Tyler, T. R. (1990). *Why people obey the law.* New Haven, CT: Yale University Press.

Tynan, D. (n.d.). 25 ways to reward employees (without spending a dime). *HRWorld.* hrworld.com.

Tziner, A., & Eden, D. (1985). Effects of crew composition on crew performance: Does the whole equal the sum of its parts? *Journal of Applied Psychology, 70,* 85–93.

U.S. Department of Health and Human Services. U.S. Food and Drug Administration. (2009, May 12). *H1N1 Flu: FDA Responds Quickly to Protect the Public's Health.* fda.gov

U.S. Securities and Trade Commission. (2008, September 16). *Statement regarding Madoff investigation.* sec.gov

U.S. Senate Select Committee on Intelligence. (2008, June 5). *Senate Intelligence Committee Unveils Final Phase II Reports on Prewar Iraq Intelligence.* intelligence.senate.gov

U.S. Small Business Administration. (2010). *Customer service—An imperative.* sba.gov

United States Department of Defense. (2010). *Operation Iraqi freedom military.* siadapp.dmdc.osd.mil

United States Department of Labor, Bureau of Labor Statistics. (2009, June 24*). American time survey—2008 results.* bls.gov.com

United States Department of Labor. (2010, January 21). Usual weekly earnings summary. *Bureau of labor statistics.* bls.gov

Uzzi, B. (1997). Social structure and competition in interfirm networks: The paradox of embeddedness. *Administrative Science Quarterly, 42,* 35–67.

Uzzi, B. (2010). Leadnet web site at http://www20.kellogg.northwestern.edu/leadnet/teamnetcover.asp

Uzzi, B., & Dunlap, S. (2005). How to build your network. *Harvard Business Review, 83*(12), 53–60.

Uzzi, B., & Gillespie, J. J. (1999). Access and governance benefits of social relationships and networks: The case of collateral, availability, and bank spreads. In H. Rosenblum (Ed.), *Business access to capital and credit.* Washington, DC: Federal Reserve Bank.

Uzzi, B., & Spiro, J. (2005). Collaboration and creativity: The small world problem. *American Journal of Sociology, 111,* 447–504.

van Avermaet, E. (1974). *Equity: A theoretical and experimental analysis.* Unpublished doctoral dissertation, University of California, Santa Barbara.

Van de Ven, A. H., & Delbecq, A. L. (1974). The effectiveness of nominal, Delphi, and interacting group decision making processes. *Academy of Management Journal, 17*(4), 605–621.

Van der Pool, L. Survey: (2009, May 7). Office meetings often a waste of time. *Boston Business Journal.* boston.bizjournals.com

Van der Vegt, G., & Bunderson, S. (2005). Learning and performance in multidisciplinary teams: The importance of collective team identification. *Academy of Management Journal, 48,* 532–547.

Van Dyne, L., & Saavedra, R. (1996). A naturalistic minority influence experiment: Effects on divergent thinking, conflict and originality in work groups. *British Journal of Social Psychology, 35,* 151–167.

Van Ginkel, W., Tindale, R. S., & van Knippenberg, D. (2009). Team reflexivity, development of shared task representations, and the use of distributed information in group decision making. *Group Dynamics: Theory, Research, and Practice, 13*(4), 265–280.

van Ginkel, W., & van Knippenberg, D. (2008). Group information elaboration and group decision making: The role of shared task representations. *Organizational Behavior and Human Decision Processes, 105,* 82–97.

Van Ginkel, W. P., & Knippenberg, D. (2009). Knowledge about the distribution of information and group decision making: When and why does it work? *Organizational Behavior and Human Decision Processes, 108*(2), 218–229.

Van Kleef, G. A., Homan, A. C., Beersma, B., van Knippenberg, D., van Knippenberg, B., & Damen, F. (2009). Searing sentiment or cold calculation? The effects of leader emotional displays on team performance depend on follower epistemic motivation. *Academy of Management Journal, 52,* 562–580.

van Knippenberg, B., & van Knippenberg, D. (2005). Leader self-sacrifice and leadership effectiveness: The moderating role of leader prototypicality. *Journal of Applied Psychology, 90*(1), 25–37.

van Knippenberg, D., van Knippenberg, B., Monden, L., & De Lima, F. (2002). Organizational identification after a merger: A social identity perspective. *British Journal of Social Psychology, 44,* 233–262.

Van Maanen, J. (1977). Experiencing organization: Notes on the meaning of careers and socialization. In J. Van Maanen (Ed.), *Organizational careers: Some new perspectives* (pp. 15–45). New York: John Wiley & Sons.

van Oostrum, J., & Rabbie, J. M. (1995). Intergroup competition and cooperation within autocratic and democratic management regimes. *Small Group Research, 26*(2), 269–295.

Van Prooijen, J.-W., Van den Bos, K., & Wilke, H. A. M. (2005). Procedural justice and intragroup status: Knowing where we stand in a group enhances reactions to procedures. *Journal of Experimental Social Psychology, 41,* 664–676.

van Swol, L. M., Savadori, L., & Sniezek, J. A. (2003). Factors that may affect the difficulty of uncovering hidden profiles. *Group Processes & Intergroup Relations, 6*(3), 285–304.

Vandello, J. A., & Cohen, D. (1999). Patterns of individualism and collectivism across the United States. *Journal of Personality and Social Psychology, 77*(2), 279–292.

Verberne, T. (1997). Creative fitness. *Training and Development, 51*(8), 68–71.

Verespej, M. A. (1990, December 3). When you put the team in charge. *Industry Week,* pp. 30–31.

Veronikis, E. (2008, August 21). Not your average office. *Central Penn Business Journal, 24,* (35).

Von Glinow, M. A., Shapiro, D. L., & Brett, J. M. (2004). Can we talk, and should we? Managing emotional conflict in multicultural teams. *Academy of Management Review, 29*(4), 578–592.

von Hippel, E. A. (2005). *Democratizing innovation.* Cambridge, MA: MIT Press.

Vroom, V. H., & Jago, A. G. (1978). The validity of the Vroom-Yetton model. *Journal of Applied Psychology, 63*(2), 151–162.

Vroom, V. H., & Jago, A. G. (1988). *The new leadership: Managing participation in organizations.* Upper Saddle River, NJ: Prentice Hall.

Vroom, V. H., & Yetton, P. W. (1973). *Leadership and decision-making.* Pittsburgh, PA: University of Pittsburgh Press.

Wade, J. B., O'Reilly, C. A., III, & Pollock, T. G. (2006). Overpaid CEOs and underpaid managers: Fairness and executive compensation. *Organization Science, 17*(5), 527–544.

Wageman, R. (1995). Interdependence and group effectiveness. *Administrative Science Quarterly, 40*(1), 145–180.

Wageman, R. (1997a). Case study: Critical success factors for creating superb self-managing teams at Xerox. *Compensation & Benefits Review, 29*(5), 31–41.

Wageman, R. (1997b, Summer). Critical success factors for creating superb self-managing teams. *Organizational Dynamics, 49–61.*

Wageman, R. (2001). How leaders foster self-managing team effectiveness: Design choices versus hands-on coaching. *Organization Science, 12*(5), 559–77.

Wageman, R. (2003). Virtual processes: Implications for coaching the virtual team. In R. Peterson & E. A. Mannix (Eds.), *Leading and managing people in the dynamic organization* (pp. 65–86). Mahwah, NJ: Lawrence Erlbaum Associates.

Wageman, R., & Donnenfeld, A. (2007). Intervening in intra-team conflict. In K. M. Behfar & L. L. Thompson (Eds.), *Conflict in organizational groups: New directions in theory and practice.* Northwestern University Press.

Wageman, R., & Gordon, F. (2006). As the twig is bent: How group values shape emergent task interdependence in groups. *Organization Science, 16*(6), 687–700.

Wageman, R., & Hackman, J. R. (2005). When and how team leaders matter. *Research in Organizational Behavior, 26,* 37–74.

Wageman, R., Hackman, J. R., & Lehman, E. V. (2005). Team diagnostic survey: Development of an instrument. *Journal of Applied Behavioral Science, 41*(4), 373–398.

Wageman, R., & Mannix, E. A. (Eds.). (1998). *Uses and misuses of power in task-performing teams. Power and influence in organizations.* Thousand Oaks, CA: Sage.

Wagner, G., Pfeffer, J., & O'Reilly, C. (1984). Organizational demography and turnover in top management groups. *Administrative Science Quarterly, 29,* 74–92.

Wajcman, J., Bittman, M., Johnstone, L., Brown, J., & Jones, P. (2008, March). *The impact of the mobile phone on work/life balance.* Australian Mobile Telecommunications Association. website: amta. org.au

Waldzus, S., Mummendey, A., Wenzel, M., & Boettcher, F. (2004). Of bikers, teachers and Germans: Groups' diverging views about their prototypicality. *British Journal of Social Psychology, 43,* 385–400.

Walker, R. (2002, August). Hook, line, sinker. *Inc.,* 85–88.

Wallach, M. A., & Kogan, N. (1961). Aspects of judgment and decision making: Interrelationships and change with age. *Behavioral Science, 6,* 23-31.

Walton, R. E., & Hackman, J. R. (1986). Groups under contrasting management strategies. In P. S. Goodman (Ed.), *Designing effective workgroups.* San Francisco, CA: Jossey-Bass.

Walumbwa, F. O., & Schaubroeck, J. (2009). Leader personality traits and employee voice behavior: Mediating roles of ethical leadership and work group psychological safety. *Journal of Applied Psychology, 94,* 1275–1286.

Wang, H., Law, K. S., Hackett, R. D., Wang, D., & Chen, Z. X. (2005). Leader-member exchange as a mediator of the relationship between transformational leadership and followers' performance and organizational citizenship behavior. *Academy of Management Journal, 48,* 420–432.

Wang, J. (2008, January 8). Why you (yes you!) need a cool office. *Entrepreneur.* Entrepreneur.com

Wann, D., Grieve, F., Waddill, P., & Martin, J. (2008). Use of retroactive pessimism as a method of coping with identity threat: The impact of group identification. *Group Processes and Intergroup Relations, 11*(4), 439–450.

Wanous, J. P. (1980). *Organizational entry: Recruitment, selection, and socialization of newcomers.* Reading, MA: Addison-Wesley.

Wards Cove Packing Company, Inc. v. Atonio, 109 S. Ct. 2115 (1989).

Warner, R. (1988). Rhythm in social interaction. In J. E. McGrath (Ed.), *The social psychology of time* (pp. 63–88). Newbury Park, CA: Sage.

Wartzman, R. (2008, August 29). Organizations need structure and flexibility. *Business Week.* Busines week.com

Wash, W. (2009, September 6). A Dream Interrupted at Boeing. *The New York Times,* p. BU1.

Wason, P. C., & Johnson-Laird, P. N. (1972). *Psychology of reasoning: Structure and content.* Cambridge, MA: Harvard University Press.

Watkins, C. (2009, January 20). Sources: Dallas cowboys often tardy, undisciplined in '08. *The Dallas Morning News.* Dallasnews.com

Watson, W. E., Kumar, K., & Michaelsen, L. K. (1993). Cultural diversity's impact on interaction process and performance: Comparing homogeneous and diverse task groups. *Academy of Management Journal, 36*(3), 590–602.

Waung, M., & Highhouse, S. (1997). Fear of conflict and empathic buffering: Two explanations for the inflation of performance feedback. *Organizational Behavior and Human Decision Processes, 71*(1), 37–54.

Webber, S. S., & Klimoski. (2004). Crews: A distinct type of work team. *Journal of Business and Psychology, 18*(3), 261–279.

Weber, M. (1958). *The protestant ethic and the spirit of capitalism* (T. Parsons, Trans.) New York: Scribner's.

Weber, M. (1978). *Economy and society: An outline of interpretive sociology* (G. Roth, & C. Wittich, Trans.). Berkeley, CA: University of California Press.

Wegge, J., Roth, C., Neubach, B., Schmidt, K., & Kanfer, R. (2008). Age and gender diversity as determinants of performance and health in a public organization: The role of task complexity and group size. *Journal of Applied Psychology, 93*(6), 1301–1313.

Wegner, D. M. (1986). Transactive memory: A contemporary analysis of the group mind. In B. Mullen & G. Goethals (Eds.), *Theories of group behavior* (pp. 185–208). New York: Springer-Verlag.

Wegner, D. M., Giuliano, T., & Hertel, P. (1995). Cognitive interdependence in close relationships. In W. J. Ickes (Ed.), *Compatible and Incompatible Relationships* (pp. 253–276). New York: Springer-Verlag.

Weick, K. E., & Gilfillan, D. P. (1971). Fate of arbitrary traditions in a laboratory microculture. *Journal of Personality and Social Psychology, 17,* 179–191.

Weingart, L. R. (1992). Impact of group goals, task component complexity, effort, and planning on group performance. *Journal of Applied Psychology, 77,* 682–693.

Weingart, L., Cronin, M., Houser, C., Cagan, J., & Vogel, C. (2005). Functional diversity and conflict in cross-functional product development teams: Considering representational gaps and task characteristics. In L. Neider & C. Schriesheim (Eds.), *Understanding teams* (pp. 89–100). Greenwich, CT: IAP.

Weisband, S. P. (1992). Group discussion and first advocacy effects in computer-mediated and face-to-face decision making groups. *Organizational Behavior and Human Decision Processes, 53,* 352–380.

Weisberg, R. W. (1986). *Creativity, genius and other myths.* New York: Freeman.

Weisberg, R. W. (1993). *Creativity: Beyond the myth of genius.* San Francisco, CA: Freeman.

Weisberg, R. W. (1997). Case studies of creative thinking. In S. M. Smith, T. B. Ward, & R. A. Finke (Eds.), *The creative cognition approach.* Cambridge, MA: MIT Press.

Weisbuch, M., & Ambady, N. (2008).Affective divergence: Automatic responses to others' emotions dependent on group membership. *Journal of Personality and Social Psychology, 95,* 1063–1079.

Weitzman, M. (1984). *The share economy.* Cambridge, MA: Harvard University Press.

Welch, J., & Welch, S. (2005, April 4). How to be a good leader. *Newsweek,* p. 45.

Wellens, A. R. (1989, September). Effects of telecommunication media upon information sharing and team performance: Some theoretical and empirical findings. *IEEE AES Magazine,* p. 14.

Wellins, R. S. (1992). Building a self-directed work team. *Training and Development, 46*(12), 24–28.

Wellins, R. S., Byham, W. C., & Wilson, J. M. (1991). *Empowered teams* (p. 26). San Francisco, CA: Jossey-Bass.

Werner, D., Ember, C. R., & Ember, M. (1981). *Anthropology: Study guide and workbook.* Upper Saddle River, NJ: Prentice Hall.

West, M. A. (1996). *Handbook of work group psychology.* Chichester: John Wiley & Sons.

Wheelan, S. A. (1990). *Facilitating training groups.* New York: Praeger.

Wheelan, S. A. (1994). *Group processes: A developmental perspective.* Boston, MA: Allyn & Bacon.

Whetton, D. A., & Cameron, K. S. (1991). *Developing management skills* (2nd ed.). New York: Harper Collins.

White, J. (2008). Fail or flourish? Cognitive appraisal moderates the effect of solo status on performance *Personality and Social Psychology Bulletin, 34,* 1171–1184.

Whitehead, A. N. (1929). *The aims of education.* New York: MacMillan.

Whitte, E. H. (2007). Toward a group facilitation technique for project teams. *Group Processes & Intergroup Relations, 10*(3), 299—309

Whole Foods Market. (2010). *Whole Foods Market benefits.* Wholefoodsmarket.com

Wholesaler profile Suma. (2008, June 14). Theg rocer .com

Wicker, A. W., Kermeyer, S. L., Hanson, L., & Alexander, D. (1976). Effects of manning levels on subjective experiences, performance, and verbal interaction in groups. *Organizational Behavior and Human Performance, 17,* 251–274.

Wicker, A. W., & Mehler, A. (1971). Assimilation of new members in a large and a small church. *Journal of Applied Psychology, 55,* 151–156.

Wild, T. C., Enzle, M. E., Nix, G., & Deci, E. L. (1997). Perceiving others as intrinsically or extrinsically motivated: Effects on expectancy formation and task engagement. *Personality and Social Psychology Bulletin, 23*(8), 837–848.

Wilder, D. A., & Allen, V. L. (1977). Veridical social support, extreme social support, and conformity. *Representative Research in Social Psychology, 8,* 33–41.

Wilkerson, D. B. (2009, August 18). *MGM's CEO out in reshuffle.* MarketWatch.com

Williams, C. L. (1992). The glass escalator: Hidden advantages for men in "female" professions. *Social Forces, 39,* 253–267.

Williams, K. D. (1981). The effects of group cohesiveness on social loafing in simulated word-processing pools. *Dissertation Abstracts International, 42* (2-B), 838.

Williams, K. D. (1997). Social ostracism. In R. Kowalski (Ed.), *Aversive interpersonal behaviors* (pp. 133–170). New York: Plenum.

Williams, K. D., Harkins, S. G., & Latané, B. (1981). Identifiability as a deterrant to social loafing: Two

cheering experiments. *Journal of Personality and Social Psychology, 40*(2), 303–311.

Williams, K. D., & Williams, K. B. (1984). *Social loafing in Japan: A cross-cultural development study.* Paper presented at the Midwestern Psychological Association Meeting, Chicago, IL.

Williams, K. Y., & O'Reilly, C. A. (1998). Demography and diversity in organizations. In L. L. Cummings & B. M. Staw (Eds.), *Research in organizational behavior* (Vol. 20, pp. 77–140). Greenwich, CT: JAI Press.

Williamson, B. (2009, June 17). Managing virtually; First get dressed. *Business Week.* businessweek.com

Wilson, D. C., Butler, R. J., Cray, D., Hickson, D. J., & Mallory, G. R. (1986). Breaking the bounds of organization in strategic decision making. *Human Relations, 39,* 309–332.

Wittenbaum, G. M. (1998). Information sampling in decision-making groups: The impact of members' task-relevant status. *Small Group Research, 29,* 57–84.

Wood, W., Lundgren, S., Ouellette, J. A., Busceme, S., & Blackstone, T. (1994). Minority influence: A meta-analytical review of social influence processes. *Psychological Bulletin, 115,* 323–345.

Worringham, C. J., & Messick, D. M. (1983). Social facilitation of running: An unobtrusive study. *Journal of Social Psychology, 121,* 23–29.

Wright, S. C., Aron, A., McLaughlin-Volpe, T., & Ropp, S. A. (1997). The extended contact effect: Knowledge of cross-group friendships and prejudice. *Journal of Personality and Social Psychology, 73*(1), 73–90.

Wu, J., Tsui, A., & Kinicki, A. (2010). Consequences of differentiated leadership in groups. *Academy of Management Journal, 53*(1), 90–106.

Wuestewald, T. (2010, January). The changing face of police leadership. *Police Chief Magazine.* police chiefmagazine.org

www.boeing.com

Yaniv, I. (2004). The benefit of additional opinions. *Current Directions in Psychological Science, 13,* 75–78.

Yukl, G. A. (1981). *Leadership in organizations.* London: Prentice-Hall International.

Yukl, G. A. (2002). *Leadership in organizations* (5th ed.). Upper Saddle River, NJ: Prentice Hall.

Zaccaro, S. J. (1984). Social loafing: The role of task attractiveness. *Personality and Social Psychology Bulletin, 10,* 99–106.

Zajonc, R. (1968). Attitudinal effects of mere exposure. *Journal of Personality and Social Psychology* (monograph supplement, No. 2, Part 2).

Zeleny, J., & Cooper, H. (2010, January 6). Obama says plot could have been disrupted. *New York Times*, p. A11.

Zellmer-Bruhn, M., & Gibson, C. (2006). Multinational organizational context: Implications for team learning and performance. *Academy of Management Journal, 49*(3), 501–518.

Zellmer-Bruhn, M., Maloney, M., Bhappu, A., & Salvador, R. (2008). When and how do differences matter? An exploration of perceived similarity in teams. *Organizational Behavior and Human Decision Processes, 107*(1), 41–59.

Ziller, R. C. (1957). Four techniques of group decision-making under uncertainty. *Journal of Applied Psychology, 41,* 384–388.

Ziller, R. C. (1965). Toward a theory of open and closed groups. *Psychological Bulletin, 64,* 164–182.

Zolin, R., Hinds, P. J., Fruchter, R., & Levitt, R. E. (2004). Interpersonal trust in cross-functional, geographically distributed work: A longitudinal study. *Information and Organization, 14*(1), 1–26.

Zurcher, L. A. (1965). The sailor aboard ship: A study of role behavior in a total institution. *Social Forces, 43,* 389–400.

Zurcher, L. A. (1970). The "friendly" poker game: A study of an ephemeral role. *Social Forces, 49,* 173–186.

NAME INDEX

SUBJECT INDEX